Th

A CENTURY OF HEROES

America's First High School Football Dynasty

Foreword by

Chris Spielman

College Football Hall of Fame, 2010

By Scott H. Shook

Author of *Massillon Memories*

For information:
Massillon Memories Publishing Company, 100 Stevens' Landing Drive, Suite 403, Marco Island, FL 34145.
239.394.6615

A Century of Heroes website: acenturyofheroes.com
email at acenturyofheroes@yahoo.com

ISBN 978-0-9667027-2-9

§

To Leanne. I couldn't have done it without you.
9.12.21

Acknowledgement

I have not attempted to cite in the text all the authorities and sources consulted in the preparation of this book. To do so would require more space than is available. This list would include many newspapers, magazines, libraries and individuals.

A special thanks goes to John Bartholomew, Gene Boerner, Bruce and Jo Campbell, Herb Campbell, Lori Campbell, Darylle and Rick Connelly, Mark Creighton, Judy Crone, Ruth Dunkle, Matt Fox, Susan Gamble, Becky and Goose Gatsios, Kelley, Molly and Jason Gatsios, Nancy Halter, Arvine and Joyce Hamilton, Jamie and Julie Hamilton, Gary Hauze, Barbara Hope, Connie Hope, George Hope, Karin Hope, Leanne Hope, Ginger and Laci Csernohorszky-Hope, Robert "Doc" Immel, Scott Knudsen, Paul Koch, Pat McRee, Mike Nastoff, David Nelson, Adam Pavkov, Pastrami Dan's, Sue Repp, Dave Rossiter, Jim Rossiter, Niladri Sarkar, John Soto, Mike Sowards, John Spencer, Ron Styer, Junie Studer, Randy Thorne, Bill Vellios, George Vellios, James Vellios, Lu Wallace, Barb Wolfe, Michelle, Bryce, Zach and Victoria Wolfe.

Cover design by Adam Pavkov. InDesign technical consultant John Soto. Proofreaders: Barbara Hope, George Hope and Leanne Hope.

Unless otherwise credited, photographs are provided by Washington High School, Massillon, Ohio, The Massillon Tigers Football Booster Club and Massillon Memories Publishing Company.

Preface

A Century of Heroes is the story of the Massillon Tigers, and in many ways is the story of Massillon, Ohio, itself. It is Americana at its best. Through profiles of the players, coaches and other key members of the community, you are exposed to many of Massillon's life-dramas from the past century.

Like Massillon, *A Century of Heroes* revolves around the Massillon Tigers football team, who started as the first professional football power in 1903 and continues as America's most famous high school football program, winners of 22 state championships and 9 national titles.

A Century of Heroes tells the behind-the-scenes stories of Massillon, a former steel town whose population has fluctuated between 30,000-35,000 over the century. Some stories are happy, some sad, some celebratory, some disturbing—much like life itself.

I interviewed hundreds of players, coaches, sportswriters, school superintendents, principals and sports historians in writing a book that will entertain not only diehard Massillon fans but anyone who enjoys slice of life stories about a community with a resolute commitment to excellence that has withstood the test of time.

I benefited greatly from the work of two Massillon men, Robert "Doc" Immel and Junie Studer. Immel provided me access to taped interviews of Massillon coaches who passed away before I began my work. Studer's personal stories and his cataloging of every Massillon high school football game makes him a researcher's best friend.

Foreword

Massillon Star, Ohio State All-American and College Football Hall of Famer

My first memory was at a Massillon-McKinley game. I was living in Canton at the time and I had no idea I would be attending Massillon. But for some reason I was rooting for Massillon. Probably because my dad was head coach at another Canton high school. I just remember it felt like the biggest thing in the world at that time. I think I was in the third grade. Massillon won. I was impressed. It just seemed so much bigger than any high school game that I had ever been to. And with my dad being a coach, I had been to a lot of high school games. This one seemed bigger than high school football.

Chris Spielman went from being the USA Today Player of the Year at Massillon to the College Football Hall of Fame.

PHOTO: OHIO STATE ATHLETICS

That game stuck with me. I wanted to play at the best school I could play at. Fortunately it worked out that we moved to Massillon when I was a freshman and I was able to play at Massillon. I was glad to have that opportunity. I wouldn't trade it for the world. It's a great experience being a player there.

Winning is important to the Massillon players. Winning is very important. Winning is important to the whole town. They understand the tradition. They understand what tradition is. They're raised in a belief that they win and they *should* win and they always will win.

"Winning is important to the Massillon players...Winning is important to the whole town."

Chris Spielman

One of my best friends in the world was Steve Studer. Steve was a star player for Massillon in the early 1970s. Steve took me in at his house. I knew he worked out. I'm 15, I'm not even driving yet. I walked by his house every Saturday night trying to get up the nerve to go in there and ask him if he would teach me. And finally I did. He took me in and I guess I became like a younger brother to him, or protoge or whatever you want to call it. But to this day, without him, I wouldn't be where I am today. I really believe that.

Usually when people find out that I'm from Massillon they'll ask me what it was like. A lot of people shake their heads and can't believe the things I say about all the different booster clubs, how many people go to the games. I remember when I was a sophomore in 1981 they couldn't pass the school levy. Then, finally, whoever makes those decisions said, "The stadium needs repaired and it's not safe to play games in it anymore. If you don't pass the school levy we'll have to play our games in the Rubber Bowl." They had a vote and sure enough the school levy passed. Stories like that. Stories about how many kids go out for football. And how when a boy is born there he gets a football in his crib. All the little traditions. The Obie pins, the live tiger mascot, the swing band. *Everything*. There's nothing like it. And the fact that the whole town enjoys it makes it special. In Columbus you go over six blocks and there's another high school, go over another 10 blocks and there's another high school. There's nothing like Massillon.

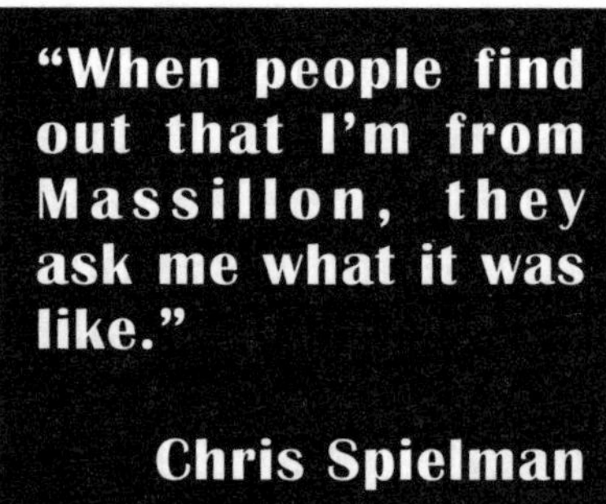
"When people find out that I'm from Massillon, they ask me what it was like."

Chris Spielman

I met my girlfriend, who became my wife, in Massillon. She was from Jackson Township. We would walk on Brookside golf course. We would talk about what we were going to do. That's the great thing about her, she knew me through all that stuff. She knew me like no other person.

Playing at Massillon taught me to have belief in your team. And confidence. It teaches you confidence. I think that's the biggest thing that's stuck with me. And loyalty. I always tried to represent not only myself and my family, but the city the best way I could. And I think people understand that.

I'm proud to have been able to have the opportunity to play there. I'm proud to say I played at Massillon. That's the biggest thing. Every time they ask where I played high school football, I say Massillon, and a feeling of pride comes over me.

It's like something you've never seen or heard of before.

People have to understand how unique it is. I think in *A Century of Heroes* Scott Shook does a nice job of capturing that. It makes you remember the games, playing in that stadium. Any time you have great times somewhere you almost wish you could go back to it sometimes.

54

Chris Spielman

College Football Hall of Famer, 2010

Four-Time Pro Bowler, Detroit Lions, 1988-95

Two-time All-American, Ohio State, 1984-87

Two-time All-Ohioan , All-American, Massillon Tigers, 1981-83

ESPN Color Analyst, Since 2001

Table of Contents

Introduction

Massillon's Proud History Includes Rockne and Brown, Pro and High School Championships

Massillon, Ohio is a city of heroes. Most of them are well-muscled teenagers who don shoulder pads and helmets for Friday night battles every fall. For over a century these post-pubescent warriors have made Massillon the most tradition-rich football town in the USA.

Massillon fans jam Lincoln Way, the town's main thoroughfare, in a snowstorm, to honor their gridiron heroes in 2005.
PHOTO: JOE NAGY

Massillon is located in the southwest corner of northeastern Ohio, about an hour south of Cleveland, on the Tuscarawas River. Through its early days as a wheat port, and its heyday as a world leader in the steel industry, Massillon has forged its identity as a football town. And while the steel industry has died, football remains the lifeblood of the city.

It begins at birth when each baby boy is given a football, and it ends at the grave when diehards are buried in Massillon Tiger coffins.

Luther Emery, Massillon's great sportswriter and newspaper editor expressed it best.

"Football is bred in Massillonians," Emery said. "The native citizen has heard it talked about from the time he opened his eyes in the cradle, and new residents have frequently been bored to tears with the boasts of the old guard until they, too, become convinced that there's something more than usual about the game as it is played here. The whole community enters into the spirit of the thing."

The reason for this undying devotion to their gridiron heroes dates back to the turn of the century when the Pro Tigers were dominating professional football. By the time Massillon was producing its first steel in 1909, its high school was producing its first undefeated football team. A century later, Massillon's high school team has enjoyed 23 undefeated seasons.

"You can go back as long as you want to go back," University of Michigan coaching legend Bo Schembechler said of Massillon's tradition. "That's one school that has been a consistent, traditional powerhouse down through the years. That's one of the greatest high school programs in the nation."

Schembechler, who coached the Michigan Wolverines from 1969-1989, may be looked at as an outsider by many Massillon fans, but he grew up with a great respect for Massillon football and the players who played there.

"What do I know about Massillon? I was born and raised in Barberton, Ohio. Yes, I know all about Massillon. I *know* Massillon, I know Canton McKinley. That's my home.

"Massillon kids were always in a program where they were well coached, well trained. I've coached Massillon kids at Ohio State and Michigan. I've coached 'em everywhere. Back in the '50s when I was with Woody Hayes at Ohio State, I coached linemen Jim Schumacher, Jerry Krisher and Jim Reichenbach. They all came down at the same time. Mike Takacs was already there. They were the Massillon Middle. When you come out of a program like that, these guys are guys who have been around. They know how to play, they're highly competitive, they're used to winning. They know what they're doing."

Massillon teams have maintained a standard of excellence for over a century. When the high school team started playing in 1894, their debut was inauspicious. It was the Pro Tigers who started Massillon's championship tradition.

The Pro Tigers won pro football's first five professional football championships, from 1903-07. In 1915 they shared the title with Canton.

In over 100 years of playing football, whether on the professional, semi-professional or high school level, Massillon has produced All-Ohioans, All-Americans, All-Pros, college head coaches, National Football League head coaches, general managers, and owners.

Massillon has 22 high school state championships, 9 high school national championships, 6 professional football championships, and who knows how many semi-pro championships.

Seven football stadiums in the USA are named after Massillon players and coaches. Paul Brown is probably the only person to have *two* stadiums named after him, Paul Brown Tiger Stadium in Massillon and Paul Brown Stadium in Cincinnati, home of the Cincinnati Bengals.

Lori (Liebermann) Miller with a tray of Tiger Tails. The orange and black striped cream sticks are big sellers at the century-old bakery—Liebermann's—in downtown Massillon. It's an example of how Massillon football permeates the community.

Knute Rockne starred for the Pro Tigers before becoming Notre Dame's legendary coach. He has a stadium named after him in Chicago.

Bill Edwards played during the early years at Massillon and went on to achieve great coaching success. The stadium at Wittenberg University bears his name.

Edwin "Dutch" Hill was Edwards' teammate at Massillon, leading Massillon to its first state championship after starring in Burgettstown, Pennsylvania. The stadium in Burgettstown, where he grew up, bears his name.

Lee Tressel, father of Ohio State coach Jim Tressel, was Massillon's head coach from 1956-57. He left Massillon to begin his legendary coaching career at Baldwin Wallace University, where he had been a star running back. The stadium at Baldwin Wallace is now named Tressel Field.

Bob Commings, Massillon's head coach from 1969-73, has a stadium named after him, too, at GlenOak High School in Canton. Commings coached GlenOak after head coaching stints at Massillon and the University of Iowa.

Earle Bruce, Chuck Mather and Don James probably *should* have stadiums named after them. Both Bruce and Mather are members of the Ohio High School Coaches Hall of Fame. Bruce and James are members of the College Football Hall of Fame. Bruce was selected for his coaching success at Ohio State, Iowa State, University of Tampa and Colorado State. James was elected to the Hall of Fame after his legendary career at the University of Washington, where he led the Huskies to six Rose Bowls and a national championship. The impressive glass-enclosed Don James Center is a vital feature of Huskie Stadium in Seattle.

Massillon may be the most productive coaching cradle

in football history. Two of the most famous coaches of all time, Brown and Rockne, played in Massillon.

Brown, who grew up in Massillon, won championships at the high school, college, and pro levels—14 in all—and may just be the greatest football coach of all time.

Through the years, Massillon has produced hundreds of college players, dozens of NFL players, four NFL general managers and three NFL head coaches.

The College Football Hall of Fame in South Bend, Indiana, has 11 Massillon players or coaches as enshrinees. The Ohio High School Football Coaches Hall of Fame counts 12 Massillon members on its roster.

Six Massillon players have been elected captain at Ohio State. Three Ohio State head coaches were former Massillon coaches. Four former Tigers are Cleveland Browns Legends. Massillon players are often captains of their college teams.

Massillon's love of its football team shows no sign of waning. The tradition just grows stronger with each succeeding generation.

Some say Massillon is a town stuck in the 1950's because of their unbridled enthusiasm for their team and their adherence to tradition.

Maybe that's not such a bad thing.

"Alma Mater"

C.M. Layton

Oh, Alma Mater Massillon,
We stand to sing thy praise
With hearts that thrill with worthy pride
At thoughts of high school days,
Thy friendship true, thy Spirit too, a part of us shall be,
Oh, Alma Mater Massillon, We're true to thee.
And through the long, long years to come,
Wherever we may be,
Oh, Alma Mater Massillon, We're True To Thee

"Carry On For Massillon"

George T. Bird

Carry on for Massillon, fight square,
We ask no odds of any one, that's all,
We ask no odds of any one, play fair,
Play ball!
We're all for one in Massillon
and when the game is won,
we will march with proud hearts ever on
For Mas - sil - lon ....Mas - sil – lon!

The Early Years

Massillon's Tradition Rooted in Pro Tigers Success

Football tradition is woven into the very fabric of life in Massillon, Ohio.

Everywhere you look downtown you see signs—and plenty of them—proclaiming the Massillon Tigers. Storefront display windows contain elaborate football motifs and a painted banner stretches across the town's main thoroughfare encouraging the Tigers. Orange and black flags that proudly inform visitors of Massillon's 22 state championships line both sides of the street all the way through town.

J. J. Wise was a founding father of the Pro Tigers.

Massillon's football tradition goes back so far that even today's most ardent Tiger fans don't realize just how deeply-rooted the tradition is.

The tradition *didn't* start with Paul Brown, the town's favorite son, whose coaching legend at Massillon, at Ohio State, with the Cleveland Browns, and with the Cincinnati Bengals make him, arguably, the greatest football coach of all time.

Sportswriters were already heralding the *Massillon Tradition* when Brown moved to town in 1916. Brown was a childhood fan of the Pro Tigers, and many of the semi-pro teams that flourished in the area.

This 1906 cartoon shows the Massillon Tiger guarding his "bones," symbolizing the professional football championships of 1903-05.

The founding fathers of the 1903-07 Pro Tigers were J. J. Wise, E. J. "Doc" Stewart and J. W. McClymonds.

Yet in Massillon, where anyone in town can regale you with stories about Massillon teams from yesterday and today, you would be hard pressed to find anyone who has heard of Massillon football's founding fathers.

Wise was well respected in Massillon at the turn of the century. He organized a group of 35 local businessmen who met in the Hotel Sailer in downtown Massillon, most likely at the behest of McClymonds. McClymonds was the head of Russell and Co. and one of Massillon's wealthiest and most influential individuals. His residence remains a local landmark today, serving as the site of the Massillon Women's Club on Historic 4th Street.

The Hotel Sailer meeting, on September 3, 1903, laid the groundwork for the Massillon football tradition. Prior to that meeting, Massillon's only football win was a dubious 30-0 victory by the high school team over the Massillon Business College in 1899. Worst of all, the high school team was 0-5 lifetime against Canton Central. These flagging football fortunes are believed to have led to the Hotel Sailer meeting.

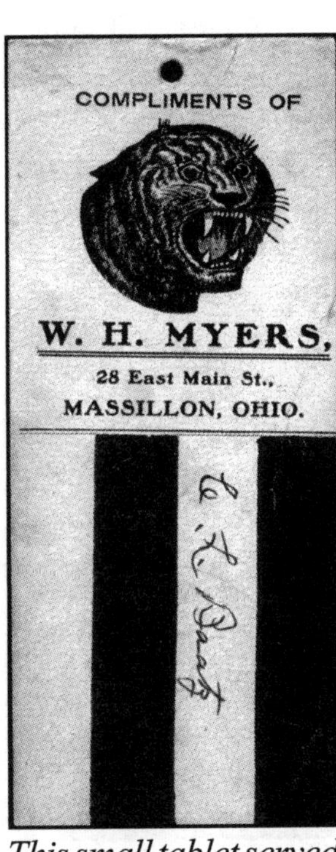

This small tablet served as a program for the 1905 Pro Tigers.

The meeting led to the formation of the original Massillon Tigers.

Legend has it that Massillon became the Tigers because a local sporting goods store had matching jerseys with stripes. The founding fathers bought up the striped jerseys and named the team the Massillon Tigers.

McClymonds was the chief money man, Wise the financial wizard, and the team's manager.

Stewart was the coach and

quarterback. Stewart was also editor of the Massillon newspaper, *The Morning Gleaner*. Stewart's presence ensured the team would have comprehensive media coverage.

Little did anyone know that the seed that sprouted from the Hotel Sailer meeting would still be flourishing in Massillon— and across the USA—over 100 years later.

The original Pro Tigers were comprised of mostly local talent who played for the love of football.

TIGERS

MASSILLON TIGERS.

Wise	(Mgr.)
Wittmann	RE (Capt.)
Stewart	QB (Coach)
Schrontz	LE
McNulty	LT
Kerchoffe	LG
McFarland	LG
Shiring	C
Haag	C
Botoner	RG
Lang	RT
T. Nesser	LT
Merriam	RE
McChesney	RE & RT
Hayden	QB
Bast	QB
Riley	LHB
Matthews	LHB
Moran	FB
Salmon	FB
Miller	FB
J. Nesser	RHB
Featheringham	RHB
Clapper	FB

Roster from 1905 tablet program.

The Pro Tigers were 41-2-1 through their first five seasons, winning the championship each year. They never lost a home game. In 1904 they beat Marion, 148-0.

Legendary sportswriter Luther Emery, who started covering Massillon's high school team in 1923, had many first-hand accounts of the Pro Tigers.

"The Pro Tigers in 1903 got quite a rivalry going with Canton and had pretty good backing," Emery said. "In 1905 it became very hot, the rivalry between the two teams. They say some people would mortgage their homes on the outcome of the games. I don't know about that. My dad saw the game in 1905. I have a program of it. It was like a little penny tablet. It had the pictures of the players in it.

"Irv Whitman, the son-in-law of Jakey (J. J.) Wise told me this story," Emery said. "The story is this: Willie Heston—the University of Michigan star—Massillon thought they had him signed up. But Canton had him signed up. So Mr. McClymonds brought Mr. Wise in and asked, 'Who do you need to beat Canton?' Wise said, 'Well, I think Red Salmon of Notre Dame.'

"McClymonds asked, 'Where is he?' Wise told him that Salmon was working as an engineer on the Holland Tunnel in New York. 'Well, go get him,' replied McClymonds.

"So Wise went to New York. He came back without Salmon," Emery said. "McClymonds was at the railroad station with his best rig, horse and carriage. 'Where's Salmon?' McClymonds asked. 'He wanted too much money,' Wise said. 'Did I mention money?' McClymonds asked. 'No,

The 1905 Pro Tigers were the best of Massillon's champion professional teams.

you didn't,' Wise answered. 'Get on the next train to New York and sign him up for whatever he wants,' McClymonds said. So he did. They paid him $900 to play in the game. Red Salmon didn't come until after he saw the Tigers when they were playing in Cleveland to see what kind of football they were playing. He came to Massillon and they won the game, 14-4. They played on a field in front of the state hospital.

Canton's professional team, represented by a gladiator, and Massillon's by a tiger.

"Canton came over to Massillon with an ambulance carrying a Tiger on it, and they returned on the back roads," Emery chuckled. "In Canton, when they won the game, all the whistles in the manufacturing plants would blow in triumph. So the headline of the Massillon paper the next day was 'The Whistles Were Not Blown.'"

After a seven year hiatus, the Pro Tigers returned in 1915. Emery was also familiar with the second generation of the Pro Tigers.

From 1915-17 the professional game saw Knute Rockne leading Massillon against Jim Thorpe and his Canton teammates. The Tigers were 17-6-2 overall and 2-3-1 against Canton during that stretch.

"They used to come in here Friday night or Saturday morning without their team intact," Emery said. "They usually only practiced Saturday night, maybe in the high school gymnasium or Sunday morning on one of the practice fields. I saw them practice on the Agathon field. The high school team moved from the Meadows field to the Agathon field when the Pro Tigers moved."

In 1909 it was the high school team that was making all the noise. It was the first of Massillon's 23 undefeated high school seasons.

Ducky Schroeder played high school football for Massillon in 1923. He was also an assistant coach from 1948-1970. He had a good feel for why Massillon football has stood the test of time.

"I think it's tradition," Schroeder said. "It started with the old Massillon Pro Tigers. Then the fans transferred their loyalty to the Massillon high school football

The original Massillon Maroons of 1917. The Maroons were probably Massillon's most famous semi-pro team. Relatives of many of these players still reside in Massillon. Front row, Russ Hall, Chet Featheringham, Poss Kannel, Louie Seimetz, Maury Griffith, Hap North, Tink Ulrich. Center row, Jim Graybill, Emmit Graybill, Walt Liebermann, Heck Silverthorn, Bow Liebermann, Bob Featheringham. Back row, Joe Graybill, Walt Hamilton, Vern Giltz, Leo Baus.

team. There seems to be a special breed of people here in Massillon who take a deep interest in their schools and their activities, and they want to be winners. From way back, I've always felt that way. The Massillon people, lots of times, were not satisfied. But they're really a high class of people. They give their kids lots of support. Make good in everything they do. I don't know if that causes a good football team or if that's a result of a good football team. I think it's the fact that the community backs the football program. It's more of a community effort than it is in any other town, possibly. That's the reason Massillon High School's become famous across the United States."

KNUTE ROCKNE

Knute Rockne had not yet gained his greatest fame when he arrived in Massillon with Notre Dame teammate Gus Dorias in 1915.

Quarterback Dorias and end Rockne had just completed their Notre Dame careers when they joined the Massillon Pro Tigers.

Two years earlier the two had worked at Cedar Point, an amusement park in Sandusky, Ohio, and developed their passing game while working as lifeguards on the beach.

They made the forward pass a viable part of the game when they returned to school. In Notre Dame's 35-13 win over Army in 1913 the duo's aerial performance is considered by many to have brought the forward pass into vogue.

Rockne played for and coached the Massillon Pro Tigers.

PHOTO COURTESY OF THE UNIVERSITY OF NOTRE DAME MEDIA RELATIONS DEPARTMENT.

Rockne and Dorias brought the forward pass to pro football from 1915-1917 when they led the Tigers to the championship in 1915.

Canton, who shared the title with Massillon in 1915, was led by the great Jim Thorpe, who was just three years removed from his famous performance in the 1912 Olympics where he won the decathlon. It was at the Olympics that King Gustav V of Sweden told Thorpe, "You sir, are the greatest athlete in the world."

"Knute Rockne used to tell this story himself," said Luther Emery, the longtime Massillon sportswriter.

"Jim Thorpe came around Rockne's end. Rockne played defensive end and later on coached the Tigers.

"Rockne was never a big fella. Thorpe ran with his knees high, almost hitting his chin. They played at the driving park where the Meadows Plaza is now. That was a football field at the time. Rockne tackled Thorpe. Thorpe said, 'You better let Big Jim run.' He came around Rockne's end again and knocked Rockne out. Rockne woke up on the sidelines."

Rockne was named head coach at Notre Dame in 1918, becoming one of the most famous college coaches of all-time. In 13 years as Notre Dame's head coach, Rockne fashioned a 105-12-5 record. Notre Dame won five national championships under Rockne.

Rockne was in his prime, at age 43, when he died in a plane crash on March 31, 1931.

E. J. "DOC" STEWART

E. J. "Doc" Stewart was a true renaissance man. He was fresh out of medical school at Case Western when he helped to organize the Massillon Pro Tigers.

He also coached and quarter-backed the team and was editor of Massillon's newspaper, *The Morning Gleaner*.

"Doc" Stewart was multi-faceted.

After coaching the Tigers to a 41-2-1 record and five championships, Stewart coached football and basketball at several prominent universities across the USA. He coached basketball at Purdue and football and basketball at Oregon State, Nebraska, and Texas. At Clemson he coached football, baseball and track.

In 1923 Stewart led the Texas football team to an 8-0-1 record and the basketball team to a 23-0 finish. His overall football coaching record was 111-38-14.

Stewart founded the Stewart Motor Company between his stints at Nebraska and Texas. While coaching at Texas, he founded Camp Stewart for Boys, which operates today as the oldest continually operated private camp in the Southwest United States. He died when he was accidently shot while deer hunting in Texas in 1929.

"DUCKY" SCHROEDER

Carl "Ducky" Schroeder may be the most beloved coach in Massillon Tigers football history.

Even in a program that is renowned for its history of outstanding assistant coaches, it is Ducky's name that former Tigers players often harken to. But Ducky's introduction to Massillon football came as a player, not as a coach. In 1923, as a youth in nearby Canal Fulton, Ducky came to Massillon to play his senior season.

"I made some sort of a reputation in Canal Fulton, so that Massillon became interested in my ability and asked me if I would like to play there," Schroeder said. "Massillon was blazing a trail of glory at that time. If there was anyone I wanted to play with at that time, it was Massillon. In the area surrounding Massillon, you could say that about any boy. I was lucky enough to have a chance to do that. If I hadn't played at Massillon, I would have never received a chance to go to college."

Ducky Schroeder as a player at Massillon. Note the misspelling of his name.

After a successful playing career at

Massillon and Wittenberg College, Ducky was disappointed when he was not chosen for Paul Brown's staff at Massillon in 1932.

"He wouldn't let me in," Ducky said of Brown. "I wanted him to hire me. I liked Paul Brown and I wanted to get in with him. But I didn't get in."

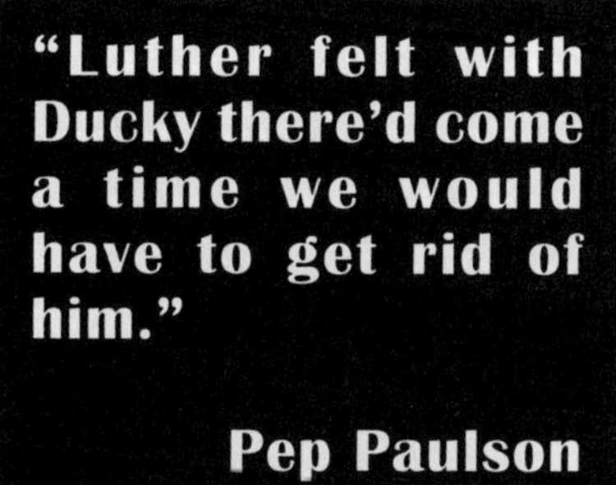

Ducky finally got a spot on the Massillon coaching staff when he was hired by Chuck Mather in 1948. The Tigers were 57-3 from 1948-1953.

Despite being an outstanding assistant under Mather, Ducky was dealt another coaching heartache. He was overlooked for the head coaching job at Massillon when Mather left for University of Kansas in 1954.

Schroeder actively sought the job. He told *Akron Beacon Journal* sportswriter Loren Tibbals that while he was interested in the job, he wouldn't campaign for it. "I'm here," Schroeder told Tibbals. "The people who will have to name Mather's successor know I'm here...I would be willing to serve."

"I had been counseled by Luther Emery," said Pep Paulson, who was on the hiring committee that hired Tom Harp as Mather's replacement. "Luther felt with Ducky there'd come a time we would have to get rid of him. Ducky was such a nice guy and such a likeable guy that it would be tough to fire him. He may have done the job very well. I dearly loved Ducky, but whether he would have done well as the head person, I don't know. I don't think he would have."

Massillon head coach Earle Bruce (1964-65) remembers when Ducky taught him a lesson in his final game as a Massillon coach. "Canton McKinley was ahead of us 14-0 going into halftime," Bruce said. "When I walked in the locker room I was *down.* To think that we're down 14 to *nothin'*. I looked at Ducky and said, 'Holy man, are we playing bad.' Ducky said, 'Coach, we've got another half.' I said, 'Ducky, you don't come back two years in a row against a team like McKinley.' Ducky said, 'Massillon can do it, coach.' I said, 'Ducky, the odds are tremendous this won't happen.' We went back out and won 18-14."

"Ducky was the best defensive end coach that I knew of anywhere."

Leo Strang

Leo Strang (1958-63) understood Ducky's importance to the program even before he accepted the head job at Massillon. "I knew Ducky's reputation, and I knew I had to keep a coach at Massillon so I would be able to know what had gone on in certain situations and who the people were that were true boosters that I could go and ask for help in any way. It's very difficult going into a new situation unless you have somebody you can rely on who knows the background and the history. I knew Ducky knew those things better than anyone. Plus, Ducky was the best defensive end coach that I knew of anywhere. I talked to Ducky before I took the Massillon job. I went to his house and talked to him about staying there. When I took the Kent State job I would have liked to have taken Ducky on, but it would have been totally unfair to Massillon. It would have been totally unfair to *him* to ask him because that would have caused a division. I knew that Earle Bruce wanted to keep him."

Schroeder was an assistant at Massillon for 23 years. During that span Massillon won 13 state championships and 5 national titles.

"For most of my career at Massillon I was considered the end and tackles coach," Schroeder said. "I coached other positions, too."

He learned the fundamentals from some of the most famous men in football history.

"In 1928 I demonstrated for Coach Knute Rockne," Schroeder said. "Coach Rockne and I were walking off the field, I'll never forget. I said, 'Coach, would you show me that block again that you were showing out on the field?' He said, 'Sure.' So in the heat of the day, everybody had gone, he stayed out there with me for fifteen minutes and showed me several different blocks that he was using. Then he said, 'By the way, where are you from?' I said, 'Massillon, Ohio, have you heard of it?' He looked at me and said, 'You know I have.' Because he used to play with the old Massillon

Pro Tigers. He asked me some questions, whether I knew Mr. McClymonds and Mr. Wise, who were the owner and general manager of the old Tigers. I told him I heard of them but didn't know them.

"Knute Rockne was the number one public speaker I've ever heard. He was sort of a humble man. When I asked him to show me those blocks, I was just a player at Wittenberg. I was attracted by his humility. When he got up to speak in the Wittenberg Chapel, the place was just jammed, and you could hear a pin drop. He had a way of saying words that was just magnetic."

The next summer, Schroeder also learned from Jim Thorpe and Pop Warner. Pop Warner had Jim Thorpe with him at the same coaching school.

Warner was one of the early coaching legends. He coached Thorpe at the Carlisle Indian school. He won four national championships in a career that spanned 43 years.

Ducky remembered, "Pop Warner was a very fascinating person. I watched Jim Thorpe giving exhibitions on punting, place kicking and drop kicking. I can look back and feel that I really got a good basic knowledge of football from famous men like that."

Ducky passed his knowledge on to Massillon players.

"He was on his way out when I was coming up," said Jeff Huffman, a standout receiver for Massillon in the early 1970s. Huffman later returned to Massillon as an assistant coach. "Ducky was always giving me little tidbits. 'When you catch the ball, try not to make any sound. Make it soft so you don't hear that *smack*.' He always gave me little nuggets like that."

Huffman was able to pass along those lessons to his son Brett, who was All-Ohio at Massillon before becoming a starting tight end at Duke University.

"I tried out with the Cleveland Browns," the elder Huffman said. "I made it to the second round. I had a chance to be a graduate assistant at Bowling Green, because I wanted to get into coaching, but I turned it down so I could try out with the Browns. I thought, 'I've got to give this a shot. I've gotta know. I'm not going to sit back and say, 'what if.' So I gave it a shot and I got cut. When I got home I called Ducky Schroeder and said, 'Ducky, I just got cut. Do you know anybody who needs a coach? And, if they have a teaching job that's even better.'

"Bill Boran was a coach at Steubenville and just got the job at Portsmouth. He called me up and offered me a coaching job. Never even met me. He said, 'If Ducky's recommending you I know you're a good coach.' So I owe everything to Ducky."

Among the honors Ducky has received is his inclusion in the Ohio High School Coaches Association Hall of Fame, one of 12 Massillon coaches so honored.

Ducky Influenced Players/Coaches

Ducky Schroeder embodied the role of the veteran Massillon assistant. Ducky counseled head coaches throughout his 23 years as a Tiger assistant coach.

A head coach at Wittenberg College, Ducky is the standard-bearer for the fine line of Massillon assistants who were formerly head coaches.

Ducky Schroeder, 1967.

"On any good coaching staff, all the coaches must have input," Ducky said. "My experience as a head coach helped along those lines. It makes you a better assistant."

"Ducky'd tell you just what he had to tell you, then he'd take you out there and you would *do* what he wanted you to do," said two-time All-Ohioan Hase McKey."

Another Massillon Tiger, tough lineman Jim Houston, who starred at Ohio State and with the Cleveland Browns, recalls Ducky. "I can still see Ducky giving us the cadence and hollering, 'Hit, hit,' the saliva coming out of his mouth. I didn't like it at all, he worked our buts off."

JOHN SNAVELY

John Snavely is a man of firsts in Massillon football history. Starting out as a high school football player in 1907, Snavely played right end for the first Massillon team to tie Canton. The 0-0 tie was greatly celebrated as a "moral" victory for Massillon, who had lost their first 11 games to Canton. It was not until their 15th try, in 1908, that Massillon finally beat Canton, 12-6. Snavely was the starting right halfback on *that* team. Snavely was involved in two more firsts in 1914 when he became the first former Massillon player to become the team's head coach. That appointment also made Snavely the first head coach of the newly christened Washington High School.

Perhaps his most famous *first* came when he coached Massillon's first undefeated, untied team in 1916. Snavely proclaimed his 10-0-0 Tigers state champions in 1916 after they finished the season with a 16-9 win over Canton.

Massillon historians, however, consider the 1922 squad Massillon's first state champions. Ironically, Snavely was also a central figure in *that* Massillon first.

Snavely proclaimed his 10-0-0 Tigers state champions in 1916.

Snavely left Massillon after the 1919 season and was coaching Cleveland Shaw—who was considered a state power when they visited Massillon in 1922. Massillon's landmark 7-6 win over Snavely's Shaw squad that day led to the Tigers first state championship.

Snavely was a very active student at Massillon High School. In addition to playing football, he was a pitcher and left fielder on the baseball team, a member of the debate team and a writer for the yearbook.

After high school Snavely attended Otterbein College. He returned to Massillon as an assistant to Sidney Jones in 1913, becoming head coach the following season.

Snavely was a young, hands-on coach at Massillon, who would often mix it up with his players during practice. In Snavely's first three years the Tigers posted a 24-3 record with 18 shutouts, while outscoring their opponents 623-72. His overall record at Massillon was an impressive 41-8-2 from 1914-19.

Snavely's 1916 charges

scored 318 points while yielding only 38.

A year earlier, his 1915 team started with eight straight wins and were unscored on before losing a heartbreaker, 7-6, to Canton, in the season finale.

Among Snavely's pupils was Harry Stuhldreher, who quarterbacked Snavely's last Tiger squad in 1919. That team finished 8-1, beating Canton McKinley 21-0, despite playing with its third team quarterback after Stuhldreher and back-up Chuck Hess were injured. Snavely's only loss that season was to state power Toledo Scott, 21-14. Stuhldreher went on to fame as the All-American quarterback of the Four Horsemen of Notre Dame.

Snavely as a Massillon player in 1908. Snavely became Massillon's high school coach in 1914.

Snavely created a groundswell of interest in the high school Tigers, who had long played in the shadow of the Pro Tigers.

"Jack Snavely was a good coach," Massillon sportswriter Luther Emery said. "I'd say the build-up of high school football in Massillon came in his days. They had football before, but the interest started to take over then."

When Snavely brought his undefeated Shaw team to

Massillon in 1922, Massillon's squad was being touted as its strongest since Snavely's 1916 squad. The 1922 Massillon-Cleveland Shaw battle is considered one of the great games in Massillon's glorious history.

Shaw scored in the second quarter and led 6-0 with two minutes remaining. Only a super-human effort by Massillon's star running back, Edwin "Dutch" Hill, saved the day for Massillon. Hill's touchdown with seconds remaining tied the score at 6-6. Another Massillon legend, Bill Edwards, kicked the winning extra point to give Massillon its landmark win. Edwards went on to an outstanding coaching career with the Detroit Lions, Vanderbilt University and Wittenberg University, where he achieved legendary status.

Late in his 17-year coaching career at Shaw, Snavely again played Massillon. This time he was humbled by the legendary Paul Brown 46-0 in 1934 and 66-0 in 1935.

DAVE STEWART

"Dave Stewart was a big, long lanky guy from Pennsylvania. He was a bachelor," said Bud Houghton, describing Massillon's head coach from 1921-25. Houghton, a former Massillon head coach himself (1941, 1946-47), played under Stewart.

"Paul Brown and I were a couple of his favorites. He used to take us around with him. He'd take us to movies, stuff like that. We were kind of his kids, I guess."

Stewart as Massillon coach.

Stewart coached Massillon's first state championship team in 1922. Perhaps more importantly, Massillon's lanky leader gave Brown his first chance as a player *and* as a coach.

"I could throw, and that's what intrigued Dave," Paul Brown said. "Throwing the ball then was a little more daring than it is today."

Stewart's first introduction to Brown came during Brown's freshman year. Stewart was holding a football camp at Turkey Foot lake. Brown's father took his diminutive son to the try-outs.

"In those days it was the custom of the coach to take his quarterback around with him. Rockne set the style. He used to take Stuhldreher up to Cedar Point. That started this trend. Dave used to take me around with him. That was an education for a young guy. My mother and father thought if I happened to be with Dave Stewart, everything was in good hands.

Dave Stewart.

"We'd ride and talk about, 'what would you do here, what would you do there.' It was helpful."

"Dave made me enjoy coaching. I used to go over to Sharon before I went back to college in the fall and help him out. I was just obsessed with it. I enjoyed it. I was a goner. He recognized this."

Stewart came through for Brown again in 1930 after Brown had graduated from Miami University.

"Dave took the trouble to tell Severn Prep about me," Brown said. "I was one of the few guys in college to get a job coming out.

"Then, when the job at Massillon came open, Dr. Bell, the president of the school board, called Dave and said, 'Who do you think we should hire here?'

"Dave said, 'That's easy—Brown.' Dr. Bell had a lot of faith in Dave Stewart. I got the job."

Stewart was 38-9 in his five years at Massillon. He had a 4-1 record against arch-rival Canton McKinley. He is also noted for recording the highest point total in Massillon history when his 1922 championship squad beat Akron North 94-0.

Stewart may have had a second undefeated state championship team in 1924 if not for a forfeit at Youngstown South.

Stewart pulled his team off the field after a series of bad calls against the Tigers. Harry Gorrell, Superintendent of Schools, was at the game and backed his coach. Gorrell severed relations with Youngstown South saying the officiating "makes impossible games between the two schools for some time to come." The rival teams did not play again until 1934 when Massillon won, 45-0.

Stewart left Massillon and coached Sharon, Pennsylvania, High School for 20 years. He squared off against his old pupil Brown twice while at Sharon.

In Brown's second year at Massillon he beat Stewart's Sharon team 27-0. Stewart led his 1937 team to an unbeaten record and hosted Brown in 1938. This time Brown turned back his former mentor's team 37-20.

ARVINE "TINK" ULRICH

To know about Arvine "Tink" Ulrich, you need only look at his early childhood in Massillon's west side, circa 1912. Ulrich was part of a tough bunch of neighborhood kids who were always playing sandlot football games. But amongst the group, no one had a football. "I got started rather young in football," Ulrich said, "we played with just a stick and we would throw it."

Arvine "Tink" Ulrich, quarterback of Massillon's first state championship team in 1922.

From those skirmishes in his under-privileged neighborhood, Ulrich graduated to semi-pro football at the tender age of 13—suiting up for perhaps the most famous semi-pro team in Massillon history.

"I was on the original Massillon Maroons football team," Ulrich said. He shared the center position with Walt Featherington. Ulrich played on the line because of his toughness, not his size.

Ulrich said, "I wasn't very big."

Young Ulrich wasn't trying to make a living by playing football, nor were his adult teammates. "The only money we got was what money was gathered by passing the hat down at the field."

Young Ulrich wasn't trying to make a living by playing football, nor were his adult teammates.

Ulrich, a future Massillon leading citizen as head of the water company, was a troubled youth. In 1918 he entered Massillon High School, hoping to play football there. Harry Gorrell, who became an outstanding Superintendent of Schools in Massillon, was the high school principal when Ulrich first strolled in. "The secretary for Mr. Gorrell stopped me in the hall and said, 'Mr. Gorrell wants to see you in his office.'" Ulrich's reputation had preceded him.

"I walked in and Mr. Gorrell was sitting there reading a pamphlet and he didn't seem to be paying attention to me, so I got up to walk out. He said, 'Where are you going young man? You were asked to come up here to see me.' I said, 'Yes sir.' He said 'I just wanted to have a conversation with you and warn you. The first wrong move that you make in this school, out you go. We have a report of your record from Mr. Bowers at Lorin Andrews, and you were somewhat of a little problem down there. We're hoping to straighten you out.'"

Gorrell was not an immediate success with Ulrich, who

struggled in school and was ineligible to play football in 1918 and 1919. Fortunately, another important figure was about to enter Ulrich's life. John Snavely, Massillon's head coach, was shooting pool at the Brunswick Pool Hall when he encountered Ulrich, who was skipping school.

"He said, 'Tink Ulrich, what are you doing here?' I said, 'I just dropped in to watch you play billiards, Coach.' Snavely said, 'Aren't you supposed to be in school?' I said, 'I had study hall this period.' He said, 'Don't you go to study hall?' I said, 'I'm supposed to, but I didn't go today.' He said, 'You don't go to class sometimes, either, do you?' Sheepishly I said, 'No, I guess not.' He said, 'You like to play football, don't ya? Well, you know you're never going to play with the high school if you keep behaving like you're behaving. You just seem to be going in the wrong direction.' After he talked to me for about 10 or 15 minutes, he had me bawling. I got up off that chair and I went back down to the high school. From that day on I never missed a day in school. He just turned me around. I owe everything I became in life to those two men, Gorrell and Snavely. Without them I may have ended up digging ditches for the water company instead of running it."

Snavely planted the seed, but he didn't get to see Ulrich grow under his tutelage. "Snavely left in 1919. He went to Shaw High School in Cleveland," Ulrich said. "We all hated to see him go."

When Ulrich finally played football for Massillon, in 1920, his head coach was a tremendous disappointment. "They hired a man named Elmer Snyder, who I don't think had any coaching experience at all. And it's a shame, because we had some real good material. Half of the time he wasn't even out to practice. One game (Akron West) he was supposed to meet the team in Akron. Mr. Gorrell went with the team. Snyder never showed up until the middle of the third quarter. Mr. Gorrell had to do the coaching for us."

"I owe everything I am to those two men, Gorrell and Snavely. Without them I may have ended up digging ditches for the water company instead of running it."

"Tink" Ulrich

Things improved dramatically in 1921. "Mr. Dave Stewart came in and he was one of our great coaches," Ulrich said.

While Stewart started turning things around in 1921, the Tigers still took their lumps, enduring a 5-4 season. Their most stinging defeat was a 68-0 loss to state power Dayton Steele. "I remember I went down on crutches and Chuck Hess came back on the same crutches."

Hess and Ulrich, lifelong friends, were Stewart's captains, Hess in 1921 and Ulrich in 1922.

Everything came together for Ulrich and the Tigers when they won Massillon's first state championship in 1922. Ulrich, considered one of the fastest backs in the state, led the championship squad to a 31-0 win over Steele as its quarterback *and* captain.

The win over Steele got Massillon statewide attention. "We were prepared for them," Ulrich said. The 1922 Tigers ripped through the majority of their schedule. "We were undefeated that year, we won 10 games. We set some records. We scored 379 points and we only had 28 scored against us. We beat Akron North 94-0."

The biggest game of the year came in Week 7 against Cleveland Shaw. "Our closest game was against Shaw. Jack Snavely was the coach there. We beat 'em 7-6. It was odd playing against Coach Snavely. In fact after the game I went over and talked to him. I said, 'Coach, I'm happy we won, but if there was any one coach in the world I didn't want to see get beat, it was you. I hated to see you lose.' He put his arm around me and gave me a good hug and said, 'I'm happy that you straightened out and are going to school now and doing such a good job.'"

Ulrich played college football at Grove City, in Pennsylvania, but he left there after two knee surgeries. That's how he got his start at the Massillon water company.

"I went to work at the water company for a whole year. In 1925 Wittenberg College took a whole group of us from Massillon down to play."

"Bill Edwards came in when I was a junior at Wittenberg. He came over from Ohio State. They just didn't take good care of him down there. Bill apparently skipped some classes and ran around with guys like Tarzan Taylor and some other guys who had graduated. So Bill didn't make his grade and was ineligible to play. He entered Wittenberg as a freshman during my junior year." Another Massillon legend joined Ulrich at Wittenberg. "Ducky Schroeder went down with us, too. Ducky played fullback. Edwards played center and linebacker. He was one of the greatest linebackers I've ever seen for his weight."

"I told Jim Thorpe I was from Massillon and that I'd seen him play when he was with the Bulldogs in Canton...he was everything they claimed he was."

"Tink" Ulrich

Ulrich's leadership abilities off the field were recognized at Wittenberg. "I was president of my senior class in college. I was in charge of camp fire activities. I got Jim Thorpe to come over, he was playing professional football at Marion, Ohio, at the time. I told him I was from Massillon and that I'd seen him play when he was with the Bulldogs in Canton. He came over and did a terrific job. He wore a big helmet he had brought along. The Indian pants. And he sat cross-legged like an American Indian at the camp fire and talked to the boys. He was everything they claimed he was. He was firmly built."

After college, Ulrich returned to his job at the Massillon water company. "I made superintendent of the water company when I was just 10 months out of college. I never went through anything like that in my life. People would come in during the depression, they couldn't pay their bills. They had no money. I'd say, 'Just pay me *something*.' I had people who owed 18-month delinquent water bills. Watson Dark called me up to his office and said, 'Your accounts receivable are about the worst in our system. You're gonna have to collect these bills or we're going to have to have somebody collect them for you.' That's just a nice way of tellin' ya to do it or else. I knew all these people. Women would come in cryin'. I got tough. I sent a letter to every one of the delinquent accounts and said they'd have to pay something on their account or I would have to shut them off. I don't think I lost any friends. I got the accounts paid up."

Ulrich was the first president of the Massillon Booster Club in 1934. "The Booster Club was the result of a request by Paul Brown. We got the enthusiasm started and we had some wonderful members. It cost you 25 cents to join—it was depression time. I think we had around 100 members, and $25 doesn't go that far, but it did go a long ways in those days and it helped a lot. We were able to provide the needs that were required using our membership dues, a game program and extra help from our more prosperous members. I think the Booster Club is the most successful and one of the first in the state of Ohio and this part of the country."

ELWOOD KAMMER

Elwood Kammer's influence is interwoven throughout the history of Massillon football in a way that is perhaps the most unique of all Tiger greats.

From All-Ohio running back, to junior high head coach, to state championship head coach, to semi-pro coach and back to assistant coach, Kammer's gridiron resume at Massillon spans five decades.

Kammer first gained fame in Massillon as a hard-running ball carrier and an outstanding defensive back.

Elwood "Cannonball" Kammer, Massillon's first All-Ohio selection, circa 1925.

In fact he was the first Massillon player to be named All-Ohio in 1925, the inception of the award.

He returned to his hometown of Massillon as a junior high coach for Paul Brown after a great playing career at Grove City College.

In Massillon's highly competitive three junior high system, Kammer developed his coaching legend as head coach of the west side school, Lorin Andrews.

Barney Wallace was the second of three brothers to play under Kammer at Lorin Andrews.

"That was our coach all through Lorin Andrews," Wallace said. "This guy was a friend of the family. My mother talked to him more than I ever talked to him. She had three kids who were comin' up under him."

In the late 1930s there was a great rivalry between Lorin Andrews and the northeast side school, Longfellow. A socioeconomic divide was felt by the players and their coach at Lorin Andrews.

"We used to get tee'd off because we thought he was working us too hard," Wallace said. "But he wanted us to be the best. He was trying to be better than Longfellow. Bud Houghton was up there. He didn't like Bud Houghton. And Bud Houghton didn't like him. When it comes to a fight, Kammer could beat Bud Houghton. He slugged him a couple of times, one time when they got into it. Kam was a type that he didn't take nobody's crap. He was a tough old guy. Houghton thought he was a tough guy but he found out he wasn't. But Kammer treated his players good. We loved Kammer. The poor people liked him, because he had all their kids. We didn't like Houghton, we thought he was a rich guy. The rich people didn't like Kam. He didn't care for them, either. He used to call the Longfellow players the cake eaters. He said 'We've gotta play the cake eaters on the east side so you'd better be ready.'"

Houghton acknowledged the rivalry with Kammer. It was a rivalry that came to a head when Paul Brown took the head coaching position at Ohio State following the 1940 season. The three finalists for the Massillon post were his three junior high coaches; Houghton, Kammer and Mel Knowlton, who coached at Jones Junior High.

> **"Kam was a type that didn't take nobody's crap.""**
>
> **Barney Wallace**

"It created so much tension between the three junior high coaches," Houghton said. "Really, I never applied for the job. It ended up they selected me over the other two guys. Kammer stayed on with me as an assistant in 1941. Mel wanted to be a head coach and took the job down at Steubenville.

"Kammer was slipshod. He was a heck of a nice guy, but his teams were not real organized. Kammer had been quite a star in high school and college. I think that sometimes those guys who were outstanding themselves don't make as good a coach. They don't realize how important it is to learn the little details. To stick with it, to work on things. If you have a lot of natural ability, which he did, you don't have to work on those things."

Houghton's relationship with Kammer started in childhood. Houghton thinks Kammer's mother influenced his development.

"He was a hardnosed kid," Houghton said. "He lived right across the street from me on Woodlawn. We used to play a lot out on the side lot. I remember next to Kammer's house was an alley. He and I used to go out there and play fungo bat. I remember one day I hit one too hard and it went through his mother's window. She came running out and really started raising heck with him. I ran home. She was rough on him. I think she helped make him tough."

Losing the competition for the head job at Massillon was a great disappointment for Kammer. Making it even more unpalatable perhaps was that Houghton—who was a back-up player at Massillon and a less accomplished junior high school coach—was given the job.

"Kammer made quite a push for the job," Houghton said. "He had a lot of people backing him, because he had been a heck of a lot better player than me in high school. He had followers in Massillon. Kammer really campaigned for the job. I didn't think he'd stay on as an assistant. Mel and I got along a lot better than Kam and I. I don't think he resented me getting the job as much as Kam did. At the time I would have been happy if Kammer had gone somewhere else, but he didn't. I was really surprised when I got the job."

Houghton won the state title in 1941. When he entered the military the following season, Kammer was given his chance at the top spot. As head coach, Kammer stretched Massillon's state record unbeaten streak to 52 straight games before a 35-0 loss to Canton McKinley in the 1942 season finale.

Bob Graber was the quarterback and star of the 1942 team. Over 60 years later, memories of the McKinley loss remain painful.

"Don't ask me about that game," Graber said. "That was an experience where you can't do nothin', nothin' works for ya. When I had a bad ankle for the McKinley game Kammer had me tape one ankle high and keep the other one down. The good leg he taped high, figuring they'd go after it. It didn't help me runnin' any. They had a doctor who wanted to shoot it with novocaine because I couldn't run on it or anything. My dad wouldn't let 'em. I wasn't worth a darn. I got to play, but it wasn't the same. I was off two weeks with a bad ankle. I shouldn't have played at all. It was bad."

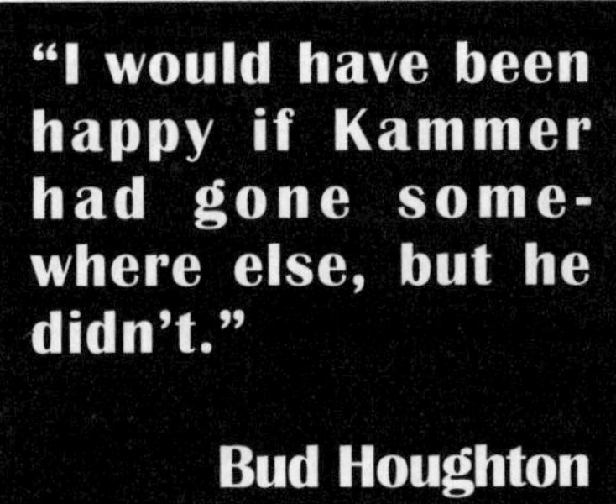

Graber liked Kammer as a coach, but he didn't care for Paul Brown. As one of the few sophomores on the 1940 team, Graber was a third stringer on Brown's last Massillon squad. In practice, Brown would have him square off against Horace Gillom, Ohio's player of the year. "He put me in some tough situations," Graber said. "I guess I weighed 125-130 pounds, and he always had Gillom coming out clipping me. I was always the guy he put on with Gillom. But I liked Elwood Kammer. He really knew his football. If he cussed you out or something he'd just say 'You ain't worth a pint of owl pee.' "

Kammer came back from the disappointing loss to McKinley with one of Massillon's finest defensive teams. Captained by running back Bob Wallace, the 1943 Tigers ran the table, finishing 10-0 and winning the state championship. The '43 Tigers gave up only 12 points all season. A season-ending 21-0 shutout of Canton McKinley helped ease the pain of the 1942 loss to their hated rival. The future looked bright heading into the 1944 season for Kammer and the Tigers.

The 1944 season got off to an auspicious start with a 60-7 win over Akron West in the opener. It looked like another championship season was at hand. But a 6-0 loss in Week 2 to Cleveland Cathedral Latin and a disappointing 27-0 shutout loss to Canton contributed to the Tigers 7-3 record and led to Kammer's ouster prior to the 1945 season. His replacement, Augie Morningstar, had starred as captain of Paul Brown's first state championship squad in 1935.

Rampant rumors made it appear that Massillon's flagging football fortunes were not the only reasons why Kammer was fired. Morningstar was serving as Kammer's assistant coach in basketball when the axe fell on Kammer.

"We were coaching a basketball game. And I was really shocked, because I was Kam's assistant and we were sittin' there talkin', tryin' to win the ball game," Morningstar said. "One of the board members come down and said, 'Come on, I want to talk to you.' I said, 'We've got a ball game. I can't leave,' and I sat back down. He got a hold of me and said, 'Come on with me. We've got to talk to you.' So they were having a board meeting and they took me up and asked me if I'd take over. I thought, 'Oh, something's happened, maybe Kam's got another job or somethin'. I said 'Yeah,' rather than have someone else come in and change everything.

"So they hired me that night and that was it. I never knew what happened. There were a lot of rumors going around. But you know rumors, they'll kill ya sometimes. Kammer, he was a happy-go-lucky turkey. He had a lot of fun. We'd go to a coaching clinic together and he'd say, 'You take notes, I'll be back in a little while.' Well, I might not see him for four or five hours. I couldn't figure it out because he wasn't a poker player. If he'd have been playing cards someplace I would have known about it. He liked to play."

Kammer with Henry Mastrianni after the 1943 McKinley game, a 21-0 Massillon win.

Junie Studer, who worked as a statistician with the basketball team when Kammer coached, remembers Kammer coming into his father's waffle shop late at night. "He was different," Studer said, "and I think all of the stories that remain about Kam are off-beat. He was noted as being a ladies' man. We were open all night at the waffle shop and he'd come in at two in the morning and he'd have lipstick on his cheeks...it was obvious."

Wallace acknowledged the rumors. "Everybody was always on him because he was always going with these women and he was married. A lot of people was teed off about that. They criticized him for that. The things he did probably shouldn't have been done where he did 'em. The kids never thought nothin' of it. The kids all liked him. But he was a womanizer."

Kammer moved on to the Massillon Chevrolets, then the Tigertown Stars, two successful semi-pro teams made up of former Massillon high school players. The Tigertown Stars also featured former NFL players. "You had guys like Maurice Basset who were over the hill. He was a fullback with the Cleveland Browns," Studer said. "We had some guys with names. But I really think the Billy Stones and the Joe Jones'—the Massillon guys—were the most dependable and probably the best football players.

"I remember Kam coming in after the game and everybody's sitting there and it's pretty quiet for this group, because it's different, it isn't high school anymore," Studer said. "Kam walks in and everything gets real quiet. And Kam says, 'Football team my ass.' That was the after-the-game speech. That's all he said."

Kammer may be best remembered for his stint as an assistant coach, starting during Chuck Mather's regime.

Lee Nussbaum, a bruising running back on the 1951 and 1952 teams, remembered

Kammer as a bit of an outlaw.

"He was from the old school," Nussbaum said. "He said 'You stick the fist in 'em, you don't use the stiff arm.' He was the guy, if you wanted to use a knee, an elbow, you go right ahead. If you want to use the heel in the guy's jaw, that's all right. He was from the old school, he played thc old way. Now, he didn't teach biting, but he wouldn't have minded. He was a tough coach. Between Mather and Kam it was a whole different philosophy. There was no conflict between him and Mather. But I know one thing, he would have never gotten away with it if Mather would have caught him. When we were working one on one, he'd say, 'Now here's how we did it back in Grove City.' He was the only one who taught hardnosed, tough football. Mather taught football, but he taught technique, timing. Kam just said, 'Blast 'em. Anyway you can get him. Hook him, trip him.' Just hard-nosed football."

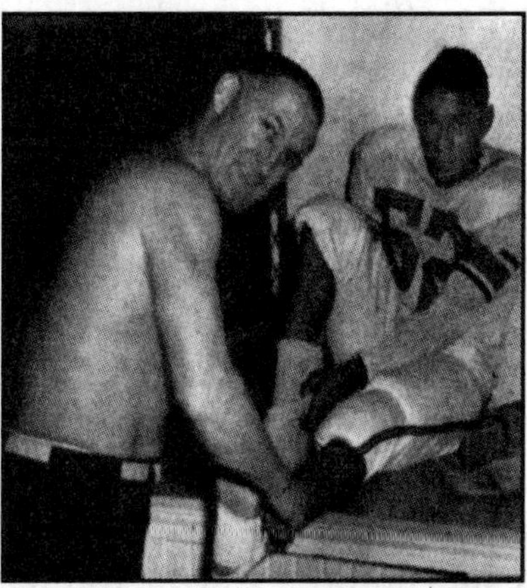

Kammer tapes the ankle of star running back Johnny Traylor in 1953.

Ivory Benjamin, a star running back under Lee Tressel (1956-57), remembers tips he received from Kammer.

"Elwood Kammer was a little crooked, but he was a

smart man," Benjamin said. "He knew how to do it. They made silk pants for me. And I never wore the long socks. My legs would be full of grease. He greased me up. All you could do is grab and slide. Someone on the other team told the officials they couldn't hold on to me. So the officials stopped the game and checked me out. They made me wipe the stuff off me. Coach Tressel didn't even know it."

Kammer also knew how to get players ready mentally.

"Kammer told me before we went to Barberton, 'I'm going to tell you somethin', these guys are in for you. They're going to say they've been to bed with your mother. Your sister. They're going to call you a black so and so. So look for this, because they're going to try to get you out of the game. He told me exactly what was going to happen. Well, I made 500 yards that night, they took about 200 yards of that back. I was on the sideline laughin', because I couldn't help myself. He told me *exactly* what was going to happen.

"He'd show us what to do. 'Now you don't do this 'til Friday night. You don't do this in practice, coaches ain't goin' for it.' But on Friday night you'd go and do what he showed ya. You hurt somebody. He showed ya how to hurt people. That's the way he taught us. He was the best."

Kammer and His Sidekick "Duke"

Those who knew Elwood Kammer also knew his basketball-dribbling dog Duke.

"He spoke with a bit of a lisp," Junie Studer said, "I don't know that he even realized it.

"He had a dog. The dog's name was Duke. But Kam couldn't pronounce Duke. It was always "Doot." Somebody in practice would drop a pass and Kam would yell, "Doot could catch a ball better than that."

"That dog could dribble a basketball," Augie Morningstar said. "The kids couldn't catch him. He'd throw the ball out on the basketball court. He'd hit it with his nose and he'd dribble that ball all over the place. The kids would chase him. Kammer would sit there and laugh."

Kammer and "Duke."

"He used to go to the Alibi bar after he was older," Lee Nussbaum said. "Take his dog for a walk. He'd take Duke and go to the Alibi. Kam loved his booze."

EDWIN "DUTCH" HILL

Massillon's first state title was delivered upon the broad shoulders of Edwin "Dutch" Hill.

Hill possessed movie star good looks with the personality to go with it. But his tragic death robbed us of the chance to know just how brightly his star would have shone.

Edwin "Dutch" Hill was a triple-threat back.

Hill arrived in Massillon in 1922 from the tiny hamlet of Burgettstown, Pennsylania, where he is so legendary that the football stadium bears his name. And despite playing only the 1922 season for the Tigers, he was the unquestioned star of the team.

"That was the year of Dutch Hill," said Arvine "Tink" Ulrich, who was the team's quarterback and captain. "Pennsylvania had a 20-year age limit in high school and Ohio had a 21-year limit. The coach at Burgettstown was a friend of Dave Stewart's and they wanted to see Hill get a chance to play because he was an outstanding athlete and had a chance to go to college on his athletic ability. So he came to Massillon and stayed with teammate Junie Weirich in the Weirich's home. Hill was about 175 pounds and he was the most perfect physical example of a young high school athlete that I've ever seen. He had a wonderful physique. Broad shoulders, powerful legs."

"He was a big star," said Bud Houghton, a former Massillon player and head coach. Houghton was a youngster when he and childhood friend Paul Brown—who became Massillon's legendary coach—watched Hill dominate Massillon's opposition. "He was just a big burly guy. Kind of had a swaggering walk," Houghton said.

"Dutch Hill was a powerhouse," classmate Tom McConnaughy said. "He would take the ball and plow through the other team, knocking them right and left."

Hill was best known as a line plunger—a pure power runner. "He normally plowed over everybody," Houghton said. "They didn't pass much in those days. It was mostly running and defense."

Ulrich concurred, "We very rarely threw the ball. You couldn't grip the ball, it was like a basketball."

But Hill was a true triple threat at Massillon. In addition to his running skills, Hill was considered the finest punter in the state. And it was his passing ability that was key in Massillon's landmark come-from-behind win over Cleveland Shaw.

Hill was so ill that he had to leave the game near the end

of the second quarter, not to return until late in the fourth quarter. With Massillon trailing 6-0, and less than two minutes left to play, Hill summoned up his last bit of strength.

Starting from his 36-yard line, Hill fired a 15-yard pass to Harry Potts on the first play. Another pass to Potts brought the ball to the Shaw 19. Then Ulrich, who later became a pioneer Booster Club leader, called on Hill for six straight running plays.

Ulrich recalled a time when Hill grew a little tired of his workhorse role.

A gain of three, then a 10-yarder gave the Tigers another first down. With less than a minute remaining and the ball on the six yard line, Hill smashed through for three yards. On second down Hill battled for another yard. A third down plunge left the ball resting on the one yard line—fourth and goal from the one. On his final line plunge Hill disappeared into the line and a huge pile-up ensued. When they unpiled the players, Hill was lying on the ground, a full yard inside the end zone. Twenty-seven seconds remained on the clock and the game was tied 6-6. Then Bill Edwards became the hero. Edwards, the Tigers offensive end, kicker and defensive stalwart, drop-kicked the final point, giving Massillon a 7-6 win.

The crowd of 6,000 fans at Massillon's Pearl Street field swarmed the field, carrying several of the players off the field.

In the Canton McKinley game, Ulrich recalled a time when Hill grew a little tired of his workhorse role.

"McKinley had a real tough ball club," Ulrich said. "We didn't score until late in the third quarter, and in the fourth quarter we scored 24 points against them. I scored the first touchdown and Dutch scored the next three. Whenever we got down close to the goal line we gave the ball to Dutch. We used him a lot. We got down there and he was running in there against Butch Gibson at linebacker. He was one of the toughest, best linebackers they've ever had. Butch was hittin' Dutch and ooh boy. Finally, Dutch came back to the huddle, and I was quarterback, and he said, 'Why don't you run somebody else with the ball once in a while? What's the matter with you or Midge Thomas running with the ball?'"

Edwin "Dutch" Hill.

"I said, 'All the rest of the season you wanted to carry the ball. What's the matter, now you don't want to carry it anymore? Too big a guy over there?' I said it in a kidding way. But Dutch was terrific."

Hill scored 34 touchdowns in 1922—still a Massillon record. His eight touchdowns against Akron North is also a record. He scored five times against Cambridge, three times each against Warren, Canton McKinley, Barberton and Youngstown South.

At his funeral, Chick Meehan said that he had planned to build the 1929 backfield around Hill.

Hill played a year at Bellefonte Academy prep in Pennsylvania before rejoining his high school coach from Burgettstown, Dale Sprankle, at Adrian College in Michigan for a season. He then moved to New York University, a football power at the time under legendary coach Chick Meehan.

In an era where an athlete's college eligibility was not tracked as fastidiously as it is today, Hill entered NYU as a freshman. That year he rushed for four touchdowns, passed for two more and kicked two extra points in a single game.

He spent the next two seasons blocking for NYU's All-American running back Ken Strong, who was inducted into the Pro Football Hall of Fame in 1967, along with Massillon's Paul Brown. According to Jim Dallara, a Pennsylvania sportswriter, Strong praised Hill's blocking in his induction speech, saying "If it were not for Dutch Hill, I'd have been an ordinary halfback."

Following his junior season at NYU, Hill was killed. An Associated Press story dated May 8, 1929 said Hill was "shot and killed in a playful struggle for a policeman's revolver." The policeman, Joseph Green, told the AP that Hill and teammate John Bunyan had stopped at the police booth to talk to him. Hill tried to grab the officer's nightstick, then his revolver. During what was described as a "friendly tussle" the revolver discharged. "The bullet pierced Hill's left breast, killing him instantly," the story said.

Bunyan was quoted in another article saying the two players had "nightly conversations" with Green, who was popular with the student body. In a statement, the university said, "It was a well-known fact that the student was a good friend of Patrolman Green whose pistol was responsible for the fatal shot in what apparently was a moment of joking and playing."

At Hill's funeral, Meehan said that he had planned to build the 1929 NYU backfield around Hill. New York sportswriter Joe Williams said, "The team had been built around Hill in the spring, and the prospects for a winning team were bright. Without Hill in the fall it was necessary to rebuild the team."

The *Pittsburgh Press*, prior to Hill's death, named Hill to its NYU All-Timers team. Press reporter George Trevor described Hill as "a wild, untamed spirit who blocked with an unselfish zest that smoothed the path for others."

HARRY STUHLDREHER

"Outlined against a blue, gray October sky, the Four Horsemen rode again. In dramatic lore, they are widely known as 'Famine, Pestilence, Destruction, and Death.' These are only aliases. Their real names are 'Stuhldreher, Miller, Crowley, and Layden.'"

Harry Stuhldreher, quarterback of the Four Horsemen of Notre Dame.

PHOTO COURTESY OF THE UNIVERSITY OF NOTRE DAME MEDIA RELATIONS DEPARTMENT.

Sportswriter Grantland Rice's famous lead paragraph, inspired by the biblical Four Horsemen of the Apocalypse, would never have been written without Massillon's Harry Stuhldreher, the All-American quarterback of The Four Horsemen of Notre Dame. Stuhldreher led Notre Dame to a 28-2 record from 1922-24 and was the only member of the celebrated backfield to be named All-American.

Stuhldreher led Massillon's 1919 team to a 9-1 record before joining Knute Rockne's charges at Notre Dame. Rockne himself had starred on the gridiron at Massillon as a member of the Pro Tigers—the most dominating team in the fledgling years of the Ohio Professional League—just a handful of years before Stuhldreher joined him at Notre Dame.

Stuhldreher actually spent a year at Kiski Prep, a college preparatory school in Saltsburg, Pennsylvania, before beginning his career at Notre Dame.

"We were kids in high school together," said Chuck Hess, who was a sophomore at Massillon when Stuhldreher was a senior. "Harry never played against Canton McKinley, he always was hurt for one reason or another. But he was a great football player. He went to Kiski one year, but he only went there for one reason. He made up his mind that he was going to be the quarterback at Notre Dame. And he was, of course."

While at Kiski, Stuhldreher honed his football skills and met another individual who would have a great impact on Massillon football. Dave Stewart was an offensive line coach at Kiski who made an impression on Stuhldreher. Stuhldreher informed Massillon about Stewart and Stewart got the job as Massillon's head coach in 1921. Stewart led the Tigers to their first state championship in 1922.

Massillon's longtime sportswriter, Luther Emery, delivered newspapers with Stuhldreher as a Massillon youth.

"I carried newspapers with him," Emery said, "only he

had a pony cart, so he didn't have to carry them on his shoulder.

"He was a very jovial sort of chap," Emery said, "He wasn't very big. He was 5'7" tall and weighed 151 pounds, but he was a good player. He was a pretty good forward passer and a shifty runner. He and Chuck Hess shared the quarterback job in 1919. They were lifelong friends.

"When he was at Notre Dame, the Tigers would start their summer practice before Notre Dame. Stuhlie would come down and work out with the Massillon team."

Stuhldreher was All-American at Notre Dame in 1924.

PHOTO COURTESY OF THE UNIVERSITY OF NOTRE DAME MEDIA RELATIONS DEPARTMENT.

At Notre Dame Stuhldreher was described in a newspaper article dated November 24, 1924 as "the general of the outfit, a veritable Rockne on the field. This keen little player knows the Rockne system upside down and backwards. He possesses rare judgment—especially when within the scoring zone, which presents the real test of a field general."

Rockne once said of Stuhldreher, "Harry made an error of judgment in his sophomore year. He never made another."

Both of Stuhldreher's losses at Notre Dame were to Nebraska. In 1924 Stuhldreher led Notre Dame to their first national championship.

Stuhldreher became head coach of Villanova in 1925, where hc compiled a 65-25-9 record in 11 years. Hess often attended Stuhldreher's games at Villanova.

"When my wife and I lived in Wilmington we used to go up there every Saturday," Hess said. "I remember his wife used to sit next to me with her rosary beads in her hand and say, 'If anything happens, let me know.'"

Stuhldreher became Wisconsin's athletic director and head football coach in 1936. Although he had highlights there, his overall record was a subpar 45-62-6 in 13 years. His finest season was 1942 when his Badgers finished 8-1-1 and finished third in the nation. He also handed Brown the only loss in his march to the 1942 national championship at Ohio State.

Emery covered the 1941 Ohio State-Wisconsin game. It was the first time the two coaches from Massillon coached against each other. Brown prevailed, 42-39.

"My assignment was to go to the Wisconsin locker room after the game and get Stuhldreher and bring him back to this reception we were having for the two coaches," Emery said. "I went in and said, 'I'd like to meet Coach Stuhldreher, where is he?'

They said, 'He's sitting back there cryin'.' I said, 'Cryin'?' They said, 'Oh he always cries when he loses.' So I went back there and sure enough he had his head in a towel crying."

Stuhldreher's friend, Hess, arranged for the Massillon band to play at halftime in place of the Wisconsin band.

"On the way back from a vacation at Yellowstone we went to Hezzy Stuhldreher's house in Madison," Hess said. "I said, 'I understand you're playing Ohio State this year. Are you going to bring your band along?' He said, 'I don't know.' Then he went and rang up somebody on his phone. He came back and said, 'No we're not, it's too far away.' I said, 'Why can't the Massillon band be your band?' He said, 'Wait I'll find out.' He went and rang up the same person on the telephone and came back and said, 'That would be wonderful.' That's how George Bird's band got into the Ohio State-Wisconsin game."

Following his college coaching career, the gregarious Shuhldreher joined U.S. Steel in Pittsburgh as vice-president in charge of industrial relations.

He made appearances with the other members of the famous Four Horsemen backfield. They appeared in Massillon in 1963, visiting the locker room at halftime of the Cleveland East game.

"It may have been their last appearance together," said Tom Straughn, president of the Massillon Tiger Football Booster Club in 1963.

The Four Horsemen were in the area for the opening of the Pro Football

Hall of Fame in Canton.

Stuhldreher wrote two books, *Quarterback Play* and *Knute Rockne: Man Builder*.

Stuhldreher's wife once said, "Harry has become a football legend. No matter where he speaks or what he says, he is always remembered as the quarterback of The Four Horsemen of Notre Dame."

Four Horsemen's Last Ride?

This is believed to be the last photograph taken of the famous Four Horsemen of Notre Dame, at the Massillon Club in 1963. The front row is the Four Horsemen of Notre Dame: Elmer Layden, Don Miller, Harry Stuhldreher and Jim Crowley. Back row: Chuck Hess, Rip Miller, Tink Ulrich, Creighton Miller and Tom Straughn. Hess, Ulrich and Straughn are all former Massillon Tiger Booster Club presidents. Rip Miller was one of the Seven Mules who blocked for the Four Horsemen. Creighton Miller was an All-American running back at Notre Dame in 1943.

PHOTO: TOM STRAUGHN COLLECTION.

BILL EDWARDS

How good of a coach was Bill Edwards? Good enough that he has a famous coach *and* a football stadium named after him.

New England Patriots head coach Bill Belichick is named after Edwards, who employed Belichick's father as an assistant coach at Vanderbilt University.

As for the stadium, Edwards' name is on the stadium at Wittenberg University, where his fame as a player is only overshadowed by his fame as a football coach and athletic director. Edwards was hired by Wittenberg University when he was 50 years old. He felt he could make a difference there. And what a difference he's made. Edwards was already a graduate of Wittenberg (1931) where he captained the football team for two years and was considered the best center in the nation in 1929 by sportswriter Grantland Rice, who

Bill Edwards is a legend at Wittenberg University.

PHOTO: WITTENBERG UNIVERSITY

picked an annual All-American team. "Edwards is the best center in the nation, but I can't name him All-America because of his team's schedule," Rice said.

It all started for Edwards in Massillon, Ohio, where he grew up in the tiny berg of East Greenville, just west of the city limits.

Edwards had dropped out of school at age 13 and was playing semi-pro football for the famous Massillon Maroons. He was a starter on the 1921 Massillon Maroons team that finished undefeated and claimed the Ohio semi-pro championship.

Another Massillon legend, and Maroons player, Tink Ulrich, was told to stop playing for the Maroons immediately after Dave Stewart became Massillon's head coach in 1921. Ulrich was instructed to talk to Edwards.

"He was working in the coal mines in East Greenville and we got him to come in to Massillon."

Tink Ulrich

"I talked Bill into coming to school," Ulrich said. "Dave Stewart asked me to talk to him. Bill was eligible. He was young, very young. He had just gotten out of elementary school, and he was out of school one year. He was working in the coal mines in East Greenville and we got him to come in to Massillon high school. He was about 165 pounds at that time. That was the first year they had Longfellow Junior High School. Bill had to spend his first year at Longfellow. He wasn't at Washington High School, but he practiced and played with us his freshman year. And that was a little difficult to be going to a junior high school when the other players were at the high school. But Bill stuck with it."

Edwards' extra point won the state championship for Massillon in 1922.

Edwards was one of the stars of Massillon's first state championship team in 1922. Augie Morningstar, who went on to captain Paul Brown's 1935 state champs, remembers watching Edwards play.

"He couldn't stand the headgear on," Morningstar said of Edwards, "But the rules said you had to wear headgear, so when he went out to start the game, he had his headgear on. It wasn't more than a couple of plays 'til he threw it off to the sidelines and played without it. He was a tough linebacker. He was one of my heroes. I'd tear a hole in my pants sliding under the fence to get to see him play."

It was an Edwards' extra point that sealed Massillon's most important win in the 1922 state championship season. Playing against Cleveland Shaw and former Massillon coach John Snavely, Edwards kicked the winning point in a 7-6 game.

Following Edwards' playing career at Wittenberg he was a finalist for the Massillon head coaching job when Paul Brown was awarded the position in 1932.

Bill Edwards, 1923.

Edwards coached at Springfield High School and Fostoria before joining the staff at Western Reserve in 1933. Edwards ended up as head coach at Western Reserve in 1934 and led them to a 49-6-2 record, including three undefeated seasons. He also led Western Reserve to a win over Arizona State in the 1941 Sun Bowl.

Edwards was head coach of the Detroit Lions from 1941-42. He took the Lions from a last place finish to third place before entering the Navy as lieutenant commander.

He even coached with Paul Brown in Cleveland following WWII as tackle coach.

Back in the college game at Vanderbilt, Edwards was athletic director and head football coach from 1949-52. Six times while at Vanderbilt he was named national "Coach of the Week" as a result of upset victories.

But building the Wittenberg program into a dynasty is Edwards' legacy. He led Wittenberg to five unbeaten seasons, five Ohio Conference titles and two national titles as head coach. Good enough work to be elected into the College Football Hall of Fame in 1986, a year before his death.

Wittenberg built upon Edwards' blueprint for success. His longtime assistant, Dave Maurer, succeeded Edwards and won three more national championships for Wittenberg.

The Wittenberg program was at rock bottom when Edwards took over in 1955, having suffered eight losing seasons in the previous 10 years. Since 1955, Wittenberg has an NCAA record 50 winning seasons.

Don Snavely

Massillon's All-Ohioans

1933

Steve Birkish

1934

Heine Krier
Wendell Lohr
Cloyd Snavely

1935

Augie Morningstar
Howard Dutton
Bob Glass
Neri Buggs

1936

Charley Anderson
Mike Byelene
Bob Glass
Don Snavely
Jim Miller

1937

Bob Glass
Don Snavely
Junie Anderson

1938

Lin Houston
Vince Snyder
Fred Toles
Bud Lucius

1939

Horace Gillom
Jim Russell
George Slusser
Earl Martin
Ray Getz
Gene Henderson

TEAMS 1930s RECORDS

78 17 5

WINS LOSSES TIES

5 State Championships
3 National Championships

1930
6-3-1

Head Coach: Elmer McGrew

M	Key Games	Opp.
0	Steubenville Wells	19
27	Warren Harding	0
14	Canton McKinley	6
142	***Season Totals***	***52***

1931
2-6-2

Head Coach: Elmer McGrew

M	Key Games	Opp.
0	Toledo Scott	27
0	Steubenville Wells	68
20	Canton McKinley	6
39	***Season Totals***	***152***

1932
5-4-1

Head Coach: Paul E. Brown

M	Key Games	Opp.
0	Barberton	0
0	Dover	18
0	Canton McKinley	19
79	***Season Totals***	***98***

1933
8-2-0

Head Coach: Paul E. Brown

M	Key Games	Opp.
0	Barberton	6
13	Niles	0
0	Canton McKinley	21
311	***Season Totals***	***52***

1934

9-1

Head Coach: Paul E. Brown

M	Key Games	Opp.
46	E. Cleveland Shaw	0
27	Sharon, PA	0
6	Canton McKinley	21
427	***Season Totals***	***21***

1935

10-0-0

National Champions

State Champions

Head Coach: Paul E. Brown

M	Key Games	Opp.
46	Portsmouth	0
6	Canton McKinley	0
483	***Season Totals***	***13***

1936

10-0-0

National Champions

State Champions

Head Coach: Paul E. Brown

M	Key Games	Opp.
13	New Castle, PA	0
21	Canton McKinley	0
443	***Season Totals***	***14***

1937

8-1-1

State Champions

Head Coach: Paul Brown

M	Key Games	Opp.
6	Mansfield	6
0	New Castle, PA	7
19	Canton McKinley	6
228	***Season Totals***	***50***

1938

10-0-0

State Champions

Head Coach: Paul Brown

M	Key Games	Opp.
31	Steubenville Wells	0
52	New Castle, PA	7
12	Canton McKinley	0
302	***Season Totals***	***60***

1939

10-0-0

National Champions

State Champions

Head Coach: Paul Brown

M	Key Games	Opp.
40	Cleve. Cath. Latin	13
20	Canton McKinley	6
460	***Season Totals***	***25***

Story of the Decade 1930s

Birth of the Booster Club May Have Saved Coach Paul Brown's Job

It would be hard to overestimate the importance—or power— of the modern day Massillon Tiger Football Booster Club. The organization that was formed in 1934 is now a 2,000 member machine with far-reaching power.

The popular party line states that the Booster Club "was formed at the request of Paul Brown to help feed and clothe the many indigent players during the depression years and to be able to inform the public of the data pertaining to the high school football team."

Program from the 1933 Massillon-McKinley game.

Don't believe it.

While those *were* important missions of the original Booster Club, there was a more urgent reason why the club was formed.

Paul Brown had just concluded his

second year as head coach of the Tigers. "In his second year, you could begin to see him building up, sportswriter Luther Emery said. "The team was playing better. They only lost two games. One was to Barberton. But they were beaten by Canton McKinley, 21-0. That made for an interesting episode. We didn't look good. A lot of Massillon people thought the Tigers should have done better in 1933 against McKinley. There was a little movement on, including one board of education member, to replace Brown after the McKinley game. I think we only scored two first downs. This little movement prompted the organization of the Massillon Tiger Booster Club.

"The idea of organizing the Booster Club was to help Brown," Emery said flatly. "A member of the board of education—his name was Karl Young—conceived of the idea. The idea was to give Brown an opportunity to talk to the bunch and tell them why such and such happened. Why he did such and such.

"Brown organized the Booster Club and Tink Ulrich was elected president. There was just a small group of us who got together to start with, but we called a public meeting in the high school gymnasium. That was the first time they went public with it. We had good attendance. Brown stripped the boys down to shorts and had them run through plays on the gymnasium floor. I never missed a meeting for years.

"We'd meet on Monday night. Brown would do a chalk talk. He'd let the boosters ask questions. They'd ask plenty of questions and he'd answer them.

"We also figured we needed

a project. The project was right there. It was still in the depression. Brown figured that some of his players weren't getting enough to eat. So we decided that any player that was not getting enough to eat would get a noon lunch at the YMCA. And we checked them. I know I checked one and the kid had nothing to eat that whole week but potatoes. And by the end of the week they were boiling potato skins and making soup out of the skins.

Paul Brown at Booster Club Meeting.

"So that was our project. And I assumed the project by beating the drums."

Edgar "Echo" Herring, a star back for Brown from 1934-36, benefited from the Booster Club's efforts. "I was in that program," Herring said. "There were quite a few of us. I really enjoyed it. Because I knew I was going to get a good, solid meal. I used to love that. You had your choice. When you went home you had to have what mom cooked. What mom cooked was all right. Mom had repetition. It was good to go out and get something different. I think Brown picked out us guys he figured things were pretty rough for at home. That was depression days. We weren't gettin' the right kind of food to eat at home all the time."

Ulrich recalled another project that was initiated during his year as president of the club. "Back in those days there was no Fairless High School, there was no Tuslaw High School, no Jackson High School, no Perry High School, there was no Northwest High School," Ulrich said. "All of those kids came into Massillon for school. They'd come in by bus and street car.

Booster Club Meeting, 1940.

"Fellas that came in from these areas were farm boys. After practice these kids had no way home. Most of these kids walked home. Ducky Schroeder used to tell me how he walked home to Canal Fulton on a few occasions. That's terrible. I know some of the kids that lived out of the city that played for Paul Brown back in 1934 had a terrible time getting home. Their parents were complaining about the kids getting home late. So Paul wanted to have people volunteer to take these boys home.

"Brown would always give a report about how the boys were doing and how they were getting along. One kid got sick on the practice field and threw up and it was nothing but tomatoes. Paul said, 'What's wrong, what is this?' And the kid said, 'That's all I get to eat is a tomato out of our garden once in a while.'

"Fortunately we had guys like Cart Albrecht. I'd say, 'Cart, by golly, we don't have any money, do you think we could solicit among some of you fellas to get some money?' He'd say, 'How much do you want?' Then he'd fork out whatever I asked for. Fork 'er right out and we'd take care of the kids. It was a wonderful thing.

"Our membership never really got large until the mid-40s. But we were able to provide the needs that were required from our membership.

"After the formation of the Booster Club, all of Brown's reports were favorable because he was tickled to death. From then on he talked more about how good things were getting and didn't have to talk about bad things in the past."

Emery told of a story of a group of workers overheard at Massillon Steel Castings.

"The boys were eating. One fella was criticizing D.C. McCants, the big fullback. He said, 'He don't knock 'em down. He's not a good blocker.' Another worker, said, 'You don't know your football. That was brought up at the Booster Club meeting last night. Brown said he wasn't supposed to knock him down, he was supposed to brush block and then go through and get somebody else.' That's the ways things worked."

And the Booster Club's work had just begun.

Games of the Century

1934 Massillon-McKinley Game was the First "Big One"

There have been a lot of big games in Massillon Tigers history, but there was none bigger than the 1934 Massillon-McKinley game.

How big was it? Well, can you name another football game—at any level—that a stadium was enlarged for *during* the season?

SOUVENIR BOOKLET
22nd ANNUAL FOOTBALL CLASSIC
Massillon Washington Hi Tigers
vs
Canton McKinley Hi Bulldogs
Massillon Field - Saturday, November 24, 1934
PRICE 10c

Program from 1934 Massillon-McKinley game.

The outcome of the game, a 21-6 win for McKinley, has become a footnote to the events leading up to the game. Like the 100th Massillon-McKinley game 60 years later, the 1934 game took on a larger than life aura.

Workers literally labored around the clock to enlarge the seating capacity of Massillon Field from 10,000 to 22,000.

Massillon's longtime sportswriter, Luther Emery, was instrumental in the stadium enlargement.

"The board of education in late October had a meeting

and was wondering whether they should enlarge the stadium," Emery said, "and if they did, how large should it be.

"I told them they couldn't build it big enough to hold the crowd that wants to come. So they decided to go ahead and build seats according to demand."

Workers had less than a month to enlarge the stadium to over twice its size.

"They worked night and day, they had flood lights, continuous work. The stadium was constructed with all wood, of course," Emery said.

Robert "Doc" Immel remembers the stadium enlargement project. The future team dentist and school board president was a student manager for Paul Brown at the time. Immel was particularly impressed by the feats of the father of Massillon's big fullback, D. C. McCants.

Before expansion

Massillon Field, October, 1934. Note height of bleachers in background. Capacity 10,000.

"They were putting in temporary seats," Immel said, "and I remember D. C. McCants' dad. I looked over and I saw this big man picking up all these big planks for seating. All the other guys had two men—one on each end—lugging these things. He'd go over and pick one up under each arm and take off. I never saw a big man or a strong man do something like that before. That was fantastic. It's something what makes an impression on a young kid."

After Expansion

Massillon Field's capacity was increased from 10,000 to 22,000 in one month.

As if the game wasn't already big enough, a dastardly act made things even more interesting. As fans started pouring into the stadium, it soon became obvious that a duplicate set of tickets had been printed.

"Someone counterfeited tickets," Massillon sports writer Luther Emery said. "People would come in and find their seat taken. There were quite a few scraps went on before they identified the problem. Fortunately, before too many bogus tickets got in, they discovered they could tell by the signature on the back of the ticket—if it didn't correspond with the signature of the ticket manager. They never found out who did it."

Games of the Century

Glass Touchdown Gives Brown First Win Over McKinley in 1935

Before the 1935 season, Massillon head coach Paul Brown's luck against Canton McKinley had all been bad. The Massillon coach lost all three match ups between his Tigers and Jimmy Aiken's Bulldogs. But this time his team was favored to win the season finale.

Program from 1935 Massillon-McKinley game.

The Tigers were led by a handful of stars who would become Tiger legends—All-Ohio captain Augie Morningstar, future All-American Eddie Molinski, and All-Ohio end Charlie Anderson. But the player who earned star billing for the 1935 Tigers was a bruising sophomore whose name belied his strength and durability.

Bob Glass was a boy in a man's body—had been that way since junior high. If stats for rushing yards had been kept in his era, it's sure that Glass would be among the Tigers all-time leaders. Glass was the featured running back for three straight state championship teams from 1935-37.

Brown was taking no chances that a mistake would cost his team a chance to beat Canton McKinley for the first time in 1935. This conservatism became evident as the game unfolded.

"It was tight, awful tight," said Augie Morningstar, Brown's 1935 team captain. "Normally we'd throw, we'd run reverses. In that game we were driving off tackle and holding the ball, trying to keep it away from them Just try to make first downs. Run, run, run."

Aiken (l) and Brown.

On a cold, snowy day at Lehman field in Canton, the strategy worked. After a scoreless first half, Charley Anderson recovered a Canton fumble on the 21. On fourth down at the three yard line, Glass was given the ball. He drove through the line, crossing the goal line by a foot.

The crowd roared, as if they knew those points would be enough to deliver Massillon its second state championship and its first under Brown. They were right, Massillon prevailed, 6-0. Brown would not lose to McKinley again, finishing with a 6-3 mark against Massillon's arch-rival. As for Aiken, it was his last game as a Bulldog coach. He became head coach at the University of Akron in 1936.

Tiger Skin Brought to Life in 1938

Massillon head coach Paul Brown and superintendent of schools L. J. Smith were attending a University of Pittsburgh football game in 1937 when Brown had a brainstorm.

"Between halves," Smith said, "out came a Panther. Two fellas in uniform with three socks on and something over their head. It was the lousiest thing you'd ever seen, with all due respect to the University of Pittsburgh.

Pep Paulson was Massillon's first Obie from 1938-39

"Paul turned to me and we had quite a little discussion and he said, 'Why can't we have a tiger skin, L. J.? A *real* Tiger skin.'

"I said, 'Why not?' He said, 'Do you know where we can find one?' I said, 'I think I do.'

"So I wrote a letter to the Jonas brothers, who were taxidermists in Denver, Colorado, and told them what we wanted, described it the best I could. They wrote back and said, 'We've got the nicest tiger skin here. A beautiful tiger skin. This is the first one we've put out to a high school. We'll build it to your specifications and to your satisfaction.'

"Down at the bottom there was a price: Five hundred dollars. Five hundred dollars, way back then, when we had band instruments and uniforms to buy...somebody was going to be bankrupt. The athletic board passed a resolution and we had it there in a couple of weeks."

Paulson gets make-up treatment for a school play.

George "Red" Bird, Massillon's new band director, tabbed Harry Burkhart as the first Obie. Pep Paulson, who later became a Massillon Municipal judge, took over for Burkhart after just one game. "Well, he wasn't the first Obie," Paulson objected. "He *tried out* to be Obie and he couldn't get along with George 'Red' Bird. Harry was a kind of a zany kid, pretty likable, but he wouldn't do what George Bird wanted him to do. George Bird was a stickler for that kind of stuff. If he said he wanted you to go over there, you went over there. George must have said something to Paul Brown. I had Paul for History. One day, as class ended, he said to me, 'Pep, go down and see George Bird, he wants to see you.' So I did. George wanted to know if I wanted to be Obie. Who wouldn't? So from the second game on I did the Obie thing for two years."

Paulson, who had a flair for drama, appearing in school plays, was a natural in the tiger skin. But it wasn't the most comfortable outfit he ever wore.

"All it had in it was a pair of tennis shoes that were sewn into the feet. The head gear thing was up on the top. You looked out of the tiger's mouth. So it wasn't the easiest thing to see out of. You kind of had to raise your head to look forward. And it had no liner in it. And that thing was hotter than all get out, and it stuck to ya. Later on they put a liner in it, some kind of slick material, so that you could move around pretty good."

Paulson climbs a ladder to the crossbar of the goal posts in his tiger skin.

Sherlock Evans, the husband of Brown's sister, Marian, had a circus background and helped Paulson bring the tiger skin to life. One of Evans' ideas was to have Paulson stand on the goal posts.

"Sherlock was a good, funny guy and a good showman, so he knew what appealed to the people," Paulson said. "They used a ladder to get me up there, then they had a rope tied between the goal posts. The goal posts at that time were four-inch cast iron pipes, so you could get up and walk on them. You could get up there and that rope was about underarm high. The people in the stands couldn't see much of the rope. I could lead the band as it comes down the field and I was okay because my arms were over this rope. I worked my way from the post side where I got up the ladder to the middle and then at a certain time it was time for me to get down and start workin' with the band and I had to swing down off of the cross bar, run out and become part of the band show. That was a good gimmick."

Like Obies through the years, Paulson enjoyed relating to kids.

"Kids react a couple of different ways," Paulson said. "Some little kids would be frightened when you'd go over to them. We did a lot of that. You'd go over to kids and put out your paw and that sort of stuff. Some of them would be old enough and sophisticated enough to know that there's some kid in the costume. The little ones weren't too sure and they'd cry and try to get away. The public liked it. We did street stuff, marches and parades. And even today, a lot of the tiger's activity is working the sidelines."

HEINIE KRIER

Heinie Krier was a rebel. A smoker and a drinker. Pudgy. And he was all of this while starring as a running back and defensive lineman for one of the finest teams in Massillon Tigers history. And who was the coach of this incorrigible star? Well, it was none other than legendary Paul Brown.

A rare action photo of Heinie Krier ripping off a big gain against Canton McKinley in 1934.

Krier might not have looked—or acted—the part, but he was *magic* with the football tucked under his arm. Brown's first marquee back, Krier is Massillon's second all-time leading scorer with 248 points. But we'll never know how much damage Krier may have done to Massillon's all-time rushing record, since rushing statistics weren't kept in the 1930s.

Krier was the unquestioned star of the 1934 team, and he enjoyed the celebrity that came along with it. He would often invite underprivileged children to enter the stadium with him before games. It was a trait he learned, perhaps, from his father.

"Heinie was a heck of a ball player. He was the greatest at that time," said Barney Wallace, a cousin of Krier's who played for the Tigers himself, from 1941-42. "He was a bundle of muscle, he loved to hit guys. He loved to run into them. He would run over guys and we thought that was great. Nobody runs over guys like Henry did. He also had speed. His old man was mayor of Massillon," Wallace said. "That was my grandmother's brother. I'd say 'Hi Uncle Hen,' and he'd say, 'Come on in with me.' We couldn't get in any other way, unless we went over the fence. You didn't have the money. That was the depression. We'd wait to see him comin' and we'd come in with him."

"Heinie was a heck of a ball player. He was the greatest at that time."

Barney Wallace

"Heine's only problem, he and Brown didn't get along too well," teammate Edgar 'Echo' Herring said. "Some of the guys would sneak around and smoke. Heinie was one of 'em."

Like most things, Krier's transgressions were not lost on the head coach. "Brown would get him out there sometimes before practice and run him, because he knew he smoked. He'd make him pay for it. Sometimes he'd be out there vomiting, he run him so much. Brown was tryin' to break him of the habit."

As undeniable as Krier's running skills were, so was his disdain for training—and authority. But Brown kept his star running back on the field. Bob Immel was Brown's student manager in 1934. He later became a school board member and the team's dentist. He remembered Brown's relationship with Krier. Immel said Brown had an interesting way of dealing with Krier and other unruly stars. "Brown was funny," said Immel, "He was strict. And he would kick guys off the team at times. But he never kicked a regular off the team. Henry was quite a guy, he wasn't very big. He was short. He was a powerful guy. But he was a rounder. We had several of 'em on that team. Sometimes he'd make a long run into the end zone and stand down there and throw up because he had a hangover from the night before."

Heine Krier.

While Brown couldn't break Krier—or win without him—Canton McKinley found a way to stop the Tiger star.

In the 1934 landmark Massillon-McKinley game, Krier ripped off a 37-yard touchdown run. Krier's breakaway run gave Massillon the momentum, but he was soon forced from the game with an ankle injury. "Heine got his ankle twisted," said Immel. "He said Red Haas twisted it in a pile-up. I don't know whether that's true or not."

Without Krier, Massillon lost, 21-6.

H. W. "DOC" BELL

"Doc" Bell was known as "Mr. Football" during the halcyon days of the Massillon Tigers.

"The people of this community owe a lot to this man," Paul Brown said of Bell. "Not for what he did with me, but because of what he did for the school system. He was far-sighted."

Doctor H. W. Bell.

Bell was a physician in Massillon for 50 years and school board president from 1936-42. He did great things for Brown, the citizens of Massillon and for Massillon football.

"He was a tremendous fella," Brown said, "He delivered our children. He was my doctor as well as my friend."

Bell not only delivered children, he committed himself to helping them as they grew up.

In addition to his 15 years on the school board, Bell was instrumental in founding the Massillon Boys Club in 1936 and served as their president for 17 years.

Bell was on the school board when Massillon Field, the predecessor to Tiger Stadium, was enlarged from a 10,000-seat facility to a 20,000-seat stadium during the 1934 season.

Longtime Massillon sports-writer Luther Emery and Bell were part of a group that congregated at the Rider's Drug Store in downtown Massillon.

"It was kind of a hang-out for some of the top boosters," Emery said. "One night when they were in the process of enlarging the stadium, Dr. Bell and I were wondering if they were leaving enough elevation between rows so the person behind could see over the person in front of them. So at 11 p.m. we went down to the field. Workers were hammerin' away. Old Doc Bell would sit in a seat and say 'Now Lute, you're short, so you sit behind me. Can you see the field?' We'd move to another section and do the same thing. That would go on until we'd worked our way around the entire stadium."

> **"My dad got credit for building the football stadium, but Dr. Bell was the driving force on that."**
>
> **Mike Brown**

Bell was largely responsible for the construction of Tiger Stadium in 1939. He insisted that it be included in a federal building program in the late 1930s and was responsible for convincing the WPA and PWA to work together on the project. He donated his time between office hours and patient visits to supervise the building of the stadium.

Brown is often credited with the building of Tiger Stadium, which now bears his name, but he always deflected the credit back to Bell. His son, Mike Brown, owner of the Cincinnati Bengals, remembers the respect his father had for Bell.

"My dad had great faith in what Dr. Bell would say or think," Mike Brown said. "My dad got credit for building the football stadium, but Dr. Bell was the driving force on that. You have to give him credit, it's certainly the best high school football stadium in the state of Ohio. I've never seen a better one anywhere, even to this day. When my dad returned to Massillon they were talking about his foresight. He joked about that because he said all that he was thinking about was having enough football fields and having the football team taken care of right."

"My dad had great faith in what Dr. Bell would say or think."

Mike Brown

Bud Houghton, Massillon's head coach in 1941 and 1946-47, appreciated Bell's contributions to the program.

"We had a good fairy on the board of education in Dr. Bell," Houghton said. "He was a great football enthusiast, a heck of a nice person. He was crazy about football. He was for anything that would make Massillon football good. He was the guy who piloted the whole thing. If you wanted more assistance, Dr. Bell was the guy you went to."

Shirley Bird, daughter of Massillon band director George "Red" Bird, remembers how her father and Bell loved Tiger Stadium.

"Dad always called the football field the sacred sod because Doc Bell would get out there on the field after every football game, put his hands behind his back and cry over every bent blade of grass. I guess he wanted that football field to look perfect. It killed him that they had to play football on it and mess it up. The sacred sod meant the world to Doc Bell."

"The sacred sod meant the world to "Doc" Bell."

Shirley Bird

"I'll never forget when I was given the job at Ohio State," Brown said. "Dr. Bell said, he always called me 'P, P Brown'. He said, 'P, I don't know. You may be wound too tight for that kind of a job. I hope you don't explode on it.' I said, 'I can't think of any better way to go.' That was the send-off I got from the good doctor."

Emery's memory of Bell's final hours of life exemplify his dedication to Massillon football.

"On his death bed he had me calling him from the press box during a football game, telling him the score by quarters. The last time I called, Mrs. Bell said, 'He's in a coma.'

That was Emery's send-off from the good doctor.

ROBERT "DOC" IMMEL

Robert "Doc" Immel is a shining example of what is good about the town of Massillon.

From student manager, to dentist, to school board president, to circus historian, to Massillon Tiger football historian, Immel's gracious hands touched Massillonians for eight decades.

Immel had humble beginnings. As a youngster he once tried out for the Longfellow Junior High School football team, a move that ironically led to his first significant service to the town of Massillon.

Bob Immel as school board president.

"When I was in junior high my mother said, 'You're going over to Longfellow this morning. They have football try-outs over there.' I only weighed about 80 pounds but I said, 'Okay,'" Immel said.

"Head coach Carroll Widdoes looked at me and said, 'What are you doing here?' I said, 'My mother says I'm trying out for football.' He said, 'I'm afraid you can't do that, but I need a manager.' So he made me the team manager."

Doc Immel's experience with Widdoes at Longfellow paid off when Immel became a team manager for the legendary Paul Brown in 1934.

> **"We managers were like bellboys in a hotel...They hear everything."**
>
> **"Doc" Immel**

"Widdoes went down to the high school the same time I did," Immel said. "He told Paul Brown I was a good manager, so I got a job as manager there."

Brown was a young 24-year-old coach at Massillon when Immel served as his manager. Immel remembers that he wasn't awed by his first introduction to Coach Paul Brown.

"It was nothing special," he said, "of course he wasn't that old—he was just a kid himself, really. It wasn't different than meeting anybody else, because he didn't have that reputation yet. He was just another coach. But it didn't take long until I found out that he was a pretty qualified person."

Immel had a rare opportunity to observe Brown from his vantage point as student manager. "We managers were like bellboys in a hotel," Immel said. "If you want to know something that's going on in a hotel, ask the bellboy. They hear everything. And people talk in front of them thinking that they're being ignored. And they often say things that they don't realize might get out."

Brown struggled through the second half of his first season at Massillon, losing his final four games. Brown's second year he went 8-2, but was beaten 21-0 by Canton McKinley at the end of the season.

"We got over there and we had forgotten to bring socks and jock straps."

"Doc" Immel

"I was very fortunate to have been there when Brown started making his real moves. His first two years he was afraid of being fired. Those first couple of years there was quite a bit of pressure to get rid of him. He was just a young kid and he didn't come in and turn it around immediately. He certainly was able to save his job."

Brown saved his job in a big way. In his final seven seasons at Massillon, Brown's record was 46-2-1—and the Tigers won six straight state titles.

Immel remembers Brown as a coach who was far ahead of his time. "It was easy to see when you were around it, how far ahead he was. People think we had great athletes. We had some good athletes. But most of 'em were just average kids. They were well-trained and well-conditioned. Brown was just so far ahead of everyone else in organization and training. He was so far ahead that he used to give clinics for the area coaches. He would have them come in and he'd teach them to coach. That's how far ahead he was. With his organizational ability, I don't care what he would have gone into, he would have been a tremendous success."

Immel also got to see the hard side of Brown. "Paul was someone—he could look at you and you'd cringe. He could say something, three words, cut right into ya, then turn around and walk away. He was tough.

"Paul used to chew some butts out," Immel said. "He was good at chewin' out. I know he chewed mine out one time about a football. Someone walked off with a football. You know you have footballs all over the place, no boundaries any place. I wasn't watching and some kid walked off with a football. He ate my fanny out for that. I got the thing back the next day."

Immel as student manager, 1936.

Immel found it was sometimes better to solve problems without letting Brown know there was ever a problem. When Massillon traveled to play McKinley in 1935—a game Brown desperately needed to win—Immel had to avert a disaster.

"We got over there to play and we had forgotten to bring socks and jock straps," Immel laughed. "We had to run back to Massillon and get them. We didn't let Brown know. We found out early enough that we could remedy the situation. Fortunately we were over to Canton McKinley real early."

As school board president Immel was responsible for hiring some of Massillon's finest coaches. He also developed an effective method for hiring a coach that is still being used today.

As school board president, Immel was responsible for hiring some of Massillon's finest coaches.

"When we hired Bob Commings I put in the selection procedure that they use now. Up until that time, it was kind of a little committee—the superintendent would ask Tink Ulrich, Chuck Hess and myself and maybe one more, and we'd interview the coach and make our recommendation. I was president of the board when we needed a new coach so I set up this procedure.

We'd get the applications in and select several people that we thought we'd be interested in. We'd contact them and they'd send in two films: a loss and a win. The committee would get together and look at the films and grade 'em, pick 'em apart. Then we'd interview 'em. Later on when all the interviews were over we'd get together and discuss the pros and cons, not only football, but on their teaching abilities, their disposition. Then we'd send two teams to the coach's home town and ask questions of the town's people. I was always quite proud that I created that system. When Bob Commings, went to Iowa, he told them if they wanted to hire a football coach, go talk to them in Massillon. Other coaches have said that. They said they've been interviewed other places and they've never had an interview like they did in Massillon."

The Immel Circus, a 100-square-foot miniature circus, is an enduring gift from Immel to the city of Massillon. Immel spent almost 50 years working on the circus that is now on permanent display in the Massillon Museum. Immel carved a total of 2,620 figures, including circus animals, people and tents.

Immel at the controls of his recording equipment. He spent untold hours interviewing Massillon coaches and Booster Club presidents.

Another labor of love for Immel was an exhaustive series of recorded interviews with former Massillon coaches and Booster Club presidents.

"I tell many people that I was so lucky, when I look back, to be born in Massillon and go through the things that have happened in Massillon. The football, to see that develop, and to see Brown's philosophies, how he handled people, it was really an experience."

The city of Massillon was pretty lucky to have Immel, too.

AUGIE MORNINGSTAR

It's hard to overstate Augie Morningstar's contributions to the city of Massillon: captain of Paul Brown's first state championship team in 1935, All-Ohio end in 1935, head coach in 1945, longtime Washington High School administrator.

But for all his contributions to—and love for—Massillon, it was, ironically, a win over Massillon in 1949 that stands as Morningstar's shining moment.

Augie Morningstar's banquet program as head coach, 1945.

Morningstar was head coach at Massillon for just one rocky season—probably the most unusual season in the program's history. Augie's 1945 Tigers went 5-0-5 and he was relieved of his coaching duties after the season.

His job was given to Bud Houghton in 1946. Houghton had won the state championship as Massillon's head coach in 1941 before serving in WWII for four years. Upon his return from the war, he was given his old job back.

"They wanted me to stay here as an assistant coach," Morningstar said, "But it would have been too difficult, being the ex-head coach with Houghton coming back as the head coach. People talkin', you've got that underground constantly babbling. I said 'No.'"

> **"I wanted a shot at Massillon, having played and coached there."**
>
> **Augie Morningstar**

Morningstar landed on his feet, accepting the head job at Portsmouth High School in 1946. He spent two years as head coach at Portsmouth, but the fire to beat Massillon was burning in him. When the Mansfield job opened in 1948, he jumped at it.

"I went to Mansfield because Portsmouth didn't play Massillon, but Mansfield did," Morningstar said. "I wanted a shot at Massillon, having played and coached there."

And probably most importantly, having been fired from there.

Morningstar's first shot at Massillon didn't go so well.

"When Massillon came to Mansfield in 1948, they whipped us good (33-7). So when I walked in the locker room after the game, I put "365" on the chalkboard. Each day we took one day off. We were one day closer to beating Massillon."

Beating Massillon became an obsession for Morningstar, his players, and the city of Mansfield. It's no wonder why. In 16 previous meetings, all Mansfield had to show for their efforts was three 6-6 ties in 1937, 1941 and 1946. In 13 losses to Massillon they were outscored 411-32. Six times Mansfield failed to score.

It's easy to see why Augie's 16-12 win over Massillon brought hysteria to Mansfield.

Morningstar as Paul Brown's captain, 1935.

"We had six thousand people waiting for us to come back from Massillon out on the square," Morningstar said. "They hit our team bus and I opened up the door and screamed and hollered, 'Don't upset the bus.' They were rockin' that bus, the wheels were starting to come up. They never even heard me. They just pulled me out of the bus and they passed me hand over hand and up to the podium. We had beaten the Tigers for the first time in 40 years."

Mansfield and Massillon split the 1949 state championship in the two wire services.

And that's the way it was for Augie Morningstar, the All-Ohio, captain, and head coach at Massillon who came back to town to play the role of spoiler for one glorious night.

MIKE BYELENE

Paul Brown had big plans for Mike Byelene. Byelene's father wanted Brown to just butt out.

Brown's bond with Byelene was so strong that the coach named his son after the 16-year-old quarterback. Byelene was just a junior in high school when Brown's son Mike was born.

Mike Byelene, All-Ohio quarterback of the 1936 state and national champions.

Brown wanted the soft-spoken Byelene to use his fleet feet and powerful arm to produce a college scholarship. But Byelene's immigrant father, a steelworker, wanted to forge a different future for his oldest son. He was violently opposed to Brown's meddling.

"My dad got Mike Byelene to go to college," said Mike Brown, Cincinnati Bengal's general manager. "Byelene's dad got angry about this. "He was going to do some damage to my father for having his kid go to college. He thought his kid should go to work in the steel mill."

But Byelene's mother, who worked as a seamstress to help make ends meet for Byelene and his six younger siblings, understood and appreciated what Brown was doing for her son.

"Mike's mother brought my mother pillowcases she had embroidered," Mike Brown said. "My mother cherished that. She kept them for many, many years."

Byelene held the Massillon record for career touchdown passes for 65 years.

Paul Brown told his story of the pillowcases in a late-in-life letter to Byelene's wife.

Brown wrote, "His father was more than a little irritated with me because I wanted Mike to go to college. He believed in doing things like they did back in the old country. His mother went along with me and you might tell Mike that I still have the pillowcases and sheet that she embroidered and gave to us as her way of expressing how she felt. We only use them on special occasions because they are special to us."

On the day of his funeral, Brown's second wife, Mary, told Byelene that Brown wanted to wait until his death to return the pillowcases and sheet. Brown used those "special occasion" linens for over 50 years.

In another letter, written for Byelene's retirement party, Brown called Byelene his greatest all-around back at Massillon.

Besides being an outstanding runner, Byelene held the

Massillon career record for career touchdown passes (34) for 65 years until Justin Zwick eclipsed the record in 2001 (63). His single game record of five touchdown passes against Niles as a sophomore in 1934 also stood for 65 years before being topped by Zwick's six touchdown passes against Fremont Ross in 2001.

"We were predominantly a good passing team," Byelene said. "You look through Paul Brown's history and you'll see that he's won by passing. He used to be a passer himself."

Byelene was named All-Ohio in 1936. Many consider the 1936 Tigers among Massillon's best ever.

Following his record-setting career at Massillon, Byelene had an unpleasant experience with legendary Harry Stuhldreher, the former Massillon quarterback who gained notoriety as the All-American quarterback of the famous Four Horsemen of Notre Dame.

Stuhldreher was head coach at the University of Wisconsin when Byelene visited campus. Stuhldreher wasn't impressed and said so in a letter to Brown.

Augie Morningstar, captain during Mike's junior season at Massillon, read the letter.

"Stuhldreher wrote, 'If you're going to send someone up here, send someone with size so I can make something out of them. I'm afraid he's too small,' " said Morningstar.

Bylene resented Stuhldreher's treatment. "He talked to *me*, I didn't talk to *him*," Byelene said, "He said I was too small. But he was smaller than me and he played for Notre Dame."

Byelene got revenge.

"Mike joined me at Purdue," Morningstar said. "We played Wisconsin and were behind. We put Byelene in at tailback and he practically won the game by himself."

Byelene threw a 16-yard touchdown pass and ran 73 yards for another touchdown, leading Purdue to a 13-7 come-from-behind win.

Mike Byelene (55) follows Bob Glass (22) around left end in 1936. Byelene was All-Ohio and team captain in 1936, Glass in 1937.

"I went through the middle and was gone, 73 yards," Byelene said of his long touchdown run. "I shocked 'em."

Following the game Stuhldreher, Morningstar, Byelene and Jim Miller, a Massillon player who became captain at Purdue, were sharing stories about Massillon when a Western Union telegraph delivery arrived.

"The Western Union boy handed Stuhldreher this thick letter," Morningstar said.

"Stuhldreyer opened it up and this long scroll of names came out. At the top it said, '*Is Mike Byelene still too small?*' It was signed by all of the boosters in Massillon."

EDDIE MOLINSKI

Before he was an All-American lineman at the University of Tennessee, Eddie Molinski was a tough Massillon kid. He enjoyed playing football in junior high, but his first love was boxing.

"He was a pretty hefty kid for junior high," longtime Massillon sportswriter Luther Emery recalled, "they were counting on him at Washington High."

Eddie Molinski as an All-American at University of Tennessee.

Molinski's father had other ideas. He wanted his son to concentrate on boxing.

"His dad didn't want him to play football because he had aspirations of Molinski being a professional boxer," Emery said. "He was pretty handy with his dukes even as a young kid. So his dad made him quit football."

Molinski came out for the first couple of practices during his sophomore year in 1933. When he quit showing up, Head Coach Paul Brown was concerned. Brown went to his childhood friend Emery for help.

"Brown called me up and told me about it." Emery said. "He asked me if I'd talk to Molinski."

So Emery had to decide how to convince this tough kid—and his father—that football was important for Eddie.

"I thought about it a long time," Emery said, "I finally thought about Neil Brogan, who had done a lot of professional fighting in his day and about all he came out of it with was a pair of bad eyes. Brogan's career was over with, so I called him up and gave him the story. I asked if he would go with me out to the Molinski's and talk to Eddie's dad and tell him his experiences in boxing. He agreed. We arrived under the worst conditions. Molinski was working out on a sand bag that was hanging in the back yard from a limb of a tree. His dad was sitting on a limb coaching him.

"I told him the story about how Brown would like to have him out for football. I told him how Neil Brogan had fought some of the best in the ring, how he wound up with his bad eyes.

"We kept talking. They were a good Catholic family, so I finally said, 'If Eddie makes good in high school I'll write to Elmer Layden at Notre Dame and recommend him.'"

Layden was the highly successful head coach at Notre Dame at the time. "I didn't know Elmer Layden from anybody else," Emery said, "but I said I would do it, that was part of the deal.

"I could see his father weakening a little bit. Finally, his father said, 'Do you think he'd let Eddie box in the off season?' I said, 'Well, I'm not talkin' for Paul Brown—I'll have to ask him.' His father said, 'If he'll let Eddie box in the off-season, okay.'

"Of course I called Brown and he was tickled to death. He said, 'Sure he can box in the off-season.' The next day he was out to football practice."

While Molinski became a key member of the Tigers from 1933-35, he never forgot Emery's promise.

"I never had a word with Eddie until his last practice, the night before the Canton McKinley game. Eddie saw me standing on the sidelines and came over and said, 'You know you told my family if I made good you'd write a letter to Notre Dame? Well, do you think I made good?' I said, 'I think you did. Now I'll write the letter.'"

Emery wrote the letter to Layden, who answered the letter and sent alumni representatives to meet with Molinski. But instead of signing with Notre Dame, Molinski ended up with Major Neyland at Tennessee.

"Eddie was a heck of a good guard and linebacker ," said Augie Morningstar, captain of the 1935 Massillon squad. "He became an All-American at Tennessee."

Molinski also found success off the field. "He was a doctor," Morningstar said. "He got an infection in his leg, in his ankle. They wanted to take it off. He said, 'You can't take it off—I'm not going to let you take it off. You're either going to cure it or this is it.' So, that's the way he died. He knew it was going to happen. He had studied it."

Eddie Molinski was a tough guy to the end.

BOB GLASS

You won't find a more revered player in Massillon football history than Bob Glass. Widely considered the greatest fullback in Massillon's illustrious history, Glass was that and so much more.

"I don't remember anybody as good as Bob Glass," said former Massillon head coach Bud Houghton. "He was kind of a one-man gang. Punter, passer, drop kicker, linebacker, runner. He just had a perfect bodybuild. Good strong legs."

Massillon players wanted to wear number 11 after Glass made it famous.

Already a star as a sophomore, Glass was what sportswriters of the day called a line plunger.

"He was a straight ahead runner," 1936 captain and quarterback Mike Byelene said of Glass.

In Massillon's landmark victory over Canton McKinley in1935, it was

Glass who coach Paul Brown counted on to ground out the tough yardage. It was in that game—a 6-0 win for Massillon—that Glass scored one of the most famous touchdowns in Massillon history.

But while Glass was a star on the field, he could be a challenge off the field.

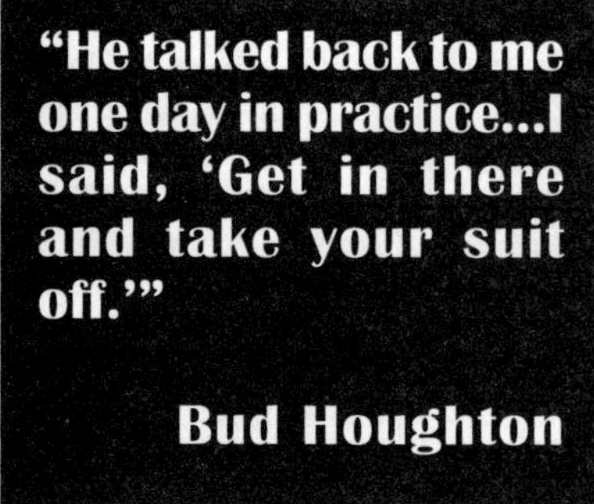

Houghton, who replaced Brown as head coach in Massillon in 1941, coached Glass in junior high. "He was my first big star," Houghton said of Glass. "He was also my first opportunity to discipline somebody. He kind of got out of line. He was a rambunctious kid. Heck of a nice boy. A real muscular kid. As an eighth grader he probably weighed 185 pounds. Good legs. Just a strong kid. He lived with his grandparents. I don't know what ever happened to his parents. He talked back to me one day in practice, about the second or third day of fall practice. I said, 'Get in there and take your suit off.' He went in and took off his suit and came back and he was standing on the sideline. I told the kids just before the practice was over, 'Glass is standing over there, I don't want anybody talkin' to him. I want everybody to walk right by him like he wasn't even standing there.' That worked. He came over to my house that night and apologized. I never had any more problems with Bob. He did my punting and passing and backed up the line on defense. I don't remember anybody in my time that was as good. I think he could be wild, but he was a good boy for me."

Earl Martin, who was a three-year starter for Massillon's state champion teams of 1937-39 and captain in 1939, played with Glass during Glass' senior season.

On the 1937 team, Glass was the senior hero, Martin was the promising sophomore. While Martin had been identified by Brown as a future star, Glass was already an established Massillon Tiger legend.

Bob Glass was the star fullback for three straight state championship teams from 1935-37.

Glass at His Best Against McKinley

Bob Glass was the star of three Massillon-McKinley games—and all three games ended up bringing Massillon state titles.

In 1935 Glass scored the game's only points. In 1936 he scored 15 points and in 1937 he scored 13.

"Bob Glass was 80 percent of the 1937 team," Martin said. "He was a powerful runner. He wouldn't go around you, yet he was fast. He ran low to the ground. I think he was one of the best football players I can remember playin' at Massillon."

You have to realize Martin's not a casual Massillon fan—his memory of Tiger stars goes back over 60 years. And Martin not only played with some of Massillon's best ever, he *was* one of Massillon's best ever. Of course he realizes that other players get more recognition than Glass does in modern day Massillon.

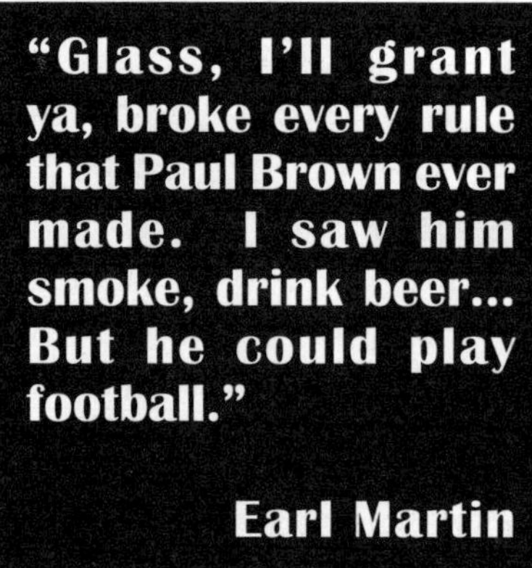

"People may differ with me about Glass' greatness because they look at what a player did after they left Massillon. Like Tommy James, for instance. If Massillon had been the extent of his football career, you'd never have heard of Tommy James. The same thing with the Houston brothers, Lin, Jack, Walt and Jim. Think of what Glass did on that '37 team: First of all he kicked off. He was the left halfback—which is equivalent to the quarterback now. He did the passing, he carried the ball 80 percent of the time. He did the punting. He kicked the extra points and he backed up the line on defense. The guy did all that. That '37 team, you take him out of there and we're 5-5 or something like that." Instead Massillon finished 8-1-1 and won the state champion.

Teammate Edgar "Echo" Herring recalled Glass' punting ability.

"Glass could kick the ball

the way Brown wanted it," Herring said, "He wanted it as high as you can go. It gives the defense time to get down and hit the man before he gets started."

Massillon's famous sportswriter Luther Emery remembers Glass' performance on the 1937 team. "Bob Glass was the mainstay of that team. He carried the ball about every play," Emery said with a laugh.

Glass was a star as a sophomore running back.

Even though Massillon relied heavily on Glass, Brown had a trick up his sleeve when the Tigers played Canton McKinley. "Glass was the leading scorer and ground gainer all season," Emery said. "Brown changed his offense. He had the play start off to the right, which is the direction Glass usually carried, then they'd immediately switch to the left and give the ball to Red Snyder."

The strategy of using Glass as a decoy worked. Snyder ended up being the leading ground gainer and the Tigers beat the previously undefeated Bulldogs 19-6.

Martin, though two years younger, quickly became friends with Glass. He admired Glass' free spirit.

"We were real good buddies," Martin said. "We'd go frog huntin'. He was one of those who liked to have a good time. And regardless of what they say about how the whole town disciplined the players, Bob Glass, I'll grant ya, broke every rule that Paul Brown ever made. Glass was just a fun-lovin' guy who didn't care. But he could play football. Had he been a lesser player, Brown would have had him out of there."

"The next thing I knew I got a letter from home that Bob Glass had been killed... He got killed on the Green Islands..."

Earl Martin

The fun-loving, hard-living Glass went on to star at Tulane University after leaving Massillon. Then WW II called. Martin stayed close with Glass while he was in the Marines.

"He and I corresponded," Martin said. "The last letter I got from him I could tell by his spec number where he was. I had talked with a few pilots from our outfit, and I was going to try to make a hop down there to see him. The next thing I know I got a letter from home that said he'd been killed. He was second lieutenant in the line company. A lot of misreports said he got killed on Iwo Jima. He got killed on the Green Islands in New Guinea."

Emery was in the service when Glass was killed. He remembers visiting Brown, who was coaching the Great Lakes naval station team. "I said, 'Did you know that Bob Glass was killed at Iwo Jima?' Brown said, 'Yes, and I bet it took a big bullet to stop him.'"

LUTHER "LUT" EMERY

The sage of Massillon Tigers football, Luther Emery, may have been the greatest sports writer of them all. True, Red Smith and Grantland Rice enjoyed a larger, national stage, but "Lut" may have been better.

Luther Emery recalls details from the Tigers past.

Emery's words had impact. They packed emotion. They inspired. They built buildings. And, above all, they were fair.

"I never tried to take advantage of a player who might have made a mistake or something like that," Emery said, in describing his journalistic style. "They didn't do it on purpose."

Massillon coaching legend Paul Brown often said Emery, with his sports writing, was more important than Brown was in bringing Massillon football to national prominence. Chuck Mather, who won six state championships as Massillon's head coach, agreed.

"Luther was the very best. I don't know of *anyone* who's equalled him of all the sportswriters I've ever met," Mather said. And Mather met plenty of sportswriters in a coaching career that led him from Massillon to the University of Kansas as head football coach and to the Chicago Bears as offensive coordinator for George Halas, the legendary head coach.

"He was probably the most knowledgeable and fairest sports editor in the state of Ohio," Mather said. "If he thought there was a better team than we were, Massillon didn't automatically get a first place vote from him. But Luther was a great, loyal supporter of Massillon football.

"Luther would write articles that put the team in the right frame of mind." Mather said. "His writing was always just *exactly* what you liked to hear as a coach."

"Luther was the very best. I don't know of anyone who's equalled him of all the sportswriters I've ever met."

Chuck Mather

Tom Harp, Massillon coach from 1954-55, appreciated Emery.

"Lute Emery had to be the most loyal sports writer that any coach could ever hope to have," Harp said. "I don't care, Lute would always have a bright spot for ya. He never was critical. He reported things honestly. He never got abrasive. He was not like some of these guys that have to find controversy in everything they report. I was always comfortable with him. I knew whenever he asked me a question it would be reported honestly and clearly."

Emery's memories of Massillon football ran deep.

"I was about eight years old when my father said, 'It's about time you see a football game.' He was a fan of the old Pro Tigers of 1903-05. Massillon High School was playing Canton. They played in back of North Street School. That was the football field. It wasn't long enough to have two goal posts. They just had a goal post at one end of the field. The score was 13-13. That was in 1913.

"They didn't sell tickets to the game. The high school girls had little tags and they stood on the street corners and they'd take any contribution you had and give you a tag. Most people, I think, would probably walk by. But some would give money and that's how they got support for the team. I didn't miss a whole lot of games after

This graphic accompanied Emery's popular sports column. Emery rose from newspaper delivery boy to editor of The Evening Independent.

that. I didn't see the 1914 game, which was played at Canton. Massillon won it, 3-0. Joe Eckstein kicked a field goal right at the end of the game. They had a round ball—almost—a lot more round than it is now."

Emery got his first sports-writing job in 1923, on his 18th birthday. "I started on my birthday, September 13. I was a correspondent. I would catch the 10:30 electric car to Canton. They had a late deadline there at the *Canton Daily News*. I worked 365 days a year. I worked Christmas Day, too.

"I was offered a job at the Independent in 1926, a full-time job as a reporter. And I took it. I covered every game until 1956, with the exception of a period during World War II, in 1943 and 1944."

Even then, Emery managed to see a game every year.

"When I was on furlough, I saw the Canton-Massillon game in 1945. It was played in a sea of mud. It was a scoreless tie.

"I missed football during the war. I was still pullin' for 'em. I was out in training in the Mojave desert. The Booster Club sent me a Massillon pennant and I tied it to a Joshua tree."

Some of Emery's favorite Massillon Tiger game memories came on road trips. "We took a special train to New Castle in 1936," he recalled. "It was rainin' when we got on the train, it was rainin' when we got off. The lights in the stadium began poppin'. By the end of the game you couldn't hardly see at all. It just poured rain. My wife had a blue suit and a white rain coat. Her raincoat was blue when we got back home.

"Charlie Anderson got off the longest punt I have ever seen in football in that game, with a wet and soggy ball. Bob Glass was the punter, but he had one blocked and we were backed up in the shadows of our goal posts. It was fourth down. Glass said, 'You punt it Charlie.' Anderson dropped back and he kicked the wet, heavy ball 70 yards. And he didn't get much of a roll because the field was just a quagmire. Charlie played for Paul Brown at Ohio State, but he broke a training rule and Brown cut him.

Luther Emery (l) with childhood friend and Massillon coaching legend Paul Brown.

"I used to carry a portable typewriter along on road trips. I wrote the game story on the way home on the train."

Another favorite of Emery's was a road trip to Erie, Pennsylvania. "The Erie East game in '40, the 74-0 game," Emery said. "The crowd wouldn't let Massillon's band off of the field after the game. They played and played and I stayed and watched. Finally I went out to catch the bus. The buses had gone. I saw one come down the road empty. I flagged it down. The gang at Watts Confectionery, they had the 33 Club, a little booster club that rented a bus and went to all the games. It was named after the number of seats on a bus. Their bus passes the bus I was in by myself. We pulled up beside them at the traffic light. Somebody yelled, 'Look, Lut chartered a bus for himself,'" Emery recalled with a laugh.

Emery was close with both of Massillon's great coaching legends. Brown he knew since childhood, Chuck Mather he got to know when Mather coached Massillon. There was little doubt who Luther Emery was closest with.

"I liked him, yeah," Emery said of Brown. "We associated a good bit. I probably associated more with Mather. Chuck and I are good friends. He calls me every other week or so. And I get a letter from him every week, at least one. For no apparent reason at all. He called me the other night to tell me he'd won the tennis championship at his club. You'd have thought he'd beaten Canton."

EARL "ICK" MARTIN

All-Ohioan and three-year starter Earl Martin almost became the greatest Tiger who never was.

Earl Martin with head coach Paul Brown. Martin was Brown's captain in 1939, but he was not a big fan of the legendary coach.

Martin, who captained Paul Brown's 1939 state and national championship team, almost never got his chance to shine at Washington High School.

"I had the misfortune up at Longfellow Junior High School of having a confrontation with a woman teacher," Martin said. "She came up behind me in study hall and smacked me upside the head. I got up and hit her in the nose. I got thrown out of school for a couple of days. My coach, Hugh McGranahan, came and talked to me and got me back in school."

Martin said his action wasn't planned. "It was just a reaction on my part. She didn't say a word to me, she just came up behind me and hit me."

The incident did not escape

the seemingly all-knowing high school mentor Brown.

"Our Longfellow team came down to the high school to scrimmage against Massillon's third team," Martin said. "I remember I was playing defensive tackle and the runner came through and dragged me a few yards. Paul Brown said, 'That's the guy who's so tough with the woman teacher—he's not so tough when he gets down here on the football field.'

"I thought, 'Because of this, I'll never make the football team,' Martin said. "But I turned things around."

In those days the Massillon varsity played a team comprised of former Massillon players, called the Ex-Highs. It was in that game that sophomore Martin got his break. Brown had decided to move his All-Ohio center, Don Snavely, to end. Martin was second team center heading into the spring contest.

Things went better than Martin expected. "After halftime Brown put me in at center," Martin said. "We did pretty well in the second half. I can remember real well, he said, 'Son, you've just made this ball team.' So I overcame the battle with the teacher and won his respect."

But another event, at the end of his sophomore season, almost convinced Martin to give up the game. Massillon was playing Canton McKinley at Lehman field in Canton.

"It was a sea of mud," Martin said. "It was a day of snow storms. The ground was thawed, then this storm came through, the temperature was 15-20 degrees. The field was just mud, no grass on it. When we played on one end it'd be muddy. The next time you came down there the mud would be frozen it was so cold.

"We only had one ball. You can imagine what it'd be like with that mud on the ball. At half-time my two fingers were frozen—frostbitten.

"We washed 'em off in cold water and I finished the game. We beat 'em (19-6)."

Earl Martin dives in an attempt to block a punt against Canton McKinley.

"That's where I almost lost my desire to play football," Martin said. "We played over there—went over in a bus. We came back on route 30. I lived right on the corner of Hankins Road. When we came back from the McKinley game, one of the coaches asked if there was anybody there to meet me. I said no—at that time my mother and dad had never been to a football game. I said I didn't have a way. Well, they let me out on the corner. I'm telling you it was snowing; we had just played the game, taken a shower and I walked two miles down 27th street to Hankins Road. That's how I celebrated winning the Canton game."

GEORGE SLUSSER

George Slusser was not only one of Massillon's greatest players, he may have been Massillon's most handsome star.

A great passer and elusive runner for Paul Brown's 1938 and 1939 teams, Slusser was awarded a scholarship to Dartmouth, played for Brown at Ohio State, and later became a fighter pilot who sadly lost his life in the Pacific during World War II.

Classmates said George Slusser was so handsome that some teachers had a crush on him. This photograph, with a high school teacher on his lap, lends credence to those stories.

"He was a good looking kid," said Earl Martin, 1939 team captain and Slusser's center in 1938 and '39. "He had all the girls after him. Anybody who would meet George would like him. He wasn't real fast, wasn't real powerful," Martin said. "He was a true passer. He could throw that ball. He would have been a good pro quarterback.

"He and I used to put a show on in front of the fans before the game. I could pluck the ball out of the air with either hand. He'd get through running a play and he'd throw it back to me. He'd stretch me as far as he could just to see me stretch out and pluck the ball. The fans would always holler. Every time he'd throw it, he'd throw it about three feet over my head. I'd go up with one hand and pluck it."

Slusser knives through the Mansfield defense in 1939.

Slusser has the distinction of being the only quarterback to lead Massillon to back-to-back 10-0 seasons, in 1938 and '39. Those teams were also state champs. The 1939 Tigers were national champs.

In his final high school game, against Canton McKinley, Slusser ran for 159 yards and two touchdowns—one a 51-yarder, and threw a 21-yard touchdown pass in a 20-6 win. He was rewarded by being picked as the state's first team All-Ohio quarterback for 1939.

Slusser transferred from Dartmouth to Ohio State after his freshman season when Paul Brown got the job as head coach. He played at Ohio State for two years before being drafted into the Army.

He received his wings and

was commissioned as a pilot in 1944.

"I was home from the service after he had joined the air corps," Martin said. "I stopped over to see his mother. She was so worried about him. He had just got out of flight training. I told her, 'Mrs. Slusser, they lose more of those people in flight training than in combat.' I was trying to make her feel better."

Paul Brown (l) with George Slusser at Ohio State University. Slusser transferred from Dartmouth to play for Brown at Ohio State.

Slusser piloted a P-47 fighter plane in the Pacific. In letters to his wife and mother, mailed the day he died, he said, "I've been getting plenty of flying over Japan and I'm looking forward to returning home to lead a normal life again."

He was shot down over the Ryukyu Islands in the Pacific.

"I hadn't seen Slusser's mother," Martin said. "Two days before the war's over he got shot down. I never did go and see her. After that happened I couldn't face her. They never did find him. He was just lost in the Pacific."

PAUL E. BROWN

Any serious discussion of Massillon Tigers football begins and ends with the man known as "Father Football."

Paul Brown, arguably the greatest football coach of all time, is the only coach to win national championships at the high school, college, and professional levels. And through all his successes and all of his championships—14 in all—Brown always harkened back to his hometown of Massillon, Ohio.

Paul Brown pioneered football film study while at coaching at Massillon.

Brown won six state championships and four national championships at Massillon between 1935 and 1940. He won Ohio State's first national championship in 1942. He led the Cleveland Browns to 11 championship games, winning it all seven times. Brown coached the Cincinnati Bengals to the playoffs quicker than any other expansion team. His Bengals also reached the Super Bowl faster than any other team.

Brown's childhood was spent playing on Massillon's playgrounds. In high school he was a Massillon quarterback, a pole vaulter and a star basketball player. As head coach he brought Massillon to national prominence.

Brown's coaching success at Ohio State and with the Cleveland Browns—with rosters dotted with Massillon players—brought Massillon even more fame. And when he was laid to rest, he again put his hometown in the spotlight as national media descended, making Massillon look like a Hollywood movie set.

It was the perfect environment for Brown, who was already totally immersed in sports.

The game of football, still in its infancy, was bursting at its seams in Massillon when Brown moved there with his family in 1916. While the high school team was reaching new heights with its first undefeated, untied season, the real noise was coming from the professional gridiron. Notre Dame's legendary Knute Rockne was starring for the Pro Tigers against the Canton Bulldogs and their star, Jim Thorpe. Meanwhile, numerous semi-pro teams were playing throughout the city.

It was the perfect environment for the nine-year-old Brown, who was already totally immersed in sports. Memories of those early years stayed with Brown throughout his life.

Mike Brown recalled his

father telling him about the early days of semi-pro football in Massillon.

"One day, it was odd, he was in his 80s," said Mike Brown, "we were driving in the car and he started talking about when he was a young kid going out to watch the semi-pro teams back then in Massillon. He could remember the names of the players on the teams. He could line 'em up as though it were yesterday."

Brown's younger sister, Marian Brown Evans, recalled attending a Massillon-Canton McKinley high school game with her brother in 1919. "I remember the first game I saw," she said, "It was over at Myers Lake. It was a Massillon-Canton game. Paul was in grade school. My mother and Mrs. Buttermore drove us over in the old Ford. Stan Buttermore was a neighbor of ours, he became a Massillon policeman. So when we got over there, Paul and Stan went off by themselves. I remember watching the game and having no idea what was going on. After the game was over they came back to the car and we asked them who won. Paul and Stan sure knew what was going on." Massillon won that day, 21-0.

Brown was born in Norwalk, Ohio, where his first football memory was formed. "When I was in Norwalk," Brown said, "I had a little football, I must have been four or five years old. Then the bladder went the way of all bladders and we stuffed it with leaves and rags. We played with my little boyhood friends, football, or at least we thought we did."

"I remember when he first got to know Dave Stewart," Evans said. "Dave was the head football coach in

Massillon (1921-25). They were at the Longfellow Junior High School yard and they were pole vaulting. Paul wasn't even in high school yet. Paul went up to Dave and said 'I can do better than that.' Dave said, 'Let's see you do it.' And he did. Paul had done it in Norwalk and knew he could do it better than they were doing it. He and Dave kind of got acquainted that way."

"The Brown Family didn't have a whole lot of money...they lived close to the buck."

Tom McConnaughy

Luther Emery, longtime sports writer and editor of Massillon's *Evening Independent,* was a childhood friend of Brown's in Massillon. He remembers Brown showing up at one of their neighborhood football games. "We used to play in back of Lorin Andrews school," Emery said. "Paul lived in the back of the school yard on Green Avenue. He came wandering up and was leaning up against a tree watching us. This was just a pick-up neighborhood game and one of the boys got called to dinner. Paul asked if he could take his place. We finally said, 'Okay.' We thought he was too small. We found out he wasn't."

Another boyhood friend, Tom McConnaughy, also recalled the neighborhood gang's first meeting with Brown. "We told Paul how we played. He said, 'I'd like to play quarterback on one team.' We said, 'Okay.' The first time they hiked the ball back to him, he threw the ball way high in the air and then ran like crazy, caught his own forward pass and ran for a touchdown. We said, 'You can't do that.' He did it two or three times and we had to outlaw it. When he'd get the ball you couldn't catch him. He'd go for a touchdown about every time he got the ball. He was fast."

McConnaughy was two years younger than Paul and lived two doors down from the Browns. "They didn't have a whole lot of money," McConnaughy said, "they lived pretty close to the buck."

The McConnaughy family, on the other hand, were the wealthy owners of the Ideal Company, a thriving business in downtown Massillon. They had a clay tennis court in their back yard.

"Kids from all over Massillon came there to play tennis," McConnaughy said, "We liked to have 'em come. One day here comes Paul. He said, 'Could I learn to play tennis? I've got a racket.' He had a wood-framed racket with a broken string in it. We taught him how to serve and receive. Inside of a week he beat everybody in the area with that broken racket. He was a better player than anybody else we'd ever had. He could cover that court like you wouldn't believe. What an athlete he was. Quick and fast. We'd never seen an athlete who could cover

"Paul said, 'Could I learn to play tennis? I've got a racket'... Inside a week he beat everybody."

Tom McConnaughy

the court like that. You just couldn't beat him. He wasn't a good tennis player. There was no form to him. But, boy, when the ball was in play, you couldn't get it away from him. He'd get it no matter where you put it. You tried to drop one over the net and he'd get it and put it right past you. He never did get a better racket. He had a very humble beginning. He made a lot out of nothin'.

> **"The only reason he took me up there was I couldn't eat and I couldn't sleep."**
>
> **Paul Brown**

Evans remembers Paul playing tennis. "I remember he and a friend, Ralph Williams, won the city doubles' championship."

Evans, Brown's only sibling, remembers the family's early days in Massillon. "My father was moved to Brewster to work at the Wheeling and Lake Erie railroad. He brought us to Brewster over the weekend and took us to Massillon on that little tram that was called the Hootle Bug. We got off the tram at Lincoln Way at the base of the viaduct there. There was a huge sign across the street that said, 'Massillon Invites Industry' all lit up at night. We moved into an apartment that was right across from the post office downtown. It was upstairs. We lived up there for a year."

As a youngster, Brown persuaded his father to take him to a tryout with the Massillon Tigers. "I went out," Brown said, "I was full of vim and vigor. I wasn't very big. I can remember my father brought me up to Turkey Foot, it was my freshman year of high school. The only reason he took me up there was I couldn't eat and I couldn't sleep. I had talked myself into the fact that I was going to go up to the football camp at Turkey Foot. And it never entered my mind that I wasn't going to be allowed to go. My mother and father felt I was too small, too young. My dad finally relented and drove me up."

Brown at Massillon, circa 1936.

Stewart was Massillon's coach on that fateful day. He told the Hall of Fame Luncheon Club in Canton in a 1967 speech that he didn't invite Brown to the football camp at Turkey Foot, "because he was just a little colt with knobby knees." He said that Lester Brown brought Paul to the fourth day of practice after Paul hadn't eaten or slept for three days. "The boy thought he belonged in camp and I told his dad that I'd keep him and see to it that he wouldn't get hurt."

Stewart was busy putting together the 1922 Massillon Tigers, a team that would become Massillon's first state champions. To Stewart, Lester's son, Paul Brown, looked more like a manager than a player.

"It was just the beginning

of it," Brown said of his first practices at Massillon. "Dave became a little intrigued by me, and it was just the beginning of my story here."

Stewart took Brown under his wing and actually became quite fond of his pint-sized quarterback. Brown learned from his mentor and as a 120-pound sophomore back-up quarterback he saw his first varsity action.

"I could throw, at least I thought I could, and that was the thing that intrigued Dave," Brown said. "The first game I ever went in, he told me what the pass would be and I just threw it—and it was a touchdown. I walked out and my father would have liked to have fallen over in the stands. He couldn't believe this could happen to me. It really made Dave Stewart take more of an interest in me. Of course, throwing the ball was more daring than it is today. As time went on I played all the time at quarterback."

Evans remembers watching her brother play for Massillon. "I was scared a lot, hoping he wouldn't get hurt," she said. "He was always so little. But he always did well, never had a serious injury of any kind. He was always smaller than everyone else out there. He used his brains instead of his brawn.

"I don't know where he got all his smartness when it came to athletics. My father was never into anything like that. Father was all work and no play. When Paul played father went to the games and when Paul coached he went to the games. He was very proud of him. I don't think he ever went out and tossed a ball with him or anything. My mother was sports-minded. Paul always said he got his aggressiveness from his mother. Mother had to win and so did Paul. Whether it was cards or what."

The diminutive Brown went on to play quarterback as a junior and senior. He was known as an intelligent field general whose speciality was short, accurate passes. Emery compared Brown to Stuhldreher, who quarterbacked Massillon in 1919 and later became an All-American quarterback at Notre Dame.

"I don't know where he got all his smartness when it came to athletics. My father was never into anything like that."

Marian Evans

Bud Houghton, who succeeded Brown as Massillon's head coach in 1941, was a childhood friend of Brown's.

"Paul Brown was a real serious kid," Houghton said. "He played the piano, I played the drums. I remember one time, Paul and I played for a dance at St. Timothy's church. He wasn't a great football player, but he was a good player. A very intelligent guy, Paul had a very good mind. He developed himself into a good forward passer. In fact I think he was the first good passer that Massillon ever had. He was a good basketball player. In fact he was a better basketball player than he was a football player. He was excellent. He was a good athlete."

Brown started only one football game as a junior in 1924. It was a humbling experience. "I remember one time Dave started what he called his 'pony' backfield. Pauley Smith and a couple of us little guys got to start against Akron South. We got into trouble. They finally had to put the men in to pull it out. Massillon was getting licked for a while. I couldn't believe that we couldn't do what those other guys did. I was so obsessed with it, I think I didn't really know my own limitations. But, anyway, the team finally won the game (33-20). We sure gave them about a 20-0 deficit."

> **"I don't think father ever went out and tossed a ball with him...he always said he got his aggressiveness from his mother."**
>
> **Marian Evans**

Brown saw more action at quarterback as a senior, but he was still the second choice to Vince Define, who was Stewart's captain.

A highlight of Brown's senior year came in an historic road game against a strong Erie Academy team in Pennsylvania. When Define was ejected for fighting, Stewart turned to Brown's passing and Elwood Kammer's running to lead the Tigers to a 17-10 win.

With the game tied 10-10, Brown completed a 35-yard pass to give Massillon the ball at Erie's one-yard line. Two plays later Kammer, Massillon's star running back and the school's first All-Ohioan, smashed over for the winning score.

Brown's fondest memory

as a player at Massillon involved a pass. "We beat Toledo Woodward on a forward pass, I threw it to Paul Storrie," Brown said.

McConnaughy crossed paths with Brown again in high school. "I was in high school with Paul. He was dating a girl called Katie Kester, her folks ran a greenhouse. I was attracted to Katie also. But she wanted Paul. Well, he went off to school. I didn't go to school at first, I went later. I thought, 'Now's my chance to get in with Katie.' I asked her and she said, 'Sure, I'll go out with ya.' We went out and we had a real nice time, so I asked for another date. And we went out again. And I was really encouraged with her. Then on the third date all she wanted to talk about was Paul. Everything had to do with Paul or she didn't talk. I could see that there wasn't any chance for me. She was wrapped up with Paul. So I bowed out of the situation. But I liked her real well. She was a really nice girl. But I can still remember thinking, 'I wish she would talk about something else.' Then she married him, of course."

Before Brown married his high school sweetheart, he enrolled at Ohio State, where he planned to continue his football career. His father approved of his college choice.

"It was the state university and my father thought that's where I should go," Brown said. "He wasn't interested in whether I played athletics. He wanted me to play if I wanted to, but football in particular, he didn't think I was big enough to do it."

The coaching staff at Ohio State shared Lester Brown's opinion.

"They wouldn't give me a uniform for football, which was quite a blow for this 'great' player," Brown said, using the term 'great' facetiously. "They just took one look at me. I weighed about 150 pounds."

Brown transferred to Miami University after his first year at Ohio State. He did so with his father's blessing. "I had taken a trip down to Miami University in Oxford and I fell in love with that place. I thought it was just what college should look like. So I asked my father and at first he was reluctant. But he said, 'Since your grades are satisfactory, and it's a state school, you can transfer.'"

> **"They wouldn't give me a uniform for football, which was quite a blow..."**
>
> **Paul Brown**

At Miami, Brown was welcomed on the football squad and actually made a name for himself at quarterback.

During summers he would reunite with Stewart, who had moved from Massillon to Sharon, Pennsylvania. Brown said, "Dave made me enjoy coaching. I was just obsessed with it. I enjoyed it, I was a goner. He recognized this."

After graduating from Miami, Brown felt lucky to land a coaching and teaching job at Severn Prep in Maryland. "I was one of the few guys to get a job in coaching right out of college in 1930," Brown said. "I was not gonna be 21 'til I started work there at Severn."

Interestingly, Brown was not hired as the head football coach for the military prep school.

"He wanted to get a job coaching," Evans recalled. "I just remember he said that he was going there to coach a game he never played—lacrosse. He went out there and learned it and taught 'em."

Brown also assisted Severn's football coach, Bill Hoover.

"He was dying of cancer," Brown said. "This man was in bad shape. It was an opportunity. I became an English grammar teacher and History teacher and coached. We had success. I think we lost one game in two years."

Brown as a quarterback at Miami University.

After Brown's 12-2-1 stint at Severn, the Massillon job opened up in 1932. Brown's major competition for the Massillon job was another former Massillon player, Bill Edwards. Edwards became a great coach himself. His legendary career at Wittenberg University landed him in the College Football Hall of Fame.

When Brown returned to Massillon, he inherited a program that was down. The team's equipment was in deplorable condition.

"I remember them putting on

the equipment, even shoes that had been worn before by someone," Brown said, "I don't think the public realized the condition of football when I first came here."

Massillon had finished 2-6-2 under Elmer McGrew in 1931. About the only highlight was a 20-6 win over Canton McKinley.

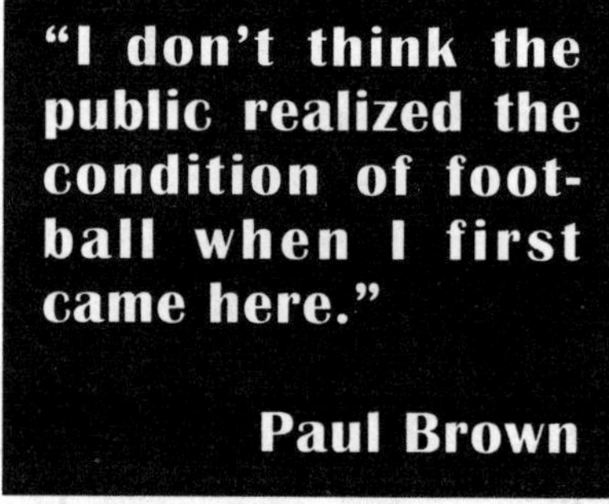
"I don't think the public realized the condition of football when I first came here."

Paul Brown

"The first time I ran into Paul after he got the job was down in Lincoln Park, at the Bottoms there," old friend Emery remembered. "There was a football game. I met him on the sidelines and we walked home together. He was telling me what his plans were. He was going to copy from Chic Meehan, the New York University coach. They were real hot at the time.

"Chic Meehan's offense was a military shift. Paul would have them line up like that, hup, two, three, kind of military-like. They gave that up after one year.

"I remember asking him what was going to be different. He said 'We won't be using the water bucket.' It used to be every time out someone would run with the water bucket and a dipper. 'And the team will stand during all intermissions. They will not get down and rest. Meehan also had them jump over a rope in front of the bench when they came off the field, but I'm not going to do that.'

"Paul started having three teams, first, second and third. He'd rotate them at desirable times. It might have been Chic's idea, it might have been Paul Brown's. He'd take a whole team out and put another in if he was far enough ahead — which wasn't very often his first year."

Brown actually won his first five games as Massillon's coach. Things changed following a 0-0 tie with Barberton. The Tigers were shut out in four straight losses, including a season-ending 19-0 loss to Canton McKinley.

"We gathered very slowly," Brown said of his rookie campaign. "We won five games, then we lost four games."

Brown at a snowy Tiger Stadium.

Evans recalled her big brother's return to Massillon. She was 21 at the time. Brown was 23.

"He started rebuilding things the minute he got here," Evans said. "He taught English and History in high school. One of my good friends was in his history class. She said the girls were all so impressed because he always called them, 'Miss' so and so. It was always very formal. It made them feel very grown up.

"It was just something so

new in town, the things he did. It seemed extra special. He seemed to be able to figure out things that nobody thought of before. Massillon football was all he thought of, I think. He *lived* it."

Brown led the 1933 team to an 8-2 record. "One loss was to Barberton," Emery said. "Barberton's Jumpin' Joe Williams ran 50 yards backwards and 100 yards forward. That's an exaggeration, but he was quite a star. The score was 6-0. He scored the only touchdown, Jumpin' Joe. He starred later on at Ohio State."

"She said the girls were all so impressed because he always called them 'Miss' so and so..."

Marian Evans

But the dagger for Brown was a disappointing 21-0 loss to Canton McKinley to close the 1933 season. The loss to McKinley and their head coach, Jimmy Aiken—who started at McKinley at the same time Brown started at Massillon—almost led to Brown's firing.

"The people were a little bit anxious because primarily we didn't beat Canton right off the bat," Brown said. "I remember one of them who was on the school board was always very questioning of the various formations and everything. Then he was one of the big rooters when things began to go better. I'll never forget when I was coaching at Ohio State a few years later and we were at Pittsburgh. Who's seated out there in the front row of Pitt Stadium, it was this guy. He became a big rooter, a personal rooter. The public, you've got to understand, they get disappointed. They want to get there in a hurry."

The 1934 Tigers were Brown's first powerhouse at Massillon, outscoring their first nine opponents 421-0. Then came Brown's third match-up with McKinley's coach, Aiken.

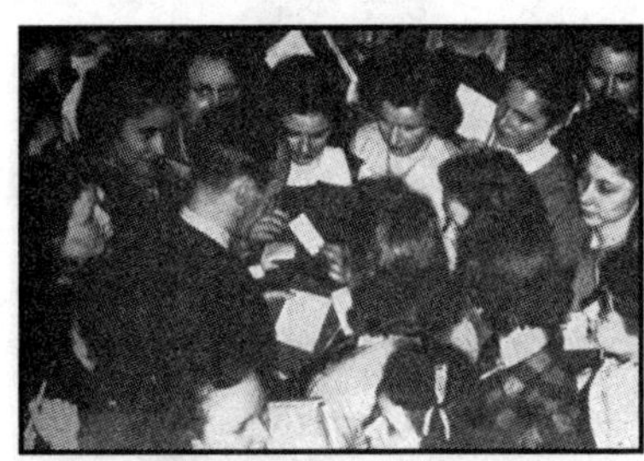

Star status: Brown is besieged by students seeking his autograph in 1940.

The 1934 Bulldogs are still considered among the very best Canton teams of all time. McKinley had outscored its first 10 opponents 466-12.

The anticipation for the game couldn't have been bigger. Massillon worked during the season to expand the stadium to accommodate the frenzied crowd. The stadium capacity was more than doubled—to over 20,000.

Aiken prevailed again, 21-6, ending Brown's bid for an undefeated, unscored-on season.

"He was shattered," Mike Byelene said of Brown. Byelene was a sophomore in 1934. He would become one of Massillon's finest quarterbacks. Due to injuries, he played extensively in the 1934 McKinley game. "I played three whole quarters," he said. "It was a tough game."

Brown came back with even more resolve in 1935. Augie Morningstar was his captain.

He penned a six-page letter to Morningstar, detailing what he expected for the 1935 season.

"He really didn't leave anything to the imagination," Morningstar said. "I read it and tried to follow it. I just didn't know if I *deserved* to be captain or not. I went down and talked to him. He told me I was his choice. If I didn't want it then don't worry about playin'. Because he was runnin' the team."

Brown at Massillon, just prior to his move to Ohio State.

Brown started the letter by saying, "Dear August, you are my choice to be Washington High's 1935 captain. It is a big honor, but it carries many responsibilities. It takes a super boy to carry out the responsibilities that I have lined up for you—but I expect you to do it."

Brown's letter gave Morningstar a list of players and whether they got a tackling dummy or a football. "Burlap charging sack, piled full of sand and sawdust," Morningstar said, "we knocked that. Hung it up as a tackling dummy and worked at it all summer long."

The letter enlisted Morningstar to canvas the town,

making sure the players had their dummy hanging from a tree in their yard. He had to work with center Don Voss all summer. "Drop by and see Voss every couple of weeks and work on his passing with him—make him do it every day, as it means 'make' or 'break' to your team," Brown told Morningstar.

Brown ordered Morningstar to "See that the players abide by the rules that I set up for you and you will have captained the State Champions. You must:

A) Be the first man dressed and on the field (Check that they all do their exercises until I get up on the field.)

B) Be the first to respond to my whistle or any call from me. Call out, 'Hurry up gang.' They must like you, be glad to jump in behind you. You must expect to lead, then they will expect to be led. Remind them to hand in their plays monthly this summer.

C) Be cheerful and spartan-like in your attitude no matter how hard the work-out has been or no matter how tired you are. Constantly remind the boys of this axiom: 'Drive yourself in practice and you won't have to in games.'

D) See that, if I am particularly sharp in my criticisms, the boys understand the idea that it is to make a ball club—allow no sour pickles to develop.

E) Sing and have fun in your showers. Keep your talk clean.

"Here is the code a Massillon Captain must live up to:

1. The team comes first.

2. Set an example not only as a football player but also as a gentleman, scholar and school citizen.

3. Be alert for opportunities to better the team.

4. Be in all instances a sports-

man and a gentleman.

"Hang this little book I am enclosing up by a string in your toilet and read it every time you go in there," Brown concluded.

Brown's attention to detail paid dividends in 1935. His highest-scoring team at Massillon scored 483 points and gave up just two touchdowns all season. Best of all, Brown turned the tables on Aiken, beating McKinley, 6-0, to win his first state and national championships.

Brown (l) finally beat McKinley head coach Jimmy Aiken in 1935 after three tries.

"'Jake 'em' Aiken," Emery said. "Aiken was a tough guy. He played tough football. I liked him. Brown liked him. Paul came up with the good team, the better team in 1935."

Aiken left McKinley after that game to become head coach at the University of Akron. He later led programs at Nevada and Oregon. His 1948 Oregon squad played in the Cotton Bowl.

Brown followed his historic 1935 season with another of the best teams in Massillon history in 1936.

Byelene was back as the starting quarterback after splitting the job with Howard Dutton in 1935. Byelene was a dual threat. But he was also an outstanding runner. He teamed up with two-time All-Ohio running back Bob Glass and speedster Edgar “Echo” Herring to make the 1936 backfield as potent as any in Massillon history.

“Echo” was a nickname that spoke to Herring’s blazing speed. “Brown called him, ‘Echo,’ because he was so fast,” Morningstar said. “He called him, ‘Echo,’ because he’d say, ‘Here he comes, there he goes.’ He was just an echo.”

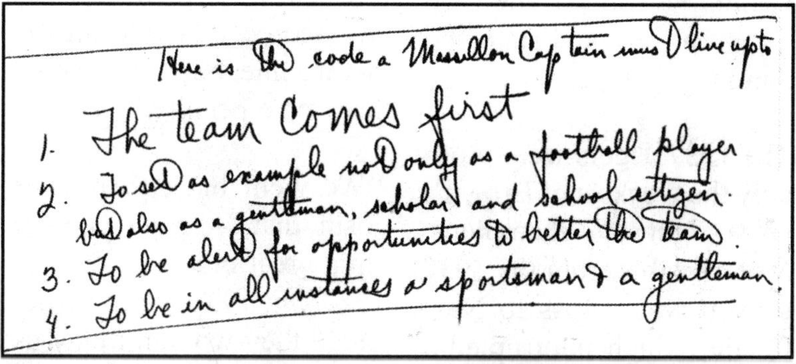

Here is the code a Massillon Captain must live up to
1. The team comes first
2. To set an example not only as a football player but also as a gentleman, scholar and school citizen.
3. To be alert for opportunities to better the team.
4. To be in all instances a sportsman & a gentleman.

Excerpt from a letter from Brown to 1935 captain, Augie Morningstar, outlining “The code a Massillon Captain must live up to.”

Herring may have been the fastest player in Massillon history. “I could outrun most guys,” Herring said, “I don’t know of any I couldn’t outrun. I weighed 142-145 pounds. I usually faked ’em out. Fake one way, then go the other. I had a good side step, a good stutter step. Throw ’em off balance.”

Byelene was fast, too. He was a noted speedster in the Big 10 when he played halfback at Purdue.

“I was a lot faster than Mike,”

Herring said. "I always thought Mike Byelene was a little slow, but maybe it was because I was so fast."

The 1936 Tigers were never challenged, posting eight shutouts in 10 games, including a 21-0 decision over Canton McKinley. The 1936 Tigers were voted state and national champs.

The 1937 Tigers were probably the weakest of Brown's six straight state champions. Most notable from the 1937 season was a loss to New Castle, which interrupted a pair of incredible unbeaten streaks.

Massillon had a 26-game unbeaten streak stopped when they lost, 7-0, to New Castle in 1937. They immediately started a 52-game streak that didn't end until the final game of the 1942 season. That remains a state record, almost 70 years later.

Brown said, "I took my players to a movie in the afternoon, which is my custom to get 'em away from it. And we all of a sudden had guys who were vomiting and what not. I called Dr. Bell. He told me they couldn't play against New Castle. We lost on a forward pass. We scored earlier from the 8-yard line, but it was called back on a penalty.

"We went back then after losin' that 7-0 game and ran up a great big score on 'em (52-7) in 1938 and they decided they wouldn't play us anymore. So that ended the series."

Emery recalled with a laugh the only words he ever had with Brown.

"I walked in the locker room and Brown said, 'And you, too. You thought that we were going to run all over New Castle.' I said, 'Yeah, but I didn't know the right side of your line was going to be out.' That's the only words I ever had with Paul. He was madder than a hornet."

Brown won the rest of his games at Massillon, winning state titles in 1938, '39 and '40. His 1939 and '40 teams were also voted national champions. Brown shut out 60 percent of his opponents at Massillon.

Brown's success put Massillon on the map nationally. "I'll never forget *Life* magazine," Brown said. "They spent more time taking pictures. I often wondered how they selected the very few they used. It was a phenomena to me. They took hundreds of pictures. I think that was the first time a big magazine ever did that for a high school. Whenever people think of Massillon, to this day, they think of football right away.

After Brown's 1940 team dominated their schedule, outscoring opponents 477-6, including shutouts in their first nine games, Brown interviewed for the head coaching position at Ohio State.

"Mr. St. John, the director of athletics at Ohio State, called me and asked me if I would drive to Wooster to a professor's home where he would like to talk to me. St. John wasn't sure about putting a high school coach in down there. But he came to our home and he was taken with my wife Katie, he liked Katie. From that point onward we began to negotiate. And when I say negotiate, it was when would I go there. I never asked them how much they paid. I don't think it was a whole lot more than I was making at Massillon. I had received my Master's there, so I knew quite a few of the professors in education as a result. I told them I wasn't so concerned about the money as I would like to have a full professorship because it would put me in standing with the faculty. I didn't realize it at the time but that pleased St. John and they made me a full professor."

Brown had not quite reached star status, he found out, when he arrived at Ohio Stadium for his first game as Ohio State's head coach.

"Our opening game, we're playing Don Faurot, who had been a candidate for the Ohio State job. I'm riding in with the buses with our players and as we're going in the gate I see a bunch of Massillon guys there. Tink Ulrich and Swig Thomas, people that I had been with for the last ten years. So I jumped out of the bus and talked with 'em. I then went into the game and would you believe I couldn't get in the game. The gatekeeper wouldn't let me in without a ticket. He didn't know me. I told him who I was. He said, 'Yeah, yeah,' just like, 'Get away, boy, you're botherin' me.' I went over, picked up some pebbles and I was throwin' 'em up to where our training room was. I hit the window and somebody came and looked out. It was one of the players and he said, 'Coach, what are you doing down there?' I said, 'Have somebody come down here and get me in.' And the trainer came down and got me in the ball game."

Brown's Ohio State team beat Faurot's Missouri team, 12-7. It was the first time Brown had seen a Split-T formation. His friends from Massillon expressed concern to their former mentor.

"I ran into some of the same

guys in a little affair of Massillon's after the game and I'll never forget Tink sayin', 'Hey P, if you can't beat that team anymore than 12-7, this is gonna be a long season for ya.' He didn't know it, but they ended up playing in the Sugar Bowl. They were a great team and we didn't even know it. That was my introduction to Ohio State. Those were exciting days."

Brown with Ohio State athletic director Lynn St. John.

Brown finished 6-1-1 his first year at Ohio State. The loss was to Northwestern, where Brown was beaten by Otto Graham, the quarterback who would eventually lead his Cleveland Browns teams to all of their championships.

"He was a tailback in the single wing," Brown said, "I don't think I've ever seen anybody do anything quite like it. He ran to the left and he did a great big cross sashay. For a righthanded quarterback to throw on the run all the way to the other side of the field like he did... that was some coordinated man. He made a believer out of me. They beat us 14-7 on that one play."

The final game, a 20-20 tie at Michigan, was one of Brown's all-time favorites. It was in that game that Brown invented the technique of freezing the kicker, albeit that was not his intention.

"I was always given credit for being smart in that

game," Brown said. "It wasn't that. I just didn't want to see it happen. The score was 20-20 and there were just seconds to play and they had to line up for an extra point which would have made it 21-20. And every time they'd get ready I'd send in another substitute and they'd wave it down. I actually just hated—couldn't stand—to see the guy kick the ball and beat us after we had fought. We were big underdogs. Finally the kid that was doing the kicking was getting a little tight under his chin. He just flubbed it. We came home from the game on the train as if we'd won the game."

In 1942 Brown won Ohio State's first national championship. The only loss was to fellow Massillonian Harry Stuhldreher, who was coaching Wisconsin.

"The same kind of thing happened to us like happened in high school," Brown said. "The water we took on the train made people sick. We just had tremendous diarrhea and we had people sick.

"We were voted national champions. It was a high honor and we were on our way from this point on."

Brown was named the national Coach of the Year in 1942. His team he had assembled for 1943 was thought by some to be the finest collection of college talent ever assembled.

"It could have been the best team ever," Brown said. "It was organized. I knew where the players were because I had been in high school football, and the high school coaches were my friends. The state of Ohio was the boundaries of our campus. We were after anybody in the state. And they were almost all in-state people."

World War II had different plans for the intended stars of Brown's 1943 team.

"The 1943 team, Brown's boys, were shipped out," Emery said. "He was left with just remnants."

Brown said, "They had to be 17-years-old or younger. They called us, 'The Baby Bucks.' It was hard for me to handle losing because I wasn't used to it."

A highlight of the 1943 season came at the end of the game with Illinois. Time had expired with the game tied 20-20.

Brown using classroom techniques to teach football at Ohio State, a practice he introduced at Massillon.

"The official came rappin' on my door and said, 'Coach, could I see you a moment?"

It turns out the game had ended on a defensive penalty.

"The official said, 'You've got one more play.' I said, 'We'll take the play.' So we walk out there and some of the players have their shoulder pads off. The crowd, there's only about a third of them left. It never entered my mind that we were going to kick a field goal and win the game. I remember everybody was standing on the sideline. I've got my arms spread out tryin' to keep everybody back. It was about a 30-yard field goal. John Stungis kicked it and I said to (assistant coach) Carroll Widdoes, 'I think that bloomin' thing went over.' It surprised me and at that point I'm up in the air on people's shoulders. It was an amazing end."

Brown's next stop was at Great Lakes Naval Training Center where he was a junior grade lieutenant.

"We had played Great Lakes with our Baby Bucks," Brown said. "The Admiral there sort of liked us and he had asked Mr. St. John if I went in the service if he'd let him know. I got to Great Lakes and they had a place for us to stay. It was all set up. And of course I coached the football team and became athletic officer. We had some outstanding teams."

While serving at Great Lakes, Brown was approached by Arthur "Mickey" McBride, who, among other interests, ran taxi companies in Cleveland, Akron and Canton.

"John Dietrich, the writer for the *Cleveland Plain Dealer*, told McBride to get me," Brown said. "Arch Ward, the sports editor for the *Chicago Tribune*, was starting this league with the idea that, like in baseball, there would be a National League and an American League. At first I wasn't interested in the proposal.

"I finally talked with Mr. St. John. He said, 'Paul, you have the right to come back, it's your job. You'll have to work something out with Widdoes because he's had a good year.' Well, I was a little tender on the subject, I guess. I thought, 'Well, I'll make this easy for everybody.' And they were talking about building a franchise in Cleveland. I could do it pretty easily because I knew the players that were going through Great Lakes that I wanted. It wasn't like starting up a new league. Some of the players had been in the service for three or four years and there were no contracts left anymore. They were null and void. So I went after my own people. I actually signed my contract to coach the Cleveland Browns in the *Chicago Tribune* offices.

Brown as a Naval officer, circa 1945.

"Mr. St. John took some abuse because of the fact that I made this decision. He was a grand man. I liked St. John. Some people always had the idea I didn't, but that wasn't true at all."

Over the years there has been controversy concerning the naming of the Browns. Brown put the rumor to rest.

McBride ran a contest to name the Browns. The contest ended with the Panthers being chosen as the team name. After it was discovered that there had been a semi-pro team named the Cleveland Panthers, another contest was run.

"They decided to run another contest," Brown said. "It was decided that they would use whatever name appeared the most. Whatever word it was that came in on most of the letters. Since I had been coach at Ohio State and Massillon, and was right at home, the name 'Browns' came into play more often than any of them. 'The Cleveland Browns.' We were a success right away."

"Mr. St. John said 'Paul, you have the right to come back, it's your job...I was a little tender on the subject, I guess."

Paul Brown

The Browns dominated the fledgling All-American Football Conference. They won the championship all four years the league existed. Their dominance may have been the reason for the league's demise.

"We won too much, they said," Brown deadpanned. Indeed the Browns were a staggering 52-4-3 from 1946-49. At one point the Browns won 29 straight games. In 1948 the Browns finished 15-0. The only other undefeated, untied team in professional football history is the Miami Dolphins of 1972. Brown said his team was at its peak in 1948.

"I thought the peak was about two years before we got into the NFL," Brown said. "That's when Marion Motley was young. Otto Graham was young—real young. We were better then than when they merged us in 1950. We had great personnel."

The NFL schedule-makers decided to pit the Browns against the Philadelphia Eagles, NFL champs from

1948-49, in their first game in the league in 1950. The Browns won, 35-10. Eagles Hall of Fame coach Earle "Greasy" Neale chided the Browns, even in defeat.

"After we had won the game big, Greasy Neale said, 'Brown should be a basketball coach.' The game really was not a close contest," Brown said. "After the game, Commissioner Bert Bell came in our locker room. He stuck out his hand and said, 'That's the most intensely coached football team I've ever seen.'

"We had worked on the Eagle defense for about a year. Those were pretty fun days. It was a pretty good dissecting, or surgery, as we used to call it."

After Neale's "basketball" comment, referring to the Brown's reliance on the pass, Brown decided to play the second game against the Eagles without passing. He was successful, leading the Browns to a 13-7 win without throwing a single pass.

The Browns won the 1950 championship 30-29 over the Los Angeles Rams. The Browns were in the NFL championship game their first six years in the league, winning three times.

Brown's life changed drastically when 38-year-old advertising executive Art Modell bought the team in March of 1961.

Bad blood between Modell and Brown started almost immediately. The situation quickly deteriorated, with Modell firing Brown in January of 1963, less than two years after he bought the team.

"I never dreamed of such a thing," Brown said. "I was under contract for eight more years. When Modell came he said he was buying the team primarily because of yours truly."

Evans saw the writing on the wall when Brown made a visit to Massillon.

"Paul came to Massillon, my mother was very ill at that time, it was shortly before he was fired. Paul said, 'Things aren't going well at all. I don't know what's going to happen.' Paul figured Jim Brown and Art Modell were together. I remember Paul saying that just before he was fired he had gone over to Modell's home to talk to him and he said when he pulled up, Jim Brown was just coming out. He always figured they were together on that deal.

"Modell wanted to be the top man and Paul had been the top man. They just clashed, that's all. And Modell owned the team. After that Paul said he'd never be put in a position again where he could be fired."

Brown lended his name and image to a board game in the 1940s.

The news of Brown's firing shocked the sports world. *Cleveland Press-News* sportswriter Frank Gibbons said Brown's firing was "Like the Terminal Tower Toppling." The Terminal Tower was Cleveland's tallest skyscraper in 1963. Brown, too, was a towering figure, considered the top coach in the history of professional football.

The Cleveland newspapers were on strike when the firing occurred. A 32-page magazine, *Paul Brown, The Play He Didn't Call*, edited by legendary Cleveland sportswriter Hal Lebovitz, was produced because, "people openly admitted they hungered to read what their favorite writers had to say about the toppling of Brown."

The Cleveland writers collectively were aware that problems existed between Brown and Modell, but didn't think a firing was imminent. They quoted several disgruntled players who voiced displeasure with Brown and felt the change was good.

It was well known that Hall of Famer Jim Brown, who many consider the finest running back of all-time, did not see eye to eye with Brown.

There was also controversy surrounding Ernie Davis, the Heisman Trophy winner from Syracuse who was acquired by Cleveland after being the first pick of the 1961 NFL draft by Washington. Cleveland traded future Hall of Famer Bobby Mitchell for Davis. Davis was diagnosed with leukemia before he ever had the opportunity to play for the Browns. When his leukemia went into remission, there was disagreement between Brown and Modell about whether to play Davis. Brown, with backing from NFL Commissioner Pete Rozelle, chose not to play Davis. Davis died in 1963.

Because of his success at Cleveland, a 167-53-8 record in 17 years, and his long-term contract, many thought Brown was untouchable in spite of his differences with Modell.

"I don't have any use for Modell, myself" Evans said.

"It was just the way he fired Paul without notice or anything. He just took Paul's stuff out of the office and locked the door."

Modell's firing of Brown crushed the veteran coach. "Paul was very depressed for those six years before he started the Bengals," Evans said. "I didn't see much of him. I think he was kind of a recluse at that time. Without his football, he was lost."

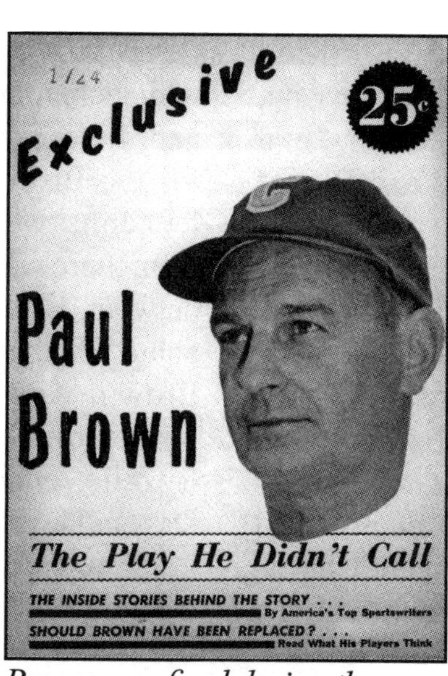

Brown was fired during the Cleveland newspaper strike in 1963. Cleveland sportswriters published this 32-page magazine dedicated to the story.

During his exile from coaching, Brown was involved in bringing the Pro Football Hall of Fame to Canton.

"I think I was somewhat helpful in getting it here in Canton," Brown said modestly. "What I did was line up some of my friends as owners, like Art Rooney, Sr., of the Pittsburgh Steelers and people of that nature, and I simply said to them something that I thought was very logical. 'The National Football League started in the front window of somebody's automobile dealership in Canton.' George Halas (owner and head coach of the

Chicago Bears) was one of the people who was a party to it. And if it started here I can't think of anything more appropriate than to put the Hall of Fame here.' I think I convinced some people. We had rivals, Detroit wanted it. Latrobe, Pennsylvania wanted it. They put it in Canton and I must say that the National Football League people are very glad they did."

Brown was inducted into the Hall of Fame in 1967. "It's an emotional thing," he said, "It's something they can never take away from you. It was in the early days of the Hall of Fame that I had this happen to me."

Pete Rozelle wanted Brown back in professional football.

"Rozelle told me that he would like me to come back into football," Brown said. "He was helpful. He had tried to dissuade Modell from doing what he did to me. I knew that I could get the franchise, so I had a family meeting out in La Jolla, California. The three boys (Mike, Robin and Pete) were there with their wives and babies. I was in the process of getting a radio station in San Diego and also one in Escondito. We did some financial figuring and what not with people of finance and I said, 'Now we'll all go to bed tonight and sleep on it and decide in the morning if we want to buy these radio stations or whether we'd go back into football.' So we get up in the morning, eat our breakfast and go into the living room. I said, 'I guess we have to make a decision.' Katie said, 'We made the decision, we'll go back into football.' I don't know if she even asked the kids."

Mike Brown said his mother was the one person who could

handle his father. "My mom was a pretty special person," Mike Brown said. "She had an ability to take some of the bite—smooth things out—for my dad was always running hard. If he would get off on some tangent, she could settle him down. It was just a gift that she had. I saw that throughout their lives. If he would say something that was outrageous or overstated, she would put it in perspective. That would settle him down and he would not pursue the thoughts he was onto. Instead of making things worse, she would make it better. And not many other people *dared* try that."

Brown founded the Cincinnati Bengals in 1968.

"The first years were difficult," Brown said. "We had poor players, all the castoffs that they could give us, we had 'em. There was a war going on. You could draft a guy out of college but you couldn't necessarily get him to play because the military might end up takin' him.

"Rozelle told me that he would like me to come back into football."

Paul Brown

"I'll never forget a coach up at Western Reserve University, Tommy Davies, wrote me a letter. He said, 'How can you dare do this to your record, with the things that you've done in football, knowing you don't have a chance and your record can't be good, by taking this thing up in Cincinnati.' I told him, 'Tommy, that really doesn't bother me. I look forward to what we can do.'

"As time went on we did get to a Super Bowl quicker than any other team. I have no regrets. Records, wins and losses, are just part of the game. I don't like to lose, but I suffered through it."

Brown retired after the 1975 season, after the Bengals finished 11-4. "We played and lost to Oakland in a great playoff game, 31-28.

"I quit coaching and stayed as general manager," Brown said. "When I started the Bengals I elected to coach, and I said publicly I'd do it for two or three years and get it underway and absorb the knocks and losses that go with starting a new franchise—then turn it over to somebody. And I ended up coaching the Bengals for eight years, which went beyond what I had thought about. It began to weigh a little heavily. Although my health was fine and all my life I could go to sleep the night before a game or afterwards. Actually to go out on the field on the day of the game and call signals and be part of it was intriguing to me. But we had come full cycle and I had no regrets about remaining as an owner and general manager."

Mike Brown was at his father's side throughout his career and reflected on his father's life and how much Massillon football and the town meant to him.

"The thing he did in Massillon was he got the whole town behind it, which is a very extraordinary thing," Mike Brown said. "It was a most remarkable thing that this town of about 26,000 people then was able to come up with a football team, a band, something that held the interest of the whole town, and it has never lost its grip. I've always been proud of the role my father played in that. And I think of all the things he did in his life, that's what pleased him most. I *know* that. He'd talk about his career, and it was a long and successful one. But he'd always say his happiest days were when he coached at Massillon. He thought he could help those kids. He would take them around and they'd visit colleges. He would work to get them into school. He believed in education. He believed in working hard to better yourself. It always pleased him that so many of those kids went on to do good things with their lives.

"He believed in himself," Mike Brown said. "Most of us have self doubts. I'm not so sure that he had so many as the general person. He had very good judgment. Had it all his life. He could take a situation and analyze it and get it down to what was really important and he could do it succinctly. People always marveled at that. That was true throughout his career in the NFL. As years went on, he would go to the meetings and when he would talk, people would pay attention to him talk. Give him credence. He never was bombastic. At that stage of his life he was disciplined.

"It's funny, people had different images of him because they knew him at different stages of his life. The theme that carried throughout his life, the intensity, that was always there. The organizational ability. The ability to express himself forcefully and succinctly. That impressed players over a 50-year span. They'd remember things he said to them, and I doubt that he remembered any of those things. He could be very sharp and cutting and he could do it in about a word and a half. It made the guys around him toe the line. They were on their toes, literally. There wasn't much daydreaming going on. They were paying attention. Those words, "Pay attention," that would have been his phrasing.

"He had this standard and if you didn't live up to it, it didn't matter who you were. There was never any remorse with him about it. If a player didn't live up to his duty he cut 'em."

Brown died in 1991 at age 82. His sister made the trip from Massillon to Cincinnati to visit her brother on his death bed.

"He was very seriously ill," Evans said. I went down about a week before his death. He was so pleased. He said his baby sister came to see him. He was 82 and I was 80—the baby sister.

"He loved Massillon," Evans said. "Massillon was everything to him. He said, 'When I'm gone, I want to come back to Massillon.' That's where he came back to. He's buried at Rose Hill cemetery. There are no stones out there. It's hard to find. My whole family is buried there.

"When Paul's funeral was in Massillon, I think it was the biggest thing that ever happened around here. The television equipment was all around the funeral home and across the street. The yards were full with television equipment. The town was just solid with people. It just was amazing. I think people came to see all the old celebrities. Even Art Modell came for Paul's funeral, of all people."

Brown Disciple Don Shula Ended Up the Winningest Coach in NFL History

Who knows where Hall of Fame football coach Don Shula would be today if not for Paul Brown? Shula considers Brown the biggest single influence on his coaching career.

Like Paul Brown, Don Shula was a teacher.

Shula, whose father was a Hungarian immigrant who worked on a fishing boat in tiny Grand River, Ohio, fell in love with the Cleveland Browns.

"I became a Cleveland Browns fan in 1946 when Paul Brown started the Browns," Shula said, "I was 16 years old and in high school."

Shula was a pretty good high school running back and ended up with the opportunity to play college football.

"I went to John Carroll University in Cleveland. We would sit in the bleachers for 50 cents with our letter sweaters on and watch the Browns play," Shula said. "Our coach at John Carroll, Herb Eisele, went to every Paul Brown coaching clinic.

"That's the way I got started in football," Shula said, "in Paul Brown terminology and the Paul Brown playbook."

Shula was taught Brown's system by Eisele as a two-way player at John Carroll. The experience proved to be valuable.

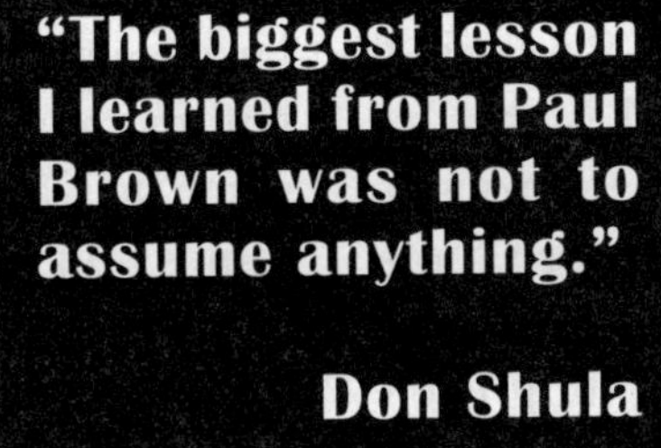

"I got drafted by the Browns in the ninth round along with my teammate from John Carroll, Carl Taseff. It was certainly an advantage knowing the terminology."

Despite the advantage of knowing Brown's system, Shula still had his work cut out for him trying to earn a spot with the NFL's champions from 1950 as a low-round draft pick. "I think the squad size was only 33 then. At that time you were just happy to be given the opportunity to make the team. I went in there wide-eyed and eager and enthusiastic. I was the only rookie to make the team that year. Carl Taseff came in later when somebody got hurt."

Shula was nervous when he finally met Brown after being drafted. "Maybe a month or two after we were drafted we got a call from his secretary inviting us down to his office to sign our contracts. That's the first time my teammate and I got to meet him personally. He walked into the room and introduced himself. It was a big thrill for sure. He said,

'Here are your contracts. You can sign here.' Shula laughed, "We didn't hesitate. We signed as quickly as possible, thinking he might change his mind."

Shula soaked up everything Brown did and said as an eager rookie in 1951.

"The thing about Paul that I think was special is that he was a teacher. He brought the classroom into pro football. Before Paul you had big burly guys hitting each other. And Paul taught 'em how to do it step-by-step in the classroom, on the practice field, and on game day. He used the classroom more than anybody else ever had. Everyone wrote their own playbook. You sat in the meetings, no matter how hot or sticky it was. He dictated and you wrote down every word he dictated."

Shula was impressed with Brown's deportment. "He was in charge," Shula said. "He was a great teacher."

Of all the lessons he learned from Brown, Shula said one stands alone.

"The biggest lesson I learned from Paul was not to assume anything. Just because a player had played before, you shouldn't assume he was going to do the things you wanted him to do next time. You wanted to make sure you covered everything in detail before you evaluated the player on the practice field."

When Shula got his first opportunity to be an NFL head coach at age 33 with the Baltimore Colts, he found himself using Brown's methods.

"A lot of my football was based on the Paul Brown playbook and Paul Brown football. When I went into coaching it was the Paul Brown system. His terminology, the numbering of the holes—everything.

"I just think he was a great teacher. He surrounded himself with great assistant coaches. I think he did a great job with the playbook. His practices were short but every detail was covered. That's something I tried to incorporate."

"When I went into coaching it was the Paul Brown system. His terminology, the numbering of the holes—everything."

Don Shula

Shula has a favorite quote that he's famous for that relates to teaching.

"As a teacher, it's not what you know, it's what you can transmit to the people you're responsible for," Shula said. Shula managed to transmit enough information to his players to win a record 347 games in the National Football League.

Shula felt *his* teacher had no weaknesses. "Not really," Shula said. "You evaluate a coach by his record and his accomplishments. Paul Brown, certainly in high school, his brief time in college, Great Lakes Naval Training Center and professional football, always had produced championship teams."

Shula had the chance to coach against his mentor.

"It was a great experience

being a young coach and looking across the field and you're coaching against the master," Shula said.

Brown ran into a buzz saw when he played Shula's Dolphins in a first-round playoff game in 1973. The student beat the teacher that day, 34-16. Shula was in the midst of an historic two-year run. "The back-to-back Super Bowls," Shula said, "17-0 and 15-2 are two great years."

Shula didn't have many memories of the win. "The handshake pregame and afterwards," Shula said. "But there really wasn't a lot of socializing or dialogue. I really got to know Paul when we served on the NFL Competition Committee."

The Competition Committee was a four-man committee when Shula became a member in 1970. He served until 1995, his final two years as co-chairman. The committee was like a Who's Who of NFL royalty when Shula joined.

"When I went on the committee I took Vince Lombardi's place," Shula said. "They wanted a coach on the committee. Paul Brown, Al Davis and Tex Schramm were the other three members. So it was a real honor for me to be asked to come on the committee."

Al Davis was the owner of the Oakland Raiders and Tex Schramm was the founder and owner of the Dallas Cowboys. The group represented 15 professional football championships as coaches and owners.

Shula's relationship with Brown flourished as they worked together. "We spent so much time together on the committee," Shula said.

"We'd spend two weeks—morning, noon and night together—talking about football and how to open the game up, make it more exciting and safer for the players. It was a really interesting time in my life working with Paul, Al Davis and Tex Schramm.

"Paul was very intelligent," Shula said. "Great football background. Very interested in doing whatever he could to continue to improve the game. I think everybody respected Paul for what he accomplished in coaching and what he brought to the game.

"There's a lot of his assistants that went on to head coaching jobs and a lot of his players went into coaching," Shula said. "There was that Paul Brown influence."

"It was a great experience being a young coach and looking across the field and you're coaching against the master."

Don Shula

Brown and his proteges make up six of the 21 coaches inducted into the Pro Football Hall of Fame: Shula, Bud Grant (Vikings), Chuck Noll (Steelers), Bill Walsh (49ers) and Weeb Eubank (Colts, Jets) all coached or played under Brown. Half of the head coaches in Super Bowls I through XVIIII played or coached under Brown. Brown disciples have won nine Super Bowls.

Brown's Dream Day at Massillon

It was during the middle 1920s, a time when passing was in its infancy. But Paul Brown loved to throw the football. In fact, his shining moment as a quarterback came during his senior season at Massillon in 1925.

Paul Brown at Massillon.

Massillon was playing Toledo Woodward Tech on a muddy field and Brown was hot, connecting on touchdown passes of 19, 35 and nine yards. He was a nifty 7-15 for 133 yards passing in leading Massillon to an 18-0 victory. All three touchdowns were to Brown's favorite target, Paul Storrie. The muddy conditions were blamed for three unsuccessful points after touchdown attempts.

The Tigers finished 7-2 in 1925, including a tough 6-3 loss to Canton McKinley in the season finale. It snapped a five-game winning streak in the series for Massillon, who had shut out McKinley in the previous three match-ups.

Brown's Massillon Staff Endured

Paul Brown had two coaching mainstays who were with him from his early days in Massillon through his successful days at Ohio State: Carroll Widdoes and Hugh McGranahan. The three developed a winning chemistry while at Massillon.

Widdoes, McGranahan and Brown at Massillon.

"Paul was tough," remembers Robert 'Doc' Immel, a student manager for Brown from 1934-36. "Brown was a bad man—what I mean is it was built that way. McGranahan and Widdoes were the pals of the players. Paul would go in and chew somebody out—chew the team out. Then he'd turn around and walk away. Then the pacifiers would come in. McGranahan or Widdoes would say, 'Now boys, now boys, the old man's mad. But this is what we're gonna do. Let's make the old man happy.' It was beautiful to watch work. They were a beautiful pair, the two of them. Widdoes was so clean, and McGranahan so gruff and everything. They were just handpicked to be together."

Firing Impresses Future Star

Mike Byelene was just a junior high kid watching the Tigers practice at Jones Junior High in 1934 when he saw an image of Paul Brown that he'd never forget.

"Ohhhh, I remember this distinctly," said Byelene, who went on to become an All-Ohio quarterback and captain of the 1936 Tigers.

Wallace Clay.

"Coach Clay was a farmer. He was a teacher, he taught chemistry. Well, Coach Clay came a half hour late for practice. Brown came up to him and said, 'Where you been, what's the trouble? You were supposed to be here at three o'clock. We don't need you now. You get out of here. Get dressed. We don't want you anymore.' He fired him right now. Fired him right off the bat."

Byelene was standing just across the street and watched the scene unfold. It made an impact on him.

"That straightened me out. I thought, 'Man, this guy means business.' He was the boss man and what he says goes. And the assistant coach better know the difference. There were no excuses."

Brown Signaled Plays at Massillon

When Paul Brown was the head coach at Massillon he found a creative way to control the game from the sidelines through a series of inconspicuous signals.

Ray Getz, an All-Ohio running back and a co-captain on Brown's famous 1940 team at Massillon, remembered the signals his coach employed.

"He called every play by signal," Getz said. "If he crossed his leg, it was 16. Hold his toe, it was 18. That's why he wore the bright coat. If he got down in front of the bench, it was a punt. It was a pass if he put his hand on his shoulder. It was a reverse if his hand was on his hip. The center and the quarterback would watch him. He always had two players watch him. He'd call every play."

Brown in a familiar sideline pose. According to Ray Getz, co-captain of Brown's 1940 Massillon team, this pose was a signal for the team to punt.

Brown Introduced Many Firsts

It's doubtful that any one person introduced as many firsts to professional football as Paul Brown. Many of the innovations began during his coaching days in Massillon.

He was the first to use game film to analyze his team's performance and to grade his players. He was also the first to use classroom techniques to teach football.

He started playbooks at Massillon and introduced the concept to professional football years later.

Brown was the first to hire a year-round coaching staff while at Cleveland. "Brown made it a year-round job for them," said Tommy James, who played for Brown at Massillon, Ohio State and Cleveland. "They graded film all winter long."

Brown also made timing players in the 40-yard dash a standard. Prior to Brown the 100-yard dash was how a player's speed was measured. Brown reasoned that the 40-yard dash related better to football.

Paul Brown also invented the facemask. "I said to the Riddell people," Brown said, "make me something no bigger than my little finger with tensile strength enough that it will take away the inclination for someone to swing at a guy or catch a stray heel flying through the air. Save the nose and the teeth. And no more than an ounce in weight. They came up with it and what happened is it just spread. For a while I was doing better with the rights and royalties for that than I did in coaching."

L. J. SMITH

L. J. Smith was the Godfather of Massillon Tigers football. As superintendent of schools, L. J. presided over 18 state championships at Massillon. His stern, no-nonsense leadership played a major role in the program's success.

L. J. Smith, the Godfather of Massillon Tigers football.

Paul Brown was already the head football coach when Smith began his reign as superintendent in 1935; Leo Strang was the grid boss when L. J. stepped down in 1961. The 1935 and 1961 squads were bookend state and national champions for Smith's voluminous 26-year career as Massillon's superintendent.

Despite his firm hand, it was L. J.'s cooperative spirit that allowed Brown to implement many of the programs that helped to make Massillon football the juggernaut it quickly became in the 1930s. But Smith's cooperation was not limited to his dealings with Brown. The cooperative spirit of L. J. Smith spread throughout the community.

"Everyone has had a definite part in making us what we are," Smith told the crowd at a banquet honoring George "Red" Bird in the twilight of his life. "It is the Massillon spirit. Every church, office, home and street corner contains that spirit."

"It is the Massillon spirit. Every church, office, home and street corner contains that spirit."

L. J. Smith

L. J. often took a tough stance that was tempered by his desire to do what was right for Massillon. Nowhere was that more evident than when he negotiated the hiring of legendary Massillon coach Chuck Mather, who was responsible for six of the state titles won during Smith's reign.

Mather remembers his meeting with Massillon's "Godfather."

"L. J. Smith said, 'We're willing to pay you $4,800.' I said, 'I'm making $5,200 in Hamilton. Why would I want to move to Massillon for $4,800? I don't think there's any point in talking about it.' L. J. said, 'Okay.'"

Just that quickly, Mather could have become just a minor footnote in Massillon history, instead of one of its leading men. He walked out of the room.

"Doc Clunk came out—he was president of the Board of Education at that time. He said, 'Now wait a minute, wait a minute.' Doc went back in to the meeting and he came back out."

Clunk delivered the "Godfather's" final offer. "We'll give you $5,800," he told Mather.

"That's how I got started in Massillon," Mather said. "L. J. was saying what an honor it is to coach in Massillon. I guess I should have been willing to take a cut in pay to come to Massillon. It was just a matter of chance, Clunk going back in and raising $1,000—which back then (1948) wasn't too bad."

Smith and Chuck Mather on Mather's hire date in 1948.

Mather respected Smith. "I always liked L. J.," Mather said. "He was very cooperative. The type of guy who could kind of play all sides. He tried to keep everybody happy. L. J. had a lot to do with Paul Brown's success and with my own, too. He was a very cooperative guy. We got along real well. He didn't want to fight with anybody. He'd always try to smooth things out."

In 1953, Mather left Massillon for the head coaching job at the University of Kansas. Smith picked a young head coach from Carrollton, Ohio, Tom Harp, to replace Mather.

"L. J. Smith was a throw-back to the old-time super-intendent that ran the school programs with an iron fist," Harp said. "He was not afraid of anybody. Any decision he wanted to make, he made."

Leo Strang loved his tenure at Massillon as much as any coach has. Of course he had great success, winning three straight state championships (1959-61) and two national championships (1959 and 1961). Ironically, Strang almost never took the job to begin with.

"We had to talk him into even coming down for an interview," said Robert "Doc" Immel, a former Massillon school board president who was involved in Strang's hiring. "Leo was the hardest sell we ever had. He was hard to convince."

"L. J. Smith was a throwback to the old-time superintendent that ran the school programs with an iron fist."

Tom Harp

But if Strang was the immovable object, Massillon superintendent L. J. Smith was the irresistible force.

"I didn't apply for the Massillon job," Strang said. "L. J. Smith called me after the job was open for about five, six weeks. They were picking a successor to Lee Tressel. And Lee had given them five names of coaches he thought they should interview. I was the only one who didn't apply for the job. I think that raised their curiosity.

"L. J. called me one night. He said, 'Coach Strang,'—and he was a man who got right to the point—'are you interested in this job down here?' I said, 'Oh, L. J., I've got a real good job up here. I've known about Massillon for a long time, but I don't think I'd be interested.' He said, 'Well, you *could* spend an evening and come down and talk with us at least, couldn't ya?' I said, 'I could do that.' I went down, it was supposed to be an hour interview and it ended up being a two and one-half hour session.

"The next morning, about 9:30, I'm in my office and I get a phone call and L. J. says, 'Well, what'd ya think of the interview last night?' I said, 'Oh, I learned a lot of things about Massillon I didn't know, that I didn't realize...' He said, 'Well, based on what you've heard and what we've told ya, are you ready to sign a contract?' I was stunned and I blurted out, 'No!' I said 'There's a lot of other considerations. We didn't talk anything about money or we didn't talk about a lot of things I'd need to talk about.' He said, "All right, Mr. Kemp and I will be up at your place this afternoon about 3:30.' I said, 'Okay, L. J., come on up.' We talked for about an hour and a half, I had a lot of questions. At the end we came to an agreement. We had to give Massillon's principal a raise in pay. They had a ruling at that time that they wouldn't pay the head coach and athletic director more than the principal. What we settled on was more than what the high school principal was making, so I got the high school principal a raise, too."

So the immovable object, Strang, succumbed to the irresistible force, L. J. Smith, and made the move to Massillon.

Dr. Jim Snively was a school board member at the end of

Smith's career. He said the superintendent had worn out his welcome.

"He was only there one year," Snively said, "He had promised to retire. I went on the board with an open mind. I heard an awful lot of people didn't like L. J. *A lot.* Fortunately I wasn't down on him. I wasn't in his camp or anything. If you're a preacher or you're a school superintendent or you're president of the United States, if you stay too long, you're going to make some enemies. And L. J. Smith had been here 25 years. He was a good superintendent. But if you are in a spot that long, you're going to step on some toes. Just like when I was on the school board, you have to make decisions that you know are going to make half of the people mad at times. And you just have to do what you think is right. And the longer you're on the school board or the longer you're superintendent the more people you're going to make mad, and they're not going to forget it. I went on the school board and I didn't have anything against or for L. J., but the one year he was there I slowly gained a lot of respect for him. I also realized it was time for him to retire."

Snively stopped short of saying that Smith was forced out.

"He had a dictatorial style," Snively said. "He did things that you couldn't do now. And I think the longer he was there the more dictatorial he became. But he did an awful lot of good things, too. It just worked out great. We got him out of there at just the right time. Or he quit at the right time. I especially liked the way he quit, the way he broke free and didn't try to keep his hand in things.

GEORGE "RED" BIRD

When George "Red" Bird's Massillon Tiger Swing Band turned halftime into a "show" in 1938, it set a high standard that Massillon bands continue to strive for today.

Mike Brown, president and general manager of the Cincinnati Bengals remembers the relationship between his father Paul and George Bird.

Shirley Bird, Massillon majorette, helps her father, Massillon band director George "Red" Bird, circa 1945. Bird created the board as a miniature Tiger Stadium, with band members represented at scale size. It was at Massillon that Bird turned the halftime show into a "theatre in the round."

"Dad and George Bird were a great team," Brown said. "Of course George went with my dad to Cleveland and they connected up again with the Bengals. George lived next door to us in Massillon. George was a very talented guy. He got that Massillon band up to the standard that it has maintained since—and it's a very high standard.

"So much of what they did then was extraordinary," Brown said. "The team was far, far ahead of its time. The band was far, far ahead of its time in the standard to which they performed. It was a most remarkable thing that this town of 26,000 people was able to come up with a football team and band that held the interest of the entire town. It's never lost its grip."

Brown was instrumental in getting Bird to Massillon, even though the famous coach had never even heard of the famous band leader. But Superintendent L. J. Smith had a background with Bird.

"Paul Brown opens the door to my office and says, 'L. J., I understand you're going to have to find a band director," Smith said. 'I'll tell you what I have in mind. I am going places in football. Why can't we have somebody that can put a good marching band down on the field? Put a little entertainment down there and have a good show?' I said, 'I agree with you 100 percent.'

"So much of what they did then was extraordinary...the band was far, far ahead of its time in the standard to which they performed."

Mike Brown

"As Paul Brown walked out the door my mind went back to George Bird. I had become acquainted with George when I was a teacher in the little town of Fayette in the northwest corner of Ohio. George was a likable sort of young lad. He had a little four-member band they called a scrap iron quartet. He came from a home that was full of music. His mother was a beautiful pianist and his father could play any instrument in the hometown band. George went along and played when he was a little kid."

L. J. tracked down Bird at Steele High School in Dayton.

"I called him and said, 'I have an opening for an instrumental man. I want a good symphonic band. And I want a good marching band. I want somebody who can put on a good show.'

George Bird was as important as Massillon's band leader as Paul Brown was as Massillon's football coach.

"He said, 'You're not looking for a real man, you're asking for a Superman.'

"I said, 'I know what you can do.'

"He said, 'I'm not interested in the job at all. But I'll tell ya, I'd like to come and see ya.'

"George came down and we had a long conversation. He said, 'You know, I've heard a lot about Massillon. I've heard a lot about this football team you have. I'd like to see the stadium. Where does the band work?'

"We went down to the old field, and it wasn't much. But we talked about what we anticipated doing, building a new stadium, which we did in 1939. We sat there and talked for quite a little while. He said, 'What are you selling, anyhow?' I said, 'Well, I'm trying to sell Massillon to you strong enough so that you'll come up here. We have an opening, we have a real challenge for you. And I think you're the man to do the job.'

> **"He said, 'You're not looking for a real man, you're asking for a Superman."**
>
> **L. J. Smith**

"He said, 'Hmmm. What kind of instruments do you have to work with?' I said, 'None.' He said, 'Well, what do you use?' I said, 'The kids furnish their own.' He said, 'What do you have in the way of uniforms?' I said, 'None.' He said, 'What do you use?' I said, 'The kids come out in their daily clothes and get what uniforms they can and we do the best we can. Now, are you interested?' He said, 'I don't know if I'm interested or not. Do you think you can do what I ask?' I said, 'I don't know. What do you want?' He said, 'I'd like to have 64 new musical instruments. Then I want new uniforms for the band.' I said, 'All right. Take a piece of paper, sit down, write out what you want, total it up. Put the addition at the bottom. Do the same thing for the instruments and the uniforms.' Then I saw the flash. I said, 'I don't know George, that's a pretty big order, isn't it?' He said, 'Well, not very much. I've got to have it. What do you think I'm going to work with?' I said, 'Tell you what we'll do. Let's call a board meeting tonight. Are you interested in coming, really, if the board of education would furnish the instruments and the band mothers would furnish the uniforms? Are you really interested in coming up here?' He said, 'Let me talk to Paul Brown first.' So he went in and talked to Paul. I think Paul helped to sell him as much as I did—may-

Mrs. Bird: A Reluctant Massillon Fan

It wasn't love at first sight for Marie Bird, the wife of Massillon's famous band leader, George "Red" Bird. "My mother refused to move to Massillon," said Shirley Bird, daughter of George and Marie. "They sent me to camp for the summer and Dad moved us. Finally we moved to Massillon. When we got there all the furniture was in the wrong rooms. It was a disaster. Mother told the story. She had only been there a couple of days when Paul Brown came over. He said, 'Mrs. Bird, we're so glad you and your husband are here. I have a couple of season football tickets for you.' Mother looked at Paul and said, 'Mr. Brown, I've never been to a high school football game in my life. And I really think I'm a little too old to start now.'

But things changed quickly. "She never missed a game," Shirley Bird said. "She said, 'I was dumb. I was stupid.' But unless you're in Massillon you cannot begin to imagine what Massillon is."

be more. Anyhow, we had a board meeting that night and Doc Bell was president. We talked about this problem for about an hour and Doc Bell said, 'We've talked long enough. Let's do something, let's act.' He said, 'I make a motion that we employ George and buy him all the equipment that he needs. We made a motion and they voted unanimously. I thought George was going to fall off the chair. I said, 'What are you going to do now?' He said, "It looks like I'm coming to Massillon.'

"You know what he's done at Massillon. His story is known all over the country."

"That story of me plinking the piano all night, that wasn't any lie, that really happened."

George "Red" Bird

Massillon's signature song, "The Tiger Rag," became a standard when Bird started the Tiger Swing Band in 1938.

"Paul Brown's the one who said, "'The Tiger Rag' would be a good tune for the Massillon Tigers,'" Bird said. "He had a lot of ideas I used. He was a guy with an imagination.

"So I made this arrangement of 'The Tiger Rag.' That story about me plinking the piano all night, that wasn't any lie, that really happened.

"We had a rehearsal. The kids straggled in. The kids had very little technique. They were lousy sight read-ers. We started in and we rehearsed twice a day. Mornings and afternoons. The birth of that band was a hot, sweaty, painful experience. The kids would depart at night with bruised and sore lips, sore hands from clappin' rhythm, sore feet from stamping down on the floor trying to maintain a steady beat. I would say to myself, 'I don't think they'll show up tomorrow.' If somebody'd worked me like that I don't know if I would or not. But, my golly, the next day they'd come in, their faces shining and bright and have another go at it. Sweat and work.

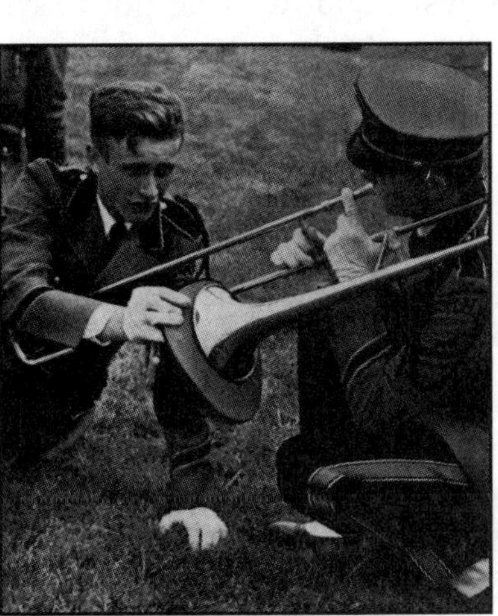

George Bird had his band natilly attired in 1939.

"The Booster Club was having a meeting down in the gym and we had to play for them. We played 'The Tiger Rag.' I never got so sick of a song in my life," Bird said with a laugh. "We played 'Tiger Rag' for the Booster Club and they thought it was good. The kids thought, 'Hey, this is all right.' It was the first time they'd ever gotten a big hand about anything. So that pleased them very much. They wouldn't give up. I think that's when I realized there's a different spirit about this town. They *wanted* to be good."

Another song that Bird started

at Massillon that has become part of the tradition is "Carry On for Massillon." Writing the song wasn't so hard. It was the *naming* of the tune that gave Bird trouble.

Shirley Bird was a majorette in her father's last band at Massillon in 1945. She later succeeded her father as entertainment director of the Cincinnati Bengals. She remembers her father struggling to come up with a name for the song.

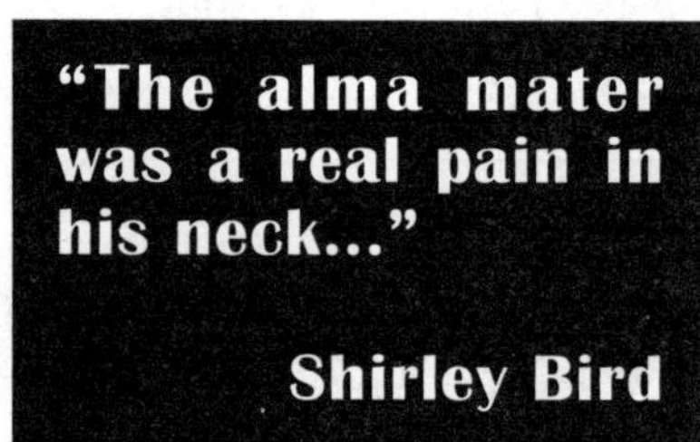

"I just remember what he told me about trying to find something that rhymed with Massillon," Shirley Bird said. "He said, '*Nothing* rhymes with Massillon.' Mass-ill-on. Car-ry On. That's how he got that. I know Massillon was giving him fits trying to get something that would rhyme with it.

"The Alma Mater was a real pain in his neck because it had never been sung until he got to Massillon," Shirley Bird said. "He thought that *everybody* should sing The Alma Mater. So he made an arrangement of it, and you know how everybody sings The Alma Mater today. But after about five years, he said, 'This is the dumbest thing I ever did.'

"It had to do with how when it ends it goes back through. 'And through the long, long years...' He said, 'That makes it too long, I'm going to cut that part.'

"Well there were newspaper articles, *George Bird is tampering with tradition.*" It had only been going on for five years. But they *would not* let him shorten The Alma Mater.

"He said, 'I don't know *why* I didn't cut it when I first did it.' Nobody had ever even heard the song until it came out in the football season of 1938. And it was probably 1943 when he wanted to shorten it. And all these people were going on about tradition. You'd think they'd have been singing this song for 50 years the way they were carrying on."

The other song Bird is famous for in Massillon is "Fanfare." "The Tiger Rag," "Fanfare" and "Carry On" are inseparable for Massillonians.

"When I wrote the "Fanfare," they played it when they went on the field. I put a high C in it," Bird said. "They'd never heard of anybody blowin' a high C. I said, 'There's nothing to it.' I'd take out a horn and blow a high C. And they'd say if old so and so can do it, I can, too. So Don Bushman and I would bet a milkshake whether or not he'd get a high C or whether he wouldn't get it. Later on we had some leather-lipped guys who thought nothing of it—they could really blow."

"It was things like that which made the whole thing such a wonderful experience for me being here in Massillon. Massillon was the first town I ever got involved with any kind of a community life. I got more involved in the community life until, truly, Massillon seemed home to me. I wish I'd never left it."

Maestro Bird Turned Out Champion Beagles and Bands

While George "Red" Bird was renowned for turning out the very finest marching bands during his stops at Massillon, Ohio State, Cleveland and Cincinnati, the maestro also had a strong pedigree outside of the music business.

Bird with a prize Beagle.

"Dad was in the Massillon Beagle Club," daughter Shirley Bird said. "We had as many as 18 beagles at one time. He raised them. And the only thing that was important to him when we rented a house was to have a garage with room enough for his dogs. The first thing he'd do was build a kennel and a way for them to get in and out of the cold.

Bird's famous discipline crossed over into his canine training.

His daughter remembered, "The people next door to us half the time didn't know we had dogs. Dad could not stand dogs that barked. And he made sure they didn't, even when there would be 18 rabbits running up to the fence."

CARROLL WIDDOES

Carroll Widdoes' coaching ascent may be the fastest in major college football history. Widdoes went from assistant coach at Massillon Washington High School in 1940 to head coach at Ohio State University in 1944.

Widdoes was an assistant to Paul Brown at Massillon, then came to Ohio State with Brown in 1941.

Carroll Widdoes as Ohio State Head Coach, Circa 1945.
PHOTO: OHIO STATE ATHLETICS

When Brown left Ohio State to serve in the Navy during World War II, Widdoes was named his replacement.

Like many coaching jobs during WWII, Widdoes' job was expected to last just until Brown completed his military service at Great Lakes Naval Training Center.

Widdoes made the most of his two years at Ohio State, leading the Buckeyes to a 16-2 record, including an undefeated season in 1944. It was Ohio State's first undefeated season in 20 years.

Widdoes coached Ohio State's first Heisman Trophy

winner, Les Horvath in 1944. Widdoes' creative use of Horvath—moving him from wingback to quarterback midway through the season—helped lead the Buckeyes to a 9-0 record and the number two ranking in the nation. Included in that record was a 26-6 win over his mentor Brown's Great Lakes squad and an 18-14 conquest of Michigan.

Army won the 1944 national championship, their first of back-to-back championships under Earl "Red" Blaik.

Brown decided to forego his return to Ohio State for the 1945 season to pursue his professional football coaching career, due in part to Widdoes' success in 1944.

Widdoes led the Buckeyes to a 7-2 record and a twelfth-place ranking in 1945. Paul Bixler, an assistant under Brown and Widdoes at Ohio State, took over for Widdoes in 1946. Widdoes remained at Ohio State as an assistant before accepting the head job at Ohio University in 1949. He coached there for 9 years, compiling a 42-36-5 record, including a Mid-American Conference championship in 1953.

Widdoes was the nation's Coach of the Year for his impressive performance as a rookie head coach at Ohio State.

Widdoes was the nation's Coach of the Year for his impressive performance as a rookie head coach at Ohio State. His MAC conference championship at Ohio University earned him the Ohio College Coach of the Year award.

While Widdoes complemented Brown as an assistant, his style was quite different. Brown was the stern taskmaster; Widdoes' style was marked more by kindness.

"I was the manager when Widdoes was coach at Longfellow," said Robert "Doc" Immel, a student manager at Massillon who later became school board president and served as team dentist.

"Widdoes was one of the finest men I ever had the pleasure to meet. He was the son of people who were missionaries over in the Philippines. I never saw Wid take a drink of alcohol. Or smoke. He wouldn't swear. He was just a wonderful, wonderful person. He used to, in the locker room, sing this song to us at times about Abdul Aboo Boo Amir, or something like that. And he'd get up and dance around. He was something special."

"I never saw Widdoes take a drink of alcohol. Or smoke. He wouldn't swear. He was just a wonderful, wonderful person."

"Doc" Immel

Earl Martin, captain of the 1939 Tigers, also held Widdoes is high esteem.

"If you ever had a boy playing football, that's who you'd want him playing for," said Martin, who was coached by Widdoes at Massillon and at Ohio State. "He'd never call you a name like Brown might. He just had to look at ya. He never swore, but he could get his point across."

Chuck Mather celebrates the 1948 state championship with captain Al Brown.

Bill Wallace

Massillon's All-Ohioans

1940
Horace Gillom
Tommy James
Jim Russell
Bill Wallace

1941
John Hill
Fred Blunt
Joe DeMando

1942
Fred Cardinal
Vern Weisgarber

1943
R.C. Arrington
Tom Jasinski
Bob Williams
Bob Wallace

1944
Bill Gable

1945
Brutus Webb

1946
Tony Uliveto
Jim Young
Gene Zorger

1947
Julius Whitman

1948
Jack Houston
Al Brown
John McVay

1949
Irvin "Ace" Crable
Dick Shine

TEAMS 1940s RECORDS

80	12	8
WINS	LOSSES	TIES

5 State Championships
1 National Championship

1940
10-0-0
State Champions
National Champions
Head Coach: Paul Brown

M	Key Games	Opp.
28	Toledo Waite	0
34	Canton McKinley	6
477	***Season Totals***	***6***

1941
9-0-1
State Champions
Head Coach: Bud Houghton

M	Key Games	Opp.
28	Marblehead, MA	6
6	Mansfield	6
32	Canton McKinley	0
314	***Season Totals***	***37***

1942
9-1-0
Head Coach: Elwood Kammer

M	Key Games	Opp.
40	Lincoln, Nebraska	6
13	Erie East, PA	6
0	Canton McKinley	35
282	***Season Totals***	***80***

1943
10-0-0
State Champions
Head Coach: Elwood Kammer

M	Key Games	Opp.
12	Alliance	0
20	Warren Harding	0
21	Canton McKinley	0
278	***Season Totals***	***12***

1944

7-3-0

Head Coach: Elwood Kammer

M	Key Games	Opp.
0	Cleveland Cath. Latin	6
19	Steubenville	6
0	Canton McKinley	27
175	***Season Totals***	***92***

1945

5-0-5

Head Coach: Augie Morningstar

M	Key Games	Opp.
7	Steubenville	7
0	Warren Harding	0
0	Canton McKinley	0
168	***Season Totals***	***38***

1946

6-2-2

Head Coach: Bud Houghton

M	Key Games	Opp.
35	Dayton Chaminade	12
6	Toledo Waite	40
6	Canton McKinley	6
166	***Season Totals***	***103***

1947

6-4-0

Head Coach: Bud Houghton

M	Key Games	Opp.
7	Revere, MA	6
12	Barberton	26
0	Canton McKinley	14
138	***Season Totals***	***107***

1948

9-1-0

State Champions

Head Coach: Chuck Mather

M	Key Games	Opp.
44	Cleveland Cath. Latin	13
0	Alliance	14
21	Canton McKinley	12
271	***Season Totals***	***95***

1949

9-1-0

State Champions

Head Coach: Chuck Mather

M	Key Games	Opp.
63	Steubenville	13
12	Mansfield	16
6	Canton McKinley	0
395	***Season Totals***	***93***

Story of the Decade

1940s

Brown's 1940 Team, Massillon's Best *Ever*

It's rare for sports fans to agree on much of anything. That's as true in Massillon as it is anywhere else. But there is one consensus in Massillon. Virtually everyone recognizes the 1940 team as being Massillon's best ever.

Now you're likely to get an argument about which team is *second* best.

Minutes after his 1940 team dispatched of unbeaten Canton McKinley, 34-6, Paul Brown put to rest any question about where this team ranked.

Programs from the 1940 Massillon-McKinley game.

"This is without question the finest Massillon team I've ever coached," Brown said. "Its ability to come back in the fashion it did, after leading by only a single point at halftime, is proof enough to me that this is really a great team."

The 1940 aggregation gave

up their first—and only—points in the final game of the season. Athie Garrison, one of Canton McKinley's all-time great running backs, scored on a 32-yard run—putting Canton ahead. Massillon responded with 34 unanswered points.

Just how dominant was Paul Brown's greatest team? One wire service named Massillon's entire starting 11 All-Ohio. The Associated Press named Horace Gillom, Tommy James, Jim Russell and Bill Wallace to first team All-Ohio. Gillom was the A.P.'s Player of the Year.

One wire service named Massillon's entire starting 11 All-Ohio.

The 1940 Tigers scored 477 points, making their average margin of victory a dizzying 47.7-.6. Along the way they withstood a much-ballyhooed threat to their dominance of Ohio prep football. Toledo Waite, winners of 19 straight games, were claiming to be the new state "power." Instead, Massillon won easily, 28-0, on a rain-soaked field. Only the slippery conditions kept the outcome from being much worse for Waite.

The win over Waite increased Massillon's unbeaten streak to 31 straight games and bolstered the Tigers reputation as the team to beat in Ohio.

Four members of the 1940 Tigers were already making big noise for the Tigers as sophomores in 1938. Russell, Gillom, Gene "Red" Henderson and Ray Getz were all sophomore starters. James, Wallace, Eli Broglio and Gordie Appleby also saw frequent action for the Tigers in 1938.

Gillom and James went on to become NFL stars while playing for Brown at Cleveland. Gillom is considered one of the greatest punters in NFL history and James is considered one of the Browns' all-time best defensive backs. Both are members of the Cleveland Browns Legends, along with Brown, their coach at Massillon, Ohio State and Cleveland.

None of the 1940 seniors tasted defeat at Massillon, finishing a perfect 30-0. The senior-dominated starting 11 were comprised of nine seniors and just two juniors.

Brown left Massillon to become the head coach at Ohio State after the 1940 season. His 1941 Buckeyes team finished 6-1-1 and 13th in the nation.

The 1940 team is considered the best team in Massillon history. Paul Brown is the first person in the fourth row.

"I've often wondered whether my Ohio State team, which only lost one game that year, 14-7 to Northwestern, could have beaten our Massillon

1940 team," Brown said.

"Our 1940 team here in Massillon was much faster. Ohio State would be bigger. I had both teams. I used to wonder about it because some of our Massillon players became fine pro players.

"Pokey Blunt was the most deceiving little fella with tremendous jet speed. If I had compared him to the guy who was playing for me at Ohio State it'd been no contest as far as being a long-shot running back was concerned. It's a thing that's crossed my mind more than once."

"I've often wondered whether my Ohio State team, which only lost one game that year, could have beaten our 1940 team."

Paul Brown

Massillon scrimmaged a college team, Kent State, before the 1940 season started. The Tigers were winning 47-0 when the Kent State coach pulled his team from the field. Kent State finished the season 8-1, their best season ever.

Two members of the 1940 team were elected captain at Ohio State. Center Gordon Appleby was captain at OSU in 1944. Tommy James was captain-elect for 1946 after returning from serving in the military during WWII. James never became Ohio State's captain, choosing instead to join the Detroit Lions.

The 1940 team played before 180,500 fans in a 10-game

season. They were the first high school team to play in the Akron Rubber Bowl when 33,000 fans packed the brand new stadium for Massillon's game with Alliance. The Tigers shut out the previously undefeated Aviators 40-0.

Massillon shut out an undefeated Alliance team, 40-0, in the first high school game played in the Akron Rubber Bowl. The Massillon band is featured on the program cover.

At Erie, 22,000 witnessed Massillon's 74-0 win over Erie East, who lost only one other game that season, 6-0, to Erie Academy in Week 10. Erie sportswriter Dick Peebles wrote, "It wasn't a football game, it was an exhibition of sheer power, speed and deception the like of which never before had been unfolded before a local football crowd."

The 1940 team handed Warren it's worst defeat ever, 59-0, and only played the starters in the first half.

Brown paid the 1940 team the ultimate compliment when he told reporters before beginning his first training camp with the Cleveland Browns in 1946 that his 1940 Massillon team "came nearer to perfection than any team that I have ever coached."

Domination of Kent State in Spring Game is Part of 1940 Team's Lore

Adding to the mythological greatness of the 1940 Massillon Tigers is their thorough domination of a Kent State University varsity squad that went on to be the best team in the Division I college's history. Massillon won 47-0 in a game that ended when Kent State coach Donald Starn pulled his players late in the contest.

Massillon got a surprise when they arrived at Kent State's stadium, dressed in their practice gear. "We get there, and they have their game uniforms on," said Ray Getz, co-captain of the 1940 team. "The referees were in striped shirts. Brown looked, then he said, 'They want a football game, you give it to them.'"

"We beat 'em so bad they walked off the field in the fourth quarter. They wouldn't play us anymore," Getz said. "They went on to win the league championship that year."

Akron Beacon Journal sportswriter Jim Schlemmer summed things up pretty well after the game.

"This Kent team will never be fast enough to play Massillon, but it may go against some college 11s which are likewise heavy and slow and not too well conditioned and not overly educated in the value of good blocking...and if and when it does, it may win by a decisive margin."

The University of Akron, scuttled plans to scrimmage the 1940 Tigers after seeing the result of the Kent State scrimmage.

Games of the Century

Massillon Defends Challenge to State Supremacy in Rain

The Massillon Tigers had won 30 games in a row and 74 of their last 77 games. But Toledo Waite and their football coach, Jack Mollenkopf, the future legendary coach at Purdue University, disputed Massillon's dominance. In fact athletic officials from Toledo Waite claimed that their team was too strong for the competition in Ohio and the midwest and had to look to Massachusetts, Oklahoma, Texas and elsewhere for teams who could give them a battle.

FRIDAY, NOVEMBER 1st, 1940

Official Program

Price 5c

Schedule 1940

	Mass.	Opp.
Sept. 13—CATHEDRAL LATIN	64	0
Sept. 20—WEIRTON	48	0
Sept. 27—WARREN	59	0
Oct. 5—ERIE EAST	74	0
Oct. 11—ALLIANCE	40	0
Oct. 18—STEUBENVILLE	66	0
Oct. 25—MANSFIELD	38	0
Nov. 1—TOLEDO WAITE		Here*
Nov. 8—YOUNGSTOWN EAST		There
Nov. 16—McKINLEY		Here

*Night Games

Day Games start at 2:00 Night Games at 8:00

MASSILLON HI TIGERS

VS.

TOLEDO WAITE

Program from the 1940 Massillon-Toledo Waite game.

Waite challenged Massillon to a championship game following the 1939 season, which Paul Brown, Massillon's head coach, declined. What Brown did, though, was go to work on his schedule for 1940.

Massillon's schedule was already full for 1940, but Waite had an open date in the eighth week of the season.

"We had Canton Lehman scheduled for that date," Massillon sportswriter Luther Emery said. "We paid them $1,200 to get off the schedule so we could play Waite."

The battle line was drawn.

Both teams were 7-0 coming into the game, which was a quick sellout. The demand for tickets was so strong that Massillon school officials opened an exchange office downtown to buy back tickets that could not be used. Only four tickets were returned, despite torrential rains that preceded the game.

In fact, 3,000-4,000 fans showed up at Tiger Stadium looking for tickets before the game. Many reportedly were angry when they were turned away.

The heavy rain actually *encouraged* more fans to show up looking for tickets to the game, which had been sold out for a week. A rain-drenched Tiger Stadium was packed with 22,000 fans an hour before kick-off.

The rainy weather was supposed to favor Waite, who greatly outweighed the Tigers. But the Tigers had an interesting ace in the hole.

"We had rubber pants we put on in those days," Massillon halfback Ray Getz said. "Most teams in those days had regular uniforms. Our rubber pants got slick and when Waite slowed down, we got faster."

Massillon dominated from the start, blanking Waite 28-0. So dominating were the Tigers that Waite, who brought a 19-game winning streak into the game, managed only one first down and 21 yards of offense all night. Massillon rang up 16 first downs and 286 yards. It turned out the rainy weather was the only thing that kept things close for Waite.

Following the game, Brown addressed Waite's pre-game boasting. "Let them go to Honolulu or the South Seas for their opponents from here on out," Brown said, "and let them claim the international championship if they want. We didn't win as decisively as the boys wanted, but in view of the playing conditions, which were so definitely against us, we should be satisfied."

Ray Getz is Hero of Waite Game

Halfback Ray Getz was a 1940 team captain, three-year starter and second team All-Ohioan. But against Toledo Waite, he was Massillon's secret weapon.

"They were laying for Tommy James," Massillon sportswriter Luther Emery said, "Massillon used Tommy as a decoy."

"We had a play where you go three steps right and you barrel back the opposite direction," Getz said of the decoy play. "We just tore 'em apart. I was down in Myrtle Beach in 1996. I went into a store to write a check and the guy recognized my name and said, 'Do you know I went from Toledo down to Massillon to play in the pouring rain and *you* beat me.'" After 56 years, it seems Massillon's secret weapon was a secret no longer.

Games of the Century

Could Dynasty Continue without "Miracle Man" Brown?

There were still questions about whether the Massillon dynasty could carry on without "Miracle Man" Paul Brown as the 1941 Massillon-McKinley game approached.

Program from 1941 Massillon-McKinley game.

Massillon was riding a 42-game unbeaten streak that dated back to a 7-0 loss to New Castle, Pennsylvania, in 1937. They hadn't lost to an Ohio opponent since McKinley turned the trick in 1934.

Bud Houghton needed some miracles himself, inheriting an inexperienced team from Brown, who became head coach at Ohio State University following the 1940 season. It was Houghton's first varsity head coaching job.

"Since they had lost Brown, a lot of people figured all was lost," Houghton said. "His starters all graduated, except for Fred 'Pokey' Blunt and Herm Robinson—and we lost Robinson the first day of practice."

But the Tigers had a stout defense and an offense that got better as the year went on. "We were strong enough defensively that we thought we could stop anybody and then get the ball and move it on offense," Houghton said. Massillon had quick backs. Dick Adams, who shared the passing role with Bob Graber, was a shifty runner. Blunt was an All-Ohio running back and team captain. But Massillon's passing attack had been erratic all season.

The Bulldogs' strategy was to take away the run by stacking eight men on the line of scrimmage and playing their three-man secondary close to the line.

Bob Graber is on the run during the 1941 Massillon-McKinley game. Graber started at quarterback from 1941-42.

"I had two quarterbacks at the time," Houghton said. "I sent in Graber and told him,

'I don't care where you are, we're going to throw this pass.' They only had two men deep and there was no safety man.

"It was the second or third play of the game and I threw a pass to Pokey and he scored a touchdown," Graber said. "That opened everything up.

"We just went wild through the air that day," Houghton said. "We had 432 yards of offense that game—266 yards passing. Once we started throwing, there was no stopping us."

Adams and Graber were both effective throwing the ball. Adams was equally effective on the ground, picking up 113 yards on just eight carries. The result was a 32-0 win for Massillon.

Dick Adams shared quarterbacking duties in 1941.

"We ran up the largest margin of victory Massillon had ever scored against McKinley until that time," Houghton said. "They were happier than larks—everybody in town. I was invited to everyplace to celebrate. The country clubs, all of 'em... when I'd walk in the door everybody would jump up and down and cheer. I was the toast of the town."

Games of the Century

Crable Stars in Mather's First Win Over Canton McKinley in 1948

No one gave Massillon much of a chance against Canton McKinley in 1948. The Tigers hadn't beaten the Bulldogs since 1943, Canton McKinley was unbeaten, number one in the state and had beaten Alliance—the only team to beat Massillon—46-6.

"We were supposed to have been beaten pretty severely by McKinley," Mather said. But Mather felt his team's 14-0 loss to Alliance in Week 5 may have helped his team.

Program from 1948 Massillon-McKinley game.

"We naturally felt pretty bad about the thing. Even though I felt we played well, we couldn't beat 'em. They were just so determined to win.

"The loss really got our attention and put a little fear in us about McKinley. If we had gone into the end of the season undefeated, like they were, they might have beaten us. Sometimes it pays to lose a game some-

Ebbert was Tigers Secret Weapon

"Pat Ebbert had a lot to do with us winning the McKinley game in 1948," said Head Coach Chuck Mather. "John McVay was hurt, so about all we were going to let him play was offense. We created a defense around Pat, who only weighed about 140 pounds. We had him three yards back of the line of scrimmage. He was in a position where it was hard for them to block him. He created about three fumbles that game by hitting the center just as he was making the exchange to the quarterback. So Pat won his letter just on the McKinley game. He was our third string fullback, so I don't know that he even got in another game. He was tough."

Pat Ebbert earned a varsity letter in McKinley game.

where along the line to get yourself focused again.

"We didn't have a very big team," Mather said. "Our biggest guy was 160 pounds, or something like that. McKinley averaged about 210 pounds. It was just unbelievable the way we played. John McVay was our center and he had the Pucci brothers (Ed and Ralph) to block. They played guard on defense. Both of 'em went on to play at Southern Cal. Ed Pucci was Frank Sinatra's body guard. McKinley really had a lot of really great football players."

The McKinley game was especially tough for McVay. "I was hurt," McVay said. "I had hurt my leg and they didn't think I was going to play. The muscles in the back of my leg were in a spasm. I remember laying on the training table for more than an hour with a local doctor massaging my legs. They didn't think I was going to play because I didn't practice that week. He got my muscles relaxed enough that I was able to play in the game."

Although the Pucci brothers were bigger than McVay, he felt he had an advantage. "We were taught better techniques," McVay said. "We didn't rely on brute force. The coaches taught us techniques for blocking big guys. Even though we would often be playing against bigger teams, we'd be okay. because the coaches had the patience to teach the techniques."

Massillon quarterback Jack Hill credited a new defense the coaching staff put in before the game.

"The Friday night before the McKinley game you usually have a light practice. But we said we wanted to run this thing full tilt. A couple of the guys said, 'Let's make sure we've got it.' Chuck couldn't get us off the field. We were up there two and one-half hours. He was upset. But we wanted to make sure we had it right."

Both teams were without star running backs. McKinley's All-Ohio back John

Colceri was out with a separated shoulder. Massillon's Clarence Johnson, who averaged almost three yards a carry more than Colceri, was out for Massillon. Fortunately for Massillon, Irvin Crable played magnificently in Johnson's backfield spot.

Crable raced for 112 yards and scored all three of Massillon's touchdowns. Captain Al Brown ran for 105 yards and provided leadership.

"Al Brown was tough," Hill said. "He wanted a state championship. He was a real strong leader, emotionally, but mainly physically. He was a street fighter. There wasn't a guy on that football team that wanted to take on Al Brown. And that's *anybody*. He had the reputation from junior high school that he'd take anybody on. He always came out a winner. After McKinley scored to make the score 14-12, Chuck grabbed Al and told him that we had to hang onto the ball. We couldn't give the ball back to McKinley. I remember Al came back in the huddle and said, 'Here's what we've got to do. And if you guys don't do it, I'm going to take every one of you on after the game.' Now that was probably an exaggeration, but that's the way he came out. Chuck will tell ya, it was the greatest drive he's ever seen in a football game. We just took the ball for the last eight minutes, starting on the 20-yard line, and drove right down the field."

Crable scored his third touchdown and Massillon held McKinley for the final 36 seconds for a most improbable 21-12 win.

Games of the Century

Offensive Giants Battle to 6-0 Finish in 1949 Massillon-McKinley Game

It looked like offensive fireworks were in store when Massillon and Canton McKinley squared off in 1949's battle for the state championship.

McKinley was undefeated, number one in the state and had scored 383 points in nine games.

Massillon, meanwhile, was fielding one of their most explosive offensive teams, scoring 389 points in nine games.

Program from 1949 Massillon-McKinley game.

Surprisingly, when these offensive powerhouses tangled, just the opposite occurred—a 6-0 defensive struggle.

"In 1949 we had a team that was extremely fast and had three backs who averaged 11 yards per try," said Massillon head coach Chuck Mather.

"They were the speediest team we had. Probably the best offensive team we had for breaking away and making long runs."

Crable was star of McKinley wins

Irvin "Ace" Crable receives the WHBC Stark County Player of the Year award from announcer Jim Muzzy.

Without Irvin "Ace" Crable, the legend of Chuck Mather would not shine as brightly. Crable scored four touchdowns in two games against Canton McKinley.

Massillon head coach Mather held Crable in high esteem. "An Akron sportswriter inquired about how I regarded Crable's ability," Mather said, "I said, 'He scored all our touchdowns against Canton McKinley in 1948 and 1949 and we won two state championships—what do *you* think?'"

Don James, who achieved national fame as head coach of the University of Washington, was the quarterback of the 1949 Tigers. But he realized that he was the supporting cast to the 1949 Massillon team's headliners.

"The three backs were the stars," James said. "Dick Jacobs, Clarence Johnson and Irvin 'Ace' Crable were all Division I-type players. "Crable was the center of the basketball team at 5'8". He was one of the real fine athletes. He had speed and quickness. Johnson was big and fast. Jacobs was fast. We just had a tremendous yards-per-play average. Tons and tons of big runs for scores. Those guys would get out in the open with such great speed."

McKinley's offense was led by All-Ohio quarterback John Rogers and a pair of dynamic running backs. Lou Mariano was a unique talent, a deaf mute who ran with reckless abandon. It was Mariano's second season as a mainstay in McKinley's backfield. Sam Parks was McKinley's leading rusher with 1,062 yards.

With all of the attention being paid to the powerhouse offenses, it was easy to overlook two outstanding defenses. McKinley had given up just 51 points and Massillon 93 coming into the showdown.

As good as Crable was on offense, he was just as good on defense. Assistant coach Dave Putts appreciated Crable's contributions on the defensive side of the ball.

"I would say he helped win the 1948 and 1949 McKinley games with his defense," Putts said. He was an excellent defensive back."

Jacobs was also a playmaker in the secondary. "Jacobs was probably a better defensive back than offensive back," said Jack Hill, quarterback of the 1948 Tigers. "He was a great open-field tackler. He hit people so hard. He just had a knack for nailing people. He was unreal."

Both defenses were unreal. It was a scoreless tie for three and a half quarters. That's when Crable scored the game's only touchdown.

"I'm gonna tell ya what happened on the touchdown run," Crable said. "It was a 33-cross. We ran that in the first half. Donnie James. handed me the ball at the 25-yard line and all I could see was daylight...and I fumbled it. So we let that one go and now it's the third quarter. The coach sent in a play and I told Don, 'No, let's run 33-cross,' and he changed the play. The way it was set up the first time, that's the same way it was the second time. That line blocking was beautiful, nobody had a chance. Nobody laid a hand on me, either. I was amazed. My instincts said 'It's going to be there again.' And I just waited and waited, and I said '*Now's the time.*' And it was right there again. Put me right in the end zone."

Late in the fourth quarter Crable made one of the most famous defensive plays in Massillon history. Both Putts and Mather recalled the play clearly.

"Crable makes the tackle that causes Lou Mariano to fumble," Putts said. "He was on the six-yard line. He was going to score."

"By the time he got to Irv he had already made about 20 yards," Mather said.

Crable said his play wasn't as heroic as it seemed. "Mariano was something, you should have seen him," Crable said. "We watched their line block on film all week. This guy was *exceptionally* good. There was something different about him—the way he ran. When he ran he didn't try to duck ya. He had a habit of running over ya. They said I knocked him out and everything, but actually I couldn't get away from him. I'm telling you, if I could have moved or ducked I probably would have. I didn't have no choice, I looked up and this guy was on top of me. He was on his way in. That fumble turned that game around completely."

But the drama wasn't over yet for the Tigers. "We're ahead 6-0 with about two minutes to play," Mather said. "I just wanted to run the game out. I sent the play in with Don James. He was very good. I was thinking, 'Nobody's going to fumble, nothing's going to happen.'"

"I'm telling you, if I could have moved or ducked I probably would have."

Ace Crable

"We had an audible system for our passing game," James said. "I'd come up to the line and I'd shout out the tackle's name to the side I was going to throw it to. I'd say, 'Come on Jerry, *get up, get up*.' That was the signal to the rest of the team that I was going to throw the look-in pass to the tight end. We were really backed up around the six-yard line and I threw a couple of passes coming out. The coaches about had a heart attack. I didn't think, I just ran the audible."

"They threw up an eight-man line on us," Mather said. "A goal line defense. Part of our audibles was the quick pass to the end when we had eight men up on the line against us. We didn't want to try to run the ball. So when they threw this defense up there, Don, instead of running the play I sent in, calls this audible to Don Slicker. I about died. It went for about 10 yards, but at the same time, I did not want to pass down there. If it had been incomplete there'd have been no time used. Boy, I was trying to get somebody in the game to get to Don. Before I could get a guy into the game, they lined up for another play. I would have *never* audibled in that situation. But Don did it, and could have saved the game. He just did what we trained him to do. It wasn't his fault."

"Chuck said years and years later that any time he'd mention me he'd say, 'I learned one thing about our audible system, you've gotta tell your quarterback what part of the field you want to use it on.' But it was good, it got us out of the hole and we won the football game," James said.

James, who has experienced more than his share of exciting games, coaching the University of Washington to six Rose Bowls and winning the 1991 national championship, remembers the excitement surrounding the 1949 McKinley game.

"I was never so up for a game in my life," James said. "You'll never forget it. You'll go to your grave remembering this game."

Games of the Century

Mather's Debut the Stuff of Legends

Opening night is an exciting mixture of anticipation and renewal. And Massillon's 1948 season opener was everything that is good about opening night.

It was Chuck Mather's debut as Massillon's head coach and no one was sure what to expect.

Program from 1948 Cleveland Cathedral Latin game.

The Tigers opponent was Cleveland Cathedral Latin, a team Massillon had failed to beat in their previous three meetings.

"Massillon hadn't beaten Latin for a long time," Mather said. "Being the first game, we didn't know anything about 'em at all."

The Tigers didn't know much about themselves, either.

"We had a couple scrimmages, but we didn't know how good we were," said Jack Hill, Massillon's quarterback in 1948. "Cathedral Latin—they were like a Cincinnati Moeller or Cleveland St. Ignatius of their time. They were *the* Cleveland power. The year before they beat us 16-12 and we played one of our better games against them in front of a huge crowd at Cleveland stadium (25,000)."

But it didn't take long for Massillon players to find out how good they were and for Tiger fans to find out that the good times were back.

"We ran four plays and scored four touchdowns," Hill said. Chuck thinks it's a record that will never be broken."

"That was an unusual situation scoring like that," Mather said. "You can imagine the elation of the fans over a start like that."

On Massillon's first play from scrimmage, running back Irvin "Ace" Crable ran for a 49-yard score. The next time Massillon had the ball Al Brown motored 61 yards for a score on second down. The next Massillon possession saw Crable breaking away on first down for a 55-yard touchdown. On Latin's next possession Massillon's Jack Houston recovered a fumble in mid-air and returned it for a 22-yard touchdown. At the end of the first quarter Massillon led 25-0.

"The runs in that game were unbelievable," Mather said, "how long they all were. It wasn't a mater of working it inch by inch down the field on any of those. They were boom, strike, away we go."

Massillon scored three more times to make Mather's opening night debut a 44-13 winner. It was just the beginning of a wonderful relationship between Mather and the city of Massillon. The Tigers went on to win the 1948 state championship.

THE WALLACE BROTHERS

Barney, Bill and Bob Wallace (l-r) all starred for the Tigers.

Massillon football was held in the highest regard in the household of Urban and Clara Wallace. Raising three boys during the great depression, football became a healthy obsession.

"That was our life," middle son Barney Wallace said, "that's all we were thinking of." Urban put Bill, Barney and Bob through daily calisthenics. His "gym" was conveniently located. "We played football right in our living room," Barney said. "We fought, we boxed, we wrestled—right in the house. We'd put holes in the wall. Mom would get mad at Dad. She wouldn't get mad at the kids.

"Dad was always gettin' us together. He'd put the boxing gloves on us. He was the referee. We fought until he saw that one guy was gettin' beat up—then he'd have to stop it. Dad was buildin' us up to be athletes. He wanted us to play for Massillon. He got what he wanted. We all got there. He made us football players."

Clara Wallace was no shrinking violet herself. During World War II, when Urban was sent to work in Baltimore by the B&O Railroad, she joined the workforce. "Mom became a crane operator at Republic Steel," Wallace said. "She was also a bartender at night at Ehret's Grill. She was a tough old gal."

She made sure her boys were tough, too. "I'll never forget one time when I was coach at Massillon," former head coach Bud Houghton said, "It was raining after practice. So finally, I told Bobby and Barney, 'I'll drive you on home.' It was really wet. Their mother came out and said, 'What are you trying to do, spoil these boys? They can walk home in the rain.' She was a tough old gal. She was just a little woman, but she was tough. They were tough kids. But nice kids."

Bill Wallace was one of four Tigers named first team All-Ohio in 1940.

Bill was the oldest of the Wallace brothers and served as a role model—and hero. "Me and Bob felt so proud of Bill," Barney said. "He was so quick and so strong. He was strong built. And he could pick those guys up and throw 'em down. He was a tough son of a gun."

As a senior, Bill Wallace was one of four players from the famous 1940 Tigers team to be named first team All-Ohio.

Bill made a memorable play against Toledo Waite in the 1940 match-up between two Ohio powers with long unbeaten streaks. Massillon's streak was 30 games; Toledo Waite's, 19. "He scored a safety," Barney said. He blocked a punt and it rolled out of the end zone." Wallace's two points accounted for the only scoring in the second quarter of the 28-0 Massillon win.

Barney and Bob followed Bill, playing together in 1941 and '42. Bob was a three-year starter, and captain of the 1943 state champions. Barney started in 1942, before being drafted into World War II later in his junior year. They started next to each other in 1942, Barney at center, Bob at guard. "I was always getting a bloody nose," Barney said. "I had to put my head down and when I'd look up, 'Boom.' Every game I'd be bleedin' in the nose and in the mouth." Finally, the brothers worked out a plan. "I said, 'Bob you have to do something to the guy who's doing this to me.' The next thing I knew the guy that was over me was going out of the game. Bob put him out of the game. Bob just hit him. He was bleeding out of the nose and mouth. He never did come back in the game. That saved me."

They call that brotherly love, Massillon style.

TOMMY JAMES

The great Paul Brown epitomized the potential that Tommy James held as an Ohio State running back. "He will make football forget about Tommy Harmon," Brown said, comparing James to perhaps Michigan's most famous player of all-time.

Tommy James as a Cleveland Brown, circa 1950.

The story of James began in a Genoa (now Perry Township) sandlot. A friend tipped off Massillon junior high coach Bud Houghton about James: "A fellow named Dick Shrake told me, 'You ought to go out to Genoa. This little guy out there can run like the devil,'" Houghton said, "'He's thinking about goin' to Canton Lincoln now.'"

Houghton followed up on the tip and drove out to the James' home.

"We were playing touch football that turned into

tackle football," James said. "He said he thought I could make the team at Longfellow Junior High with what he had seen, with the speed I had."

"At that time those Genoa kids could either go to Canton Lincoln or Massillon," Houghton said. "I think I sold his father more than anything else. I told him his potential for going to college was better at Massillon.

"His first day of practice he got hit pretty good. He didn't come back for the afternoon practice."

Bud Houghton

"His first day of practice he got hit pretty good. He didn't come back for the afternoon practice. I went out and talked him into coming back out there. Fortunately he turned out pretty good."

Saying James turned out "pretty good" is a colossal understatement. James was All-Ohio as a star runner and passer for Paul Brown's 1940 Tigers—widely considered Massillon's best team.

"My junior year I was named startin' right halfback," James said. "I had a couple touchdowns against McKinley my junior year. My senior year I got moved over to the left halfback position in the single wing. I liked the left half because you did the passing and the playcalling."

James scored the first two touchdowns in the newly constructed Tiger Stadium in 1939. The humble James was never comfortable talking about himself. "It was a new stadium, we were playing Cathedral Latin, which was the power of Cleveland," James said. "With all the hoopla and everything of the new stadium it was supposed to be a great game. For years I never realized that I was the first one to score over there. In fact someone told me the other day that I scored the first two in the stadium, but I'm not even sure about that. Those things never entered our minds back in those days. We were interested in winning the ball game. I don't know if it was off a fake punt or not, to tell you the truth. It might have come off a fake punt."

James scored twice in the 1940 Massillon-McKinley game.

It was indeed a fake punt, from 39 yards out. Later in the first quarter James scored the second touchdown in Tiger Stadium on a 31-yard run. Massillon won the stadium opener 40-13.

James led Massillon's prolific offense to 477 points in 1940. He was also a key to Massillon's stalwart defense that allowed only six points.

James joined Brown at Ohio State after the 1940 season. At a time when freshmen did not play on the varsity, James made a big splash as a sophomore on the 1942 national championship squad.

An offensive highlight from 1942 was a two-touchdown performance against Illinois. In a game played in Cleveland Municipal stadium, James scored on runs of 33 and 76 yards.

Ticket from 1942 Ohio State-Illinois game where James scored on two long touchdown runs.

Defensively James turned in a performance that was being hailed as one of the greatest in Big 10 history. Playing against former Massillon star Harry Stuhldreher's Wisconsin team, James made four touchdown-saving tackles against All-American Elroy "Crazylegs" Hirsch. Hirsch is a member of the Hall of Fame in both college and professional football

James was then drafted into WWII, where he served for three years. After the war James was elected captain at Ohio State in 1947. James turned down the captaincy to play professional football in Detroit.

"I had planned on finishing school there," James said, "but then Wes Fesler came in. He said he wouldn't let me play unless I told him I definitely was not going to go pro. I told him, 'Wes, I came back, I could have gone with the Browns in 1946. I came back to finish school.' But he gave me an ultimatum. That just teed off the old redhead, so I went up to the fraternity house and called the Detroit Lions that night. They came down and signed my contract in downtown Columbus. I'd been given too many ultimatums in the service for three years and I just didn't go for it. For a long time I wished I'd stayed and been a captain at Ohio State."

James was featured in this cartoon for the College All-Stars-vs-NFL Champions game.

Luther Emery, the legendary sports writer from Massillon's *Evening Independent*, reported on the turn of events in his popular "Emery Wheel" column. Emery wrote, "Tommy resigned his football captaincy at Ohio State Monday to accept a flattering offer from the Detroit Lions after turning down the Lions when they drafted him last winter."

Things didn't go so well in Detroit. "I got my arm broke the second game against the Chicago Cardinals. Marshall Goldberg's knee came in and hit my arm above the elbow and I was out for the season. I got immediate wrist drop, I couldn't lift my wrist. They had to do surgery from my elbow to my shoulder to see if the nerve was severed in that bone fracture. It ended up it was just so badly bruised that it took six months, even with electrical therapy, to get a twitch that went through the nerve into my fingers. But once it went through it came back good. I really thought I might go the rest of my life with a crippled hand. I had surgery in Chicago and every two weeks I'd catch a train in Massillon and go to Chicago with my arm in a cast to see the doctor."

While recuperating, James talked to Brown at a New Year's Eve party in Massillon. "He talked me into coming out for the Browns in the 1948 season," James said. "I told him if my arm came along I'd report to training camp."

James reunited with Brown in 1948 and was a starting defensive back on one of the greatest teams in pro football history. Playing in the All-American Conference, the 1948 Browns were 15-0, the first professional football team to finish a season undefeated. It was Brown's first undefeated team since 1940 in Massillon. The 1972 Miami Dolphins are the only other undefeated team *since* the 1948 Browns.

Don Shula, the coach of the Dolphins' undefeated season, was James' back-up. "He played the same position I played," Shula said, "or I played the same position he played, I should say. Because he was the starter."

"I'd help him out in practice, show him a few things," James said of Shula who was a rookie in 1951. "But you didn't have that much time when you went into camp, the way Brown ran the camp. You'd try to help 'em out if you could. But you didn't want to help 'em out too much until you were sure you made the team," James said with a laugh.

"Tommy was a great teammate," Shula said. "You had Tommy James on one side and you had Warren Lahr on the other. Two good corners." James was a star defensive back for the Cleveland Browns from 1948-55. He finished his NFL career with Baltimore in 1956. The speedy James had 34 career interceptions and has been named to the All-Time Cleveland Browns team.

"He played the same position I played. Or I played the same position he played, I should say. Because he was the starter."

Don Shula

"That's what a defensive back lives for," James said, "to intercept passes."

He honed his skills in practice by covering two of the best receivers in pro football history. On one side was Dante Lavelli, the Hall of Famer. On the other side was Mac Speedie, who many feel should be in the Hall of Fame. "Speedie was harder to cover as far as I was concerned," James said. "Mac was a great end. He'd be in the Hall of Fame except he went in to negotiate his contract with an agent. Brown kicked 'em both out. He ended up playing Canadian ball. That was before the players got organized."

James was also noted for his ability as the holder for Hall of Fame place kicker Lou "The Toe" Groza. "I held the ball for Lou for eight years," James said. "I always kidded Lou, 'If you missed it you always blamed it on the holder.' I always kidded him that way. But he didn't miss many of 'em."

> **"I jumped about five feet in the air when I saw the ball going through the uprights."**
>
> **Tommy James**

The most famous kick of Groza's career was a 16-yarder with 28 seconds left on Christmas Eve in the 1950 championship game. "We worked our way down the field and got close enough for the field goal," James said. He said he wasn't nervous with time running out and the championship on the line. "Didn't bother me a bit," James said. "I told Frank Gatski, Cleveland's center, 'Just get the ball back to me to where I don't have to get off my knee to get it.' He put it right where I needed to get it. Gunner Gatski, he centered for extra points and field goals. He was great. He's in the Hall of Fame."

"I jumped long before it even went through the uprights because I knew it was going through. It was hit direct, and I was right behind it. I had the best seat in the house. I jumped about five feet in the air when I saw the ball going through the uprights."

James had a good season in 1950 and decided to ask Brown for a raise. "You had to represent yourself when you talked to Paul Brown," James said. "I had a good year in 1950, our first year in the NFL. I thought I'd ask for a raise. Brown said, 'Tom, you had a good year. But you know, the steel mills are on strike, and we don't know if we'll have anybody coming to the games. However, how much school do you have left?' I said, 'I've got one quarter and I get my diploma from Ohio State.' And he said, 'Tom, if you come back this summer at the beginning of practice and show me your diploma, I'll give you a $500 bonus.' I said, 'Put it in the contract.' So he gave me that nudge to finish college. I thought that was great because I'd been puttin' it off for four years."

"My wife handed me the Cleveland Plain Dealer. The headline read, 'Browns to Release James Today...'"

Tommy James

James' career with the Browns ended on a heartbreaking note when he was released on the day before the regular season opener in 1956.

"My wife handed me the *Cleveland Plain Dealer*," James said. The headline read, 'Browns to Release James Today Before Leaving for Opener in Chicago.'"

James was disappointed that Brown didn't tell him in person. "He admitted in front of my 1942 teammates at a reunion of the 1942 Ohio State National Championship team that he made a mistake by putting me on waivers my last year. The two guys he kept in my place only lasted two games and he got rid of them. But I'd already gone to Baltimore. It made me feel real good that he admitted that. But the damage had been done. That's the way pro ball is. You're good 'til they're done with ya. And I'd had a good year in 1955. Somebody probably had fed him the old line, 'It's better to get rid of players before they're past their prime.' That's what he did with me. I had him as a high school coach, a college coach. He didn't show any partiality when it come time to..." James' voice trailed off. "But those things happen."

James was a treasure in the city of Massillon, where he lived his entire life.

James finished his career with the Baltimore Colts where he was coached by another future Hall of Famer, Weeb Ewbank, who had coached under Brown. Ewbank is famous for being the only coach to win championships in the NFL (Colts) and AFL (New York Jets).

James spent his entire life in Massillon, where he was very much a part of the city's social fabric.

IRVIN "ACE" CRABLE

Sportswriters couldn't settle on just one nickname when describing the man who was possibly Massillon's all-time best running back. "They called me Irvin 'Ace,' 'Crazylegs,' 'Swivel Hips,' 'Jackrabbit,' Crable," Irvin Crable said. Opposing defenders probably just called him *impossible to catch.*

Ace Crable uses the stiff arm as he turns the corner in this 1949 action.

To many who saw him play, Ace was Massillon's finest running back. Crable combined a sprinter's speed with an elusiveness and toughness that also served him well as one of Massillon's all-time best defensive backs. Former Massillon coach Chuck Mather, who coached both players, said that Crable reminded him of Chicago Bears Hall of Famer Gale Sayers.

Ace raced through opposing defenses for 1,129 yards in just 100 carries in 1949. His incredible 11.3 yards per carry average is the all-time best among Massillon's impressive history of 1,000 yard rushers.

But Massillon football almost wasn't in Crable's future after moving from Massillon to Akron as a young teenager.

Although he didn't follow the Tigers as a youngster in Massillon, he was excited when he heard that Massillon was going to be playing in the Akron Rubber Bowl. He quickly got a job as a refreshments vendor so he could see the game.

"Massillon was playing," Crable said excitedly, "it was really thrilling." The young soda pop vendor decided in the stands that night what his future held. "I said to myself that I wanted to play football, that I wanted to play football for Massillon. I wanted to come back home."

Crable had already had a setback at Akron East, where he was coveted for his speed. Coveted, at least, by the track coach. "I was trying to play football there," Crable said, "and this coach told me, 'You're too small to play football.' But I knew what it was; they wanted me to *just* run track."

Akron East was noted for their strong track program. "Them boys were runners," Crable said, "some of the fastest kids I'd ever seen in my life. But I wanted to play football, so I came back to Massillon."

Crable had a history of trouble as a youth growing up on the streets in Massillon.

Mather had to enlist the help of the mayor when Crable got arrested for stealing hubcaps in 1948. Assistant coach Dave Putts recalls another incident when Crable was in trouble.

"We had trouble with Irvin Crable once in a while," Putts said. "One time he got in trouble at a little candy store that was on the corner across from the school. The proprietor really wanted to stick it to him. Apparently he picked up six candy bars and only paid for four. It wasn't a really big thing. The store owner wanted to put the pressure on us. Mather went and talked to him, and then he went to the mayor, Junie Weirich, and Weirich talked to this guy and he decided to drop it."

"When I was small we had gangs," Crable said. "We lived in what you call the Bottoms. The houses were so close together you could step off one porch onto the other porch. And we always had conflict with the hill."

Crable on the loose in 1949.

Crable attributed his elusive running style to his troubled childhood. "All the city runners were on the top 10 most wanted list," he said with a laugh. "That's the city boys. That's how I learned to run, running from the police. I'm serious.

"I was in all kinds of trouble when I was a kid. I was what you would call a menace to the community. Football got me straightened out."

"'Irvin Crable was an excellent running back," Putts said. "I thought he was an excellent defensive back, too. He was a little cocky, but he had a right to be. He was a real good athlete. He just wasn't tall enough to be a major college prospect."

Crable recalled a time when he was disciplined by Mather.

"We were playing Steubenville Big Red and I was on the sideline," Crable said. "I had missed class and Coach Mather wasn't going to play me that Friday night. Steubenville went up 14-0. Me and Freddy Grier, in high school we were running mates. Everybody had a sidekick and Freddy was my sidekick. I hunched Freddy. I said, 'Freddy, watch this, he's on his way down here to see me.'

"Coach Mather kept looking down. We're down 14-0—he doesn't want to lose that game. He sent Coach Elwood Kammer down there. Kammer said, 'Come on up here.' I acted all nonchalant, but I was anxious to get in the game. By halftime it was 21-14, Massillon."

Crable relished his days in the spotlight at Massillon. "There were so many happy moments," Crable said. "Beatin' McKinley was one of them. Especially afterward. A lot of nice things happened. Take my word for it. When they say Massillon takes care of their players, Massillon takes care of its players. Wasn't nothin' too good for 'em. Those were the most joyous times, beatin' McKinley. That was a thrill I'm tellin' ya. It was just like I imagined when I was in Akron. It was just like that. It was just like a dream come true. I was playing for the Massillon Tigers."

JOHN McVAY

Football has been very good to John McVay. Starting as an under-sized All-Ohio center at Massillon and finishing as Vice-President and General Manager of the San Francisco 49ers, McVay's is a football success story.

But it was a tragedy that brought him to Massillon and started him on his stairway to football success.

This early photograph of John McVay as a high school head coach foreshadows his future as an NFL Executive of the Year and five-time Super Bowl winner with the San Francisco 49ers.

"We lived in Belair, Ohio," McVay said. "My father was an attorney. He was killed in an automobile accident when I was six. My mother had been brought up in Massillon, so we moved back with grandma and grandpa."

McVay's first coach at Massillon was Bud Houghton, a no-nonsense coach who had won a state championship at Massillon in 1941. When he returned as head coach after a tour in WWII he had lost something.

"He taught a lot of us fundamental football," McVay said. "He was a strict disciplinarian. When Bud came back from the service he probably just did what he did when he left. I don't think he coached anywhere during the war. Some guys did, and that gave them an edge.

"He really got mad at us one time," McVay said. "Our sophomore year after the big games on Friday night a bunch of us third stringers would take our equipment, football pants, helmets and shoulder pads, take it out the back door, throw it over the fence at the stadium, then go around and pick it up.

"Then we'd go down to the Bottoms on the west side, and we'd be fully decked in our Massillon uniforms and we'd be playing against pick-up teams. We were frustrated because we weren't playing in the games.

"The coaches found out about it and we were in huge trouble."

Chuck Mather replaced Houghton for McVay's senior year.

"When Chuck came in 1948, all the pieces fell together," McVay said. "That's when I really came into my own as a high school player."

McVay got the most out of his 5'8" frame. "I was 165 pounds soaking wet," McVay said. "If I achieved, I certainly was an over achiever. I certainly wasn't big. But the coaches taught us how to block, how to play, how to approach the game, how to prepare for the game."

"The first guy I was responsible for at center was John McVay," said Dave Putts, an assistant under Mather. "He wasn't big, but he was fast. He was a fine athlete."

McVay wanted to impress Putts, who was a hero to him.

"Putts was a young stud," McVay said. "He was just out of the Marine Corps, a big, good-looking guy. He had played college football at Miami. I looked up to that guy. It was sort of a combination of hero worship and a big brother kind of deal. Chuck had a good blend on that coaching staff, and knowing him, it didn't just happen. He did it on purpose."

"I was 165 pounds soaking wet. If I achieved, I certainly was an over achiever. I certainly wasn't big."

John McVay

Mather recalled McVay's courageous play against Canton McKinley in 1948. McVay was injured, and it was feared that he wouldn't play at all.

"John McVay was hurt all week leading into the McKinley game," Mather said. "Didn't practice. We didn't have any center at all that could do the job he could do. Then he goes in there and plays a game against the big Pucci brothers that you couldn't believe. He was very conscientious, tough and strong."

"I remember laying on the training table for more than an hour with the doctor massaging my legs. They didn't think I was going to play because I didn't practice that week. He got my muscles relaxed enough that I was able to play in the game. The Pucci brothers were good players. They were big. But we were taught better techniques. We didn't rely on brute force. They taught us techniques for blocking big guys." McVay said. "I played like I had good sense.

"The older I got, going into my senior year, the more I appreciated what Massillon was. It was really the total package. It was the fans, the band, the cheerleaders. Instead of being isolated, just a football team, you were part of a total package. There was a great camaraderie between the guys on the football team and the kids that were in the band and the kids who were cheerleaders.

"The coaches set high standards and goals for us and pushed us toward those goals."

The expectations of the town fueled the players, too. "In 1946 and 1947 they were expecting more than we delivered," McVay said of the community. "It was ugly. It wasn't a feeling like you'd let your teammates and coaches down. It was like you let the *whole community* down. It was a real community effort. Everybody in the community was involved. When you went to the grocery store or the barber shop people would say, 'We're going to be good this year, aren't we?' I'd say, 'Oh yeah, sure.'"

McVay left Massillon and became a key player at Miami University. "I wound up, through Chuck's efforts, getting the last scholarship at Miami from Woody Hayes. So, I played on the freshman team the first year. I played my sophomore year for Woody. Then Woody left for Ohio State and Ara Parseghian took over. So I played for Ara for two years. I was his captain my senior year."

After a couple of coaching stops, McVay landed at Canton Central Catholic as head coach. It was a successful stint.

"I got the job at Central Catholic," he said. "We had lots of athletes, everything was great there for five years (1957-61). I had future Hall of Famer Alan Page. We were 41-7-2 there."

McVay used his success at Central Catholic to move into the college game.

"I went to Michigan State with Duffy Daugherty for three years. Then I went to Dayton in 1966. I was the head coach at Dayton until 1973. Then I became the athletic director."

"I played for Ara Parseghian for two years. I was his captain my senior year."

John McVay

Frustrated over an underfunded athletic program, McVay saw an opportunity to get back into coaching in the upstart World Football League.

"I went into the WFL," he said. "We started in Toronto, and then we moved to Memphis. The first year there we were 17-3. We had Massillon Tiger running back Willie Spencer. Willie was a piece of work. Nice guy. He was an awesome football player. We had him there and. gee, what a pleasure it was. When we got him, he was just a big old roughneck."

McVay added some serious star power to the franchise

in year two. In fact he made the biggest headlines in the history of the league when he raided the NFL's reigning Super Bowl champions of three of their star players.

"We are the team that signed Larry Csonka, Jim Kiick and Paul Warfield away from the Miami Dolphins," McVay said. "I don't think (Dolphins coach) Don Shula ever forgave me for that."

> **"We are the team that signed Larry Csonka, Jim Kiick and Paul Warfield away from the Miami Dolphins. I don't think Don Shula ever forgave me for that."**
>
> **John McVay**

John McVay's Memphis Southmen were one of the most successful teams in the fledgling league. Unfortunately, by the end of the second season, the league folded. "When the league shut down, I went to work for the New York Giants," McVay said. "I was coaching special teams, doing some scouting. We started off 0-7.

"I walked into the front office one day to talk with the general manager, Andy Robustelli. Andy said, 'John, come in. Coach Bill Arnsbarger is leaving, you're it.' I said, 'Oh no, Andy, not me.' He said, 'You're the only guy who has any head coaching experience. You've got to do it.' So I talked to Bill and he said, 'You've got to take it, keep the staff together.'

"We finished that year, we finally won a few ball games. The next year we were a little bit better, and the third year we were a little better, but we were still just 6-10 and I was discouraged, and I'm sure management was discouraged. So I left and went with the San Francisco 49ers."

It would be a colossal understatement to say it was a good career move for McVay.

"It was great," McVay said as he reflected on his career with the 49ers.

McVay was a key figure in the 49ers dynasty of the 1980s and 1990s. He was named NFL Executive of the Year in 1989. He retired from the 49ers in 1996.

"I had a chance to work with 49ers owner Eddie DeBartolo, Hall of Fame Head Coach Bill Walsh, and Head Coach Bill Seifert. We had a great run here. We won five Super Bowls and I don't know how many division championships and conference championships. I was the general manager and the vice president for football operations. I've had all kinds of titles, but I've been doing the same kind of work. I started in 1978 and we came out of the blocks 2-14. Then the next year we were 6-10 and the next year we won the first Super Bowl. There are a lot of National Football League coaches that came through our graduate school. There were Seifert, Sam Wyche, Mike Holmgren, and Mike Shanahan. They were all assistants who came through our program."

BILL WALLACE

Bill Wallace received his greatest compliment from a man who was famous for *not* passing out compliments. Unless, of course, they were richly deserved.

"Bill Wallace was the best player, pound for pound, that I ever coached," Massillon coach Paul Brown said. Wallace, an All-Ohio guard on Massillon's 1940 state and national championship team, was *unblockable*.

Bill Wallace was a small, but quick and powerful lineman on Massillon's famous 1940 squad. Wallace developed his physique by walking on his hands using flat irons.

All-Ohio teammate Ray Getz said that Wallace was legendary in practice. A run-in with All-Ohio center and team captain Earl Martin in 1939 got everyone's attention. "I'll never forget," Getz said, "Martin was the center, we were on the practice field. No one could block Billy. Couldn't keep him out. Martin hook-blocked Billy right in the face. He was bleedin' and everything. It about knocked him out. Martin had to hook block to get him. No one could block Bill Wallace."

Wallace, the oldest of three Wallace brothers who starred at Massillon, was small by *any* standards, standing 5'6" and weighing just 149 pounds. But what he lacked in size, he made up for with quickness and strength. Twice during the1940 season he crashed through the line to block punts—one a key play that resulted in a safety in an important win over Toledo Waite. Wallace also beat the odds by winning first team all-state honors, despite starting for the first time as a senior.

Wallace had a bodybuilder's physique, although he was not a weightlifter. His father, Urban, had Bill and brothers Barney and Bob perform exercises on a daily basis. There was one unusual exercise Wallace excelled in... walking on his hands.

Using flat irons, thick slabs of cast iron with a handle that predated the modern clothes iron, Wallace would constantly walk around on his hands for exercise. Family members said he could walk up and down stairs on his hands as well as most people could on their feet.

"He had irons," brother Barney Wallace said. "He'd just grip on them and walk. He'd walk up stairs and down stairs on his hands. It was just natural to him. I tried it. I could never get the balance. He walked all over on his hands.

"He was always doing things to build up his body. He used to do push-ups with me and (youngest brother) Bob on his back. Bob would get on his back and he'd do so many. He'd get off then I'd get on. He'd say 'I want some weight.' He said one day that he could keep pushing up as long as he wanted to, he just stops because he gets bored."

Tommy James, an all-time great with Massillon, Ohio State and the Cleveland Browns, was a teammate with Wallace from 1939-40. "Bill Wallace was one of the small guards, good strong upper torso, and he was quick," James said. "I would say he was strong in his arms and he had quick moves. Back in the old single wing, pulling guards had to pull out and do the blocking on the sweeps."

Wallace was perhaps most famous on defense where he had a knack for breaking into the opposition's backfield.

"He was just quick," James said. "At the snap of the ball he had a quick charge. He got a good jump on the snap of the ball. Back in the old single wing, you had to snap the ball back three and a half yards. And of course if he could time it, he'd get there when the ball got to the ball carrier."

Wallace was as tough as they come—a fact that Horace Gillom learned one day in the locker room.

Gillom, the outstanding player in the state of Ohio in 1940, was one of Wallace's bigger teammates at 6'2" and 189 pounds. "He took Horace Gillom," Barney said of his brother. "Gillom was one of the great football players from Massillon. He got in a fight with Bill in the locker room. Bill threw him down and he jumped up and grabbed Bill, and Bill threw him down again. Bill never picked a fight, but he never got beat in a fight."

AL BROWN

The toughest guy on a team of tough guys. A street fighter. That's Al Brown, captain of the 1948 Massillon state championship team.

Head Coach Chuck Mather hugs his captain, Al Brown, after the 1948 Massillon-McKinley game.

"Al Brown was a rough, tough, mean, nasty football player," said John McVay. McVay, who played center on the 1948 team. Brown's other teammates—and coaches—echo McVay's sentiments.

Brown wasn't big, but he was a starting running back for three years at Massillon who inspired teammates with his toughness. "My sophomore year I went 130, my junior year I was 135, my senior I gained about ten pounds," Brown said.

"When I was a captain my senior year, I kept those guys in line. I said, 'If you guys get out of line you've gotta fight me.'

"I used to have a meeting every Thursday before a football game down at the basketball court. I told them what I thought they did wrong.

"One time, after we played Toledo Waite, we had on white uniforms, and this guy wasn't even dirty. At our next meeting I told him right to his face, 'Buddy, you're the only guy who didn't have to get his shirt or *nothin'* cleaned. And if you don't like it, take a poke at me.' He didn't say a word. I think most of those guys respected me. They knew I wouldn't take no crap. I guess it worked anyway, we won. I used to be bull-headed. I used to get in a fight about every day."

Brown's toughness was developed during his childhood. "My grandparents raised me," Brown said. "I played football in the yard about every day—played with guys older than me, too. A couple of times my grandmother got mad at me and sent me upstairs. I climbed out the window to get out and play with those older guys. I was an ornery son-of-a-gun, I guess."

Brown figures he got his toughness from his friends. "I ran with guys older than I was. These guys would get in fights and I'd help them. When I was little I lived in a tough neighborhood. These guys used to push me around all the time. Then some big guy got hold of me and said, 'Don't take that stuff off of these guys.' His name was Parnell, I'll never forget him. So, when they started pushing me around, I'd push 'em back.

"I remember the first game Coach Mather coached here. Some guy really put the bangs to me. I told the guys, 'You've gotta set this guy up.' They set him up and I creamed that guy. Mather pulled me out of the game.

I said, 'Hey buddy, you're in Massillon now,' and I went right back into the ball game. He chewed my tail out after the game was over. I said, 'Hey coach, if they play dirty, we've gotta get 'em back.' He didn't believe in that.

"Mather was a heck of a guy, though. Seemed like he never raised his voice. When he chewed you out, you felt terrible. He didn't have to raise his voice."

Captain Al Brown was featured on the cover of the banquet program.

Brown was Mather's captain in 1948, but it was actually Bud Houghton, his coach in 1946 and '47, who selected him. "That was really a shock, because me and Houghton had gotten into it.

"My senior year, we were state champs, I was the captain and made All-Ohio. That's probably the happiest time of my life." The saddest time? "When I graduated. I missed football."

BUD HOUGHTON

Bud Houghton was old school. He was a high school teammate and friend of Paul Brown and became Brown's successor as head coach at Massillon in 1941. He was a stern disciplinarian.

"I'll tell you one thing, he didn't take nothing off nobody," Al Brown said of Houghton. "Sometimes he wouldn't say anything, he'd just come up and boot you," said Brown, who started for Houghton in 1946 and 1947. "He told it the way it was—he told it *exactly* the way it was.

Bud Houghton succeeded Paul Brown as Massillon's head coach in 1941.

"I remember one time my junior year, he and I got into it. I told him, 'You can take this team, I quit.' After the Barberton game he told me I left my guts up at my girlfriend's house. I took my helmet and slung it at him. I said, 'I quit.'" Al later came back to the team.

"He told one guy, 'Your dad

ain't nothin' but a banana peddler,' Brown said. "I told them, 'If that son-of-a-gun ever says something like that to me buddy...' He wasn't a bad guy, though, really.

"I'll say one thing about Houghton; there was nobody in any better condition than we were. He believed in calisthenics—he worked your tail off. He did 'em right with ya."

"I was strict with those guys," Houghton said. "I really made them toe the line. If they got out of line, I'd let 'em know. I would give them a second chance to come back. I was pretty stiff with them about paying attention and working hard and givin' their all and not monkeying around. If they didn't behave we didn't keep 'em, that's all. They had to behave themselves, listen, be courteous with their teachers and keep their studies up."

Houghton figures he got the Massillon job on Paul Brown's recommendation. He was in competition with fellow junior high coaches Elwood Kammer and Mel Knowlton.

"I think in the final analysis Brown made the difference. They pinned him down as to who would be the best organizer, because that's what he was famous for."

Houghton rose to the challenge in 1941, winning the state title with a 9-0-1 record. The only blemish was a 6-6 tie with Mansfield.

Houghton was called into service in WWII after the 1941 season. He returned to coach Massillon from 1946-47, finishing with 6-2-2 and 6-4 seasons.

HORACE GILLOM

Horace Gillom was perhaps Massillon's greatest player ever. He was the best *player* on the best *team* in Massillon history. Whether catching passes, making big gains on the end around, punting balls above the stadium lights, or pounding opposing runners as a linebacker, Gillom was a star nonpareil.

Horace Gillom may have been the greatest football player in the Tigers illustrious history.

Not only was Gillom the unquestioned star of *his* team, he was recognized as the best player in the state of Ohio for 1940.

Head Coach Paul Brown depended heavily on Gillom, who caught passes and ran from his right end spot on offense, played defensive fullback, punted and kicked off. "There's nothing much else left for him to do unless we tie a lawn mower on his back and let him mow the grass while he runs," Brown told reporters in 1940.

Gillom scored 108 points in 1940, a Massillon record for ends.

"Horace was one of the great receivers," said Tommy James, who threw passes to Gillom in 1940. One of the most famous pass plays in Massillon history was a James-to-Gillom touchdown in the McKinley game. McKinley had just scored the only points scored against Massillon all season. "We went in at halftime ahead 7-6," James said. "I threw a touchdown pass to Gillom right before the half. Horace could jump, and I just threw it up there and he went up after the ball and got it. He was a good receiver, I think he got that from his basketball and track. He had good leaping ability, "

Autographed Horace Gillom high school photo, 1939.

Luther Emery, Massillon's famous sportswriter of the era, remembered the 55-yard play well. "Gillom caught the pass with one hand," Emery said. "He batted it with one hand, got it with the other hand

and scored a touchdown. It was a cold day. In fact it was in the 30s, a little snow once in a while. All the boys hadda pee, and they didn't think of Massillon scoring. They were back in the restroom. They heard this shout go up from Massillon and they came running out with their peckers in their hands. Half of the stands came running out of the lavatory."

> **"Everybody always talked about Horace Gillom and how long that ball stayed up there."**
>
> **Don Shula**

Gillom still ranks among the all-time great punters in NFL history—and many who saw him play say there was none better.

"Horace could put the ball out of sight as a punter," Notre Dame coaching legend Ara Parseghian said. "He still would be great in today's game. He would put that thing up there and it would just soar. He could kick it up high above the lights and turn it over. He was really something." Parseghian watched Gillom play in high school. He also was a teammate of Gillom's at Cleveland.

"Horace Gillom and I were friends," Parseghian said. "We used to drive back and forth together when we both played at Cleveland. He came up from Massillon and I lived in Akron."

Legendary NFL coach Don Shula was a teammate of Gillom with the Cleveland Browns.

"Horace Gillom was probably one of the great punters who's ever played the game," Shula said. "He was a fantastic punter. His hang time had to be as good as anybody who's ever punted in the NFL. Everybody always talked about Horace Gillom and how long that ball stayed up there. That gave the coverage team a chance to get down there underneath it and cover it."

James said a football catch phrase was developed because of Gillom's punts. "After he quit punting they talked about hang time. When he was punting, the ball always went high and far. The term hang time was more or less developed because of the height of his punts. That's when the term started."

Shula remembered Gillom's contribution to the Browns' offense, too.

"Aside from his punting, Horace was a good tight end," Shula said. "He didn't start, but there was times he went into the game when someone was hurt and made a lot of big plays on offense, catching the ball and blocking and playing the tight end position."

The baby brother of Jake and Odell Gillom—Massillon stars in their own right—Horace became the star of the Gillom family and a Massillon legend.

Odell recalled the Gillom household. "My oldest brother Jake was the teacher," Gillom said. "We broke more things in the house throwing the football. The old lady would yell. 'Get that football out of here.' The old man didn't like it at first. But the longer we played it the more he liked it. He'd get ready for our games like *he* was gonna play."

Gillom was discovered by Brown when he was in grade school. In addition to coaching football, Brown also served as Massillon's first recreation director. It was during a tour of Massillon's grade school playgrounds that Brown discovered Gillom punting the football. Brown took time to teach young Horace punting techniques. By the time he was in junior high, Gillom's punting was already gaining notoriety.

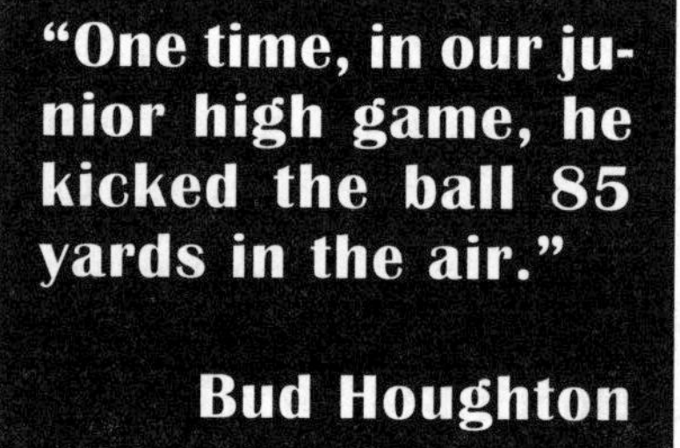

"One time, in our junior high game, he kicked the ball 85 yards in the air," said Bud Houghton, Gillom's coach at Longfellow Junior High. Houghton succeeded Brown as head coach at Massillon in 1941.

"I had him in seventh, eighth and ninth grade," Houghton said. "He wasn't very polished. He was skinny, he only weighed about 125 pounds. He was very poor. I helped him out. I wouldn't just give him money. I would have him up to the house to wash windows or cut the lawn.

"When he was in the eighth grade Brown came up and watched practice. Gillom took three long strides when he punted. I told Brown, 'I tried to teach him a step and a half to punt, but he can't kick it.' So Brown said, 'Well, keep on doin' it.' So I kept workin' with him, and finally I said, 'If you want to use him as a punter you have to let him take three steps. Just put him back further.' So we put him back 15 yards. That extra five yards didn't make any difference to him."

Gillom joined Brown briefly at Ohio State.

"Paul Brown called me up, he said 'Lute, I'm gonna have to get rid of Gillom,' Emery said. "This was in January. He said, 'He isn't in school, he hasn't come back from Christmas vacation.' I said, "Maybe he's sick or somethin'.' He said, 'I don't think so.' I said, 'Have you told anybody else this?' He said, 'No.' I said, 'Paul, don't do anything and I'll go down and call at the house and see whether he might be sick or somethin'.' So I went down to the house. I don't know whether Paul knew that he wasn't going to come back or not. I went down to the house and said, 'Horace, why aren't you down at Columbus?' He said, 'Well, I haven't been able to find a way.' I said, 'You haven't found a way?' He named a fella that promised to take him at five o'clock in the morning. So I called Paul and told him. He said, 'Well, I won't announce it. I'll wait and see if he comes.' About nine o'clock the next morning he called me. He said, 'Lute, put it in on Horace. He hasn't shown up.' While he was talking to me Horace walked into his office. But

Gillom was a menacing sight on the end around.

then he didn't go to class so he suspended him."

Luther Emery was able to help Gillom again when he ran into former McKinley head coach Jimmy Aiken, who was the head coach at the University of Nevada.

"After the war, Jimmy Aiken was the principal speaker at the McKinley Booster Club banquet. I knew Jimmy real well. He said, 'Can you tell me where I can get a good football player?' I said, 'Jimmy, I saw Horace Gillom the other day.' He said, 'Could you tell me where he lives?' So Jimmy got him to go out to the University of Nevada. Of course Marion Motley, the Canton McKinley star and future Hall of Fame running back with the Cleveland Browns, was at Nevada, too."

Gillom had just returned from the Army where he earned three bronze stars.

Gillom played one year at Nevada before joining Brown with the Cleveland Browns.

Gillom starred for 10 years with the Browns where he was used primarily as a punter. With another team, he may have had a bigger impact at receiver. At Cleveland he played behind Hall of Fame receiver Dante Lavelli and Mac Speedy, who had Hall of Fame ability. Gillom finished his career with 1,083 yards receiving.

As a punter, Gillom led the NFL in net punting average in five of his seven seasons. He also led the NFL in yards-per-punt twice. In 1954 he nailed an 80-yard punt.
"He was an end on the right side and I was the right halfback, so we used to stand next to each other in the huddle. We were together a

lot," Parseghian said. "We used to joke around. And there were times when Horace would take a drink or two before practice, or the night before, and it would start to sweat out. And you could smell it. Paul Brown used to walk into the huddle. Horace would grab me to make sure there was no area for Paul to pass through to get in the huddle because he didn't want Paul to smell the booze on him."

Gillom as a member of the Tigertown Stars semi-pro team.

Emery remembered Gillom had a reputation for drinking. "Paul finally let Horace go from the Browns," Emery said. "I went to a party at Sherlock Evans' home (Brown's brother-in-law). Paul invited everyone that was there to go up to a Browns game on Sunday. The Browns' new punter was terrible. He couldn't get off a good punt at all. After the game, we were sitting at a card table eating lunch. I said to Paul, 'Where did you ever get that punter?' He said, 'Why, don't you like him?' I said, 'No. Gillom *drunk* would have outpunted him.' He told that story at the Hall of Fame luncheon club.

"Horace Gillom was over the hill, and I guess he was drinkin' a little bit. That isn't why he was fired. It might have been a contributing factor. I just got my little punch in on Brown. He said I wasn't far from being right."

Gillom returned to Massillon after his career with the Browns and played semi-pro football with the Tigertown Stars.

The Tigertown stars were made up primarily of former Massillon High School stars, many of whom were All-Ohioans. Gillom and former Cleveland Browns fullback Maurice Bassett gave the team some name recognition.

"It was a fun thing," said Junie Studer, Massillon historian, who was a statistician for the Stars. "The bus always had a case or two of beer in the aisle for the trip home."

The Tigertown Stars were successful, winning the Ohio semi-pro championship in 1959 with a 7-1 record. In 1960 they were runner-up with an 11-3 finish.

Gillom died in 1985 at age 63 in Los Angeles, where he was the city's assistant athletic director. He was buried in Massillon.

MIKE TAKACS

Chuck Mather said Mike Takacs was his best lineman at Massillon.

Mather coached 13 All-Ohio linemen in his six seasons with the Tigers.

"I guess you really have to put Mike at the top," Mather said.

At Ohio State, Takacs acheived All-American recognition as a senior in 1952.

Jack Hill was Massillon's quarterback in 1947 and '48.

"We always ran off of Mike Takacs, the right tackle," Hill said. He was 178-180 pounds. He was a guy that tied the other guy up right away because he was so quick."

Takacs was an All-American guard at Ohio State in 1952.

"We were playing McKinley and they thought he was going offsides all the time," Mather said. "But he was just going quicker than all the other linemen, so it made him look like he was offsides. He would be that far ahead of everybody else."

DON JAMES

At The University of Washington, Massillon's Don James is a coaching legend. Of course the lofty title of "legend" also describes James' stature in the Pac-10 conference.

James, National Coach of the Year in 1984 and 1991, won Washington's first and only national championship in 1991. His 12-0 Huskies are considered one of the top teams in west coast football history.

Don James is the winningest coach in Pac-10 history. He coached at the University of Washington for 18 years.

James is the winningest coach in Washington *and* Pac-10 history. He led the Huskies to a 153-57-2 record —with 99 Pac-10 wins among them.

In 18 years as head coach, James led the Huskies to 15 bowl games, winning 10 of them—including a Pac-10 record nine straight bowl appearances from 1979-87.

Want to talk Rose Bowls? James led the Huskies to six, winning four. He's one of four coaches to win four Rose Bowls. Heady stuff for the former Massillon quarterback.

For all of that James was elected to the College Football Hall of Fame in 2000.

James was a product of good role models. As a youngster he dreamed of being a player while watching brother Tommy, one of Massillon's greatest halfbacks.

In 18 years as head coach, James led the Huskies to 15 bowl games, winning 10 of them.

"When you grow up in Massillon with an older brother playing, seeing him in uniform, it made me want to do that." James said. "Watching Tommy just got better, from Massillon to Ohio State to the Browns. He could run."

As a teenager James caught the coaching bug from the tremendous coaching environment he was exposed to in Massillon. James' coaching influences were many.

"I just idolized those coaches. In fact, that's when I decided to coach. Bill Muir at Longfellow, he was just an impressive guy. It was football at a different level. It wasn't swearing, kicking you in the butt. It was just being a teacher—a positive teacher on the field. Chuck Mather was extremely organized. Being a quarterback, I got to spend a little more time with him. Guys like Tommy Evans, Paul Schofer, Lauri Wartenian, Dave Putts, Dick Piskoty, guys like that. Watching them, being around them, that's what I wanted to be like."

James was a master ball handler as quarterback of Massillon's 1949 state championship team.

"I was efficient, not great," James said. "We didn't have to throw much with that backfield. Ace Crable was one of the real fine athletes. Clarence Johnson was big and fast. Dick Jacobs was fast."

Don James led on one of the most potent offensive attacks in Massillon history in 1949.

James was modest in describing his quarterback play. After accepting a scholarship to The University of Miami, he proceeded to set five school passing records.

"We weren't a very strong team, so we had to throw a lot," James said with a laugh.

While James was exposed to positive coaching role models at Massillon, his coaches at Miami showed him a different side.

"My college coach was a little unique in that he was an alcoholic. He presented himself to the team dead drunk on at least two occasions. He's dead now, his name was Andy Gustafson. And he was just an exceptional speaker and he had so much going for him. But he had an alcohol problem. And that tainted me a little bit. A young guy. He came in the locker room before our big game with Florida and he was drunk. I was shocked. But I learned so much. There's a way to coach in this business. You can never let players know that you drink, or drink when you're gonna be around 'em."

"My college coach was a little unique in that he was an alcoholic."

Don James

"It's like having a good teacher and a bad teacher. A bad teacher's not bad for you. It's going to be uncomfortable for a semester, but you learn that you don't ever want to be a bad teacher and why they are bad teachers. You take the experience and learn from it."

After a year as a graduate assistant with Mather at Kansas and two years as a high school assistant at Miami Southwest, James got his first break.

"I had a chance to get on the Florida State staff," James said. "I was at Florida State for all of Biletnikoff's career." Fred Biletnikoff was Florida State's first All-American and a Hall of Fame wide receiver with the Oakland Raiders.

James tried to move to the University of Florida, but his head coach Bill Peterson blocked the move.

"Ray Graves offered me a job to come and coach his defense. Bill Peterson contested that. There's a rule in the state of Florida that you can't move from state school to state school unless you're given a raise in responsibility. For about a month I didn't know where I was coaching. So, I came close to being a Gator.

James interviewed for the head coaching job at Florida in 1979, when he was head coach at Washington.

"I interviewed for the job there when Charlie Pell got it," James said. "I wasn't about to leave Washington, though."

James went from Florida State to the University of Michigan, where he coached under Bump Elliott for two years. Then he moved to the University of Colorado for three years. There he met Mike Lude, who later offered him the head coaching job at Kent State University.

"That was the best thing that ever happened to me," James said. "I think the good Lord was looking out for me then. We won a conference championship our second year. The only one they've ever won. They haven't won one since.

"I got the Washington job...they were all complaining about them hiring me."

Don James

Lude moved to the University of Washington and soon recruited James to join him there.

"When I got the Washington job, they were all complaining about them hiring me," James laughed. "They had never heard of me out there."

No one was complaining after James turned the program around. James has many good memories of his days as the head man at Washington.

James was elected to the 2000 College Football Hall of Fame.

"The six Pac 10 championships, taking the team to the Rose Bowl six times. If you'd have told me that when I started coaching, I'd say you're nuts. And the Orange Bowl. We beat Oklahoma in the Orange Bowl. That's the year BYU got the National Championship (1984) and they beat a real weak Michigan team in the Holiday Bowl. So they came up first, we got second. But it was still exciting to get second. If I went to my grave never winning a national championship, that wasn't going to bother me. But then to win it in 1991, that was a thrill. That would have been a real disappointment if we didn't win a share of it. Those were exciting times. Any time you beat an LA school, it's just incredible. We beat USC and UCLA my first year there. UCLA went to the Rose

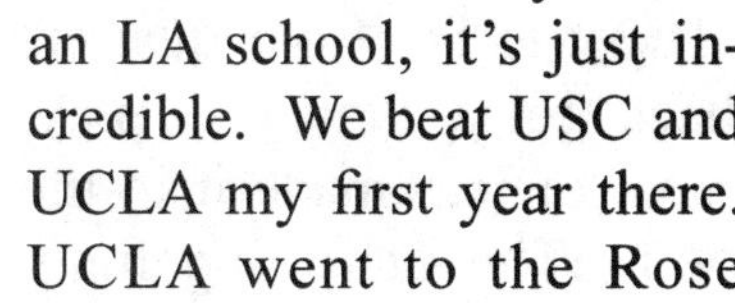

Bowl and we beat them. We beat USC coach John McKay's last team.

James coached some famous players at Washington.

One of his star pupils was Hall of Famer Warren Moon.

"We went out and got Warren Moon," James said, "then we started cranking out some quarterbacks."

Among James' quarterbacks at Washington to play in the NFL are Mark Brunell, Steve Pelluer, Hugh Millen, Cary Conklin, Chris Chandler, Billy Joe Hobert, Damon Huard and Tom Flick. At one point the University of Washington had more quarterbacks in the NFL than any other school. It wasn't always like that.
"It got to be if our quarterback got a chance to play, most of 'em made it in the NFL. The interesting thing, my first year out there, high school coaches were telling the kids that with my offense you'll never be able to make it in the NFL. It really made me mad. I let some coaches know that. Then we started cranking out some quarterbacks and that was the end of that stuff."

James also had a number one overall pick in the NFL draft. "Steve Entman went out as the first pick," James said. "He came out of a small school. He wanted to show people. It bothered him that he wasn't a Blue Chip player. He competed in the weight room, competed in practice. He was going to go out and kick butt every day. He just got better and better."

James credited a philosophy that he learned at Massillon for much of his success at Washington.

"Never waste a day," James

said. "We've got 365 days. I'd tell our recruits, we've laid out every day of your life for the year. We want you to think in terms of getting better every day. Sunday may be rest and church and study, but we've got a plan. And we counted days to the next big event."

"I was a great believer in organization. I hated to ever have anything go wrong—it would kill me. It was a matter of focusing your time on things that really contribute to winning.

"I was a disciplinarian. I wouldn't let anything slide. If I even heard a rumor about a player I'd have him in my office that day. Just saying, 'Here's the rumor, man, this is the image you're projecting.' If a player did something wrong, we never let it slide. A lot of people think problems will go away if you don't deal with them. That's an easy thing to do, but that doesn't work.

"We went out and got Warren Moon, then we started cranking out some quarterbacks."

Don James

"We tried to make all game decisions on Thursday. Tried to look ahead with our game plan. Do we go for one, or go for two. Fourth and one in the middle of the field, do you go for it? When do you go for the win? Do you need to be kicking field goals or scoring seven? We had a pregame checklist we'd go through and it gave every coach an opportunity. I wanted to eliminate all the emotional decisions I could on game day, because you know what the fans want you to do. They always want you to go for it. Sometimes that's okay, but a lot of times that's dumb."

James was comfortable with his strengths as a coach.

"I think I'm good at molding a staff and a team," he said. "That was the fun part each year. Putting it together and staying on top of things."

James enjoyed his run, but he doesn't miss coaching.

"I had a great run, and I had great support. I don't look back. After 38 years you start to wear down a bit. It's only glamorous one day a week. It's hard, long work."

Today much of James' income comes from public speaking. He speaks on discipline, motivation and success.

"I've done, and still do, a lot of speaking," James said. "I'm always introduced as being from Massillon, Ohio. It's not an especially large town, but one in which football's extremely important. And you start throwing out names like Paul Brown, you know that gets people's attention."

Jim Reichenbach

Massillon's All-Ohioans

1950
Jim Reichenbach
Bob Howe
Jerry Krisher

1951
Bruce Brenner
Glenn Tunning
Ace Grooms

1952
Bob Khoenle
Jim Geiser
Lee Nussbaum

1953
Jim Letcavits
Bruce Schram
Ronnie Agnes
John Traylor
John Francisco
Tom Boone

1954
Homer Floyd
Bob Williams

1955
Jim Houston
Dave Canary
Don Duke

1956
Mike Hershberger
Jim Mercer

1957
Clyde Childers
Ivory Benjamin
Chuck Beiter
Leaman Williamson

1958
Bob Vogel
Hase McKey
Bill Zorn

1959
Joe Sparma
Hase McKey
Terry Snyder
Gary Bednar
Art Hastings

TEAMS 1950s RECORDS

90	7	2
WINS	LOSSES	TIES

6 State Championships
4 National Championships

1950
10-0-0
State Champions
National Champions
Head Coach: Chuck Mather

M	Key Games	Opp.
29	Alliance	7
33	Canton McKinley	0
407	***Season Totals***	***37***

1951
9-1-0
State Champions
Head Coach: Chuck Mather

M	Key Games	Opp.
13	Steubenville	6
13	Warren Harding	19
40	Canton McKinley	0
316	***Season Totals***	***65***

1952
10-0-0
State Champions
National Champions
Head Coach: Chuck Mather

M	Key Games	Opp.
27	Alliance	21
41	Canton McKinley	8
437	***Season Totals***	***93***

1953
10-0-0
State Champions
National Champions
Head Coach: Chuck Mather

M	Key Games	Opp.
27	Warren Harding	6
48	Canton McKinley	7
399	***Season Totals***	***55***

1954
9-1-0
State Champions
Head Coach: Tom Harp

M	Key Games	Opp.
7	Alliance	19
12	Warren Harding	7
26	Canton McKinley	6
295	***Season Totals***	***66***

1955
8-1-1
Head Coach: Tom Harp

M	Key Games	Opp.
22	Alliance	6
12	Mansfield	12
7	Canton McKinley	13
262	***Season Totals***	***99***

1956
8-2-0
Head Coach: Lee Tressel

M	Key Games	Opp.
6	Mansfield	14
35	Barberton	6
7	Canton McKinley	34
237	***Season Totals***	***104***

1957
8-1-0
State Runner-up
Head Coach: Lee Tressel

M	Key Games	Opp.
20	Warren Harding	14
30	Barberton	0
25	Canton McKinley	7
221	***Season Totals***	***46***

1958
8-1-1
Head Coach: Leo Strang

M	Key Games	Opp.
8	Alliance	8
0	Warren Harding	6
38	Canton McKinley	16
220	***Season Totals***	***45***

1959
10-0-0
State Champions
National Champions
Head Coach: Leo Strang

M	Key Games	Opp.
90	Barberton	0
20	Canton McKinley	0
431	***Season Totals***	***46***

Story of the Decade 1950s

1955 Snow Bowl Loss to Canton McKinley Was Tigers Biggest Heartbreaker Ever

After over 100 years of gridiron wars, can one loss be singled out as *the most* heartbreaking? It would have to be a very close game. Historically significant. Controversial. Gut-wrenching to recall. Well, the 1955 Massillon-McKinley classic was all of that—and more.

Program from the 1955 Massillon-McKinley game.

"They beat the Bulldogs everywhere but on the scoreboard," Luther Emery wrote in Massillon's *Evening Independent* after the game. "But it is the score that counts and in years to come, the score, not the statistics, will be remembered."

Emery was right for the most part. Massillon *did* dominate statistically. McKinley's potent offense, led by quarterback Nap Barbosa, was averaging over 400 yards a game. McKinley gained just 62 yards—56 of them on runs by Barbosa. Massillon gained 194 yards, but the 52 yards they lost on errant center snaps—and the ensuing scores—doomed them.

Emery underestimated people's memories of the game. While many may forget the final score, it's the *events* of the game that are indelibly imprinted.

David Canary, an All-Ohio end for the 1955 Tigers, remembers watching a film of the game with teammates decades after graduating from Washington High School.

"It had been devastating to all of us," Canary said. "But we thought, 'Well, we're grown ups now, it's been 30 years for crying out loud, let's watch the tape.'

"So we went in to John James' basement, we got a little drunk in the process—to make it easier—we were drinking a lot of beer. Well, we were laughing and carrying on. We were laughing until about the end of the first half. We stopped laughing. It was kind of like watching a train wreck. We couldn't take our eyes off of it. By the end of the game we just were so depressed—as adults—it destroyed the party.

"We should have outscored them. We outgained them 3-1. The second half you couldn't move. There was no movement. It was just a bunch of guys wallowing around in this wet, snowy, whitish, blackish, muddish thing."

Canary believes that the attitude that is born—*and drilled into*—Massillon players has a lot to do with the disappointment the players felt after the game.

"You have to come up in that

environment, to run up the hill to kiss the blarney stone 6,000 times, get in shape, suffer the pain. In Massillon you win. You don't lose. You win. That's what you do. It's not a choice. You don't break even with the season and think, 'Well, we did pretty good.' No, in those days you won *every* game, or you failed. And that loss just decimated a lot of people.

"We just felt...that we had been cheated by the fates... as if God had conspired to humble us."

David Canary

"We just felt, partly, that we had been cheated by the fates," Canary continued, "It was as if God had conspired to humble us or something. We just felt powers that were stronger than us had come down and played a hand in that. Because the weather is what won that game for them. No question about that. Plus the two passes from center, but that was all part of the mess that we were dealing with. That wasn't a good day."

The impact of two errant center snaps on the lives of the two centers who snapped them in the 1955 Massillon-McKinley game was profound.

One center, Tom Spicer, was an outstanding athlete and a Massillon co-captain for 1955.

The other center, Jim Dowd, lacked Spicer's athleticism, but excelled in the classroom, graduating as class valedictorian and Outstanding Senior Boy.

It would be fair to say the two centers came from different worlds.

"The two centers came from totally different backgrounds," Canary said. "Spicer was a great big guy (6'1", 192) came from not any money, they were rather poor. He wasn't a great student. Tom was terribly torn up by what happened that game. He centered one of those passes from center and Jim Dowd centered the other. The Dowd family, his brother's a judge. That whole family became district attorneys and lawyers.

Massillon coaches, players and fans never blamed the centers for the loss.

Massillon coaches, players and fans never blamed the centers for the loss. In fact head coach Tom Harp takes the blame for the bad snaps.

"It all goes back, probably, to overcoaching," Harp said. "On the practice field we had a spot that we kept water in—a little mud spot. Every night we'd have the centers go over there and snap the ball out of the mud 10 times for long snap practice, so in case we got into a sloppy game it wouldn't be something new to them. But the managers put water in this hole. We probably weren't watching them close enough. They just filled it up and kept filling it up. And when they put the ball in there it would just float. So the managers would shove it down so it was stuck in the mud. So when the center went over there to center the ball, instead of making his normal, smooth snap, he would jerk it out of the mud, then snap it. And so here they are out on this muddy field, two different guys, and they remember snappin' it out of that mud hole. And they jerk it up and they snap it. They just snapped it right over his head. If we had overlooked that sort of drill and weren't trying to be complete in our coaching, that probably never would have happened."

Jim Dowd (left) was selected Outstanding Senior Boy. Tom Spicer was co-captain of the 1955 squad.

"Nobody blamed them," Canary said. "It was like trying to pick up a mud ball and throw it back 20 yards to somebody. It was a quagmire by that point. We all felt badly for losing the game."

Dowd remembers the events, 50-some years later. "It was my senior year," he said. "Massillon had won seven straight titles in football and our team did not. I played football from seventh grade all the way through. I had watched my brothers Dave and Jack play. That was a huge ambition for me.

"Tom Spicer started out as the starting center. He and Dave Canary were co-captains. I backed Tom up. As of the third game of the season, Harp started alternating us. Tom would start and play the first possession, then I would be the center for the second possession, Tom the third and me the fourth and so on. Against Barberton, which would be the eighth game of the season, Tom injured his wrist. He was also the starting middle guard on defense. At halftime the decision was made that he could continue playing on defense, but should probably not continue playing on offense. So I played center the rest of the season, which is to say the second half of the Barberton game, then we played Akron Garfield, then we played Canton McKinley.

"Because he was team captain, he played the first series of the Canton game at Fawcett Stadium. Tom muffed a punt formation center and the punter wasn't able to get it off and McKinley recovered the ball inside the 10 and pushed it in for a touchdown. We were all feeling a little sick to fall behind so quickly. It was the very beginning of the game. It had snowed the night before and that morning, so the field got progressively more muddy as the game went on.

"After falling behind 7-0, shortly thereafter we drove the length of the field and Don Duke scored and John Kausnick kicked the extra point and we were tied 7-7. We went that way through the rest of the first half and well into the second half. We were well into the fourth quarter and still tied 7-7.

"I had played center ever since the first series. We were in punt formation and on my previous punt snap the ball had slipped out of my hand such that the punter had to sort of scoop it up at his knees instead of where he *should* get it. So I made darn sure I didn't throw the snap too low. Instead I held on too long and it went over the punter's head and bounced into the end zone and McKinley fell on it. So we lost the state championship."

Players in the Massillon locker room were devastated following the loss. Emery was there. "A good many Massillon boys there were crying," Emery recalled. "Dave Canary was just sittin' down wiping his eyes with a towel. They had built up their hopes and nerves. This was quite a letdown for them. It didn't show any weakness on their part to cry. It was a nervous letdown."

"I made darn sure I didn't throw the snap too low. Instead I held on too long and it went over the punter's head."

Jim Dowd

"I remember crying;" Canary said, "those were bitter tears after the McKinley game."

Dowd remembers how he felt after the game. "After the game I went into the locker room and just sat. I just couldn't do anything. Dave Canary came over and put his arms around my shoulders and just held onto me until I regained my emotional stability. That's the kind of kid he was. I was crying like crazy."

Dowd got a surprise when he returned to school on Monday.

"I had no idea what to expect when we went back to school except that I knew there would be a rally in the gym and all the football players would be recognized. I didn't know what kind of response I would get. In fact it turned out I got a very positive response from the students. None of my teammates ever said anything to me that year about how I had screwed up their season. However, three years later I'm at the Akron Rubber Bowl before the season started. A buddy and I had gone to watch the Browns in a preseason game. A fellow named Jerry Hofacre, who had been a teammate, came walking into the stadium and my friend and I were sitting about five rows up. He came walking by and suddenly looked up and saw me. He waved and said, 'Bad snap.' He was bein' funny. That was fine. That didn't bother me. You've got to put that kind of thing in perspective."

Dowd had great respect for Spicer. "Tom was a great player," Dowd said. "He was an All-Ohio kind of player. He was tough. He was big. He was stronger than I was. He was a very aggressive football player. As a middle guard he was very important to the defense.

"When you're playing the same position, but also competing against each other, it's an interesting dynamic. I never questioned that he was the better player, so I think that we got along just fine.

"Tom and I had a conversation when we went up to play in the Rubber Bowl against Barberton, when he got his wrist injured. On the way up, we sat together on the bus and we had a conversation. He said to me, 'Ah, I wish I had your brains.' And I responded to him, 'I wish I had your skill as a football player because it would have meant so much for me to start for Massillon.' At that point I had not started a game.

"I was never quite sure whether he *really* injured his wrist all that bad. Which is to say I'm not that sure that he didn't make that possible in response to me saying how much it would have meant to me to start a game for Massillon. I think that really says a lot about Tom. Now Tom was a rough guy. We both centered away a touchdown. Okay, if his wrist was that badly injured, centering a punt formation snap means you're going to throw it back 12 yards or so at that point. I'm not sure whether he didn't make it possible for me to start the last couple games of the season."

"David Canary came over and put his arms around my shoulders and just held onto me until I regained my emotional stability. I was crying like crazy."

Jim Dowd

Canary was philosophical about the effect the snaps had on the two centers.

"Well, Tom didn't respond to it well, I'd have to say," Canary said, "I haven't seen him much since, but he was really crippled up by that game. And Jim, instead of going and doing what everybody *knew* he was going to do—he was going to be a lawyer—the tradition of his family, go into politics. Well, he became a minister. And I don't think there's any doubt in his mind or my mind that game had a good deal to do with that."

While Dowd *did* become a minister, he doesn't feel like memories of his errant snap played a part in his decision.

"I don't think that was a factor in my decision to go into ministry instead of into law or politics," Dowd said. "I felt that God was calling me to go into ministry and was *not* calling me to law and politics. My brother Dave is a federal judge and has been one for 25 years. My father went into law. My brother Jack was also a lawyer with a big firm in Cleveland. So yes, that was very much a family tradition. I broke the family mold. I was a pastor for 40 years."

Dowd then spoke slowly and deliberately, sounding like a man reflecting on whether the events of the 1955 Massillon-McKinley game *could have* influenced his career choice. "I don't think that game, per se, or the *outcome* of that game affected it that much," he said, "If anything, it may have shortened my football career."

Games of the Century

1957 "Clock" Game Most Famous in Massillon-Warren History

All the ingredients were in place for a football masterpiece. Start with two arch rivals. Mix in a 6-0 start for Warren and its new head coach, Gene Slaughter. Sprinkle in a Massillon

"You'd better get that clock fixed," Warren head coach Gene Slaughter tells Massillon coach Lee Tressel following the famous "Clock Game." Sportswriter Charlie Powell is in the middle of the action.

squad that was smarting from its only loss of the season, 13-7, to Cleveland Benedictine. Pack 21,384 frenzied fans into Tiger Stadium. Bring it all to a boil with a 14-14 tie. Wind the clock down to 1:00. Shake things up with a clock malfunction that gives Massillon an extra minute. Then finish it with a "Hail Mary" pass that is tipped, then caught for the game winning touchdown in a 20-14 game.

It was a recipe for success for Massillon. For Warren, disaster.

Clyde Childers awaits the game-winning touchdown pass from Joe Sparma.

Senior running back Ivory Benjamin, Massillon's star player, remembers the final minutes well.

"The score was tied 14-14," Benjamin said. "I'd just ran the ball. Joe Sparma comes into the game. He's sayin', 'Ben, Ben, get up. We've got time.'

"Well, the clock says 59 seconds (laughs). That's where the clock got messed up. I saw it. And I'm pretty sure everybody in the stadium saw it right along when I did."

Massillon assistant coach Ducky Schroeder remembered things differently.

"The men who ran the clock, Bill Archibald and John Morgan, said there's no way there was anything wrong with that clock. Yet, when we ran it, twice out of 16 times it showed that it wasn't right.

"I was spotting from the top of the stadium and of course when it gets that close you're watching the clock. I never saw anything happen to the clock."

During Massillon's final drive, some say an extra minute flashed onto the clock. What we know for sure is that the clock read 0:04, with the ball on the Warren 38, when sophomore Joe Sparma, Massillon's third string quarterback, dropped back for a final desperation pass. Sparma found All-Ohio end Clyde Childers streaking down the sideline. The 6'4" Childers caught the ball—which he leapt to deflect at the four—then grabbed at the two and scored. The clock read 0:00. Delirious Tiger fans swarmed the south end zone where they mobbed Coach Lee Tressel, Sparma and Childers.

Warren coach Gene Slaughter looks forlornly at the scoreboard following Warren's 20-14 loss to Massillon in the famous "clock" game.

After the game Massillon faculty manager Roger Price tested the clock while Warren coach Gene Slaughter and a group of Warren fans looked on. During the first test the clock malfunctioned. The second time the clock functioned properly. Slaughter told Price, "You'd better get that thing fixed," as he headed to the Warren bus.

Games of the Century

Homer Slams McKinley with Record Performance in 1954

In the pre-playoff days of Ohio high school football, every game was like a playoff game. A single loss often meant your season was over. This grim fact was not lost on Massillon's young first-year mentor Tom Harp.

A loss to Alliance in Week 3 made Harp's bid for a state championship tenuous. One thing was certain, Massillon had to win out and hope things fell into place elsewhere in the state.

Program from the 1954 Massillon-McKinley game.

"The first thing we had to do was win the rest of our football games," Harp said. "I believed we could do it but we were going to need some help.

"All the things we needed to happen, happened. And we won all the rest of our games. We came down to the McKinley game. They're ranked one and we're ranked two. They were favored by seven points."

All of Massillon was in a fervor over the big showdown

with Canton McKinley. "Every store in town was going crazy," Harp said. "The kids in school all week, every time class changed they were playing 'The Tiger Rag' and screaming 'Go Massillon, hold that Tiger.' Cheers all over the place. It was just electricity all week."

The heart of Massillon's attack was Homer Floyd. Floyd, who ranks among Massillon's all-time greatest running backs, had a career day against McKinley.

Harp knew McKinley would be focusing on Floyd. "All year long we always ran a criss-cross on our kickoff. Regardless of whether Andy Stavroff got it or Homer Floyd got it, they'd criss-cross and Floyd would end up with it—except for the opening kickoff in the McKinley game. The kickoff came to Floyd and he gave it to Stavroff—which is what we planned. Stavroff broke into the open and ran all the way to the 15-yard line."

That play seemed to set the tone for the game.

"Homer Floyd gained 263 yards as halfback. The other halfback, Jerry Yoder, gained 125 yards," Harp said.

Massillon completely dominated the game, picking up 21 first downs to McKinley's six and outgaining the Bulldogs 446 yards to135.

Floyd was surprised at how easy the yards came. "It was a lot easier than I expected it to be because the holes were there—our line was making the holes," Floyd said,

"We beat 'em 26-6," Harp said, "and it could have been 40-6."

Games of the Century

Warren, Paul Warfield, No Match for 1959 Tigers in 38-8 Route

"We held Paul Warfield to minus-seven yards gained," said Ducky Schroeder, remembering Massillon's surprisingly-easy 38-8 Week 7 win over Warren Harding in 1959. "To me, that was one of the greatest games we ever played. I don't recall another time where our team was more fired up for a game."

Programs from the 1959 Massillon-Warren game.

Schroeder would know. He played for Massillon in 1925 and was an assistant coach there for 22 years. "They came in here to Tiger Stadium undefeated, we were undefeated," Schroeder said. "At the half we had 'em beat 30-0. A great exhibition of football."

Warfield followed his All-Ohio prep career at Warren with an All- Big 10 career at Ohio State and an eight-time Pro Bowl and Hall of Fame pro football career with the Browns and Dolphins. He won two Super Bowl rings with the Miami Dolphins.

Leo Strang, Massillon's head coach, remembers the scene in the locker room before kickoff.

"I never saw a locker room like that one before the game," Strang said. "You could hear a pin drop. And Dick Scholem, who did our play-by-play on the radio, came to the locker room to ask me a few questions before the game. He looked around and looked at the team and he said, 'Coach, what's wrong?' I said, 'I don't know. I've never seen anything like this. Well, I don't know what's going to happen. But if I were to guess, I think a real good football team is going to get the crap kicked out of them.'

"Hase McKey was outstanding. The Warren center couldn't handle him at all," Strang said of his two-time All-Ohio noseguard.

"They came to Massillon and switched jerseys," said Marty Gugov, a junior cornerback. "Warfield switched jerseys with Marvin Howard, another running back. We didn't know beforehand," Gugov said. But by kickoff the Massillon players knew of Warren's trickery.

"I personally knocked Paul out of the game two times in the first half," Gugov said. "We knocked him out of the game about eight times—just rocked him. I truly believe that game enhanced my chances of getting a scholarship to Ohio State."

Massillon went on to win the state and national championship. Warren finished 9-1.

Games of the Century

Tigers 90-0 Route of Barberton Sets Off Poll Controversy in 1959

After the final gun sounded, Barberton head coach Tom Phillips refused to shake hands with Massillon mentor Leo Strang. He felt the Tigers had gone too far in their 90-0 win over Barberton.

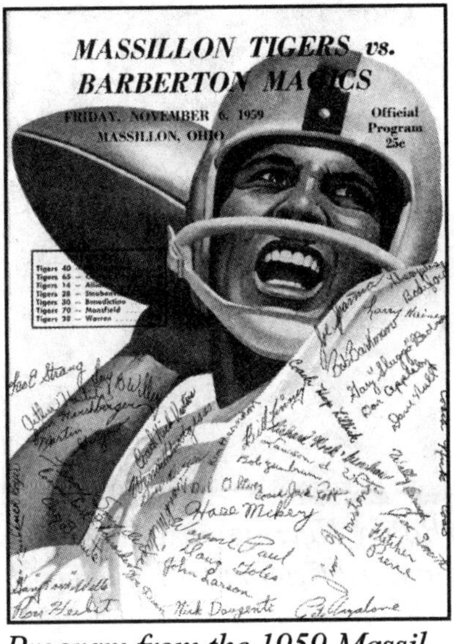

“I couldn’t do anything about that game,” Strang said. “I substituted all of the kids.”

Program from the 1959 Massillon-Barberton game.

Indeed nine Tigers scored on the evening. “I got into the juniors, who were state champs the next year, and they were better, more inspired than the starters. What are you gonna do? Bobby Herring, one of our wingbacks, weighed about 135 pounds. He came up to me and said, ‘Coach, I’m the only one who hasn’t carried the ball.’ There were only 28 seconds to go in the game.

“We have the ball on our 35-yard line. I only had one running play for the wingback—an inside reverse. I said, 'Okay, Bobby, get in there and run your play.

"So he went in and I'll be darned if he didn't go 65 yards for a touchdown. That made it 90-0. We weren't trying to score. What can you do? You can't tell 'em not to play."

Bobby Herringmakes a tackle against Canton McKinley in 1959.

AP Poll voters, who decided the state championship in the pre-playoff days, responded to Massillon's win by dropping them in the ensuing poll.

Fritz Howell, AP sports editor, responded to the snub by suspending the poll.

"Ratings of Ohio's high school football teams will not be moved this week," Howell said. "Of the 46 sportswriters participating in the weekly poll, 14 ignored completely one of the high ranking, unbeaten untied teams and awarded high spots to its chief rival. Thus the poll fails to give a true statewide picture."

The team that was ignored was Massillon. The poll turned around, however, with Massillon reclaiming the top spot and the 1959 state championship. Massillon was also voted national champs.

Obie Pins Are an Enduring Tradition

In 1952 Massillon head coach Chuck Mather came up with the idea for an Obie pin. "It was something that people could have that basically costs nothing," Mather said. "It was a plaster copy of Obie. People seemed to like that kind of stuff. Things seem more sophisticated today, whether it would appeal to people today like it did 50 years ago, I don't know."

Obie pins come with membership to the Booster Club.

Mather would be pleased to know that the Obie pin is still going strong. "A lot of people have their ball caps full of Obie pins for every year they've been a Booster Club member," said Bill Dorman, Booster Club President for 2005. "My mother-in-law just passed away, and when my wife was going through her things she found a bunch of Obie pins. It's a tradition. They're issued with the membership card. I know when I was president people made sure they got 'em. They didn't just want the card, they wanted the pin. I think it was more important than the membership card."

Junie Studer, Massillon's famous artist, has painted Obie more than anyone else. He knows the history. "The first pin in 1952 was made in white," said Studer, Booster

Club president in 1972. "The next year it was orange. The next year they decided to spray it copper. Then it got to where each year was different. Today each Booster Club president is responsible for painting 1,500 to 2,000 pins. They have to see that they are painted and are different than any other Obie pin. You can get somebody to help—but you have to see that it gets done. It's a chore."

"A lot of people have their ball caps full of Obie pins for every year they've been a Booster Club member."

Bill Dorman

"I took 'em with me to Nag's Head on vacation to finish them up," Dorman recalled. "We had to issue them to the players to sell when we got back. Each player gets a packet of membership cards and Obie pins and is asked to assist in selling them."

Dorman's favorite Obie pin memory? "I pinned coach Tom Stacy when he was announced as coach, that was the first thing I did." It must have brought good luck. Stacy led the 2005 Tigers to a 13-2 season and an appearance in the state championship game.

Massillon's Famous Tradition of Placing Footballs in Baby Cribs Started in 1954

One of the most famous Massillon traditions is the presentation of a football to every baby boy born there. But like many traditions, it's difficult to trace the origin of this practice.

Baby boys born in Massillon receive a football in their crib from the booster club.

Tom Harp had already heard of the Massillon tradition when he took the reigns as head coach in 1954. But he's sure Massillon's baby boys didn't receive footballs prior to his arrival.

"They talked about footballs when babies were born," Harp said "But they never gave footballs when babies were born 'til I got there. I asked them about that and they said, 'That's just something they *said* that they always did but they never *really* did."

So, as Massillon coaches have done for years, Harp approached the Booster Club for help. "A guy at the Booster Club was an administrator at the hospital. So the Booster Club formed a committee. Every month the administrator at the hospital would provide the committee with a list of the baby boys that were born that went home from the hospital. We bought a big box of small footballs. One fella would paint on the footballs, 'Congratulations to a future Tiger.' This committee would go to the homes and deliver these footballs.

"These footballs were sitting on mantles around the city. One of the proudest things was for the father to get one of these for his baby son."

Tom Harp

"These balls were sitting on mantles around the city. One of the proudest things was for the father to get one of these for his baby son. Even though the footballs weren't part of the tradition before we got there, that tradition still prevailed. 'My son, I wanted my son to be a football player. This is something he had lived for and dreamed about since he was a little boy. He got in the junior high, he came down as a sophomore, became a junior, and now he had his shot as a senior. If he was one of the ones who made it, he achieved one of the greatest things ever.' You didn't have to worry about 'em. You didn't have to worry about their dedication to the game. Or to Massillon. Or to anything you wanted them to do."

And it all starts with that football in their crib.

Victory Bell Tradition Was Started by Tressel

Massillon embraces their traditions. One of the favorites started in 1957 when Massillon head coach Lee Tressel purchased a locomotive bell to be exchanged between the winner of the Massillon-Canton McKinley game each year.

Maria Protos and Obie (Dick Fink) ring the victory bell and display a Massillon championship flag in 1972.

Massillon controlled the bell for the first nine years. McKinley finally got to keep the bell for a year when they knocked off the Tigers in 1966.

Since then the bell's been passed back and forth between the schools an amazing 19 times.

When the playoffs began in 1972, a decision had to be made about what to do with the bell when the two teams meet in the playoffs. The decision was made that the winner of the regular season game keeps the bell regardless of who wins the playoff game.

The victory bell has become a very important symbol for players, coaches, cheerleaders and fans alike.

It becomes all the more important when one school establishes a winning streak in the series.

The love of the bell became so pervasive that during McKinley Week when Canton held the bell, the Massillon cheerleaders used to cheer, "We want our bell back, we want our bell back."

The longest streak for keeping the bell was Massillon's initial reign. Since then neither team has kept the bell more than four straight years—a testimony to the fierce rivalry between the two schools.

The Victory Bell was rather nondescript in 1961. McKinley's bulldog appears to be protecting the bell in this photograph. Today the bell gets a new coat of paint and elaborate graphics every time it changes hands.

Willie Spencer, Jr., learned the importance of the Victory Bell during his senior season in 1994 when the Tigers played the Bulldogs in the 100th game.

"Up until that point I didn't think that much of it. But after that game, Coach Steve Studer and I sprinted across the field and both grabbed the bell and took it back over to the Massillon sideline. It felt great. It brought tears to my eyes."

THE HOUSTON BROTHERS

Lin Houston

Jack Houston

Walt Houston

Jim Houston

Family Lands Three Brothers in NFL

Three were first team All-Ohio. Two were All-Americans at Ohio State. Three played professional football. And one—who they say may have been the best of all—never got to prove himself because of a tragic childhood accident.

The Houston brothers' football legacy looms large in Massillon history. The sons of an Illinois sharecropper, the Houston boys knew nothing about football when they arrived in Massillon in the fall of 1936.

While walking down the hallway at Washington High School, Lin Houston's stocky build caught the eye of an assistant basketball coach named John Tannehill. Tannehill introduced Lin to assistant football coach Carroll Widdoes who quickly brought Lin to Paul Brown. Brown recognized Lin's powerfully built legs and started training him to play guard. In the fall of 1937 Lin Houston played in the first football game he ever saw.

A certain gentleman named

Homer Williams is responsible for bringing his cousins to Massillon. Depending on which story you believe, Williams either: 1) Was drinking at the Massillon bus depot and missed his bus but met a supervisor at Union Drawn who offered him a job. Or 2) Williams had married a girl from New Brighton, PA, and had worked at Union Drawn there. When Union Drawn moved to Massillon, Williams moved along with them.

The story we are sure of is that Williams called for Mr. Houston, telling him he could get a job for him in Massillon.

The Houston family was poor. In southern Illinois they lived in a three-room house. Mrs. Houston cooked breakfast, lunch and dinner on a wood stove.

"She made everything from scratch," recalled son Howard Houston. "How she did it, I still can't believe this hardly now. She made everything from scratch, like the bread, the biscuits in the morning and maybe cornbread for lunch and biscuits again for supper. And she'd can 800 quarts of fruit and vegetables every year. We only had hogs for meat. And Dad would kill six in the fall. We'd put 'em in the smoke house and make sausage and smoke the hams and all that stuff.

"People have so much room today. We had three rooms: A kitchen, living room and a bedroom. And us boys, there were four of us, slept in one bed. Three long ways and one at the foot. The littlest one slept at the foot. But we managed."

Mr. Houston got a job at Republic Steel in Massillon where he worked until the steel strike in 1937. Interestingly, Homer Williams' brother, Lester Williams, was arrested for carrying dynamite during that strike.

"He was going to blow up the building down there," Howard said. "The police caught him. He had the dynamite under the back seat of his car. He served the rest of his life in the penitentiary."

While serving in WWII, Lin signed a contract to play for Brown with the Cleveland Browns.

About that time, Lin was graduating from high school and had offers to play football from all over the United States. He decided on the University of Michigan. According to his brother, Howard, University of Michigan arranged for Lin and his father to get jobs at Ford Motor Company, and the Houston family moved to Michigan until Republic Steel picked back up.

Lin spent just one semester at University of Michigan, then bounced around at several schools until Paul Brown became the head coach at Ohio State. Lin joined his old high school coach there and became an All-American guard for the Buckeyes.

Then, while serving in the Army during WWII, Lin signed a contract to play for Brown with the Cleveland Browns. "Paul Brown sent him $200 a month while he was in the service," Howard said. "That was big money back in those days. His first salary was $11,000 a year."

Lin was a star guard for the Browns from 1946-53.

Brown, in his autobiography, *PB: The Paul Brown Story,* described Lin Houston as one of his all-time greatest guards and the *fastest* guard he ever coached.

Jack Houston was an All-Ohio guard for Massillon in 1948 and played collegiately at Purdue. Knee injuries kept him from playing professional football.

"Walter went to Purdue University, graduated from there, and was signed by the Washington Redskins," Howard said. "He played with them only one year. The coach out there had brought in a rookie and was paying him $100 a year more than Walt was making. Walt told him to shove it and he quit. He owned Superior Container in Cleveland for many years.

"Jim was the Cleveland Brown's top draft choice in 1960," Howard said.

Massillon sportswriter Luther Emery remembers the Houston brothers fondly. "They were all good football players. All of them. They weren't cocky. Just down to earth fellas. They always said that their brother Howard would have been the best of all."

Howard lost the use of his legs when he was run over by a truck while hitchhiking.

This Houston is Glad to be Alive

A walk into *Houston's* was like a walk back in time.

Time was inescapable at *Houston's,* a business that Howard Houston owned and operated for over 50 years. *Houston's* was a combination jewelry store/ watch and clock repair shop. The ever present ticking of the clocks marked the time.

Howard Houston and his clocks.

Generations of Massillonians have appreciated the fair shake they got from Houston.

It would be easy for Houston to feel like he didn't get a fair shake in life. He never had the opportunity to star on the high school, college or professional gridirons like several of his famous brothers did. And many say he would have been the best of them all.

Brothers Lin, Walt and Jim all played professional football. Another brother, Jack Houston, was selected to the All-Ohio team.

"Myself, I was headed in the same direction," Houston said from behind the counter in his shop. "I loved the game. I played it hard. I guess I was pretty good at it."

Houston was the quarterback at Jones Junior High as a seventh and eighth grader. "I played first team," Houston said. "I still have a lot of friends around town that played. Milan Chovan, the Wallace brothers, Bob and Barney, the Lukes, the Demises. All those guys."

By the time Howard was playing junior high football, brother Lin had finished his All-Ohio career at Massillon and had gone on to pursue his All-American college career.

"He'd come home from college in the summer and we'd go down to Lincoln Park and work out together. I could outrun him in the 100-yard dash when he was in college."

So, was it true that Howard would have been the greatest of the Houston brothers?

"How would you know," Houston said. "I've heard all kinds of speculation, but how are you going to prove anything like that?"

Howard's proving ground in sports ended after his eighth grade year at Jones.

It was the summer of 1941, school was out, and jobs were hard to find for teenagers in Massillon. So Howard and a friend decided to do something daring. They headed to Texas to try to land a job on a ranch.

"We hopped freight trains and hitchhiked and got to Texarkana, Arkansas. The war had been declared on December 7, 1941. A lot of troop trains were heading in that direction. We were riding the freights.

"We were going across this railroad bridge and a railroad detective caught us. He pulled a gun on us. He thought we might have been sabotaging this railroad bridge where the troop trains kept going by. He gave us a stern warning. We had a hunting knife that we carried. He took that away from us. Took our matches away. He said 'You guys get off of this railroad and never come near it again.'

"So we did. We were scared to death. I was only 16 years old. My friend was the same age. So we decided then we'd come on back home. On the way back, why, we were thumbing, and we got outside of Memphis.

"Then, for some reason—I can never explain this—why that truck...my friend was thumbing and I was settin', my feet pointing toward the highway, I was leaning against the guardrail. And that truck hit my friend. Then he jackknifed the truck and I couldn't get out of the way."

"It killed my friend. And of course I ended up in the hospital."

Howard Houston

The driver of the truck ran over both of Houston's legs. He drove away without helping the boys.

"It killed my friend. And of course I ended up in the hospital."

Houston laid in pain, waiting for help.

"I laid on the road for 45 minutes, bleeding. Finally a

sheriff came by and put tourniquets on my legs. I never passed out all this time."

The sheriff took Houston to a Memphis hospital where he heard words that he'll never forget.

"When I got to the hospital I heard the doctor say, 'I'll give him 10 minutes to live.' Blink—I went out."

Houston didn't come to again for two weeks. "I was unconscious, due to the lack of blood. I think at the time if they would have dressed my wounds properly I might have not got all this infection. He patched 'em up and said I wasn't going to live anyway so what's the use. But I came through it. I survived that."

Houston spent four months in that Memphis hospital. During that time his weight dropped from 180 pounds to 90. Doctors decided to send Houston back to Canton Mercy Hospital. The trip was not easy.

"They brought me back to Canton in a baggage car on a freight train on a little short bed. They put me in a cast. It was really miserable. I nearly died in Chicago before I got here. I had to go from Memphis to Chicago and back to Canton."

Back at Canton Mercy, Houston got weaker and weaker, trying to fight the infection. Finally, a week after Christmas, they amputated the first leg.

"Boy, I felt 100 percent better." After the first of the year they amputated the second leg. "If I had it to do over now, I'd have waited. Waited to see if maybe that other one might have healed, maybe, with the right nutrition."

Houston took an immediate upturn in his health, physically and mentally.

"I started perking up, feeling great. I was running all over the hospital in a wheelchair after I got healed up a little bit."

Houston said he was never depressed after losing his legs after nearly nine months in the two hospitals.

"After laying there all that time in the hospital I was so glad to get out of there that it never bothered me. I wanted to get out and do things."

Houston remembers when he first got fitted with artificial legs. The room had a very low ceiling.

"When I stood up I hit my head. I'd been down so long. That was quite a sensation. From then on I was on the go. I never backed up at all.

"The guy who made my artificial legs, the guy who owned the place, Spivak Artificial Limb Company, he really encouraged me. I found out that I didn't have to be a handicapped. He was older—Mr. Spivak was his name. I was so glad to get going that I didn't have any problem learning to walk with them.

"At first I walked behind my wheelchair, then pretty soon I got a cane."

The moment of truth for Houston came when he was walking back from getting the mail at his house. "We had a fairly long driveway. One day I walked out to the mailbox. On the way back I stuck the cane in the mud and it broke off. I just left it there and kept on going. Never used anything since."

Houston says he never felt sorry for himself. Instead

he forged ahead after getting his artificial legs. "I went to watchmaker school. I finished my schooling and I apprenticed for two years down in New Philly . From then on I've been on my own. That was over 50 years ago."

Houston has also worked as a farmer. "I have a 170-acre beef farm that I actively farm. I've had several different farms over the years. I did dairy. I milked cows for 28 years. Every day. I enjoyed it. I still enjoy the farm and the cattle."

"On the way back I stuck the cane in the mud and it broke off. I just left it there and kept on going."

Howard Houston

Houston remains philosophical about the accident that changed his life.

"I just feel gratitude, great gratitude, that maybe this accident was for a purpose. I would have gone to the war and maybe gotten killed. I don't know how *that* would have turned out. I just count it as a blessing and go on. God was good enough to me to let me live. Maybe that was how it was planned. I don't know any other reason. That's the way life is, I guess."

CHUCK MATHER

"He was a hero, an absolute hero," David Canary said, describing Chuck Mather, who coached the Massillon Tigers for six dream seasons.

Canary was in grade school when Mather won the first of his six straight state championships in 1948. Canary played under Mather as a sophomore and went on to become an All-Ohio end under Tom Harp. Canary later gained fame as a television and movie actor.

Chuck Mather, with six state titles in six seasons, may have been Massillon's finest coach.

"Mather was terribly big and important and impressive to me," Canary said. "There was an awesome gentleness to him somehow. He was very contained, almost always very calm. He spoke—he didn't have to speak loudly. Everybody jumped when he talked. He was a very awesome figure to me. I've seen him as an adult and there's a wonderful sense of humor about him. A wry sense of proportion about life.

Canary's words express Mather's effect on Massillon. A 57-3 record only added to Mather's allure.

Massillon fell in love with Mather, who arrived when all seemed lost to a populace that had tasted the fruits of victory and feared they may never have it so good again.

"He won the town over because of his charm. You immediately liked him."

John McVay

"He won the town over because of his charm," said John McVay, the San Francisco 49ers Vice President and General Manager, who starred at center and linebacker for Mather at Massillon. "You immediately liked him. He didn't have to work on selling himself. He was well received right away."

The Massillon faithful were hungry for a return to the championship days Paul Brown pioneered a dozen years earlier. Fans had suffered through four sub-par seasons before Mather started his state championship streak.

But no one knew what to expect from Mather, who came to Massillon after successful stints at Ohio high schools in Brilliant, Leetonia and Hamilton.

His playing days certainly gave no hint to his impending success as a coach. In fact Mather didn't even play football in high school. His alma mater, Hopedale High School in Unionport, Ohio, dropped football the year he enrolled in school as a sophomore. At Ohio Northern University, his only football action was spot duty at tackle at the close of his senior season.

Chuck Mather is mobbed after beating Canton McKinley.

But *coaching* football was something Mather certainly had a knack for. His first job was at Brilliant, a small town outside of Unionport. Like Hopedale, Brilliant had abandoned its football program several years earlier. Mather was 0-7 in his first year of coaching at Brilliant in 1937. "They hadn't played any football and I hadn't coached any football," Mather said, "You can see what a combination that is." By his third year, Brilliant had improved to 6-2 and Mather accepted the head coaching job at Leetonia.

At Leetonia Mather experienced great success, sandwiching 27 wins, one loss, and three ties around a three-year hitch in the United States Coast Guard during World War II.

Mather honed his football knowledge while in the Coast Guard.

"At Leetonia, we had a bunch of players who loved to play football. They were sort of like Massillon guys. I only lost one game up there." Leetonia was 10-0-1 in 1940 and 7-1-1 in 1941. "Then I went in the service for three years," he said. After three years in the Coast Guard, Mather was itching to get back to coach the kids he had left behind at Leetonia. "The war was over in August of 1945. I told my commanding officer that all the kids I started with at Leetonia were seniors and 'Boy would I like to coach them.' Danged if he didn't go to Washington and get me out of the service. He managed to get me out the first week of September so I could coach."

Mather honed his football knowledge while in the Coast Guard. "He became associated with two future professional football Hall of Famers," said Carl "Ducky" Schroeder, a longtime Mather assistant at Massillon. "Clarence 'Ace' Parker and George McAfee were coaching in the Coast

Guard at Norfolk." McAfee was a young Chicago Bears halfback at the time. Mather took advantage of his friendship with McAfee and contacted the Bears and asked for their game films, which they were happy to send.

"During the service I had seen lots of Chicago Bears movies and they were using a T-formation," Mather said, "I would break down the movies and the plays. I had the whole Chicago Bears offense down by the time I got out of the service."

"Thorney told my brother Don that Massillon ought to check in on Chuck Mather."

Luther Emery

A Coast Guard coaching assignment provided Mather with an opportunity to implement what he had learned. "I was elected to coach a community football team, which was basically eighth and ninth graders. So I put in the T-formation. We just killed everybody. Back in those days most people hadn't even seen the T-formation offense."

The T-formation was just as successful at Leetonia when he returned in September of 1945.

"In one week's time I put this offense in at Leetonia," Mather said. "Against one of our toughest opponents, East Palestine, we won 7-0. Leetonia was a Class B school and seven of our opponents were Class A schools. We went on to win the Class B school state championship. Then there was another school, Copley, that was undefeated. So we had a challenge game with them that we won 46-6.”

Mather’s success at Leetonia led to his ascension to coaching Hamilton, a Class A school. “I almost didn’t go at all because I was making about as much money at Leetonia as they wanted to pay me at Hamilton,” he said. “Anyhow, I went to Hamilton and we had some great players. We were third in the state, beat Toledo Waite, beat Middletown twice—which was like beating McKinley—so I got to apply at Massillon.”

Mather is pictured on the cover of the football banquet program from 1948.

Mather’s record was 16-3-1 at Hamilton. But it wasn’t his record so much that attracted interest from Massillon, it was the recommendation of a friend of his wife, Mildred. “Mildred, who had gone to school at Barnsville, had a friend named ‘Thorney’ Thornberry who followed us very closely,” Mather said. “He worked with ‘Lut’ Emery’s brother Don. Don constantly talked to ‘Lut’ about me as a coach.”

Emery, Massillon’s longtime

sportswriter, had played a pivotal role in much of Paul Brown's success at Massillon, and was at the forefront in Mather's hiring.

"Thorney told my brother Don that Massillon ought to check in on Chuck Mather," Emery said. "He said 'He's at Hamilton now. When he coached at Leetonia his team won the small school state championship by beating Copley in a challenge game.' So I called Chuck Mather up at Hamilton. I said, 'Have you applied.?' He said, 'No. I didn't think I had a chance. Are they considering me?' I said, 'They haven't said who they are thinking of.' He said, 'Do you think I have a chance?' I said 'You won't if you don't apply. I never met you but I do know about you beating Copley—and your Hamilton team did pretty good.'"

The board heeded Emery's 11th hour plea, delaying the hiring and sending a delegation to watch Mather's Hamilton team practice.

Mather and Emery met in Columbus during the state basketball tournament, following a party thrown by sporting goods representatives. "I got to the party and bumped into Larry Strobel who was the head coach at Barberton and at that time was coaching at Ohio State," Emery said. "He said, 'Who's going to get that job at Massillon?' I said I didn't know. He said, 'You know I'm an applicant.' I said, 'I know you're an applicant.'

"About that time Ducky

Schroeder comes along. He asks me the same thing. I said, 'I don't know, Ducky.' He asked who some of the prospects were. I mentioned Strobel and I said 'I heard Chuck Mather down at Hamilton might apply.' He said, 'Oh, why I'd come as his assistant. I'll bring him around.'

"The next morning at eight a.m. there was a knock at my hotel room door. There was Ducky with Chuck Mather. He introduced me. I said, 'If you're going to apply, you'd better apply this morning, because the board of education is going to meet this afternoon, and they may make an appointment.' So Mather called the superintendent of schools, L. J. Smith, and applied. I called Fred Beckman, the editor of the *Evening Independent*, and told him what I'd found down there. I said 'The board is meeting at one p.m. and they're going to make a choice, but I think we ought to postpone it and consider Mather.'"

The board heeded Emery's 11th hour plea, delaying the hiring and sending a delegation to watch Mather's Hamilton team practice.

Schroeder knew of the plan and tipped off Mather. "Ducky told me there was a group coming down from Massillon to watch me practice," Mather said. "Four well-dressed men, Chuck Hess, Tink Ulrich, Rudy Schaidnagle and Bob Wilson, were over by the side of the fence. So rather than practice away from them, we moved over pretty close so they could hear and see the whole thing.

"They introduced themselves after practice. I invited them up to the house. Over the years they always kidded me a lot because I didn't offer them a drink. I offered them a Coke. They all kidded me. They said, 'You almost didn't get the job because we all wanted a drink.'"

Mather remembered his first look at the team he inherited in Massillon.

"The first thing I noticed was that they weren't too big," Mather said. "But the most *impressive* thing was when we had them run 100 yards. I wanted to find out who the fastest guys were.

"I couldn't believe it—none of us coaches could. They were running from one goal line to the other and they were diving to be the first guy to cross the goal line. We'd get a whole bunch of guys running, and not just one guy was doing that. It was just unbelievable to see that type of thing."

Mather is carried from the field after a big win.

While Mather was developing his impressions of his new players, his players were developing their impressions, too. Irvin "Ace" Crable was a speedster who caught Mather's eye early on.

"Everybody heard they were

firing previous coach Bud Houghton and we had a new coach coming in," Crable said. "He was just a long, lanky man. And that stride that he had was out of sight. I used to try to make fun of the way he walked. Ever see a rabbit walk in the snow? That's how Mather walked."

"He was just a long, lanky man. And that stride that he had was out of sight."

Irvin 'Ace' Crable

"We were all excited about Chuck coming in," said Jack Hill, Mather's quarterback in 1948. Hill started four games at quarterback for Houghton in 1947.

"Those years were kind of a low for Massillon football," Hill said of Houghton's 1946 and 1947 seasons. "The 1947 team had enough talent, especially on the offensive and defensive line," Hill said. "We should have been better than we were. The entire backfield was made up of underclassmen. Al Brown, who became the captain the next year, Dick Jacobs and Clarence Johnson—who was probably the best physical specimen of anybody on our team. He was a natural. That group, combined with Crable, provided an extremely talented backfield for Mather to work with in 1948."

"I don't think we had a man on the team that weighed 200 pounds," Crable said. "We were really snots, I'll tell ya. But we were tough. We were *really* tough. We were what you call street fighters. Mather made a team out of us. He put that team together beautifully. When Houghton was coach our offense was like Woody Hayes, three yards and a cloud of dust. When Mather came in it was more streamlined—like a Cadillac. We went to the T-formation. Spread out the field and everything. Traps, counters, reverses, the whole works, it was really beautiful. That's how we beat those teams. Almost every team we played outweighed us from 25-50 pounds a man. We were just that small."

"Mather was laid back, relaxed," McVay said. "He used to coach in his golf shoes. We all said, 'That's different.' All the other coaches had worn kind of knickered pants and football shoes and here's Chuck with a pair of long slacks and golf shoes."

Fullback Al Brown compared his coach to Massillon's legendary coach Paul Brown.

"As far as I'm concerned, Mather wouldn't have to take a back seat to Paul Brown. Really. That's how I feel about it. It was just the way he talked to you. He'd put his arm around you. He was chewing you out, but it was in a nice way. You didn't really know you were getting chewed out."

Mather was the first coach to field large squads at Massillon. "Paul Brown usually confined himself to 33-35 players," Emery said. "The coaches who followed him probably did the same because he was so successful. They copied him any way they could. Chuck for some reason or other opened the gates of the temple," Emery said with a laugh. "Anybody who wanted to play football—he might end up sittin' the bench—but Mather was the first one to break out the large squads. And it might have been the reason for his success along the line because he pretty well had experienced boys every year. I had a mother of a boy, I never thought of the boy being a football player myself. She called me up and said Teddy wants to play football but she didn't think they'd let him play. When he went out Mather let him play. I don't think he ever got in, but he sat on the bench and was fodder for the practice. I think Mather sometimes carried a squad of 100. My thinking always was that if the kid had any ability at all and wanted to go out, he was entitled to it. They could make some use of him."

"Chuck, for some reason, opened the gates of the temple...and it might have been the reason for his success.."

Luther Emery

"We always tried to keep at least 20-some guys from each class," Mather said. "I always wanted to play all seniors. Seniors had more size, experience and everything. I always thought you had about 22 guys who were seniors to choose from. Naturally you'd have a few juniors. I don't think we ever had a sophomore play, although I did have our sophomores practice with us all the time. So even if they weren't doing anything but holding the bag, they were there with the varsity and they went though the same drills that the varsity did.

"I'd say we let anybody come out who wanted to come out," Mather said.

"Sometimes the suits didn't fit very well. We tried to suit up everybody who wanted to play football. I think we treated everybody well. We never kicked anyone off the football squad. If they broke a training rule, they just didn't play. The only way you missed football is if you didn't come to practice. Then we took your suit."

Bob Kraus was a success story.

Onc player whose "suit" Mather took was an offensive lineman who ended up being one of his biggest success stories.

"Bob Kraus didn't particularly care for football," Mather said. "Bob was a good, strong boy. His dad was real forceful behind him. I always defended it. A lot of mothers forced kids to practice the piano. So what's wrong with a father giving the kid a hard time for football? Particularly in Massillon, because this is a college education to anybody that is intelligent. We got scholarships for anyone who got the grades. Bob, when he was a sophomore, missed practice and we took his suit. About the next day his dad's there with him. 'He's not going to miss any more,' he said. I think this only happened about twice—I think he missed once again. Bob became good enough that he got a scholarship to Purdue in 1952. When I went to Kansas he transferred there. His senior year, Bob was one of my captains. He married one of the richest girls in Kansas and still lives out there. The point of the story is the old man, by forcing him, really put him into a great life. Education and everything.

Another Mather tenet was footwork. "We had what we called agility drills," he said. "Running through tires...footwork kind of things. That would lead to everybody hitting a sled. Not just linemen, but backs and everybody. A lot of coaches only have their linemen hit that sled. But I felt it was just as important for the backs. When I got to the Bears as offensive coordinator, George Halas agreed with me."

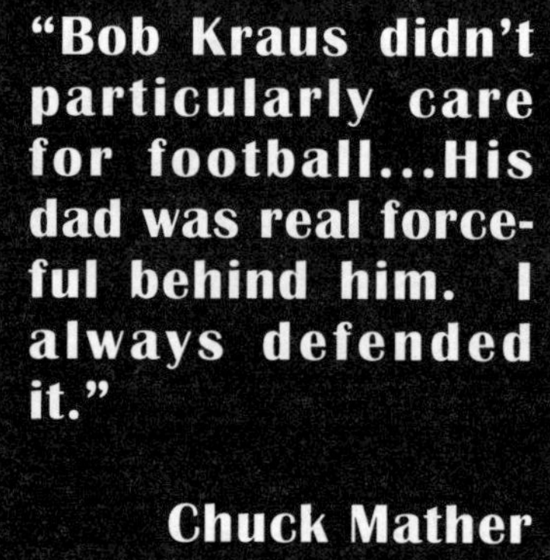

Mather had to teach his two Pro Bowl running backs, Rick Casares and John Arnett, how to hit the sled. "It was unbelievable," Mather said, "These guys had played football all their lives and had never hit a sled. It was almost pathetic to see them hit it and get knocked down. In all the time I coached with the Bears, we never had a knee operation. The only knee operation we had at Massillon was Jack Houston, and he stepped in a hole at Toledo Waite. When I quit coaching with the Bears in 1965, they quit using the sleds. In two years Mike Ditka, Johnny Morris, Gale Sayers and several others had knee operations."

Mather said hitting the sled developed footwork. "Just running doesn't really extend you very much compared to digging in there and pushing somebody," he said. "I used to say you had to be like a squirrel. There's no way you can get close to a squirrel. His feet are moving all of the time. On a football field you have to be like a squirrel and move to avoid being cracked. Footwork is the essence of any sport."

Mather's system worked at Massillon right away.

"Mather was a smart coach," Emery said. "A stickler for detail. He'd do it over and over and over again. He produced a good team the very first year because of that."

Mather was 9-1 in 1948 and won the state championship by knocking off heavily favored Canton McKinley in Week 10. McKinley was undefeated, untied, and ranked number one in the state. Massillon prevailed 21-12.

A year later the Tigers found themselves in the same situation, facing an undefeated, untied McKinley team. Massillon rose to the occasion again, beating McKinley 6-0 behind a stout defense and a 35-yard touchdown run by Crable. McKinley would never seriously challenge Mather again.

"After 1948 and '49 McKinley was never the same," Mather said. "Outside of those first two years they were never really a challenge for us—to the point where you're afraid you're gonna lose. We felt in '48 and '49 that they could beat us. We were very fortunate to win both years. You might say it started our whole program. It got everybody behind us." In Mather's next four wins over McKinley the Tigers outscored the Bulldogs 162-15. In six years Mather was 6-0 against McKinley.

But McKinley wasn't the only team to be dominated by Mather's Tigers. Only Warren, in 1951, beat the Tigers between 1950 and 1953. Mather never lost more than one game in a season, and never lost two games in a row at Massillon.

In Mather's next four wins over McKinley the Tigers outscored the Bulldogs 162-15.

Of his three losses, two were to coaches who were former Massillon players. Mel Knowlton of Alliance, who was Brown's first quarterback when he began coaching at Massillon in 1932, beat Mather in 1948. Augie Morningstar, who captained the state and national champion Tigers of 1935, handed Mather his only loss at Tiger Stadium, in 1949. Morningstar's Mansfield Tygers trimmed Mather's Tigers, 16-12.

The loss to Warren in 1951 was bitter. "We were all, naturally, very disappointed," Mather said. Consistent with his style, Mather did not criticize his team.

"The game's over. We never had any crisis after we lost. It's over. Play next week."

Lee Nussbaum, a junior running back in 1951, was in the middle of the action in the Warren loss. "Total confusion," Nussbaum said. "We were down 19-13 with about 20 seconds left and Mather sends me into the game at halfback to lead the play to the right. I got out there and it was mass confusion. People running in every direction. I don't think we ended up blocking at all hardly. That was the only time I ever panicked. There was no more time and it was the last play of the game. And I don't think I made a block. Our guards were running one way and the backs were running the other way. And the ball carrier runs out of bound on the two-yard line. Mather said to him, 'What did you run out of bounds for?' The player said, 'There was no place to go.' Mather said, 'Then you lower your head and run. You might get in.'

Lee Nussbaum, All-Ohio fullback, 1952.

"Everybody felt so sad in the locker room," Nussbaum said. "Because we had 'em on the ropes and let 'em slide off. Mather had 'em scouted. I think they were just too strong for us. They beat us at the point of attack. The only time in my life I've ever been beat at the line of scrimmage."

Nussbaum appreciated Mather as a coach. He had a couple of legendary coaches to compare to Mather. He played college ball at Ohio State and signed with Green Bay in the NFL.

Nussbaum was a big, strong country boy who ran with the ball like a run-away steer. He was more likely to plow under a defender than try to elude him. "There wasn't anybody I didn't think I could run over," Nussbaum said.

He butted heads with Hayes at Ohio State.

"Mather wasn't one for a big speech. Woody Hayes would cry. He really laid it on. He preached. I didn't like him. If I would have worked with him as an adult one of us would have ended up on his ass," Nussbaum said.

"The two greatest coaches I had in my life were Mather and Vince Lombardi."

Lee Nussbaum

When Hayes was struggling in his first two seasons at Ohio State, it was rumored that Mather was going to take his place as head coach.

"The only reason I went to Ohio State was because it was rumored that Mather was coming down in 1953," Nussbaum said. "When I heard that, I was going to Ohio State. I was enrolled at Purdue, but when the word got out that Mather would be goin' to Columbus, that's when I switched. They wanted to hang Woody in 1953. How he hung in there I don't know. But when Woody won that 1954 national championship there was no gettin' rid of him."

Nussbaum admired his coach at Green Bay, however. "The two greatest coaches I had in my life were Mather and Vince Lombardi," Nussbaum said.

As a highly recruited high school star, Nussbaum met many of the great coaches of the day. "I met Frank Leahy at Notre Dame, Biggie Munn from Michigan, Stu Holcomb and Jack Mollenkopf from Purdue and Duffy Daugherty at Michigan State."

Schroeder and Mather were closely linked since Mather's days at Brilliant. "We first met in 1937," Mather said. "Ducky was the guest speaker at my first year's banquet at Brilliant. When I was coaching at Leetonia, Ducky was coaching at nearby Salem. Ducky became athletic director at Springfield when I went to Hamilton, so we were always close."

Chuck Vliet was one of Massillon's all-time great linebackers.

Ducky Schroeder joined Mather as an assistant coach at Massillon in 1948. He felt Mather was one of the first football coaches to practice positive thinking and positive coaching.

"I never heard him yell at a boy on the field," Schroeder said. "He always was offering encouragement to the boys and coaches. I really think he was a leader in that field. He felt you could win better by encouraging boys rather than degrading them. He never cut anybody. Occasionally he'd tell a boy, 'You might never be a football player, but if you put as much energy into another area of high school you're bound to be a success in that.' A lot of times the boy would just break down and cry. And Chuck would say sympathetically, 'Why don't you just be a manager?' Usually the boy would end up being a manager."

"I never let the coaches yell at anybody," Mather said. "Out on the field or anywhere. Often times you hear of coaches yelling, screaming, stuff like that. I always made a point that we don't want any of that. The coaches all spoke quietly when they had criticisms. After every game we always had the players evaluate what they thought about the team. We had it in printed form. They had to put their name on it. They could criticize us or anything."

"Dick Woolbert bit his tongue. He bit it real bad...he came up to me at halftime, bleedin' bad. He said, 'I'm gonna play. I want to finish the game.'"

Chuck Vliet

Chuck Vliet was Mather's defensive captain in 1951. He also started at linebacker on the undefeated 1950 state and national championship team.

"We had great talent on the 1950 team," Vliet said, "Both on offense and defense."

Vliet remembered Mather honoring his word with his childhood friend Dick Woolbert.

"Dick and I went to grade school together," Vliet said. "Dick was a good athlete. He just had the natural ability. But when we got to high school I don't think he quite had the heart. Dick had the *ability* that he could play any time he wanted to play. Chuck always told every one of us guys that anybody can play any Friday night when they make up their mind they want to play. He'd say, ' You show me on the practice field and I'll start ya.' And he would do so. If somebody was loafin', and somebody beat 'em out during the week, he'd start. That kept everybody enthused.

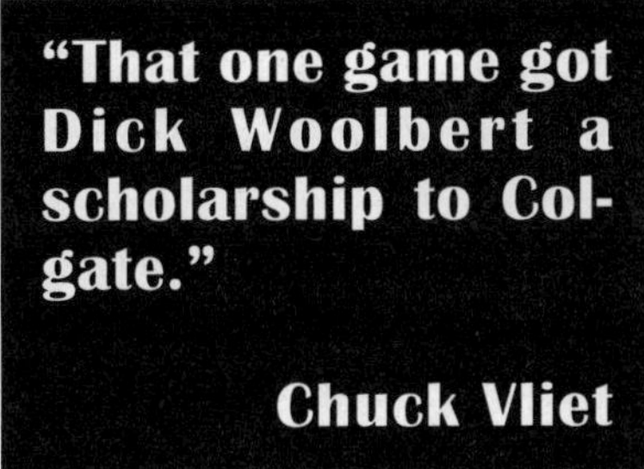

"So we got to the McKinley game in 1950. I remember Dick sayin' something to Chuck about wanting to play in that game He said, 'It's my last game, I'm a senior and I want to play in that game.' Chuck says, 'Okay, I'm going to start you at nose guard if you show me all week that you want to play in the game.'

"So Dick worked real hard all week and he did a good job. We got to the McKinley game and Chuck started him. He was doing a great job until somebody hit him in the mouth real hard and he bit his tongue. He bit it real bad. They took him in the locker room and put a couple of stitches in it. His tongue swoll up real big and he couldn't talk—could hardly breath. He came up to me at halftime, bleedin' bad. He said, 'I'm gonna play. I want to finish the game.' He did. He played a great game all day. That was one of the best examples of a kid wantin' to play. That one game got him a scholarship to Colgate. That game alone. When they looked at those movies they saw that he did such a wonderful job over the center at nose guard."

Dick Woolbert earned a scholarship to Colgate by playing well in one game at Massillon.

Mather was proud of the number of Massillon players he sent on to play college football. From 1948-50 alone Mather sent 32 players to college.

"At Ohio State we had Mike Takacs, Jerry Krischer, Jim Reichenbach, Jim Schumacher," Mather said. "At Cincinnati we had Jack Hill and David Canary. Miami of Ohio we had John McVay. We had several at Purdue: Jack Houston, Bob Khoenle, Bob Kraus and Russ Maier. Clarence Johnson and Ray Lane were at Northwestern. Illinois had Ace Grooms and Frank Gibson. Don James was at the University of Miami and he set several records down there. Anybody that wasn't good enough to get into a major college we got 'em into a smaller school."

It was too hard for Mather to pick the best of his six state championship teams. Three teams, 1950, 1952 and 1953 were undefeated state and national champs.

"I think that each team had its own personality," Mather said. "Probably as tough a team as we had was 1948. All of these kids were rough and tough. They all had gone through junior high together. Houghton was good on sled work and stuff like that. His kids were fundamentally good football players. So it wasn't just us. We had some kids who liked to play football and who wanted to play.

"In 1949 we had a team that was extremely fast and had three backs who averaged 11 yards per try. They were, you might say, the speediest team we had. Probably the best offensive team we had for breaking away and making large runs.

"The 1950 team was the biggest team we had. No one was too speedy or anything like that. Everyone was just good...and sound football players. Guys like Krisher and Jim Reichenbach, Jim Schumacher who went to Ohio State. I just think of how big and strong that team was.

"Then of course in 1951 the biggest thrill was winning the Steubenville game. That was the most dramatic point that year (a 13-6 last second win). We didn't have much trouble with McKinley that year (40-0)."

"I can't think of any game in 1952 or 1953 that we had much of a problem."

After almost being named head coach at Ohio State in 1951, Mather turned down offers to become head coach at the University of Minnesota and Arizona State while at Massillon. Finally, Mather accepted the head coaching job at the University of Kansas in 1954.

"When Kansas came and asked me to come and coach, that's when I decided to make a move," Mather said. "I had the feeling there in Massillon that we could go on and maybe never lose a game. We had the players and the organization and I even felt it sort of good for Massillon to get a new coach in there. It would have been much easier to stay coaching at Massillon. I think I always realized that Massillon was the type of town that liked their coaches to come in for two or three years and move on somewhere. They were known for kind of pushing their coaches on."

Mather inherited a messy situation at Kansas. He encountered a faculty who was loyal to his predecessor, Jules Sikes. The experience was so bad that Mather actually quit before he started.

"The faculty was very upset that they hired a new coach," Mather said. "They liked Jules Sikes. So what did they do but flunk 26 football players. Guys like Bob Allison, who became Rookie of the Year with the Minnesota Twins. He was the leading ground gainer.

"So what did they do but flunk 26 football players."

Chuck Mather

"I resigned. They said, 'You've not started.' I said, 'There isn't any way I can win. If the faculty is going to flunk guys like this, there isn't any way I'm going to coach here.

"The president, Mr. Murphy, said, 'Let me think about this.' He came back to me and said, 'I'm going to plan faculty for academic advancement of athletes. You're going to be in charge of the athletes.' As a result I never lost another guy from flunking out in four years."

But the damage was done. In his first season, with a depleted roster, Mather lost every game in 1954. The losing streak stretched to 17-straight before they knocked off Washington State, 13-0 in 1955.

Another low point at Kansas came at the end of his third season when he was hung in effigy following a season-ending loss to rival University of Missouri.

The Jayhawks had lost by a safety, 15-13. Mather had blamed his own play-calling for the loss.

A dummy was found hanging by the neck from a rope tied in a tree in front of the campus library. Mather's record in 1956 was 3-6-1.

Mather and his staff resigned during the 1957 season at Kansas. A series of incidents led to the resignation.

"The president came to me at mid-season and wanted me to hire a former coach. I said, 'Fine.' He said, 'You have to get rid of one of your coaches. I said, 'Dr. Murphy, no way will I let one of my guys go to put a new guy on. If this is the way it is, I want no part of it.'

"There isn't anybody who could do a better job than we did that last year at Kansas, finishing second in the conference.

"To me, I accomplished all I could at Kansas. To go from nothing to second place, I never worked so hard in my life. Kansas was such a struggle that you didn't have time to think about anything. You were just trying to stay alive. When you're playing teams like Oklahoma, Colorado and Nebraska, those teams that have two or three players drafted each year and you don't have anybody like that..."

Dave Putts, who coached with Mather for 10 years, was on his staff at Kansas. "Paul Schofer (who came to Kansas with Mather from Massillon) said we should stay and make 'em fire us. Mather didn't want to do that. So we finally decided we'd resign. The whole coaching staff resigned. We won the rest of our ball games and we were second in the Big 8. I'd say that's the saddest I saw Mather."

"Kansas was such a struggle that you didn't have time to think about anything. You were just trying to stay alive."

Chuck Mather

Don James, who was Mather's quarterback at Massillon in 1949, rejoined Mather as a graduate assistant at Kansas following his career as a quarterback at the University of Miami. James went on to become one of the all-time great college coaches based on his outstanding record at the University of Washington. He has a unique perspective in looking at Mather's fate at Kansas.

"Mather did a great job at Kansas," James said. "It just took a while to get it built. It was a really tough job. When you lose that much early, people get down on ya. When people are down on ya, the press is down, the alumni, so much negativity, it's just hard to get 'em back. Then you get into a place—I see it all the time in college football—it's almost like they want you to lose enough so they can fire ya so they can get you out and bring in someone else. A lot of coaches have gone through that. A lot of good coaches. It happens to about everybody, Paterno, Schembechler, or even myself. I was 1-3 in my third year in Washington and they wanted me out of there. But then fortunately we turned it around."

"It's almost like they want you to lose enough so they can fire ya so they can get you out and bring in someone else."

Don James

James reflected on how things would have been different for Mather had he landed the Ohio State job in 1951. "It would have been light years ahead of the Kansas job. And he'd have done well there. He'd have done extremely well."

After resigning from Kansas, Mather decided he had enough of college football.

"I was very discouraged with college football," he said. "The way you have to recruit, constantly recruiting, time consuming, talking to these kids. You might liken it to trying to keep 50 women on the line. The attention you have to give in order to keep their interest. Constant communications with them.

"We enjoyed Kansas. Great people out there. I used to kid the basketball coach. Wilt Chamberlin was there. He was a great athlete. He liked to play football, too. He'd be out there when we were practicing. It'd drive you crazy seeing this big, seven-foot tall guy out there, 280 pounds. Running, catching the football. So I used to kid the basketball coach, 'You let him play football, I guarantee we'll double his salary.' He'd say, 'Don't talk like that.' Turns out many years later Wilt said publicly that he was makin' $4,000 a year when he played for Kansas. I was just kidding when I'd say that. But at the same time I knew he was getting help. Wilt would have played football if they would have let him. If you had a seven-foot guy who could run the 440 in 48 seconds, put the shot 56 feet. A tremendous athlete. They talk about Jordan flying, I saw Wilt take off at the foul line and dunk the ball.

Mather as offensive coordinator for the Chicago Bears.

Mather got a call from Chicago Bears head coach George Halas after leaving Kansas.

"Chuck came back to Massillon after Kansas," Emery

said. It was during that time that Halas contacted him about coming to Chicago. He had read about Chuck's use of motion pictures to grade his players and how good they were."

Mather served as Halas' offensive coordinator for several years, including 1963, when the Bears won the NFL championship. He had a few overtures for head coaching positions while he was there. "He almost got the Pittsburgh Steelers job," Emery said. "I was going to go as his assistant. "He was up for the Washington Redskins job, too, but he didn't have much of a chance there. Otto Graham got the job."

Mather decided to give up coaching when Bears defensive coordinator George Allen left to take the Los Angeles Rams job. He wanted Mather to join him. Mather would only do that if he could continue his work as an insurance executive.

"Halas, because Chuck was thinking of giving up the coaching, he took him off the coaching and made a scout of him," Emery said.

After stepping down from active coaching with the Bears, Mather spent 10 years scouting for the Bears. He worked as a successful insurance executive in Wilmet, Illinois until his death at 91 in 2006.

"I like to be remembered in Massillon as a coach who tried to do things we should do," Mather said. "You'd like to be remembered as a winning coach. We never lost to McKinley. We always tried to think of Massillon as being the top high school in the country."

Teaching "Papa Bear" George Halas How to Run the Quarterback Sneak

Chuck Mather got a big surprise after he was hired as offensive coordinator by famous Chicago Bears head coach George Halas. Halas didn't know how to run the quarterback sneak.

"I told Halas, 'You don't run the quarterback sneak right.' He said, 'What do you mean?' I said, 'Well, this is the way it should be run.' I said, 'This isn't original. I got this from Jock Sutherland in 1937 at one of his clinics in Pittsburgh.' So Halas said, 'What is it?'"

"I told Halas, 'You don't run the quarterback sneak right.'"

Chuck Mather

Mather explained, "When you're down near the goal line, you either have an even type of defense or you have an odd type of defense. One or the other. The whole essence of the sneak is if this man is uncovered he can run out, if he were to block he might not move. So the guy that's uncovered does not in any way try to block anyone. You're always gonna get a yard.

"A big strong guy can move a yard without anyone over him. For example, if no one's over our center, he doesn't block anyone. If he tries to block, he might not move anywhere.

"We scored on two quarterback sneaks in one game with the Bears."

Mather Was Ohio State's First Choice as Ohio State's Coach, not Woody

What if? How many coaching careers have been dramatically altered by "what ifs?" In Chuck Mather's case, the "what if" was a huge one.

In 1951 Mather came within a whisker of becoming Ohio State's new head coach. In fact, he was assured that he had the job.

> **"They were impressed with the success we had at Massillon."**
>
> **Chuck Mather**

Mather won over Ohio State's Athletic Board of Selection. "They were impressed with the success we had at Massillon for one thing," Mather said. At the time Mather was 28-2 at Massillon with three state titles. "They also liked the approach we took by grading the players and approaching the game from somewhat a mechanical way."

Fritz Howell, *Associated Press* sports editor for the state of Ohio, covered the process. He kept the details secret until 1979, when Woody Hayes' career at Ohio State ended in his firing after he punched a player from Clemson University during the 1978 Gator Bowl.

"The first vote by the Athletic Board of Selection, a vote that had to be approved by the trustees, Chuck was named coach at Ohio State," Howell said. "John Bricker, the former governor and senator from Ohio, was on the board of trustees. He was in California at the time. He heard the result of the balloting and he wired back and told them to hold up the approval of it until he got back. When he returned he told the Athletic Board of Selection that he didn't think the trustees would approve another high school coach moving in after the experience we had with Mr. Brown, meaning Paul Brown, from Massillon. Brown was looked upon as a tyrant during his three years at Ohio State. Here was another coach, Mather, from Massillon. He didn't think that they'd approve it. He suggested that they take another vote and select a more established coach. So Woody Hayes got the job. And it's pretty well authenticated that Dick Larkins, the athletic director, called Mather after the first vote and told him that he had the job and that it would be announced at the end of the week. By that time they met again and Woody got the job."

"He heard the result of the balloting and he wired back and told them to hold up the approval..."

Fritz Howell

It's amazing that a story like this could be kept secret for 28 years.

"I imagine everyone was sworn to secrecy there," Howell said. "I knew it at the time. Of course Chuck knew it after Larkins had called him. I can see where Chuck wouldn't come out with it, it would look like sour grapes on his part if he said something about it. I was told in confidence, which shut me off from using it. Once Mr. Hayes was fired down there I figured all bets were off and it was a story that needed to be told, just to complete the record."

"When Woody found out I was hired, he went right to Governor Frank Lausche," Mather said.

Mather figures Lausche sabotaged his hiring. "I told him, 'You cost me the job.' He said, 'What do you mean?' I said, 'You voted for Woody.' He said, 'I didn't know Woody, I voted for you.' He was basically lying," Mather said.

> **"It was probably the dumbest thing I ever did. I felt old Woody wasn't going to make it and maybe the next time the Ohio State job opened up I'd be the coach."**
>
> **Chuck Mather**

Another vote that likely went against Mather was cast by Bricker. "Bricker came all the way back from California to the trustees meeting to vote against me," Mather said. "I lost by two votes. That was a disappointing thing at the time."

Mather had a shot at another high profile job when the president of Arizona State flew to Massillon with a job offer. Mather turned the job down.

"It was probably the dumbest thing I ever did," Mather said. "I felt old Woody wasn't going to make it and maybe the next time the Ohio

State job opened up I'd be the coach. Woody was the type of coach that never had any imagination or anything. Three yards and a cloud of dust. His personnel was such that he could get away with that kind of a thing. No one felt that he was very much of a coach. They wanted to fire him that first year."

Howell confirmed Mather's story. "After Woody's fourth game, a 32-10 loss to Indiana, Ohio State athletic director Dick Larkins told assistant coach Ernie Godfrey, 'We hired the wrong guy,'" Howell said. "He asked Godfrey to coach the team for the rest of the year."

Godfrey refused the temporary position and Hayes went on to coach 28 years at Ohio State, winning three national championships and 13 Big Ten titles.

Mather's Magnificent Stay at Massillon "Couldn't Have Been any Better"

Chuck Mather's popularity in Massillon knew no bounds. He was one of the few Massillon coaches who was never on the "hot seat." Even Paul Brown had to fear losing his job after starting his career with three straight losses to Canton McKinley.

"Naturally, if you don't beat Canton McKinley, they want to fire you," Mather said of Brown's predicament. Mather was 6-0 against McKinley and never lost more than one game in a season. Mather appreciated his treatment in Massillon.

Chuck Mather may have been Massillon's most popular coach. He's also in the Ohio Athletic Association's Hall of Fame.

"It couldn't have been any better," he said. "It might have been different if we hadn't won. Winning takes care of almost everything.

"I think I probably had a relationship with the Booster Club and Massillon residents that Paul never quite entered in to. I think I did bring in an openness that he never had, except with intimate friends."

Mather's Creativity Leads to Tackles Record for Vliet in 1950 Warren Game

Chuck Vliet wasn't one of Massillon's biggest line-backers—just one of its best.

And that was never more true than when Head Coach Chuck Mather made a last minute change to his game plan prior to the 1950 Warren game.

That night Vliet set a single-game Massillon record for tackles. Thirty-two times when the Warren runner went down, it was Vliet pinning him to the turf. His tackle record stands today, 60 years later.

Chuck Mather with his defensive captain for 1951, Chuck Vliet.

"Right before the game Chuck said, 'We're going to change our defense. I found out their quarterback turned his ankle and is not going to be able to play tonight. All they're going to do is run the ball. We're going to play a 7-1-2 tonight. I'm going to put Vliet in as our roving linebacker. All I want you guys to do on the defensive line is keep the blockers off of him.' They did a great job. If they hadn't done a great job, I couldn't have made tackles that night. Chuck was a smart man, he was a great coach."

Vince Lombardi Learned Famous Sweep Play from Chuck Mather

The most famous play that Vince Lombardi ran as coach of the Super Bowl Champion Green Bay Packers was the sweep play. But few realize that Lombardi learned the fine points of the sweep from Massillon Chuck Mather.

Mather's Massillon teams were famous for their sweep plays. "Our main offense was actually a sweep," Mather said, "a pitchout to the fullback and then faking back a trap to the halfback or vice versa. I think every year our fullback made All-Ohio. They were our number one runners.

Due to his incredible success at Massillon, Mather was invited to speak at the National Coaches' Convention.

"I made a couple of speeches at the National Coaches' Convention on this offense with movies and charts," Mather said.

Mather noticed a bespeckled coach taking copious notes while he spoke.

"Vince Lombardi was an assistant coach at Army at the time. I can remember him sitting in the front row. He was intrigued with the sweeping.

"You go back to Lombardi at Green Bay," Mather said, "that was his offense."

LEE TRESSEL

They say you only get one chance to make a good first impression. Well, in Lee Tressel's case, "Better luck next time" might have been a more appropriate saying.

Tressel's first impression when interviewing for the Massillon job in 1953 could have been better.

"He had trouble with his film—it got off the track and went all over the floor," quipped Massillon sportswriter Luther Emery. "He didn't have as good an interview as he should have had because of that."

Lee Tressel as head coach at Massillon, circa 1956.

Young Tom Harp, a 26-year-old from Carrollton, Ohio, got the job—partly because of his outstanding highlight film.

Harp had great success at Massillon, winning the state title in 1954, then accepting an assistant coaching job at the U.S. Military

Academy at West Point after the 1955 season.

But Tressel, a young man of 28 himself, must have made a favorable impression on the Massillon interview committee. No sooner than Harp resigned his post at Massillon, Superintendent L. J. Smith was thinking about Tressel as his successor.

Of course Tressel did nothing but enhance his attractiveness as a candidate, winning all of his games at Mentor during the two seasons following his interview at Massillon.

"When Harp quit, L. J. Smith immediately contacted Lee Tressel," Emery said. "He called me up and said, 'Who was that candidate we had whose film went all over the floor?' I told him. He said, 'I think we'll hire him.'"

Smith must have had great confidence in T[illegible] make such a quic[illegible] sion. Two years earlier, [illegible] search for a Massillon coach involved over 100 applicants and a three-month selection process.

Tressel accepted the job with as impressive a resume as any coach in Massillon history. He was riding a 34-game winning streak at Mentor High School—the longest in the state at the time—when he was contacted by Smith.

Tressel's first season at Massillon was challenging.

"In 1956 he was 8-2 and I thought he did one of the greatest jobs of coaching that year of anybody I had been in association with," longtime Massillon assistant Ducky Schroeder said. "To me that was the year that we had the poorest material of any year I've been here."

Tressel's captain for 1956, star running back and defensive back Mike Hershberger, saw things differently than Schroeder. He felt his coach's offensive approach was too conservative.

"We felt we had a very explosive team that year," Hershberger said. "But Lee would never let us turn it loose. He was always saving it back for the next week. As long as we were winning the ball game it was like he was holding everything back. I'll never forget, the option play was one of our better plays. We didn't run it that much because we didn't want to show it to teams."

"In 1956 he was 8-2 and I thought he did one of the greatest jobs of coaching that year of anybody I had been in association with."

Ducky Schroeder

Tressel's second and final season at Massillon almost ended with a state championship.

"In 1957, we were 7-1-1," Schroeder said. "Cleveland Benedictine beat us out of the state championship. That was the year we had to cancel a game because of the flu. In fact in the Cleveland Benedictine game, we only lost 13-7, but a lot of our kids had the flu."

Hase McKey was a sophomore starter for Tressel in 1957. McKey went on to be one of Massillon's rare two-time first team All-Ohioans.

"He was strict," McKey

said. "He believed if you had pride, if you put out all you had, you would succeed in whatever you wanted to do. He kept saying that over and over. I owe a great deal to him for giving me the inspiration of going on through school from there. I ended up playing first team for him. Really, the first sophomore to play first team. Coach Tressel was a beautiful, beautiful coach. A beautiful man, a gentleman all together. Like his kids."

Tressel's son Jim, who is now Ohio State's head coach, was a youngster when his dad coached the Tigers. Legendary Massillon running back Ivory Benjamin had a special relationship with the coach and his young son.

"Mr. Tressel, my coach, Lee, boy he was a great guy to me," Benjamin said. "He was a great guy to all of us, let's put it that way. Yes, sir. And his son down at Ohio State is a great guy. He probably don't remember me but I knew him when he played on his knees here. I lived in the same house as him three weeks out of the year during football season. I lived with them. Jim wouldn't let me out of his sight. Nooo, I couldn't get out of his sight."

Lee Tressel left Massillon after the 1957 season and began his legendary career at Baldwin-Wallace that landed him in the College Football Hall of Fame. Tressel was head coach at Baldwin-Wallace for 22 years, finishing with a 155-52-6 record at the Division III college. He led the Yellow Jackets to the 1978 national championship.

IVORY BENJAMIN

No one's life epitomizes the saga of the Massillon Tiger football hero better than Ivory Benjamin's. Ivory has savored the highs that come with being Massillon's football idol; and he's experienced life's lows, crashing a few times along the way. Massillon's townspeople have known Ivory at his best *and* at his worst. And after he fought back from adversity—like a Tiger—to put his life back together, he found that the town of Massillon had been with him all the way.

Ivory Benjamin.

Benjamin was the toast of the town during his two glorious years as Massillon's star running back in 1956 and '57. It was a role he relished. In fact, through 50 years of good times and bad times since his glory days, Benjamin remains secure in his place among Massillon's legendary running backs. He puts himself right up at the top.

It's a fact that whenever longtime Massillon fans discuss the greatest running backs in Massillon Tiger history—and the list is long and impressive—Ivory's name is prominent. "My name comes up all the time when they're talkin' about running backs," Benjamin said. "In my time, I was the best, I don't care," he said with a laugh, "I wouldn't put *nobody* in front of me. No no, no, no no. That don't work."

Benjamin's unabashed story telling might come across as egotism from someone else, but Ivory doesn't project the veneer of a braggadocio. It's just Ivory being himself, telling his story the way he sees it. Or, as pitching great Dizzy Dean said, "It ain't braggin' if you can back it up." And Benjamin certainly "backed it up" during his career at Massillon.

Ivory was "The Show" for the Tigers in 1956 and '57. But Massillon fans almost missed seeing Benjamin perform in high school. He was given an alarming wake up call during his first spring practice against the high school players on the band field, adjacent to Tiger Stadium. The lesson was delivered by a teammate who would go on to be All-American at Ohio State and All-Pro with the Cleveland Browns.

"They gave me a dummy," Benjamin said. "I don't know what the play was, all I know is I was a dummy, holdin' a dummy. I'm a freshman, so big Jim Houston—he's about as big as a door—he comes around and hits me. I went one way, the dummy went the other. When that day was over, I was through with football. I made my mind up—now I was a big star in junior high, right. I didn't want to be no big star no more. I'd done been hit by the big boys. Oh, nooooo..."

Benjamin quit going to practice. "Head Coach Tom Harp didn't see me for two days. He comes up to Lorin Andrews Junior High. I was in study hall. Harp comes up to talk to me, chewing that chewing gum of his, (imitating Harp). 'Ivory, I want you to be like Homer Floyd.'

"I told him, 'I don't *want* to be like Homer Floyd. You know, this ain't my thing. If I'm going to be like anybody, I'm going to be like my brother-in-law, Irvin Crable. But I'm not going to hold no dummy. Jim Houston isn't going to hit me no more.' He told me I didn't have to hold no dummy no more. This was fine. I didn't have to hold no dummy the rest of spring practice."

Ivory Benjamin won All-Ohio and Stark County Player of the Year awards in 1957.

Harp left after Benjamin's sophomore season and Lee Tressel became Massillon's new head coach. Benjamin liked Tressel and his young son Jim, who grew up to be

Ohio State's head coach.

"I tell people I knew Jim Tressel and they say, 'Get out.' I said, 'I *know* the kid, why wouldn't I know him, his dad was my coach.'

Benjamin respected the elder Tressel, but that doesn't mean he didn't have a few run-ins with his mentor. The biggest one came after one of his crowning achievements.

Tressel's tough stance brought the world crashing down for Benjamin.

"I got cut the week before the McKinley game," Benjamin said. "That was the night I made high school All-American. I got a telegram from California telling me I'm a high school All-American and, well, I'm happy."

Benjamin celebrated by running wild against Barberton in a 30-0 Massillon win. He was so happy that he made a big mistake. "I wanted to hurry up and get home," he said. "I wanted to show off because I'd done something a lot of people haven't done. I came home with the wrong people. Coach Tressel's worried. He's got a right to be. If something happens to me he's responsible."

Tressel laid down the law to Benjamin on Monday morning. "He called me into his office and told me I'm *done*."

Tressel's tough stance brought the world crashing down for Benjamin. "I was sick. I'm cryin'. I was a big shot, but I'm still cryin'. He told me that I'm out. And I beg and I beg. I don't mind tellin' ya I begged. 'Cause I wanted to play in the McKinley game like anybody else would. He let me come back, but he let me know who the boss was."

Tressel made Benjamin earn back the respect of his teammates. He ordered Benjamin to do laps around the blarney stone. The blarney stone stood at the top of a steep hill adjacent to the old practice field outside Tiger Stadium. The blarney stone was used for conditioning and also for punishment. "I paid for it out on the football field. The blarney stone's not out there any more. But I got a lot of mileage around that. I believe I got more mileage running around the blarney stone because of that episode than I had out on the field."

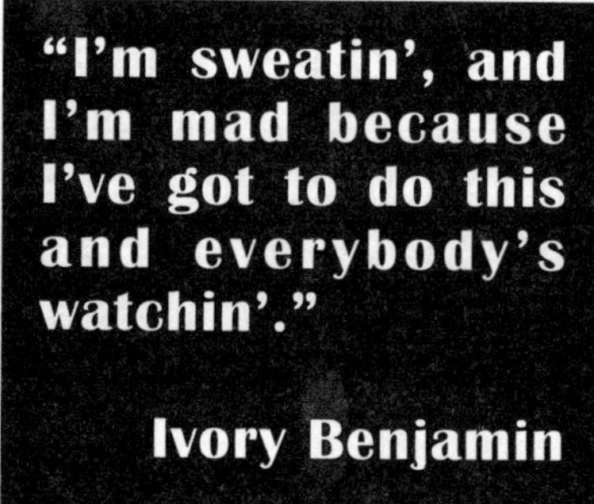

Benjamin recalled another run-in with the coaching staff that involved the blarney stone. "It was the first day of practice our senior year. I came out on the football field and I didn't have a shoe tied up, I wasn't fully dressed." Assistant coach Don Boothe delivered a stiff punishment to the team's new captain. Benjamin was told to make seven trips around the blarney stone—but not in the normal fashion. "I've got to do seven, crawlin'

up and down this hill on all fours," Benjamin said. "Well, I got five of 'em. It was 90 degrees of heat and I ran like a wild man for two hours, now I have to crawl on my hands and knees. All these people are lookin' up there. I'm sweatin', and I'm mad because I've got to do this and everybody's watchin' me do this."

Ivory Benjamin today.

Boothe shouted to Benjamin's teammates, "This is the captain of your football team."

Benjamin snapped.

"I told him what he could do with his football team and everything else. I took my helmet and threw it at him and I went in and took my shower. They didn't see me for two days."

Tressel wasn't aware of the incident. "Tressel didn't know what happened. He thought I was sick. My mom thought I was goin' to practice. I wasn't goin' to practice, I was goin' somewhere else. Tressel came by the house and found out what was goin' on. I was back on the field the next day. Then

I paid for it again. Blarney stone, here I come. Tressel was a good man. I learned from it. I was not the boss. Just because I was a big shot, I was not the boss."

When Leo Strang took over as head coach at Massillon after Benjamin's senior season, he had a running back in Jerry Allen that he said was going to be "the next Ivory Benjamin."

"Ah, I was the people's choice then."

Ivory Benjamin

Benjamin scoffed at the suggestion. "There'll only be one Ivory Benjamin," he laughed. "That's my opinion. There'll only be one of them, believe me when I tell you ."

Benjamin scampered for 1,157 yards in just nine games in 1957, just under eight yards a carry. His career total of 2,300 yards puts him among Massillon's elite. But above all, Ivory Benjamin had star power. And no one enjoyed being in the spotlight more than he did.

"The greatest thrill I ever had in my life was running through the goalposts when they called my name before kickoff. When you're in junior high you see the big boys do it; you always want to hear your name announced up there. The announcer would say 'Ivory Benjamin' and I'd run through that goal post. It's the greatest thrill I ever had in my life. My junior year when they called my name out, you couldn't tell

Benjamin: "I Just Wanted to See if the People Were Still With Me."

Massillon was leading Canton McKinley in 1957 when Ivory Benjamin scored on a spectacular 26-yard run. "I carried a guy about 18 yards on my back," Benjamin recalled. "They called it back. Then I faked like I was hurt. 'Oh, I'm hurt.' The crowd says 'Ohhhhhhh.' The trainer came over and messed with my leg. I get up and run back and forth for about 10 yards. And then the crowd goes crazy. I felt like a new man. I just wanted to see if the people were still with me. What am I supposed to say? That's the way it was."

me *nothin'*. I felt like I was a God or somethin' running through those goal posts. They saved me for last, that's what was good about it. Ah, I was the people's choice then."

Local merchants couldn't do enough for the likeable Benjamin when he was starring on the gridiron.

"You got everything you wanted," Benjamin said, "I could go anywhere and get clothes. I'd tell 'em what I needed. And I'd get it. A lot of guys, they'd come with me because they couldn't give something to me and not to the guys. Everybody got clothes. My teammates got clothes right along with me. Shirts, slacks, underclothes."

After high school, Strang had Benjamin practice against his varsity. "I was what you call the scout team," Benjamin said. "He only got me out there if it was a big game. When Paul Warfield come in to town, whoever was a big shotty shot, whoever the back was, that's who I was. I'd run rings around 'em for a while, then all of a sudden the defense would pop up. Then I'd quit. Hase McKey and all them boys would light my behind up and I'd say, 'That's enough.'

Benjamin started to let alcohol get the best of him after high school. "I was about 21 when me and one of my best friends, George Matie, got into a fight. I don't really know what it was about. But he whupped me up pretty bad. I went to my car, couldn't find what I was lookin' for, so I got a tire iron. Went back and I commenced to beatin' him with that. The cops come, they put me in jail, and I done three and a half years down at Mansfield Penitentiary for that. We don't know what we got in a fight over to this day. We were drinkin'. We're the best of friends. He didn't press charges on me. The state took it over. That's the way it went."

"Every week I was in trouble."

Ivory Benjamin

Things weren't much better after he got out of the penitentiary. "Every week I was in trouble," Benjamin said. Benjamin credits Massillon Municipal Court Judge Richard Kettler with helping him to turn his life around.

Benjamin had gotten in trouble again, and Judge Pep Paulson had warned him the last time he was in front of him. "Paulson said he was going to give me all of this time if I ever came up in front of him again. I pleaded not guilty and got a court date.

"Kettler wasn't a judge at the time, he was a public defender. And he kind of liked me. Kettler kept postponing and postponing until Paulson went on vacation. I ended up only going to jail for three days. I was in the AA program in the care unit up at Massillon City Hospital. I was 47. I went 20-some days in there without a drink. After that, I hadn't had a drink in a week, I was getting back into my prayer thing. And I go two weeks. I thought I needed a drink to make it. I went up there and made it 20-somethin' days without a drink. I said, 'I'm quittin', I ain't drinkin' no more.' I went to jail for three days, got out, and I haven't had a drink since. I'd be dead now if I'd a kept drinkin'. There's no doubt."

Benjamin has been sober for 22 years. He quit smoking 20 years ago.

Benjamin's been sober for 22 years. He quit smoking 20 years ago. "I'll say it again, I'm the luckiest black guy to ever come out of this town. I don't care what anybody says. I'm very fortunate. I've got friends. That's what it is. They've gotta be friends because they remember back when we were coming up. I finally straightened my life out."

Ace Crable Was Benjamin's Teacher

Two of Massillon's all-time great running backs, Irvin "Ace" Crable and Ivory Benjamin, share more than their gridiron fame. They are former brother-in-laws who share a special teacher-student bond.

"Ace" Crable.

Crable starred for the 1948 and '49 Tigers, earning All-Ohio and Stark County Player of the Year honors. He became Benjamin's hero. "I wanted to be like Irvin Crable," said Benjamin who played from 1955-57. "I played like he played. I wore his jersey number, I done it all. Just like him.

"My brother-in-law more or less taught me how to play the game," Benjamin said. "He'd get off work and I'd meet him, I was 11, 12 years old. We'd run every night. We'd stay 'til I beat him in a 100-yard dash. He'd tire out. That's the only reason I'd beat him. Age would get him. He'd show me how to go in and out of those posts," Benjamin said. "We called it the jungle when we were at the stadium. They had cement poles you could run in and out of—without touchin' 'em. That's how I learned to do some of the things I did in my time. Crable taught me how to go down the field and keep yourself wide open. He also taught me how to go through the line. I was gifted through him. I wanted to do everything that my brother-in-law did. And I did. He taught me the game."

TOM HARP

Tom Harp was 26 years old when Chuck Mather was named head coach of The University of Kansas after winning six straight state titles at Massillon.

The search for Mather's replacement ensued, with over 100 coaches applying for the job—including well-known and well-respected coaches from around the state.

Tom Harp was 17-2-1 as head coach at Massillon.

Harp was inspired by a newspaper article listing him, along with a dozen local coaches, as possible candidates for the job. "I got excited," Harp said. "They were talking about Tiger Ellison from Middletown, Bob Brownson from Portsmouth, and Chuck Thacker from Hamilton. They were all big-name coaches in big schools. I decided there was no reason I shouldn't at least write them a letter and submit an application."

A few weeks passed before Harp received a phone call. "It was on April First," Harp said, "I know April the First is April Fools' day. And it was late at night. The party on the other end said to me, 'This is L. J. Smith, superintendent of schools in Massillon. We've heard some fine things about you and we wonder if you'd be interested in coming up to Massillon for an interview.'

"I said, 'Yeah, yeah, April Fools'.' I thought it was my next door neighbor, because I kidded back and forth with him. L. J. laughed, 'It is April Fools' Day, but this *is* L. J. Smith.' I had no choice but to go along with him. So I said, 'Yes, I'd be delighted.' So we set a date and time. When we hung up I checked with the operator—Carrollton was a small town—I said, 'This is Tom Harp, did I just receive a long distance call?' She said, 'Yes you did Tom, from Massillon.' So I knew I got the call."

"L. J. laughed. 'It is April Fools' Day, but this is L. J. Smith.'"

Tom Harp

After Harp's first interview, L. J. Smith pulled him aside. "L. J. said, 'You made a fine impression. But you're a little young yet. Would you be interested in coming up here as an assistant?' I said, 'I appreciate that and I appreciate the interview. But I don't think I'm going to lose a football game in Carrollton the next three years with the team we've constructed. If I can come to Massillon as the head coach, that's great. If not, I'm just going to say thanks for the interview.' I figured it was over at that point.

"Ten days later he called. 'You're really hanging in there better than I thought you would. In fact there are only four candidates left. We're going to have a final interview and we want you to bring scouting reports and game films.'"

Harp decided to bring a highlight film instead. His gamble paid off. The handsome young Harp wowed the selection committee with a superb, touchdown-filled highlight film of his Carrollton team.

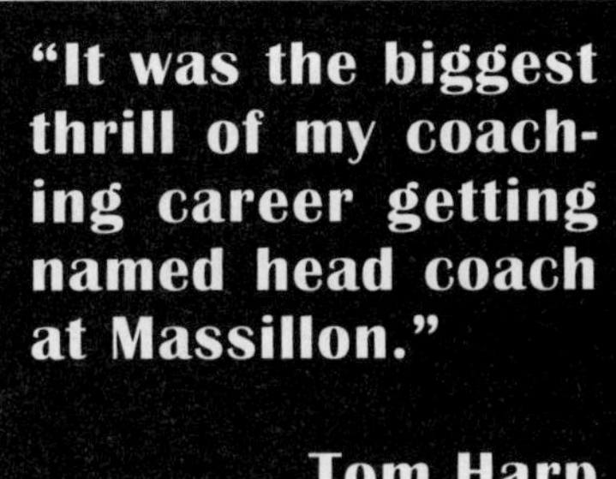

"The highlight film was impressive," Harp said, "I could hear the committee saying 'Ooh, aaah, look at that.' I could hear all this mumbling as I was showing it, so I knew it was going over good.

"I got up and said, 'I realize and understand that there's a concern about my age. I might point out that I'm a year older than a guy you hired here some time ago by the name of Paul Brown.' They went, 'um, hmmm.'"

Pep Paulson, a Massillon municipal court judge for many years, was the Booster Club president and a member of the committee when Harp was hired. "Tom Harp is a very personable guy, a good talker, somebody you like right off the bat," Paulson said. "He's kind of funny. He had put together an excellent movie. That got him hired."

Harp, like all new Massillon coaches, was a bit overwhelmed when he was first installed as head coach. "At Carrollton I had two coaches. I said to myself, 'I'm going to have 12 there. What am I going to do with 12 coaches?'

"I remember being introduced as head coach. It was fantastic. The band was playing 'The Tiger Rag,' and 'Carry on for Massillon.' All the students were there. And the enthusiasm for football. The way they reacted when I was introduced. I remember I said how happy I was to be there. I said, 'I'm replacing a guy that's done pretty well. But they've brought me in here to get this program straightened out and I'm going to do everything I can.' And everybody laughed. It was the biggest thrill of my coaching career getting named head coach at Massillon. Without any question the biggest break I've ever had. You had great kids, great town support, great school support, great tradition."

Tom Harp is carried off of the field after a victory in 1954.

Harp inherited a 23- game unbeaten streak from Mather. It lasted until his third game.

"Alliance came in and beat us (19-7). I was horrified. I didn't know what the town's reaction was going to be. 'Were they going to fire me?'" But he didn't panic. Instead he laid out a road map to put Massillon back in the state championship hunt.

"I remember getting up in front of the squad on Monday night. I said, 'Okay, we lost a football game. We shouldn't have lost. We didn't play well. We didn't deserve to win. Give them credit. Our goal now is to win the state championship. Here's what we have to do in order to win it.

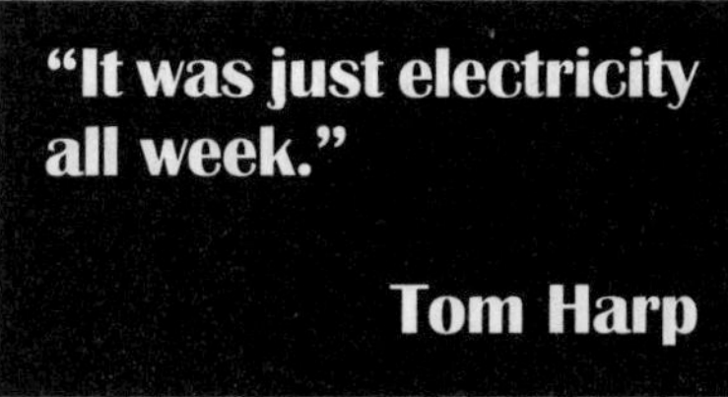

"I knew how they'd react. All the things that I said had to happen, happened. We won all the rest of our games and we came down to the Canton McKinley game and they're ranked one and we're ranked two.

"I remember that every store in town was going crazy. The kids in school all week, every time class changed they were playing 'The Tiger Rag' and screaming 'Go Massillon.' Cheers all over the place. It was just electricity all week. And that year we just kicked the tar out of 'em. I mean, we beat them 26-6 and it could have been 40-6. We dominated them. It wasn't even close. I've never had kids any sharper for a football game than they were for that McKinley game. They were ready to go."

Harp was rewarded with the state championship—Massillon's seventh straight.

He had no idea the heartache his second season at Massillon would bring.

The heartaches started early. Mike Hershberger, a running back and defensive back who went on to captain the 1956 team, went down with an injury in training camp. "I was counting an awful lot on Mike Hershberger that '55 season," Harp said, "and a kid by the name of Donny Humes."

Hershberger was expected to be the next star running back until a training camp injury ended his junior season before it started.

"Humes and Johnny James were competing for the quarterback job," Harp said. "Humes had kinda won it. In the senior game that year he broke his neck. He had a fractured vertebrate and couldn't play. So it became James' job."

Then it looked like James' services might be lost. "Johnny was painting that summer and he was overcome by fumes," said Humes. "I remember Harp saying, 'My first quarterback breaks his neck and the other one is in the hospital overcome by fumes.' He was wondering what he was going to do for a quarterback."

"I remember Harp saying, 'My first quarterback breaks his neck and the other one is in the hospital.'"

Don Humes

On the field, two heartbreaking games kept the Tigers from winning their eighth straight state championship. First came a 12-12 tie against Mansfield.

"We missed an extra point that would have won it," Harp said. "We were behind 12-6 and we got the football back, deep in our own territory, with less than two minutes to play. I remember James bursting up to me and saying, 'Don't worry coach, we're going to win it.' They went out and drove it down the field. I remember Don Duke going off the right tackle for the touchdown to tie it with two seconds left in the game. It turned out we missed both extra points. It wasn't a very happy night."

But the real heartache came in the final game against Canton McKinley, who Massillon had beaten seven straight times. "We played 'em in a snow storm," Harp said. "At McKinley. For the state championship. They don't cross mid-field under their own power. We lose the game because we snap two balls over the punter's head. One went into the end zone and one to the three-yard line and it took 'em three downs to score. That's how they got their two touchdowns and beat us 13-7. Other than that we beat 'em in all departments."

Harp was lured away from Massillon after the 1955 season by Earl "Red" Blaik, who in 18 years at West Point coached two national champions and six unbeaten teams.

Harp enjoyed 15 years as a Division I head coach at Cornell, Duke and Indiana State, posting 61 career wins.

"Massillon was probably my best job," Harp said. "Any time you've got a job that when you go on the field you figure seven out of 10 games you're better than the other guy, you've got a good job."

Veteran Assistants Guided Harp

Experienced assistants have been a cornerstone of Massillon's success through the years. Tom Harp felt fortunate to have a pair of Massillon's finest assistants at his side.

Front: Dick King, Tom Harp. Back: Ken Wable, Elwood Kammer, Ducky Schroeder and Lee Hasslinger.

"Ducky Schroeder was a legend. Elwood Kammer was the same way. They knew Massillon inside and out. They had some stability, they were a little older than the coaches I was bringing in. They were older than I was, they knew the traditions. Consequently I didn't make many mistakes because of stupidity. I didn't do something stupid and then find out 'You don't *do* that at Massillon, you don't *say* that at Massillon.' They were kind of like father figures to me. 'Just stay with us, these kids will be all right.' They kind of kept me calmed down a little bit. I got all excited when I was that age. Booster Club meetings were an example of where a Ducky Schroeder and an Elwood Kammer would say, 'Now don't go in there and get mad when they start criticizing—because they're going to do a little criticizing. But don't fly back and say 'I don't care what Paul Brown did.'"

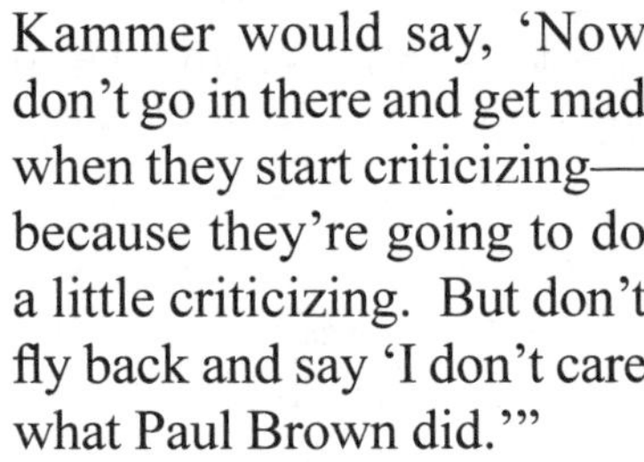

Broken Neck Didn't Break Humes

"It happened in the spring game when we played against the graduating seniors," said Don Humes, describing his life-changing injury. "It was near the end of the game. I was rolling left to throw a pass and I was brought down from behind. I cradled the ball in my arms while I was going down so I wouldn't fumble and I landed on three points with my knees on the ground and my head on the ground. One of the defensive players was not sure that I was down or couldn't control himself, I don't know which. He hit me and my neck just rolled under. I broke my neck. Fortunately, it didn't touch the spinal cord at all, so I got up and wobbled off the field. The game ended a few plays later."

Don Humes in 1955.

A scene in the locker room made Humes realize something was seriously wrong. "I didn't know what was wrong. It hurt when I took the shoulder pads off of my head. I told one of the equipment managers that I was really feeling bad. The coach (Tom Harp) said 'We'd better take him to the hospital.'

"They put me in a bed and they put sand bags all around my head to immobilize it. I later learned that they were waiting for the swelling to go down a little bit before they set it and put a cast on.

"I saw the paper the next morning and it said 'Don Humes' Neck Broken in Grid Tilt.' That was the first I knew about it. I was very shocked when I saw the headline. I hadn't realized that my neck had been broken."

The injury ended Humes' football career, but he remained with the team. "I was in a cast for 100 days," Humes said. "I had a cast around my waist and it went up and over my head. I got out of the cast in the summer, but I was not released to play football. I knew I couldn't play. I stayed with the team, I went to practice every day. Traveled with 'em. I felt a part of the team. I just didn't get to play."

Prior to the injury, Humes won a tight contest with Johnny James for the starting quarterback position for the Tigers, who were vying for their eighth straight state championship in 1955. Johnny was the youngest of the famous James brothers at Massillon.

"Johnny did a great job at quarterback," Humes said, "he had some of his brother Tommy's good moves."

Humes never felt sorry for himself following the injury. "I was very accepting of it," he said. "I never felt any anger about missing the season."

Humes' destiny was to gain notoriety as a pioneer in the U.S. Space Program. "I spent 44 years as a research scientist for NASA," Humes said. "It was really great because I got in there when it was just getting started."

HENRY "ACE" GROOMS

The story of Henry "Ace" Grooms is kind of like a Massillon fairy tale.

The way the story goes, Grooms was a star running back from Pennsylvania who showed up on the coach's doorstep saying, "I want to play football for Massillon."

Henry "Ace" Grooms, 1951.

Like in any good fairy tale, Grooms became a hero for the 1951 Tigers. A great runner and passer, Grooms provided the feature back that was otherwise missing from Chuck Mather's fourth straight state championship team.

Mather's championship squads in 1948, '49 and '50 were loaded with exciting runners. The original "Ace," Irvin "Ace" Crable, Dick Jacobs, Al Brown, Clarence Johnson and Bob Howe were all star running backs. Brown, Crable and Howe were all first team All-Ohio backs.

But the 1951 team didn't have an "Ace" until Grooms showed up just before the beginning of the season.

"Ace came up on my porch and said, 'I'm Ace Grooms and I'd like to go to school in Massillon,'" Mather said.

"He was 19 at the time. In Pennsylvania you weren't allowed to play when you were 19, and he wanted to play his senior year.

"He said he was an all-state end. I said, 'Ace, we just couldn't do that, it would be impossible.' "Well, he said, 'I'm going to Steubenville.' I knew how Steubenville was loaded, so I said, 'Just wait a minute.' I went in and called our commissioner. I said, 'Mr. Emsweiler, I want to tell you what happened here. This young man came up and said he wants to go to school here. I've never even heard of him. I don't know a thing about him other than he said if he's not going here he's going to Steubenville.' Emsweiler said, 'Well, you know Chuck, there's going to be a lot of folks investigating this. If this is all the truth, I don't think you have anything to worry about.' So it *was* the truth and actually nothing happened."

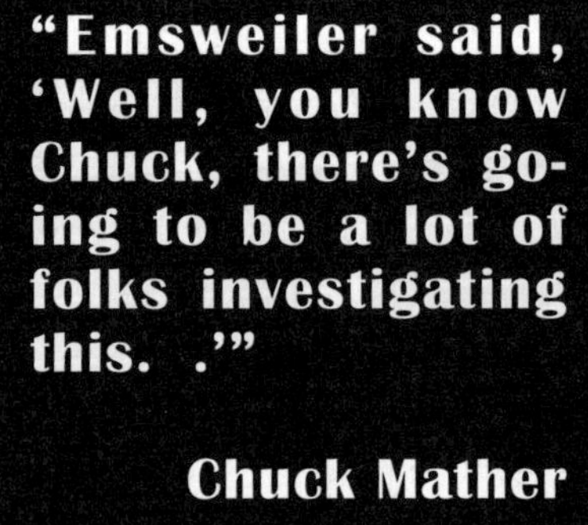

Well, nothing happened except for Grooms rushing for 1,062 yards, earning All-Ohio recognition and leading the Tigers to the state title. The game of the season? A 13-6 win over Steubenville, with Grooms picking up 55 yards and scoring with 10 seconds left in an 88-yard game-winning drive.

BOB VOGEL

Before becoming a first-round draft choice and an All-Pro with the Baltimore Colts, Bob Vogel was a high school junior whose father was looking for the best place for his boy to play his senior year of high school football. His search led him to Massillon.

Bob Vogel was selected to the Pro Bowl five times in his 10-year NFL career.

Vogel, whose father was a heavy equipment operator, played through his junior year of high school at Toronto, a small town on the Ohio river. "His father wanted to move his son to a high profile high school to increase his ability to earn a scholarship to a big name college," said Leo Strang, Vogel's coach at Massillon. "Bob's dad was a uke driver—one of those great big earth movers. Bob had been at two different schools along the river. Prior to his senior year, he went over to look at Steubenville to see the Big Red play—that's when they had their great teams. The mistake that was made was the night they went over, Steubenville played Massillon. Massillon's crowd and band, 'Hold that Tiger' and all that stuff...Bob told his dad he wanted to go to Massillon for his senior year.

Bob Vogel makes a pass reception at Massillon.

"Now that all happened before I accepted the Massillon job. They got in touch with one of the Booster Club members in Massillon. The Booster Club member told me there was a big, good-lookin' kid coming to Massillon. They arranged that on a Sunday I'd be out at the stadium to meet him. They drove up from Belair, Ohio, and when they drove up at the stadium and he got out of that car, I about flipped. He was a handsome guy with a crew cut, 225-230 pounds, six foot four. I could tell he was an athlete just the way he carried himself. So they came to Massillon, his father got a job there in Massillon.

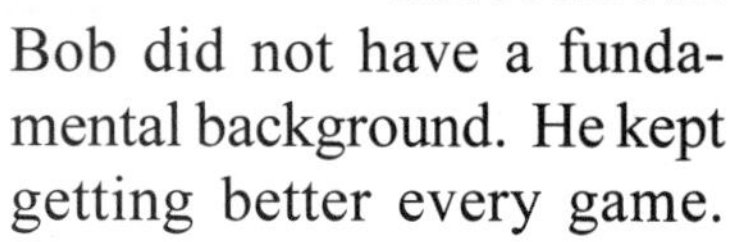

Bob did not have a fundamental background. He kept getting better every game.

He just got better and better and better as he learned fundamentals and techniques. The schools he had played at before, he didn't need 'em. He was just so big and strong and fast.

"I remember Woody Hayes wanted to speak at our football banquet pretty badly, and I knew why. He came and got Bob Vogel and Joe Sparma. I recommended that Vogel go to Ohio State. I recommended Sparma go to Michigan State or Purdue."

"Vogel was...a master technician at offensive tackle."

Bo Schembechler

Legendary Michigan coach Bo Schembechler was Bob Vogel's position coach when he was an assistant under Hayes. "I coached Vogel and Darryl Sanders, both of 'em," Schembechler said. "Vogel we moved from tight end to tackle. Both those guys, interestingly, were drafted number one. One by Detroit, the other by Baltimore. Because they were so close, they negotiated the contracts for the two guys at the same time. Detroit and Baltimore were going to give the exact same contract. So Vogel and Sanders kept calling me because they didn't have agents. I'd tell 'em, 'That ain't enough, hang in there.' Sanders would call back and say, 'Vogel is weakening, he's weakening.' And it was like 11 p.m. Then after midnight they finally agreed to contracts. That's how those guys were drafted and signed. There were no agents, so what were they going to do but end up calling me, because I was their coach. There were a lot of Massillon kids that I coached.

"Vogel was a good kid, a real good kid, very fine. He was a master technician at offensive tackle. Beautiful technique. Quick feet. Both of those kids, one of them weighed 229, the other weighed 231. They were both about exactly the same size, they were both about 6'4". They were good."

Bob Vogel's football resume was very impressive. With the Massillon Tigers, Vogel was first team All-0hio in 1958.

Vogel at Ohio State.

After starring at Ohio State, he was the fifth player chosen in the 1958 NFL draft by the Colts.

In half of his 10 seasons with Baltimore, Vogel was chosen to play in the Pro Bowl. In 1969 he was named first team All-Pro.

Vogel played the valuable left tackle position in Baltimore, protecting Hall of Fame quarterback Johnny Unitas. It was Vogel protecting Unitas' blind side in Super Bowls III and V.

JIM REICHENBACH

One of Ohio State's all-time greatest linemen, Jim Reichenbach, almost bypassed Columbus altogether. A soft-spoken country boy, Reichenbach was sure Columbus wasn't going to be for him.

Jim Reichenbach as an All-American at Ohio State.

It all started with the recruiters—who came at Reichenbach from all directions. "The pressure I felt to go to Ohio State I didn't like at all," Reichenbach said. "Pressure from my coaches, area businessmen who were Ohio State recruiters and the Ohio State coaches."

To understand his trepidation, you need to consider his childhood. He grew up on the same farm he lives on today. He attended a one-room schoolhouse through eighth grade. Jim Reichenbach deadpanned, "My eighth grade class had three kids in it."

Visits to downtown Massillon offered some of his only

socialization. "We went to town once a month to buy groceries," he said. "When I went to Massillon it was like going to New York City. My social life was very, very sheltered."

Entering Lorin Andrews Junior High School was traumatic. With no orientation, finding his classes in the three-story junior high was overwhelming. "I remember trying to find the restroom and I walked in the girls' restroom by mistake. My teacher saw me and mentioned it in class. He said, 'Some dumb farmer walked into the girls' bathroom.' I was so embarrassed. He didn't need to say that." The teacher's insensitivity did nothing to bolster Jim Reichenbach's confidence.

"To me it was just like throwin' a calf down in the barnyard, which I'd been doin' for years."

Jim Reichenbach

Fortunately, the football field became a perfect refuge. He was still attending the one-room schoolhouse when his friend Jim Schumacher told him about Roger Price, who was coaching football at Lorin Andrews. "My Dad and I went down to Lincoln Park and Lorin Andrews was playing football. It was half time. We walked right in the middle of the huddle, which was kind of unusual for my dad because he was a farmer and sort of a bashful kind of guy. He asked Roger Price if he needed a football player. He said, 'Yeah, we can use one.'

"The first time they put me in—it was probably more lucky than anything else—but Jones had this big running back, Clarence Johnson, and I made a couple of good tackles on him. Everybody thought that was great. But to me it was just like throwin' a calf down in the barnyard, which I'd been doin' for years. So it wasn't that much of a task. This impressed Mr. Price and I started the next week."

Captain Jim Reichenbach leads the 1950 Tigers onto the field for the Canton McKinley game. Massillon won, 33-0.

As the farmer's son, Jim Reichenbach, moved on to the high school, he was still backward. "It's unbelievable," he said of his high school experience, "but I attended Washington High School for three years and didn't know they had a cafeteria. We weren't very wealthy people and my mom would give me a quarter and I'd go over to that pool hall next to the Lincoln Theatre and I'd get a lemon blend and a hot dog and that was my lunch."

But Reichenbach fit right in on the high school gridiron, where it didn't take him long to earn his starting spot as a sophomore on the 1948 varsity squad. "Probably a week or so into two-a-days, I think some of the guys resented that a sophomore was going to start. But when I was the highest graded player on the team my first game, I earned their respect. Up until that point if they had a chance in practice to take a good shot at me, they would. And that's all right, that's the way it should be."

Reichenbach, in addition to learning from the coaching staff, learned in the huddle from 1948 team captain Al Brown. "Al Brown was the captain of the team and probably one of the toughest guys I ever knew. Tough as nails. A great competitor. A great captain. The type of captain that Massillon should have. He was the kind of a leader that if you weren't doing well, he'd give you a couple of words right in the huddle. As a sophomore it happened to me a couple of times."

He still remembers his first great block, it came in his first game. "The second play of the game they ran a 61 trap, the fullback up the middle, and I did the trapping. I executed the block and got up and looked and he was in the end zone. That was pretty exciting. But that happened a lot. We had a lot of long runs at Massillon."

Starting three years at Massillon was a great thrill for Jim Reichenbach. The Tigers lost only two games in his three-year career, winning the state championship all three years. "It was very exciting for a kid that lived out in the country all his life. I was so impressed. I was a kid that seldom got off the farm and here I am playing in front of a crowd of 19,000 people. The crowd never bothered me. I never had any sense of how many people were in the stands in high school or college."

Reichenbach was named captain of the 1950 Tigers—a team considered to be one of Massillon's all-time best. His fine high school career was recognized when he won All-Ohio and All-American honors following his senior season.

College offers poured in. "I got a lot of offers. I liked Northwestern and Purdue. I was turned off by the pressure to go to Ohio State. I didn't want to be pressured into going someplace. I wanted to decide on my own." Inevitably it was his old friend who finally delivered Jim Reichenbach to Ohio State. Reichenbach piled into the car of Jim Schumacher to drive to Columbus for summer school. Reichenbach was nervous. "I was afraid of going down there and getting lost," he said. "I didn't want to stop at Columbus. I pleaded with Jim to drive on to Purdue. He wouldn't listen to me, so we ended up at Ohio State."

"I didn't want to stop in Columbus. I pleaded with Jim to drive on to Purdue."

Jim Reichenbach

What ensued was a legendary career at Ohio State. The Buckeyes had a new coach, Woody Hayes, and Reichenbach found he was ready to perform for his new boss. "When I got down there, I didn't find the competition much harder than it was in high school. It probably took me longer to establish myself as a starting football player at Massillon than it did at Ohio State."

Reichenbach credits the coaching he received in Massillon for his quick start at Ohio State. "As far as me learning the game, Massillon assistant coach Dave Putts contributed more to me than anyone else. Massillon football was just as fundamentally sound and as state-of-the-art as it was at Ohio State University. The coaching I got at Ohio State was mostly a review of what I had learned in high school. To go in there and start as a freshman I had to have some awfully good coaching."

Reichenbach started for four straight years at Ohio State. He was exposed to a different coaching approach there. "There was a big difference between Massillon coach Chuck Mather and Woody," he said. "I never heard Mather raise his voice. I heard Woody raise his voice quite a few times, but I don't mean that disrespectfully. I'm sure there were times Woody *should* have raised his voice. But I'm sure there were times when Mather was at the end of his rope, too, and he never allowed anyone to know it. Woody didn't care who knew it. But I admired him, because there was never a time when you didn't know where you stood with Woody."

In his final year at Ohio State, Reichenbach was selected as All-American. The award didn't mean much to him at the time. "It never really seemed that significant," he said. "I guess I'm a little more proud of it now than when it happened."

MIKE HERSHBERGER

Mike Hershberger spent 11 years in *The Show*, playing major league baseball alongside Hall of Famers Reggie Jackson, Luis Aparicio, Early Wynn, Jim "Catfish" Hunter, Rollie Fingers and Nellie Fox.

Mike Hershberger was an 11-year major leaguer.

But in spite of his success on the baseball diamond, Massillon's former All-Ohio football player still wonders if his skills were better suited to an NFL gridiron.

"Looking back, maybe I would have liked to have given it a shot and seen what I could have done in football," Hershberger said. "Wayne Fontes always said he thought I'd end up being a pro football player at defensive back."

Fontes, the former Detroit Lions head coach, starred on Canton McKinley state title teams in 1955 and 1956. Both players, Massillon's Hershberger and McKinley's Fontes, were named All-Ohio while playing running back and defensive back in high school.

Hershberger's football career had its share of heartache. As a sophomore in 1954, he dressed with the varsity, but saw little action. His best memories were of *watching* legendary running back Homer Floyd. "He was the best I've ever watched play the game at Massillon," he said.

Hershberger did enough as a sophomore to make a believer out of second year head coach Tom Harp. "Mike Hershberger was going to be the guy who replaced Homer Floyd as a running back in 1955," Harp said, "He didn't have Floyd's speed, but he had great balance and he was illusive. Then he stepped in a hole and broke his ankle in camp."

The injury was difficult for Hershberger to deal with. "It was tough when you sit on the sideline and you don't do anything," he said. "When you walk around on crutches the entire year it isn't a very pleasant experience."

But he came back in 1956 ready to make up for lost time. "I was determined to come back strong. I worked out hard. But it wasn't just me. *Everybody* worked hard in Massillon. It was a tradition."

Massillon had a new head coach in 1956. Lee Tressel took over for Harp after a brilliant stay at Mentor High School.

The Massillon Tigers went 8-2 in 1956, losing to the Mansfield Tygers and the Canton McKinley Bulldogs.

"We lost to Mansfield in a foot of mud," Hershberger recalled. "Chester Brown ran one back about 89 yards and it got called back. We ended up losing 14-6." Hershberger did his part, rushing for 143 yards on seven carries, including an 83-yard touchdown run where he outran the Mansfield defensive backfield.

Another great highlight of Hershberger's senior year came against Canton Lincoln. "When we were tackled, they were scratchin' eyeballs and punchin'." After Lincoln tied the game at 13-13 late in the third quarter, a determined Hershberger lined up deep for the kickoff. "I was just prayin' they'd kick the ball to me. You were just so mad, because they were playin' so dirty that you just wanted to go after 'em. I wanted the ball kicked to me, and it was. I ran it back 79 yards for a touchdown. That was a highlight. It was just the way that they played the game that challenged us. It was a delight when we beat 'em."

But heartache returned when he suffered torn knee ligaments in Week 7 against Warren. "I missed three games up to the McKinley game. I wasn't even sure if I'd play in the McKinley game. I ended up getting in the game. We got beat (34-7), but it was probably one of their all-time great teams."

Teammate Ivory Benjamin remembers Hershberger as an unselfish player. "Mike was a great guy," Benjamin said, "we'd get down to the five- or 10-yard line and they'd send Mike in to run the ball. But Mike wouldn't run it. He'd change the play. He'd give it to someone else to run it in. That's the kind of guy Mike was."

Hershberger got the most out of his time on the gridiron at Massillon, turning a career that saw him only able to start a handful of games into a college scholarship at the

University of Cincinnati.

"Just earning the scholarship to play college football was the big excitement," Hershberger said.

Hershberger was assigned to the freshman squad at Cincinnati. "At that time freshmen weren't eligible to play varsity," Hershberger said. But he was able to impress Cincinnati head coach Wayne Blackburn as a freshman. "They were counting on me to be a starting halfback my sophomore year," he said. "But I signed a pro baseball contract at the end of my freshman baseball season."

Hershberger signed with the Chicago White Sox. "I spent three years with the Chicago White Sox, from the end of the 1961 season through 1964. We ended up in second place three times."

In 1965 Hershberger was part of a famous three-team, eight-player trade that brought a Cleveland Indians icon back home. "I was involved in the Rocky Colavito trade," Mike Hershberger said. "Cleveland traded John Romano, Tommy John and Tommie Agee to the White Sox. Kansas City received Jim Landis, myself and Fred Talbot. The White Sox sent Cam Carreon to the Indians. Colavito was sent to Cleveland by Kansas City."

Being traded to the Kansas City Athletics was disappointing to Hershberger. "I went from a team that was a contender to a last place ball club," he said. "The total atmosphere was just completely different."

But things quickly turned interesting with the A's, who won three straight World Series titles from 1972-74.

"The nice part with the A's is that I was there in the beginning," Hershberger said. "I was one of the veterans of the ball club—and I was only 25 years old. These guys ended up as a great, great ball club."

As a member of the A's, Hershberger was a part of Hunter's perfect game in 1968 and Jackson's breakout 47-home run season in 1969.

"Reggie was great. He was just a young kid. He'd hit the ball so hard. We would actually get up, get out of our seats in the dugout and watch him hit because you didn't know how far he was gonna hit it. He hit some tape measure shots and you didn't want to be where you weren't paying attention."

Hershberger played with another Hall of Famer who was on the other end of his career. "To play with Nellie Fox back then was the thrill of a lifetime. I caught him at the end of his career."

Hershberger's skills allowed him to play at baseball's pinnacle for over a decade. "I was a good contact hitter," he said. "I hit the ball fairly well. But my strength was defense, my speed and my arm. I had terrific speed back then."

"It was just the thrill of a lifetime to be there," Hershberger said "To play on the same field against Mickey Mantle and Roger Maris and the great superstars of that time was quite a thrill. I ended up spending three years in the minor leagues and ended up in the major leagues when I was 21 years old. I had 10 years in the big leagues when I was 31 years old. Not a lot of guys can say that."

JOE SPARMA

If there was ever an All-American boy at Massillon, it was Joe Sparma. A good looking, strong-armed quarterback, Sparma went on to play quarterback at Ohio State before becoming a starting pitcher in the major leagues.

Sparma pitched for the World Series champions in 1968.

"Joe was a real good student," said Leo Strang, Sparma's coach at Massillon. "A real fine young man to work with. He was a good lookin' guy, too. All the girls were after him. But he had a favorite one he married." In keeping with his All-American image, Sparma wed his high school sweetheart, Connie Huff.

Following his All-Ohio career at Massillon, Strang encouraged his star quarterback to join Duffy Daugherty at Michigan State, where his big league arm would be showcased. But Sparma was wooed by Woody Hayes.

"Woody was a salesman," Strang said. "He didn't want Joe to go to a school in the Big 10 and pass against him."

Strang felt that Sparma's college choice kept him from becoming an NFL quarterback instead of a major league baseball pitcher.

"I don't think there's any doubt about it that Sparma could have been a great pro football player," Strang said. "He was a great, pro-type dropback passer. That's the reason I wanted him to go to a school and pocket pass. Woody didn't throw much at that time. He'd throw on third and long. So that's about all Sparma got to play was third down and long."

Sparma managed to lead the Buckeyes in passing in 1961 and 1962, but undoubtedly was limited by Hayes' famous Three Yards and a Cloud of Dust offense.

He still holds the record for the longest touchdown pass in the Ohio State-Michigan rivalry, an 80-yarder to Bob Klein in the 1961 classic, a 50-20 Ohio State win. Sparma was 7-10 for 200 yards against Michigan. Sparma also hit future NFL Hall of Famer Paul Warfield in stride with a 70-yard bomb in that game. Warfield was knocked out of bounds at the 10-yard line, preventing Sparma from having *two* 80-yard touchdown passes in the game.

Sparma left Ohio State after his junior season to pitch for the Detroit Tigers. He won 52 major league games, three times winning 10 or more games in a season, including a 16-9 slate in 1967.

Sparma enjoyed a seven-year career in the big leagues, mostly with Detroit. He ended his career with the Montreal Expos in 1970.

Sparma's most famous moment came when he pitched a complete game in the pennant-clincher for Detroit in 1968. The Tigers went on to upset the St. Louis Cardinals in the World Series that season. Sparma was in the starting rotation with a couple of famous pitchers—Denny McLain and Mickey Lolich. In 1968, McLain was the last pitcher in major league baseball history to win 30 games, with a 31-6 record. Lolich, Detroit's lefty ace for many seasons, is a 200-game winner who was the MVP of the 1968 World Series.

Sparma at Ohio State.

Sparma was successful against the New York Yankees. "Joe wound up beating the Yankees three or four different games," said Dave Null, a football and basketball teammate of Sparma's at Massillon. "At that time there was a label on Joe that he was kind of a 'Yankee Killer'."

Bill Freehan, the Detroit Tigers all-star catcher, was a roommate with Sparma and wrote about him in his book *Behind the Mask."* Freehan recalled an incident Sparma had with Hall of Famer Mickey Mantle. Sparma was the starting pitcher for Detroit on Mickey Mantle Day. Sparma left the mound to shake hands with Mantle. According to Freehan, Sparma told Mantle, "I've never had a chance to meet you in person, and I've always admired you." Joe Sparma returned to the mound and struck out Mantle. Freehan said that Mickey Mantle turned to him and said, "They have a day for me, and your manager's got to put some hard-throwing kid out there. Couldn't he have put in some soft-tossing left-hander for me to hit off of so I could look like a hero in front of all of those people?"

"Joe wound up beating the Yankees three or four different games... he was kind of a 'Yankee Killer.'"

Dave Null

It was no secret in Massillon that Sparma was destined for sports greatness. He showed early signs of greatness as a sophomore quarterback at Massillon. In the famous Clock Game against Warren Harding in 1957, Sparma flung the game-winning touchdown pass to All-Ohio end Clyde Childers in the final seconds of the game.

The pass and catch in the Clock Game have become part of the magical history of the Massillon Tigers. Warren supporters blame a malfunctioning scoreboard clock for giving Massillon extra time at the end of the game to rally for the victory. Over fifty years after the fact, many Warren fans still become emotional when the Clock Game is mentioned.

"Joe was one of the better athletes Massillon's had in the last 50 years," Null said. "He was not only a great quarterback, Joe was a good basketball player on some good teams and was a tremendous baseball player, obviously."

Vrotsos, who coached Sparma in football and basketball remembered his versatility. "Joe Sparma probably threw the ball as good as any quarterback as far as arm strength. If he had gone on to a college where they threw the ball, he probably would have gone into the pros as a pro quarterback. Everybody knew when he was going to throw at Ohio State. If he had gone to a program that was throwing the ball, like Michigan State or Notre Dame or down south, he probably could have played in the NFL."

Joe Sparma led Ohio State in passing in 1961 and 1962.

Ivory Benjamin, the star running back of the 1957 Tigers, played with Joe Sparma during the quarterback's sophomore year. The young quarterback's arm was already mature. "He could throw that ball any way that he wanted to throw," Benjamin said. "He could thread it."

Sparma is remembered in Massillon as a confident athlete—bordering on cocky.

"Joe had a lot of self-confidence," Vrotsos said. "He was confident that he could take a baseball and throw a no-hitter. He was confident that he could quarterback a football team and win. He was confident that he could play basketball and get the job done. He was a three-sport star here. A lot of people thought maybe he might be cocky. Joe was sure of himself, not cocky."

"I thought he was very confident, very outgoing," said Null, who was a back-up quarterback to Sparma as a sophomore and junior. He was a leader. Personally, I thought he had a right to be a little bit cocky. I learned a lot from Joe. It was awful fun playing back then. We were one of the premier programs in the state and just to be part of it was a great experience. Personally I enjoyed learning a lot about throwing the football and playing the quarterback position from Sparma. Joe was an All-State quarterback and it was a great opportunity for me to be an understudy to somebody like that."

Marty Gugov was Sparma's catcher in baseball and a running back on the football field.

"I had a long history with Joe," Gugov said. "We played on the same Little League team when I was nine years old. We were good friends. He wanted to have a good time, all the time. And he did. Joe wasn't a tough guy; Joe just liked to have a good time. He always laughed. Life was not so serious that he couldn't laugh all the time and enjoy what he was doing.

Sparma, as fate would have it, died a young man, succumbing to heart disease at age 44 in Columbus.

Gugov "Jacked Up" Sparma in 1959 Canton McKinley Game

Marty Gugov felt Joe Sparma had the physical tools to be a great quarterback.

"Joe could throw the ball and he could hand the ball off," Gugov said. "I don't think football was his best sport."

Gugov remembers challenging Sparma during the heat of battle in the final game of the 1959 season. It was the game that would cap a state championship and national championship season for Massillon.

Game program, 1959 Massillon-McKinley.

"We were in the Canton McKinley game his senior year. We had a great season going. The McKinley defenders were beatin' on him and he couldn't handle that very well. We were having a hard time getting the handoff from him. I'd just about had enough. We weren't deserting *him*. We tried to keep the defenders off him. McKinley wasn't really that great that year, but in that game they really got after him pretty hard. I was really concerned about his level of play."

It was at that point that Gugov took things into his own hands.

"Quite frankly, I jacked him up. I had to. I was emotional. I said, 'Just give me the ball! Don't fumble it! Just get it to me!' He was pretty well upset from getting hit so much."

Joe Sparma.

Did Gugov sense his quarterback was scared? After a long pause he said, "I hope not. I just think he didn't want to get hurt. And that's what was happening. They hit him after he handed the ball off, and I don't think he liked that very well. But I wanted to make sure he kept handing the ball off. That was a tough game. We were only up 8-0 at the end of the first quarter."

Did Gugov feel he got through to his rattled quarterback?

"Oh yeah, no doubt. And we were still friends after that. It didn't make any difference. We were there for each other. We were trying to help each other out. And when you get into a game like that, where you're being challenged physically, and on the scoreboard, and it's a game like the Canton McKinley-Massillon game, it goes way beyond the normal things. We had a lot to lose that day. And they weren't showing us very much respect. So you have to fix those things."

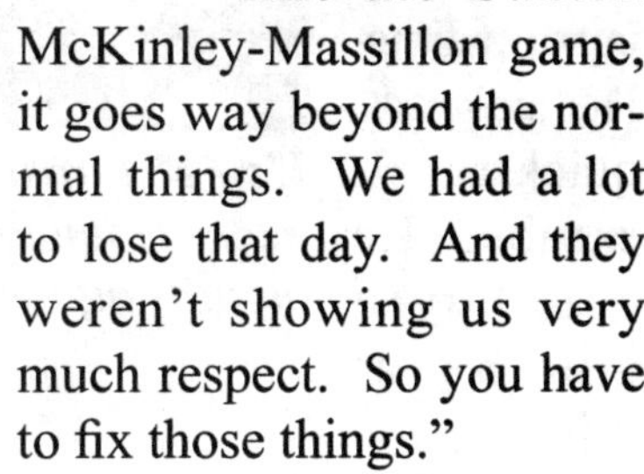

HOMER FLOYD

Homer Floyd was ballet in football cleats, a Ferrari with an extra gear. "He just looked like a thoroughbred," Floyd's Massillon mentor Tom Harp said.

"When he walked it was like twinkle-toes or something. Nice looking, streamlined kid.

"Homer ran like the wind, cut on a dime. He had great, quick acceleration. He could turn and be at full speed in nothin' flat. He'd kind of run along at what looked to be full speed, making these moves, and be looking for an area. Then all of a sudden he'd spot what appeared to be a hole and then boom, he'd kick it into high gear and be gone. He was amazing."

Homer Floyd often left opponents, teammates and fans with mouths agape.

Floyd not only left opponents befuddled, gasping for and grasping at air, he left the same impression on teammates.

"Homer was a year ahead of me," said All-Ohio end David Canary (1955). "In the spring we played a game against the graduating seniors, so I was playing against Homer Floyd. I knew he was good, I'd seen him in the films, watched him on the field, but I never tried to tackle him before. During the spring game I had a bead on him a couple of times, then he'd give that 'hooof', and I'd see him swing into that gear where he'd sink a little lower and almost stop, and then 'pfft', he's gone. It's like when you go for a target and it's gone. He had an amazing, relaxed change of pace about him that made him incredibly deceptively hard to tackle.

"I saw people missing him for a couple of years at Massillon. I felt sorry for 'em, then I felt sorry for myself when I tried to catch him. Of all the halfbacks I ever played against, he was the best. I played against Dick Bass (a three-time Pro Bowl player and 1,000-yard back with the Los Angeles Rams), who was quite a good player, but Homer was the best."

Floyd had a unique upbringing in Massillon, living in several different areas, with different families. "In some respects I was a community project, because my mother was ill a lot," Floyd said. "My sophomore year I lived in a foster home because my mother was in a sanitarium, she had tuberculosis. My mother came out of the hospital for a short time, then had to go back in. I lived with Mr. Dandridge my junior and senior years in high school. We were very active in the Friendship Baptist Church. That was a support system. I just had a lot of people to touch my life in a variety of ways. I think all for the good. Because even though I wasn't a model student and a model citizen, I never got into any serious difficulties."

Floyd did have some troubles as a sophomore on the varsity at Massillon. "I recall that I had somewhat of a temper," Floyd said. "One of my coaches wanted to kick me off the team. It was one of the backfield coaches. I had a confrontation with Coach Paul Schofer. The sophomore game was on a Saturday and I had played quite a bit that Friday night. I, for whatever reason, thought I should not have to go play with the sophomores."

"We played him in some of our Friday night games when he was a sophomore," said Chuck Mather, Massillon's head coach during Floyd's sophomore season. "On Saturdays we usually had the sophomores play against a smaller school's varsity squad. Homer said he wasn't going to go."

It was decided that Floyd would either suit up with the sophomores on Saturdays or be dismissed from the team. "I said, 'Homer, you're gonna play,'" Mather said. "He had played with the varsity so he didn't think he should go play with the sophomores. He was developing, and playing would be to his advantage. He was a strong-willed guy. But he did it."

"Mather saved me," Floyd said. "He kind of pulled me out of the fire. Looking back, I didn't handle it very well. I think I had made some assumptions about my importance. That was a lesson for me. I learned a number of lessons along the way. Ultimately, I still had to play."

When Mather was nearly 90 years old he reflected back on the stance he took with Floyd. "I've often thought about what a difference it would have been if Homer would have said, 'Okay, I'm not going to play with the sophomores.'" Fortunately for everyone involved, Mather was able to get through to the strong-willed sophomore.

As a child Floyd dreamed of being a star running back at Massillon. "In the sixth, seventh and eighth grade we were all striving for that. You could see the Irving Crables and the Al Browns and the other outstanding football players we were watching as we were growing up, we all wanted to be like them. To that extent, we were all broken field runners, always playing football and trying to be like the stars, but you didn't necessarily feel that you were going to be that.

"When I was young they had a semi-pro league that was going on. We used to go out on Sunday afternoons and watch the semi-pros. There was just so much history we were exposed to. Many of the Massillon stars that were older were playing in that league. I remember Bert Webb, he played quarterback in the semi-pro league. He was incredible. He certainly was a hero of mine. So was Clarence Johnson. I always liked Al Brown. He was so small and just so tough. He would get hit so hard and he was up in your face and at 'em again. I had a great deal of respect for him."

"I always liked the shiftiness of Irving Crable, but I could never do it. He could change, reverse fields and make you miss. Stop on a dime. But I could never do that. I don't think I ever tried to run like any particular player. I just admired the abilities of many of them.

"It was such an exciting era, because from my sixth grade year on through my senior year, we won state championships."

Floyd remembers arriving at the high school as a sophomore. "I just looked up to Mather with awe. I was not a starter as a sophomore, but I came off the bench quite frequently."

As a junior, Floyd was installed as the starting fullback. He had good company in the backfield. "The two halfbacks at the time were All-Staters that year," Floyd said. "John Traylor was pretty fast. He had great hands. He didn't overpower you, but he would try to finish the play. John Francisco, by contrast, was a lot more shifty and had very strong legs. He would fake and dodge and just break tackles because when you try to hit him you're off balance a lot."

Floyd learned a lot about the craft of running from Francisco. "I learned a lot about keeping the defender off balance when he hits you. And therefore they don't get a clean shot at you."

Floyd enjoyed a successful college career at the University of Kansas, where he was reunited with Mather. He was captain of the 1958 team. He led the team in rushing all three years (freshmen could not play varsity at that time). He started every game of his career. He was All-Conference as a senior.

Mather paid Floyd the ultimate compliment. "I've always said I wouldn't have won a game at Kansas without Homer."

Floyd has enjoyed a long career as Executive Director of the Human Relations Commission for the state of Pennsylvania.

HASE McKEY

Hase McKey may be the finest lineman in Massillon history. In 1959 he became the first Tiger to be named first team All-Ohio twice, at different positions.

McKey became an impact player as a sophomore. In fact, some believe that it was an injury to Hase against Cleveland Benedictine that cost Massillon the 1957 state championship.

Leo Strang shows off his innovative uniform design and his star player, Hase McKey, circa 1959.

"Hase McKey is the reason we weren't state champs my senior year," said co-captain Ivory Benjamin, an All-Ohio running back.

Benjamin remembers how Benedictine, who won the state championship in 1957, exploited the hole that was left at middle guard when McKey was forced to leave the game.

It was late in the fourth quarter, Massillon was clinging to a 7-6 lead, when McKey broke through the line. "George Sefcik had the ball and somehow I got in there and made a shoestring tackle," McKey said. "His foot kicked me in the face." Sefcik, Benedictine's star running back, went on to be a three-year starter at Notre Dame and a longtime NFL backfield coach.

"Hase got a bloody nose and Coach Lee Tressel took him out of the game," Benjamin said. "I called Hase 'Big en.' I said, 'Big en, you all right?' He said, 'I'm all right, I'm all right.' I said, 'Well, come on.'" Benjamin took him over to Tressel to plead his case for getting McKey right back into the game. "The coach said, 'No, his nose is bleedin'.' I said 'What do you mean his nose is bleedin'?' I said, 'Put cotton up in there, let's go.' They took him out and they beat us. Benedictine ran right up over center all the way down the field for a touchdown." Benedictine won 13-7, the only blemish on a fine season by the Tigers.

Starting as a sophomore at Massillon was extremely rare in the 1950s. "I was the only sophomore to play first team," McKey said, "so I got harassed by the team. As a sophomore you had to shine shoes and stuff like that. So I refused to shine shoes, because I played first team." McKey was big enough—and tough enough—to impose his will, even as a sophomore. "I was the kind of guy if you wanted to get it on, well, we'd get it on. So I never had to shine shoes."

His junior year brought a new head coach, Leo Strang. McKey had to adjust to the new head man. "That was a little bit of a change," McKey said. "Leo, his tone of voice, you had to get used to it. He believed in you doing *exactly* what he told you to do. And that was point blank." McKey and several of his African-American teammates had a showdown with Strang in 1959.

"It was after spring practice," Strang said. "I had just named Gary Sluggo Bednar team captain. I was sitting in my office and Hase came in with three other prominent black players. He told me that they wanted a black captain. I said, 'What do you mean a black captain? I don't pick the captain because he's black or white. Do you have a problem with Sluggo Bednar? Don't you think he'd be a good captain?' Hase said, 'No, we don't have any problem with Sluggo. But Coach Tressel named a black captain and a white captain. We want a black captain or we're going to quit.'" Strang said, "I told them, 'I've been watching you guys since practice started. There's not one of you that could get a group of kids to follow you to the malt shop if you had a pocket full of quarters. But if you want to quit the team, we'll have to get some paperwork together and we'll have to go see the vice principal.' Well I took them into Augie Morningstar's office and told him, 'Augie, these kids want to quit the football team. And I told them there was some paperwork they had to fill out.' Well, Augie's jaw just dropped, because he knew these kids were good players.

"Anyway, the next morning when I arrived at my office, Hase and the others were waiting at my door. They told me that they had changed their minds and decided to stay on the team."

McKey remembers the incident. "At first I kind of resented that," he said. "Art Hastings was there. Jim

Houston, the black one, was there. He was rough just like the other Jim Houston."

Hastings was Massillon's all-time leading rusher. Houston had a reputation as one of Massillon's most feared hitters. The *other* Jim Houston was All-Ohio at Massillon in 1955 and went on to become an All-American at Ohio State and an All-Pro with the Cleveland Browns.

"We felt that we should have had equal representation back then," McKey said. "When Strang made me captain for the McKinley game, he united the team. So when we won they took a picture of Leo, Gary and me. We hadn't won a championship since 1954. In 1959 we won the state championship and the national championship."

McKey was one of Strang's favorite players. "Hase McKey was a tremendous football player," Strang said. "He was as good as they come. He was quick. He was a middle guard and an end."

Hase McKey grew to love Strang. "What he taught me on the field stayed with me," McKey said. "I didn't get in a whole lot of trouble. The things he told me and the discipline he put on me, it stayed with me. He was a very super man in my life. I had a lot of friends who fell by the wayside, who got in trouble. Evidently what he taught me kept me on the right path."

Strang got McKey's attention one evening at Tiger stadium. McKey, who kicked extra points for the Tigers, was practicing, with mixed results.

"Hase was out there, he had two or three footballs and he was practicing place-

Sweet Ending for McKey, Strang, Tigers

"Leo knew that I thought that I should be a captain," Hase McKey said. "I felt I had what it takes and that I earned it. And I never got the chance until my senior year, and then I *still* didn't have it through the whole season. I really respected him when he did make me captain for the McKinley game. And I played an exceptional ball game in that one, too."

Hase McKey, Leo Strang and Sluggo Bednar following the McKinley game, 1959, a 20-0 Massillon win.

kicking," Strang said. "He would set the ball in the tee and kick it. And set another one in the tee and kick it. About the third one, I saw him miss. I went out and said, 'Hase, how could you possibly miss it? How can you miss an extra point on the tee with no one rushing you?' 'Oh, coach,' he said, 'you can't make 'em all.' I said, 'Hase, set that football up there.' He set it up. I turned around and kicked it through with my heel. I had done this since I was in high school, just foolin' around, because I was the extra point kicker. You do kind of a dance step and turn around and kick it through with your heel. You have to have it on a tee to do that. In that time tees were legal.

"Hase looked at me and his eyes got big. He said, 'Let

me see you do that again.' I said, 'Oh no Hase, I just do that once.' Because I could just make one out of three of them like that. That story spread all over Massillon. This new coach down there, he kicks the ball with his heel.'"

McKey played under legendary coach Frank Kush at Arizona State.

McKey went on to a successful college career at Arizona State University, playing under legendary ASU coach Frank Kush, who is so revered that they've honored him with a statue. McKey also spent time with the New York Jets in the NFL.

He credits one man for much of his success. "Russell Ramsey was my coach in junior high," McKey said. "He was the guy that talked me into going as far as I went. He's the one who really got me on the road to playing football." Ramsey taught McKey the importance of education. "I really didn't have the grades. My motivation for getting the grades to go to college just wasn't there. But I kept going, and I kept improving. I really stress today, do your studies first, then football. Because when football's over, you're on your own."

FRANK GIBSON

The bond between a football coach and his team captain can be very close. The coach puts a lot of faith in the player he names captain. He sees in this player leadership qualities he wants other players to emulate. The team captain accepts this responsibility and sets out to please his coach and become a role model for his teammates.

Frank Gibson, co-captain of the 1951 State Champion Tigers.

Head coach Chuck Mather gave Frank Gibson the thrill of a lifetime when he named him a team captain after Massillon had just defeated Canton McKinley, 33-0, in 1950.

"Right when we won the state championship and came into the locker room," Gibson said, "he put his arms around me and he told me, 'Frank, you're going to be my captain for next year.' That was one of the greatest honors and thrills I've ever had. It was tremendous."

Gibson served his captaincy well, helping to lead the Tigers to the 1951 state championship.

Gibson, who was hotly recruited coming out of Massillon, first accepted a scholarship to play for the University of Illinois.

Gibson and Massillon teammate Henry "Ace" Grooms were being courted by both Michigan State and Illinois. Grooms was the star running back in 1951. After visiting both schools, they made a decision.

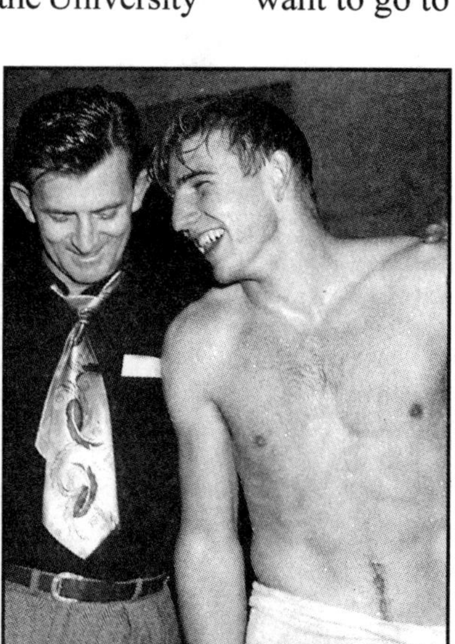

Frank Gibson celebrates a victory over Canton McKinley with head coach Chuck Mather.

"Ace and I had decided we were going to Michigan State. Then Mather called me into his office. He said 'Illinois wants to fly down to the Akron-Canton airport in a private plane. They want to fly you and Ace to Illinois one last time just in case you want to go to Illinois.'"

"They took us out to a baseball game. After the game they took us out for steaks. Illinois head coach Ray Eliot was such a motivator, a great talker. We had never seen anything like that before. He swept us right off our feet."

JIM HOUSTON

A review of Jim Houston's remarkable football resume reveals the evolution of a star athlete. All-Ohio at Massillon. Two-time All-American at Ohio State. First round draft pick at Cleveland. All Pro linebacker. Four Pro Bowls. Thirteen-year NFL veteran.

Jim Houston as a Cleveland Browns All-Pro.

Houston was a champion at every level. At Massillon he was part of two state championships in 1953-54 and one national championship in 1953. At Ohio State he was a contributor to Woody Hayes' 1957 national championship team. At Cleveland he starred on the Browns' last NFL championship team in 1964.

But when Houston reflects on his career, he sees himself as someone who was lucky.

"I had unbelievable luck," Houston said, "that's what it takes to have played as much as I have and to be able to culminate everything—to finish it. And for the amount of times I've run into people, it's amazing that I have never been seriously injured."

Houston grew up as the baby of one of Massillon's most storied football families.

Imagine being the little brother trying to measure up to your big brothers on the football field when two of them played in the NFL.

"I was cut when I was in seventh grade...at the time, the earth came falling down around me."

Jim Houston

"I remember the competitive levels of my brothers," Houston said. "Lin was 17 years older than I was. Massillon was a hotbed for football, and Lin got us started playing. What it meant to us was a chance to get a college education at little to no cost. So we pursued it that way. All the tradition started there. I was in awe of my brothers' abilities as I was growing up."

Lin was an All-American at Ohio State and starred for Paul Brown's championship teams with the Browns. Brothers Jack and Walt both played college football at Purdue. Walt played in the NFL for the Washington Redskins.

Jim played mainly touch football as a youngster before trying out for the junior high team at Lorin Andrews. It was a heartbreaking experience.

"Roger Price was the head coach at Lorin Andrews Junior High when I tried out in seventh grade," Houston said. "Roger said, 'Jim, why don't you wait until next year to come out?' He said, 'Jim, you're not big enough yet, you're not fast enough.'

Houston as a high school junior in 1954.

"I don't know if he knew I'd grow up to be big like my brothers, who came along ahead of me. But he actually cut me. Absolutely. I was cut when I was in seventh grade. I guess it was good for me that he cut me like that. Actually it was. But at the time, the earth came falling down around me.

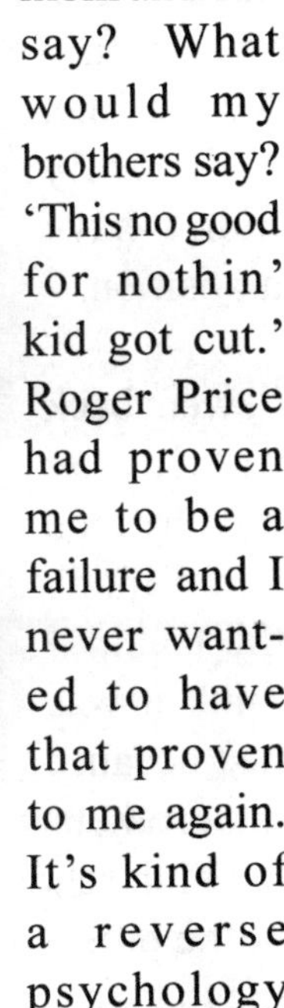

"I was so devastated about that. It was a very, bad, sick feeling. What would my friends say? What would my mom and dad say? What would my brothers say? 'This no good for nothin' kid got cut.' Roger Price had proven me to be a failure and I never wanted to have that proven to me again. It's kind of a reverse psychology thing. 'Put the kid down and he'll fight you back harder and harder every time.' I was determined I'd never get cut again.

"I went home and talked to my mom about it. She said, 'Don't worry about it, try next year.' My brothers said the same thing.

"I had tried out at running back and I was too slow, too small. I was too small for the line. So I really didn't have a position.

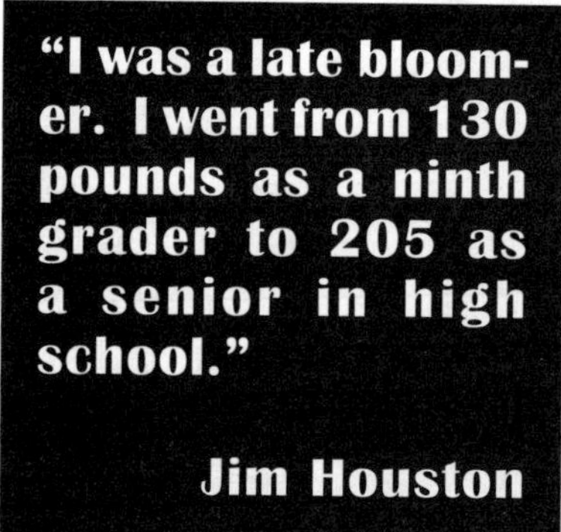

"I went back out in the eighth grade and I made the team. I think it was just because my brothers were playing at the high school and Lin was in the pros, so they allowed me to stay. I guess that was it. In the ninth grade, I had grown quite a bit and had the determination that I would never get cut again."

Despite his family pedigree, Houston didn't feel he was preordained to play football at Massillon.

"You know what, in seventh grade I didn't *like* to play football. You get hurt. In those days the seventh, eighth and ninth graders were all together, so you had a wide range of physical development. It was one team. I weighed 130 pounds as a ninth grader. I was a late bloomer. I went from 130 pounds as a ninth grader to 205 as a senior in high school, to 220 in college to 240 in the pros.

"When I was a child, my brother Lin was playing for

the Browns. His wife would take me up to the games. That's when I got interested in pursuing it. I could watch the pros play, I could meet all the pros. Going into the Browns' locker room. Watching all of those guys running around on the field. I wondered, 'Will I *ever* be able to do that? Will I ever have the opportunity to be there? What will it take to get there?'"

Houston was a two-time All-American and captain at Ohio State.

By ninth grade, while he hadn't added a lot of weight, he had grown taller. "I played offensive tackle," he said, "That was more to my liking because I knew what to do. My body action was good. I could block guys that were a lot heavier than I was and keep 'em out of the path of the back."

Houston continued to blossom in high school, where he gained notoriety as an offensive and defensive end.

"Being named All-Ohio was exciting. I really found out how important Massillon was. The other kids on the all-star team had a strong respect for Massillon. We all want respect in business and life."

Houston earned the respect of his teammates at Ohio State and was elected captain his senior year.

"I assumed they were going to name a couple of captains," he said.. "They voted to name one captain and I was it. I was very happy about that. And I made All-American as a junior—that was my *real* goal because my brother Lin had made All-American as a junior in 1942 before he went into the service."

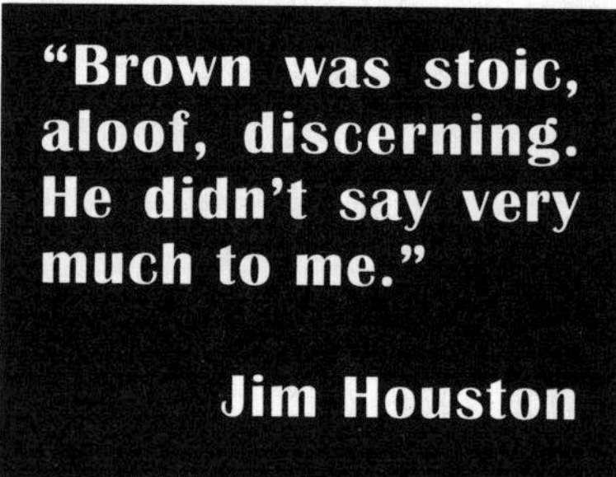

Houston is a member of the exclusive Massillon-Ohio State-Cleveland Browns family. He sees a common thread between the three organizations.

"One thing that's remarkable to me is the dedication of the Massillon fans. And the dedication of the Ohio State fans. And the Browns fans. I've lived the part in Massillon, that of the rabid fan. And Ohio State—are there any more rabid fans than at Ohio State? And here, to have the luck to be able to play for the Browns after having watched them since I was nine years old. And to meet the great fans of the Browns from all over the world. It's just unbelievable the luck I've had my whole life."

Those who know Jim Houston will tell you that his remarkable career wasn't just lucky. In Houston's case it took outstanding careers at Massillon and Ohio

State to put him in position to become the fifth player selected in the first round of the 1960 NFL draft by Paul Brown and the Cleveland Browns.

"There was a lot of hoopla going into the pros because I was drafted high. It was Jim Brown's fourth year. He was a nice guy. Me, I was a rookie, I kept my tail between my legs and kept my position. Played against and *with* a lot of fine athletes. I went from being cut in seventh grade to starting my rookie season in the pros."

Houston was one of the finest linebackers in the NFL from 1960-1972.

Despite being a high draft pick from his hometown, Houston didn't enjoy a close relationship with head coach Paul Brown.

"Brown was stoic, aloof, discerning. He didn't say very much to me," Houston said. "He communicated through his assistant coaches. He didn't have to say anything to you, he'd just look at you and you'd know you got your but in trouble. I remember one game, it was an exhibition game my rookie season, I've just gone in to play defensive end. San Francisco ran a sweep. The tackle I was playing against was future Hall of Famer Bob St. Clair. I moved out one position but he still hooked me. When we went off the field, you should have seen Paul Brown look at me. He looked at you like he could look right through you. He actually *did* look right through me. I felt bad. Kind of like that Roger Price feeling. He didn't say *anything*. Just looked at me like I was an idiot or something."

Through all of his successes on the football field, a lesson Houston learned from his playing days in Massillon always stuck with him.

"It was an attitude that we could always win," Houston said. "It didn't matter what the circumstances were, how many points we were down or anything. We could always do it. We had the same feeling at Ohio State. You don't give up. You *cannot* give up. You do your best all of the time. You do what you have to do to be successful. If you were an end, you had to do certain things to increase your capability against a tough opponent. You know you can beat anybody who isn't at the same standard that you are. But when the guy across the line from you is All-Ohio, you have to know your skills to the utmost degree, and you must be able to use them. You have to do it when you're out of breath and in the fourth quarter. That's the kind of thing that was instilled in us in Massillon. Just the attitude. 'We can do it.' Massillon had the Nike slogan before they did. 'Just do it guys. Just do it.' In Massillon it is understood that you go the extra mile and do what you can to be successful on that football team. Extra training, extra work, extra effort."

An amusing anecdote from

Houston's playing career came in the 1969 NFL championship game against Minnesota. The Vikings' quarterback, the rough-and-tumble Joe Kapp, was running in the open field.

"He was 6'4", about 215 pounds," Houston said. "He tried to hurdle me and I caught him with my arm. Well, he did a 360-degree turn in the air. The shock of his knee hitting my helmet knocked me out and I went right into the ground. You know, I'm a 255-pound linebacker being knocked out by a quarterback. It doesn't matter how big the quarterback was. Here I am, asleep in a championship game on national television. Talk about getting cut in the seventh grade, this was just as embarrassing.

"You have to do it when you're out of breath and in the fourth quarter."

Jim Houston

"I was at the Pro Bowl with Joe after the season. He and I were standing right next to each other, taking a shower, and he says, 'Hey Jim, boy oh boy, your head really hurt my knee.

"Five years after I'd retired, I flew into the Washington airport to watch an exhibition game for the Browns. There were six cabbies standing outside the airport. They were talking about the exhibition season. I said, 'Hey, do one of you guys want to take me to Baltimore?' One of the younger guys stepped out of the crowd and said, 'Yeah, I'll take you. And aren't you Jim Houston?' I thought, 'Oh, they do still remember me, don't they?' He said, 'You're the guy Joe Kapp knocked out.' That's exactly what he said."

Houston cares about how Massillon fans remember him. "I'd like to be remembered as a good, dedicated football player and as a good person," he said, "and I think I am. How can a guy have the luck that I had. Going from the time I was nine years old, watching the Cleveland Browns play, seeing Massillon and being caught up in Massillon and having enough success in the program to go on to a great university and to have the success there.

"Then to go to the Browns, the team I loved, I met those guys when I was young—very young. And now to have the luck to play with the same team. It was unbelievable.

"Just unbelievable luck in my whole life. I've been blessed with the experience and the capability of responding to those challenges which they always gave you at Massillon, Ohio State and the Browns.

"To go from looking over the fence or looking from the seat when you were a young kid to the fact that you were there, too.

"It was kind of unbelievable and it is luck. How many guys make it to the pros out of all the kids who start playing football? Not too many."

JIM HOUSTON

The name Jim Houston is a famous one in Massillon Tigers history. Even casual fans know of Jim Houston, the All-Ohioan, All-American and All-Pro. But people who saw the *other* Jim Houston play—often referred to as the *black* Jim Houston—will tell you that he didn't take a back seat to his famous namesake.

Jim Houston was one of the greatest Tiger linebackers.

"You could throw Jim Houston up in the air, twist him around, and he'd land on his feet running," said Leo Strang, Houston's head coach at Massillon. "He played an offensive guard and linebacker for us. He was tough. He *hit* people."

Venerable Massillon assistant coach Nick Vrotsos had great respect for Houston.

"Jim's gotta be right up there with Chris Spielman and Paul Marks as a linebacker," Vrotsos said, "He was very tough. He had a try-out with the Cleveland Browns. He was about 6'1", 210 pounds, quicker than a cat. He could strike a blow like nobody else could strike a blow. He had a nose for the ball just like Spielman. We've had some great linebackers. He ranks right up there in the top five."

Marty Gugov was a running back who benefited from Houston's blocking.

"He had a heckuva physique," Gugov said. "He was very, very agile. Very quick. He was mean. You always wanted him on your side."

Hase McKey, a two-time All-Ohioan at Massillon (1958-59) played next to Houston on the offensive line.

"Me and Jim Houston, we had a thing going," McKey said. "We would go up on the line and when they'd throw up some kind of funny defense I'd look at Jim and say, 'You take that Cat and I'll take this Cat. They couldn't figure out what we were talking about.

This Warren defender probably still feels this block by Jim Houston in 1959.

That's the way we'd do it. We called it Cat Blocking. Leo ended up calling it Cat Blocking. At banquets he'd say, 'We've got a new kind of blocking. Cat blocking.'"

LEO STRANG

Leo Strang was hardworking, creative, inventive and colorful. But most of all he was loquacious. "Loquacious Leo." "I am a complete extrovert," Strang said in describing himself. "I guess I was a colorful coach. We always did things a little bit different."

Like white shoes. "The Massillon football team was the first team in the United States to wear white shoes," Strang said. "Joe Namath and Billy 'White Shoes' Johnson copied that."

Leo Strang won three state titles and two national titles at Massillon.

A college art student, Strang's uniforms were his canvas. His uniforms had tiger stripes long before former Massillon coach Paul Brown made waves in the NFL by putting tiger stripes on the Cincinnati Bengals' uniforms.

But it was Strang's idea to put decals on helmets that had the most universal appeal of all.

"At that time Chevrolet had billboards with a leaping tiger on them," Strang said. "I told them we wanted to use the emblem on our helmets. They said they'd get back to us.

"A couple days later they sent a letter saying we could use that tiger. I found an outfit in Pennsylvania that made decals—not for helmets, but for other purposes. He told me he could make it, that he'd get to work on it right away, as long as I gave him permission to do others...bears, lions, a lot of other things. Foolishly, I agreed. I should be getting a nickel for every decal on every helmet in the United States right now."

"I should be getting a nickel for every decal on every helmet in the United States right now."

Leo Strang

Strang's decal ideas didn't stop there.

"We started the helmet award system that year, too. We started putting stars on the helmets. That was a result of a grading system we set up. We put the star right on the end of the grade sheet. And then later we put a star on the helmet." Of course the helmet award system has spread across the nation, too.

The players responded to Strang's flashy style.

"Leo was one of the best coaches I had," said David Whitfield, who went on to captain Ohio State under the legendary Woody Hayes.

"Leo was able to talk to the guys and the guys could talk to Leo. We just loved his style. The way he used to like the guys to dress. Everybody loved that. Not only did you play good, you looked good doin' it. Everybody wanted to go out and play. Because on Friday night, those guys *looked* good. And you know what, they *played* good.

"Then Earle Bruce came in and changed that around—took everything away that was flashy—that color. All that beauty and everything. He went to that white and whatever. No name on the back. Do you know how important it was for a guy to go out there and get a great hit and for people to say, 'Who was that?'—and to look on the back of his jersey and see '*Whitfield.*' Do you know how much that makes you want to go out and do that again? Well, Bruce came in there thinkin', 'No, we should all be a team. Team oriented, we shouldn't be standin' out.' No, that was wrong.

"Strang had the right idea...showmanship."

David Whitfield

"In Massillon always, growin' up, everybody knew who you were from what you did. You were standin' out. If you screwed up you stood out. If you did good you stood out. That's what you played for—to be recognized. There's fans out there that don't hear nothin' except what that announcer says. The announcer doesn't always call out the right name. If your name's on that jersey you're getting credit for what you do. Somebody's lookin'.

"When he took away the guy's ability to go out and show what he can do, to be known to the fans, I thought that was bad. I understood what his purpose was, but I didn't go along with it. Strang had the right idea. He loved that showmanship. He felt that if they look good, they're going to play good. Give them something to live up to. To be vanilla? No. Everybody blends in together."

Strang's Tigers traveled in style.

"We had a lot of different uniforms and combinations," Strang said. "We had the orange pants, the white pants and the black pants. And we had the white shoes and the black shoes. And we had the orange jerseys, the white jerseys and the black jerseys. So we could change 'em around to any combination. Got a lot of attention out of the uniforms. We got a lot of attention about how a kid dressed on a trip. On game day, they all had blazers, tiger ties and white shirts."

Appearance was important to Strang. He felt strongly about the mental affect that appearance had on his team—and on their opponents.

"That's part of our organization," Strang said. "We even organized our team photos. We had those kids placed way before we took the photo."

Strang was concerned about how his players looked on and off of the field.

"We took the 1959 team down to Ohio State and they went in with their blazers, jacket, black pants, white shirt and we sat in the upper part of the end zone. I got phone calls and letters from Ohio State fans who were sitting around them and saw them come in. Nothing but praise for how they looked, how they acted and behaved."

But looks aren't everything. The best looking, best dressed team is not worth much if they're not winning. Strang's teams were among the winningest in Massillon history. His 1959 team is considered one of Massillon's best ever. And during his run of three straight state titles from 1959-61 the Tigers won 31 games and lost just once. The Tigers outscored their opponents 1,111 to 203 during that span. The 1959 and 1961 teams were also national champions.

During Strang's run of three straight state titles from 1959-61 the Tigers won 31 games and lost just once.

His 1959 Tigers were a combination of talented skill athletes and hardnosed blue collar players. All-Ohio quarterback Joe Sparma was special.

"I don't think there's any

doubt that Sparma could have been a great pro football player," Strang said.

Art Hastings, Massillon's all-time leading rusher, was the star running back on the 1959 team, rushing for 1,245 yards at an amazing 10.6 yards a carry average—and he was just a junior.

Leo Strang gets carried off the field after beating Canton McKinley in 1963.

When asked to name the most hard-nosed player from the 1959 squad, Strang rattled off a half dozen candidates.

"We had a number of hard-nosed players on that team. Jim Houston, not *the* Jim Houston who starred for the Cleveland Browns. This is another Jim Houston. He played a guard and defensive end for us. He was tough. He hit people. Of course there was Hase McKey, he was All-Ohio. Jim Wood was another guy that'd knock the livin' jock off of you. Boy could he block. He had no fear at all. None. Virgil Buckuts, Lawson White, Gary Wells—they would hit you. The hardnose award would probably be between those guys."

The success of the 1959 team brought nationwide fame to Strang. Eastman Kodak selected him to be part of a prestigious coaching clinic that traveled across the United States. Strang had no illusions as to why he was selected to the panel. "It was because of Massillon, because of that 1959 team, that national championship team," he said. "I was the only high school coach."

Strang traveled with some of the legends of college football: Paul "Bear" Bryant of Alabama, Bud Wilkinson of Oklahoma, Duffy Daugherty of Michigan State and Jake Gaither of Florida A&M.

"We used to have some great times at those coaches' clinics," Strang said. "I'd get in poker games with Bear Bryant. Bear thought he was a pretty good poker player, but he couldn't play at all."

Strang said there really wasn't a common thread among the famous coaches he traveled with. "They were all as different as day and night. Bud Wilkinson was a sophisticated, thinking coach. Bear Bryant was a tough, no nonsense coach. Duffy Daugherty was a coach every player loved. Just an absolutely great guy."

Strang got a big surprise during a clinic in Texas. "The strange thing about it," he said, "I always got the most attention and the most questions and everything else. The reason for that was because I was from Massillon—it wasn't me. They just wanted to know about Massillon, how we did things in Massillon. The Texas High School Coaches' Convention I spoke at had 2,700 high school coaches.

We would take the morning session and the Florida college coaches would take the afternoon sessions. We outdrew 'em at every session. I got letters for years and years after that asking me about different things. They were totally fascinated with the Massillon program."

People's fascination with Massillon's program followed Strang throughout his life. Strang recalled, just months before his death, phone calls he'd received from reporters about Massillon.

"I still get questions today asking how Massillon can maintain good teams year after year after year," Strang said in 1996. "I tell 'em today a good team in Massillon is 9-1 or 8-2. When I was coaching there, that wasn't a good team. You had to be *undefeated.*"

"I tell 'em today that a good team in Massillon is 9-1 or 8-2. When I was coaching there, that wasn't a good team. You had to be UNDEFEATED.

Leo Strang

"Things have changed. I understand things have changed at other schools, too. Paul Brown and Chuck Mather set such a high standard at Massillon. Mather was there six years and he's the only other coach to go 6-0 against McKinley (along with Strang). Mather was 57-3. But I tell him, 'Hey, I only lost three games in five years, too. Let's forget about that one in 1962 (when the Tigers went 6-5 under Strang in an injury-plagued campaign that saw 21 Tiger starters go down with injuries)."

Accepting the job at Massillon was a move that Strang thought he might not have been wise to make—especially when he first saw his prospective squad.

"The most shocking memory was the team meeting," Strang said, "standing in the gym and watching the football players come in after school. Looking at them and how young they looked and how small they were in comparison with the kids I had at Cleveland Shaw. Most of the kids I had at Shaw were like Tom Matte, who played for the Colts. Tom was a running back, about 6', 210 pounds—we didn't have anybody like that at Massillon. I remember going home and telling my wife Betty, 'Boy, I'll tell ya, I made a big mistake. These kids don't look as mature, as big, as the kids at Shaw High School."

"They were dead serious and wanted to do what you told them to do.

Leo Strang

What Strang couldn't see in that initial meeting was the size of the heart and the determination and commitment of the Massillon players.

"When I got them out on the football field and started working with them, I could see the difference," Strang said. "I could just tell. They were dead serious and wanted to do what you told them to do."

The inherent power that comes with the head coaching job at Massillon and the creativity that Strang possessed was a mix made in heaven. Strang's ideas were endless—and his freedom to create was unencumbered.

"Having all the facilities we needed at Massillon. Being the athletic director and being able to run the show...there was nobody I had to go to say we want to do this or do that," Strang said. "I'd just say, We're gonna do this, we're gonna do that.'"

This freedom and Strang's inventiveness spawned a rather interesting "first" for Massillon.

Leo Strang, 1958.

"We went to the *Akron Beacon Journal* and bought an old camera—one of those big box cameras. We took it apart and put a Polaroid back on it. Then we put a zoom lens on it. We cut a hole in the scoreboard at the end of the field. I had a phone connected to the press box and a phone connected to the scoreboard. As soon as we'd get information—maybe it was a spread formation—I'd say, 'Take,' and they'd snap a picture of it. Immediately they'd put the picture in a little can and with a string lower it to the sideline. My youngest son would be waiting for it. He'd grab that photo and it would be developing as he ran up the sideline. Before the next play, we knew exactly how they were defending us. We had a Polaroid picture of it. We knew exactly where they were. Whereas before this, looking down, we weren't sure whether the guy was cheatin' ya on the inside or cheatin' ya on the outside."

Strang had a great relationship with the Massillon fans. After a loss to Warren Harding, he wasn't sure how the crowd at the Booster Club meeting would react. In fitting with his personality, he did something creative.

"I dressed up with an old slouched hat, dark glasses, a big beard and some sloppy clothes."

Leo Strang

"We had won 20 games in a row and we got beat at Warren (19-18 in 1960). I knew there would be some tough questions at the Booster Club meeting on Monday night when I showed the films. So I dressed up with an old slouched hat, dark glasses, a big beard and some sloppy clothes. I went in and sat down with the rest of the boosters down in front. Nobody recognized me. Nooo. No way they could recognize me with the outfit I had on. Nick Coso was up there and did the preliminary stuff and got everything started. I could hear the people around me saying,

'Where's Strang, anybody seen Strang? Where's he at? I bet he doesn't show up.'

"Nick Coso says, 'Coach Strang put me in charge of getting things started tonight. The first thing we'll do is show the movies then we'll entertain questions and go over our scouting report.' Coso showed the movie. Then they turned the lights on in the auditorium and I got up and started walking down the aisle and took off my beard and glasses. Everybody just starts roaring. That took the edge off of it and I didn't get those hard questions you get when you lose."

Marty Gugov, Virgil Bukuts, Leo Strang and George Demis "rescue" a hanging Tiger following Massillon's win over Alliance in 1960.

Strang was always looking for ways to motivate his players. Sometimes his tricks backfired.

"One time before the McKinley game we were trying to get the kids fired up by asking a booster group called 'Reese's Raiders' to act like they were from the other team spying on practice. They got up in the trees up in the park behind the practice field. At a given time an assistant coach yelled, 'Look up there!' We started up the hill and they got out of the trees and got in their car and sped away. The kids all thought it was Canton

McKinley spying on us. The only difficulty is some of the other people sitting out there watching practice weren't in on the deal. So they jumped in cars and started chasing these guys from our booster group out of town at about 80 miles an hour. They went around one of those curves and ran off the road and into a ditch and smashed up their car. So the best laid plans..."

Coaching at Massillon was the highlight of Strang's career.

"The best pay. The best treatment. Best side benefits—I can't tell you some of them. One of them was the new automobile every year. All of the theatres for nothing, a pass to the swimming club, the Elm's Country Club, the Massillon Club. We were invited to all kinds of things. I know I took a cut to come to Kent State."

The paycheck wasn't the only thing Strang missed when he arrived at Kent State.

"When I left Massillon and took the Kent State job, our practice fields were terrible in comparison to Massillon's practice fields. I didn't get a new car ever year like I did at Massillon, even though I was running all over the country recruiting. We couldn't put three men in the spotting booth at Kent State. We didn't have the room for it—and we didn't have the three men to put there because our coaching staff was much smaller than at Massillon. Now I'm talking about going from a top-notch high school program to a major college program.

"I didn't have the administration that knew what they were doing. The people in Massillon are a great advantage in that they know the game and support the team.

"The people of Massillon, the fans, are a great help. If I needed to have a banquet, I could get on the phone and get the money in nothin' flat at Massillon. At Kent State you couldn't do that. So the atmosphere was tremendously different. Massillon is a football town.

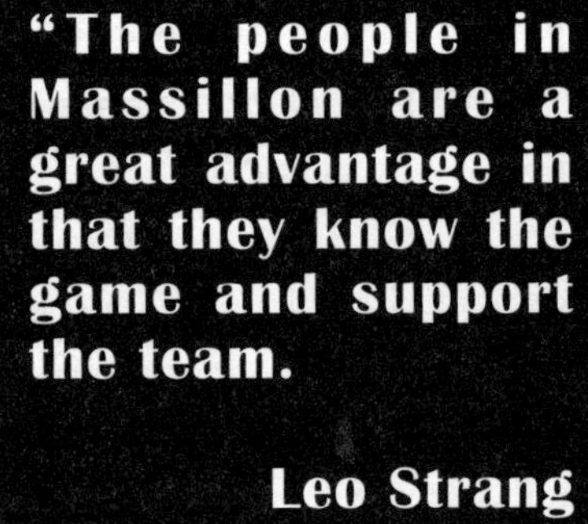

"When I came to Kent we played Xavier the first football game. It was before school started and we upset them. We had no cheerleaders. We had no band. I was really upset. I went into the athletic director's office the next morning and I told the director, 'I can't be a part of this. If this doesn't change, I can't be a part of it. Have you ever seen a Massillon football game?' He said, 'No, I haven't.' I said, 'Well, when you approach the Massillon stadium—and even before you approach it, you see the flags waving downtown. And as you get near the stadium you see the search lights going around. You hear the calliope playing, you hear the hawkers hawking, you see the tiger in his cage. Then rockets go off at 'The Star Spangled Banner.' And the Tiger roaring from the scoreboard. You know that something is happening. You get the feel. I never got that feel here at all. We had none of that. We had no hawkers hawking, no bombs bursting in mid-air.'

"It was just like I had taken a step backward in time. I think that's one of the things that makes the Tigers football team so much better than they should be. Because they get that adrenaline running, they get the atmosphere and the feel. The crowd gets the atmosphere and the feel."

Strang was 19-21 in four years at Kent State (1964-67).

"He came within just a small amount of making it real big at Kent State," said Ducky Schroeder, a longtime Massillon assistant who served under Strang. "I asked Don James why he took the Kent State job in 1971. He said, 'I watched the movies and Leo Strang came within one inch of making it real big at Kent State University, and that was the reason I was interested in taking that job."

James parlayed his success at Kent State (25-19-1) into the head coaching job at the University of Washington, where he became a college coaching legend.

Strang always looked back on his career at Massillon with fondness.

"I'd like to be remembered for having some of the best teams ever at Massillon. The old saying, 'Once a Tiger always a Tiger' is true.

"There was no place that was as great to my wife and I since leaving Massillon. And that is very much appreciated by both of us."

ART HASTINGS

The lofty title of "Massillon's All-Time Leading Rusher" has been resting next to the name of Art Hastings since 1960. Impressive? Especially when you consider Massillon's glorious history of star running backs. All counted, 44 Massillon running backs have been named All-Ohio. But only Hastings, with 3,090 yards, has eclipsed the 3,000 yards plateau.

Art Hastings, Massillon's all-time leading rusher.

"I had great runners, but I don't know that I ever had any better than Art Hastings," said Massillon head coach Leo Strang. Strang coached Tom Matte at Cleveland Shaw High School. Matte starred at Ohio State and became a Pro Bowl running back with the Baltimore Colts. Matte ran for 116 yards in Super Bowl III.

"Hastings looked like his hips went out of joint,"

Strang said. "He was like trying to catch a dog in the middle of an open field."

Strang remembers joking about Hastings' skills at a Booster Club meeting.

"I remember telling the Booster Club one night, 'I'd like you to look at this play.' We were on our 40-yard line. We ran a belly pitch-out to Hastings. Well, the defensive end didn't do what we thought he'd do. He came straight across. And about the time Art caught the ball, he hit Art. Almost knocked him down. Art went down to one hand, spun around and he just got straightened out when the linebacker hit him, then the cornerback hit him. Then another linebacker hit him and the safety hit him. He cut back inside the safety man and went 60 yards for a touchdown. I shut off the projector and I told the Booster Club, 'Gentlemen, I'm gonna tell you some thing about that play. That's great coaching."

Only Art Hastings, with 3,090 yards has eclipsed the 3,000-yards plateau at Massillon.

Strang feels Hastings deserves a spot among Massillon's finest running backs.

"Art Hastings was just a great, great runner," Strang said. "Art had great moves. I don't know if Massillon ever had anyone as great before or since. Maybe Homer Floyd (1952-54) and Ivory Benjamin (1955-57). They were in an elite class."

Dave Null, who quarterbacked the 1960 team, appreciated Hastings' skills. "Art was the premier back of that era," Null said. "He wasn't real big. He was about 5'9", 165, but very, very strong, with great balance. Art had the ability to run over people, but he also had the ability, and was shifty enough, to go around people. Art was the kind of guy who didn't appear to be a blazer, but when he was on the football field with his equipment on, he appeared to be extra fast. Art Hastings was what I would call a 'gamer.' Art would probably be one of the best backs we ever had. For his size he had a lot of strength and was able to take a lot of hits."

Art Hastings making a move, 1959.

As great as Hastings' accomplishments were at Massillon, they could have been even greater had he been given the opportunity to start in 1958.

"I told Leo, 'I have better backs on my sophomore team than you have on the varsity,'" said Nick Vrotsos, a longtime Massillon assistant who spent his first two years coaching the sophomore team. Vrotsos was referring to Hastings and Marty Gugov, who captained the 1960 Tigers. Vrotsos never lost a game as sophomore coach. He did, however, lose this argument with Strang.

"Leo said, 'You know Nick, for every sophomore you play on the varsity, you lose a game.' I said, 'Uh uh, Leo. Art Hastings is older than your starting tailback, which was Jim Snively." Vrotsos feels Strang made a mistake. "He went 8-1-1 and it could have been 10-0 with Arthur Hastings," Vrotsos said with a laugh. "Sometimes coaches make mistakes, you know."

There was no mistaking Art Hastings' talent as a running back. "Picture a bowlegged guy at running back— strength, quickness, speed, toughness," Vrotsos said, "You couldn't put him on the ground. He didn't have blinding speed. He'd take a tackler on, forearm him, hit him with a shoulder, stiff arm him, knock him off. He was sort of like Jimmy Brown when he had the ball. You couldn't bring him down. It took more than one guy to bring him down. He was a power guy with quickness."

Would Vrotsos rank Hastings as Massillon's greatest? "I'll tell you what," he said, "Art Hastings would be hard to beat. We've had some good ones. He's the greatest running back we had for a long while. I'd rank him right up there. He was one of the best."

Running mate Gugov, a talented running back himself, had the utmost respect for Hastings.

"Art Hastings was by far, *by far,* the best back I ever saw," Gugov said. "He was fabulous, just a terrific athlete.

"Every time you hit him, you got this dead leg to hit. I tried to hit the heck out of him when we practiced. If you grabbed him you were all right, but you had to hang on. Even if you hit him in the waist, it didn't seem to help any. He was just a truly unique back. He was all muscle. He could run fast, he was very shifty, but he always gave you that deal with his leg that would make you miss. Either leg. He was shifty and he was determined. He just had the ability to run the football. We were really lucky to have him. He had three years to play. They let him play as a sophomore. And he truly deserved to be there. He never rubbed it in anyone's face. He was a good guy to us. We were friends."

Gugov first discovered Hastings' toughness when he noticed Hastings looking listless during practice. "We're in the early part of the season and Art's not wantin' to practice. I said, 'What's the matter with you? Why don't you want to practice?' He said 'Look at this leg man.' He had a spot on his leg that was probably four inches in diameter and it took over his whole calf. He said 'I don't know what's wrong with me, but something's wrong.' His leg got infected to the point where he had a red line from his crotch all the way down to his ankle. They got him some help and got that infection cleared up. That's how tough he was."

What was probably even tougher for Hastings was his home life. An abusive, alcoholic father made Hastings' life at home a battle for survival.

"I had no clue he was in as bad of shape home-wise as he was," Gugov said. "I never really knew that.

"He come from a real bad home life. His father was notoriously abusive with the family. He was a drinker and a lot of bad things happened as a result of that. Very abusive, very much so. His dad used to chase him around the house with a gun. It was awful. Art didn't bring that to school with him. Leo knew about it. We talked about it so I could give him a little hand occasionally."

But as bad as things were at home, Hastings was able to put it aside when he stepped on the football field. He rushed for 1,245 yards as a junior and 1,274 as a senior. "On Friday night he was just phenomenal," Gugov said.

"I don't know if Massillon ever had anyone as great."

Leo Strang

Hastings' struggles at home, and in school, helped to doom the future his athletic ability made seem so promising. "I tried to help him in class. If he'd only gotten good grades in class he could have gone anywhere in the country to school," Gugov said. "I tried to help him."

So instead of being recruited by schools like Ohio State and Michigan, Hastings landed at Morehead State University. He was never to realize the success he seemed to be destined for.

"I went to Art Hastings' funeral," Gugov said. "I was the only white guy there. I loved Art Hastings. You have choices to make in life, and Art made some bad choices. I hadn't talked to him in several years before he died. He had awful troubles with drinking. He got it honestly."

DAVID CANARY

David Canary is a quintessential hometown boy-makes-good story. An undersized over-achiever who becomes a football All-American and a multi-Emmy award-winning actor.

David Canary.

And through all the years of fortune and fame, Canary has stayed connected with his hometown—and its people—who relish the successes of their hometown heroes.

Through the years Canary has made a habit of returning home, whether it's for a theatre performance, a class reunion, or to visit his father. He acknowledges the importance of the values he learned while growing up in Massillon.

"The values were learned there," Canary said of Massillon. "In my business I meet a lot of people who have wealth, some of them are genuinely sophisticated, worldly people. They've been all over the world, they speak four languages. They've gone to Harvard, they've gone to the eastern establishment schools, they've gone to school in Paris. I meet people like this on a fairly regular basis. They talk to me and say, 'You're a nice guy.'

"That nice guy came from Massillon. If I was from somewhere else I would have been a different person. And I'm real glad it's the way it is. I think values and that common touch are something Massillon taught me. The people in Massillon are as good as anybody anywhere in the world. That's why I like it. I feel like David Canary from Massillon every day of my life.

"The values that were instilled in us in Massillon..." Canary reflected, "I couldn't possibly enjoy something that I felt I hadn't earned—and certainly not if I cheated to get it or bent the rules somehow. The values I learned in Massillon were that I want to earn something or I don't feel it is mine. And I think that's a good thing. I think that keeps the playing field level and the game interesting.

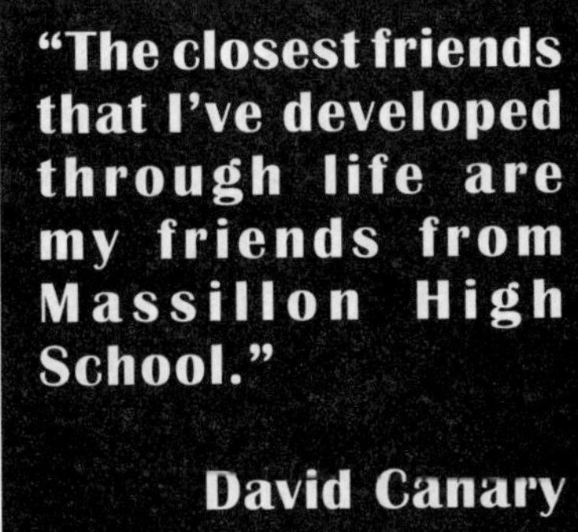

"My closest friends that I've developed through life are my friends from Massillon High School. I don't have those feelings about the University of Cincinnati, I haven't maintained any friends there.

"The fact that the town has something to rally behind,

something as clean and fair as football is. To have that be the rallying cry. That gets the people out and gets them together. It affects everything else in that school. Everyone else has a standard of excellence to which they aspire.

"The Massillon football team infects and invades the whole town. If there were not something like that team, it would be a different place to live. It affects so many kids at a very early age. That spirit is there. Everybody wants to be as good as they can be. I don't think there's anything at the school level that's quite as all-pervasive as an athletic program. In terms of the town and the school. It's in the papers. It's something that everybody can get behind and root for. If you lose, the world doesn't come to an end, but you don't *want* to do that. You can have a wonderful mathematics program, you can have the best math teachers in the state or country, but it doesn't have the same pizazz to it that a football team will. And for that reason it's good press. It's all pervasive, it's everywhere, it's good. I like it.

"It was always a tremendous challenge to me. I was always one of the smallest guys on the team..."

David Canary

"I like going back. If I say 'home', I'm usually talking about Massillon. I have a very, very strong feeling about Massillon. A lot of people do."

Canary first gained notoriety while playing football for the Massillon Tigers, but it's his work as an actor that has brought him nationwide fame. Canary's credits include Broadway theatre, Hollywood movie roles, a starring role in the legendary western TV series *Bonanza*, and his signature dual roles of Adam and Stuart Chandler in the soap opera *All My Children*. Canary has won six Emmy awards and 16 Emmy award nominations as Outstanding Lead Actor.

David Canary, 1950.

Surprisingly, Canary's success on the gridiron seems rooted in insecurity. He describes himself as an "undersized" and "slow" football player. But his gridiron achievements offer a more flattering biography. He was an All-Ohio end in high school and a scholastic All-American end at the University of Cincinnati.

At Massillon, Canary and Jim Houston were arguably the greatest defensive end tandem in school history.

"That's what they've said," Jim Houston said with a laugh. "Dave and I, we took a lot of pride. I was a little bigger than he was, I weighed 205, but boy he was scrappy. He played defense very well and he could catch the ball. He was smart—knew what to do."

Ducky Schroeder, a legendary Massillon assistant, coached Canary and Houston, who were bookend All-Ohio ends in 1955. "That was really great," Schroeder said. "Jim Houston was an All-American at Ohio State and a famous Cleveland Brown. And David Canary, every coach he ever played for told me he was the hardest hitter they ever saw. He was a great guy to have on a football team. I don't think there ever was a high school team who had two better ends. Not only great players, but they were great people, too. I don't think it took too much coaching with them. I could make up jokes for the banquet circuit while I was coaching those two."

> **"If you just try hard enough, you try harder every moment, you'll make it. You'll squeak through."**
>
> **David Canary**

Becoming successful in football was hard work for Canary, who stood 5'10 and weighed 145 pounds in high school. "It was always a tremendous challenge to me," he said. "I was always one of the smallest guys on the team no matter where I was. In high school, I think Dick Roan was about my size, he was a guard, and John James was smaller than I was, he was the quarterback. But in college, forget it, I was the smallest guy on the team, on offense or defense—*including* the quarterback.

"You've gotta work harder. I had to try harder because I was a little runt. Fear. I wanted to make that team. My dad, God love him, was always telling me he was proud of me. I wanted to make him even prouder. And my mom...I just couldn't stand the idea of either not being out there or not being first string in whatever I was playing. And when you're as small and as little as I was, you've *gotta* try harder. I sometimes joke—and it is a joke—that when you're coming up through the grades in Massillon, you either play football or you're just like out of it. There was only one choice—you tried to play football. At least you *tried*.

A student trainer fixes a cleat on Canary's shoe. Note the mask on Canary's helmet.

"The first time that head coach Chuck Mather sent me into the game I couldn't quite imagine that I would be good enough to play out there with those guys the next two years. I was a sophomore. I remember he turned around and said loudly 'Canary.' I said, 'Huh?' He said, *'Get in there.'* I remember they were all so much bigger and faster and *olde*r than me. It was really a frightening moment. That vivid, vivid memory—and the magnitude of it I guess, more than fear, the *magnitude* of it. I was stepping into my manhood to *dare* to go out on the field with these guys.

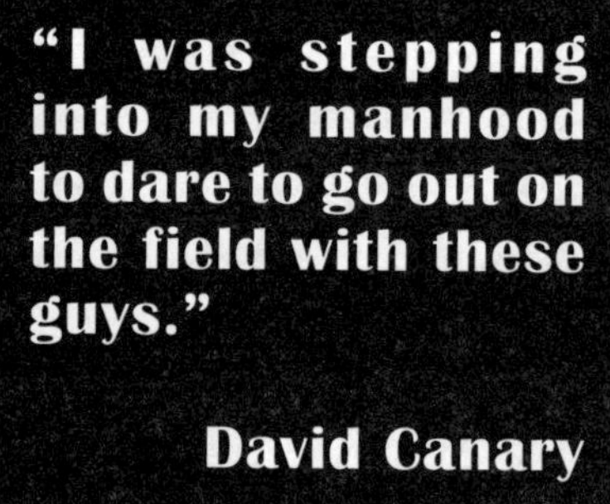

"It was just a goal that almost seemed unattainable. I've had dreams for years—I don't have them much anymore. The dream generally is that I can't run fast enough. That was the curse. I could have been a *real* good football player if I'd have been faster. I wasn't pokey slow. By halfback standards—and for as small as I was—I wasn't very fast. They used to tease me in junior high school that I ran too long in the same place. That was kind of true. In this dream that recurred over the years, I'd go out the day of the game, I'd be on the first team. They'd send me in. They'd snap the ball. The worst nightmare is then they're trying to throw me a pass. And I'm trying to...I'm just running in tar. I can't get those legs going fast enough. That was not good. It sort of haunted me for a long time.

"I'm not sure I ever felt I was good enough. I just thought if I just keep moving fast enough and keep hitting as hard as I can, as long as the coach keeps sending me in I'm going to keep doing the job. A lot of actors have that feeling that they're going to get fired tomorrow. They can't quite see themselves objectively. A lot of insecurity. And a lot of us are insecure, in a lot of areas, if we're absolutely honest about it. But I would have been surprised, I guess, if in the middle of my senior year they suddenly said, 'Oh, you're not good enough, get off the field.' That would have been a surprise. Up until about then, I was struggling. There's something to be said for a certain perseverance and grit that can be gained by not feeling you're quite good enough. But if you just try hard enough, you try harder every moment, you'll make it. You'll squeak through. I felt I was squeakin' through."

Canary possessed another trait that helped him excel against bigger and faster opponents.

"David Canary might be the toughest kid I ever coached," said Tom Harp, Canary's coach during his junior and senior seasons at Massillon. "The hardest-nosed, toughest kid I ever coached. One night he blocked an extra point against Mansfield that preserved a 12-12 tie. He blocked it with his face. He ruptured a blood vessel in his eye. His eye was shut. He just kept right on goin'. He was solid as a rock and tough. Intelligent. Polite."

Homer Floyd was one of Massillon's all-time best running backs, winning All-Ohio honors in 1954. He was one year ahead of Canary at Massillon. Floyd recalls the punch Canary put behind his tackles, even as a youngster. "Dave Canary wasn't very large but he would hit you," Floyd said. "As a matter of fact, Dave hit me one time when I was in junior high school and I had bruised ribs for the rest of the season."

While football was his first love in high school, his interest in the arts was flourishing.

"I loved music, I loved the choir," Canary said. "I got to do the leads in the musicals that we did. Our senior class musical was *Brigadoon*. And I really liked it. I had great fun. But I remember being incredibly shy.

"I was in debate with Jim Dowd, who's a wonderful man. He's a minister up in Cleveland now. Jim was the brains of the outfit. I wasn't very good at debate. I did it because my older brother had done it. Jim usually did most of the research and most of the leg work. Then he would hand me some notes and I would get up and sort of perform. I was always more of a performer than a debater. Somehow the shyness didn't matter on the football field. You hit the guy harder than he hit you and he'd fall down—you didn't. It's pretty simple logistics.

"I remember the Struts and Frets was the drama group. It wasn't cool for the football players to be in the Struts and Frets—the drama club. That was sort of for strange people, I think. The little guys who couldn't make the football team. I'm sure we sort of thought that in those days. It was very cool for football players to be in the choir. It wasn't cool to be in the drama club, but being in the choir was a very butch thing to do.

"I really didn't think of myself in terms of being an actor until my senior year in college. I was taking voice lessons. I had done a musical. I remember they said, 'You sing well.' I said, 'Well, I hope I sing well, I sure can't act.' I remember saying that to somebody and meaning it at the time. But I did like it and I got much more involved in that in college.

"It turned upside down at that point. Football became secondary to me. And I started doing professional stock (theatre) when I was in college. I started wanting to play football less and less and less. As a matter of fact, I had a tough time getting through my senior year. I kept wanting to be off in New York somewhere doing my thing, and I was still playing football at 172 pounds. And I just *knew* that wasn't where my future was."

"I knew full well that I wanted to go to New York and be an actor. And I could. So I did."

David Canary

Despite being named All-American, Canary was surprised to be drafted into professional football by the Denver Broncos.

"It amazes me," Canary said, "I'm not putting myself down — I was a fairly good college player—but I don't know what they were thinkin'. I was 172 pounds. I wasn't a pass receiver. I don't know what they thought they were going to turn me into. It was the first year of the Denver Broncos, and they weren't winning in those days. And now I know why (laughs). But, by that time I knew full well that I wanted to go to New York and be an actor. And I could. So I did."

Canary spent two years in New York, landing jobs as a singer in off-Broadway chorus, then off-Broadway leads. After two years he got his first big break, an on-Broadway play starring Colleen Dewhurst and directed by Jose Quintero. But while the play was in production, Canary was drafted into the Army.

"That was not a happy day," he said. Canary was able to perform in the play before joining the Army, but it was terribly disappointing none-the-less.

"The show actually ended before I had to report," he said, "but with momentum like a Broadway show with these people—these were the best people in the business—and with credit like that, it was momentum that certainly could have helped me in my career. But I went off and handed out tennis shoes for two years for the U.S. Government. A total waste of their time and mine as far as I could tell."

Canary did have a touching experience during his time in the service. It reminded him of a story line from the epic WWII movie *Battle Cry*.

"Well, I'd been drafted, I wasn't a happy pussy cat," he said. "I was on my way down to Fort Knox to basic training. On the train I sat next to this young kid. I don't think he knew who I was because I hadn't been in television at that point. We got to talkin', I was about 25 and he was about 17. And we talked. He had enlisted and he was just ecstatic. I just liked the kid—he was the kid from *Battle Cry*. He was *that* story. And he couldn't wait to get into the Army. We were in basic training, and we all had to jump into a fox hole with the sergeant and pull the pin out of a grenade. They'd given us some training of course, first. You'd pull the pin, you'd count, then you'd throw the grenade out of the hole. I did it, everybody did it. Well, his exploded in his hand and it killed him instantly, and badly injured the sergeant. I went over to the church, over to the chapel, usually, on Sunday mornings. And the pastor approached me. He heard that I was a singer and he wondered if I would mind doing a memorial service for this young soldier. I had heard that a young kid had been killed, but I didn't know who he was at that point—until I got to the service and saw his picture. I hadn't even remembered his name, we had just talked about stuff. And I realized it was this kid—it was this *Battle Cry* thing all over again. And it just broke my heart. And to this day I don't remember his name, but I'll never forget his face."

"I auditioned, talked to the director, and got the part. So that was good."

David Canary

After leaving the Army, things started happening for Canary. A big break came when he appeared in the movie *Hombre*.

"I got *Hombre* basically

because I met the director, Martin Ritt. It was a Paul Newman film, of course. I was offered this role of Lamar Dean, which was very much a secondary role to Richard Boone's role, who was the head bad guy. And Lamar Dean, basically, gets killed in the first reel. There were a few nice scenes. I auditioned, talked to the director, and got the part. So that was good. It was basically footage from that which got me the audition for *Bonanza* and led to me getting the role that I'm best remembered for."

David Canary joined *Bonanza,* one of the first color television shows, in 1967, after Pernell Roberts left the show. Canary played the role of Candy Canaday, the Ponderosa's ranch foreman. Candy was treated like one of the Cartwright sons.

Canary recalled, "I ended up with a new Corvette every year while I was there. That was Michael Landon's doin'. I would say I was there four years, that's about 120 shows. I probably did 90 of 'em."

Bonanza was the second-longest running western in television history. It was also the second-most popular television western. Canary's work on *Bonanza* was routinely viewed by television audiences of over 15 million.

Only *Gunsmoke* tops *Bonanza* in both categories. Interestingly, Canary also appeared in two episodes of *Gunsmoke* in the role of George McClaney.

Canary remembers, "I thought James Whitmore was a wonderful man. He came back and appeared on the set of an episode with a whole bunch of kids, about half black/half white. And I went over and he introduced me to them. He was teaching an acting course down in Venice, which is kind of a ghetto, sort of an artsy colony slash ghetto. Not an all black, but mostly black area of Los Angeles. He taught an acting class to these kids. I said, 'Could I help in some way?' And he said 'Sure you can, come on.' So for about a year and a half I was down there with James Whitmore trying to teach acting. I learned more than I taught, certainly. You learn how little you know sometimes. But, I had tremendous respect for James Whitmore. He's a wonderful man, a wonderful actor."

"I ended up with a new Corvette every year I was on Bonanza. That was Michael Landon's doin'."

David Canary

Canary also played a role in the wildly popular prime time series *Peyton Place*.

"I wasn't happy in LA. I didn't like the business out there, I didn't like the town. So, after about 10 years of it I worked up the courage to come back to New York. New York is real to me. L.A. is La La Land. They don't call it 'La La Land' for nothin'. I liked a lot of the actors I met out there. But basically, the day to day existence is a fantasy. You're building on a fantasy, or trying to. On appearances, on image. And your image determines how much you are worth. Dollars and cents. What I wanted to do was to be an actor. I totally lost track of why I wanted to be an actor when I was in L.A. And that's why I wanted to come back to New York."

Canary found the soap opera world and living in New York much more to his liking. But that wasn't his original plan.

"I came back to New York not wanting to do soap opera," Canary said. "I wanted to do theatre. And I did. I did about five years of regional theatre. I got poor as a church mouse. But I got some of the best training and experience. What I know about acting I learned during those five years. I did Shakespeare, Cherkov and a lot of it. I did plays, I did musicals, stretched all aspects of my being. I explored a lot of things and learned an awful lot about acting.

"I kind of changed my mind about soap operas because I was asked to do a short skit on *The Doctors*. It was a daytime soap opera. I was playing a guy named Farwind. Farwind was sort of a Charles Manson figure. I had a wig and a robe, my hair came down to my shoulders. I came into this hospital and there was this very young girl in there who was one of my chosen pupils and I was chanting and carrying on like a nut. I was a total imposter. And I ended up taking over the hospital, holding people hostage. Killed a few. Just an awful, evil evil man. I had a ball. I had such a good time. They all seemed to like what I was doin', they gave me free rein. There was this one scene where I was walking through this group of people, these hostages in a room. Of course I had my gun in my hand and I was just being as nasty as I could possibly be to these poor frightened people. Of course they usually block you to within an inch of your life because of the television camera angles and stuff. Well, this director said, 'Just go. We have three cameras here. We'll follow you.' I've never had anyone say that to me. 'Just go, live it up, have a good time.' I was carrying on. Well, I had such a good time.

"A year later I had another hole in my schedule, and they asked me to come back. I dressed up in a three-piece suit and a briefcase. And I do the same kind of stuff. The second time is when I took the people hostage. Again, I worked about six weeks doing this and I had a great time. I said, 'I'm an actor and this is like doing a big improv. It's great fun.'

"Bonanza was one of the first color television shows."

David Canary

"Sometime later I had a real bad experience trying to do a musical. I hated the director. These things don't happen to me. I always have a wonderful time when I go out on a regional. I went out and did *Man Of La Mancha,* and this director was a monster. Part of it was my fault, I was having trouble, I was flatting a little bit, and so it was a very unpleasant experience. So somebody hit me to come do something on *Another World.* A contract player. That means you sign for a couple of years.

You don't just go in for a few weeks. It's a serious move. So I decided to do it. I was there for a year and four months and I got fired, I got written out. It was the first time I'd got fired in my life—and the last time. So I went out and I did five plays in nine months.

"Then I got an audition for *All My Children* in 1983. I don't regret it at all. I sometimes say it's hack work, and I mean that in the best sense, if there can be a good sense to that. It's very quick, it's done for the money, it's mass entertainment, it's melodrama. But for the actors to take these scenes...some of them are well-written some of them are pretty terribly-written, they keep churning it out every day...and make something out of them, to look for something in there. 'Oh that's good. What if we did this, that would change the whole angle of the scene.' To work with other good actors trying to make these things work. That's the craft. That keeps me happy. I'm working with real good people. We have good actors working hard to make the best show they can. I've worked with many good actors on the show. It pays very well. I don't have to audition for stuff (laughs). I don't have to go on the road. I get to stay home with my family, of course, except when I'm working. I don't have to travel a lot. It's worked out well for me. I've won six Emmy awards. I've been nominated about 16 times. It's just been fabulous to me. No complaints."

Art Hastings

Massillon's All-Ohioans

Art Hastings
1960
Lawson White
1960
Ken Ivan
1961
Charlie Brown
1961
Larry Strobel
1961
Ben Bradley
1962
Bill Blunt
1963
Larry Larsuel
1963
Will Perry
1963
John Muhlbach
1964
Larry Larsuel
1964
Tom Whitfield
1964
Paul Marks
1965
David Whitfield
1965
Will Foster
1966
Bill Porrini
1966
Ron Ertle
1967
Tom Hauser
1967
Jim Smith
1968
Pat Midgley
1969

TEAMS 1960s RECORDS

83	18	2
WINS	LOSSES	TIES

4 State Championships
1 National Championship

1960
10-1-0
State Champions
Head Coach: Leo Strang

M	Key Games	Opp.
8	Cin. Roger Bacon	0
18	Warren Harding	19
42	Canton McKinley	0
348	***Season Totals***	***93***

1961
11-0-0
National Champions
State Champions
Head Coach: Leo Strang

M	Key Games	Opp.
21	Parma	20
7	Canton McKinley	6
332	***Season Totals***	***64***

1962
6-5-0

Head Coach: Leo Strang

M	Key Games	Opp.
0	Alliance	46
8	Steubenville	14
7	Warren Harding	20
269	***Season Totals***	***164***

1963
9-1-0
State Runner-up
Head Coach: Leo Strang

M	Key Games	Opp.
6	Akron Garfield	13
24	Canton McKinley	20
22	Canton McKinley	6
324	***Season Totals***	***47***

1964
10-0-0
National Runner-Up
State Champions
Head Coach: Earle Bruce

M	Key Games	Opp.
14	Niles	8
20	Canton McKinley	14
297	***Season Totals***	***48***

1965
10-0-0
National Runner-Up
State Champions
Head Coach: Earle Bruce

M	Key Games	Opp.
20	Warren Harding	14
18	Canton McKinley	14
247	***Season Totals***	***78***

1966
4-5-1
Head Coach: Bob Seaman

M	Key Games	Opp.
6	Upper Arlington	21
12	Steubenville	0
16	Canton McKinley	25
142	***Season Totals***	***135***

1967
9-1-0
State Runner-up
Head Coach: Bob Seaman

M	Key Games	Opp.
26	Steubenville	16
6	Upper Arlington	7
20	Canton McKinley	15
200	***Season Totals***	***79***

1968
7-3-0
Head Coach: Bob Seaman

M	Key Games	Opp.
0	Mentor	19
16	Niles	8
6	Canton McKinley	26
226	***Season Totals***	***135***

1969
7-2-1
Head Coach: Bob Commings

M	Key Games	Opp.
20	Niles	33
0	Steubenville	0
7	Canton McKinley	14
298	***Season Totals***	***107***

Story of the Decade 1960s

Quarterback Controversy: In 1964 It Was Kanner and Sheegog and Everyone Had an Opinion

Head Coach Earle Bruce led the Tigers to 20 straight wins and two state championships during his two seasons in Massillon. It must have been all peaches and cream in Massillon for the coach who never lost a game...right?

Steve Kanner.

In Massillon, life is never *easy* for the head coach. And Bruce had his share of stress as Massillon's head man, to be sure. But the biggest issue of Bruce's tenure—by far—had to do with his choice of quarterback in 1964.

Steve Kanner was the senior starter. His father owned Kanner's Men's Store in Massillon.

Junior Dave Sheegog was a natural—a quick and shifty triple threat quarterback. Sheegog was black, and his father worked in a steel mill.

They were the central figures in the quarterback controversy of 1964. It was a controversy that was not lost on the coach.

"Yeah, that got back to me,"

Bruce said, "But there was no pressure to play Sheegog. You'd have to understand a couple of things. First of all, Steve Kanner was not a great, talented athlete, as such. But he was a good leader. He led our team to victory.

"It's tough to replace a guy at quarterback who's taken you to victory every week. How can you take the winning quarterback of a 9-0 football team and change the quarterback? You can't do that. That's kind of a no-no," Bruce said. "How can you bench a guy who's doing so good?

Dave Sheegog delivered perhaps the most heroic performance in the history of the Massillon-McKinley game.

"I had my doubts about who should start, too. I could question that. But I wasn't going to make any changes that would hurt our football team. And there weren't any pressures. I never felt any pressures. I think that was talked about by people, I'm sure.

"The fact that Kanner was a good person. He worked hard in practice. He did everything he was asked to and everything he was supposed to do."

Teammate David Whitfield, who was captain at Massillon in 1965 and Ohio State in 1969, had strong feelings about Bruce's choice at quarterback.

"Earle's offense was more conservative than previous coach Leo Strang's offense," Whitfield said. "Leo was wide open. Earle was more the Woody Hayes Three yards and a Cloud of Dust type of football. That's why he went with a quarterback like Kanner. He was a little more settled. Then Bruce found out he had a quarterback like Sheegog who can scoot this way, scoot that way. Throw the football. And then scoot up the middle. But that's too wide open for him. It should have been Sheegog all the way.

"We had grown up to believe that if you do well in practice, you're going to be the starter. But Sheegog never got that opportunity."

David Whitfield

"Sheegog proved it on the practice field," Whitfield asserted. "We had grown up to believe that if you do well in practice, you're going to be the starter. You prove yourself on the practice field. But Sheegog never got that opportunity. We kind of resented Bruce a little bit for that. We got in some jams sometimes, and we knew we had the most mobile quarterback sittin' on the bench.

"Kanner was a little slow handing off, a little slow getting back. He's kind of slowin' down the backs. If you've got somebody who's a little more mobile, you're going to make those backs look a little better. There was a little animosity. We brought it to Bruce's attention.

"I remember it was Larry Larsuel, my brother Tom and Brock Herring, they explained a couple of things to him. They said, 'Wait a minute Coach, you came in talkin' that if you proved yourself on the practice field, you'd start. It almost looks like you're getting some push from some outside forces. Because we see some people that should be starting. Like Sheegog and Jim Lawrence. Those two guys proved themselves out there. Nobody can stop those two guys from doing what they want to out there on the practice field. And now we come to the games and you've got some other people out there in front of them.' He put 'em in there. At least Lawrence went in. Sheegog was subbing in more."

Massillon-McKinley game program, 1964, signed by Earle Bruce.

The quarterback controversy came to a head in the final

game of the season against Canton McKinley, a showdown between the state's top two teams for the state championship.

"I would have to tell you, I really don't think that we would have won the McKinley game the last game of the season if Kanner hadn't gotten hurt at the end of the third quarter and Sheegog had been able to perform the way that he did," Bruce said.

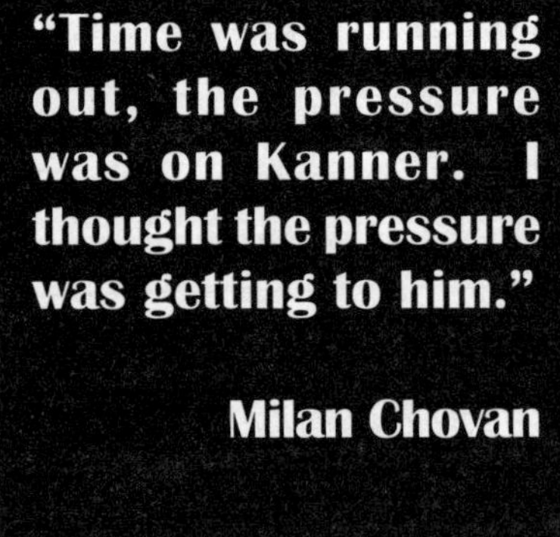

There was even controversy in regard to Kanner's third quarter injury. The Tigers trailed 14-0 with 3:30 left in the third quarter when Kanner came to the sidelines after running a quarterback sneak. Milan Chovan, a longtime Massillon assistant coach, was alongside Bruce at the time.

"Time was running out, the pressure was on Kanner. I thought the pressure of it was getting to him," said Chovan, who coached Sheegog in junior high. "I could see it when he came off the field. I never saw a kid so excited. I'm not going to say he had fear—it could have been the fear that he knew he couldn't do it—and it's so important that it is done.

"If that's what he thought he probably took himself out," Chovan reasoned. "I think Earle Bruce saw something in him that wasn't clicking just right. His execution wasn't 100 percent. Maybe Earle took him out for that reason and put Sheegog in."

Whitfield questions whether Kanner was hurt at all.

"No. Nope. I think he was getting talked to in the huddle," Whitfield speculated. 'I think it's time you get out of here. We got something we've gotta do. And we can't do it with you in here.' His teammates worked on him. McKinley had a good team. They were second in the state. It picked our team up when Sheegog came in."

"The first play I was kind of nervous. Going in there, it's late in the game."

Dave Sheegog

But Bruce insists that Steve Kanner *was* injured. In fact, he says he would not have substituted Sheegog otherwise.

"No, I don't think so," Bruce said emphatically. "You know why? You know what, I think we would have gone down to defeat. But then again, maybe Kanner would have been the person who scored the winning touchdown. Who knows? He was a very good passer. You can't ever fault his talent.

"I think Sheegog was a much better athlete than Kanner and probably contributed more to our football team as far as talent goes to run the ball and do things that we needed going against a great football team like Canton McKinley.

"I even predicted that if we were going to win, that Sheegog would be the quarterback. I predicted it. Talkin' all week. The real option was the inside belly play where he kept the ball. That was a special play for him. Kanner could have never run that. But that was a heckuva play for us."

Sheegog, who was a starting cornerback, entered the game at quarterback at the end of the third quarter. He naturally had butterflies.

"The first play I was kind of nervous," Sheegog said. "Going in there, it's late in the game. A lot of times you might have a missed snap, you might fumble. That could have happened in a game like that when you go in. I was used to playing *defense*."

Dave Sheegog on the run.

But Sheegog, who was nicknamed "The Magician" because of his slight of hand work on the field, started working his magic immediately. And it was with the belly play that Bruce alluded to that Sheegog took center stage.

"It was the 58 Option," Sheegog said. "It goes around to the right. You fake to the fullback up the middle. When the defensive end gets sucked into the fake, you pull the ball out at the last second. Then you've got another back coming around that will lead you. Usually you'll pick up some yards."

The first play picked up 10 yards—and helped Sheegog get rid of some of those butterflies. Six plays later Sheegog had Massillon in the end zone for the first time.

Then Sheegog worked his magic on a punt return after McKinley's drive stalled on its next possession. Sheegog received the ball at his own 17 and motored 22 yards to give the Tigers a first down at the McKinley 39.

Sheegog mixed the run and pass and quickly moved the Tigers to a score with 3:32 left in the game. A Sheegog keeper on the two-point conversion tied the game at 14-14. The Tigers defense then shut McKinley down and set the stage for more Sheegog heroics. But Bruce warned Sheegog to be careful when fielding McKinley's punt.

"They were punting deep in their own territory," Bruce said, "and we told Sheegog, 'If the ball hits in front of you, get away from it so it doesn't hit you.' Well, the ball hit the ground and bounced up in the air. He jumped up as high as he possibly could and grabbed the ball with one hand and returned it down to the 17 yard line. I said, 'What a play.' He returned that punt—it was unbelievable."

Sheegog's unbelievable 30-yard punt return put Massillon in prime position to score with just 1:27 remaining in the game.

Four plays later Sheegog weaved his way 14 yards through the McKinley defense for the winning score.

Sheegog's magic moves that day made him an instant Massillon Tigers immortal. But for Sheegog, after the postgame celebration, it was all "no big deal." His parents weren't even at the game.

"My parents didn't watch the games, and I'm not one to talk about the games," Sheegog said. "Everyone was cheering and yelling. It was like having a party in the locker room. The coaches and the boosters were in there cheering. It was bigger than just a victory. State champs and all that goes along with it. After the game I just went home."

"Why did it have to be a $64,000 question?"

Dave Sheegog

The next day all of the newspapers were raving about Sheegog's performance. One paper trumpeted "Tigers Agog Over Sheegog." Friends were telling Sheegog they had read about him in the *Akron Beacon Journal* and *Cleveland Plain Dealer*. That was fun for Sheegog.

But a headline that followed was sobering. "The headlines came out—'Bruce Answers $64,000 Question, Sheegog Will Be Quarterback next season.' Why did it have to be a $64,000 question?" Sheegog asked. He felt the headline smacked of racism, something he had not experienced on the team. But race was a volatile issue in America in 1964.

"It was the '60s, I'm sure it was there," Sheegog said. "You could feel it. I always say that was part of it. I don't think there had been a black quarterback before then."

Actually, in 1941 Dick Adams was Massillon's first black quarterback, sharing the job with Bob Graber.

But Sheegog would become Massillon's first full-time black quarterback in 1965.

"People were saying I didn't start my junior year 'cause they didn't want a black quarterback. There could have been some truth to that. A lot of people were saying that Massillon wouldn't start a black quarterback. I said, 'That won't change me any.' I got my chance in the McKinley game. Being in the '60s, they didn't really want to get into the race thing. They'd say, 'Well, he's a junior, he doesn't know the plays yet,' or, 'He's screwing up on the plays.' But still, do you want to put *that* person in the most important game, not of my life, it was the biggest game of the coach's life. Now, I can play the last minutes of the third quarter and the fourth quarter, but I'm not good enough to start? That's why people would always say to me, 'Well, Kanner's store is the reason you don't start because your dad works in the mill. His dad was buying the coaches shirts and stuff like that. Who knows? I didn't let it bother me. You go out for a sport to play. If they don't want to play you because of that, then they don't want to be fair. My senior year, with me as starting quarterback, we won every game."

Games of the Century

Massillon Ends Niles' 48-Game Streak Before 30,000 at Rubber Bowl

Earle Bruce learned a lot about the Massillon Tigers during his second game as head coach.

"It was proven to him what we've always known," assistant coach Milan Chovan said. "The Tiger spirit comes through. They'll pull the unbelievable when it's least expected. The big play."

Program from 1964 Massillon-Niles game.

Chovan was alongside Bruce on the sideline during the 1964 Niles-Massillon game. "The defensive back on Massillon receiver Rick Paige's side also started on offense," Chovan said. "Bruce told us, 'We're going to wear that guy out by sending Rick down and out, down and out. We're going to make him cover Rick Paige.' Rick had a reputation as a good receiver. He was tall, about 6'2"—and he could jump like a kangaroo. The idea was, Rick would get down in his stance and this kid would play off of him because Rick could beat him deep. He was giving Rick a lot of cushion. He was backpedaling. Then all of a sudden he would have to come up and make a play. All that movement was going to tire this kid out. Well, it proved to be the right thing."

With time running out in the first half and Massillon trailing 8-7, Bruce remembers showing Paige the route he wanted him to run. "We were running an out and I had to draw an out and up," Bruce said, "I said, 'Can you do this? You just gotta come out like you're going to run the out, then go up and you'll catch the ball.'"

The possibility of a Niles-Massillon match-up was the talk of Ohio football...

Paige came to Chovan confused. "Rick comes to me and says, 'Coach, what do I do?'" Chovan used his right index finger to diagram the play on the open palm of his left hand. "I didn't have time to go into detail, so I said, 'Rick, it's here, here and here.' He said, 'I got it, I got it.' And the kid did it. He caught the pass for a touchdown."

Paige's 16-yard touchdown catch ended up being the game winner in a 14-8 defensive struggle.

"Our defense played like you wouldn't believe," Bruce said, "No one had ever kept Niles McKinley to eight points."

The possibility of a Niles-Massillon match up was the talk of Ohio football in those days—especially with Niles

Tom Whitfield was Fifth Man in Niles' Backfield

A lot of Massillon Tigers played great games against Niles in 1964. But the greatest game of all may have been turned in by a lightening-quick nose guard named Tom Whitfield.

Tom Whitfield in 2002.

"Niles had an All-Ohio center," assistant coach Nick Vrotsos said, "and Tom was the fifth guy in their backfield. He played a great game. I don't know how many tackles he got. He was sortin' 'em out. He had their center goin' gun shy. It was somethin'."

on the verge of breaking Massillon's record 52-game unbeaten streak. As Niles' unbeaten streak swelled to 48 games, a game between the two Ohio football powers became a priority.

"We wanted to schedule Niles," said Leo Strang, who was Massillon's head coach from 1958-63. "But Niles would not schedule us unless it was at their home. Tony Mason was the coach up there. I had always told Tony that there's no way we could possibly play you in your place. You only seat about nine thousand people and I would get shot in Massillon—we would not have enough seats for that game.

"We had a little rivalry going

back and forth and got quite a bit of publicity out of it," Strang said. "We were actually friends. We pretended to be enemies as far as getting the most publicity out of it.

"The Akron Rubber Bowl committee contacted us about playing Niles in the Rubber Bowl," Strang said. "We got together for dinner in Akron and after much discussion we came up with an agreement to play Niles in the second game of the next year. I signed the agreement. I handed it to Tony and he signed it. I grabbed the paper out of his hand and I said, 'You just lost the first game.' About five or six weeks later it was announced that Tony Mason took an assistant job at the University of Michigan. And a week after that it was announced that I took the Kent State job."

So Massillon was facing one of the program's biggest games ever at the beginning of the 1964 season, and it didn't even have a head coach lined up. Interestingly, it may have been the importance of the Niles game that led to Bruce's hiring at Massillon.

Robert "Doc" Immel was part of the committee that hired Bruce.

The committee's final three choices were Bruce, 33 at the time, and two younger coaches.

"The feeling was," Immel said, "if we hired one of the young kids, and they lost that Niles game, it might be bad, the way this community is. It might ruin the guy. So we hired Earle, who was seasoned, and we knew he was a good coach."

Bruce came to Massillon with a 62-12-3 record after coaching stops in Salem and

Sandusky.

Bruce got off to an inauspicious start at Massillon. The Tigers were heavy favorites to beat Cleveland East in the opener.

"It's hard to believe it was nothin'-nothin' with about a minute and 50 seconds left," Bruce said. "They had a chance to run out the clock on us. They ran a little counter play and fumbled. We drove it in on fourth down. Then they threw a pass and we intercepted it and Paul Marks ran it back to the one-yard line. We scored 16 points to win the football game.

"I just kept quiet about it. I didn't want to draw any attention to the fact that we were going to have to shoot our guns the next week against Niles in the Rubber Bowl. It was like, 'Oh golly, we're the underdogs.'

"It was a rainy, misty night. This is hard to believe, but the two players who scored our 14 points against Niles were not on the football team the week before. Imagine that.

"Jim Lawrence was having troubles at home with his step-father. He left the week of the opening game to go live with his grandmother in Washington, D.C. Fortunately that didn't work out, so he came back right after the first game. Someone came to see me and said if I would take Jim Lawrence back on the football team there would never be a problem with him from this day forward. I said, 'How can you guarantee that?' He said, 'I guarantee it.' His name was Charlie Anderson."

Anderson was the star end for the '36 Tigers. He played for Brown at Ohio State but, unfortunately, was kicked off the team. Perhaps he didn't want to see Lawrence make the same mistake he did. Bruce smiled. "I said, 'Okay, Lawrence is back on the football team.' We played Niles and he only knew two plays. He knew the trap and the sweep. He scored on a 45-yard sweep that we pitched to him.

"The other kid, Rick Paige, was actually in jail the week of the opening game. He got in a real situation in the neighborhood. He was charged with something. The prosecuting attorney here and juvenile probation officer came to see me and he said, 'He was not guilty of that, it was not a problem. We'd like you to take him back because it would help him.' So I took him back and he caught the winning touchdown pass that I had to draw up on the sideline that night for him to score."

Marks, a two-way starter who ended up being named a Parade All-American after his senior season, was a junior on the 1964 squad. The Niles game was a blur to him.

"I don't know where my mind was that game. I think I must have done pretty good. I must have been on an adrenaline high. It was pumped into us how bad we needed to stop them and end their streak and protect our streak. That whole week leading up to the game I would say it was drummed into us. And you get so high on emotion. By all rights they should have just whipped the livin' snot out of us, because they were so dominant."

Perhaps Chovan said it best: "The Tiger spirit comes through when it's least expected."

Bruce: "The Night I Became a Tiger"

Earle Bruce was worried heading into the famous Week Two showdown between Niles and Massillon in 1964.

"We were supposed to romp all over Cleveland East and we barely won," Bruce said. "Were we worried about our team? Absolutely."

"Earle got orange jerseys and had *Beat Niles* put on the back of them," assistant coach Nick Vrotsos said. "We went out with our game jerseys on. He had everybody come back in the locker room and he said, 'Take those jerseys off,' like he was mad at 'em. We gave 'em the new jerseys. Jim Binge, a tackle, looked at his jersey. He said, 'Look what it says, *Beat Niles*.'"

Earle Bruce with memorabilia from the Tigers famous win over Niles.

Massillon edged Niles 14-8. Nick Pribich remembers how the players felt. "When we put on those *Beat Niles* jerseys, I don't think any team in the country could have beaten us that night."

"I said that's the night I became a Tiger," Bruce said, "because I couldn't believe how hard they played."

Paisley's Kicks Saved 1961 Titles

In 1961 the Massillon Tigers were steamrolling through their first nine games, heading toward a third-straight state championship and a second national championship in three years. Only Parma and longtime nemesis Canton McKinley stood in the way.

Wilbur Paisley's kicks saved 1961's final two games.

Little did anyone know that a junior place-kicking specialist would play a pivotal role in the season's outcome.

"Wilbur Paisley, our place-kicker, certainly was an unsung hero," Head Coach Leo Strang said. "He kicked the extra points when we needed 'em." Massillon trailed Parma 20-8 at Cleveland Municipal Stadium. Two touchdowns by Ken Dean made the score 20-20. "We went down and scored and Paisley kicked the extra point," Strang said. Massillon held on to win 21-20.

The following week, against McKinley, Paisley was called upon to repeat his heroics. This time, in a defensive struggle, Massillon edged McKinley, 7-6, with Paisley's extra point winning it.

Massillon finished first in the UPI poll, splitting the state championship with Niles, who won the AP poll. The national title, however, was Massillon's alone.

THE WHITFIELD BROTHERS

"Leadership." Tom and George Whitfield said simultaneously. It was *leadership* that led three Whitfield brothers to be captains of the Massillon Tigers.

"We probably get it from our dad," Tom Whitfield said. "The respect and leadership that he had in the community. We watched that and admired that and we developed it. He was the one that we could depend on. He was our role model. He provided for 10 people in the family. We never wanted for food or clothing or anything. And he made sure we got us a good education and everything.

David Whitfield

"He also instilled in us to follow in each brother's footsteps, from the big brothers on down," Tom said.

"I remember sitting over there in Section 4 when my brothers were playin'," said George Whitfield, the baby brother, and a captain for the 1968 Tigers. I remember Charlie, with Jim Houston and all those guys—and they knew how to hit. I remember when Leo Strang came out with those beautiful uniforms and white shoes. As kids we saw that when we were watching David and Tommy, watchin' 'em in those comeback games against McKinley when we were down and Sheegog comes off the bench. And

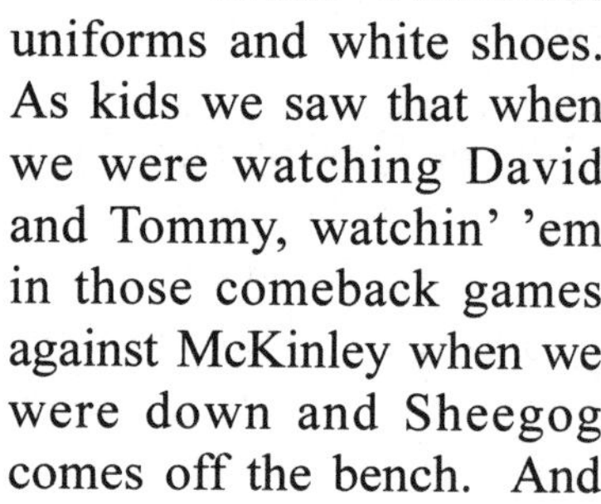

you hear, 'Whitfield on the tackle.' Hey, that's what made us want to play."

David Whitfield, captain of the 1965 Tigers, remembers the Altoona (Pennsylvania) game in 1964. Brother Tom had a great game. "The best game I ever saw Tom play was against Altoona when Mike 'Freight Train' Reid came into town," David said. "He ran into Chico (Tom), little bitty Chico, 145-pound middle guard. And Freight Train Reid got stopped, for no gain. Several times."

Charlie Whitfield

Tom squared off with Reid prior to kick-off. Reid went on to become an All-American at Penn State and an All-Pro with the Cincinnati Bengals. "I told him he had something coming today," Tom said. "I told him when we hit you you're gonna know it."

The Whitfield home wasn't large. But it was a home, in the truest sense of the word. "It was a home that was full of love," David said, describing the home that produced five Massillon Tigers football stars.

There were four sisters and five brothers. Their home had four rooms.

"You hear people talking today about going out and buying a house that has four bedrooms," David said, "We had four *rooms*. No shower. It was back when plumbing facilities weren't the greatest. You think, 'Wow, that must have been the '20s.' No, that was in the '50s. We might have had the indoor toilets, but we didn't have the showers and the bathtubs. We had to make some things happen. We had 11 people who had to sleep and eat in a four-room house."

The Whitfield home wasn't unusual in the neighborhood that was known as "The Bottoms." The Bottoms was located in downtown Massillon, adjacent to the Tuscarawas river.

"We weren't the largest family on the street. There were other families that had 13 kids," David said. "The average, I'd say, was about six kids. Count mom and dad and how many have you got? There were about 12 homes and each of them averaged about six kids.

"So we had a village. You had to learn how to get along with people. And how to mingle. How to do things. And stay out of trouble. There was lots of love there. My dad worked at Republic Steel, like a lot of the fathers down there. You'd watch mom and dad work themselves to the bone to make things happen for you. There had to be a lot of love there—and a lot of respect. They were good role models."

George Whitfield.

Tom, son number three, said "I wanted to be like big brother Richard and Charles when I got in high school. David and George followed after me."

The Whitfield's gridiron legacy started with the oldest son, Dick, a captain on the 1956 Tigers, who was named after his father. David remembers looking up to his older brothers. "Charlie was my idol," David said. He was a real good football player. That was a trademark there, you see them come home from playing. You *had* to do what they did. They were part of the team that was out there training you in the streets. If you got hurt or fell down, you better not cry—because big brother was watching you. Big brother also taught you how to play football. The proper stance. The proper way to fire out—those kind of things. That kind of passed down.

Tom Whitfield.

"Richard passed that down to Charlie. Charlie passed it down, too, " David said, "They were the best coaches I ever had in my life." A lot of the Whitfields' football acumen can be credited to the games they played in the Bottoms, where they actually played on asphalt streets. Those were among David Whitfield's earliest memories.

"It's the first thing you remember when you're learning how to walk," David said, "You're lookin' out in the street and seeing people having fun playing football. I'd see guys out in the middle of the street. All summer long. They're out there playing football and everybody's having a good time. The older guys were like the coaches. The younger kids were allowed to get in now and then. They wouldn't get 'em in there enough to hurt 'em, just kind of break 'em in to the game. The real good younger kids would play a little more. The other young kids had to sit on the side and watch.

"You were playing with those older guys, so you had to be on the line. You learned how to block. You might be the fastest thing out there, but you ain't playing the backfield. That's reserved for the older guys."

Dick Whitfield.

Maybe those early days playing on the streets decided the Whitfields' fate as linemen. On Friday nights in the fall the youngsters got to see some of their "street football" role models in action at Tiger Stadium.

"After you saw them playin' out there on the street, you saw them gettin' older and going down to the high school," David said. "The stars started to show up—the ones that were able to make it that far and hang on. You started seeing their performances and thinking, 'I want to be just like that guy. I played with him down on the street.'"

Father Time has caught up with the Whitfield brothers. "Just me and George are left," David said. "We lost Richard in 2006, we lost Tom in 2005. I lost Charlie my senior year of high school, 1965. I've just got one left now."

"First Hit" Legacy Was Passed Down to Brothers from Big Brother Richard

A hardnosed principle of football was handed down through the Whitfield family tree.

"The first play of the game, everybody gave the guy across from them the hardest hit they had in them," David Whitfield said. "To let them know that they came to play Massillon.

"It was a psychological ploy that we used. That was passed down. My brother Richard used to tell me that.

'The first play of the game, I don't care what your coach told you to do, you step across and hit that guy as hard as you can. It's psychological. He's going to be thinking about you all day.

"Give him your hardest hit.'"

David Whitfield, Captain, Ohio State University, 1969.

DAVID WHITFIELD

Lessons from legendary Massillon assistant Carl "Ducky" Shroeder helped to mold David Whitfield, a player who was captain at both Massillon *and* Ohio State.

"Ducky Schroeder was my position coach," Whitfield said. "Ducky was great. He taught me everything there was to know about playing football. I mean from the techniques to the attitude—everything. He was the first coach that I had that was truly a football coach."

Massillon captain David Whitfield, 1965.

Whitfield remembers his first practice in 10th grade. "You knew you were going to be out there in the midst of giants because they put you out there against the varsity the first day. The boards came out. The boards were six-foot planks that were about one-foot wide. Somebody gets on one end, somebody gets on the other end. You start from the down position and you run into each other. One guy's supposed to block the other guy off the plank. The coaches wanted to see how tough you were."

Whitfield also benefited from a double-dose of tradition—Whitfield tradition and Massillon Tigers tradition.

"The Whitfields always had the heart. That good old Massillon history and the mentality of the Tiger. Just go out there and fight 'til you win and don't give up. When it gets tough you just think of what it is to be a Massillon Tiger football player. Something down in the pit of your stomach comes up, and it swells up in your throat. That's the pride of the Massillon Tigers.

"Ducky knew that he could teach you the technique that you could get around and do the things you needed to do as long as you had the heart. That was the thing that he was concerned about."

Whitfield recalled a road game against Steubenville in 1965 that Massillon won 20-14. Both teams were undefeated and a record crowd was packed into Harding Field.

"People talk about going to Steubenville and getting hosed by the referees," Whitfield said. "But I never saw a game that was so out of whack. It was obviously poor officiating. It was tough to get cheated, and *know* you're getting cheated and then have the referee say, 'You'd just better shut up or we'll make it rougher than it already is.'

"I was assigned to a guy named Franklin—he was a wide receiver. My task was to keep him in, not let him out. Well, I did a pretty good job. After the game he came at me with a knife, ready to cut me because that happened on the field. He confronted me. We had a few unkind words for each other. My teammates said, 'What's that all about? You already whupped him on the field.'

"We got on the bus and had to go through that tunnel and have stuff thrown at us. You think, 'This is only high school football.'"

Whitfield played for two great Massillon coaches, Leo Strang and Earle Bruce. Strang brought Whitfield up to the varsity squad when he was a sophomore in 1963.

"We should have been undefeated three straight years," Whitfield said, "We lost to Akron Garfield in 1963 (13-6). I got on varsity after that. I got to play back-up guard and defensive end. I got in mostly on the kick-off team. They called us 'Chico's Headhunters' (after his brother Tom, whose nick-name was 'Chico'). It was an honor to be on that squad.

"I remember the two McKinley games in 1963. Massillon won both games, 24-20 and 20-14. I ran down on the kickoff team and ran into that big wall Willie Hall. I also recall that by the fourth quarter Willie Hall wasn't running like he normally does. He was kind of tiptoeing. He was definitely a little shy about touching the ball. The second time we played them he wasn't the same Willie Hall."

Whitfield's second head football coach at Massillon was Earle Bruce. Bruce led the Tigers to two straight unbeaten seasons that were punctuated by state titles and a second place national ranking.

"When Earle came in, things started to change a little bit," Whitfield said. "His philosophies were a little different. Earle played the Woody Hayes type of football. But he did one thing that was real smart. He always played the open side and the closed side of the field on defense. And he'd flip-flop the players. He took his quicker guys and put them on the wide side. He felt if you protected the wide side of the field on defense you're going to stop most of the big plays. He took that with him to Ohio State and talked Woody Hayes into doing that. That was Earle's stuff.

"He gave the greatest locker room speech I've ever heard. He'd get on people who weren't doing their job properly. Then he'd give a sermon. And you never heard a sermon like this guy would give. We came out and we were a different team. It wasn't that he tore people down. He built people up. He was a motivator. He got the leaders charged and the leaders charged the rest of the team."

Whitfield and Bruce ended up going to Ohio State together after the 1965 season.

Whitfield played defensive end for the Buckeyes, earning a team captain spot in 1969. He started for the 1968 national championship team that beat USC and O. J. Simpson in the Rose Bowl, 27-16.

Whitfield delivered the hardest hit of his career during that game. "We knew that 'The Juice' liked to do a wide sweep and then cut back. We had a game plan for that. On this play, when he got ready to stop and make his cutback,

I was full speed ahead and *bam* (laughs). O. J. fell right into my trap.

"O.J. got up and said, 'That was a very good hit.' And I'm thinkin', 'Hmmm.' That opened my eyes real wide. This guy is really tough. He can take everything I put on him, he is tough. I mean I hit him square, too. Because he had just turned and was getting ready to make his cut back and he was wide open to me. I was going full speed ahead.

"The next play he got an 80-yard touchdown run. He went to the other side of the field."

In 1969 the Buckeyes appeared to be on their way to another national championship until they were upset by Michigan. Ohio State was undefeated and top ranked going into the game and riding a 22-game winning streak. It was the rookie season at Michigan for head coach Bo Schembechler. He remembered Whitfield. "The little defensive end," Schembechler said. "Very good player. He was a very, very quick, tough kid. Very good player."

Ducky Schroeder was proud of his protege at Ohio State.

"Dave Whitfield was a very fine defensive end," Schroeder said. "He played guard on offense. He only weighed 175 pounds. I asked the Ohio State coaches, 'How can you play a guy that small at defensive end?' They said, 'Listen, if we had all Dave Whitfields we'd win every football game.' I said, 'Why?' They said, 'Because he doesn't know what it is to loaf. He plays with intensity every game. Every play of every game.'"

JOHN MUHLBACH

John Muhlbach epitomizes the athlete who could not be measured by the typical standards of height, weight and 40-yard dash time.

Muhlbach, could best be judged by the size of his heart.

"Johnny was one of the smallest centers in the game," said David Whitfield, a teammate of Muhlbach's at Massillon and Ohio State.

John Muhlbach in the Massillon locker room.

"He was an overachiever," Whitfield said. "He was a good leader—all the way from junior high through Ohio State. He would never say die. Sometimes he'd play hurt. He'd make *you* want to do the same thing. He got beat up quite a bit at Ohio State, but he was always out there."

Earle Bruce, Muhlbach's head coach at Massillon, was an assistant coach at Ohio State during Muhlbach's career there.

"He was one of the best-conditioned athletes I've ever coached," Bruce said. "I've coached Chris Spielman, who was very good, too. But Muhlbach had the ability to keep playing all the time, every play. John Muhlbach, Chris Spielman, Dave Whitfield, they were unbelievable."

Muhlbach was Woody Hayes' center for three years at Ohio State.

"Woody was always such a physical guy," Muhlbach said. "At practice I used to come back and we'd huddle. I'd say, 'Huddle.' Woody'd say, 'Huddle?' that was the worst play you guys ran all day.' And he'd hit me in the facemask. He'd just haul off and hit me, *boom, hard.* It had to hurt his hand. He'd grab ya. He'd grab big guys and shake 'em up. He was pretty aggressive.

"Woody often said that in the three years that I snapped punts, extra points and field goals, we never had a bad snap."

John Muhlbach

"One thing I do remember, and Woody often said that in the three years that I snapped punts, extra points and field goals, we never had a bad snap. I didn't keep that statistic, Woody did. I did take a lot of pride in snapping the football and making good snaps, not just the quarterback-center exchanges, but the long snaps, the short snaps for the extra points and the field goals."

Muhlbach was ready for Hayes when he got to Columbus. Bruce had been a physical coach, too.

"Earle was a raving maniac on the sideline," Muhlbach said. "He was in everyone's face, grabbing and shaking.

"Earle was one of the great Ohio high school coaches of all time. He was my position coach at Ohio State. He and I would always run on Friday. We had a light practice in sweat clothes and when practice was over he and I would always hook up and run some 50-yard dashes. It was always a competition, we had a bet on it. Earle was a runner.

Muhlbach as a junior center and linebacker at Massillon.

"David Whitfield and Earle came to Ohio State as a package deal," Muhlbach said. "There was no way Earle was going to come to Ohio State with me as a package deal. I wasn't that good. David was a great player. Of course he was the team captain at Ohio State the year after we were national champs. He was one of the great athletes, high school or college, that I ever had the chance to play with."

Muhlbach had a pair of great bookend games during his Ohio State career.

His first collegiate game was against Texas Christian in 1966.

"It was a very close game," Muhlbach said. "I intercepted two passes. It was the first game I played. They gave me the game ball. It was my dad's birthday and I hadn't gotten him a birthday present. So I gave him the game ball."

Muhlbach's final football game couldn't have been bigger.

"The last game I played was the 1969 Rose Bowl, the one where we won the national championship. I got the game ball."

The 1968 National Championship game was a pleasure and pain experience for Muhlbach.

"I broke my leg in the Rose Bowl," Muhlbach said. "I got clipped on a punt return. Just before they took me to the hospital Woody gave me the game ball. We were in the locker room. I had met O. J. Simpson, because we did a lot with the Southern Cal team prior to the game. We were number one in the nation and they were number two. So we were playing for the national championship. He came into our locker room after the game. It was the only time I ever saw anybody do that. He said, 'I just wanted to let you guys know that you're a great team. You're the best in the country and I wish I'd had a chance to play for your head coach.' Then he left. I thought that was really quite a gesture for him to come over and congratulate us. Because you're usually really disappointed or upset after losing in a game like that. O. J. Simpson was such a great athlete. Just to watch him run. When he ran that 80-yard touchdown against us it was like he was in one gear and everybody else was in a slower gear."

Muhlbach was the smallest center in the Big 10. "Woody liked small centers," Muhlbach said. "I was 5'10", 190 pounds. My greatest accomplishment was making the first team All-Big Ten academic team. We had some great centers in the Big Ten at that time, but the only thing I can figure is those guys didn't have as good a grades as I did," Muhlbach said with a laugh. I was one of the smallest guys on the team. Only a couple of wide receivers were smaller than I was. Being in the center of the line I was usually blocking guys who were much bigger. Back then we couldn't use our hands to block. You led with your head and shoulders. I took some poundings. Fortunately I was quick enough to block linebackers and get downfield on defensive backs."

Muhlbach appreciated Hayes' concern for his players off of the field.

"Woody was always disappointed in me for not going into the ministry. My senior year, after the season was over, he took me up to Yale Divinity School. He made a recommendation for me.

That was his plan for me. To help me pay my way through he had arranged for me to be a freshman football coach up there. He flew me up there and I visited with them. Back then Yale Divinity School was a great, theological school—and it still is. But I'll never forget going in and talking to him about that and saying, 'Coach, I'd really prefer at this time to stay at Ohio State and get my master's degree and help coach football. He finally understood and allowed me to coach as a graduate assistant. But that's the type of thing a lot of people didn't see in Woody Hayes. And that was not just for me, he did that for every kid on the team."

Muhlbach made his career in Massillon in the insurance business. He also held an interesting side job as Chairman of the Professional Football Hall of Fame Board of Trustees. He got his start from a Massillon football star from the early years, Tink Ulrich.

"When I moved back to town after college I got to know Tink and he got me involved in the Hall of Fame."

Muhlbach has become friends with many NFL luminaires over the years. A conversation with New England Patriots coach Bill Belichick was particularly interesting.

"All he wanted to talk about was Massillon," Muhlbach said. "He said, 'I hear there's a big debate about who was the best coach, Paul Brown or Chuck Mather.'"

CHARLIE BROWN

Before he was an All-American at Syracuse or an NFL defensive back, Charlie Brown was an impressionable little boy on the southeast side of Massillon. His heroes were running backs.

"There was Homer Floyd and the Francisco Brothers," Brown said. "There was a whole group of guys."

But one stood out above the rest.

"An aspiring back would have to have this kind of super hero," Brown said. "That was Homer Floyd. By my opinion, Homer wasn't the fastest guy out there. Wasn't the *fanciest* guy, but he got it done. His persona was very positive.

Charlie Brown as a defensive back for the Chicago Bears.

"Us young kids didn't dare to have conversations with those super heroes. But we saw them. Everything we saw of them on the southeast side of Massillon—they were God-like. They carried themselves in such a way that it allowed us to admire them. We never heard anything bad about them. The Homer Floyds, the Willie Longs, the Chuck Beiters. We never heard anything but positive stuff about them. So it was very easy to aspire to be like them. My early memories of Massillon were centered around those types of personalities."

Charlie Brown didn't see himself as an outstanding talent. "If you're not the fastest guy on the field, you had to figure out a way to do what you want to do. You had to learn how *not* to take a beating. You had to figure out how to strike a blow instead of being struck. You're not an Ivory Benjamin. You're not a Willie Long, who was bulkier and quicker. What you are is a skinny kid who is kind of gutsy.

"I was kind of aggressive. I wasn't afraid. I figured out a way to make it hurt as much as it hurt me. It was learning a style. A slasher is what I think I was. It's about angles. Leo Strang's offense was designed for a guy who understood about cutting back. And a guy who wasn't afraid to run inside. Who kind of *liked* to run inside.

"You have to know when you're going to get hit, then you explode into the guy. You might get an extra two or three yards or break away as opposed to being stopped in your tracks. Whether you're conscious of it or not, it starts to become part of your running style.

"Homer Floyd was very good at dropping his shoulder and exploding into you. I liked that. I could do that. I couldn't do what Art Hasting and Ivory Benjamin did. Naw. I couldn't do that. Art was probably one of the most phenomenal athletes I've ever seen, in terms of raw gifts. It was so easy for him. He had all these tools to work with. He had great body balance and great leg strength. He was very quick and adaptable. That is a gift for a running back to have in your bag of tricks. I don't think Art ever appreciated how good he really was.

"Sometimes there are moments in your life when you have to ask for all you've got—and then some. And *hopefully* that will get you through. I don't think Hastings *ever* had to call for that. He had so much. He had such a surplus of gifts and talents, he never had to scrape the bottom of the barrel to excel. I had to on a regular basis. I think I had pretty good discipline. I had more than my fair share of drive. I think I *wanted* to be a part of something good. Something that would win."

Longtime Massillon assistant coach Nick Vrotsos remembers Brown coming up through the ranks.

"I told Hastings and that bunch, 'Charlie Brown is going to make a lot of people forget about you guys.' They'd say, 'You mean scared Charlie?' They were older and he was scared of 'em.

"Charlie was a big running back," Vrotsos said. "He was about 6'2". He looked like Eddie George, the Ohio State Heisman Trophy winner. Had that same run over ya style.

Brown was co-captain of the 1961 Tigers, along with Ken Ivan. "Charlie Brown was an outstanding leader," Massillon head coach Leo Strang said. "When we needed a boost, Charlie would get up on a chair and really get into 'em. The Roger Bacon game, down in Cincinnati.

We were both undefeated. Charlie made a couple of outstanding runs, one was 60 yards."

Brown gained 165 yards on 23 carries in that game.

"Part of your job as a co-captain of this team is to lead by example. And part of leadership is to be able to articulate what needs to happen," Brown said. "You have to do your part. I was paid the honor to be a co-captain. That means you have to figure out what you need to do to make it happen. You've got to work as hard, if not harder, than anyone else at practice. You've got to be first in sprints. If not first, you *can't* be last. If you can't be first, you can sprint *longer*. I was always in excellent condition. I ran those stairs, and I often would take an extra shot at it on my own. I wasn't alone. There were other guys doing that. I was really familiar with those stadium steps."

Charlie Brown turns the corner during his Massillon career.

A 19-18 loss to Warren in 1960 inspired Charlie Brown and his teammates in 1961. "The most painful high school experience I can remember was the loss to Warren. That was excruciating. The lights went out. They called a touchdown back. We deserved to win. We played well enough to win. We did everything we were supposed to do to win. Yet, the records say we lost. On the way back home on the bus we committed that we weren't going to lose anymore.

"We were ashamed to go downtown. We were ashamed to show our faces that next day. Doesn't matter that they called one back. We lost. We were visibly ashamed. We understood that we were representing our town, our way of life, our everything. We were carrying the aspirations of our town. We understood when guys looked at ya, even if they didn't say anything, they didn't respect what you were doing. Pokey Blunt, All-Ohio 1941, was the janitor at the high school. We had guys around like that. These guys knew football. They weren't guessin'. They *knew* when you got your butts whipped and you didn't do your part. They just *knew*. And to come back to town havin' lost and havin' to face those guys. They didn't say much. But they didn't have to. You knew you had failed them. How much worse could it get? Losing is for those other guys, not us.

"There was a great pressure because of that," Brown admitted. "All these guys *knew.* They expected you to give the best that you could give. They didn't *care* about your talent level. They cared about what you were willing to give and what you were going to put into it.

"In preparation for life, I think it's a good thing. As a high school athlete, it's a lot of pressure for a town to put on a kid. But if you make up your mind that this is what you want to do, I don't think it's too much pressure. It could be overwhelming for a kid who is a third string quarterback and can't get to play quarterback, and he's willing to come out and do everything. There were guys that were victims of that. I knew them. Grew up with them. I remember how hard they worked."

Brown as an All-American at Syracuse, 1965.

Brown had a lot of college offers after leading the 1961 Tigers to state and national titles.

"That was really kind of like fun and a vacation," he said of the recruiting process. "It was my first plane ride when I went to visit the University of Cincinnati. I was treated like a rock star, going to all of these places. I remember Ohio State, Michigan, Michigan State, Indiana, Wisconsin. Different schools created different impressions.

"When I visited Syracuse I met my lifelong friend, James Solomon Nance. The running backs coach said, 'If you come to Syracuse Jim can be your fullback.' I'm going, 'This guy's a fullback?' He's like 265 pounds. He's a heavyweight wrestler, a two-time All-American.

"Woody Hayes and I, we never hit it off. He said to me that I owed it to my state to go to Ohio State. That didn't sit well. Plus Woody was kind of a high-pressure kind of guy. Leo Strang was not a high-pressure kind of guy. I was looking for a coach that I could find a comfort level with. I think that's why Syracuse head coach Ben Schwartzwalter and I could get along so well. He was low-key, and, first of all, he was a teacher. I could relate to that. I didn't need somebody yelling and screaming at me for motivation. I could provide that.

"I met Ernie Davis and John Mackey at the same time. Ernie Davis was very low key."

Davis had just won the Heisman Trophy as a star running back at Syracuse. Mackey was about to embark on a pro football Hall of Fame career with the Baltimore Colts.

"Syracuse had just won a national championship," Brown said. "I thought of myself as a running back and I was recruited as a running back. Syracuse ran the same kind of offense we ran at Massillon, so I know this offense intimately."

Charlie Brown was impressed by meeting Davis, but it was tempered by his love of Massillon.

"I appreciated meeting him," Brown said, "But I appreciated it more a year later. When you come from Massillon, there's Massillon football, then there's the world. He was part of the world. Massillon was focusing on Massillon being Massillon. You could read some of that other stuff if you sought it out, but if you didn't seek it out, it went right past ya. The *Massillon Evening Independent*, *Canton Repository, Akron Beacon Journal, Cleveland*

Plain Dealer talked about Massillon. So, we were consumed with that.

"I was a pre-freshman and Ernie is now going to the Cleveland Browns. They acquired him and a tackle named John Brown. John got to play, but Ernie never got to play. It was awesome meeting him. He was very humble. He didn't have much to say. You got the sense of his humility. You also got a sense of his ferocity because he was ferocious when carrying the ball. We saw a lot of that on film."

As a freshman at Syracuse, Charlie Brown thought he was destined to follow in the footsteps of Ernie Davis. "I was the starting tailback on the freshman team and I did well," Brown said.

After his freshman year he learned that his destiny lay on the other side of the ball. "It was apparent that not many sophomores were getting to start on anything," Brown said. "The coach said to me, 'You know, as a sophomore tailback you aren't going to get to start or play much. But if you want to play some defense, there's a chance you will play a lot. You can letter.'

"So I'm saying to myself, 'Okay, you *may* get to play a little tailback. You *may*.' I was willing to accept that. I said, 'I want to play. I want to letter.' It was part of the expectation. My expectation was that I was playing defense to pay my dues. I got to return some punts. I remember fumbling one. It became apparent to me that I wasn't going to be a great college punt returner."

By his junior year, Brown was starting at defensive back. As a senior he was selected All Big-East and

All-American at defensive back.

Brown's highlights at Syracuse include playing in the 1965 Sugar Bowl with LSU and being selected to play in the East-West Shrine game. He also received the Joe Alexander Award for Excellence in Football, Scholarship and Citizenship at Syracuse.

> **"When you come from Massillon, there's Massillon football, then there's the world.'"**
>
> **Charlie Brown**

As a senior, Brown met future Hall of Fame Coach George Allen who was then the defensive coordinator for the Chicago Bears. The meeting gave him a glimpse of a pro football future.

Because of Allen, the Chicago Bears selected Brown with the 28th pick in the 1966 NFL draft.

"I was still basking in the glory of being the number two pick of the Bears when I found out Allen was going to the Los Angeles Rams. The guy who drafts you has a plan, right? Well he goes to Los Angeles and his plan goes with him. I thought I was being drafted to play the fifth back. I think he was trying to take me as a safety who can fill on the run and take the back out of the backfield and run with him if he needs to."

Allen's departure drastically changed Brown's NFL career. "The Bears went back to the Mike linebacker," Brown said. "They had two All-Pro cornerbacks and an All-Pro safety. They put me outside to see if they could make a corner out of me. But I wasn't a corner. A corner is a different kind of mentality. Corners are kind of born, not made. They had a couple other guys who were natural corners. So they moved me to strong safety backing up Richie Petitbone.

Brown's biggest contribution at Chicago was on special teams. "Special teams were just fun and crazy," he said. "You get to use your speed, your ability, and you get to hit somebody."

He did get to start with the Bears at Green Bay. "Richie got hurt and I got in and made an interception. Man, it was the first time I'd had my hands on the ball in so long. An interception against Green Bay—is there anything greater with the Chicago Bears?

"I got to run a reverse once in a while. One reverse I got to run, I'm breaking clear. I'm about at the 50 and my own guy trips me up from the back. I was en route to scoring a touchdown."

Charlie Brown tried to catch on with the Cincinnati Bengals after his two years with the Bears.

"I left Chicago and got to Cincinnati with Paul Brown. I think Coach Brown needed a cover guy. And I wasn't it. I was there about three weeks. You don't have conversations with Paul Brown. He has conversations. You get to answer, yes or no. He and I probably wouldn't have gotten along. I'm a give and take guy. That wasn't my impression of him. My impression of Paul Brown is, 'It's my way or the highway.' And that's fine. But not necessarily for me."

As Charlie Brown was returning home from Cincinnati he was contacted by the Buffalo Bills. "I went to Buffalo—they needed a cover-safety-utility guy."

Brown played eight games for Buffalo in 1968. His highlight came in a game at Houston. "We go to Houston and they're beatin' us and our starting running back gets injured. The coach says, 'Is there anybody that wants to play football and knows how to run our offense?' Jack Kemp said, 'Charlie Brown does.' And for the third and fourth quarter of the Buffalo Bills and Houston Oilers I'm a running back. It's wild. I did reasonably well. I had 39 yards on three carries. Oh man, I was in pig heaven. What it proved to me is that I could operate at that level. That validated me in another way as far as I was concerned."

After Buffalo, Brown was invited to try out for the Canadian Hamilton Tiger-Cats. "They wanted to see if I could cover, and they timed me in the 40-yard dash. I stayed with the Tiger-Cats. During that season I got an interception and returned it 111 or 112 yards. I don't know if it's still a record. Can you imagine running so long that by the time you get to the other end zone you're tired out completely? I remember getting in the position to get the interception and somewhere around the 50 there wasn't anybody left. I was kind of all on my own. At the end of the season they decided how many Americans they could keep. Right before the Grey Cup, Canadian football's version of the Super Bowl, we agreed to disagree and I came home. I started out wanting to prove one thing, that I could play at that level. It's kind of the little brother syndrome. After that, I said, "*Enough.*" And that was it.

Charlie Brown Remembers Third and One

"The kinds of plays I remember are the third and ones," said Charlie Brown, who became an All-American at Syracuse after his All-Ohio career at Massillon.

"Those are the kind of things that show up. Touchdowns are kind of incidental. I remember Charlie Whitfield against McKinley saying, 'We've gotta hold 'em here. If we hold 'em here we get the ball back.' I've got this clear image of Whitfield yelling to Willie Poole what he wanted him to do. That's the kind of stuff I remember. I remember the way he held his head. Whitfield had pads all the way up under his arms."

Charlie Whitfield was a big part of short yardage plays on both sides of the ball.

Brown remembers third and one from the offensive side of the ball, too, where he starred at running back. "I remember making sure that I got the handoff clean. My head's on a swivel for the opportunity to know if I'm going to kick back if Whitfield kicks out. If he seals, I've gotta slide outside. I've gotta make the first step. That lets the fullback clear. He's running the dive to replace the guard that is pulling. The guard was Whitfield. There's the fake to Fred Philpot on the dive, then a handoff. Jim Alexander reaches and you're comfortable and confident that he's going to put the ball where it's supposed to go.

"While that's happening I'm watching Whitfield, because everything depends on what your guard is going to do. Whitfield's *going to* gct a hat on him. He kicks him out. When his half leg is going across the hole, I'm turning into the hole. I'm squaring up now, north and south. And I've gotta have enough force to break the first tackle, which gives you two or three yards. You've gotta have enough force to do that, even if the guy's in the hole. That's a defensive halfback coming up to fill. Even if he gets a hat on ya, you've got a yard. Because it's just you and him. If you want it more than him, you're going to get it. Any time you get a first down it's a good run. That's how I saw it. After a while you start to wear them down. And the one- and two-yard runs start becoming five- and six-yard runs. We were in superior condition. So as the game was getting old, you'd see other teams running out of gas. We weren't worried about running out of gas. We were in superior condition and our fundamentals were sound. We didn't have any great breakaway backs. We didn't have any great *antibodies*. But I'll tell you what, come the third and fourth quarter we were in your face. We're gonna outhustle you, outwork you. We expected to beat ya."

EARLE BRUCE

Earle Bruce has been to college football's mountaintop.

He replaced legendary Woody Hayes as Ohio State's head coach in 1979 and led the Buckeyes to the number one ranking, an undefeated regular season, and played for a national championship in his first season in charge of the Buckeyes, a dramatic 17-16 loss to USC in the Rose Bowl.

Earle Bruce was 20-0 with two state championships at Massillon. Bruce's Tigers finished second in the nation both seasons.

Bruce, who was 20-0 and led Massillon to back-to-back state championships in 1964-65, performed admirably in his nine seasons as Ohio State's head coach. He led the Buckeyes to an 81-26-1 record, 4 Big Ten championships, 8 bowl games and 8 Top 20 finishes. And he beat Bo Schembechler and his Michigan Wolverines more often than Bo beat him (5-4).

Not bad for a coach following a legend.

It's fair to say Bruce himself is a college football coaching legend.

His 2002 induction into the College Football Hall of Fame places him among the game's greatest coaches.

Bruce brought an unmistakable change of style to Massillon when he became head coach in 1964.

Earle Bruce's predecessor was "Loquacious Leo" Strang, a flashy leader on and off the field. Everything from his uniforms to his high scoring offenses. Bruce's style was in stark contrast to Strang's.

Bruce brought an unmistakable change of style to Massillon when he became head coach in 1964.

"Earle was more of an *in your face* kind of coach," said John Muhlbach, a team captain for Bruce in 1964. "He'd come up and he'd just chew you out right now, face-to-face, grab ya. Most of the guys weren't used to that. It took a little getting used to."

While Massillon players were adjusting to Bruce's intense style, Massillon fans were reacting to Bruce's low-scoring, run-oriented offense.

"It's funny," Muhlbach said, "Earle was 20-0 in Massillon and there are guys who sit around still, to this day, who criticize Earle for the offense that he ran, because it was too conservative. Yet he never lost a game. But that's Massillon."

Bruce was informed of the expectations of Massillon's fans right away.

"A couple of days after Earle Bruce was here I had the

chance to talk to him privately," said assistant coach Ducky Schroeder. "I said, 'Earle, you've got to throw the ball here. You can't just run it.' He looked at me like I'd just stuck a dagger through his heart. I thought he was gonna cry."

Bruce understands Massillon fans. "Massillon fans are great fans—but sort of tilted towards victory," Bruce said. "They're supportive, yet critical.

Did Bruce have run-ins with Massillon fans?

"When you're 20-0 you don't have much of that," he said. "You have *some* of that. 'You're not winning by a big enough score.' You don't have to jump any higher than the hurdles—just so you win. I wish we'd of won some games by bigger scores, maybe. But when you play Altoona and you play Warren and you beat 'em away from home...that's something Strang didn't do. At least we won 'em. We had an opportunity to run up some scores but we never did that. We could've gone for bigger scores. I was never into that because I always thought if we won, no one was ever going to be above us in the polls. Because we were playing good competition and we were winning."

Despite his short stay at Massillon, Bruce led the Tigers to three of the program's most famous victories.

His first big challenge came in his second game. Niles was unbeaten in 48 straight games when the teams met in the Akron Rubber Bowl. Bruce came out on top, 14-8, in front of 28,169 fans. The win kept Massillon's state record 52-game unbeaten streak safe.

In the 1964 season finale

Bruce coached the Tigers to a 20-14 come-from-behind win over Canton McKinley. Both teams went into the game unbeaten.

In 1965 Bruce again turned the trick against McKinley, this time pulling out an 18-14 comeback win.

"That guy didn't have any weaknesses," said Nick Vrotsos, an assistant coach at Massillon for 33 years. "Earle Bruce was the best. When you coach for him, you feel like you want to pad up. Not only the kids. I always say, 'Who's going to motivate the motivator?' The head coach has to be motivated to motivate the assistant coaches and the players. He was very intense. He didn't miss a trick He was just a great coach."

Bruce addresses his players during his first game at Massillon, a tenuous 16-0 win over Cleveland East. Number 77, Dennis Morgan, is in the foreground.

Vrotsos served under eight head coaches at Massillon. "Mike Currence was a good coach, yep," Vrotsos said. "Leo Strang was also a good coach. They were *all* good coaches. It's hard to say one is better than the other. I go this way. The guy who never lost a game. Earle Bruce. I give him the edge because he never lost. Then he proved it. It's a matter of record, isn't it. Won two state titles. He got the most out of what he had. His strength was that he never left a stone unturned. He went through every possibility that could happen in a football game. In every meeting, with every opponent. He was super-prepared. It was just mind boggling the football mind. He was a tough taskmaster. He had the respect of all the kids. If they didn't fear him they respected him. He didn't stand for any nonsense. It was the same with the administrators. He had a program to run and he ran it—above board."

"The guy who never lost a game. Earle Bruce. I give him the edge because he never lost."

Nick Vrotsos

"Earle's first game here we were playing Cleveland East and it was nothin'-nothin' with three minutes to play," Schroeder said. "East had the ball on their own 10-yard line. Earle Bruce was standing right next to me. He said, 'Ducky, this is a heck of a way to start the season at Massillon.' I said to him, 'Earle, the game isn't over yet.' Sure enough the Cleveland fullback ran the ball, one of our guys hit him and the ball flew up in the air. We recovered on the three-yard line. It took four downs to put it in."

The Tigers scored again when linebacker Paul Marks

intercepted a pass and returned it 40 yards. "I ran it back to the one-foot line," Marks said. "I ran out of my one shoe on around the 30-yard line. I started taping the laces of my shoes after that. Did it all the way through college."

Terry Manson scored both Massillon touchdowns and Bruce escaped with a 16-0 win.

Nick Pribich, a safety on Bruce's 1964 team, remembers East being a tougher foe than anyone expected.

"They were 9-1 that year," Pribich said. "Their quarterback would come up to the line and say, 'Is you ready to the left?' They'd say, 'Yeah man.' He'd say, 'Is you ready to the right?' They'd say, 'Yeah man.' Then he'd say, 'Well let's go tonight.' That was their cadence.

"The first play of the game they ran a sweep and I made a nice tackle and when we were watching the movie Earle Bruce said, 'Who made that tackle (excitedly). I said, 'I did.' I was afraid to say my name, but I was proud to make the first tackle of that season.

"Earle Bruce was one tough cookie," Pribich said. "He led by fear, but it was a good fear. It was a respect fear. You knew you didn't want to make a mistake because he'd chew your butt out. If you made a mistake, if you got beat or missed a tackle, you came out of the game and he put someone else in there. And you might not get back in the game."

The naysayers were laying for Bruce at the Booster Club meeting after the East game.

"After that first game I went

to the Booster Club meeting," Bruce said. "There must have been 750 people in that auditorium. There wasn't much to talk about because everybody was a little upset about only winning 16-0. I really thought our defense played exceptionally well. We didn't give up much yardage (109 yards). They had a great running back named Joe Pledger.

Bruce delivers a point during the 1965 Massillon-McKinley game.

"As I started my presentation, there began to be questions. All of a sudden one of the guys starts to attack our tackling. Three or four guys there were sitting together and were very obnoxious. They were out after me. They said, 'How do you teach tackling?'

"Well, I kind of learned a technique through the system. If you ask me a question you must have some idea how tackling should be taught if it's not being taught by me that way. So I said, 'How would *you* like to teach tackling?'

"He said, 'Well, when we played, we went in there and hit 'em low and spun and hit at the knee and they went down. You're not doing that.' I listened to him make his statement. I said,

'Well, to tell you the truth, I'd like to play your team. Right away. Because the way we teach tackling is like everybody else in America is teaching tackling. We want to gang tackle. We don't want the first guy to put the guy down on the ground. We want him to stand him up so nine other guys can hit him. Pretty soon he won't want to carry the ball. It's called gang tackling. We want to hit him, put our head on the ball and when we hit his arm, we want to freeze his arm so he drops the ball and it goes down as a fumble. We don't really want the first guy to put him down. We want to drive him back, then, boom, boom, boom.' Everybody that's around him gets a hit on him. Right at the end I said to that table of four guys, 'I've gotta tell you guys something. You know they hired me here as a football coach. I've got a three-year contract. I'm gonna be here for three years. You're not gonna drive me outta this job because I love football.' The crowd of 750 stood up and gave me a standing ovation for that. When I walked out of there I felt pretty good about that. We hadn't lost a game yet, anyhow.

"I walked out with Luther Emery, he was ready to become editor of the newspaper. He was well thought of in this community. He said, 'Earle, I want to tell you something. The day you start worrying, really worrying, is the day there's *not* 750 people there.' He said, 'When there's only 100 people, or 50 people, that's when you better start worrying. But you know what? If they ask you a question, your job as the football coach is to answer that question to the best of your ability.' He put it all in perspective. Then he looked at me and he said, 'Now we're going to the place where you'll meet with all the people who will decide your fate in football.' It was all the past presidents of the Booster Club. I've never seen a Booster Club that had so many famous people. I mean business people, successful people, doctors, lawyers, were on the Booster Club board. The people on the board knew what they were talking about. And they said all the right things."

Doc Immel, the former student manager for Paul Brown who became a school board president and the team dentist, was very involved with Bruce's hiring at Massillon.

"A fierce coach," Immel said. "I never saw a coach so fierce. I told him when he left, 'Earle, you never had the opportunity in Massillon to find out who your real friends are. You never lost a game so you think everyone in town is your friend. You should have lost one game so you could find out who your real friends were."

"Many Massillon folks thought Earle was a lucky coach," Schroeder said. "We came from behind to win quite a few games. We were behind 14-0 at the half of both McKinley games. He was able to come from behind and win. I think Earle had the ability to fire up our team more than probably any coach. But I'll say this, Earle was a different coach than many coaches we had. Earle coached with sort of a fear philosophy. Probably the same as Woody Hayes. Everybody sort of wondered what was going to happen if you ever lost a game. Some of the coaches we had were not like that. They would forget about a loss after the game. I think Earle and Woody both are coaches that use that philosophy, not only to the players but to the assistant coaches. We were afraid what would happen if we lost a game. But it brought results. We won all our games."

Bruce's 1964 team surprised him when he addressed them late in the season.

"I had never seen such an attitude on a football team. They thought they were going to win every football game," he said. "Every time they went out there. The only one that was doubting them was the football coach. Because they thought they were going to win, and they got me thinking pretty good.

"I remember when we went to Warren, it was a real test because we hadn't beaten them up there for two years. I was thinking, 'Oh no, here we are, undefeated and we go up there. So I call the team together when the polls come out. We were still ranked number one after seven weeks. And I said, 'Who would have thought this football team, when we started back in August, would be number one in the state the seventh week?' Do you know, I stand there, I made that statement, and they all yelled, *'We did, We did.'* I said, 'Oh.' It wasn't exactly what I expected, but it was what *they* expected. That just impressed me. A real attitude about the game of football."

"I had never seen such an attitude on a football team that they thought they were going to win every football game."

Earle Bruce

Marks remembered that speech. "He never thought we would reach that goal. At first I don't think he had the confidence in us. Then he started realizing the tradition and the emotion of the community that got behind the team and he started realizing that this stuff is for real. We knew we were a good ball club. We knew what we had to do to win."

Woody Hayes liked what he saw of Bruce at Massillon and brought him to Ohio State as his assistant. Who knew in 1965 that Bruce would one day be his successor with the Buckeyes?

"I'm sort of proud of that 20-0 record at Massillon," Bruce said. "There was a lot of talent in this county at that time. A lot of major college football talent."

Bruce enjoyed working with the Massillon players. "They practiced well," he said. "We had enough coaches to watch every guy. When you practiced there were a couple of eyes on you. If you do a bad job, you're told right away. And coached. Not criticized so much, but coached. So you got a chance to improve.

"Friday night, that's showtime. That's when you've gotta perform. That's when the performance tells. And they performed. They all played really hard on Friday night. They weren't all the greatest, most talented football players, but they liked the game and they worked and they took coaching. They listened and they were intelligent. And really liking the game means a lot. They like to hit. There was no baloney about that. They liked to hit ya. They didn't run to miss ya, they ran to hit ya. That's what really impressed me most about them. It was like the first time I saw that Massillon band come down the field. That's pretty impressive, too.

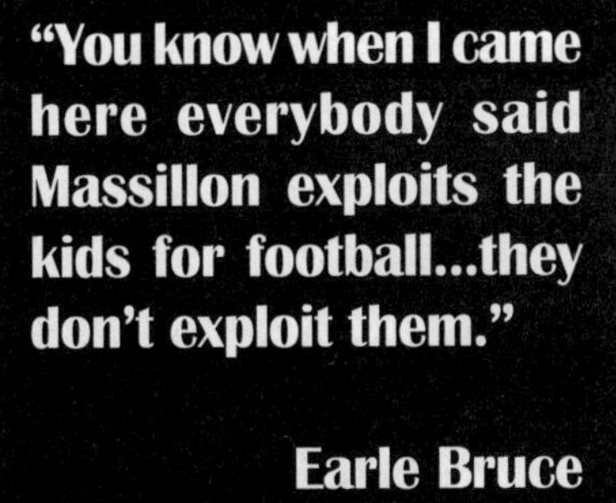

"The community spirit. You know when I came here everybody said Massillon exploits the kids for football. All over the state, when you'd hear about Massillon, they said they exploit the kids. I found out one thing. The people in Massillon care as much about their kids as anybody else does. They don't exploit them. They want them to win, and put forth effort and be well-coached and representative. But they are interested in their kids. And that's daggone important."

Bruce was recruited to Ohio State by Woody Hayes after his second season at Massillon. His overall high school record was 82-12-3. He was the Ohio High School Coach of the Year three times.

Bruce was a Hayes assistant from 1966-71, where he was part of the 1968 championship season.

In 1972 he landed his first college head coaching position, at the University of Tampa. He was immediately successful, leading Tampa to a 10-2 record, including a 21-18 win over Kent State in the Tangerine Bowl. Kent State was coached by former Massillon player Don James, who went on to become a legendary coach at the University of Washington.

Bruce had success at Iowa State before taking over at Ohio State.

Both coaches had a famous player in that game. John Matuszak was a star defensive lineman for Bruce and ended up being the first player chosen in the 1973 NFL draft. James had Jack Lambert, who went on to become a Hall of Fame linebacker with the Pittsburgh Steelers.

Bruce moved from Tampa to Iowa State after one season. Bruce spent six seasons with Iowa State, finishing 8-3, 8-4, 8-4 after struggling through three straight 4-7 seasons to start his career there.

Bruce's 1977 Iowa State team finished No. 18, losing to the top three teams in the country. Bruce was name Big Eight Coach of the Year for 1977. Bruce, who finished 36-32 at Iowa

State, is the only coach with a winning career record at the school since 1919.

When Hayes was fired from Ohio State after punching Clemson player Charlie Bauman on the Ohio State sideline in the 1978 Gator Bowl, Bruce was chosen as his successor.

It was Hayes who had urged Bruce to take the Massillon job in 1964.

"The guy that said, You better take that job,' was Woody Hayes," Bruce said. "Woody said, 'You don't pass up the Massillon job. You'll do well there.' He had heard that I was going to turn it down. He asked me how I felt about it. I told him, 'I have a great job here in Sandusky.' He said, 'You can't turn that job down. You can't turn the Massillon job down."

After being hired as head coach at Ohio State, Bruce was asked if he could handle the pressure of one of the most high profile college jobs in the country. His answer was succinct.

"If I could handle the pressure at Massillon, I can handle the pressure here."

"There's no better place like this place as far as high school football is concerned," Bruce said. "You might think there is, but there isn't. If you've been anyplace, you find out. They like football, they support football, it means something in the community. It means something to a lot of people. The pressure to win is tremendous. And I don't know if it's put on by anybody. It's put on by yourself. When you see the kids are interested in winning—they want to win the state championship. So the interest is the pressure. About the first eight or nine ball games here I used to wake up in a cold sweat in the middle of the night. I'd start pacing, I couldn't sleep. Finally I said, 'Nothing's worth this. I'm going to do the best I can, but I've gotta relax and enjoy the football.'

"There's pressure to win at Ohio State, naturally. For high school football there's no bigger pressure than Massillon. There's a great deal of pressure at Ohio State, especially when it comes to the Michigan game—it's like the McKinley game at Massillon. There's a lot of similarities between the pressures. I guess the bigness of the Ohio State program compared to the local thing about Massillon is a little greater. There's still pressure at both places. I think the pressure at Massillon prepares you to be at Ohio State, heck yeah."

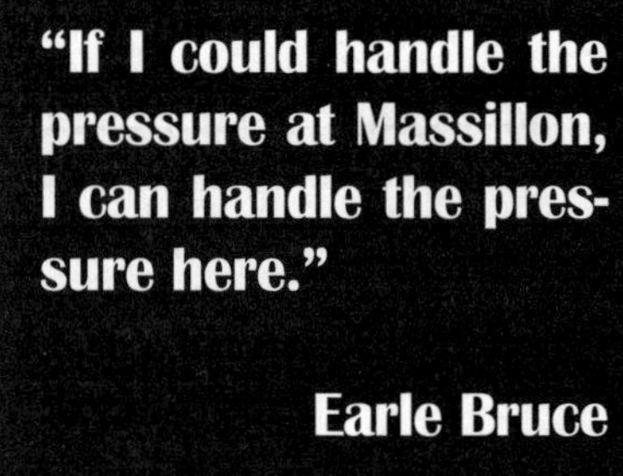

Ohio State was unranked when Bruce started his rookie season as their head coach. He was named the National Coach of the Year after leading Ohio State to an undefeated regular season and No. 1 ranking before missing a national championship by a single point in 1979.

Bruce finished 9-3 his next six seasons at Ohio State. His 1984 Buckeyes were ranked No. 6 and returned to the Rose Bowl. Again, Bruce was narrowly defeated by USC, 20-17.

Bruce finished 10-3 in 1986, after dominating Texas A&M, 28-12, in the 1987 Cotton Bowl.

In 1987, Bruce finished 6-4-1 and was fired before the Michigan game.

Bruce looks pleased as Ohio State's head coach.

PHOTO: OHIO STATE ATHLETICS

"That was really a tough week," Bruce said. "I told the kids, 'We're going to concentrate on beating Michigan. Don't you talk about the firing of Earle Bruce. Don't you even think about it. We're going to think about one thing: beating Michigan when we go up there. If you start thinking about that other crap we'll lose this ball game. They'll tear us apart. Michigan's the opponent. You want to win that game. I want to win that game. Some people maybe don't want us to win that game. So let's go do it."

"He deflected all that from the team and was able to get us ready to play without showing any change, even though he'd been fired before the Michigan game," Spielman said. "He could have easily walked out. But he hung in there with us. To me he did it the way it was supposed to be done. He held his head up high. The way he handled that whole situation, he walked out of there with so much dignity. He taught me a great lesson, not only in football, but in life.

"He's a mentally tough guy," Spielman said. "I'm sure when he was home at night he probably couldn't even sleep. He must have been sick to his stomach. But when he walked out on the field it was business as usual."

Bo Schembechler was 4-5 against Bruce.

PHOTO: U-M ATHLETIC DEPARTMENT

Bruce's players had a surprise for their head coach on game day before the kickoff in front of 106,000 in Ann Arbor.

"We went up and worked out. We had the captains ready to go out for the kickoff. I look over and all of the team is lined up. I look over and see something on their foreheads. Something written on a headband.

"I wondered, 'What the heck's going on? They don't do that kind of stuff. We don't do that kind of stuff.' I kind of try to move over like I wasn't that interested in what's going on. And I looked at the headband and it says, 'Earle.' Now I can't say anything to 'em. I can't say a word to 'em. I just gotta go up and down and play like it's not there until they put their helmets on and do what they've gotta do."

The players' sentiment touched Bruce's heart. "Oh yeah. And, you know in that game, they pushed us around for a quarter and a half. They led 13-0. And then it changed, right in the middle of the second quarter. We started to take charge. I could see it. Tom Tupa snuck it in from the one-yard line to make it 13-7. We came out the second half and threw a little five-yard pass to Carlos Snow, who turned it into a 60-yard touchdown. We took the lead, 14-13, and never looked back.

Earle Bruce was named the National Coach of the Year after leading Ohio State to an undefeated regular season and No. 1 ranking in 1979.

"It was tied 20-20. We kicked a field goal to go up 23-20. We got the ball back with about five minutes to go and ran the clock down to less than a minute. We turned the ball over on the one yard line tryin' to score. We had a good chance to score. We were just pounding it in there, running the clock. We didn't make it. But we won it when the clock ran out for them. That was it."

His players grabbed Bruce, hoisted him to their shoulders and gave him a hero's escort off of the field.

"Seeing Coach Bruce being carried off the field after he'd been fired is what stands out the most," Spielman said.

"Boy, what a game to win," Bruce said. "What a game for those kids to play. It was just one of those games that gets your heart right there.

"After the game I talked to Bo. He was a tremendous person, no doubt about it. Tremendous coach. Best coach Michigan ever had, no doubt about it. So I sit down with him after the game. Bo said to me, 'You know, Earle, how I hate to lose. I *hate* to lose. Today I didn't mind losin'.' That said a mouthful for me. What a man. What a guy."

Bruce finished his college coaching career at Colorado State, where he led them to a 9-4 record and a win in the Freedom bowl, their first bowl game in 42 years. Bruce's overall college record was 154-90-2. He led four college programs to bowl games and had an impressive 12-5 record in bowl games. Ten of Bruce's teams won nine or more games and finished in the Top 20.

Bruce was the winningest coach in the Big 10 during his tenure at Ohio State. But his record against Schembechler and Michigan probably meant the most in his storied coaching career.

"I had a winning record against him," Bruce said. "The best coach that Michigan ever had. That isn't bad. I'll take it."

Bruce's Coaching Tree is Dominating Division I College Football

Earle Bruce' coaching tree is starting to look like a Who's Who of NCAA Championship Coaches.

Former Bruce assistants have claimed national championships no less than eight times in the 2000s.

Former Bruce assistants have claimed the national championship no less than eight times in the 2000s.

Jim Tressel (2002), Nick Saban (2003, 2009), Pete Carroll (2002, 2003, 2004, 2007), and Urban Meyer (2006, 2008) have claimed outright or shared national titles in the decade.

"I had a bunch of great assistant coaches," Bruce said modestly, "both in high school and in college. But I guess the most recent ones are getting all of the publicity in coaching right now, that being Urban Meyer at Florida, Jim Tressel at Ohio State, Nick Saban at Alabama and Pete Carroll at USC.

I've had a lot of great assistants that contributed to my career—probably too numerous to mention. I might forget someone.

"I think that assistant coaches are probably the greatest ingredient of success that you could possibly have. They make suggestions that are relevant to the game of football. They become successful football coaches. They were not only good coaches but good people.

"I'm a Buckeye, naturally, but I have close connections with Urban Meyer. My grandson is a graduate assistant with him, Zach Smith."

Bruce saw two of his proteges face each other when Florida and Ohio State played each other for the 2006 national championship. "What I remember is the kickoff return and we were ahead for 16 seconds. I remember the domination of Florida in that football game, especially by the defensive line. They dominated the line of scrimmage and made it difficult for us to run."

So what is Bruce's secret for producing so many championship coaches?

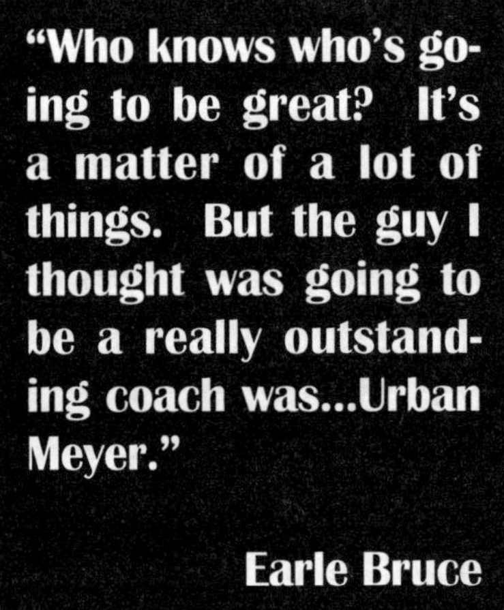

"I personally think it's great selection, in that they were great coaches where they were. Who knows who's going to be great? It's a matter of a lot of things. But the guy I really thought was going to be a really outstanding coach was a guy I recommended for the Bowling Green job, and that was Urban Meyer. And Urban Meyer went from Bowling Green to Utah to Florida and has turned out magnificent teams. He's got a lot of good thoughts about the game of football. One is speed. He wants to have the fastest team in the country, so he recruits speed. He also wants to have a good, sound program in all phases: offense, defense and special teams. When he won the national championship in 2008, his defense intercepted 26 passes. That's unbelievable. And they blocked seven kicks. Some coaches don't block seven kicks in their whole career of 20 years. I thought that Meyer would be a good coach—not that I thought Nick Saban and Pete Carroll wouldn't be.

"Pete Carroll was in a great situation. He was a California guy coaching USC. It fit like a glove. He did a great job of recruiting and coaching them.

"Nick Saban is in the element that he needs to be in. He had the number one team in LSU and won the championship. Now he's moved to Alabama where it's the same philosophy, rough, tough, rock 'em sock 'em football that he teaches. He won the championship there.

"Jim Tressel's got Ohio State and he's taken them and turned them around and headed in the right direction as far as championships and beating Michigan and doing things that make the football program successful. He's a complete football coach."

JIM SMITH

Jim Smith was a fourth grader when his mother sent him from Birmingham to Massillon to live with his aunt. "The first thing I noticed was that Massillon wasn't supposed to lose any games," Smith said.

A classic example of Jim Smith's hard running style. Smith is among an elite few to rush for 1,000 yard in two seasons at Massillon.

Massillon had a 20-game winning streak snapped and Smith remembers how dejected people were returning from Warren, where the Tigers suffered a 19-18 defeat. "I had never seen anything like that before," he said, "I thought somebody had died or something. They said, 'We lost.' It blew me away to know that the spirit was so high in this football town...and that Massillon *doesn't lose any games*. It was hard for me to believe. That made me go to the next game. And when I started going to the games, I understood why. I watched 'em play. And ever since I watched 'em play, I wanted to be a runner."

Smith's upbringing in Massillon was not rich in material terms. "My aunt already had five kids she was taking care of. I was just an extra kid. They did the best they could for us. A roof over our head, enough to eat. We didn't have a lot. Clothes and stuff like that; they didn't really have that kind of money."

The riches of Smith's childhood were found on the sandlots of his neighborhood—and in the street. "Ever since I was a kid, I knew I was going to be a runner. I could always outrun guys much older than me, even when I was six, seven, eight years old. We used to have street races. We didn't have shoes. I used to run barefooted. The street wasn't paved. Dirt and rocks. Being a kid and not wearing shoes, you get adapted to it. A lot of us didn't wear shoes during the summer. We had school shoes. If you were lucky you had play shoes."

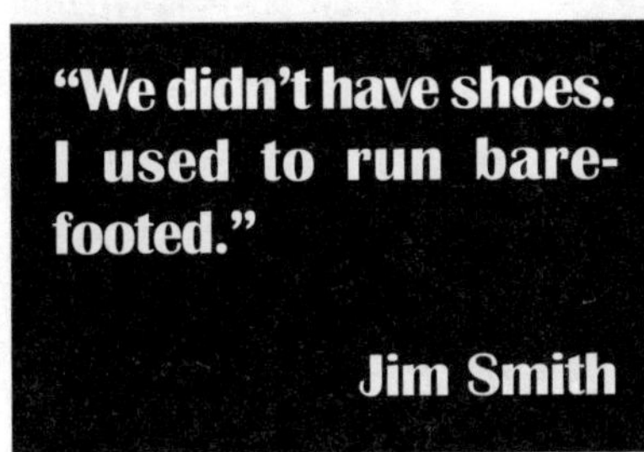

Smith dreamt of the day he would be Massillon's star running back. "When I watched Massillon play, I said, 'Yeah, I'm going to be a Tiger one day. I'm going to run that ball for Massillon. I knew it. It was like a dream come true, you know. It was like I saw it before it happened... and it came true."

The Tigers struggled through a 4-5-1 season in 1966, their first losing season in 35 years. In 1967, embattled head coach Bob Seaman made a move that probably prolonged his coaching career at Massillon.

Injury in Final Game a Sour Ending

Jim Smith wanted nothing more than to have a great game and lead Massillon to a win against Canton McKinley in 1968. Unfortunately, his fate was a knee injury on his sixth carry in the final game of his Massillon career.

When Jim Smith went down against McKinley in 1968, so, too went the Tigers hopes of victory.

"I'll never forget it," Smith said, "I always looked for pulling guard George Whitfield on my sweeps. Sure enough, he was there on time. I jumped across his back, and when I did, McKinley's linebacker caught me as I was coming down. He had one of my legs up in the air and I've got the stiff arm on him. I was just about to twist out of it, and they hit me with a cheap shot. Almost broke my leg. I cried like a baby out on that field because I couldn't play."

"My junior year they came out with the "I" formation," Smith said. "That more or less saved Seaman's career. They couldn't believe how I fit in the offense. The "I" back sits deep in the backfield. You have to have good speed to still hit the hole quick. I had the speed they needed. I had the size. That was me. That was my position. It fit like a glove."

Massillon's fortunes turned upward with Smith running the ball. In 1967 Massillon finished 9-1, losing only to Upper Arlington, 7-6. Upper Arlington went on to win the state championship.

In that game, Seaman stuck doggedly to his plan to run Smith.

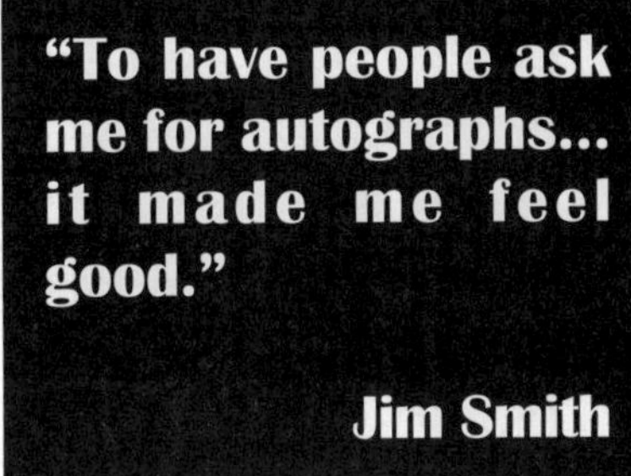

"He used to run me to death," Smith said. "He ran me about 30 times a game. I ran the ball 39 times against Steubenville. He was determined to run it. Headstrong." Smith feels Seaman's lack of imagination cost them the Upper Arlington game. "We were down on the three-yard line and all we had to do was kick a field goal and win the game. We always practiced kicking, but we never did it in the game. But he was determined he was going to run me up through there. They pounded me. They were keying on me. They had everybody up on the line and we still ran the ball. That was the only thing I had against Seaman. He was just a headstrong coach. But I loved the idea that he ran me, because I loved to run the ball."

A large, powerfully built running back, Smith stood 6'4" and weighed a solid 203 pounds. Playing against defenses that game-planned to stop him, Smith still gained

1,011 yards as a junior and 1,022 yards as a senior. His style was unique. "I don't think there were too many backs that ran the style I ran," Smith said. "I had the speed and moves of a halfback and the power of a fullback. I just didn't believe one man could bring me down. I didn't believe in running out of bounds. I believed in getting every inch I could."

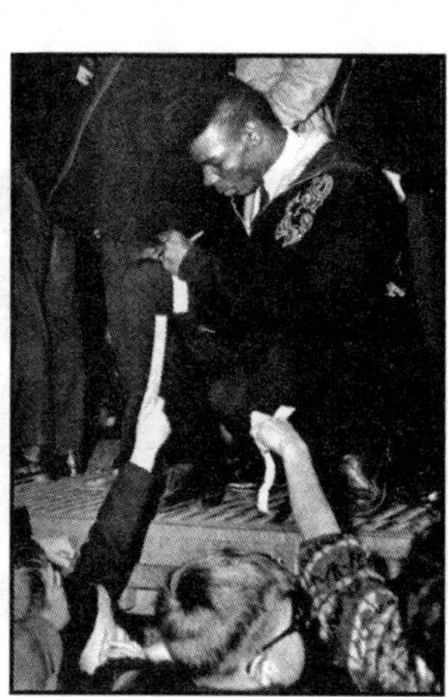

Signing autographs: Smith was a local hero in 1967 and '68.

Massillon assistant Nick Vrotsos coached Smith in football and basketball. "He was a big, slashing runner," Vrotsos said. "Tough runner. I think he's right there at the top of the list of top rushers."

Smith was fortunate enough to live his childhood dream. And along the way, he helped other Massillon youngsters to dream.

"Believe it or not, I'd be walking down the street and I'd see little kids playing sandlot football and I'd hear 'em arguing about who's going to be Jim Smith. 'I'm going to be Jim Smith.' 'No, I'm going to be Jim Smith.' It was an experience. I didn't get the big head over it. It was just something to see. And to have people come up and ask me for autographs. It was somethin.' It made me feel good."

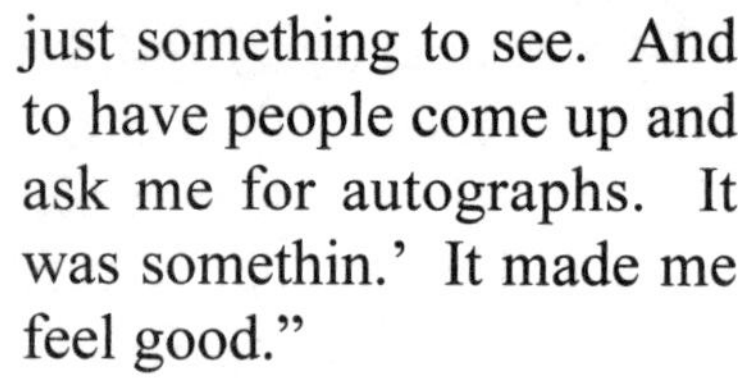

BEN BRADLEY

Big Ben Bradley is a product of lessons learned in his neighborhood—a *tough* neighborhood. Some lessons were good, some bad. But all of the lessons were important.

"Big" Ben Bradley.

Some of the lessons Bradley learned were on the streets. "I grew up on 13th street," Bradley said. "In the ghetto. Blacks and Greeks and *everybody*. We were tight. We grew up together. We were on the 'Hill.' The 'Hill' would fight the 'Bottoms.' We fought Longfellow. We fought Lorin Andrews. All of us together. It wasn't just blacks and whites. We fought as a section."

Bradley also learned lessons at home. While his parents encouraged him to play football, they also taught him to look beyond his playing days.

"I had encouragement coming from within the house and also from the church," Bradley said.

"My parents told me, 'You

have to do better. You don't want to go to the steel mills.' That was pumped into my head. 'You have to go on. You don't want to sit around here. You don't want to be a wino.' My parents pushed me. It was preached to me all of the time. 'You don't want to be like this guy, you don't want to be like that guy.'

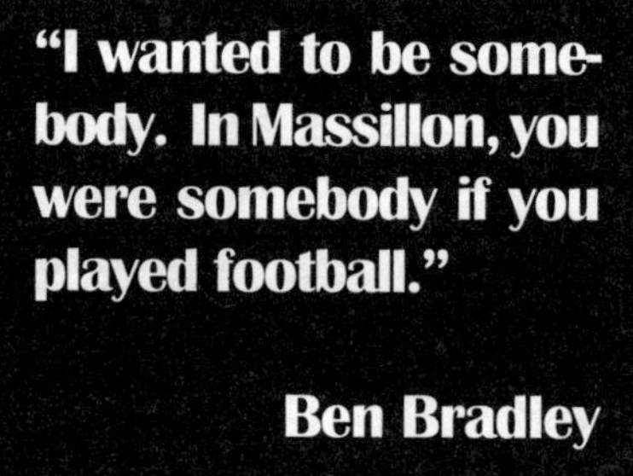

"I saw a lot of them fail. Especially black athletes. A lot of them, once they finished playing football, were finished. That's a known thing. I didn't want that to happen to me. I *definitely* didn't want that to happen to me."

Bradley was in third grade when his family moved to Massillon from Alabama, trying to improve their lot in life. "It was in 1953. My parents wanted to move up north to make a better life," Bradley said. Bradley found a great football life in his "tough" neighborhood. Many of his neighbors were football heroes at Massillon. "I always wanted to be a Tiger. A football star. I wanted to be *somebody.* In Massillon, you were somebody if you played football. We lived on 13th street, so it was the Franciscos, Homer Floyd and Johnnie Traylor—they were backs. Then I remember another back—it was always backs—I remember Ivory Benjamin in 1956. When I went to Jones Junior High, it was Sluggo Bednar, Joe Sparma, Jim Houston and Art Hastings. Those guys were two years ahead of me. I wanted to be like them."

While at Jones, Bradley discovered his inspiration; he was lining up for cross-town rival Longfellow Junior High. Hase McKey, a two time All-Ohio lineman, became a role model for Bradley. "Hase McKey was a big man. He started three years at Massillon. Quite naturally, being a big man myself, I wanted to be like him. He was my idol—where I set my standards. He was good. He was an All-Ohio player. I wanted to be like him. The guy was terrific."

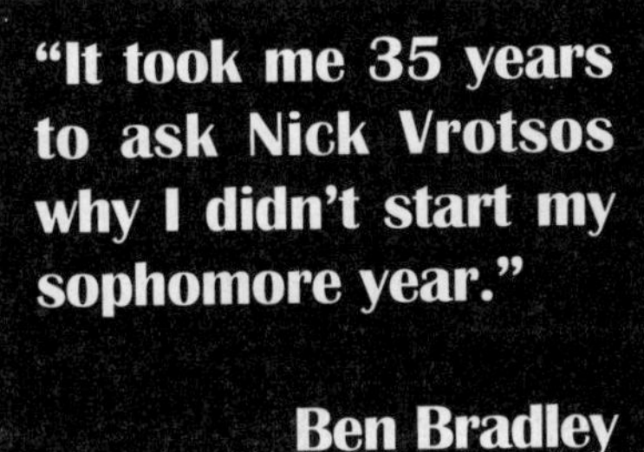

When Bradley entered high school, he was the only sophomore on Massillon's 1960 state championship team. A strapping 250 pounder, he wanted badly to start on that squad, and be a three year starter like his idol McKey.

He felt that he had earned that right. "It was hard for me to understand," Bradley said. "I had started all summer long. I cried. Hase McKey started as a sophomore—I should have started when I was a sophomore. We used to go one on one in practice. That was the measuring stick. If you beat *the man*, you were *the man*."

Bradley felt that he "beat the man" in practice, but found himself second string when the season started. He struggled with that disappointment for a long, long time. "It took me 35 years to ask Nick Vrotsos why I didn't start my sophomore year," Bradley said.

Vrotsos, a legendary Massillon assistant, counseled his former pupil about the coaching staff's decision. "Coach Vrotsos told me they had a problem playing sophomores because head coach Leo Strang would always say, 'A sophomore will make mistakes that will cost you a game.' I can understand that now. A lot of things I didn't see then, I see now. A senior isn't going to make the mistakes that a sophomore will."

Ben Bradley, All-Ohio 1962.

Bradley got his due as a junior on Massillon's 1961 state and national championship team. "I was the only junior starting on that offensive line."

Bradley's weapon was a wicked move sometimes called a *forearm shiver*. It's a quick, powerful uppercut with the forearm that strikes opponents with a sudden blow. The "forearm shiver" was Bradley's calling card. "There was no one there as effective with their forearms as I was," Bradley said.

In 1962, the individual awards rolled in for Bradley. In addition to being named first team All-Ohio, he was named High School All-American for 1962. He was named at center. Steve Spurrier was an All-American quarterback on the same team.

"If you put him in the middle they didn't run in there."

Nick Vrotsos

Vrotsos remembered working with Bradley on both sides of the ball. "I coached him as an offensive center and nose man," Vrotsos said. "He was the biggest nose man we ever had. We more or less stood him up like a middle linebacker. He made All-Ohio. He had size and strength. Back in those days you delivered the defensive blows with the forearm. He was good, he was a good athlete. If you put him in the middle they didn't run in there."

For Bradley it all goes back to his childhood and his heroes. He found out that he, too, was the idol of a Massillon youth who was to become a local legend. "Steve Studer told me I was his idol," Bradley said. "When he was a little boy, I used to work out at the stadium. In the summertime, they used to give us jobs. I never knew that's how he felt. That's why I always tell people, 'you never know who's watching you.' "

Bradley Reaches Goal as First Black Booster Club President

When he returned to Massillon in 1995, following a successful career with General Motors, Ben Bradley stated his goal: He was determined to be the first black president of the Massillon Tigers Football Booster Club.

Ben Bradley, as president of the Booster Club in 2006.

"There's never been a black president. I like being a pioneer," Bradley said at the time. After 11 years, he reached his goal. Becoming Booster Club president is not easy. It is a position you rise to, through years of service. You have to prove yourself. Bradley proved himself, just like he did on the gridiron some 45 years earlier.

NICK VROTSOS

"I coached here for 33 years," Nick Vrotsos said. "That doesn't make me the best assistant coach that ever coached here. But I coached here 33 years. That's one thing they can't take away from me. I had to be doin' something right.

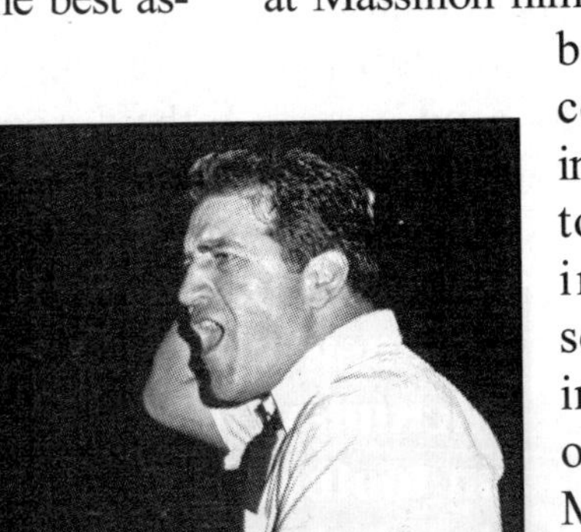

An emotional Nick Vrotsos reacts to a play in 1969.

"In 33 years I coached in 350 games," Vrotsos said proudly, "and the Tigers won 80 percent of those games."

Vrotsos was hired by Head Coach Leo Strang in 1958 and worked with eight different head coaches at Massillon. Of course he was a head coach at Massillon himself—on the basketball court—leading the Tigers to 138 wins in 10 seasons, including six wins over Canton McKinley.

"You want to know a guy who can beat McKinley?" Vrotsos said, "I knew how to beat McKinley. I beat 'em in football and basketball. When it comes to a traditional game like Massillon and McKinley, I get fired up. I coached the heck out of 'em during

McKinley week. When Mike Currence was the head coach at Massillon, he just turned me loose. Game planning and everything. I knew how to beat that defense. I knew that kind of stuff like the back of my hand."

Vrotsos loved coaching football and he loved the kids he coached—not just the star players.

> **"I knew how to beat McKinley. I beat 'em in football and I beat 'em in basketball."**
>
> **Nick Vrotsos**

"We had great players at Massillon. If I started naming players, I'd slight somebody. I thought that every kid that came to Massillon and played and got his suit on was great. Anybody that was on the team was great. Some people were a little faster, a little quicker, maybe a little stronger, but every kid that put the uniform on had a heart as good as gold.

"That's one of the things the Massillon kids have that other schools don't have. Our kids have that tradition—they're out there for a reason. They've been weaned on it. It's the most fantastic 33 years I've ever spent. And if I had to do it over again, I'd want to do it the same way."

Vrotsos loves the Massillon fans, too. "Massillon fans never change. They're with you win or die. They don't like to see you lose. They're with you and they back those kids. It's never the kids, the kids win 'em, the coaches lose 'em. And that's the way it should be. They're in love with their Tigers. The other guy might be better, but our kids give it all they've got. And the greater percentage of the time, we win. About 80 percent of the time, of all the years I've been at Massillon, we've won. And that's not too bad."

Of course football is king in Massillon, and Vrotsos knows that better than anyone. "The best thing about Massillon football is that it's always going to be there. Steeped in tradition. It's got the greatest history in high school football. It's always going to be there. They're always going to play that game in Massillon. We're always going to be a contender. There is always going to be the enthusiasm, there's always going to be the hoopla and the great fans. The people just won't let go of that. They'll demand that it stays like that. Our football is important to us. That's something that's never going to go away. The great thing about Massillon is that we're always going to have that great tradition of football. The ghosts of the past won't allow it to go.

"I thought that every kid that came to Massillon and played or got his suit was great."

Nick Vrotsos

"I still get goose bumps when I walk in the stadium. All the tradition. All the players who have played there. All the great coaches. All the great fans. There's nothing like it. It's a big turn on. It's never gonna die."

BOB SEAMAN

"I don't have nightmares," Bob Seaman quipped when asked if he ever dreamt that he was back in Massillon as head football coach.

Coach Seaman's three nightmarish seasons as Massillon's head coach ended with his firing following a 26-6 loss to Canton McKinley in 1968. It was his second loss in three tries against the Tigers arch-rival.

Bob Seaman finished 20-9-1 in three seasons at Massillon.

Whether Seaman didn't know what he was getting into when he accepted the Massillon job, or whether he was just too strong-willed to accept the role that the Massillon citizenry expected him to, is uncertain.

But one thing is certain: Bob Seaman got off on the wrong foot in Massillon.

"Seaman was named the coach of the north team for the North-South All Star game," Massillon assistant coach Nick Vrotsos said. "He played his quarterback from Sandusky instead of Massillon's Dave Sheegog, and he lost the all-star game. Massillon fans never forgave him for that. Sheegog was the golden boy in Massillon. Seaman should have burned his bridges in Sandusky."

"He made a lot of mistakes," former Massillon head coach Leo Strang said. Strang led Massillon to three straight state championships (1959-61) and a 54-8-1 record. "Starting with the all-star game. Wearing the Sandusky jacket after taking the Massillon job. A lot of things like that. Boy, you just don't do those things in Massillon. He got off on the wrong foot early."

Seaman was delivered to Massillon by Earle Bruce, who had just led the Tigers to back-to-back state championships and a 20-0 record.

Seaman was Bruce's offensive line coach at Sandusky prior to Bruce's move to Massillon in 1964. He succeeded Bruce as Sandusky's head coach and led the Blue Streaks to a 19-1 record in his only two seasons as a head coach. In 1965, while Bruce won the A.P. state championship in Massillon, Seaman won the U.P.I. state championship in Sandusky and was named Ohio's High School Coach of the Year.

"Earle asked me if I'd be interested in the job and I said, 'Yeah.' I met with the committee, it was real late in the year. I interviewed with them. Decided I wanted to give it a swing."

Seaman inherited a 28-game winning streak and the expectations of Massillon fans who wanted a 22nd state championship.

"Seaman came from Sandusky, so they thought they were going to get another Earle Bruce, but it didn't happen on the field," said Bill Dorman, a Massillon lineman under Seaman.

Seaman won his first two games in 1966, over Canton Lincoln and Cleveland Benedictine, who had a 10-game winning streak of their own snapped by Massillon.

But the foundation started to shake when Massillon returned from Mansfield with a 0-0 tie. Massillon's 30-game winning streak suddenly became a 31-game unbeaten streak.

Seaman appeared to be getting his house in order after a 24-12 win over Alliance rekindled state championship hopes. But a heartbreaking 20-14 Week 5 loss to Niles caused the walls to start crumbling around Seaman.

"This is what ruined him," Vrotsos said. "We had gotten a two-touchdown lead. We're backed up, it's late in the game. I said to him, 'Let's take a safety.' He said, 'After this play.' We ran the fullback, Will Foster, and he fumbled the ball. They recovered it, ran an option, and scored. They needed two touchdowns to beat us. Then they tried an onside kick, they recovered it, scored again, and beat us. Now, we could have won that game. It would have kept the back biters off of our back, because the banter was on the coach."

Niles coach Bob Shaw was aware of the pressure that Seaman was under at Massillon. After the game he told Chuck Hess, *Evening Independent* sportswriter, "It's a shame what they're doing to him in Massillon."

Seaman took the loss hard. "It was bitter," he said. "I thought we played well enough to have won the game, but we didn't. Niles ended up with a 63-game winning streak at home. I prayed that they waited to lose until we were there the next time."

Bob Seaman addresses the crowd at a pep rally.

The 1966 season unraveled after the Niles loss. Massillon lost four of their next five games and finished the season 4-5-1. It was Massillon's first losing season since 1931, the year before Paul Brown became the Tigers head coach.

It could have been worse if not for an upset win over Steubenville in Week 9. "We came back and beat Steubenville, who was ranked number one in the state," Seaman said. "It was an important game to me and the kids. I don't know whether the town had anything good to remember about it but I remember that win. It probably was the sweetest victory of my career. Because they were number one in the state and people weren't giving us a lot of recognition after the four losses"

Seaman remembers the losses. "I thought we played well enough to win some of those games," he said. "We just didn't do it. They were all competitive football games. Those particular games were tough, to say the least."

Seaman did not relish the tough schedule Massillon faced. And it didn't help that the competition didn't always face as tough of a schedule as Massillon did. "Kids can only get psyched up so many times a year," Seaman reasons. "It was a feather in their cap if they could play well and win against Massillon. It was a *big* feather if they won."

The 1967 season was better for Seaman and the Tigers. "What a difference a day makes," Seaman said comparing the 1966 season to the 1967 season. "We played well and we won football games. It was about the same as 1966, but the ball bounced better in 1967."

Undefeated after six games in 1967, the Tigers faced Upper Arlington, who was staking their claim as *the* "power" of Ohio High School football. Of course Massillon was trying to retain their reputation as *the* state power.

"That game, we should have won," Vrotsos said. "We had them 6-0, we're on the four-yard line. We've got a third down. Trevor Young was the quarterback. He checked off. We had the off-tackle play called. You don't check off down there. He checked off to a quarterback sneak and we jumped. We got a five-yard penalty and we didn't score. So they're drivin' late in the game and they've got a fourth down and seven. And we call down from the press box, 'Watch the reverse.' We know the reverse is comin'. They started one way, then gave the ball and came back the other way and ran 22 yards to the seven-yard line. Our kids bit on the reverse. They score, kick the point, and beat us 7-6 to win the state title."

"Number one heartbreaker in my history," Seaman said. "We didn't play as well as we could have. One point is one point.

"It really crushes the players when they don't win. If you think the community and the fans go berserk when they don't win, think about the kids. They really have problems. They oughta try to win the best they can. That's one thing I'll say about Massillon football players, they always played and they always worked and they always wanted to do the right thing in football. I think that's a positive influence that Massillon football has on the kids in Massillon. They want to do the right thing. That's a good trait."

"If you think the community and the fans go berserk when they don't win, think about the kids."

Bob Seaman

Mark Malinowski scored Massillon's only points against Upper Arlington on a 75-yard interception return. He also played quarterback in the final game of the season against McKinley. Although he would be Seaman's starting quarterback in 1968, he had not seen any action as Trevor Young's back-up in 1967.

"Trevor got hurt the first series in the McKinley game and I went in and had a great game, and we won," Malinowski said. "And the first words out of Bob Seaman's mouth to me when the game was over was 'What are you going to do this winter?' Not 'nice game, way to go.' I took it as a threat quite truthfully."

Malinowski said Seaman did not like the fact that he was on the swim team during the winter of his sophomore year and wanted him to play basketball.

Seaman's final season, 1968, started with one of Massillon's most disappointing openers. It was the first game as a starting quarterback at Massillon for Malinowski.

"Another memory that bugs the crap out of me," Malinowski said, "Mentor beating us 19-0. Nobody wants to talk about the flu shots we took Tuesday night of that week. There were a whole lot of sick kids. They won, and it was on the field, and it was fair and square, but we were sick. I was one of them.

"We did not have a great relationship," Malinowski said of Seaman. "I don't have fond memories. I just don't think he was ever the right fit for this town."

"We expected to win everything," said Mark McDew, a fleet-footed running back, of the team's attitude going into the 1968 season. McDew started three years for Seaman. He will always be remembered for returning the second half kickoff 90 yards for a touchdown in the 1967 Canton McKinley game. It was one of many dazzling plays McDew turned in during his career.

"I just don't think he was ever the right fit for this town."

Mark Malinowski

"I remember it like it was yesterday," McDew said. "Because everyone still talks about it. All I did was run straight up the middle, took two steps to the right and was never touched. It was simple. Once Willie Twiggs closed off the lane it was over."

Like Malinowski, McDew did not enjoy playing for Seaman. "Out of all the years in the history of Massillon football, I had to be playing for Bob Seaman," McDew said. "When he brought me up from the sophomore team he sat me down and told me, 'This is an opportunity for you. Don't mess it up.' And at the end of the year when he handed me an award he said, 'Do not let this go to your head.' Our relationship was not good. I respected him because he was the coach, he called the plays. Seaman was on this power trip. *I am the coach*. Well, that *I am the coach* attitude ended up getting him run out of town. He was his own worst enemy. He thought he knew more than his assistants. And maybe he did. But at least *listen* to them. He was like, *This is my team and this is the way I'm running it.* It was his arrogance that always showed with him. Nobody liked him."

Ducky Schroeder, the legendary Massillon assistant coach, recalled when he and Seaman didn't see eye-to-eye. "The thing I remember about his system was the tackle calls we had. That was a little bit different from what anybody else had here. The tackle had to make calls in order to get the best blocking angles and it wasn't too successful. There's so much noise in our stadium in a close game that the other linemen couldn't hear the calls. And the tackle calls a lot of times involved the halfbacks. So lots of times the halfback couldn't hear the calls. The crowd noise was too much. I remember the boys used to come out of the game and I'd say, 'What happened, you didn't block the right man.' They'd say, 'Coach, I couldn't hear the call.'"

Seaman respected Schroeder. "Ducky was the backbone of the program, to be honest. I think everybody looked up to him. The kids did, the coaches did, the community did. He was just a positive factor."

Seaman led Massillon to a 7-3 mark in 1968. "I think we had a pretty good football team," Seaman said. "We lost to three pretty good football teams. Didn't get blown out. Never did that. Just didn't play quite hard enough. The three games we lost were to ranked football teams."

The highlight of the 1968 season was a six game winning streak that had the Tigers ranked third in the state after a Week 5 win over Niles. "I remember that Niles waited long enough for us to beat 'em at home. That's the one I wanted, personally. Their 63-game home unbeaten streak ceased and desisted with us, which was nice."

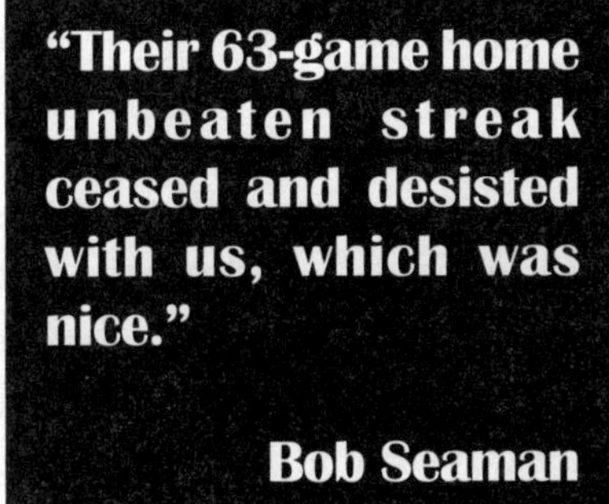

Seaman liked the Massillon players. "Not great football players, but good football players. None of 'em had big red S' on their chests, no Supermen. But they all did the best that they could. I never had a complaint with Massillon kids on that line. I think that's unusual. I've been a lot of places and there's been a lot of players at times who didn't give their best. I can't say that for Massillon kids. They always did their best."

Seaman remembers the Massillon fans giving him a hard time. "Yeah, some of them," he said. "Bad, too. I remember them calling my house after the McKinley game and telling my son, who was a young man at the time, that he wouldn't see his father alive again. That wasn't good. He remembers it to this day, I'll tell you that. The 'For Sale' signs in my yard, that kind of stuff. I think it's just dissatisfied people. I'd get some early-in-the morning calls. Those kind of aggravated the heck out of me. Two o'clock in the morning. I'd tell 'em, 'The bar doesn't close until 2:30.' They'd say, 'Why didn't you...they didn't even ask questions. Just said mean things. Ornery things. Usually you could tell they'd had a beer or two, or three or four. And those are the kind of things that aggravated me. But there wasn't a million of 'em. They would be as frustrated as I was. There's one thing a football coach doesn't like—he doesn't like to lose. Those kind of people aggravated me. If they wanted to call and talk to me, I'd be glad to talk to them. But those kind of fans—they're not fans, in my opinion."

The losses were tough to take at Massillon, Seaman said. "Because the community was behind them, win, win, or win. And there were times when they were *not* behind the kids, in my opinion. At times they weren't behind me. And when they weren't behind the coach, kids realize that. It doesn't make you happy. The people who were disgruntled and vocally saying it, that was fine. But those that were disgruntled, behind your back disgruntled, those were the kind I didn't like. I don't think they had the good of Massillon at heart. I think the kids really played well. I have no complaints about that. I know I have friends in Massillon. And I probably have enemies, too. I don't think the fans do anything as far as the esprit de corps for that football team. That's my opinion anyhow.

"I think the kids are football players because they want to be football players, not because any group wants them to be football players. Maybe their dads, but even that I don't believe. I don't believe that kind of pressure is legitimate for kids today. The pressure they put on the kids is too much. It's more than they can take. When the kids want to pressure themselves, that's good. But I think that when they started leaning on them outside, and they're hearing things that shouldn't be, that's hard on the kids. I think the game is played for the players. Not for anybody else. Not for the town. Not for the pride of Massillon, but for the pride of Massillon football. It's important for the players to win. It's not more important for the football players to win for the fans. They should be winning for themselves. I think the fan pressure is uncalled for at times with kids. I think it comes from having so much success in the past.

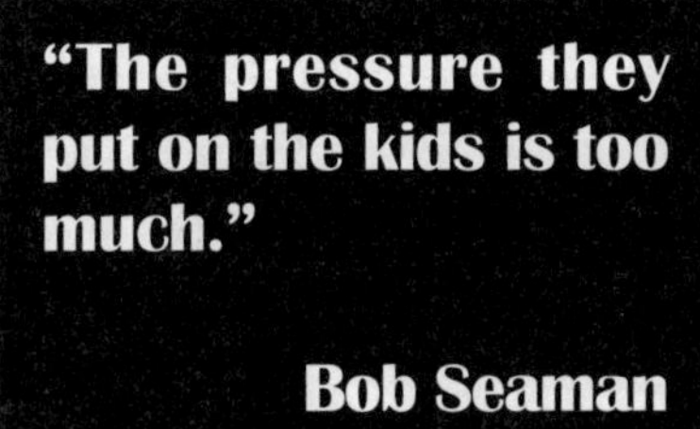

"I remember a story when we first moved to Massillon. I was at a gas station in the Tiger Wagon (the car provided for the Massillon coach), filling up the tank. A lady, an elderly lady, pulled up beside me and rolled her window down. She said, 'I just want you to know that you won't replace Paul Brown. You'll *never* replace Paul Brown.' That kind of tickled me. This is 26 years after Paul Brown. I said, 'I know.'"

Eddie Bell's touchdown catch to win the 1974 Massillon-McKinley, 20-15, is one of the enduring images in Massillon history.

Mike Mauger

Massillon's All-Ohioans

Mike Mauger
1970

Tim Ridgley
1970

Dennis Franklin
1970

Steve Luke
1970

Willie Spencer
1971

Tom Hannon
1972

Charles Danzy
1973

Charles Swann
1973

Joe Studer
1974

Bill Harmon
1975

Tom Grizzard
1975

Anthony Grizzard
1976

Tim Daniels
1977

Carl Dorsey
1977

Brent Offenbecher
1977

Brent Offenbecher
1978

Curtis Strawder
1978

Darren Longshore
1978

Jeff Pedro
1978

Eric Barnard
1978

Bob Simpson
1979

Marty Guzzetta
1979

Mark Kircher
1979

Larry Massie
1979

TEAMS 1970s RECORDS

81	16	4
WINS	LOSSES	TIES

2 State Championships
2 State Final Fours

1970
10-0-0
State Champions
National Runner-up
Head Coach: Bob Commings

M	Key Games	Opp.
22	Niles	3
28	Canton McKinley	0
412	***Season Totals***	***29***

1971
8-2-0

Head Coach: Bob Commings

M	Key Games	Opp.
6	Niles	7
7	Warren Harding	8
29	Canton McKinley	6
300	***Season Totals***	***33***

1972
10-1-0
State Final Four
State Poll Champions
Head Coach: Bob Commings

M	Key Games	Opp.
12	Canton McKinley	3
14	Cincinnati Princeton	17
193	***Season Totals***	***46***

1973
8-1-1

Head Coach: Bob Commings

M	Key Games	Opp.
13	Upper Arlington	7
0	Cleve. Benedictine	0
0	Canton McKinley	21
245	***Season Totals***	***74***

1974

6-4-0

Head Coach: Chuck Shuff

M	Key Games	Opp.
14	Upper Arlington	31
33	Steubenville	8
20	Canton McKinley	15
277	***Season Totals***	***136***

1975

6-3-1

Head Coach: Chuck Shuff

M	Key Games	Opp.
6	Nordonia	6
7	Upper Arlington	8
15	Canton McKinley	21
168	***Season Totals***	***51***

1976

8-2-0

Head Coach: Mike Currence

M	Key Games	Opp.
0	Middletown	6
0	Gahanna Lincoln	10
7	Canton McKinley	3
121	***Season Totals***	***51***

1977

8-2-0

Head Coach: Mike Currence

M	Key Games	Opp.
7	Barberton	9
21	Warren Harding	22
21	Canton McKinley	0
281	***Season Totals***	***95***

1978

9-0-1

Head Coach: Mike Currence

M	Key Games	Opp.
27	Massillon Perry	6
7	Warren Harding	7
13	Canton McKinley	10
278	***Season Totals***	***39***

1979

10-1-0

State Final Four

Head Coach: Mike Currence

M	Key Games	Opp.
16	Warren Harding	6
24	Canton McKinley	0
0	Parma Padua	12
302	***Season Totals***	***36***

Story of the Decade 1970s

Southeast Side Neighborhood Produces Four NFL Players from Same Team

The odds against a high school football player making it into the NFL are great. According to the NFL Players Association, only 0.2 percent of high school players ever make an NFL roster. It's tough enough for an elite high school player to make his mark at the *college* level, where only 2.4 percent of players make it to the NFL. Imagine the odds of four kids from the southeast side of Massillon making NFL rosters in the 1970s.

Three of the four players from the same southeast side neighborhood who played in the NFL.

In terms of demographics, the southeast side of Massillon is considered "poor." Marty Gugov, a star Massillon running back from 1959-60, grew up in the southwest side of Massillon, across the Tuscarawas River from the southeast side. The star running back remembers his neighborhood being pretty poor, too.

"In the '50s and '60s we still had a lot of the neighborhoods in town that had the old hunkeys and families that made it their business to know who played ball and who didn't," Gugov said. "They saw you wear a Massillon Tiger jacket, saw ya have your hair cut, and said hi to ya and laughed at ya. When you started getting your name in the newspaper they wanted to know how you were doing every day. They *all* wanted to know. They walked out on the porch every day as you walked home from practice. They were so strong and vehement with their passion for Massillon football that they actually contributed to the success of the football squad.

"Not all of 'em liked the same things, obviously, but they all liked Massillon football."

Marty Gugov

"My neighborhood was very ethnic," Gugov said. "My dad wanted to live there because it was close to Republic Steel and he could walk to work. We had Italians, Spaniards, Bulgarians, Romanians, Macedonians, everything you can imagine. They were all in that neighborhood. Not all of 'em liked the same things, obviously, but they *all* liked Massillon football."

"It was a tough neighborhood, but not as tough as the southeast side. The southeast side had tough people. The southwest side had a bunch of guys who played for Massillon. We had a number of kids that were pretty tough hombres. But I think the southeast side had more fire in their bellies because they were more deprived than we were."

Gugov has a term that describes the kids from the southeast side of town. "Peasant toughness," Gugov said. "That's probably the best description of someone who was tough because they had it tough. And the southeast side kids had it tough. We did, too. We didn't have much. We always had food. Always had clothes. Always had Christmas presents. The the kids on the southeast side had it tougher than we did, a lot of them. Some of 'em came from single parent families. Most of the southwest side kids came from two-parent families in those days. When you don't have *anything* it makes you get tough. If you're not tough, you're *gone*. We had a lot of over achieving kids, probably because of the community, because of inner drive, all of those combinations of things made Massillon a unique place."

"In our neighborhood, and on our *team*, we had four players who went to the NFL," Steve Luke said. "You take Willie Spencer, who was a junior when I was a senior, and Tommy Hannon, who was a sophomore when I was a senior, Dennis Franklin and I were in the same class. That's four of the 1970 team. We all played together at Franklin Elementary, Jones Junior High and Washington High School.

Their heroes were from Gugov's era. "We had a lot of neighborhood games over in the yard," said Franklin, who was a star quarterback at the University of Michigan before playing for the Detroit Lions. "We emulated all the Massillon stars. We had heroes, from Charlie Brown (1960-61), who was an All-American at Syracuse and lived right up the street, to Mike Hershberger (1955-56), who played major league baseball with Joe Sparma (1957-59), who also lived down the street. We used to always walk down the street and look at his house and say, 'That's Hershberger's house!' To us it was like going by and saying 'That's Joe Dimaggio's house.' When you're young your idols are your idols. You still look up to those people. Most of the guys who I grew up with who went on to play at the college level or were lucky enough to take it to the pros, we were all impressed as young kids. But that could have just as easily been a drug dealer who impressed us. It can go either way."

"We were all impressed as young kids. But that could have just as easily been a drug dealer who impressed us. It can go either way."

Dennis Franklin

Hannon, who was All-Big 10 at Michigan State before starring for the Minnesota Vikings, remembers playing neighborhood games on Massillon game nights.

"Growing up there and hearin' 'em shootin' off fireworks every time Massillon scored a touchdown. That was my major deal as a kid," Hannon said. "Not *going* to the games. We'd sit in the yard, just me and the neighborhood kids. We'd just listen to the bombs and we'd know Massillon scored a touchdown. On a regular basis they were shooting off eight or nine of 'em. So we always figured Massillon was winnin'. Everybody in our neighborhood who wanted to play ended up playing for the Tigers.

"Before the games we'd always play in somebody's yard. I was always Bill Blunt (1962-63), because he was my idol."

The neighborhood kids were also captivated by watching their heroes play pick-up games at the neighborhood park.

"Every Sunday, right after we got home from church, we'd all go down to Shriver Park. That's where Bill Blunt, Jim Lawrence, Bobby Hewitt, Edgar Herring, Duke Pierce, Wil Perry— everybody who played for the Tigers—used to play football right there on the street. We'd sit on the side and watch 'em play. That's when we were *real* young. We all lived on the southeast part of town and some of the guys who lived down in the Bottoms would come up and everybody would meet up at Shriver Park. And the young kids, like myself, we'd sit up there and watch them. Me and Steve Luke, Dennis Franklin, Larry Harper. All of us. We would just sit there and watch 'em."

While Harper wasn't one of the neighborhood's *fabulous four* to make an NFL roster, he was a remarkable player in his own right.

Perhaps Harper's greatest gift to Tiger fans came when he returned the opening kick-off in the 1970 Massillon-

McKinley game for a 94-yard touchdown.

Franklin had seen it all before.

"That was pretty cool," Franklin said of Harper's kick return. "He was quite a kick returner. You know, it's funny because he used to do that when we used to play those games over in the field. There must have been three or four guys on each side. I can remember that old playground field where he used to do that against us. It was neighborhood against neighborhood. So it never surprised me, the talent that Larry had. He was a very, very gifted guy. Larry was a very motivated guy, quite intelligent. Very ego driven, very tenacious. He was tough for a guy that wasn't that big. He would not be denied, he was that type of a guy. When the game was on the line and you needed somebody to go to, you could count on going to him and him giving you 110 percent."

"I can remember that old playground field where Larry Harper used to do that against us. It was neighborhood against neighborhood."

Dennis Franklin

"It's kind of funny," Luke said, "out of the whole group, Larry was the one that was most adamant about playing pro ball. He wanted to be a professional football player. All of us are still good friends. Larry didn't have the size or speed. He had great quickness, but he didn't have that burst."

Harper ended up starring at Miami University, where he is still in the record books for his accomplishments as a receiver and return man. He had a pro try-out with the St. Louis Cardinals.

The determination that helped Harper on the gridiron also served him well off-the-field where he has become a national vice-president of Nike.

"I remember the summers going up to the high school and just staying there all day watching the two-a-day football practices," Harper said. "How exciting that was. There were so many of us that the coaches saw us sitting in the hot sun, they'd invite us in and let us partake of the lunch and give us some of the juice and sandwiches that the players had. I think the coach was Leo Strang. I just remember hanging out at the practice all day long. And taking a football out there and playing while they were practicing. We were playing while they were practicing. It was just neat to be out there with the team. Just to be out there in that kind of surrounding. It was just unbelievable."

After successful high school careers at Massillon, the recruiting was heavy for three of the four neighborhood stars. Luke, Franklin and Hannon pretty well had their choice of colleges.

His popularity with colleges surprised Luke. "I remember going into my senior year of high school hopin' and prayin' that I'd get a scholarship offer from a small school. I was thinking to myself that I would take *anything.* Then out of the clear blue sky all of these offers started coming in. It just blew me away. The first time I flew on a plane was when I flew out to visit USC. USC wanted to sign me on as a tight end. I couldn't believe it. Dennis Franklin, myself and Mike Mauger received letters from 80-90 schools. It was pretty incredible."

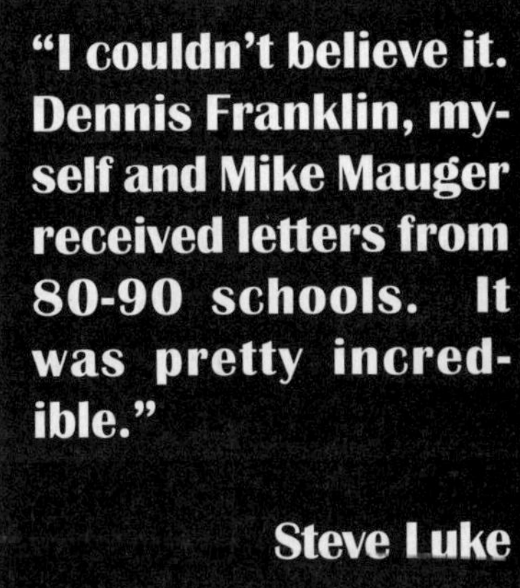

Mauger was the star of the 1970 team that produced the four NFL players. He set the single season rushing record and also handled the kickoffs and extra points. Mauger, Harper and Steve Studer, a two-way starting lineman, all had NFL tryouts after their college careers, Mauger with the Cowboys and Studer with the Bears.

Willie Spencer took a different route to the NFL. "Willie was always ornery," Luke said. "But Willie was a good guy and still is. I think that Willie sometimes let bad influences get to him. I still have a lot of respect for Willie and what he accomplished. Not everybody gets an opportunity that Dennis and I had. He just wasn't into school. But I've always admired and respected Willie for what he's done. Not everyone can say they left high school and went straight to the pros and played."

Spencer found stardom as a running back in the World Football league, where he was a teammate with Hall of Famers Paul Warfield and Larry Csonka. Spencer actually rushed for more yards than Csonka in the WFL. He also played for the Minnesota Vikings and New York Giants.

Luke enjoyed a six-year NFL career with the Green Bay Packers. Luke led the Packers in tackles in 1978. Luke intercepted 10 passes in his NFL career.

Dennis Franklin was an All-Big Ten quarterback at the University of Michigan. He led Michigan in passing and total offense every year from 1972-74. He was elected captain in 1974. Franklin finished sixth in the Heisman Trophy balloting as a senior.

Franklin was drafted by the Detroit Lions, where he was switched to wide receiver. He was the Lion's leading receiver before a season-ending injury effectively ended his NFL career.

Hannon followed an All-Big Ten career at Michigan State with an outstanding eight year career with the Minnesota Vikings. Hannon had 15 career interceptions.

Games of the Century

Biggest Upset/Most Exciting Finish? 1974 Classic Was Both

Massillon had nothing to play for. Canton McKinley had everything to lose.

Program from 1974 Massillon-McKinley game.

The Tigers were suffering through a disappointing 5-4 season under first year head coach Chuck Shuff. Canton McKinley, on the other hand, was undefeated, number one in the state and needing a win to go to the playoffs. The Tigers were in a position to be spoilers. The Bulldogs were ripe for an upset. The Tigers were heavy underdogs against the seemingly unbeatable Bulldogs. McKinley had scored 381 points, and given up just two touchdowns all season. No one gave Massillon a chance.

Junior fullback Bill Harmon was the big gun for the 1974 Tigers. In fact, for much of the season he seemed to be Massillon's *only* option. But the season finale was a different story.

"That had to be the greatest game plan we had the whole time Shuff was there," Harmon said. "We were underdogs all the way. McKinley had everything. They were 9-0, picked to go to the playoffs and probably win the state that year."

Shuff didn't change his way of game planning on his own accord.

"The game started with us two weeks before," Shuff said. "This is something that most coaches would *never* do and something that Massillon forced me to do, I'll just put it that way.

"We were gonna be playing Alliance, and I think they had only won one game. We were in our coaching meeting on Sunday. The offensive coaches are in one room in the stadium and the defensive coaches are in the other. And I'm back and forth, workin' with 'em, tryin' to get the thoughts down on Alliance. Every time I go from one room to another there's conversation in some way or the other about McKinley. And we still have to play Alliance and we've lost four games already this season. I'd have to remind 'em, 'Hey, we're playing Alliance this week. We're playin' McKinley *next* week.' This happened three, four times. Finally (assistant coach) Nick Vrotsos said, 'But coach,

"I said 'I know McKinley's the big game, but Alliance is a bigger game right now, because if we don't win this one, we're gone. We're history."

Chuck Shuff

McKinley's the big game.' I said, 'Yeah, I know McKinley's the big game, but Alliance is a bigger game right now. Because if we don't win this one, we're history. I don't care what happens with McKinley, we're *gone* if we lose this one. They're not gonna take a five-loss season. We've had enough negative press already.'

"Nick said, 'Coach, it's this way every year. These kids are gonna be out there in the streets and in the school and everybody's gonna be talking about the McKinley game.'

"I said, 'That's a big problem. We can't afford that. We just can't afford that.' Nick said, 'Well I don't know what you're gonna do about it, it's always this way.'

"Well, that's one thing you don't say to me, 'It's always this way.' So I just looked at those guys and said, 'Get Alliance figured out. Let's get this done. Figure out Alliance then we'll talk about McKinley, even if it takes talking until midnight.'

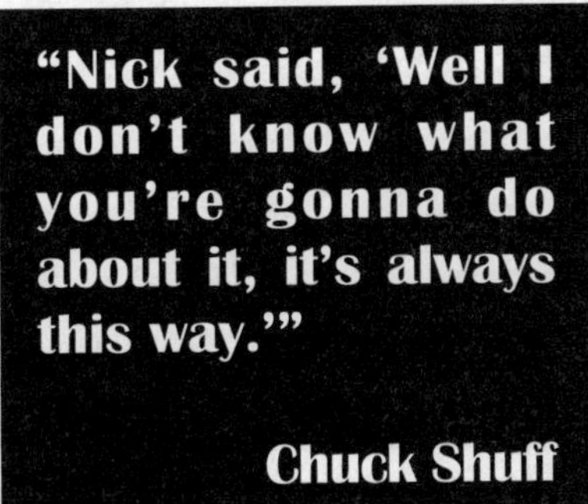

"It worked. They got the Alliance work done. I didn't hear anybody talking about McKinley. I said, 'Fine, we're ready for Alliance, now let's talk about McKinley.

"We talked about McKinley for about an hour and I'm thinkin', 'Okay, I've solved the problem with the coaches, now what about the kids? What do we do here?' Finally, I called all the coaches together. I said, 'I've got the answer on how to handle the kids.'

"I said, 'Tomorrow we're not going to look at game films.' The coaches said, 'They've gotta see what they did in the Warren Harding game!' I said, 'No, we're not gonna do that, that's past history (a 35-14 loss). We have to deal with Alliance, then we have to deal with McKinley.' The coaches said, 'Well how are you gonna do that?' I said, 'We're gonna barter with 'em. We're gonna give 'em the Alliance game plan. And when you're done with that, I'm gonna tell 'em we're gonna go out there and work for an hour and half. And we're gonna be done with Alliance. And they're gonna look at me like I'm crazy. Then, if that hour and a half has been good, and we've really worked hard, then I'm gonna tell 'em we'll work a half hour on McKinley.'

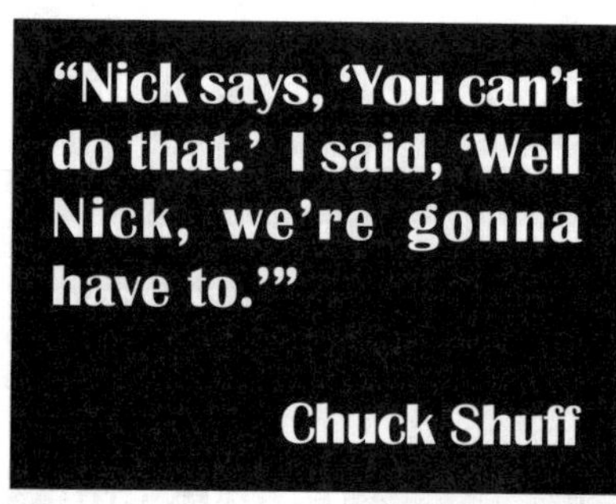

"Nick says, 'You can't do that.' I said, 'Well Nick, we're gonna have to. Because these kids are gonna be thinking about McKinley, their parents are thinking about McKinley, the boosters are thinking about McKinley and askin' questions about McKinley, so what alternative do we have?' So that's what we did.

"We had absolutely, without

a doubt the best four practices of the whole year that week. We won easily against Alliance (39-12) with our base offense and our base defense. Our best fundamental game all year.

"Then we came into the McKinley week and there's 8-10 inches of snow on the field. The field was covered. You couldn't go outside. But we had already put in our changes. We could go inside and walk through the changes. And they were substantial changes on offense and defense. McKinley had just played Harding—had a hard game. So they couldn't have worked on us very much. And they couldn't practice outside, either. They were workin' in a gym someplace, too, I'm sure. Monday, Tuesday and Wednesday all you could do was walk through stuff inside. You couldn't throw deep. You couldn't kick. Thursday and Friday we could work outside. We were one up on McKinley in that we were able to work the week before and get these changes put it. They ended up being vital changes to our success in the game. The defensive changes we made just totally baffled McKinley."

The night before the game, Shuff was introduced to a local minister.

"Jim Bryant was the Booster Club president," Shuff said. "He came to me and said, 'I want to introduce you to Father Crites. Father Crites would like a pass for the press box for tomorrow's game.' Offhandedly I made a quip to the Father, I said, 'If it takes you up in that press box to win this game, I'll give you ten passes. I asked Gene Boerner (Booster Club president, 1973) if there was any room up there. Gene said, 'Yeah, there'll be room.' So he was up there for the game.

Harmon recalled his role for the big game. "Shuff had me running left, running right, the whole first half," Harmon said. "And then we started dinking passes out to the tailback Mark Streeter.

"He started a little bit of a passing game with quarterback Greg Wood. We jumped right out ahead of them. Mark Streeter had one heck of a game. So did Woods. We'd do the belly series, where they'd fake to me into the line. They had to respect the run because I was poppin' for 4-5 yards every play. We were gettin' first downs on the ground like it was nothin'."

"Offensively we decided to go to the straight 'T' with Billy Harmon, with Streeter and Keith Harmon as blockers and let Greg Wood audible to the off-tackle play or the trap play that fits the defense that they're showin' us," Shuff said. "And it worked like a charm. We went to that because you could read their defensive tackle. Greg could come up to the line and look at it and call the audible. Billy was our primary threat. We also had several good plays from Streeter. A great pass from Wood to Streeter for a 24-yard touchdown was the game's first score.

"Everybody contributed into that offense. Joe Studer just had an outstanding game at center and gave us a little more leeway on our blocking options and adjustments. We had a 14-0 lead, partly because of some of the changes we made on offense," Shuff said, "but mostly because of the changes we made on defense.

"Their running back, Jonathon Moore, was excellent on the sweep to the wing side. Their quarterback, Roch Hontas, was great on the bootleg away from the wing side. We knew that those two plays had to be shut down. They ran them as well as anyone in the state. Defensively we moved our ends outside. Thee Lemon and Mark Streeter were our Monster backs. They were almost like linebackers. We put them in a twin strong safety situation. McKinley had never seen that before. They were trying to block guys who weren't there. That just created havoc for them. Hontas couldn't get outside because we contained him immediately. He had to throw much quicker."

Massillon led 14-0 at halftime...but a late drive by McKinley prompted Shuff to change his game plan.

Massillon led 14-0 at halftime after a two-yard touchdown run by Wood, but a late drive by McKinley prompted Shuff to change his game plan.

"They moved the ball 30-35 yards toward the end of the first half," Shuff said. "They had made a couple of adjustments. So going in at halftime I'm thinking, 'Okay, we need to get back to our basic stuff more. I outcoached myself. You stay with what's workin'. We let 'em back in the game."

Hontas flung a 35-yard touchdown pass to Reuben Floyd in the third quarter. The Bulldogs put together a 95-yard touchdown drive and

Hontas nailed a 25-yard field goal in the fourth quarter to move ahead 15-14 with 1:13 left in the game. It looked like the game was over.

Luther Emery, the longtime Massillon sportswriter, was the editor of Massillon's *Evening Independent* by this time. He was watching the game from the press box with an old friend.

"I said, 'Don't give up Reverend Crites, say a little prayer for the Tigers.'"

Luther Emery

"I sat right next to Reverend Crites," Emery said. "He practically gave up after McKinley went ahead. I said, 'Don't give up Reverend Crites, say a little prayer for the Tigers.'" Whether or not divine intervention played a role, the Tigers certainly made the most of their last possession.

Shuff remembers addressing his players after the McKinley field goal.

"When I called the kick receiving team together, I walked into the huddle. There was not one sound. It was still and quiet. The intensity in those kids' eyes told me, 'We're gonna win this football game.' I never felt that before in my life. I knew if those kids had any say in that game, we were going to win that football game. And I knew they had a lot of say. I just had no idea that something like that was going to happen. I just looked at 'em and said, 'Let's go!' Normally there's a little pep talk in there. They broke the huddle, went out on the field and returned it to about the 37.

"Greg Wood was on the sideline with me and I said, 'Greg, run the out with Eddie Bell.' It was a 90 out, semi-sprint pass. Our thinking was that we had Keith Harmon, Bill's brother, who had kicked a 47-yard field gaol against Warren Harding. We wanted to get it down to where we at least had a shot at a field goal."

"He got real antsy like he was going to try to pick it off.'"

Nick Vrotsos

Vrotsos remembers the final drive as if it were yesterday. The Massillon coaching braintrust was waiting patiently to go for the jugular against the Bulldogs.

"I was upstairs in the press box. We were behind, we needed a touchdown," Vrotsos said. "We're coming down the field. They were giving us the out. We were wondering when we could go out and up."

Wood connected with wide receiver Eddie Bell three times to move the ball into McKinley territory at the 31.

Vrotsos was watching the McKinley cornerback. "We kept playin' it and playin' it and he was getting real antsy because we were getting down there pretty good. He got real antsy like he was going to try to pick it off," Vrotsos said.

Finally, with the ball on the 34-yard line after Wood was dropped for a three-yard loss, it was time to strike.

Shuff was in constant communication with the press box as the drive unfolded. "I said to defensive coordinator Frank Thomas, 'The safety sat and covered the post.' Frank said, 'Yeah.' I said, 'So the out and up should be there. There's nobody to cover the deep out. Frank said, *'Call it.'*

Vrotsos remembers the dialog in the press box as the Massillon coaches tried to decide when the right time was to run the out and up. "We said, 'Now, no, NOW,'" Vrotsos said.

Bell took the snap with 13 seconds left and soon faced great pressure from the McKinley defense. Harmon picked up a pass rusher who probably would have sacked Wood. "Billy had a good block," Shuff said, "and the line did a good job.

"We threw it up and Bell caught it and scored," Vrotsos said. "That was a classic, because the McKinley cornerback bit on it. We went up on him and beat him."

"During the extra point and the kick-off, John Bridewiser, the McKinley head coach, was right next to me—on our sideline.'"

Chuck Shuff

"I was watchin' the quarterback," Shuff said. "After that play, pandemonium broke loose," Shuff said. "People start coming out of the stands. I'm carried onto the field. There's still six seconds left on the clock. Nick Vrotsos is running alongside of me with a couple of players carrying me. He's grabbing my hand and saying, 'Coach, we don't have to walk the alleys this winter!' I said, 'Yeah, I know what you mean. We won't have to walk the back alleys!'

Eddie Bell celebrates his game-winning touchdown catch against Canton McKinley in 1974.

"We got the field cleared to run the extra point. With all the pandemonium, I don't know who sent the team onto the field for the extra point. We didn't make the extra point. But during the extra point try and the kickoff, John Bridewiser, the McKinley head coach, was right next to me—on our sideline. He had his arm around me. His comment to me was, 'Heck of a football game. Can you believe these kids?' I looked at him and said, 'What the heck are you doing over here?' He said, 'Isn't this a heckuva game? How about these kids. I just had to be on the winning side,' was his final comment."

In the press box, Massillon play-by-play announcer Bill Caples was beside himself. "I remember when I called

Vrotsos: "Character" Won Game

Assistant coach Nick Vrotsos wrote one word on the chalkboard following Massillon's shocking 20-15 win over Canton McKinley in 1974: 'Character.'

"Character won that game," Vrotsos said. "If you're a good person, you believe in the right things, and you *do* the right things, good things happen to you. Head coach Chuck Shuff was a guy who expounded character. He was a Christian livin' man. The character he was building in the team as their leader had paid off. And it paid off in the big game, and that's what Massillon's all about."

that touchdown pass," Caples said. "It was in the south end zone. You could see it unfold. At that time we were broadcasting the game from the top of the roof. And man, from up there you had about as great a view as you could have for watching a game. It was, 'Eddie, catch the ball. Just don't drop it. That's all.' Ohhh, that whole stadium..I thought that whole stadium shook. People were grabbing each other and they were turning around and hugging each other. There were people running up and down the steps. They even got down to the field. They didn't stop, they just didn't stop."

"Beatin' McKinley and knocking them out of the playoffs," Vrotsos reflected. "That's probably one of the toughest defeats McKinley ever had. That's a magic moment."

Games of the Century

Tigers Lose Ohio's First Playoff Game

"I still can't believe that game to this day," All-Ohio running back Tom Hannon said of his final game as a Tiger in 1972. Massillon's playoff game against Cincinnati Princeton wasn't

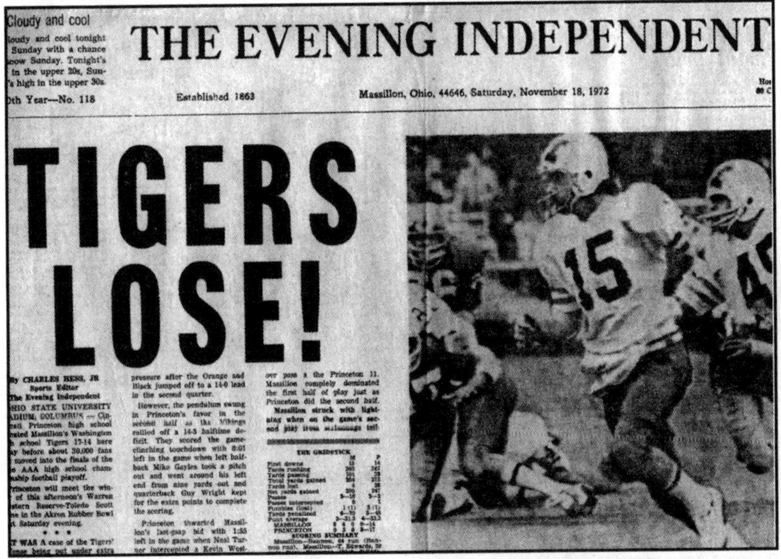

Cloudy and cool

…loudy and cool tonight … Sunday with a chance … now Sunday. Tonight's … in the upper 20s, Sun…'s high in the upper 30s.

…th Year—No. 118

THE EVENING INDEPENDENT

Established 1863

Massillon, Ohio, 44646, Saturday, November 18, 1972

TIGERS LOSE!

By CHARLES HESS, JR
Sports Editor
The Evening Independent

OHIO STATE UNIVERSITY STADIUM, COLUMBUS — Cincinnati Princeton high school defeated Massillon's Washington high school Tigers 17-14 here today before about 30,000 fans and moved into the finals of the … AAA high school championship football playoff.

Princeton will meet the winner of this afternoon's Warren Western Reserve-Toledo Scott game in the Akron Rubber Bowl next Saturday evening.

* * *

IT WAS A case of the Tigers' … being put under extra pressure after the Orange and Black jumped off to a 14-0 lead in the second quarter.

However, the pendulum swung in Princeton's favor in the second half as the Vikings rallied off a 14-3 halftime deficit. They scored the game-clinching touchdown with 8:01 left in the game when left halfback Mike Gayles took a pitch out and went around his left end from nine yards out and quarterback Guy Wright kept for the extra points to complete the scoring.

Princeton thwarted Massillon's last-gasp bid with 1:55 left in the game when Neal Turner intercepted a Kevin West… over pass at the Princeton 11.

Massillon completely dominated the first half of play just as Princeton did the second half.

Massillon struck with lightning when on the game's second play from scrimmage …

THE GRIDSTICK

SCORING SUMMARY

Massillon—Hannon, 64 run (Hannon run). Massillon—T. Edwards, 39 …

The front page headline of The Evening Independent reflects the city's shock at losing the state's first playoff game in 1972.

an ordinary playoff game, it was Ohio's first-ever playoff game.

Massillon fans among the crowd of 30,000 in Ohio Stadium thought the Tigers 14-3 halftime lead was just the beginning.

It turned out to be the beginning of the end.

After watching their team dominate the first half, many Massillon fans were amused when Princeton lined up for a 47-yard field goal attempt as the first half clock wound down. Little did anyone know that the successful kick would prove to be the turning point in the game.

Massillon fans weren't the only ones who were overconfident heading into the second half.

Massillon coach Bob Commings sensed a problem and lit into his charges at halftime.

"Coach Commings was cursing us, tellin' us, 'It's too easy guys. We should have put this game away,'" Hannon said. "Some of the players and coaches thought we had the game won. I knew Princeton was a good team."

"Coach Commings was cursing us, tellin' us, 'It's too easy guys. We should have put this game away.'"

Tommy Hannon

"Here's what happened," said assistant coach Nick Vrotsos. "We were up 14 and could have had a third one. They come out in the second half running the belly option. They come down and score. We've got 'em fourth down and seven. Larry Coyer is the defensive coordinator. I said, 'What are you gonna call?' He's gonna run angle to the field. I said, 'Oh no, Larry, no, no, no. You can't angle toward the field, they're going to run option. Just play it straight.' What happened? The end came down, all the quarterback had to do was pitch the ball. They picked up the first down and went down and scored. If we stop that play, we beat them and play Warren Western Reserve for the championship."

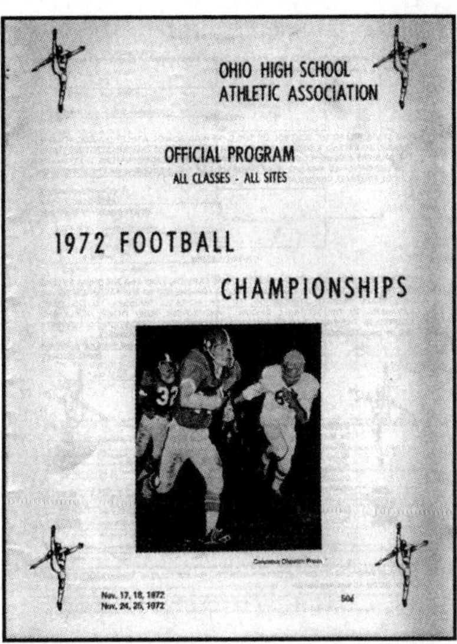

Program from first state playoff game in 1972.

Princeton scored twice in the second half while holding Massillon scoreless to win the state's inaugural playoff game, 17-14.

"Physically, talent-wise, Princeton had better talent than we had across the board," Hannon said. "We should have put the game away. We had a screen play to Alex Wood from about the four-yard line and he caught it and went all the way to the two yard line and they called it back. We had another play where we threw the ball and the receiver dropped it. So to me, it should have been 28-0, then it wouldn't have been as close as it was at the end.

"They wore our guys down," Hannon said. "They had 250-260 pound defensive linemen. Our offensive linemen were 170-180. You just eventually get worn down."

Was Game Plan Abandoned Too Soon?

Almost 40 years of reflecting doesn't make the events of November 16, 1972 less painful. Call it a game of two halves. Call it a change in momentum. One thing is certain: Tom Hannon, Massillon's Mr. Everything, disappeared from the game plan in the second half after staking Massillon to a 14-3 first half lead.

Hannon raced 65 yards for a touchdown on the second play of the game. He also ran in the two-point conversion. He totaled 135 yards rushing on 14 carries in the first half.

Cincinnati Princeton scored twice in the second half to win the game 17-14.

Did head coach Bob Commings abandon his game plan too soon? "Yep," said Nick Vrotsos, a 33-year Massillon assistant. "They got away from running Hannon. He tried to throw the ball all over the place."

Nick Vrotsos.

Hannon was beside himself. He carried the ball only seven times in the second half for 21 yards. "I love Coach Commings to death," Hannon said. "but I honestly think that we kind of panicked at the end of the game. We started throwin' the ball, throwin' the ball. I was like, 'Come on, give me the ball, *give me the ball. I'm hot, give it to me.'* It's like, I *know* we can do it, just call the right stuff. It was just so demoralizing."

Brainchild of Wilbur Arnold, Obie, the Live Tiger Mascot Started in 1970

He was sitting in the meeting-after-the-meeting at the Kendall Tavern when the inspiration hit him.

Wilbur Arnold was hanging out with fellow-members of the Booster Club executive committee when he saw LSU playing football on TV.

Wilbur Arnold with Obie I.

"We'd go up to the Kendall Tavern and meet a lot of people," Arnold said. "We did that for a lot of years. I noticed one day I was watching LSU play somebody. LSU had a Tiger, its name was Mike. I thought, you know, we can do that. I said, 'If I get to be president, we'll have a Tiger.' Little did I know what Pandora's box had in it. They put me in the line to be president and in 1969 I was vice-president and in 1970 I got to be president."

Arnold, who worked at Goodyear for 30 years as an engineer, is known in Massillon as a determined man who gets things done. He was the perfect person to launch the live tiger Obie project.

The original thought was to have a tiger that remained in Massillon year-after-year.

"We had an architect draw up a permanent facility to keep the tiger," Arnold said. "LSU developed a permanent facility. There was a little bit of resistance because of the cost. So that's when we got the idea of having a cub every year.

"There was a series of things we had to do. It is just amazing. The project's 40 years old. You don't often start a project that lasts 40 years. And there's no end in sight. The only thing that will ever kill it is some kind of regulation of some sort that just makes it impossible."

Obie I holds a special place in Arnold's heart. "I had a very personal relationship with the first tiger,' Arnold said. "It was such a close relationship that it truly was heartbreaking when it came time for her to go. She went back to the international animal exchange. They sold her to an animal park in California. He was a well-known Hollywood trainer. I made arrangements to go see the tiger. The curator took me up to the mountain and as soon as I came into view the tiger knew me. She jumped up and whined. I would not have recognized her because she had gotten so big. He took me over to the cage and I put my arm in the cage and he about passed out. He envisioned all sorts of bad things happening."

Arnold and Obie I hugged. "The problem was that I had to walk away again," Arnold said, "That was kind of sad."

Arnold was in charge of Obies I-XIII, before turning the job over to Ed Annen. Bob Hollender was an original member of Annen's Obie Crew. "When Eddy died Bob took the project," Arnold said.

"I started doing it 28 years ago with Eddy and them," Hollender said. He's been Obie's caretaker for 20 years.

It is an all-consuming commitment for Hollender. "It's a 24-7 commitment," Hollender said. "The rest of the crew helps, but you think about Obie 24 hours. I spend about four to five hours a day with Obie."

Bob Hollender has been involved with Obie since 1983.

So what's the payoff for Hollender?

"Watching how the people really love Obie. No matter where you go, even during the off season, people are always asking me, 'When are we getting Obie?' We get him around the middle of August."

Any time Hollender takes Obie out of the van he attracts a crowd, even when it appears there is no one around.

"Even when you get him out up at the stadium and

you think you're by yourself somebody drives up and says, 'Can we see Obie, can we take a picture?'

"It's more fun than being the head coach. Everybody enjoys Obie. The kids, grown-ups, people in the nursing homes. Even when we go away the away crowds enjoy him, too, Warren, Mentor, St. Ignatius. They all enjoy seeing Obie. The only time Obie has to stay behind is during OHSAA playoffs and any games played in Cincinnati.

"Kids nowadays have camera phones. Whenever Obie comes around they're poppin' those cameras out. They always want to take pictures with Obie. It's amazing how many people have camera phones. Obie draws cameras, that's for sure."

Obie XXXIII at the 2002 Massillon-McKinley game.

A thorn in the side of the Obie program has been PETA, People for the Ethical Treatment of Animals.

Hollender acknowledges that he is aware of PETA's presence. "They come around every once in a while," he said. "You never know if they are in the stands. They just think we treat Obie the wrong way.

"Obie isn't really caged up. He gets a lot of exercise. The only time he's in a cage is when we travel. He travels in a van, he doesn't travel outside. He leads a very good life. Fed three times a day. Good, fresh chicken every day, exercise."

The average Obie is 14 weeks old when it arrives in Massillon. "We generally get Obie between 18 and 20 pounds. After a 10-game schedule he's usually 90-95 pounds. Once they start eating chicken they grow pretty fast."

The tigers start out eating hamburger and ground turkey. Next come chicken thighs."

One of the best Booster Club fundraisers is when Massillon fans are called upon to help feed Obie once a year at a home football game.

"We try to pick the biggest crowd, other than the McKinley game," Hollender said. "Everybody's just too busy during the McKinley game."

Like Arnold, Hollender has trouble when it's time to return Obie at the end of the season. "It's terrible. You hate to let 'em go. They look at you like, 'Are you comin' back?' It's sad. They're sad when you let 'em go. It brings tears to your eyes."

Hollender is 73 years old and realizes that some day he will have to give up his job as Obie's caretaker. But he doesn't want to rush things.

"Right now I don't want to give Obie up. I tell the guys at the Booster Club that taking care of Obie is the best job there is."

WILLIE SPENCER

Respect. Willie Spencer wants respect. Respect in his hometown for what he accomplished on the football field. He wants to look up at Massillon's *Wall of Champions* and see a giant picture of himself. Respect.

Willie Spencer went from high school to the NFL.

What Spencer did *on the field* puts him on the short list of the greatest running backs in Massillon Tigers history. In his first—and only—season as a high school running back, Spencer was All-Ohio, rumbling for a then-Massillon record 1,251 yards. He parlayed that success into an unlikely ascent into professional football stardom.

Off the field, however, educational, employment and legal misfortune left Spencer feeling cheated. He blames a lot of that on his hometown.

"A lot of people around here didn't want to see me make it," Spencer laments, "and they didn't like the *way* I did it."

Spencer certainly didn't follow the formula of the American high school football star who is destined for greatness:
a. Star as a high school football player.
b. Receive a college scholarship.
c. Become a college football star.
d. Enter the NFL draft.
e. Succeed in professional football.

Spencer blames the attention he received as a football star at Massillon for many of his troubles.

Spencer skipped steps b through d and went straight to e. Why? Well, while Spencer was starring on the gridiron at Massillon, he *wasn't* starring in the classroom.

"Willie really wasn't into school a whole lot," teammate and childhood friend Steve Luke said. "I know he missed a lot of school. That didn't help the situation. I think that if he could have applied himself a little more in school that the sky would have been the limit for him. As much as we would talk to him, Willie just did not like going to classes."

Consequently, college football wasn't an option. Spencer blames the attention he received as a football star at Massillon for many of his troubles. He said his educational shortcomings were overlooked in high school. "I spent most of my time watching football film or I was down in the coach's office," Spencer said. "I wish they would have been more strict about my education, not just football."

The treatment he received

from townspeople was also hard for Spencer to deal with—especially after his playing days were over.

"They put you on a pedestal and as soon as the last football game's over, you're back to normal. *They* put you on a pedestal, you don't put yourself on a pedestal. They build you up around here. They have you thinking you're King. It's not you, it's *them*. Newspapers, Booster Club guys, they're the ones who do you like that. I don't understand it. This town's destroyed a lot of athletes by putting them on that pedestal and then taking it away from them. After high school football is over with, you're through around here. One day you're on top of the world. The next day you're nothin'. Massillon takes a lot of pride out of a person—especially an athlete. All these business people running up to you giving you almost anything. Once football's gone, you go to them and try to get a job and they look at you like they don't even know you. I've had that happen. But that's Massillon for ya."

Spencer was also hurt by a drug arrest in the 1970s. He feels the arrest has added to his post-football struggles. "After football, I got in this little trouble," Spencer said. "Once you get in trouble around here, it sticks with you the rest of your life. Small town. I'll be a villain the rest of my life."

Being excluded from the Wall of Champions at Washington High School is particularly hurtful to Spencer. "It seems like you don't get noticed for what you did in football," Spencer said of the selection process. "They're selecting people for the success they had *after* football. The Wall of Champions doesn't have nobody's picture in suits and ties, all of 'em have football suits on. It kind of hurts in a way. But it seems like I'm the black sheep anyway, because of the way I did it, coming up from high school and going into the pros. That was the wrong way, but it was my way. I wouldn't want no one else to try to do that. I think that's the reason I haven't been selected."

"I'll be a villain the rest of my life."

Willie Spencer

Spencer may not have gotten a shot at professional football if not for Nick Vrotsos, a longtime Massillon assistant coach who also coached Spencer in basketball. Vrotsos was the head basketball coach at Massillon for 17 years. "Willie Spencer should have been playin' running back in 1969 and we would have won the state championship in '69," Vrotsos said. "Him and Mike Mauger. Sometimes coaches make mistakes in personnel. You can't tell me that Willie Spencer doesn't belong in your starting backfield when he's a sophomore and a junior. I started him as a sophomore in basketball. You know he's *gotta* start. Those guys said, 'Willie Spencer can't learn plays.' You're not a very good teacher if you can't teach him the plays. He learned the plays in basketball."

"Nick is the one who got me moved from split end to running back," Spencer said. "My junior year when we played McKinley I was playing defensive end. I got an interception and ran it down to the four-yard line." That 42-yard interception return was all the ammunition Vrotsos needed to get Spencer inserted into the backfield for 1971.

Spencer had some experience at running back, having started at Jones Junior High as a seventh grader. "They moved me to quarterback in eighth grade," Spencer said, "Dennis Franklin and I were competing for starting quarterback. I started over him."

That's quite an accomplishment considering Franklin went on to become one of the top quarterbacks in the history of both Massillon and the University of Michigan. Spencer was on the receiving end of Franklin's passes as a Massillon Tiger split end in 1970.

Spencer was a star from the start when he was inserted into the starting backfield in 1971, picking up 126 yards in 12 carries in the opener. Spencer was a physical specimen—the kind scouts still drool over today. "I was 6'4" and 220 pounds in high school. Back then, that was unheard of," Spencer said.

"I was 6'4" and 220 pounds in high school. Back then, that was unheard of."

Willie Spencer

"I was a hard runner. I didn't look at one person bringing me down. I was a more or less reckless runner. I didn't become a total package running back until 1975, the second year of the World Football League. In high school I just ran. I didn't have no style. If somebody was in front of me I'd run 'em over."

The Ottawa Rough Riders of the Canadian Football League took notice and gave the 18-year-old Spencer a shot. It didn't work out. His coach sent him to the Indianapolis Capitols.

"I didn't have no style, I just ran. If somebody was in front of me I'd run 'em over."

Willie Spencer

"They were semi-pro, a farm team," Spencer said. "They sent me to the Hartford Knights, another semi-pro team. That was my college, those two years." Spencer's two years on the semi-pro circuit prepared him well for the fledgling World Football League, who were signing established NFL stars every day.

It was in the WFL that Spencer met John McVay, who was head coach of the Memphis Southmen. McVay had Massillon roots, having starred for the 1948 Tigers. McVay later became head coach of the New York Giants and was vice president of the San Francisco 49ers during their glory years.

"We got Willie because he played in the Canadian League and our general manager, Leo Cahill, knew him," McVay said. "Willie was a superstar in Memphis. He...was..a... superstar."

Ralph Reeves, of the *St. Paul Pioneer Press*, gushed over

Spencer in a 1975 article. "The Vikings and nine other NFL teams are very much interested in Willie Spencer, who is, beyond question, the most-sought player from the WFL. Spencer is cast as 'bigger, stronger, faster and a better blocker than Larry Csonka.'"

George Lapidus, of the *Memphis Press-Scimitar*, wrote this of Spencer during his rookie year with the Southmen: "The other players refer to Willie Spencer as a bad dude. It is a compliment of the highest order. He's but 20 years old, the youngest player in all of professional football. He is the man Larry Csonka will have to beat out next season. It may not be easy. Willie is 6'4", 225-pounds and he runs...well, you need the Marines to bring him down. Scouts from the NFL can't believe Willie is for real. Some have called him one of the best running backs in football."

"Willie was a superstar at Memphis. He...was...a...superstar."

John McVay

The WFL lasted just over a season and a half. Despite a season-ending knee injury during his rookie season, Spencer was among the league leaders in rushing (1,369), scoring (17 TDs) and yards per carry (4.9). He also set the record for touchdowns in a game with five.

The five-touchdown game was a highlight of Spencer's WFL career. "That was my first big game coming off a knee injury the year before.

I missed all of training camp that year and they tried to work me in slowly because I had a big knee operation. That's a lot of touchdowns, isn't it."

Spencer scores as a member of the Memphis Southmen.

Memphis was one of the most successful WFL franchises, finishing a league best 17-3 in 1974. In 1975 they were 7-4 when the league folded. Memphis signed Hall of Famers Csonka and Paul Warfield along with Csonka's running mate Jim Kiick away from the Miami Dolphins for the 1975 season. The signing sent shock waves through the NFL. Spencer, however, was unphased.

"Name players don't excite me. I knew who they were and everything. But to me, I was just as good as them. I wasn't influenced by their names, or who they were, or where they came from. Csonka, Kiick and I rotated. I was running fullback and halfback. I would run one series at fullback and the next series at halfback. When the league folded after 11 games,

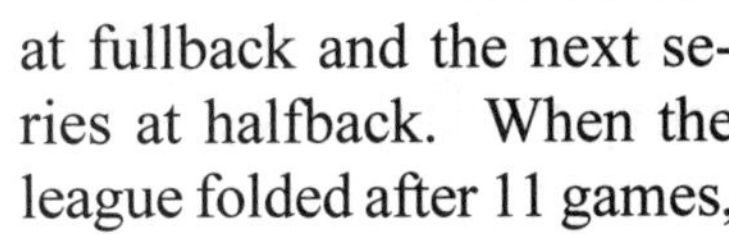

I had 581 yards, Jim Kiick had 462 and Larry Csonka had 421."

Spencer estimates that he was wined and dined by 10-15 NFL teams before he cast his lot with the Minnesota Vikings and Head Coach Bud Grant in 1976. He now feels that signing with the Vikings was a big mistake. "It just wasn't the right team for me. It was an older team. I just didn't fit in. I was 23 years old at the time."

The next season McVay acquired Spencer for the New York Giants. McVay had taken over as head coach of the Giants and had also brought in Csonka. Spencer lasted two years with the Giants, where he was used mainly as a short yardage back. A highlight of his NFL career came with the Giants, when he rushed three times for 67 yards and two touchdowns against the Cleveland Browns. "We had a third and short and I busted it for 58 yards," Spencer said. "The Massillon band was playing at halftime. A lot of my friends were at the game."

"I think he had a good career," McVay said. "He didn't make it as a big time NFL star for reasons of luck. You've gotta be lucky to have a big career in the NFL. Willie played a few years. Played well. It was like he had four years under his belt before he played in the NFL. And he had more than his share of injuries."

Those injuries took their toll on Spencer, who finally hung up his cleats for good after failing physicals with the Giants in 1980 and again with the USFL in 1983. "When you're done, you're done," Spencer said, "I enjoyed it."

Legend of "The Dive" Lives On

There are certain plays in sports history that you never forget. If you were at the 1971 Massillon-McKinley game, a 29-6 Massillon win, you witnessed one of those rare plays.

"The Dive" is one of the most famous plays in Massillon-McKinley game history.

"People make a big deal of that," Willie Spencer said. The hole was so wide open I could have walked over." Teammate Steve Studer, Massillon's center, agreed. "I can hear the band playing 'The Tiger Rag' over and over and over. We were so confident at that point. We were going in. We broke out of that huddle and it was like a bulldozer blade," Studer said, "and Willie takes it in for the score. It was really fun." And the legend of "The Dive" was born.

BOB COMMINGS

Bob Commings was the perfect fit for Massillon. A beer drinker in a blue collar town. Born and raised in steel country, Commings was tough enough to handle his players—and the tremendous pressure of being the head coach at Massillon. He also had a sense of humor that won over everyone he came in contact with.

Commings took the Massillon job under challenging conditions, replacing embattled coach Bob Seaman.

Bob Commings led Massillon to its 22nd state title in 1970.

Seaman recorded Massillon's first losing season since 1931 when his1966 team went 4-5-1. Additionally, Seaman had trouble dealing with the citizenry of Massillon. Longtime Massillon assistant Nick Vrotsos, who coached Massillon athletes for 33 years, could see Seaman's problems.

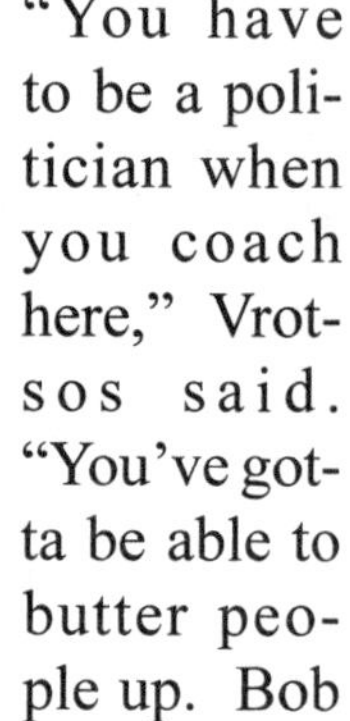

"You have to be a politician when you coach here," Vrotsos said. "You've gotta be able to butter people up. Bob

Seaman didn't have a very good knack for that.

"The guy who had charisma was Bobby Commings," Vrotsos added. "The town took to him better than the other guys in terms of his personality. He was very personable. Happy go lucky sort of a guy. Easy to be around. Liked his beer. He'd go in the bars and have a beer with the guys and that sort of stuff. He was just personable. His own man. He did things his way. He was popular."

Commings had a knack of getting the Massillon fans to fall in line, according to Steve Studer, a two-way starting lineman for Commings. "It was the same way with his players," Studer said. "When he talked, you know, you shut up. He had an aura about him when he walked into the room, in a team meeting or something, just his presence of walking into the room, everyone knew it was time to turn and look at him. He was really respected. He was a disciplinarian and he was a players' coach. He got the most out of his players. We would do *anything* for him. You know it was like a lot of times when we'd have close games and when the goin' gets tough out there in the fourth quarter and you're laying yourself down out there. We did it for *him*. We loved that guy and he knew how to talk to us and there was nothing phoney about what he said. We knew when he told us somethin' it was the truth and it was gospel."

Commings was in tune with his players. "Coach Commings was incredible," said Steve Luke, a captain for Commings' 1970 squad. "He knew people."

Tom Hannon, the star running back from Commings' 10-0 1972 team, saw Commings use a firm hand and a velvet glove—both masterfully.

Hannon was given an opportunity to run the football in an important game against Warren during his junior season. "I remember distinctly that I broke off a couple of long runs," Hannon said. "I ran all the way down to the five-yard line on a 40-yard run. Then I fumbled the ball. I just dropped the ball. That was kind of humiliating to me. I was contemplating quittin' the team.

"And he knew I was a little sensitive, so he came and he talked to me and sort of restored my confidence. He just told me, 'Everything's going to be all right. You've had a great year, you're going to be a great running back.' He was just saying some positive things that made me think, 'Well, okay, if he's got confidence in me, I'll come back and hopefully have a great year."

Hannon went on to be an All-Ohio running back at Massillon, an All-Big 10 defensive back at Michigan State and a starting safety for the Minnesota Vikings.

Hannon saw Commings' firm hand during his senior season.

"It was so strange because the next year we came out and played Sandusky in an exhibition game. The first play, they gave it to me and I fumbled. Coach Commings cursed me and cursed me and made me feel *so* bad. I guess his reverse psychology worked because I went back out and scored five touchdowns that game and after that it was smooth sailin'."

Hannon went on to break

the Massillon single season rushing record while becoming Commings' third straight All-Ohio running back.

Commings restored the Massillon spirit when he returned in 1969. The 1969 team finished 7-2-1, but showed signs of a bright future in a hard fought 14-7 loss to Canton McKinley.

His master work was the 1970 team, winners of Massillon's 22nd state championship and a team that is ranked among Massillon's all-time best. Commings liked to joke about whether it was great coaching or great talent that made the 1970 team so successful.

"The highlight of my tenure at Massillon was the 1970 season," Commings said. "We thought we were truly great, great football coaches. Come to find out four years later that six of them had opportunities to play professional football. So we weren't as hot as we thought we were."

Ducky Schroeder, the legendary Massillon assistant, recalled the 1970 Tigers. "Probably one of the best teams we ever had in Massillon," Schroeder said. "We must have had some of the greatest material. Six of those boys were selections for the National Football League after their college careers. In fact four of the 1970 team played pro football. That's Tom Hannon, Steve Luke and Willie Spencer and Dennis Franklin. Then there's Steve Studer who tried out with the Bears. Mike Mauger tried out with Dallas. So there were really six on that team that had NFL tryouts. I don't think there would be any other high school in the United States that could say that. And that's off of one team."

Commings also singled out his 1972 squad.

"The true emotional highlight was 1972," he said. "In 1972 we won 10 games and gave up four touchdowns. I don't think there was ever a team more courageous as the one who played here in 1972. I think they epitomized what Massillon stood for. Because you have guys like Tommy Balizet in there at nose guard at 147 pounds, and Brian Bash was the best defensive end in the league at 165 pounds. Our guards, Larry Mayles and Dan Guiffre, were around 150 pounds. We had some legitimate players, like Tommy Hannon, Bobby Geiser, the Edwards twins, Darius and Terry. When I say legitimate, I mean they had size and speed."

"The first year they had the playoffs we were in 'em (1972). I still think we had the best team in the playoffs, but we didn't win. It's unfortunate we didn't win." Massillon was beaten, 17-14, by Cincinnati Princeton.

"We played against a football team I think we probably should have beaten," Commings said. "They had a kid kick a 47-yard field goal who had never kicked one in his life. Never even practiced until Wednesday of that week. So I think the fates had something to do with it."

"If there was one thing, and I don't like to belabor this point, but I always felt Bob did a good job, but he didn't use his assistants enough," Schroeder said. "Because he had quite a few assistants here. But Bob was a very good football coach."

Commings' players, to a man, speak glowingly of him.

"Bob Commings was the greatest coach I've had in any sport," said Larry Harper, a star wingback on the 1970 team. "It was not only his intensity, but his love for the players. He was a players' coach. He cared for every player on that team. I don't think there was anybody better from a X's and O's standpoint, and there *certainly* wasn't a better motivator. He was also a master at preparing you for a football season. Commings was a carbon copy of Vince Lombardi. He would always talk about what Vince Lombardi would do. Commings' greatness can be seen in the love the players had for him. Everybody would call him 'Uncle Bob.' That was the closeness he had with all of the players. He was a great guy. And as tough as nails. If you ever went into a fight, you'd want to have Coach Commings with ya. No question about it."

Commings finished 43-6-2 at Massillon, with two undefeated, poll state championship teams (1970, 1972).

He left Massillon after the 1973 season to become the head coach at the University of Iowa, where he had been a star player from 1956-57.

Commings was Iowa's MVP in 1957, beating out Alex Karras, who was an All-American and the Outland Trophy winner. Karras went on to an outstanding career as an NFL football player (Detroit Lions), movie star (*Paper Lion*, *The Godfather*) and a member of the Monday Night Football team with Howard Cosell and Frank Gifford.

Karras said Commings was his best friend on the Hawkeyes.

"Probably of all the coaches at Massillon, Commings was

probably the best player of 'em," Schroeder said. "A guy his size, only about 160 pounds, he played both ways and was one of the best players Iowa ever had. Iowa Head Coach Forest Evashevski called him the Little Guard. 'He's my Little Guard.'"

Commings took over an Iowa program that was winless (0-11) the year before. He led Iowa to an 18-37 record in his five years at the helm.

Commings had some highlights among his 18 wins. In his first home game as head coach of Iowa, Commings led Iowa to a 21-10 win over 12th ranked UCLA. The Iowa faithful were so elated that they tore down the goalposts.

In 1976 Commings pulled another shocker, knocking off 11th-ranked Penn State in Happy Valley.

In 1977 Commings faced Earle Bruce, who was coaching Iowa State, in a battle of former Massillon head coaches. Iowa won 12-10.

Commings was fired after his fifth season at Iowa.

Commings returned to Ohio where he coached Canton GlenOak for 12 seasons, finishing with a 76-44-1 record. He knocked off Massillon, 9-7, in 1986. He described the win as "bittersweet."

Commings applied for the Massillon job when it was open in 1988. He came up short.

Former Massillon Superintendent of Schools Al Hennon was part of the interview team.

"With Bob coming back, I wanted everything to be perfect," Hennon said. "Bob's ready to turn to the chalkboard and I looked up and there was no chalk. We had used all the chalk. I run out and get chalk. It's still in the box and I'm fumblin', 'cause I'm nervous. I'm fumblin' to open it. Bob puts his hand on me and leans down and says, 'You must have been a lineman.' And we had a great laugh. Former superintendent of schools, Al Paris, was also part of the interview team.

"Bob had a lot of supporters," Paris said. "It did add extra stress because Coach Commings and I were very good friends. It wasn't his ability to coach and it wasn't his age or anything else that kept him from getting the job. They *did not* want to bring back somebody who'd already coached here again. They wanted to give someone else a chance for this job. I, myself, really liked Coach Commings and I possibly would have voted for him if I was one of the five board members. I was just a superintendent at the time. Bob was a good football coach."

We'll never know how Commings would have done in his second stint as Massillon coach. What we do know is that Commings became a legend as GlenOak's coach.

Dave Putts, a Massillon assistant under Chuck Mather, served with Commings for 10 years at GlenOak.

"Bob Commings could get your team ready to play. He could get his *grandmother* ready to play," Putts said.

GlenOak named its recently completed football stadium "Bob Commings Field."

BRENT OFFENBECHER

They say you're judged by the company you keep. Well, all Brent Offenbecher has to do is point to his teammates on the 1978 Parade All-American high school football team. Hall

Massillon fans will never forget Brent Offenbecher's diving touchdown against Canton McKinley in 1977.
PHOTO: BRENT OFFENBECHER COLLECTION

of Famers Dan Marino and John Elway were honored as All-American quarterbacks alongside Offenbecher. Pretty good company.

At Massillon, Offenbecher was a likable All-American. "I've always been an easy-goin' guy," Offenbecher said. "I had a lot of friends. I got along with pretty much everybody.

"I really didn't consider myself a star. I thought I was a pretty good player, but I didn't consider myself a star by any means. I played on two good football teams."

Offenbecher shares a unique "first" with another famous Massillon quarterback—Paul Brown. Like Brown, Offenbecher's first pass as a Tiger sophomore went for a touchdown. Offenbecher remembers his first touchdown toss well.

"My sophomore year, walking out on the field for the first time as a Tiger, I was in absolute awe."

Brent Offenbecher

"My sophomore year, walking out on the field for the first time as a Tiger, I was in absolute awe. If Tiger Stadium wasn't sold out, it was close to it. It was overwhelming. It was unbelievable. Ironically, the first play I threw a 60-yard touchdown pass to Mark Pringle. It was the only pass I completed on the varsity level the whole year. I think I was 1-11. But that was a thrill."

By the time he won his final game at Massillon, Offenbecher held every Massillon passing record but one. Offenbecher set Massillon passing records for yards passing (1,369) passing attempts (146) and completions (84). The Tigers were 17-2-1 with Offenbecher at quarterback.

He will long be remembered for his signature touchdown

run, an 11-yarder in a driving snowstorm against McKinley in 1977.

"It was a bad day," Offenbecher said. "It was snowing. It was supposed to be a handoff to the left. I knew it was snowing so hard they couldn't see me. I never gave the running back the ball and just kept going around the end. It was literally snowin' so hard you couldn't see from sideline to sideline. I thought I had a better chance of scoring than the running back did because of the weather situation. I went around the right side. I dove in. I remember hitting the ground. And why I dove I have no idea. I have no idea why I ended up jumping over the guy, but he never even touched me. Whether he slipped...we couldn't see it in the films. When we watched the films you couldn't see *anything*. It was whiteout. Just snowing that hard."

"Ironically, the first play I threw a 60-yard touchdown pass to Mark Pringle."

Brent Offenbecher

The win over McKinley was very meaningful for Offenbecher, a junior at the time.

"They were undefeated, 9-0. We had a couple of blemishes (7-2), but we felt we had a better football team than they did. We wanted to go out there and show 'em."

Offenbecher really mastered the snowy conditions, connecting on 7 of 9 passes for 162 yards, including touchdown bombs of 59 yards to Curtis Strawder and 48 yards to Greg Carpenter.

"Probably the biggest highlight of that season was beating McKinley, that was real intense," Offenbecher said of the 21-0 win, in front of 20,339 fans. "That was my first start against McKinley. It was my first time in Fawcett stadium. It was a big deal. When you talk about the Massillon-McKinley game, and how big it is as a player, I mean it is an intense, heartbeating, mindthrobbing deal. It's the real deal. Especially when you're 16-17 years old. No kid is going to experience what that game is unless they're actually here. Nowhere in the country. They may play in big games, but it's not in front of 20,000 people. Just the rivalry. It's just awesome," Offenbecher said. "We felt if we won that game, we still had a chance to get in the playoffs. Some things had to happen. We just *pounded 'em.* And they went to the state championship game that year. We had a good football team. We pretty much manhandled 'em that day."

"It is an intense, heartbeating, mind-throbbing deal."

Brent Offenbecher

Massillon coach Mike Currence (79-16-2) was fond of the two seasons that Offenbecher was at the controls of his offense. "Those were really great years, 1977-78, the Offenbecher years," Currence said. "Didn't get in the playoffs, but they were just great teams. It's a shame we weren't representatives in the playoffs during those years.

"Of course Offenbecher was All-Ohio and the Player of

the Year in Stark County, which is a big, big, thing. And guess who he beat out for Player of the Year in Stark County? Todd Blackledge of North Canton Hoover. He was in pretty good company. I remember Blackledge leading Penn State to the National Championship in 1982."

Blackledge was a three-year starter at Penn State. He also played in the NFL with Kansas City and Pittsburgh.

Offenbecher was literally born to be a quarterback. His father, Bill, was an outstanding quarterback under Mel Knowlton, the legendary head coach at Alliance. Knowlton, who was Paul Brown's first quarterback at Massillon in 1932, was known for developing quarterbacks.

"Offenbecher was All-Ohio and the Stark County Player of the Year...."

Mike Currence

Bill Offenbecher followed Lenny Dawson at Alliance and went on to play quarterback at the University of Illinois. Knowlton at one time had three of his Alliance quarterbacks starting in the Big Ten at the same time: Bill Offenbecher was starting at Illinois, Lenny Dawson at Purdue and John Borton at Ohio State.

Bill Offenbecher had the chance to coach his son at Massillon when he was hired as a quarterbacks coach by Currence. Brent was a freshman when his dad took the job.

"I heard that he had a young boy that he had been training as a quarterback," Currence said, "who was really an outstanding athlete. He came in as a sophomore.

"Offenbecher just didn't miss," Currence said. "He didn't overthrow ya, he always threw the nicest ball to catch, it was the easiest ball I've ever seen to catch. He had a finesse on the ball that a lot of other quarterbacks didn't have. Some quarterbacks just fire the thing, really just burn it in there, see how hard they could throw it. He'd never do that. If it was a short pass he knew not to throw it real hard and knock you down with it. He just had that touch."

Offenbecher set most of Massillon's passing records from 1977-78.
PHOTO: MIKE CURRENCE COLLECTION

In 1978, Offenbecher's senior season, the Tigers had another classic battle with McKinley.

"The biggest thing I remember is scoring our first touchdown, and then they got the ball and my future brother-in-law, Tim Reese, intercepted a pass on their 40-yard line. We got the ball back. We drove the ball right down their throat again and scored again with about a minute or so to go in the game.

"I remember we were just throwing it; I mean it was one after another after another. We were just clickin' on all cylinders. They were after our buts the whole game. And for some reason the last four minutes of the game we were just a machine, they couldn't stop us. Throwing to the right side, throwing to the left side, it was just...it was the best win I ever had. I mean we beat 'em 21-0 the year before, but my senior year was a more enjoyable win than that, because we came from behind to do it. That was probably the biggest win of my life. That was probably the most exciting thing as a player that I did. Because you look up at the clock and there's four minutes to go and we're two touchdowns behind.

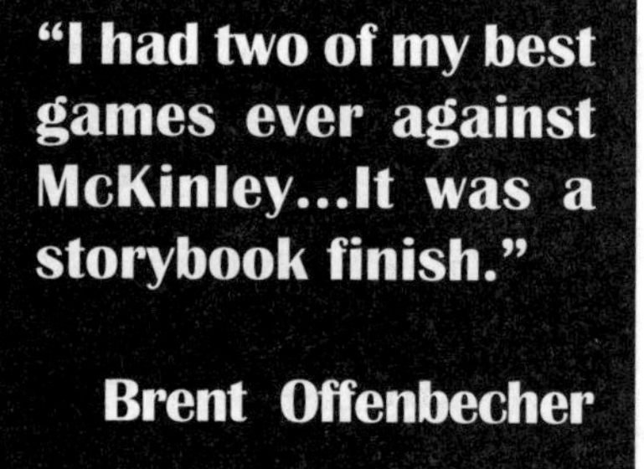

"I don't think anybody will ever match the stats in that game. I was like 17 for 20, I mean I only missed three passes the whole game. Had a couple touchdown passes and threw for 177 yards. It was like an 85% completion percentage. I don't think anybody will ever touch that (laughs). And it was against McKinley. I had two of my best games ever against McKinley, I mean stat-wise. It was a storybook finish. I couldn't have asked it to happen any other way. I remember after the game it was a rush to the field, I couldn't wait to get off the field. I was trying to get out of there. It seemed like there were 10,000 people on the field.

"That game actually had a fight in it. There was a bench-clearing brawl. Darren Longshore intercepted the ball and slid on the ground at the end of the game. He intercepted the ball, slid on the ground, got up and started running toward our sideline. One of their kids thought that he was still running and tackled him."

The confusing chain of events enraged the crowd. "Fans came out of the stands," Offenbecher said. "It was ugly. I remember that vividly, it was an ugly situation. It was scary. There were too many people—20,000 people coming out of the stands. I remember being really frightened about that. I remember people getting hit in the face, and there was blood. But the police were right on top of it and they didn't let it get out of hand. They quieted it down and within five minutes we were playing football again. But it was ugly. I remember it vividly. That was with less than a minute to go."

> **"Fans came out of the stands. It was ugly...It was scary."**
>
> **Brent Offenbecher**

Offenbecher loved the atmosphere at Massillon, but felt pressure to win. "When you go out on the field you're *expected* to win. The fans in this community are not going to accept anything but. And that's fine. That's a lot of pressure on a high school kid. You feel it, oh, yeah. *Definitely.* It will certainly make you grow. It certainly got me ready for college.

"In this town it's the real deal. Whether that's good or bad. I think sometimes it can be a bad thing. Here's a young kid who has this much pressure on him, that's pretty intense stuff. And the experience, I don't think any guy who has ever played at Massillon can say he had a bad experience here or said he regretted playing here. I certainly wouldn't."

Offenbecher was highly sought after coming out of Massillon, but he settled in on Wake Forest, a school not known for its football program. "I had the opportunity to go to a lot of different schools," he said, "I narrowed it down, at the time, to Michigan, Notre Dame and Wake Forest. I knew right off the bat that I didn't want to go to Ohio State because Art Schlichter was a year ahead of me and I knew I wouldn't start. Wake Forest, I thought, was the best opportunity for me to go and play at a young age. I really felt I could go into Wake Forest and play as a freshman. They didn't have anybody coming back that was coming in as a starter.

"I really felt I could go into Wake Forest and play as a freshman."

Brent Offenbecher

"Unfortunately, what ended up happening my freshman year down there, Jay Venuto had a career year and ended up being the ACC Player of the Year as a junior. He threw for close to 4,000 yards. That was the best record Wake ever had. And it was the first bowl bid they ever had. This guy carried them on his shoulders. He was great.

"I don't regret going to Wake Forest. It just didn't happen for me. Venuto had a great year and he was coming back the next year.

Currence didn't agree with Offenbecher's decision to leave Wake Forest.

"Ironically I ended up at Ohio State. One of the reasons I left Wake Forest—Jay had surgery on his throwing elbow the spring after that year. I was basically playing the number one quarterback that spring. He had reconstructive elbow surgery. We come into fall and he still hadn't thrown a ball yet. He was just getting released so that he could start throwin'. And I really felt at that time that I was the best quarterback on the team. And I was told that. But I was also told that I was going to redshirt and that we were going to wait for Jay and he was going to play when he was ready to play.

"I understood why I didn't play as a freshman—Jay Venuto was a better quarterback at the time. But I just wasn't willin' to sit another year when I knew I was the best quarterback. I was 400 miles away from home and it was frustrating. I felt that, 'Nah, I'm ready to go back home.'"

Currence didn't agree with Offenbecher's decision to leave Wake Forest. "I think he should have stayed there.

I don't think they would have ever found a better quarterback than him," Currence said.

Currence continued, "His girlfriend and now wife tried to go down there and live, but she was a momma's girl. Her family owned a bar in Massillon and had a booster group called Reese's Raiders. She was a Reese. They became known as the third booster club in town.

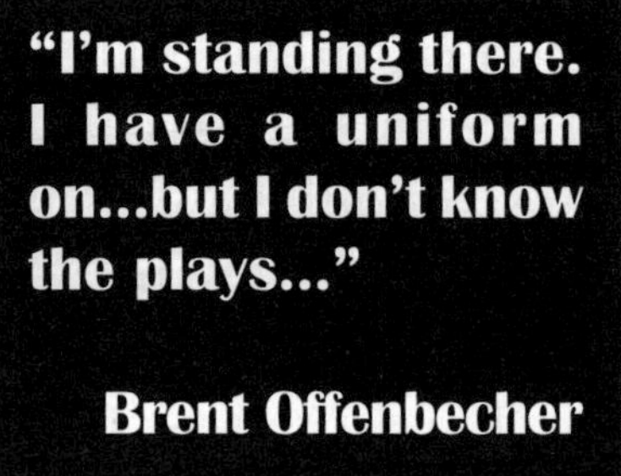

"I went to Ohio State, I called Earle Bruce," Offenbecher said. "I said that I wasn't happy at Wake Forest. I asked if I could try out for Ohio State. He was all for that. He didn't have a scholarship available. He said, 'Brent, I just don' have any scholarships. If you want to come you can walk on, we'd be glad to have ya, but I can't promise you a scholarship.' So I felt, 'Well, I'm just going to have to go earn one.'

"The first day of practice, I'm standing there. I have a uniform on, but I didn't know the plays, didn't know anything. And after that practice, the varsity practice, they were going to have a JV scrimmage with the twos and the threes. So I'm standin' behind the offense, like we normally would in a scrimmage. The quarterback, Bob Atha at the time, comes in and he throws an interception. Earle yells, 'Get out!' So he brought in a kid named Tim Stevens.

Tim ends up throwing an interception. And Earle is *hot*. I mean he's *hot*.

"I'm just standing there. I have a uniform on and everything, but I don't know the plays. He says, 'Come here.' So I walk in the huddle, not knowing what I'm going to do. He said, 'Just reverse pivot out, hand it to the tailback. It's called a 24 trap, and basically he told me what to do. I mean, it's not real complicated, reverse out and hand it to the tailback and let him run. I did that and we gained five or six yards. Did the same thing to the other side. We end up in a third and two. He called a play. He said, 'This is who you have to look at. If they jump the tight end, go deep. If they try to hang off, go to the tight end. It was a one-read deal. Well, they jumped the tight end and I just let it wing. Just let it wing.

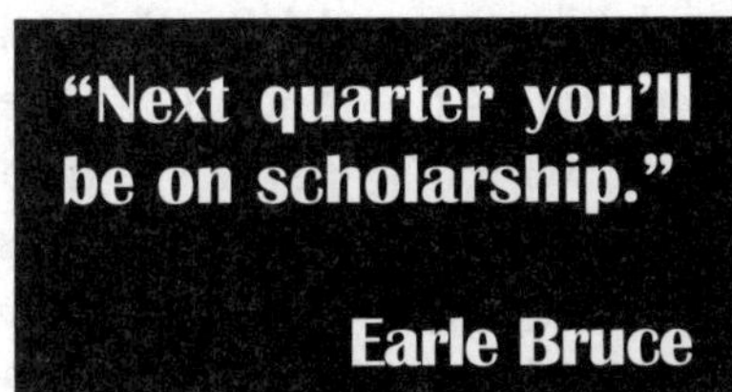

"Fortunately it got caught and ran in for a touchdown. Earle blew the whistle and everybody was running in. He yelled at me and came over and said, 'Next quarter you'll be on scholarship.' So I earned my scholarship the first day I was there. It was a real good feeling, because I didn't know what was going to happen since I went there with a lot of question marks.

"I grew up raising a family on an athletic scholarship and literally starved. You weren't allowed to work. I had two kids while going through college. We ate a lot of macaroni and cheese in college. But they were great days."

Offenbecher was redshirted his first year at Ohio State. Art Schlichter was the starter. "I felt I had an opportunity to play when Art graduated," Offenbecher said. "I knew I was going to redshirt for one year, learn as much as I could my junior year, which was my sophomore year of eligibility, and try to step in my junior and senior year and be the starter. That's the way I approached it."

Currence remembers Offenbecher starting against Schlichter in two spring games at Ohio State. "Both of the spring games that he started and Schlichter started on the other side, his team won. I remember the TV crews coming out on the field after the game and interviewing him. Schlichter just walked down the sideline. That's history. That's what happened when he was quarterbacking those spring games."

Offenbecher's debut at Ohio State came in a big game against Florida State."When I went in that game we were already getting beat, I think 14-0. That was my first opportunity. We fell short that game. I threw two touchdowns against Florida State and I had over 200 yards passing. I think I threw a couple of interceptions, too. Florida State was number one in the country. They were tough. I remember getting hit a couple times in that game.

"The next game we played Wisconsin. I started. And I really felt if we won that game my career would have been completely different. Because what happened, it was a torrential downpour. There were two, three inches of standing rain on the astroturf. We fumbled the ball four times inside our 20-yard line. We got beat six to nothin'. We fumbled the ball with two minutes to go in the game on their four-yard line. Tim Spencer on a fourth and one. If we win, I probablyget to start the next week against Illinois. I actually played pretty well against Wisconsin, I didn't have a bad game in the rain. But Mike Tomczak started the next game and we didn't lose another game the rest of the year. We ended up having a pretty good football team, and then Mike came back the next year and started. I backed up. I got to play. I lettered my junior and senior years. But Wisconsin was the only start I had. I think I threw for almost 200 yards in the Wisconsin game in the rain. But we lost. We should have beaten Wisconsin by three touchdowns and we ended up getting beat. If we won that game and I got the next start, who knows what happens? You just never know.

"We should have beaten Wisconsin by three touchdowns."

Brent Offenbecher

"I don't regret transferring to Ohio State, I had a lot of good times. I felt that I should have had a better opportunity. Mike Tomczak and I were fighting for the top spot. I felt that he got more opportunities than I did to win that spot. But Mike's a great quarterback. I think most guys would feel the same way I did. You want to play and feel you just didn't get the opportunity to do that. They say football's a game of inches."

CURTIS STRAWDER

The best receiver for one of the best quarterbacks in Massillon football history, Curtis Strawder was an all-time great for the Tigers.

Curtis Strawder scores on a 50-yard pass reception against Canton McKinley in 1977. Massillon won 21-0.

PHOTO: MIKE CURRENCE COLLECTION

"Curtis Strawder was really a fantastic athlete," said Mike Currence, Strawder's head coach at Massillon. "He won that Gahanna Lincoln game. We were actually losin' that game, too. That was a championship team they had down there. We were losin' and it was like fourth down and we had a long way to go, it was like fourth and 19. It was almost like a do or die, there was nothing else we could do. Nick Vrotsos was upstairs talkin' to me. He said, 'You've gotta get it to Strawder.' So I called for Brent Offenbecher to roll to his right and called a throwback post pattern to Strawder. He caught that thing on his fingertips divin'. *Unbelievable* catch. Kept us in the ball game. We ended up going on down and scoring and won the ball game. That's just the kind of thing Strawder did. He'd just win it for you. You could just throw it to him and he would make that catch on third down. He'd just do it. So I don't know that there has ever been another receiver that was as much of a factor in winning ball games as Curtis Strawder."

Offenbecher appreciated having a receiver like Strawder to depend on.

"Great receiver," Offenbecher said of Strawder. "Just one of the best high school receivers I've ever been around. Quick. He was very fast, but was more quick than fast. And he had great hands. If the ball was around him he was going to catch it. Great guy. Smart. Knew the game real well. He was probably the best receiver I played with. There were others, Marty Guzetta, who was a junior when I was a senior. He was Mr. Glue. You knew if you threw it at him and he was around it, he was going to catch it. I don't know if I ever saw him or Curt drop a pass."

Strawder was Massillon's career leader in pass receptions (68) when his Massillon career ended. He also held single season records for yardage (544) and receptions (42) that have since been eclipsed.

STEVE LUKE

It was spring practice, heading into his junior season at Ohio State and Steve Luke had been moved from center to defensive back. He didn't like the competition surrounding him: Doug Plank, Tim Fox, Neal Colzie—all famous names in Ohio State—and later—NFL history.

"I thought to myself, 'How in the world am I gonna start?' I'm thinking, 'I know how I can get moved up. If I can get one good lick on Archie Griffin and have the coaches go 'oooh.' I'm thinking, 'He's our best back. If I can get one good lick on him, I know that they'll move me up.'"

Steve Luke (46) celebrates a turnover with teammate at Green Bay.

Griffin wasn't just Ohio State's best back, he is the only player in history to win the Heisman Trophy twice.

"The moment of truth came," Luke said. "They passed Archie the ball. Archie's coming around the corner. I'm coming up on him to meet him. He sees me and at the last minute tries to get out of bounds.

I'm thinking, 'I will not be denied.' So I slammed into him. Knocked the crap out of him. The next thing I heard was, 'You're trying to kill our best back!' It was (head coach) Woody Hayes yelling at me. He threw me off the practice field. I couldn't believe it. I thought, 'I'll never play here. I'll never play here.' But it worked out. The following week I started."

"I'm thinking 'I know how I can get moved up...If I can get one good lick on Archie Griffin and have the coaches go Oooooh.'"

Steve Luke

Luke spent his first two years at Ohio State playing center. He started a couple of games, including the Rose Bowl his sophomore season. He couldn't understand why Hayes wanted to move him to defensive back.

"I was thinking, 'What the heck?' I thought about leaving Ohio State when they switched me to defensive back. I just came off what I thought was a good game in the Rose Bowl."

Luke conferred with his mother.

"That's where my faith and upbringing came in," Luke said. "My mom made it real clear when I called and was complaining to her. I said, 'Mom, I'm not playing. They've moved me to a new position that I've never played before.' She told me, 'You're there for one reason—to get an education. You're not there to play pro ball. You're there to play football and to get an education.' I kind of cooled my jets after that."

Luke started the rest of his career at Ohio State. One of his highlights came when he intercepted his first pass.

"When I finally got my first interception I couldn't believe I caught it, first of all. I was heading out of bounds as I caught it and I was thinking, 'Please let me hold on, please let me hold on.' It was a great experience. I think I had four or five interceptions in my two years at Ohio State."

And there were no hard feelings from Griffin for the hit that got Luke noticed.

"We were roommates at Ohio State," Luke said. "We've had a very unique friendship. He was the best man in my wedding and I was the best man in his wedding. I'm his son's godfather and he's my daughter's godfather."

Steve Luke enjoyed an outstanding six-year career at Green Bay where he was captain for three years under head coach Bart Starr. In 1977 he led the team in interceptions. In 1978 he set the Packers single season record for solo tackles. He also shared a special moment with Griffin.

"It was during my last year in the league and near the end of Archie's career. He was the captain at Cincinnati and I was the captain at Green Bay. I remember shaking hands with him at the 50-yard line and thinking, 'How often do you have two former roommates representing their respective teams in the NFL?'"

Luke was known for his hard-hitting style in the NFL. In a 1979 game against the Miami Dolphins, Luke made a diving hit on Dolphins running back Norm Bulaich as he was about to score. The hit ended Bulaich's career.

"I'll never forget the look on my defensive backs coach's face when I walked in the locker room after the game," Luke said. "All of these reporters were standing around my locker. A reporter turned the camera on me and stuck a microphone in my face and said, 'What do you thing of Norm Bulaich suing you?' I said *what?*"

"All through junior high, high school, college and the NFL I never missed a practice."

Steve Luke

The reporters thought it was a dirty hit. Luke knew otherwise. "It was just a weird, freak thing," Luke said. "I just wanted to make a good play. I was trying to cause a fumble, get something to happen because we needed a big play. But it was just one of those freak things. I remember feeling horrible about it. You don't want to be involved in anything like that, especially when it ends someone's career like that. The irony of it is that I remember watching him play when I was in high school."

Luke credits his upbringing in Massillon for his success.

"I owe Massillon a lot. I'm

just glad that I was born in Massillon. I really mean it. You have no idea. The whole experience really shaped and molded my values. That Tiger spirit was what carried me through Green Bay."

Luke was inspired by the youngest of the Whitfield brothers, who starred at Massillon during the 1950s and '60s.

"When I was a sophomore George Whitfield was our captain at Massillon," Luke said. "I really looked up to him. Through all of his high school and college days he never missed a practice."

Luke was cut from the same mold.

"I took it a step further," Luke said. "All through junior high, high school, college and the NFL, I never missed a practice.

"Massillon set such a high standard for excellence. At Ohio State I always made it a point to be the first in line for every drill. I was always the last one to leave the practice field. I learned that from Massillon. It's that terrific work ethic that you learn at Massillon."

Luke, who played linebacker and tight end, was elected captain at Massillon along with Larry Cardinal, an undersized but hardnosed fullback. They were the leaders of the 1970 team that won the state championship and finished second in the nation to Austin Reagan. The 1970 Tigers outscored their opponents 412-29.

"The thing in Massillon is they don't forget. Every time I come home I feel like it's a homecoming. I feel they're just as genuinely glad to see me as I am to see them."

BILL HARMON

There's not many places where a football player's legend begins in grade school. But there is no doubt that Bill Harmon's football legend in Massillon started when he lined up in the backfield with his 11- and 12-year-old teammates at Bowers Elementary.

Harmon *looked* like an adult. He played football like an adult, too. The adults noticed the size and weight differential and ruled that "Big Bill" could no longer run with his head down. Harmon *was* an intimidating sight crashing through the line with his head lowered. Defenders flew like bowling pins.

Bill Harmon.

"It was probably fair," Harmon said of the rule. "It was a natural thing to want to lower your shoulder.

In junior high, Harmon went straight to the ninth grade team. "I went down in the summer and met the coach. When he saw how big I was he had me come in there early. Usually the seventh graders didn't start until after school started in the fall. I didn't know nothin' and here I was playing with these guys that were older," Harmon said.

Harmon's Lorin Andrews' ninth grade school team won the city football championship with Harmon playing a key role. The championship game marked the first time

Harmon got to play on the turf at Tiger Stadium. "That was a special treat getting to do that my seventh grade year," he said.

A promising teammate on the ninth grade team was killed during Harmon's seventh grade year. "T. J. Harris broke into one of the bars down by Massillon Steel Castings, just down from the old high school. A night watchman shot him. He was a dynamite tailback. They were just droolin' waitin' to get him in the high school."

Harmon was an intimidating sight crashing through the line with his head lowered. Defenders flew like bowling pins.

Harmon's junior high school career was magical. By the time he was done he had earned nine varsity letters and won the school's outstanding athlete award. He also had a surprise visitor one day when he was in eighth grade.

"A legend came by to see me, University of Alabama football coach Paul "Bear" Bryant," Harmon said. "I was in class and they came up and got me. I guess it was during the time of year that he was on a recruiting trip. He was just in the area and my name must have come up. He had his plaid checkered hat on and everything. He just kind of looked me over. That was a real honor to meet him that early in my life."

Massillon Head Coach Bob Commings, was keeping an eye on Harmon's development.

"Bob Commings was there watching me every year throughout my junior high career. He saw the things I did, but he never talked to me. But right from the get-go when I got up to the high school as a sophomore, I mean *boom*, he had me right up front. Right with the starters. And I won the starting running back job as a sophomore. I played line-backer, too."

Harmon remembers bursting on the scene in his sophomore year—something sophomores rarely do at Massillon.

"I remember having the butterflies in my stomach big time. The first thing I remember as a sophomore was the first couple of scrimmages. I remember just having a few plays where the hole opened up and I blasted through it and I was down the field before they realized that I'd come through there. I was hearin' all the oohs and ahhs. It felt good. It was a good feeling. People stood up and noticed. When you bust off a big gain like that, they noticed right now."

Harmon also got his first media experience after that scrimmage. Veteran Massillon broadcaster Bill Caples interviewed the star sophomore. "Bill Caples was big in Tiger sports. When those first couple of early interviews came out, I thought, uh oh. It was nerve-wracking for me. I wasn't used to that. I had to kind of stammer for words. That *really* made it seem like it was big time. I knew Massillon was big time stuff, but until you got down there and you were doin' it, you don't realize how big time it is. I had people coming at me all the time."

Harmon had a productive sophomore season, despite

being injured for the equivalent of four games. The worst injury came the week before the Canton McKinley game when he sustained a deep thigh bruise.

"I remember being in the McKinley game and the plays were being run. And as a sophomore it just seemed like people were flying out there on the field. It was fast paced. It just seemed I was out of my league when I got in that game. It was different than the rest of the season, there was no doubt about it.

"I took another hit on that thigh bruise just before halftime. And it just swelled. It hurt so bad that I didn't even play the second half. I couldn't even walk. My whole right leg turned black and blue, solid, from up around the hip down to around the ankle. I mean it was solid black and blue."

Harmon, third row with coach Bob Otte, was a man among boys in grade school.

The following year Harmon lost an influence that was important to him when Commings took the head coaching job at the University of Iowa. "I was pretty sad. I really enjoyed playing for

Commings. I would have really enjoyed playing my whole time there at Massillon with him."

Instead, Chuck Shuff became Massillon's new head coach. Shuff brought in a whole new attitude, which wasn't welcomed by many of the players.

"Shuff was more of your marine-type, clean cut guy. He came in and tried to clean the act up a little bit. I would have never done (what he did). We lost some good athletes because of his changes. Like haircuts. There were a lot of different things that he changed that had been okay with Commings. And a lot of guys didn't want to adjust to that."

Harmon's junior year was successful on an individual level, but the Tigers lack of team success was frustrating. The team was 5-4 going into the McKinley game. McKinley was 9-0 and ranked number one in the state. Additionally, the Bulldogs had shut out seven opponents and had given up just 12 points going into the season finale. All signs pointed to a mismatch.

"I thought, gee, we watched Commings all those years have all those winning records. And whoa, my junior year we're 5-4. That just was unacceptable playing at Massillon."

But the McKinley game of 1974 held surprises for everyone. "We were underdogs all the way. That had to be the greatest game plan we ever had under Shuff."

The Tigers upset McKinley 20-15.

We always figured that's probably what saved Shuff's job, winnin' that game. Because we were still only 6-4 that year.

"We had all the ambition going into our senior year, but it just ended up being about the same thing. It was disappointing going 6-3-1. I just don't think we had the people in the right places."

"I visited Alabama and went right into Bear Bryant's crimson red office."

Bill Harmon

Individually, Harmon was one of Massillon's top runners. Until Travis McGuire and Folando Ashcraft came along in the '90's, Harmon was the number two career rusher in Massillon history with 2,505 yards. His 1,278 yards in 1975 puts him among the single season leaders.

Harmon was hotly pursued by college recruiters.

"I was getting letters as a sophomore," Harmon said. "They were really pouring in my junior year. There was a foot locker filled with that stuff.

"I visited Alabama and went right into Bear Bryant's crimson red office. He had that deep southern drawl. He was kind of hard to understand. He said, 'I'd like to see you here. I'd like to see you in our football program.'"

He visited several major universities, but his dream since grade school was to be a running back for Ohio State.

"In grade school we had to write essays and I wrote about that stuff. I wrote about wanting to go to Ohio State, Woody Hayes and the Ohio State-Michigan game."

Ohio State didn't turn out to be a dream come true for Harmon.

"I was like a fish out of water," he said. "It was pretty intimidating. It was the big time. You get down there and everybody's the same as you are. Same size and athletic ability. That was an adjustment. It was tough.

"Woody Hayes was still there. I had all kinds of neat experiences with him. Just seeing the way he coached. How intense he was. He'd have 300-pound linemen who kept making the same mistake. And here would come little Woody. He'd hit 'em square in the gut and just scream at 'em. They wouldn't even move. They'd just stand there and take it. I saw him get so mad and frustrated he'd stand there and he'd take both fists and he'd pound himself in the face. I stood right there and watched that. He'd take off his glasses, throw 'em on the turf and jump up and down on them. He did that a lot."

Harmon never got to play at Ohio State.

"After a while they switched me to a guard. I think that is what their plan was anyway. You get fooled as a recruit. A lot of schools will tell you what you want to hear. Woody used to be famous for gobbling up as many fullbacks as he could get. He liked changin' 'em into guards and linebackers, down linemen on defense. I think they knew that's what they were going to do with me but they didn't tell me that. That was a downfall, that was a negative. I wanted to run the ball. I left school at one point because I was upset about it. I went back, then we were getting ready for Christmas break. I came home and had a gall bladder attack and ended up in the hospital. I was included in the Orange Bowl trip, but I didn't get to go because I was getting my gall bladder out.

"I did get the ring, though. I still have the ring. I ended up leaving down there before the end of the year. I'd had enough.

"Bob Commings called me. I ended up at Iowa. That brought my spirits back up. It went really well. I had a good spring practice. Out there I ran fullback. Of course I had to sit out a year since I transferred from Ohio State. I guess at that point I knew it was over. I had really lost my desire to do it. There was a fire in me that just wouldn't quit for all those years. It just went out. I just didn't want to play anymore. I came back home."

Longtime Massillon assistant Nick Vrotsos reflected on Harmon's career.

"He was a great running back," Vrotsos said. "He was a different kind of running back. Bear Bryant wanted him in the worst way, but he wouldn't go to Alabama. He wanted him to be a wishbone fullback. He would have been an ideal wishbone fullback."

DENNIS FRANKLIN

Dennis Franklin epitomized the role of quarterback during his career at Massillon and the University of Michigan. From his confident demeanor, to his athletic ability, to his ability to lead a team, Franklin was something special whether running or passing.

Dennis Franklin's success at Michigan made him a Heisman Trophy Contender in 1974.

PHOTO: U-M ATHLETIC DEPARTMENT

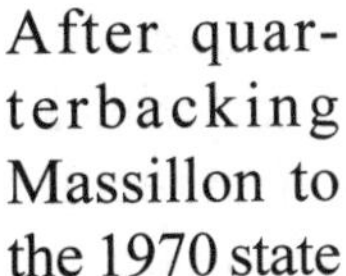

After quarterbacking Massillon to the 1970 state

championship, Franklin's star was destined to shine on a larger stage.

Legendary University of Michigan head coach Bo Schembechler brought him in and gave him the keys to the Wolverine's offense when Franklin was just a sophomore.

> **"He started as a sophomore, and for three years he won 30, lost 2 and tied 1."**
>
> **Bo Schembechler**

Franklin's only regret is that it came a year too late.

"My freshman year I couldn't play. I *could* have played, but freshmen weren't eligible. Of course, *had* I played as a freshman," Franklin paused, "it was Michigan's best senior class ever. I would have been able to play on the team that was undefeated and got beat by Stanford in the Rose Bowl. Stanford stacked the line against Michigan and the quarterback couldn't throw a six-yard pass. They lost 13-12. So I would have been a freshman on that team that had five All-Americans and four first round draft choices. I finished sixth for the Heisman Trophy as it was, but if I would have played on that team, a national championship team, as a freshman quarterback, I think I would have won the Heisman Trophy by the time I left Michigan. That's just how close I came to real stardom."

"Dennis Franklin is one of the all-time great quarterbacks we've had," Schembechler said. "We've had some great quarterbacks since I've been here. Denny Franklin was right up there. He started as a sophomore, and for three years he won 30, lost 2 and tied 1—and never went to a bowl game.

"The Big 10, stupidly, thought we couldn't beat Southern Cal in the Rose Bowl without Denny, so they voted Ohio State to go," Schembechler said. "That's why people didn't know as much about Franklin and how great he was, because he never got into a post-season game. That was the tragedy of Denny's career here. He was a great, great quarterback for us.

"In the Big 10 at that time, you either went to the Rose Bowl or you didn't go to a bowl game," Schembechler continued. "In 1973, when we were undefeated and tied Ohio State here, Denny was hit on a blitz and broke his collarbone."

Franklin with head coach Bob Commings, 1969.

Franklin first got Schembechler's attention while leading Massillon's state championship team.

A fourth and two play against Canton McKinley during his senior season epitomizes Franklin's leadership at Massillon. Head coach Bob Commings sent in a play, but Franklin had other ideas. He called a time out to plead his case.

"It was just an old-fashioned

off tackle play where you fake to Mike Mauger and the quarterback comes out—and if it isn't a good fake it's not going anywhere," Commings said. "I really was opposed to the play, but he knew he could do that well. He could fake well. And he also knew that if he got outside of the containment there was no one there. Denny came off the fake and came outside and went in for a 28-yard touchdown. It put the game out of reach."

"That play shows you how shifty he is," said teammate Larry Harper. "When you think about it, you have Mike Mauger, and Dennis is faking the ball to Mauger. You couldn't help but be tempted to go after that. You also have to credit him with the ability to make great fakes, to hide the ball from the defenders so they don't even know that he has the ball."
"I always felt that Dennis Franklin was just a special player," said teammate Steve Luke, who was co-captain of the 1970 team. "Dennis had the class and finesse of a Joe Namath. He was cocky, he was confident, he was classy."

Harper thought Franklin was the player who made the Tigers tick. "He was the consummate leader," Harper said. "Someone who was as good running the ball as he was passing the ball. Dennis wanted to be a quarterback. He didn't want to be just a running quarterback. He wanted to be an all-around quarterback. Someone who could call plays, check off plays and audibilize at the line. Someone who was a great field general. Someone who was a great athlete. He had a good football mind. He could run the ball, but he'd prefer to pass the ball. Dennis was, without question, the best all-around athlete on the team."

Mauger, by design, was the star of the 1970 team.

"No one really got a chance to truly exploit their abilities except Mauger, who was the tailback," Commings said. "It's almost unbelievable to think that Dennis Franklin was only throwing about eight or nine passes a game."

Bo Schembechler came to Massillon to honor his star pupil when Franklin was inducted into Massillon's Hall of Champions in 2000.

Despite having a great arm, Franklin's passing was limited at Michigan, too. He had more games with under 10 attempts than over 10.

Schembechler was a disciple of Woody Hayes, having served on his staff at Ohio State. Both Big 10 legends were more likely to run than pass. Schembechler considered Franklin his best open field runner on Michigan teams that featured a bevy of talented running backs.

Franklin led the Wolverines to three Big Ten Championships and he was an All-Big 10 quarterback in 1974. He led Michigan in passing and total offense for three straight seasons.

But the NFL had different plans for Franklin. A sixth round pick of the Lions, Franklin was moved to wide receiver. "Detroit didn't allow me to play quarterback," he said.

"I had to do my best to be a receiver."

It wasn't the first time Franklin lined up at receiver. He was a receiver on his grade school flag football team. "I used to play quarterback a lot when we were over in the school yard, but on the elementary school team I was a wide receiver. I learned how to catch the ball at a very early age. Those skills helped when I got to the pro level. I could catch the ball over my head, when you have to look back over your left shoulder. That's the hardest catch to make. I could make that catch with no problem."

Franklin got off to a fast start in the NFL. "I was the leading receiver for the Lions until I got hurt," he said. "I ended up starting and I got hurt in the fourth game," he said. "Tommy Nobis of the Atlanta Falcons caught me with an elbow across the middle on a high pass. They thought that I was dead. I was laying in the end zone. I thought I was dead. It was probably eight to ten days before I even got my thoughts back together. It was a major concussion. He was a tough guy."

Franklin missed the rest of his rookie season. Then a season in the Canadian League left Franklin flat: "We played in stadiums that were smaller than the stadium I played in at Massillon." He retired and became Vice President of Kingworld Productions in New York City, a company that distributes TV shows like *Wheel of Fortune*, *Jeopardy* and Oprah. He currently resides in California, where he sells real estate in Beverly Hills.

MIKE MAUGER

They called Mike Mauger "The Mailman." During the 1970 football season Mauger delivered for an even 1,200 yards, 23 touchdowns and 152 points. Mauger also kicked off, punted and kicked extra points for the team many consider to be among the top teams in Massillon Tigers history.

All-Ohio running back Mike Mauger was famous for following his blockers.

Mauger was a strong runner on a muddy field. And the turf at Tiger Stadium was just the way he liked it when Massillon played McKinley for the 1970 state championship.

"It was so muddy," Mauger said, "which I think was a big advantage to us because I ran so well in the mud. Mud never affected me, I liked running in it and it didn't slow me down. It was halfway between rain and snow. Snow flurries were coming down but the second they hit the ground they turned to mud."

Mauger rushed for 137 yards and sealed up the modern era record for touchdowns and scoring that day. "My second touchdown was the 23rd, that broke the record. I threw the ball into the stands," Mauger said. "That's the only time I ever did that. I got a penalty for that. They marked it off on the kickoff, and I of course was kicking off. I wasn't really a long kicker, I'd get it to the end zone most of the time, but I was so pumped up that I kicked that one out of the end zone, so the penalty didn't really affect us."

Mauger was a big, tough kid growing up in Massillon. And like many big, tough kids, he was always faced with situations where he had to prove himself. The opportunities manifested themselves in many ways. One instance occurred when he was in seventh grade at St. Mary's Catholic School. A famous figure in Massillon football history confronted him.

Mauger was walking down the road wearing an old Massillon jersey that a neighbor had given him when he was met by Massillon coach Earle Bruce.

"My neighbor, Dave Paulik, had graduated from Massillon and went away to college. He gave me his football jersey," Mauger said. "Now this jersey was so tore up and ripped up it looked like a rag. I was walking down Amherst Road one day and the Massillon Tiger football station wagon they used to give to the coach pulled up and Earle Bruce got out of the car. He took the jersey off my back. I was a little kid. He said, 'You're not a Massillon Tiger, you can't wear that jersey.'"

According to Mauger, Bruce

didn't *ask* him to take off the jersey, he forcibly removed it from the seventh grader.

"I was about ready to kill him," said Mauger, who at the age of 13 was already six feet tall and 175 pounds. "I wanted to fight over it. He got hired at Ohio State right after that. I swore I would get even with him."

Mauger got his chance when Woody Hayes recruited him to play at Ohio State after his outstanding senior season at Massillon. He found himself at the same breakfast table with Hayes and Bruce.

"We're all sitting at a breakfast with Woody Hayes and I told Woody the story. Earle Bruce was at the table and Earle remembered it. He didn't know it was me at the time, but he remembered vividly taking the jersey off my back. So when I got back to Massillon a few days later I got a UPS package at the high school. It was an Ohio State jersey that Earle Bruce had sent to me to make up for it. I didn't go there anyway."

Mauger found his early maturation presented challenges in his formative years of playing football. At St. Mary's he couldn't play the running back position he coveted.

"I was a guard and linebacker at St. Mary's because I was too big to carry the football. I weighed 140 in the fourth grade and you could only weigh 125 and carry the football. I played on the eighth grade team when I was in the fourth grade."

Ironically, his experience as a lineman may have developed a special skill in Mauger that served him well as a running back: the art of following his blockers.

Fans of the 1970 Tigers remember Mauger's ability to follow his blockers. His junior high coach, Milan Chovan, praised his young running back's talents.

"One thing he did real well was knew how to set up blocks," Chovan said. "He'd just slow it down and time it up, give a guard or tackle time to maneuver so they could chop that guy down for him. Mauger knew how to set blocks up for his blockers."

Chovan also remembers the physical specimen Mauger was in junior high. "Talk about physical development, he probably had the biggest set of powerful-looking legs at that age of any kid I ever saw."

Chovan also remembers Mauger's adolescent struggles. "Mike had a thing to deal with, his mother had stomach cancer," Chovan said. "She was dying day by day by day. You talk about kids going through traumatic circumstances. Now he was a big, tough, strapping football player, but you can't cope with things like that. Love goes deep. I have to believe that any of the tirades that Mike Mauger had in junior high school had to do to with the fact that his mother was worse one day than the next, and it got to him more one day than the next."

Mauger developed the reputation as a tough guy. And he had to back up the reputation constantly.

"I fought everybody," Mauger said. "I had a reputation growing up as an athlete so everybody from Canton, Tuslaw, Jackson, Fairless, they'd all come to town and want to fight. That's back when you could fight and it'd be over with and you'd be on your way. Now they shoot you. It's a different world now. A lot of the guys I'd fight ended up being friends later."

Mauger set rushing and scoring records at Massillon.

Mauger had a problem with Massillon coach Bob Seaman, who was the head coach during his sophomore year.

"I hated Seaman," Mauger said. "I didn't like anything about the guy. I didn't like his football philosophy, the way he treated people, the way he handled people. I don't know *anybody* who liked Seaman.

"Each week we had a kicking competition and I always kicked the furthest, but Seaman wouldn't let me kick because I was a sophomore. I swore I was going to transfer, I was going to Canton Central Catholic, if Seaman was still there when I was a junior.

"Seaman got fired and they brought Bob Commings in and everything worked out real well for me. Seaman's program was so bad that everybody was happy when Bob Commings came in. His whole coaching philosophy was team. His whole coaching career he would take his best athlete and make him tailback and put a fullback in front of him and then run the ball. Of course he did it with me, he did it with Bill Harmon and he did it with Willie Spencer.

"In 1969 I was a starter on defense, I did the kicking and punting and probably should have been the tailback at that time. In fact after the season was over Bob said he had made a mistake by not making me the starting tailback. We lost two games to Niles and to Canton McKinley. McKinley was 21-point favorites and they beat us on the last play of the game.

"For most of my senior year, I only played the first half of games. The only game I played in the second half was the Niles game. And that was because I was hurt the first half. We were gettin' beat. That was the only game we were gettin' beat. We were behind 3-0 at halftime.

"That was the time Commings came in and started smacking people and screamin' and hollerin'. He was going crazy.

"It was kind of weird for me because I was getting worked on. I was up on the trainer's table. Tim Ridgley stepped on me when I was running the ball, he stepped on the side of my ankle and that's how I injured it.

"Commings just came in

and started smacking people in the helmet and just going nuts."

Ridgley, an All-State tackle on the 1970 team, was in the middle of the locker room fray.

"They were filming a movie that Bob Commings was in. And he had these mikes on him," Ridgley said. "So as he was comin' through the door to the locker room he was ripping these mikes off his body. He smacked Kirk Strobel and punched me right in the shoulder pads. Willie Spencer was sittin' beside me and he was so scared he put his helmet on. If you did that to a kid today he'd have you in court. But then, I respected him for that. That told me I better get my motor runnin'."

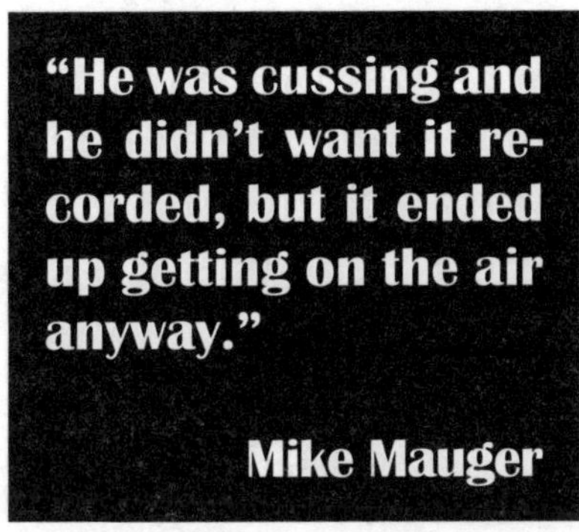

"He just was trying to get us fired up and he felt that was the best way to do it," Mauger said. "They were doing a documentary which later was on television for quite a few years. The documentary showed the whole thing. He was cussing and he didn't want it recorded, but it ended up getting on the air anyway.

"Doctor Furnace came in and looked at my ankle and said, 'I think the best thing to do is take all of the tape off of it altogether. Let's soak it in ice and see what you can do.

"I didn't think I was going to get back in the game until we came out for the second half and I started running on it to see how it felt. Even though it still hurt, I could run and we came out in the second half and I ended up rushing for 138 yards. That's the only time I didn't score a touchdown. In fact the headline the next day in the Niles paper said, 'Niles Holds Mauger Scoreless.' Niles was extremely tough."

"I have never seen a kid that had so much talent—and it was God-given. He was chiseled."

Tim Ridgley

"I have never seen a kid that had so much talent—and it was God-given," Ridgley said of Mauger. "He was chiseled. He didn't work near as hard as I did. But I had to. Because I didn't have it like he did. Mike was a team guy. He ran the ball awfully hard. Anybody that ends up getting the amount of yardage he had in one year—and the touchdowns—runs the ball real well. It's always great to see him come back home. He still looks like he can play."

"We had such a great offensive line," Mauger said. "We pulled our guards so much. We had Pete Jasinski and Dave Kulik, they weren't as fast as me but they were as quick and they could get out in front. Tim Ridgley, Kirk Strobel, Kulik, Jasinski, Steve Studer, they were all perfect technicians. That's the way Commings pushed it. And of course I had Tom Cardinal in front of me.

When I carried the ball I had a lead fullback 90 percent of the time. He was a terrific blocker."

Mauger was highly recruited following his senior season. "The three most recruited guys on our team were Denny Franklin, Steve Luke and myself. And at one point we were all going to go to the same school. We were all picking Ohio State at one point. But I didn't like Woody Hayes. I didn't like that much discipline."

Mauger's college career didn't hold the glamour many may have expected after watching him perform at Massillon.

"I went to Wisconsin," he said. "I didn't like the coach, didn't get along with him. And I got in a little bit of trouble.

"I transferred to Kent State. Don James from Massillon was our coach. I had known him all my life because his brother, Tommy James, was my dad's best friend. They switched me from tailback to fullback, which I didn't like. I didn't carry the ball much at all. But that's the way it went."

STEVE STUDER

Steve Studer may be the biggest hero in the storied history of the Massillon Tigers, where new heroes emerge on the local gridiron almost every year.

Studer was the starting center on Massillon's last state championship team in 1970, and came back home after an outstanding career at Bowling Green.

Steve Studer during a muddy victory over Canton McKinley in 1970.

Like his father, well-known Massillon Tigers artist Junie Studer, Steve Studer devoted his career to the Massillon Tigers.

He mentored Chris Spielman, who developed into a Pro Bowl linebacker. He then became Massillon's first full-time strength coach. In 20 years in that role, Studer had a profound positive influence on decades of Massillon football players.

The man affectionately—and respectfully—referred to as "Coach Stu" earned legend status in Massillon.

So it was a sad day for the city of Massillon when Studer died after suffering a heart attack at Washington High School on February 9, 2004, following a work-out. He was 51.

It was at Washington High School that Studer touched so many lives.

"I spend more time in the school building, in this weight room, than I do at home," Studer said in a 1998 interview.

It was a sad day for the city of Massillon when Studer died after suffering a heart attack at Washington High School.

"He touched so many people," Junie Studer said. "There was one incident he told me about where he had a problem with a kid. It ended up with him actually physically having to put the kid out of the weight room. This was a prominent player.

"Well, there were a lot of kids coming through the receiving line at Steve's funeral and here comes that particular kid with tears running down his face. It told me we still won. He won the kid, regardless of what had happened that day in the weight room.

"The receiving line just never ended," Junie said, "I could tell stories forever about how that week went and how the things that were brought to mind to us about how he had touched so many people. As each person came up each one of them had something to say that made you think they always knew him. There were so many things that started to hit you."

Steve's father, Junie, remembered, "I didn't go over much to the weight room, but once in a while there was a reason I'd have to go over and see Steve. One day I remember I went and Ty Partridge was there. I said, 'Where's Stu?' He said he had a class in the girls' gym. So I walked around the corner to the girls' gym and here's the team workin' out and everything's very orderly. They're doing some dashes of some sort. I didn't see Steve. Then I turned around and here he was sittin' up in the top row with this younger kid and he has his arm around him and he's just sittin' there talkin'. I think that's why Steve affected all the kids. It was just a touching scene.

Studer in the weight room that he created.

"Then the day the mayor Francis Cicchinelli proclaimed 'Steve Studer Day.' They had the rally and the people came through the museum where there was a display of his stuff. It was amazing, it really was. Then the day of the game, the whole stadium was orange and the #55 shirts were everywhere. It really struck me. If you knew Steve, he would have looked down on that. His reaction would have been, 'What is wrong with these people? Are they crazy? What are they doing?' I can just hear him saying that."

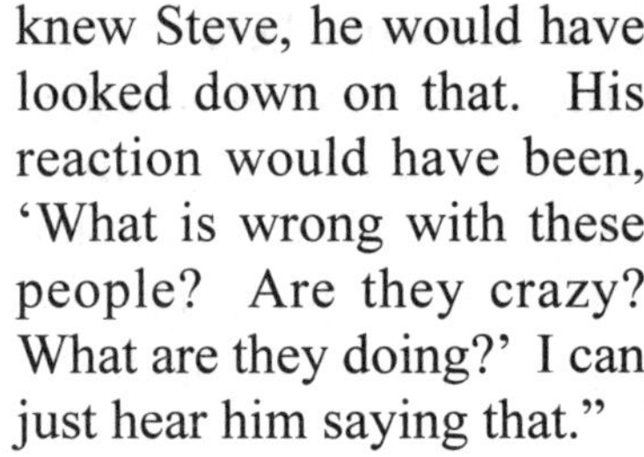

Steve Studer grew up immersed in the Massillon Tigers tradition. Junie was a big part of the tradition, painting the hoops that the Tigers burst through before each game.

"As a kid I remember him painting them in that garage next to the Massillon locker room," Studer said of the hoops, "He did that for over 30 years.

> **"The day of the game the whole stadium was orange and the #55 shirts were everywhere."**
>
> **Junie Studer**

"I'd go to the ball games with him. He used to take me to practices when I was a little kid. Being that close to the practice field and looking up to the players, it was the first memories I had."

Studer's childhood hero was Ben Bradley, a high school All-American in 1962.

"Ben Bradley was the center for Massillon," Studer said. "I don't know why, most of the other little kids would remember the running backs and the quarterbacks. But I singled out Ben Bradley, he was my hero.

"I'll never forget, I'd go to the games with my dad and he had this old pair of binoculars that he gave me and I'd sit up there and focus in on Ben Bradley the whole game. Wherever he went I'd follow him. He'd be in the huddle and I'd try to read his lips. I'd watch him break out of the huddle and come out onto the line just watch him play. I was probably in the fourth or fifth grade and I remember telling my dad, 'I want to play center for the Massillon Tigers some day because of Ben Bradley.' He was my hero."

Studer was a returning starter on the 1971 team that hoped to repeat as state champions. They came up two points short. One point losses to Warren and Niles stood between Massillon and back-to-back state titles.

"We played our hearts out those two games," Studer said. "Those game were battles, they were wars. Those losses were hard to take. Those were probably the top three teams in the state that year, Massillon, Warren and Niles. We lost those two games, but we didn't expect to lose. We had a couple of costly fumbles that kept us from winning. If you look at first downs, total yardage running and passing and all that, we won those two football games. So they were truly heartbreakers. We'd have had back-to-back state championships. I don't remember losing crossing anybody's minds," Studer said with a laugh. "That's the way it was. It was heartbreaking. Tear, tears. You know, a lot of people think, 'What kind of pressure is that for a high school kid to be under, to take a loss hard like that.' Some people might say it's a bad thing when a loss affects you that way. But, nah, I don't look at it that way. And I didn't look at it that way back then. It was hard to take those losses because we worked so hard to win. We were the defending state champions and our goal was to do that again. We weren't used to losing. We lost those two ball games and ended up with an 8-2 season. We still came back and beat McKinley 29-6 over there. It was great. It was awesome. In those days I believe that Canton McKinley really feared us and were very much intimidated by us. I could sense that. We could all sense that when we played McKinley in 1970 for the state title. We beat them pretty good in the rain (28-0). It had rained all week. They were bringing helicopters down there trying to dry off the field and all that stuff and we ended up playing in a mud bowl."

> **"In those days I think Canton McKinley really feared us and were very much intimidated by us."**
>
> **Steve Studer**

Studer chose Bowling Green to further his playing career. It was a former Canton McKinley coach who recruited him.

"Don Nehlen was the coach up there," Studer said. "He had coached McKinley in 1964. But the coach that recruited me was Ron Chismar, who was also a McKinley guy. So they knew what to say to a Massillon kid.

"At Ohio State Woody Hayes was the head coach and Earle Bruce was the assistant coach. Of course Bruce was another Massillon guy.

"But you know I think the decision came down to knowing if I went to Bowling Green that I was going to play right away, which I did. I played right off the bat. I never looked back. I loved my college days. We had some good teams at Bowling Green. My only regret of going to Bowling Green over Ohio State was

I never got to go to a bowl game and Ohio State played in four Rose Bowls during that time. I was kind of jealous of that. But in my senior year at Bowling Green I was selected to play in the East-West Shrine game. I was All-MAC at center and I was captain of Bowling Green my senior year.

"I had a try-out with the Chicago Bears. I was not good enough to make the Bears, I know that. But it was a good experience. I came home, then I got married and started a family here in town. I missed football so much and I couldn't accept that I was never going to put on a helmet and a pair of shoulder pads again. So after sitting out a year I went and played some semi-pro football. For three years I played semi-pro and then the USFL came along. Larry Coyer (who had coached Studer at Massillon) was the defensive coordinator for the Michigan Panthers. He called me up and asked if I wanted to try out with them. I'm getting older by this time, but I really felt I was in the prime of my life. I really felt good. I'd kept myself in good shape. So I said, 'Sure, I'll try it.'

"I was alternating with another guy for a first team spot. Then I had a bad situation that happened with a helmet. We were scrimmaging a team from Birmingham. We had a helmet problem that whole camp. There was a new design of a helmet. I had a busted up nose. The pad on the front of my helmet slid up and busted all the blood vessels across the front of my head. Everything. I came off the field and my head's killing me and I took my helmet off and everybody's jaws just dropped open. I missed a couple of weeks of practice where I really thought I had that team made. The Michigan Panthers. And they went on to win the daggone league that first year. But I never came back from that injury. The coach said, 'Stu, I liked you and I wanted to keep you. But you missed too much practice there at the end with your injury. The thing I liked about you so much is that a normal man would have been in the hospital, but you kept snapping to the quarterback.'

"That was the end of my football career. I didn't make the USFL."

Steve Studer

"That was the end of my football career. I didn't make the USFL. That was it. I had always been a big weight lifter. I was the strongest man on the team at Bowling Green. In fact, even when I tried out with the Bears I was the strongest man on the team. When I played semi-pro I started getting into competitive power lifting. I used that to stay in shape for football. It kept me in great shape. I know that's why I made All League at Bowling Green and had a good college career. I always felt what separated me from most of my competition when I lined up against their nose man was that I always felt physically superior."

John Maronto gave Studer his break as Massillon's strength coach in 1985. Maronto has become a high school coaching legend in Daytona Beach, Florida. He was Massillon's head coach from 1985-87.

"I had heard so much about Steve," Maronto said. "Once I met him there was no question he was the guy for the job. And I'll say since I've had Steve Studer as a strength coach, he set the bar for strength coaches. He was a guy who had such great passion. When we lost Steve, to me, we lost a guy who made such an impact. I can't *imagine* any head coach making the impact that Steve made in Massillon. He was *that* passionate about the way he coached and taught strength training. He believed in Massillon and the game of football. He was just something special. The whole Studer family's that way. You find families that are a great testimonial for a program. But I don't know if you find families like the Studers."

Studer on the sidelines.

Junie is the patriarch of the Studer family. Steve is the standard bearer when it comes to on-field prowess. But brother Joe has made his mark on Massillon football, too. Joe was a co-captain in 1974 and a key figure in two of Massillon's greatest wins over Canton McKinley.

As a player, Joe's work at center in the 1974 upset of

McKinley drew praise from head coach Chuck Shuff.

"Joe Studer was the best center I ever coached," Shuff said. "Maybe one of the best I've ever seen in high school. He did a very good job on the middle guard against McKinley. Joe told us early in the game, 'Don't worry about him coach I got him.' He handled him the whole game. Fundamentally he was sound."

Joe followed Steve to Bowling Green where the Studer brothers held down the center spot for the better part of a decade.

Joe was also the offensive coordinator in Massillon's 42-41 overtime victory over McKinley in the 100th game.

"He's the guy who called the plays in the 100th game," Steve said of brother Joe. "He said he spent that whole week in preparation to call that game. He had worked with our quarterback, Willie Spencer. They spent a lot of extra time away from the team working on the offense and what Joe wanted him to do in certain situations. They had it down."

"I can't imagine any head coach making the impact that Steve made in Massillon."

John Maronto

Steve's sons, Danny (1999) and Joey (2010) were co-captains and outstanding defensive leaders for their Massillon teams.

Al Hennon, Massillon's superintendent of schools from 1995-2005, held Studer in high esteem.

"He was my best friend," Hennon said flatly. "I looked up to Stu, and I think he looked up to me, too. We had a special relationship. It didn't grow apart, it just got tougher to maintain because I went from high school principal, where we coached the power lifting team together, to superintendent. I would see him sporadically. We would have to make time to see each other. But we still had the love in our hearts for each other.

"When Steve died, that's when I decided they weren't going to carry me out by my feet like they carried my best friend out. This job will get to you that way. I promised Stu that they'd never carry me out by my heels.

Studer (55) with former Massillon teammates Art Thompson (26) and Dave Kulik (72) at Bowling Green, circa 1973.

"No one can replace Steve Studer, it just can't happen. It's just that those bulging muscles and that bald head aren't here anymore."

LARRY HARPER

"Probably one of the most unheralded players to ever come out of this town was Larry Harper," legendary Massillon head coach Bob Commings said. "He had a great career at Miami University and he's a well-known player. We had so much going for us in 1970, but only the tailback, Mike Mauger, got to exploit his ability."

Larry Harper on the run against Cleveland Benedictine in 1969.

But to the 22,500 fans who were packed into Tiger stadium on that cold, November day in 1970, Harper was anything but unheralded. He raced untouched for 94 yards and a touchdown on the opening kickoff and Massillon never looked back, whitewashing McKinley 28-0.

"Larry Harper running the opening kickoff back for a touchdown," teammate Steve Studer said. "That was one of the loudest noises I've ever heard in my life, when that crowd went crazy."

"Larry was extremely competitive," teammate Steve Luke said. "I remember Larry's opening kickoff return. I was on special teams and I threw a block. Larry won't admit it, but it was a key block. I say it was a key block that got his but open," Luke laughed. "Once he got halfway down the field, I knew he had a chance of making it."

> **"It was just unbelievably exciting to see that open field in front of me and know that there was no one, absolutely no one, in front of me."**
>
> **Larry Harper**

Harper's return is one of those moments that has become etched in the memories of everyone who saw it. Harper himself has replayed it in his mind countless times.

"I've played that game back in my mind hundreds of times," Harper said. "I've never seen a stadium, even since that time, that was as crowded and loud as Tiger Stadium was that game. The stadium was so crowded that they actually had built temporary seats around the track area. The crowd was unusually close to the field. I remember the kickoff. I remember taking the ball and going up the right sideline on the McKinley side and remember just this kind of big gaping hole. I thought someone had come close to tackling me when I first received the ball. I remember sidestepping that individual and then just going up the sideline thinking that 'Hey, I think I'm going to get a good gain out of this.' And then all of a sudden the hole just opened up on that sideline. I cut back toward the center of the field and was amazed at how the pursuit had overrun me. It was just unbelievably exciting to see that open field in front of me and know that there was no one, absolutely no one, in front of me. All I could think was, 'I can't let anybody catch me.'

"Going into the end zone, throwing the ball up, it was as if I didn't even hear the crowd. But after I scored I could hear this thundering applause and this thundering noise in the stadium that was unlike any noise I had ever realized or have ever since. It was absolutely unbelievable. I had to stay on the field for the point after. I can remember all of the guys coming up, all the hugs and the pats on the back. It was pandemonium. As we were running off the field Coach Commings came up to me and said, 'Now that's the way you start off a game.'"

Like most Massillon boys, Harper grew up loving the Tigers. "I was a third or fourth grader when my dad took me to my very first football game. And being a small boy from Massillon, the excitement of going out to that stadium and seeing how green the grass looked and seeing all the orange and black, it was electrifying. It gave me goose bumps to walk inside that stadium and see all those people, the crowd. I got bitten by that Tiger football spirit. I remember seeing Arthur Hastings and Bill Blunt. Watching those guys. Listening to the bombs go off when the Tigers score. It's just something that never leaves you."

Not all of Harper's childhood memories are cheerful, however. He felt the sting of prejudice at a young age.

"My milkman coached the little league team," Harper said. "His name was Skip. I remember the very last cut. I remember thinking, 'Man, I'm going to make this team.' I was pretty good. Now Dennis Franklin was trying out for the same team. I can remember the very last day and my name not being called. I can remember just walking home and crying and I really couldn't understand how I could be cut because I knew I was better than at least half of the kids on the team. I was nine years old. I really couldn't understand it. Skip understood that I was crying and he told my mother, 'I'm sorry, but the league will only allow me to have one black player on the team. And Dennis was a little better than Larry and I had to let Larry go.' I remember my mother telling me that, but she didn't tell me until I was probably 15-16 years old. And I understand why she felt she should wait to tell me that many years later. It was just one of those things that happened. You don't understand why it happened, but it happened. I think getting that information at a later time in my life probably spared me from approaching things in a very negative way. I didn't really understand why my mother took so long to tell me that. But as an adult I really understood better. Those were the early 1960s and things were really turbulent at that time. She really did the right thing protecting me and insulating me from those things, protecting my feelings and my ego as a youth. But I don't think I really appreciated what she did until later in my life.

"The next year I made the Little League team. I did everything to prove them wrong. I think Skip made sure Dennis and I were on different Little League teams."

Harper made a stand against racism while in high school. "I remember staging a walk-out with a number of African American students because of what we considered unfair treatment. I remember us walking out of class one day. One of the teachers had done something and everybody just started talking about it and the discussion became a little more elevated. It became a little more heated to the point where people were saying, 'Well, what are we going to do about it?' Everybody said, 'We shouldn't take it.' I remember us going around to different classrooms and saying, 'All of the black students are walking out.' I remember vividly students walking out of the classrooms and getting together and police coming down. It was a big, big deal. I remember them shutting down the school because of the unrest. They wanted to talk to the black students and find out what the issue was and what led to the walkout.

"I remember going to Coach Commings and having conversations about this. He was actually supportive of what we were doing. He was honest and didn't bite his tongue. There were things he believed in strongly and he was very supportive of us. But he also told us, 'You've gotta be careful, guys. You've gotta be careful because you don't want to have this kind of thing on your record. To have this kind of thing on your record might prevent college coaches from coming in here and wanting to recruit you. I understand what you're talking about, just understand what this could do to you long-term.'

"I don't think that any of us, being young and naive, had thought about the long-term repercussions of that kind of thing. He basically didn't ask us *not* to do it, but he did say that, 'I want you to think about this long term. You don't want to have that kind of perception of you and maybe get passed over because one teacher or a few teachers and administrators remember these kind of things and hold it against you.' It was great advice."

Harper parlayed an outstanding career as a wingback at Massillon into a full athletic scholarship to Miami University. His size and the fact that he missed the first four games of his senior season in high school may have kept him from getting looks from upper echelon Big 10 schools.

"I had some pretty large schools recruit me. The University of Houston, Kansas, Indiana, Northwestern. I just didn't have a comfort level with their programs. All of the Mid-American schools were calling. I think missing those four games didn't give me the chance to rack up those honors and all state teams as I would have liked to have. I made All-County and was named to the All-Star game for the state of Ohio. I led the All-American conference in receiving and touchdown catches. I had a great season, but I probably could have had an even better season without the injury."

Harper had an outstanding career at Miami. He led the team in receiving and kickoff returns and even returned a kickoff 95 yards for a touchdown against the University of Cincinnati. He also made 10 catches in a game against Purdue. His name still dots the Miami University record books, over 30 years after he graduated.

His football career ended

with a tryout for the St. Louis Cardinals. "It just didn't work out for me," he said of the tryout. "And that was okay. I felt like in high school and in college I had accomplished some pretty good things and I felt that it was my time to move on to something else. And quite honestly, football has served me well."

Harper's business career has been as exciting as his athletic career. "After graduating from Miami I went to work for Procter and Gamble. The five and a half years I spent there really prepared me for the business world. It was like going to school and getting your MBA. There are fundamentals that are taught there that will carry forth no matter what company you go to."

Next for Harper was a 13-year stint at Polaroid. "I moved up the corporate ladder at Polaroid at some pretty good clips," he said. "It was pretty exciting during that time frame."

Then Nike came calling. "I had gotten a call from a headhunter asking if I was interested in interviewing with Nike." Several months and several interviews later, Harper landed at Nike. Again, he shot up the corporate ladder. He is currently Vice President of U.S. geographical business units.

Harper said, "It's been a great ride. I've accomplished more in eight years than I thought I ever would have. I have responsibility for almost two billion dollars worth of business. I have an organization of almost 200 people who report directly in to me. It's one of those companies where you've played sports all of your life and you like all of the things that sports bring to your life in terms of the energy and the excitement that is around sports. Then you get to work with the greatest sports and fitness company in the world. The fact that they're paying me and I get up every day and I'm talking about sports, and sports-minded things is a dream come true. One reward is working for a company where you don't really feel like you're working. Another reward is the compensation piece which clearly has been extremely rewarding to me and my family. The third thing is the ability to impact the lives of other folks. Help them to reach their individual goals and the ability to affect communities and people. Over the last few years at the top of my ladder, the ability to give back to the communities, to put in various athletic surfaces, whether it's soccer fields, basketball courts, the ability to give young kids shoes who can't afford a pair of shoes. To give them something happy in their lives. That brings a certain level of happiness to what you're doing. Many of the things I learned playing sports at Massillon certainly helped prepare me for some of the successes I've had in life. Working on a team, working hard, understanding one or two failures don't mean it's the end of something, it's just the beginning of something. Learning those types of lessons in Massillon helped me in the business world."

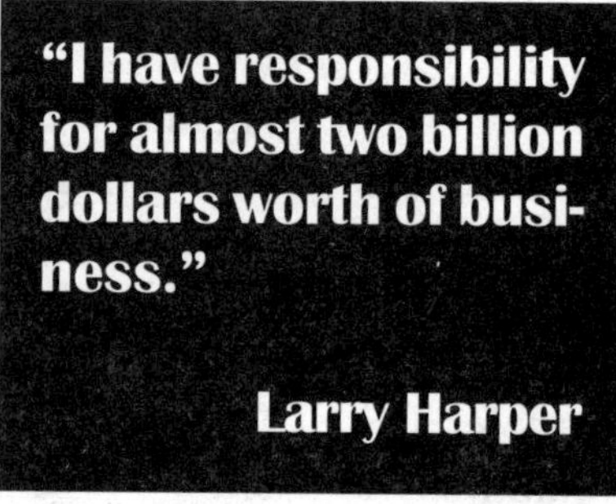

JUNIE STUDER

Devoted to the cause of the Massillon Tigers. Many Massillonians can justifiably claim such a title. But only Paul "Junie" Studer deserves the top spot.

Studer's love of the Tigers started early. Born in nearby Dover and schooled in Springfield, Ohio, as a school boy he couldn't wait to come to Massillon every summer.

For five decades Massillon players burst through Junie Studer's painted hoops.

"The day school was out, I came to Massillon," Studer said, "and I didn't go back until school started. That was always my thing, to live in Massillon."

Studer enrolled at Miami University as an art student in 1948, but those plans were soon scuttled.

"My parents moved from Springfield back to Massillon," Studer said. "That is what they always wanted, and what I always wanted."

Studer's desire to live in Massillon was stronger than his desire to finish college. "Dad opened Paul's Waffle Shop and I came back to work in the restaurant. I felt that I wasn't gettin' anywhere with this college stuff. I'm sure I was young and didn't understand what I should have been doing. I came to Massillon and fried hamburgs for nine years."

But when he was not flipping burgers, he was burning the midnight oil with an artist's brush in hand. "We had an apartment in the basement of the waffle shop," Studer said, "I started painting down there. One of the first things I did was make a football display for the shop. I made a card for each game. On Saturday I'd replace the card with a comical rendition of a Tiger beatin' up on whoever we had played that Friday, with the score painted on. I had to gamble. I made these up during the week, hoping we'd win and just put the score in."

When he was not flipping burgers, Studer was burning the midnight oil with an artist's brush in his hand.

Studer's artistic gambles usually paid off. His move to Massillon coincided with the Chuck Mather era, when Massillon was on a 57-3 tear and in the midst of winning seven straight state championships.

Those cards in Paul's Waffle Shop also marked Studer's first attempts at recreating Massillon's beloved mascot Obie. None of his early attempts at drawing Obie are still around today. "I'd probably be ashamed of 'em anyway," Studer mused.

"I can remember doing 'Dads' night' signs—the signs dads would wear on their back—in the kitchen of the waffle shop. That's the first I can remember getting involved with the football program. Then I started doing the hoop."

Studer's "hoop" is an enduring symbol at Massillon games. Tigers first burst through one of Studer's paper hoops in 1953. He hand painted each hoop through 1991, when he turned the job over to the high school art department. He figures he created over 400 hoops.

Studer tackled his responsibilities as historian with zeal.

Junie's sports exploits were modest—club level basketball success with the Massillon Buicks. "We won 19 out of 20 in the A league," he said proudly. Junie's sons, Steve and Joe, were another story all together. The Studer brothers were two of Massillon's finest centers. Steve anchored Massillon's offensive line in 1970 and '71, Joe in 1973 and '74. Every year, from 1972-78, a Studer was the starting center for Bowling Green State University. Both sons coached at Massillon, too. Steve's contributions to the Massillon program as its first full-time strength training coach have accorded him an immortal status in the town. Joe's lasting legacy as a coach at Massillon has to be his job of offensive game planning for the 100th Massillon-McKinley game, a 42-41 Massillon win.

Junie was put in a tough

spot when he was asked to become Booster Club president.

"In 1970 I got a call from Wilbur Arnold, who was the booster club president," Junie said. "He said, 'You've gotta do something for me. You're going to be vice president of the Booster Club next year.' I said, 'I'm not going to do it Wilbur. As long as my boys are playing I don't think I should be Booster Club president. He called back the next day. He said, 'I've got this all figured out, you'll be Booster Club president when son Joe is a sophomore. It won't be that big a deal being Booster Club president when your son's a sophomore.' I said, 'I guess I can live with that.'"

Studer was Booster Club president for Bob Commings' 10-0 team in 1972. That team was voted the state champion in the AP Poll, Massillon's last poll championship. They were later beaten, 17-14, by Cincinnati Princeton in the state's first playoff game.

Studer has been involved with the Booster Club in various capacities since joining the organization in the early 1950s. "It is a terrific organization," he said.

Recently, as the team's historian, Junie spearheaded a mammoth project that involved researching every game in Massillon Tigers history. By working steadily, Studer and his helpers have chronicled newspaper articles on every game the Tigers have played and posted them on massillontigers.com. Only Studer could have pulled off a project of that magnitude. That's why he stands alone, devoted to the cause of the Massillon Tigers.

Junie's Hero May Have Created Obie

Junie Studer has to be Massillon's favorite artist. You couldn't grow up there and not be exposed to Studer's terrific work—especially his Massillon Tigers stuff. But an earlier Massillon artist influenced Studer's art career, and may even be responsible for creating Obie, Massillon's beloved mascot.

YEA, TIGERS!

MOW 'EM DOWN

Tyson

TYSON ROLLER BEARING CO.
Massillon

Obie first appeared in this ad for the Tyson Roller Bearing Company in 1940.

"The guy that was capable of doing the first Obie is a guy named A. D. Small," Studer said. " I went to work for Adams Sign Company in 1957. When they'd send me to letter someone's window, I would always look at the lettering on the windows. All the really great stuff would have a little *A. D. Small* on it.

"His work was the type that fits with Obie. And I've got to think, in my mind, that he did Obie. I'll tell ya, if A. D. Small didn't do Obie, I've never run into anyone in that era that *could* have done it. But I can't prove it."

In Massillon, most people think Studer created Obie. "I would love to have done it," he said, "But I didn't."

CHUCK SHUFF

"I wouldn't even want to think about it. It would be bad. You're in a place like Massillon and you're losin'. You'd have to feel like you're a failure."—Tom Harp, Massillon Head Coach, 1954-55.

Tom Harp's description of the plight of a losing coach at Massillon is not something he experienced personally. He lost just twice in two years, while winning the state championship in 1954.

Chuck Shuff was 12-7-1 as Massillon's head coach from 1974-75.

Chuck Shuff was not a losing coach, either, if he's judged by normal standards. His two year record was 12-7-1. He was 1-1 against his arch-rival, Canton McKinley. But by *Massillon* standards, Shuff was a failure. Harp was right, Shuff's treatment in Massillon was something a coach "wouldn't even want to think about."

"My family suffered quite a bit," Shuff said. "Massillon is very hard on a coach's family."

Shuff's initiation started after he lost his opening game, 14-6, to Youngstown Ursuline. "Ursuline was not that great a team," Shuff admitted. "We got off to a rough start. We were outplayed, we made mistakes, we didn't play well. Massillon doesn't accept that. That was apparent in the letters to the editor and all the other things that started at that point."

Shuff's parents spent the night with their son and his family after the opening night loss. "My mother woke up when they were putting signs in the yard," Shuff said. "She could see figures out there, but it was dark so you really couldn't see who it was or anything. She woke me up and said, 'There are people in your yard doing something.' I pretty well had an idea what was going on. I had been told by Assistant Coach Nick Vrotsos, 'Coach, you're going to have some signs in your yard tomorrow morning.'"

"She woke me up and said, 'There are people in your yard..."

Chuck Shuff

Vrotsos had seen it before. "The Booster Club guys, when you lose, they go plant signs in the head coach's yard. It happened every time you lost. Every game. I've witnessed that. I've seen it with all of them. I think it bothered all of the coaches. It's your livelihood."

"I can't say that it didn't bother me," Shuff said. "But it was something you have to learn to put aside. Yeah, you don't like it. You want everybody to like ya, respect you. But my first responsibility was to the players and then their parents. Not the Massillon boosters, the people in town, not to the newspaper. But you don't want an opener like we had."

It didn't stop with the "For Sale" signs. "The 'For Sale' signs bothered my parents,"

Shuff said. "My family suffered quite a bit from phone calls made to the house. I didn't have an unlisted number because I wanted the kids and parents to be able to get a hold of me. So my kids, who were in second and third grade, picked up the phone a couple of times when they shouldn't have and got their ears full. Four letter words about me. After a loss we got to where we would take the phone off the hook to get a night's sleep. You'd *have* to do that. But you'd still get the signs in the yard. The signs in the yard didn't bother me. But people calling the house and blatantly... those kinds of things, they're not done by good Massillon people. They're done by what I'll just call jerks. People who have very little respect for family. Those things were hard. And they were part of my decision to move on.

"My son got in a couple of fights in school over things said about me. He was in second grade. It was hard on them in school. Our daughter came home crying several times."

"My son got in a couple of fights over things said about me."

Chuck Shuff

Mike Currence followed Shuff as Massillon's head coach. "When Chuck Shuff came in, he was really a great guy," Currence said. "Born again Christian. Nice guy. Bob Commings had left the program in a shambles. But nobody would admit it. When Shuff came in, he was really a great guy and what they had done was go to somebody who has high moral values, because Bob was just the opposite."

Shuff laughed in disbelief at Currence's portrayal of him. "I don't really see that," Shuff said, "I laugh because after I lost three games that first year there was a headline in the Canton paper that said, "Nice Guys Don't Win at Massillon." I was considered a nice guy, I guess, by some at Massillon. Yeah, we were sticklers on appearance and behavior. And Bob was definitely looser on some of those things.

"...a headline in the paper said, 'Nice Guys Don't Win at Massillon.'"

Chuck Shuff

"I think I'm a Christian person. When I was coaching and the kids were young, we were an every Sunday-type family. I think I've studied the Bible more than some and not as much as a lot. I think I have a good idea of what is expected of a Christian and a Christian life. Maybe Mike was right on that."

Vrotsos was there for the shining moment of Shuff's two years at Massillon. The Tigers were facing an undefeated Canton McKinley team that seemed poised to claim their place among the school's best teams ever. Shuff's Tigers had already lost four games.

"You aren't successful if you don't beat McKinley," Vrotsos said. "In Massillon you've gotta beat McKinley and you've got to make the playoffs. You've gotta beat McKinley first, then the playoffs are second. That's just the way it is. When you think of the tradition involved and all the people who put in years of their lives to give Massillon what Massillon has...If you don't feel that way, then, it's not worth it. What Paul Brown did wasn't worth it, what Chuck Mather did wasn't worth it, what Lee Tressel, Leo Strang, and Earle Bruce did wasn't worth it. All of 'em, that's what *make*s Massillon.

"The Massillon experience is a great experience. Some of the coaches are more successful than others. The ones that are more successful have a better experience. That's just the way it is. The losing coaches at Massillon—you say losing coach—I don't know any who lost more games than they won. All the coaches have above .500 records. But to stay with the big dogs, and achieve what the town expects... some of 'em didn't get it done, that's all."

Vrotsos continued, "Shuff was a good coach, we just didn't have a whole lot of talent. They evaluate a coach on how many you win and how many you lose. But a lot of coaches, like Shuff, if you put him in a situation where he had more talent, he would win. Now you can't tell the guys who played for Shuff that they weren't that good of football players. But the fact is any coach that has great talent is going to win in spite of himself, especially at Massillon. In a town like Massillon, where you get the support like you get at Massillon, if you've got the kids, there aren't too many games you're gonna lose. You've got the great facilities, you've got the great backing, you've got the great tradition. The town's crazy about football. How can you go wrong?"

"Nick hit the nail right on the head there with the kids," Shuff said. "Those kids just fought tooth and nail that whole game. And they were totally overmatched talent-wise. But you couldn't tell them that. And I wouldn't tell them that today. And maybe I shouldn't have said it here. I mean, you look at McKinley's kids and how many of them went on to college. And you look at what we had on the field that day. But I wouldn't have traded man for man our team for theirs. We won. That definitely was the highlight of my Massillon career, coaching-wise."

Shuff proved that he could win with great talent. At Fremont Ross he rang up three straight 9-1 seasons, paving his way to the Massillon job. He coached a couple of famous players at Ross. "Rob Lytle was an All-Ohio tailback and went on to the University of Michigan under Bo Schembechler," Shuff said. "He was drafted in the first round after being third in the Heisman voting. He played five seasons for the Denver Broncos."

Shuff also had a star on the other side of the ball. "Bob Brudzinski was a first round selection out of Ohio State. All-American. He and Rob were both selected to the Bob Hope All-American team. He was in the pros for 15 years with the Los Angeles Rams and Miami Dolphins."

Shuff retired from coaching after his short stint at Massillon, but he doesn't regret his decision to coach the Tigers. "It was a good two years of my life," he said, "I learned a lot."

TOMMY HANNON

Upholding the tradition of number 45 was important to Tom Hannon. He watched as Massillon stars Bill "Rabbit" Blunt, Tommy James, Jr., and Larry Harper brought fame to the number.

Hannon not only proved to be worthy of the number; it could be said that he became the standard-bearer for the number 45 at Massillon.

Tommy Hannon, All-Ohio 1972.

Nicknamed *The Man in the Flying White Shoes* by Massillon sportswriter Chuck "Scoop" Hess, Hannon took the number 45 to new heights during career stops at Michigan State and the Minnesota Vikings.

Hannon's reverence for the number started during childhood when he watched Blunt star as a running back and defensive back for the 1963 Tigers.

"We had a neighborhood with a bunch of kids who wanted to play for the Tigers," Hannon said. "And everybody who *wanted* to play for the Tigers ended up playing for the Tigers. Before the games on Friday night we would always play in somebody's yard. I was always Bill Blunt because he was my idol. He was number 45. After that Tommy James was 45. After that it was Larry Harper. And after that it was me."

Hannon got a glimpse of his potential when he entered high school as a sophomore. Head coach Bob Commings was in the process of building one of the greatest teams in Massillon history.

"They moved me to tailback when I got to the high school," Hannon said. "Things just started happening. I started maturing, started playing pretty well.

"Coach Commings was such a smart guy. He had me stay on the sophomore team, he didn't bring me up to the varsity team because he had Mike Mauger and Willie Spencer and Larry McLenndon. We were deep at running back. He basically let me pay my dues."

"Coach Commings was such a smart guy. He let me stay on the sophomore team...he basically let me pay my dues"

Tommy Hannon

"We had a sophomore team that went undefeated. Coach Commings would make us go against the varsity week in, week out. And they would beat our butts. But after a while we started playin' pretty good against 'em. I think we played 'em better than some teams that played 'em on Friday night. We had some guys who wouldn't back down. At first we were intimidated by 'em, but after a while we started holdin' our own against 'em. I think that's when Coach Commings thought, 'I've got a good young team that's really going to be something.'"

It was no small statement saying Massillon was deep at running back in 1970. Mauger was first team All-Ohio in 1970; Willie Spencer was the same in 1971.

Hannon probably could have started at tailback as a sophomore on many teams. Instead he made his name on the sophomore team. "Our sophomore games were always on Saturday morning," Hannon said. "I scored five touchdowns in the Steubenville game and I think they saw something special in me. We had a coach named Larry Coyer, he was a defensive coach, and he said, 'I'm going to recommend to Coach Commings that you dress varsity.' I didn't *want* to dress varsity. I didn't think I was ready for that. I had some great games as a sophomore. Coach Commings took it real slow. That was good. That's one thing I liked about Massillon, no matter how good you were, if you're a sophomore, you stay on the sophomore team. We had so much depth. Coach Commings didn't want you to get the big head. That's one thing I liked about him."

Despite his success on the sophomore team, varsity success was not a foregone conclusion for Hannon. "I was hoping it was gonna come," Hannon said. "At most any other high school I would have been playing varsity as a sophomore. But I couldn't because Mauger was a great back. Then the next year as a junior I played defense most of the time. I played running back as a junior when they put me and Willie in the backfield at the same time." So I didn't get to start as a running back until my senior year."

> **"I think the 1970 team was the best team ever assembled in high school history. I don't care what anybody says."**
>
> **Tommy Hannon**

Hannon took up the gauntlet and ran with it during his senior season. In fact he ran for a Massillon record, 1,395 yards in '72, a record that stood for 19 years, until Travis McGuire exploded for 1,976 yards in 1991.

The 1972 Tigers may have been the least talented of the three teams Hannon was with in his high school career. "One thing I'll say about our 1972 football team, we had a lot of gutsy guys. We didn't have a whole lot of talent. He had Larry Mayles and Dan Guiffre who were the guards. Todd Cocklin was the center. Mike Green and Bobby Geiser were the tackles. The offensive line was small, but like Coach Commings said, they were very gutty, hardnosed kids. *Really* hardnosed. And we outquicked everybody. A lot of teams we played, I felt had more talent than we did. But our guys played hard and we ended up winning."

"There was no doubt that we had the least talent of the three teams. I think the 1970 team was the best team ever assembled in high school football history. I don't care what anybody says.

The 1972 team *was* something. They were a perfect 10-0 during the regular season, including a 12-3 win over Canton McKinley.

The 1972 team also has the distinction of playing in Ohio's first playoff game, against Cincinnati Princeton. A 17-14 loss to Princeton ended the season on a sour note for Hannon and his teammates.

Hannon enjoyed being the star of the 1972 team and the attention it brought in school and around town.

"It was great. You walk into school and people recognize you and admire you. I thought, 'Hey, I know how a movie star feels now. People treat you real nice. It seemed like I was always the main focal point during that whole year."

Hannon was pursued by college programs throughout the country.

"I had over 150 letters," he said. "I visited Arizona. I was supposed to visit Southern California. I decline that. I liked Ohio State but Woody Hayes told me I would play behind Archie Griffin the whole time, so I didn't want to sit on the bench for two years. Michigan State said I could play there right away.

"Coach Commings told me if I wanted to play pro ball it's much easier to go as a defensive back than as a running back. I put a lot of stock in what he told me and it worked out. I was All-Big 10 for two years. Made a couple of All-American teams. I got a chance to play in the Hula Bowl, the Japan Bowl, The Blue -Gray game. I was MVP of the North-South game. I had a great college career.

"I got drafted in the third round by the Minnesota Vikings. I ended up playing for them for eight years. I started seven out of the eight years and never missed a game. I played both free and strong safety. My biggest regret is that in three separate years we missed out on the Super Bowl by one game. In all three conference championship games we were winning in the fourth quarter."

Hannon replaced NFL Hall of Famer Paul Krause at safety in Minnesota. Krause is the NFL's all-time interceptions leader.

Hannon was responsible for 26 turnovers in his Vikings career, including 15 interceptions. He intercepted a few Hall of Famers.

"I got Dan Marino," he said. "I got one from Roger the Dodger Staubach. The best quarterback I ever played against was Dan Fouts. The best running back I ever played against had to be Earl Campbell. He could run by you or run over you. Week in and week out we played a great running back every week. As far as the wide receivers go, Wes Chandler was good, so were Harold Carmichael, John Stallworth and Lynn Swann.

"I just came around at the wrong time. The money just started getting big the last two years of my career."

Scott Hendershot following Massillon's 18-7 over Canton McKinley, 1983. PHOTO: MIKE CURRENCE COLLECTION

1980s

Ramier Martin

Massillon's All-Ohioans

Dave Eberhart
1980

Todd Kausnick
1980

Doug Eberhart
1980

Mike Spicer
1980

Rick Heather
1981

George Nikitenko
1981

Charles Calhoun
1982

Chris Spielman
1982

Ty Beadle
1982

Chris Spielman
1983

Tom Gruno
1983

Craig Johnson
1983

Bruce Spicer
1984

Pat Spicer
1984

Wes Siegenthaler
1985

Jerrod Vance
1986

Lance Hostetler
1986

Mike Wilson
1986

Jerome Myrics
1987

John Woodlock
1987

John Schilling
1987

Trace Liggett
1988

Bob Dunwiddie
1988

Ramier Martin
1989

Ray Kovacsiss
1989

Lee Hurst
1989

TEAMS 1980s RECORDS

81	26	1
WINS	LOSSES	TIES

4 State PLAYOFF Appearances
2 State Finals/3 State Final Fours

1980
10-2-1

State Championship Finals

Head Coach: Mike Currence

M	Key Games	Opp.
7	Canton McKinley	16
14	Canton McKinley	6
7	Cincinnati Moeller	30
335	***Season Totals***	***166***

1981
7-3-0

Head Coach: Mike Currence

M	Key Games	Opp.
6	Cincinnati Moeller	24
24	Barberton	26
6	Canton McKinley	9
332	***Season Totals***	***64***

1982
12-1-0

State Championship Finals

Head Coach: Mike Currence

M	Key Games	Opp.
7	Canton McKinley	0
14	Sandusky	17
14	Cincinnati Moeller	35
369	***Season Totals***	***110***

1983
9-1-0

Head Coach: Mike Currence

M	Key Games	Opp.
10	Akron Garfield	14
17	Canton GlenOak	15
18	Canton McKinley	7
212	***Season Totals***	***94***

1984
6-4-0

Head Coach: Mike Currence

M	Key Games	Opp.
12	Akron Garfield	29
6	Warren Harding	18
6	Canton McKinley	17
182	***Season Totals***	***149***

1985
7-3-0

Head Coach: John Maronto

M	Key Games	Opp.
6	Akron Garfield	14
19	Austintown Fitch	21
6	Canton McKinley	21
180	***Season Totals***	***108***

1986
7-3-0

Head Coach: John Maronto

M	Key Games	Opp.
7	Canton GlenOak	9
22	Cleveland St. Joseph	17
6	Canton McKinley	23
235	***Season Totals***	***70***

1987
6-4-0

Head Coach: John Maronto

M	Key Games	Opp.
56	Warren Harding	14
7	Middletown	12
15	Canton McKinley	18
237	***Season Totals***	***146***

1988
7-3

Head Coach: Lee Owens

M	Key Games	Opp.
18	Altoona, PA	7
19	Austintown Fitch	20
10	Canton McKinley	7
236	***Season Totals***	***129***

1989
10-3

State Final Four

Head Coach: Lee Owens

M	Key Games	Opp.
24	Canton McKinley	0
42	Walsh Jesuit	24
21	Cleve. St. Ignatius	42
343	***Season Totals***	***197***

Story of the Decade 1980s

Firing of Head Coach Mike Currence in 1985 still Reverberates in Massillon

Controversy has always surrounded Massillon football. During the days of the Pro Tigers at the turn of the 20th Century the headlines were screaming about the "Fix of '06," when Massillon was accusing Canton of "fixing" games.

But through all of the decades of controversy, the firing of Mike Currence stands alone as the most controversial. Controversial enough to be featured in *Sports Illustrated* and *USA Today* and an untold number of newspapers across the nation. The coverage by Massillon's *Evening Independent* and the *Canton Repository* was voluminous.

Currence's record stood at 79-16-2 when the Massillon School Board voted 4-0 to fire him on May 24, 1985. Currence was one win shy of the Massillon wins record, held by the great Paul Brown (80-8-2).

The firing was shocking to Massillonians. "You could drop a nuclear bomb on the city and people would care more about what's happening to the football coach than the bomb," a Massillon resident was quoted as saying in the *Independent*.

The firing certainly had massive repercussions. Tom Kimmins was the president of the board of education who presided over the firing. For 40 years he's shared a law office with Jim Snively on the corner of Lincoln Way and Erie Street in the heart of downtown Massillon. Both are former Massillon football players.

Kimmins could feel the pulse of the populace throbbing when he showed up for work in the wake of the firing. "It was just boiling," Kimmins said.

"It was just boiling."

Tom Kimmins

Perhaps one reason why the firing generated so much unrest in the community was because of the board of education's refusal to tell the public why they were firing Currence.

Many thought Currence was fired because he was within a game of tying Brown's win record. There was also talk that possible changes to Currence's coaching staff led to the firing.

Whatever their motive, the school board chose to keep things private.

"I don't recall," Kimmins said, "Nobody wanted to hurt Mike Currence. Everybody liked Mike Currence."

Kimmins dismissed the threat of Currence breaking Brown's record as a reason for the firing. "I know Mike has said many times that the reason he was let go was because he was about to pass Paul Brown's win record. I couldn't tell you what Paul Brown's win record was or Mike Currence's either one at that particular time. That was not of significance. What was of significance was that we had a superintendent who was not as close to the football program as some of the superintendents have been."

School board member Bill Caples also dismissed the importance of Brown's record in the board's decision.

"One of the things Mike alluded to, one of the reasons we let him go, is the board was afraid that he was going to break Paul Brown's record for the most wins," Caples said. "He was one win away when he was let go. However, what he didn't say—and we tried to put that out and let people know it—the year before we fired Mike, we extended his contract for two more years. We extended that contract, figuring he'd be here, of course. And we thought he would win a lot more games. So how were we afraid of him breaking Paul Brown's record when he was let go? That made absolutely no sense at all (laughs). If we had been concerned at all about it we would have never extended his contract. The reason we let him go had absolutely nothing to do with football," Caples said emphatically. "*Nothing.*"

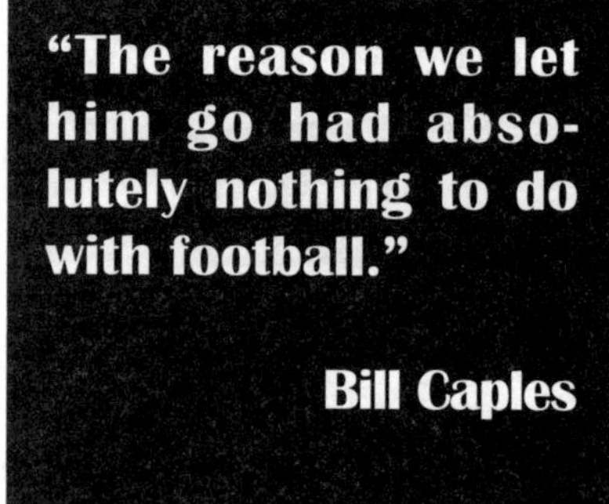

The fireworks started with a Wednesday night meeting with the school board and Currence.

It was a meeting Kimmins said was precipitated by the

school board's history of problems with Currence's hiring practices.

"We had admonished Currence on hiring coaches from the surrounding school systems," Kimmins said. "We told Currence that it was necessary for him to *not* be hiring our next door neighbors onto his coaching staff. He accepted that, except that he didn't follow it.

"I remember at the Monday night school board meeting, Dr. Darrell Cheyney (superintendent of schools) had a list of new hires for the coming school year. We were looking through them. I believe Bill Caples asked Dr. Cheyney, 'Who is this teacher who is going to be teaching up at Longfellow?' Dr. Cheyney said 'He's an applicant, he has degrees, well qualified.' 'I remember, Caples said, 'That's not why we're hiring him. He's one of our neighboring district's top coaches. Mike is doing what we told him not to do again.'

Bill Caples, Board Member.

"He was slipping one in on us," Kimmins said. "We had a little private meeting afterwards and they said they were going to call Currence in on Wednesday night for a private meeting about this, because he had a very dominant and aggressive personality. Currence thought that if he ran the football program he ran the majority of the rest of the school. That was something we had to sit on him about."

Another theory in the firing had to do with two hometown coaches who many believed Currence was ready to get rid of.

"We had a couple of guys, one of them was Butch Hose, who I think took it to an extreme by complaining to some of the board members," Currence said. "Now Butch to this day I still consider a good friend because he was always a strong supporter of me. Gary Wells at that time was one of the defensive staff. Gary was going through some problems with his family, divorce and stuff like that. He just needed to step out and get his own personal life taken care of. I think they complained, particularly to board members Joel Cunningham and Bill Caples. They never had any communications with Kimmins because he was never around. But Caples was always around and Cunningham was always around. Those two guys kind of carried the ball. Now we had on that board Jan Krofut. She normally voted against everything. So they could count on her vote (laughs). They only needed three votes, but they were going to get Kimmins' vote because they're telling him a bunch of bull about the coaches—that I was going to hire some outside coaches.

"We had a private little meeting afterwards and they said they were going to call Currence in on Wednesday night."

Tom Kimmins

"I had permission to do that. I had run it by the board and

had run it particularly by the superintendent. I had lined up Al Hennon as my defensive coordinator. And I was going to hire Fred Johnson from Minerva as my offensive coordinator. Fred was a great guy. He wanted to coach at a big-time school. He had been at a little school and wanted to coach big-time. He wanted to come bad. He had some little kids, too. And they ended up being great players. It was a win, win situation for Massillon. These two were great guys. Of course when Hose and Wells started whining about the possibility of losing their jobs because there are only so many varsity coaching positions, and they knew two guys were coming in and two guys were going out. Those two would have been the two to go out. But I don't know if that was the icing. The icing on the cake was Caples wanted me out."

Tom Kimmins, president, board of education, circa 1985.

Caples remains tight-lipped about the firing, over 20 years later. "I was on the board. Yeah. And our board decided—and I'm not going to go into all those details, I just won't do that. Yeah, he had some things that, I can say this about, they had nothing to do with football. And it had nothing to do morally. He was a fine person. But there were other things that were happening that we could not accept. You hated to see that happen. It's a shame that it had to happen like it did. But I'll always defend him as a coach. I thought

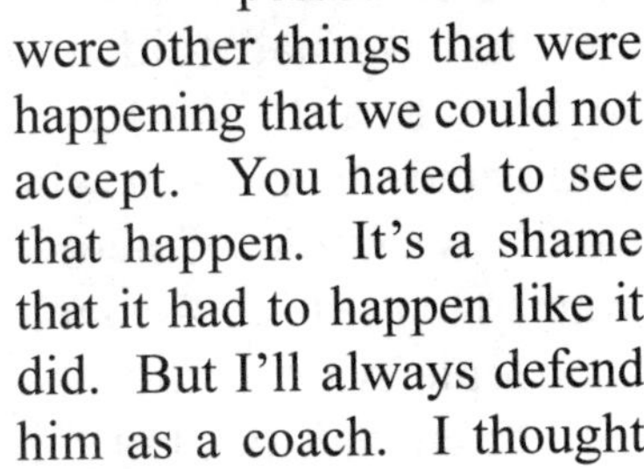

he was a great coach, a fine coach. Always. Irregardless of the record, he held his own against McKinley and overall had a fine record here. Too bad it had to happen like it happened in the end."

Kimmins didn't attend the Wednesday meeting. "That Wednesday night I was in a trap shooting league, the Tiger Gun Club," he said. "I told the board, 'Have your meeting with him and you have it out about what he has done, again, in direct violation of what we had told him to do.' I said, 'Whatever you decide to do, I'm with you.' A couple of people wanted to fire him. A couple of people wanted to move him to another position. A couple of people wanted to move him to athletic director and remove him as the head coach."

"I told the board, 'Have your meeting with him and you have it out about what he has done..."

Tom Kimmins

"It was really a surprise," Currence said of the Wednesday meeting. The superintendent called and said the board wanted to meet with me about these coaches."

Caples, Cunningham, Jo Annen and Crofut were the only board members present at the meeting, along with Cheyney and Currence.

"It was very quiet," Currence said of the beginning of the meeting. "Tense. Nobody wanted to talk. Doc Cheyney, especially, wouldn't say anything. Couldn't get him to say *anything*. I said, 'Now

Doc, you know that you had agreed on these two positions. They're two entirely new positions.' Nothing. He wouldn't say *anything*.

"Then the members of the board dropped the bombshell. "They said, 'We're going to buy your contract out.' And I said, 'Are you allowed to do that? Is that legal?' They said 'Yeah.' I said, 'I don't think that's legal for me to take that money. That's public money.' They said, 'No no, we talked to our lawyers. It's legal to pay you the contract and that's what we're gonna do.'

Jan Crofut, board member.

"I said, 'I'm not going to accept it.' They said, 'It doesn't make any difference if you're going to accept it or not. It's gonna be paid to you and we prefer that you leave, but we're prepared to reassign you.'

"I said, 'Well, I'm going to have to get an opinion on this because I don't think what you're doin' is right.' Then I tried to appeal to Doc Cheyney. I said, 'How can you let these guys do this?' I said, 'You know this is not a good time. Our summer program starts here in about three weeks. We're set to go. I think this is a real big mistake. I think you're hurtin' the kids.'"

Currence felt he had no supporters among the school board members. "I knew there was no use talkin' to Caples. I thought I could reason with Joel. And then Kimmins didn't even make the meeting. I don't remember Annen being there. She was married to the guy who took care of the live tiger, Ed Annen. Real nice guy. Real sweet woman."

The board members who were present voted as to whether to buy out Currence's contract. The vote didn't go Currence's way. "There were only four of 'em there. And it was four-zip."

"There was only four of 'em there. And it was four-zip."

Mike Currence

Currence and Caples, a local radio personality, had a contentious history. Caples was part of the radio team that broadcast Massillon's games. He was also the host of a popular call-in radio show, *Coach's Hotseat.*

Caples recalled his early memories of Currence. "I was on the school board when Currence was at Cleveland St. Edwards. So many people were after me, *'We've gotta hire him, we've gotta hire him.'* I said, 'I've got to see him, too.' And I did. And I liked what I saw. And we hired him. We brought him in here. And he lost his first two games here. So we were 0-2. 'Whoa. What's wrong here?' Then we went on to win. He had a great career here. A successful winning tradition. But other problems entered."

Currence acknowledged problems with the radio show. "Caples got back on the school board, he was off for a while, and he was upset that I wouldn't do his

Coach's Hotseat show. They didn't have a tape delay. So when I had a bad year in 1981, people would call in about one of our players, Greg Grimsley. They hated Ike Grimsley. He was a Canton Bulldog. They hated him, so they hated his kid. Greg was a nice kid. It wasn't his fault.

"And they wouldn't invest in the money for a tape delay system. And it went really bad in '81, to a point they were cussing the kids out on the radio. You can't do that. And they wouldn't tape it earlier and play it later. It had to be live. The *Hotseat Show*. That was Caples. I said, 'You either do the tape delay or I'm not doin' it.' They never thought I'd back out of that, because the coach had always done it. And I said, 'Watch me.' Well, Caples lost his job over that. So he was very vengeful about it and wanted to see me gone."

Joel Cunningham, board member.

Currence thought he had an ally on the board when Cunningham was elected. He later changed his mind.

"Joel Cunningham belonged to the Touchdown Club, the Rotary, everything like that. The Booster Club put him up for the school board. I thought it was good, because I wanted a Booster Club guy on the board, because the school board would not give us any money. Would not give me enough coaches, would not give my coaches a raise. They wouldn't give me a raise. It was tough to get anything out of them. They wouldn't do anything for football. And football runs that town. We needed somebody who supported football. So I supported him. I thought, 'Go Joel.'"

stadium tonight and they're getting the players together tomorrow? He's not gonna give that job up easily.' To make a long story short, that became a very tough battle that week."

Kimmins heard of Currence's dismissal from the media. "I got home that night from this trap shooting league about 10 o'clock and the phone was ringing off the hook," Kimmins said. "It was WHBC and the *Repository* calling me, as president of the school board, wanting to know why Currence was fired. I told them that I had missed the meeting but I knew what the subject was. And they said, for example, 'Do you know that he has called all of his assistant coaches, they've already had a meeting at the

Kimmins heard of Currence's dismissal from the media.

"I had gotten a lot of calls because this thing went out over the wire that Massillon was buying out my contract," Currence said. "It was a first, I think. Most people did not know of another case where a high school coach's contract was bought out. So I was getting calls, television interviews...And I really wanted to get the word out because the board was going to do this on the 'QT.' They didn't want it publicized. They had a meeting with me, which I thought was illegal, because it was about personnel. They're supposed to announce their board meetings. It's the law. And they didn't. And they had meetings behind my back about personnel and it was never announced. They're not allowed to do that. But, what are you going to do? They're autonomous, you can't do anything to school boards, except fire them. And they all got fired. I think they all lost elections. They cleaned house."

Jo Annen, board member.

Two days after the Wednesday meeting, a school board meeting was scheduled to seal Currence's fate. The meeting was moved to the high school auditorium in anticipation of a large turnout.

"They moved to the high school because they were going to get protesters outside their little building over there," Currence said.

Kimmins walked to the meeting, which was just a couple of blocks from his office. "On my way over—I walked from my office to there—I could see the turmoil that was building at the high school. So I stopped by the police headquarters, which is between here and there. I asked them to bring the police over."

The high school auditorium was almost full. "We went up on the stage on old Washington High School, and at that particular time he had the whole football team up there on stage, and at that time that would be about 100 kids, and they were in a riotous mood in support of their coach,"

Kimmins said. "And Currence had put the word out, because nobody—especially in Massillon—had ever fired the high school coach."

"Yeah, they called the meeting to order, took up the business, did that, then closed it," Currence said. "They were out of there. They went out the back door. They wouldn't take any questions. They wouldn't take anything. I stood up and asked if we could ask them questions and they wouldn't even recognize me."

Cameron Speck, whose son Curt was a sophomore football player, was part of the audience on that Friday afternoon. He didn't like what he saw.

"We were all astonished," Speck said. "It was all cut and dried. It was over in about five minutes. The people in the auditorium, which was darned near full, were just standing around there dumbfounded that this occurred. I became more and more enraged about it. I talked with several other people and we all felt the same way."

"I asked them to bring the police over."

Tom Kimmins

Speck decided to take action. He decided to organize a rally to petition the school board to resign. "I called city hall and arranged to use the council chambers."

Massillon mayor Delbert Demmer blessed the use of council chambers, but it turned out to be a moot point. When Speck arrived he was met with a surprise.

"We couldn't get in there because it was jam packed with people. They were standing out in the hallway and in the parking lot. So we moved it out to the park in front of city hall.

Speck estimates that 500-600 people attended the meeting. Besides Speck, former school board members Immel and Ann Lightfoot spoke to the crowd.

"The people in the auditorium, which was darned near full, were just standing around there dumbfounded that this had occurred."

Cameron Speck

The crowd eagerly signed petitions that Speck had drawn up on legal pads. "I must have had 30 or 40 legal-sized petitions signed by the people of Massillon. The crowd," Speck said, "was quite hostile."

On June 17 Speck presented the petitions, containing over 1,000 signatures, to the Board of Education.

Kimmins still keeps a copy of the petition in his desk drawer. "Every time I get to feeling too cocky, I pull that out and I look at the names of people that I had grown up—the big hitters in the community—that had signed that document for me and my board to resign, and bring Currence back, not ever knowing the facts. And that was a very difficult thing to take.

"We stuck by our guns and remained on the school board and upheld the firing. People marched around our offices here, it was not a good situation. The thing that I remember then, it got in *USA Today*. The next thing you know, I get a contact from *Sports Illustrated.* They say the coaches are a very close-knit union and organization and they defend each other. You just don't fire coaches at the high school level. You might at the pros and you might at college, but at the high school level it's never done. It was their feeling like it was one of the few times it had ever been done. They took my picture sitting here just like this with almost the same kind of background. And lo and behold there was a story in *Sports Illustrated* with my picture."

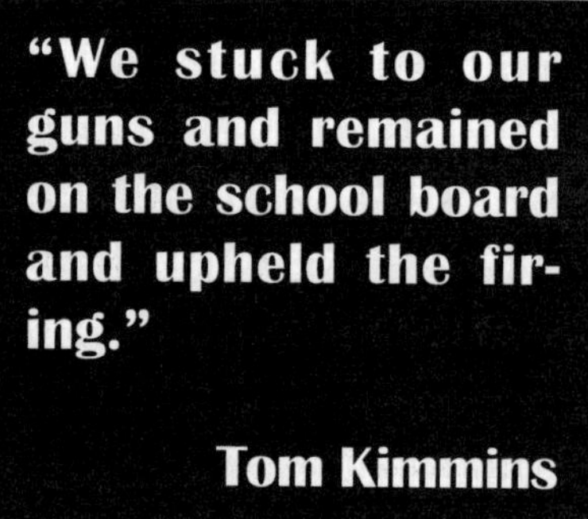

"We stuck to our guns and remained on the school board and upheld the firing."

Tom Kimmins

Currence heard from Sports Illustrated, too. "I got a call from 'em, I was quite shocked that they called and were interested. They talked to us about it, the story, and took notes. They were going to send a photographer around to take a picture. He took a lot of pictures. I hesitated to get my son involved in it, but I figured he was going to be in it anyhow. He got his picture in *Sports Illustrated*, too, because of it. It was a pretty big thing. Actually, the guy who loved it the most was Tom Kimmins. Because they pictured him as a big time lawyer in a small time town, sittin', layin' back with his suspenders on. And he really enjoyed it. I think he enjoyed the interview.

The fact that he was in *SI*. He enjoyed it. Because when we did a deposition on him, he was very cooperative. He was the guy who put us over the top. He was truthful, co-operative and the whole bit. Because he knew that he had hurt me. He knew that they were wrong, you know," Currence said.

"And lo and behold there was a story in Sports Illustrated with my picture."

Tom Kimmins

The deposition Currence alluded to was part of a $3.6 million dollar lawsuit he brought against the school board that fired him.

"We just primarily went through federal court and filed against the school board and claimed violation of a lot of things, but a violation of free speech was one of them. And I think that was the one count that came back and said that we had grounds to sue. And then my lawyers, who I got out of Akron, started runnin' up the bills on 'em. They started taking deposition after deposition after deposition and finally we were going to fly out to interview coaches who had this contract problem before and interview other high school and college coaches. Once we went to deposition their lawyers had to fly, too.

"So their expenses went well over $300,000 that they were into it. They decided to settle. Jim Delong I think helped on that. Being a lawyer in Massillon and being behind the scenes, he would talk to the board members and he'd say, 'You better settle. You're not going to win this thing. It's going to cost you more money.'"

"It was a nasty lawsuit," Kimmins said. "Two little incidents I remember significantly, because they affected me. Mike never forgave me, because I happened to be president at that time. So I became the spokesman for the board, but I wasn't at the meeting when the decision was made. But I had agreed to back them. While they were taking my deposition they said, 'There's an article in *USA Today* that says you said Mike Currence is a pariah. Did you make that statement and why would you make that statement that he was a pariah?' I remember my response to the deposition was that I do not know what the word pariah is. I know the word piranha. They said, 'Well, pariah is a third or fourth class citizen in India, who because they've been shamed, are forced to walk the alleys. They quoted you in *USA Today* as saying he was a pariah for what he had done and what he is putting this community through. That he should be treated like a pariah in India, meaning that he should walk the alleys.' I honestly didn't know the word. And there is no doubt that *USA Today* did indeed print that. I didn't even know what the word was.

The deposition Currence alluded to was part of a $3.6 million lawsuit he brought against the school board that fired him.

"In the end it was settled out of court. Mike got himself a job at a parochial school, because he had a parochial background prior to coming here. He specifically said he would not settle the contract 'unless Tom Kimmins contributed money to the settlement.' So I still have the canceled check for $5,000 that I wrote to Mike Currence, as school board president, to settle this. And I'm supposed to be immune against that. I took my $5,000 dollars—and whatever it was the insurance company paid, $200,000 I think it was—and he got $205,000. Because he believed that I was the instigator of it. I was the spokesman, I had to be, because I was president that year.

"An article in USA Today says you said, 'Mike Currence is a pariah...' Did you make that statement?"

Currence lawyer

I have seen Mike since, have played tennis on the court next to him, have spoken to him. But we have not said a dozen words since then. He went on to be successful. A lot of people in Massillon still like him. Liked him at the time.

"Probably if you look back, I blame part of that responsibility on our superintendent for not being closer to what our concerns were and having caught this situation so that it didn't come before the board. He wouldn't know a coach from an English teacher. The superintendent has to be close to the football program. But Dr. Cheyney was weak. We should not have been the ones to make the decision. I'm sure that the board felt that he wasn't capable of making that decision and backing it up. We couldn't rely on him to be a pusher in backing us in what we decided to do. Now Mr. Cheyney has since passed on, and he was an excellent superintendent, but we were left to row that boat alone. And we did it the best we could, considering."

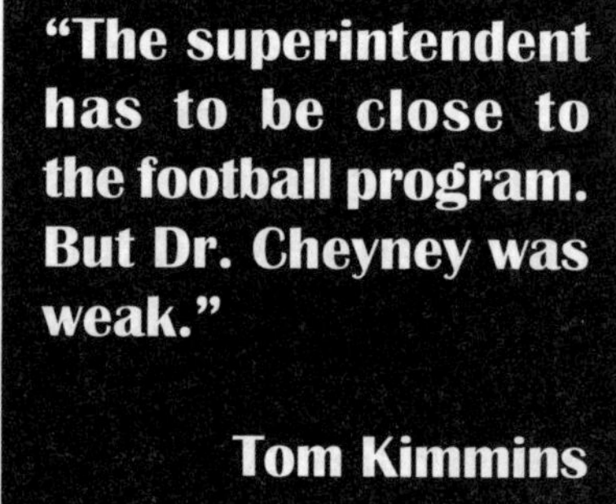

Kimmins reflected on that Wednesday board meeting, when his fellow board members decided Currence's fate.

"I think I was a little taken back that it went that far," Kimmins said. "Because they called me that night and asked me what the reason was for the firing. I was terribly embarrassed to say, 'I wasn't even there, who did they fire?' They said, 'Whatta ya mean you weren't there?' Then I had to listen to that for probably six months. 'So the president of the school board wasn't even at the meeting? He was at his trap shooting league?' That may give you some indication that I didn't think it was going to be that big of a deal, you know (laughs). I look back, I think I would have been smart enough to recognize that if I really thought they were going to fire Currence that night I would have definitely bypassed the trap shooting league to be there. That would have been my third four-year term on the school board, so I would have well recognized the significance. I honestly didn't think they would go that far.

"It was a situation where the board had a couple of mavericks—and I wasn't a maverick on that board. I was really the only really educated guy on the board. And I had been a city councilman for 12 years and I knew how boards worked. I didn't expect to get into that kind of turmoil to be very honest.

"Also, my background is, that although I was the only former football player on the board, I'm not one of those guys who used to run up and down the sidelines as an adult waving the flags. I've had my seats for 50 years and I don't miss a game. And I take my football very seriously. I understand football very well. And I support it.

"But I'm not a Massillon Tiger nut. Never have been. Was not then. I merely stepped in because the board needed a leader.

"It was a situation where the board had a couple of mavericks."

Tom Kimmins

"I was the president at that time.

"School board member Joel Cunningham was a very outspoken guy. Caples understood sports. They were pretty strong willed people."

Caples, looking back, feels the board did the right thing. "Yep, yes. The school board paid for that, though. Because within two years our whole board was voted out. All five members of the board were voted off. We knew it could happen at the time. We knew that it wasn't going to be a popular decision when we did it. But we did what we had to do, irregardless. What we did was right."

But as far as the reason *why* he felt the board was right? "I'm not going to go into those details," Caples said. "But we were right in what we did."

Kimmins, too, feels the board was right in firing Currence. "I did what I thought was good for the system at that time. You just can't have your coach run your whole school system. I think in his mind he had become too powerful. You just can't have that. He had become a little too big for his britches. Mike was a taker. That's really what it was."

Currence, for his part, thinks back on the effect his firing had not only on himself, but on the school system and the community.

"The whole ordeal was a very, very big bad thing for the school system, for the kids. It divided that community for years afterwards," Currence said. "People turned in their season tickets and have never been back. I've had guys who come and see me that have never been back."

Speck ended up running for—and winning election—to the school board following Currence's firing. Looking back, what does he think led to Currence's ouster?

"The real reason? The competition against Paul Brown," Speck said. "They wanted to maintain that so it would always be a record-setting situation."

Games of the Century

1989's 36-Point Turnaround May Be Tigers Greatest Comeback

The Massillon players were down when they came into the locker room at halftime. The favored Tigers were the top seed in their region, playing at home, but the scoreboard told a different story.

"We're coming off the McKinley game and we're playing Walsh Jesuit in the playoffs and we're down 24-7 at the half," said Nick Vrotsos, longtime Massillon assistant coach.

"We were down big," Head Coach Lee Owens said. "You expend so much energy for that McKinley win, you've gotta expect something crazy the next week. The toughest two games are the ninth and eleventh games—the week before McKinley and the week after McKinley. I went into the locker room and rattled their cages."

> **"We're coming off the McKinley game and we're playing Walsh Jesuit and we're down 24-7 at the half."**
>
> **Nick Vrotsos**

Owens wasn't the only coach trying to motivate the team.

"Vrostsos came into the locker room and said, 'If you guys don't win this game you're not Tigers," said Ramier Martin, an All-Ohio receiver for the 1989 Tigers. "That probably upset us more than anything, because he wanted to strip us of something we had worked so hard to attain. We were in the playoffs. We were the first team back in the playoffs since 1982. We beat McKinley, we're 8-2, but he's telling us we're not Massillon Tigers if we don't win this game. We're down 24-7, that's a tough deficit. It tapped into me personally. 'You're going to tell me I'm not a Tiger?' I think we all went out there with a chip on our shoulder. Probably mad at the coaches more than energized by the coaches. So that motivational trick worked."

" I got some of the other assistants out of the room," Vrotsos said. "I said, 'I want to talk to the team.' I got into 'em, I *really* got into 'em. I said, 'Tigers? You guys should take off your uniforms the way you're playin'. I really got into 'em. All of 'em. We came back and won the game 42-24."

Tom Stacy, who led the Tigers to the state championship game as head coach in 2005, was an assistant to Lee Owens in 1989.

"I saw 40 or 50 guys with tears just running down their faces."

Tom Stacy

"I remember going in at halftime and our kids just staring at the wall," Stacy said. "And Vrotsos coming in and looking at 'em all and saying, 'Hey, you're not Tigers.' I saw 40 or 50 guys, most of 'em starters and seniors, with tears just running down their face. I'll never forget that as long as I live. I didn't know if we were going to win, but I knew we were going to play a heckuva lot better in the second half."

The 36-point turnaround is the biggest in Massillon history. "We got a good spark to start the second half," Owens said. "Donnie Blake returned the kickoff for a touchdown. We started to feed off of that adrenaline."

"Donnie Blake definitely sparked us," Martin agreed, "that was the key moment. The momentum just shifted. We said, 'If we can get one, we can get two. If we get two, we can get three.'"

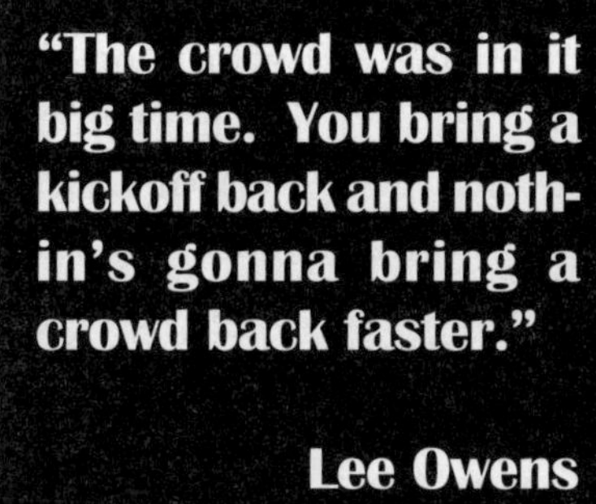

"You start making a couple of plays and the fans start getting into it and the fireworks start going off after every touchdown," Owens said. "I can always sense on the other sideline that they're saying, 'Oh no, here comes that Massillon crap again.' I can always get a good feel when the other team is coming in there with the hype—how it's affecting them. Some teams it gets them fired up. Other teams, you can see they're just looking around big-eyed. When I saw that I'd think, 'Okay, we've got these guys.' I think a little of that was starting to happen to Walsh. They came in all fired up, but then they were waiting for that shoe to drop. All of a sudden we made a couple of big plays in the second half and I knew they were just trying to hang on. We started pounding it. We started making big plays. The crowd was into it big time. You bring a kickoff back and nothing's gonna bring a crowd back faster.

"Lamonte Dixon and Ryan Sparkman were running real hard. It was going real well."

Dixon raced for 182 yards on just 10 carries.

Martin had a couple of personal highlights in the game.

"I actually scored the go-ahead touchdown," Martin said. "There was a defender on their team that was talking trash to me the whole game. He said, 'We don't know anything about you. You're no good.' So I just waited my time. There was a play in the second half that I caught an out route, turned up field and was gonna try and make a move. My whole intention was to juke, but when I saw his number, I said, 'I'm running him over.' I lowered my shoulder and ran him over and kept running up the sideline. He was dejected. When I scored, the first person I looked for was him. I remember looking back and seeing him pounding the ground in frustration. I knew that we were coming back and they were beaten. That was definitely a memorable game."

"I think it was a lot of aggression and frustation coming out," Martin said. "The memory of Coach Vrotsos' 'You're not Tigers,' him trying to strip our Tigers from us. And the brow-beating by Coach Owens. We were going to take it out on somebody."

The 1989 Tigers continued their playoff run with a 42-7 win over Akron Garfield the next week that set up a Final Four meeting with Cleveland St. Ignatius.

Ignatius ended the Tigers season, winning 42-21 in front of 18,206 fans in the Akron Rubber Bowl.

MIKE CURRENCE

The name Mike Currence elicits strong emotions in Massillon.

On one hand you have Mike Currence the hugely successful football coach—his 79 wins are second only to legendary Paul Brown's 80 in Massillon's prolific history. On the other hand you have Mike Currence, the coach who was fired, then turned around and sued the Massillon school board—and won. The circumstances surrounding his departure are still hotly debated, decades after the fact.

Mike Currence was 79-16-2 as Massillon's head coach.
PHOTO: MIKE CURRENCE COLLECTION

"Coach Currence was a great coach," said Chris Spielman, one of Currence's star pupils at Massillon from 1981-83. Spielman gained fame as an All-American at Ohio State and an All-Pro for the Detroit Lions. "I felt very fortunate that I was able to play for him. I thought he did a wonderful job. He was ahead of his time as far as offense was concerned. Precision. Teams couldn't cover our passes and reverses. Our timing was so good for a high school—they couldn't stop it. For him to be able to coordinate that among the junior high school level kids—the same offense, the same defense—was extraordinary.

"He was a guy who handled the pressure well. When we lost he took a lot of the heat. He was able to let that bounce off. He would never let that upset the team. He'd stand up and take the heat like a man. That's admirable for a guy in that position. There's no pressure level like that anywhere in high school. It beats a lot of colleges that don't emphasize winning."

"Mike Currence was a great high school coach. I felt very fortunate that I was able to play for him."

Chris Spielman

Brent Offenbecher, an All-Ohio and All-American quarterback for Currence from 1977-78, revered his coach.

"I thought he was a great coach. An X's and O's kind of guy," Offenbecher said. "He brought an offense to Massillon that was extremely hard to defend. And if you have athletes—like we did—you can win."

Currence said he had his work cut out for him when he took the Massillon job in 1976 after a successful stint at Lakewood St. Edward. "Talk about a program that was decimated," Currence said. "There were no young kids being trained to be a quarterback, which is probably one of the most crucial positions ever. I took a defensive back, Brett Traylor, and made him a quarterback in 1976, because there absolutely was no one who could throw the ball.

"I remember the first day of practice, coming out, we had an old timer there who was equipment manager. He brought like five footballs out in a bag on the field for practice. I said, 'Where's the footballs?' Because I had decided I was going to go two platoon and I had at least 15 to 20 young kids who wanted to play quarterback or receiver. I wanted 'em all to have a football for drills. He said, 'They're in the bag.' I said, 'That's it, five footballs?' And he said 'Yeah, that's all we ever bring out.' I said, 'Well, I'll tell you what, you go back and get as many footballs as you've got and get 'em out here.' And he started mumblin' under his breath. And I'm going, 'What did you say?' And he said, 'You can only carry one of 'em at a time.'" Currence laughed. "That was the mentality that they had. Because they never threw the ball.

"Currence was a guy who handled the pressure well. When we lost he took a lot of the heat."

Chris Spielman

"So we put in the run and shoot offense. When we came out all of our receivers had a football and our quarterbacks all had a football. I always wanted at least 24 footballs on the field. That was quite a shock to the equipment manager at that time.

"I started a little league program, which they had let go. They had not done anything with the elementary program. Paul Brown started working with elementary school kids back in the 1930s. It was probably one of the best things he ever did. When I got here, the first thing I had to do was study what Paul Brown had done. *Exactly* what he had done. Because he had the greatest program that high school sports ever remembered. And one of the things he did was identify these kids at the elementary level, their skills. So we started an elementary camp in the summer time specifically for that. Not for my varsity players, I wasn't interested in doing a summer camp for my varsity players at that time, I was interested in the little kids, because I had a three-year contract and I knew I needed to start developing talent because it wasn't there. And so we identified, especially, kids who could throw the ball and catch the ball at that level.

Currence recalls getting phone calls from Massillon's superintendent of schools.

"Lou Young actually played for the Bulldogs in 1934. He would call me at 5:30 on Friday night and he'd say, 'What are you doin'?' I said, 'What do you mean what am I doin'? I'm in the weight room. What are you doing?' He said, 'Oh, I'm just finishing some things up in the office.' I said 'Lou, it's Friday night, it's 5:30, what are you doing in the office?' And he said, 'Ah, I had some things I wanted to work on.' And I said, 'Lou, you gotta go home, you're gonna die of a heart attack.' He had a bad heart. And he said 'Mike, I just called to see how you were doin'. Do you think we're going to beat McKinley?' I said, 'Lou, you call me every Friday and ask me the same question. Yeah, I think we're going to beat McKinley.' I said, 'Why do you keep asking me that?' He said, 'Mike, if we don't beat McKinley, they're going to fire both of us.' He knew that he hired me and his job depended on my beating McKinley. Fortunately we beat McKinley seven out of the nine times while I was here. So it was pretty good for Lou to have hired me at the time."

"The superintendent said, 'Mike, if we don't beat McKinley, they're going to fire both of us.'"

Mike Currence

Both Young and Currence may have wondered how long Currence would last as head coach after his first two games at Massillon. "We were shut out by Gahanna Lincoln 10-0 and we lost to Middletown 7-0," Currence said of his first two games. "It rained two weeks solid. I was building a new house and I made a joke about my contractor finding out that I was coaching here and lost the first two games and he quit working on my house," Currence said with a laugh.

But it's not a joke that life can be worrisome for the Massillon coach who loses his first two games.

"That was pretty tough, because when you come to town they expect you to win.

For the third ball game they invited Paul Brown to the game. It was against, I think, Cleveland East, and we won 16-6. I don't know what we would have done if we had lost the game and Paul was in the stands. They probably would have run me out of town at that point."

Currence finished the 1976 season by winning his final eight games. Then Offenbecher led the Tigers to an 8-2 finish in 1977 and a 9-0-1 season in 1978, but it wasn't good enough. In the early days of the playoffs only four teams in the entire state qualified for the post-season. Currence said Massillon's membership in the once-proud All American Conference was to blame.

"The All-American Conference was terrible," he said. "Steubenville, Niles, Alliance and even Warren Harding were terrible. We finally convinced the school board that the best thing was to get out of the All-American Conference, which was once a great conference.

"In 1977 we shut McKinley out 21-0, which is one of the best all-time wins over McKinley. They went on to the playoffs. And we beat 'em so bad their kids didn't even want to go. It was terrible that we weren't representatives in those playoffs with Offenbecher."

Currence counts the 1979 team among his finest at Massillon. They finished the regular season 10-0, scoring 302 points and only giving up 36.

"This was probably one of the best defensive teams with Bobby Simpson at nose guard, Kevin McClelland and Tim Reese at linebacker. We had Mark Kircher at tackle. We had two defensive

ends that were unbelievable, Mike Hodson, 6'6", and Tom Mummertz, 6'5".
"This is the year I sent 25 kids to college. We should have gone to the finals with these guys.

"That team was so smooth. How bad did we beat McKinley that year (24-0). How many guys have done that? Not too many. I just remember we shredded 'em. We threw the ball anywhere and everywhere we wanted to throw it. They couldn't stop us.

"I had Billy Scott as quarterback. He ran our offense for six years, he could do it blindfolded. I really think we would have won a state championship with him, if not runner-up, if he hadn't gotten hurt. He was just a great passing quarterback. We practiced on a Thursday night before the game against Parma Padua. The coaches thought we oughta hit a little bit. Because it was muddy, I didn't want to. I gave in and let them hit a little bit. He ended up twisting his knee that night. Ended up not playing in that playoff game."

Currence's 1980 team was not expected to have the success of the 1979 squad.

"We had lost such a lot of kids," Currence said. "We knew we had a good team but we didn't have near the talent we had in 1979, I'll guarantee you of that. No way."

The 1980 team had a pair of twins leading the way: Dave Eberhart was the quarterback, brother Doug was the center.

"Dave was real steady and smart. Didn't make mistakes. We didn't make mistakes. We just didn't. My kids knew the offense.

"It was Doug, the center, not David, who was the leader. He was a straight A student. He was the kid when he spoke up, the other kids listened. And if he said, 'We're not going to party,' they didn't party."

The 1980 Tigers lost to Canton McKinley in Week 10, 16-7.

"It was a tough one," Currence said. Luckily we only had to wait a week to come back. Of course we always told our kids, 'If we lose this game we're going to have to walk the alleys for a year and we're gonna be outcasts.' The kids just cried. But then we came back around and beat them 14-6 the following week in the playoffs. I remember we were high spirited, we were coming back after them. This was vengeful, it really was. We went over with blood in our eyes. We had lived through a horrible week. The fans were doubtin' us, they were bad mouthin' us, they were doing everything. It's terrible when you lose, because they love you so much and when you lose the big one they turn on ya. They work for it. They work too hard for it. They work all year long. These kids work all of their life for their senior year and if they lose they have to live with it for the rest of their lives. A lot of these kids are gonna stay in town."

The 1980 Tigers are also known as the first Massillon team to play in a playoff championship game. Their opponent was Cincinnati Moeller.

"It was ridiculous," Currence said. "You could not believe the talent that Gerry Faust had at Cincinnati Moeller when he went to Notre Dame.

The year he went to Notre Dame, 1980, we played them in the state championship game. And he must have had half a dozen college All-Americans playing on that team. Not high school All-Americans, I'm talking college All-Americans. The one big tackle he had was amazing. I think his name was Williams. He ended up going to Kentucky, being an All-American there. He had that big fullback who went to Notre Dame, Mark Brooks.

"We thought we had a good chance," Currence said. "But when we lost running back Mike Jones and a few other players we knew we were going to have a struggle."

Massillon lost 30-7.

"Faust ended up getting the Notre Dame job immediately after they beat us. It was probably the greatest team he ever had at Moeller."

While the 1980 team over-achieved, Currence was disappointed in the 1981 Tigers.

"This was my most disappointing year of all," he said. "I really believed this 1981 team was the team. We scheduled Moeller to come back in the third ball game. We ended up losing to Moeller, getting upset by Barberton and losing to McKinley. McKinley ends up going all the way and winning the state championship. And that was really harder to live with than losin' to them. I just looked at this team and thought, man, we've got it. We've got a coach's son, Rick Spielman, at quarterback, we're ready. We're going to do it this year. This team had size, strength. I just felt that they had all the physical things. They had it. They just did not have the intensity for the big game.

"The 1981 team didn't have the leadership.

"After the season I found out they had partied themselves right out of the season, which is the first team I had that problem with. I actually took their picture down off my wall and returned it to the school and I've never put it back up.

"I felt that strongly about that team—as a team. And one of my best friend's kid was the center on the team. I loved the kids, still do to this day. They are still some of the best kids I had. But they just let me down. As hard as I worked for those kids, and as many hours as I spent with them for them to do that. And they didn't all do it, but there were enough of the leaders that did it that it killed the morale of the team. I believe it was because they let themselves mix the partyin' with the game. And you can't do it. Sometimes I really feel bad about it because I want to go back and look at those kids. I just took the team picture off my wall. I just didn't feel that the team picture belonged up there. Because they didn't pay the price to win. The dedication wasn't there for those kids. So that was my big disappointment, 1981. The saddest moment was probably when I found out what they were doing. And I didn't find that out until some time afterwards. It was kind of like, 'I can't believe this.' And it almost lost me my job. Because there were some people who felt that losing to McKinley in 1981 and having McKinley go on to win the state championship was something I was supposed to have done. We should have beaten McKinley and we probably were a better football team. The stats show we were a better team that day. They were the state champs and they only beat us 9-6. So what does that make us? They weren't going to renew my contract. I had such a hard time of it that year. With the school board and trying to get a new contract and the disappointment because I thought that team was a good team. I definitely felt betrayed. Not only with the kids but with some of the adults. They bought 'em kegs of beer. Those guys just thought they were being the buddies they were supposed to be. So I got through it, and then the 1982 team was one of my best."

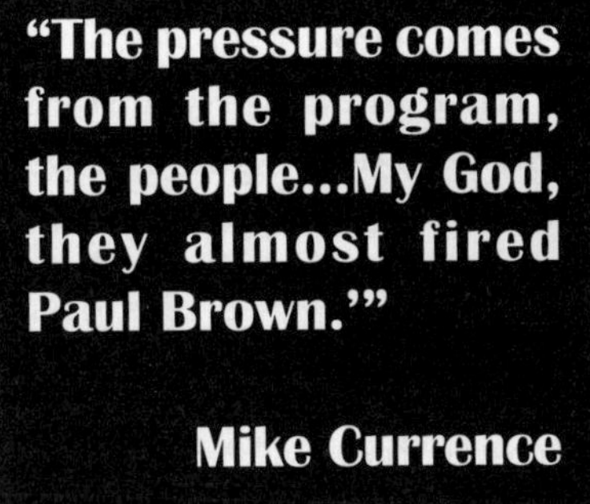

With a 52-10-2 record after six years as head coach it seems odd that Currence would need to be concerned about keeping his job. But that's the pressure that comes with being Massillon's head coach.

"The pressure comes from the program, the people," Currence said. "Nobody can coach at Massillon unless they win. That's the bottom line. That's the tradition. They almost fired Paul Brown. That's the kind of pressure you have. If you want to coach here, that's the pressure. It's inherited. It's like Ohio State. You don't put it on yourself, it's there. You're expected to win. By who? Everybody. Everybody in town.

"Going into 1982 we worked so hard that we knew that

we had to win and we knew we had to win big. And we did. That team was 12-1, state runner-up, just a great football team."

The Tigers lost to a powerful Cincinnati Moeller team in the 1982 state finals, 35-14.

"Moeller was loaded in 1982," Currence said. "They had both of the Francisco brothers. We put Hiawatha out of the game. So who do they put in when we knocked him out? His younger brother D'Juan, D'Juan Juan, whatever. They put him in the game and he was just as good. We couldn't stop 'em. It was at Ohio Stadium, it was the all-time attendance record for playoff games, 42,000 people were in there.

"I think my 1983 team was the best. Because the 1983 team was 9-1 and lost a game when we lost our quarterback, Brian DeWitz. He was a coach's son. He actually had been raised in Orrville. When his dad came to Massillon to join my staff, they moved to Massillon. He was just an outstanding athlete, not a great physical kid. But he was a skilled athlete. He could also play basketball and baseball. Very skilled kid with the ball.

"He hurt his knee in the Perry game, it was a strain and we definitely had to hold him out of the second game against Akron Garfield. And they had a great team. That was the Charles Gladman team. That Gladman kid was as good a high school back as I had ever seen. Ended up going to Pitt and getting injured and wasn't really a big college star, but man could he run. Of course they went all the way to the playoffs. They went in our place. We were 9-1 and put them in the playoffs.

"But I still believe to this day, Kenny Newlon lost it for us. He was the official. He was also the basketball coach at Canton McKinley. He was also a football official. We made a hit on Gladman and he coughed the ball up. Craig Johnson picked it up and ran all the way for a touchdown. Well, Newlon called it back. He said that he blew the ball dead. I come out on the field to have a conference. I told the official on my side 'Time out.' Apparently he didn't call it. Then Newlon threw a flag on me."That gave them the ball back and gave 'em half the distance to the goal line. Gladman went in and scored. That was a tragedy. They should have never beaten us. Ken Newlon will tell you today that he took a state championship away from me. He knew it. But he did it anyway. You have to understand that the rivalries run deep here. And there's no way that the basketball coach from McKinley should be a referee in that game. But he was. It really hurt the kids."

Of course 1982 and 1983 were Chris Spielman's junior and senior seasons.

"I think he'll end up being a Hall of Fame linebacker," Currence said of Spielman. "I think he'll make it. I think he's got a good chance of making it.

"Spielman was awesome. We had people to go with him. We had Craig Johnson, who came in from Timken, at running back. He ended up playing behind Lorenzo White at Michigan State. Bad luck.

"The 1983 team was just tough however you wanted to call it. If we wanted to run it, we ran it. If we wanted to pass it, we could pass it. Anything we wanted to do with it, we had the talent to do it. We had a great defense. We played with McKinley (18-7). We fooled around. We fumbled twice inside the 10. We would have beat 'em by five touchdowns if we had played real well that day. But we were just trying things.

"What a shame we didn't get to go to the playoffs in 1983 because they were as good as anybody I've ever had."

"What a shame we didn't get to go to the playoffs in 1983.'"

Mike Currence

Currence's final season in Massillon came in 1984. After finishing 6-4, he was fired in a controversial decision by the school board (see 1980's Story of the Decade).

Despite his abrupt firing and the ensuing fallout, Currence's record is still held in high esteem in Massillon.

"You take the winning percentage of the coaches that coached over six years here," said Nick Vrotsos, longtime Massillon assistant coach. "You take Brown, Chuck Mather, Currence. You're talking Mike Currence in that realm over the long haul, for winning football games."

"I've had a lot of young men go on into coaching," Currence said. "I don't know why, because I never encouraged any of them to do it. But I think it's because they had such great years playing for us and enjoyed it so much. Because we never brow-beat the kids. It was never a punishment type thing that we did with them. We wanted them to have fun. That was our philosophy. I wanted them to enjoy everything. Every practice that we had.

"I had a lot of happy times," he said. "Every time we beat McKinley it was just a great, great time. And we beat them seven times. That's still a record. Every year we beat them is a great year, just because of the rivalry. It's probably the greatest high school football game in the country."

Currence thought hard when asked about his legacy.

"I got knocked off by Cincinnati Moeller in the finals," he finally said. "That's probably the history of my coaching. Moeller's always been the team to beat me. I told my grandson, 'You can always put on papa's tombstone, *You know, he was a good coach and teacher and father, but he was always one game short*. Because really, I always *was* one game short of winning the playoffs. But we never got in enough. My gosh, if we had the ability to get in the playoffs all those years it would have been a different ball game. I told the people at Massillon, 'Faust has been at Moeller 19 years. He's got it down, he's got 'em comin'.' It takes time to get in and get goin'.

"I always felt like if I could have stayed in Massillon 19 or 20 years that there's no doubt in my mind we would have dominated and would have been state champions in the playoffs. That tombstone thing is really a funny thing. One game short. But really, you look at it, that's what I am, really. One game short on the championships. One game short of the all-time wins record at Massillon. It feels like a job left undone."

Tom Manion (11) and Darrel Strickling (73) carry Mike Currence off the field after a 7-0 win over Canton McKinley in 1982.

PHOTO: MIKE CURRENCE COLLECTION

Haunted by The Currence Curse?

People claimed the Boston Red Sox had the "Babe Ruth" curse for decades. Could it be that the Massillon Tigers have the "Currence Curse" as they try in vain for their first playoff-era state title? "There are some people that think I'm a curse on the program," Currence said. "They call it the 'Currence Curse.' I tell them they're crazy. They say, 'No we're not.' Massillon fans are very superstitious. I had to go over to Massillon super-fans Maurie and Katie Basler's house and make a wish and put a coin in the candle before every game. That is really bad. And my wife had to kiss Katie's ring before every game."

How Would Currence Have Ended It?

Mike Currence's brilliant career at Massillon certainly did not end like *anyone* would have chosen. But how would the coach himself have chosen to end his Massillon career? "I would like to have stayed two more years, and I think that would have been enough," Currence said, alluding to the contract extension he received before his surprise firing. But could he imagine himself finishing his career in Massillon?

Mike Currence was 79-16-2.
PHOTO: MIKE CURRENCE COLLECTION

"I wouldn't have stayed unless they really wanted me," he said. "The school board would have had to say, 'We really, really *do* want you. And here's another contract.' Then I might have stayed. I don't know. I had players coming from the junior high and elementary school programs. They were coming. John Maronto had 'em, Lee Owens had 'em after that. And I like to think it was because of my program. I think the more turnover in coaches that you have, the more the program suffers. Because a coach comes in and he doesn't have time to work with the elementary kids. Why are you going to work with the elementary kids if you're only going to be there one or two years? I had time."

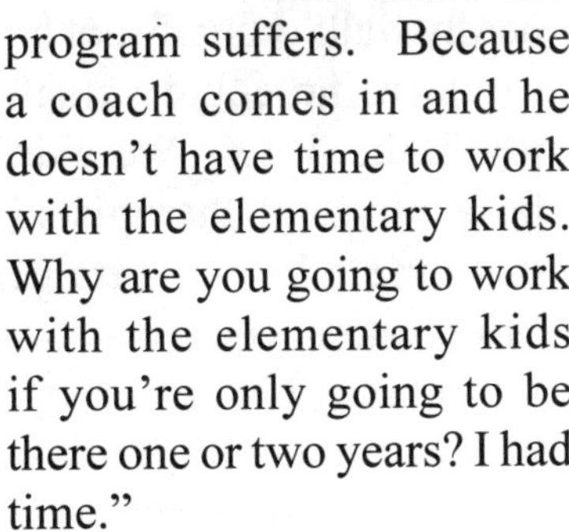

Currence Project: Dickie Cleveland

"Dickie Cleveland tore his knee before his senior year," Massillon head coach Mike Currence said. "And I lived with him. He was one of those kids that didn't have a lot of family support. But he was a real hard-nosed kid. And I kind of felt sorry for him because all he had going for him was football. I worked with him. I remember putting him in the pool, he couldn't hardly walk. I finally got him to where he could actually jog in the water. We didn't have physical therapists at that time. We had a trainer, Mike Internacola, who was a great guy, and we brought in an orthopedic guy, Doc Furnace, our old team doctor. Doc Furnace brought in Dr. Erickson, who was an orthopedic guy, a Massillon kid who had gone away to school and come back. Furnace actually recruited him to come back here because we needed him. Dr. Erickson was one of the first that when he operated on a knee, he wouldn't put it in a cast. Doc Erickson put it in a brace and he'd move that knee from time to time. He knew when that knee locked up it was going to be hard getting it back in.

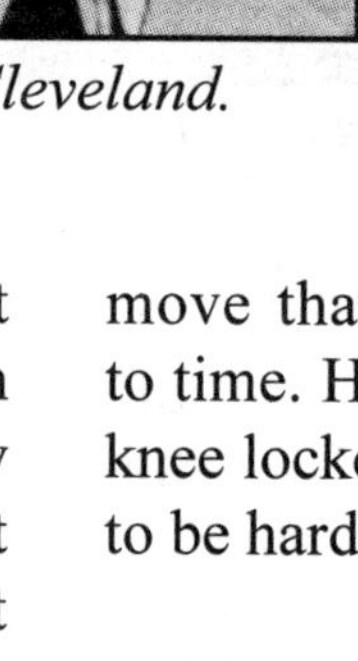

Dickie Cleveland.

"Dickie recovered and went to junior college in Virginia for two years and then went to Wake Forest."

The Amazing Bobby Simpson

"Bobby Simpson didn't have a mom or dad," Massillon head coach Mike Currence said. "Lived with his brother. He was an All-Ohio nose guard for me. A special education kid. Probably one of the best defensive linemen I ever had play the game.

Bobby Simpson.

"I wanted to send him to Ohio State so bad because Ohio State always had such good middle guards. But Earle Bruce wouldn't take him because his grades were so bad he couldn't get him in. The only junior college I could find that would take him was in California. So I bought him a ticket on a bus and got him some new clothes and gave him some money to eat on. Sent him to California. I called the coach and said 'Bobby's on the bus and he'll be there tomorrow.' So he went to the bus station and picked him up. This kid had no idea where he was goin'. He could barely read and write. He went out there and went into one of their programs and actually played for them. They won game after game. And then the coach called me up and said Bobby graduated from the two-year college. And he said, 'I'm going to send him back.' And I said, 'When's he coming back?' He said 'He's due in tomorrow on a Greyhound bus. I went downtown and brought him

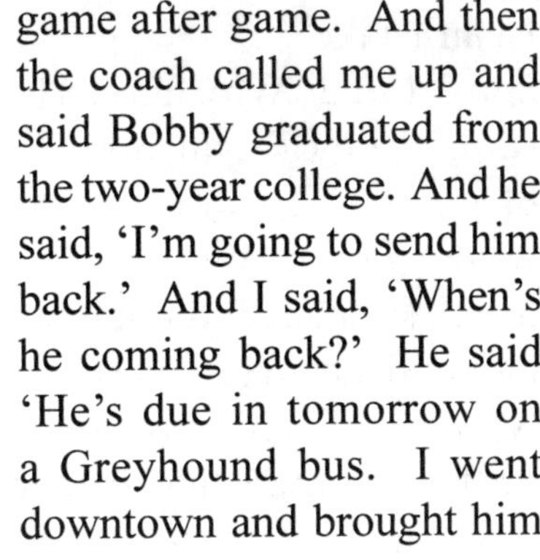

home. Then I took him down to see Earle, because by this time he weighs 235 and he could run a 4.5 40-yard dash. He was an animal. I took him down. Earle got so upset with me. He came over and got up in my face—he was like a bulldog—he said 'Why'd you bring him down here?' I said, 'Earle, he's better than anybody you've got out there.' He said, 'I know it, but I can't take him.' I said 'Why not?' He said, 'They'll run me out of town. He can't read or write.' I said, 'What do you mean, he made it though junior college.' He said sternly, 'Mike, I can't take him.' So I went back and called the coach in California and I said, 'Man, we've gotta find a place for Bobby. Earle can't take him.' And I said, 'Who do you think will take him?' He said, 'Send him out here, Fresno State will take him.' So Fresno State took him. And I'll be doggoned if he wasn't on television the next two years because Fresno State was in bowl games, once against Bowling Green.

"Earle Bruce...got up in my face—he's like a bulldog—he said 'Why'd you bring him down here?'"

Mike Currence

"Bowling Green never blocked him once. I remember them interviewing Bobby after the game. You couldn't understand a word Bobby said to the announcer. The announcer said, 'Oh that's great Bobby.'"

RAMIER MARTIN

It wasn't a given that Ramier Martin would lace up his cleats for the Massillon Tigers—let alone become a record-breaking wide receiver. Between his family tradition and his love of basketball, Martin nearly became a Canton McKinley Bulldog.

"I'm the product of the Tiger-Bulldog rivalry," Martin said. "My mother was a Massillon Tiger and my father was a Bulldog. The blood of both runs through me. I was born in Canton and raised in Massillon. My dad was a McKinley Bulldog football player."

Ramier Martin was a star receiver at Bowling Green.
PHOTO: RAMIER MARTIN COLLECTION

Ramier's father, Wrentie Martin, was a senior in 1959, when Massillon was state and national champions. They beat McKinley 20-0. "He suffered defeat to the Massillon Tigers in those days," Martin said. Canton McKinley had a lot of Martins down through the years who have played as Bulldogs."

Martin hears about it whenever he attends family reunions over in Canton. "It's surprising to them every time I go there. They still can't believe my brother and I became Massillon Tigers. We were the first from their family to put on the orange and black."

Besides his father, who started as a defensive back and fullback, there were several other Martins who played at McKinley. Paul Martin, who played at Ohio State, tops the list. "There's a lot of Bulldog blood in me," Martin said.

In addition to family history, it was Martin's love of basketball that gave him cause to debate whether he should attend Massillon or McKinley.

"There were always opportunities to go to McKinley, with my family history there. I actually liked basketball better than football," he said. "and the elite basketball school in the state was Canton McKinley. So there were real heart to heart talks and discussions about whether I'd rather play basketball and have a good basketball career at McKinley. I would have played with Eric Snow, Michael Hawkins, the Bowdins —the team that went to state and was state runner-up. The stage was set for me to be part of a great basketball tradition. But I wanted to be here and enjoy being a part of the Massillon Tigers. The fact that my brother was a senior-to-be at Massillon and went through the program and that I had a lot of friends coming up through junior high made it tough to make a decision to go to McKinley.

I always loved Massillon's football over McKinley's football."

Years later Martin had a

unique opportunity to compare the Massillon and McKinley programs while he was earning his teaching certificate in 1997. It made him realize how special the Massillon experience is.

"I actually did some observations at McKinley when I was getting my teaching certificate. They won the national championship in 1997. The biggest thing I recognized then was that the two schools are equal in terms of their general make-up, the type of athletes they can get. But the one thing I took from there was, regardless of how many games McKinley was winning, regardless of where they were in the polls, or where they were in the process, Massillon still put on a better show. In terms of fan support, community support, school support, and in terms of a program.

"I think any young player should take hold of what is being done and what has been done in Massillon and cherish it.'"

Ramier Martin

"So I think I would really have missed out on a big part of the Massillon tradition if I wouldn't have been a part of it. Massillon definitely puts on a grand show. I think any young player should take hold of what is being done and what has been done in Massillon and cherish it. Because there are many other schools across the country that do not have one inkling of a chance to know what it's all about. What goes into that Massillon tradition."

Martin's ascension to star status at Massillon wasn't easy or automatic. It was more a matter of hard work and a belief in himself—fueled by a mother who believed in him, too.

Martin was on the scout team as a sophomore and junior at Massillon. Originally a defensive back, Martin's break came when Lee Owens came in as head coach in 1988.

Martin blossomed as a senior at Massillon.
PHOTO: RAMIER MARTIN COLLECTION

"I definitely had the tools to be a player," he said, "But I think I was an undisciplined player. That's when Lee Owens came in to play. I was moved from the defensive side of the ball to offense. On the defensive side you can be reckless and your athletic ability can overcome a lack of discipline, but on the offensive side it takes a little bit more finesse. So I played JV ball and was on the scout team as a junior. I guess the coaches didn't think I had the finesse of a junior.

Playing on the JV squad as a junior can be discouraging to a player. Or it can be looked at as an opportunity to prove yourself. Martin decided to prove himself.

"I took it as a personal challenge to take every day to get better," he said. "Going against our first team as a member of the scout team, I was working against the best we had."

Martin had just one varsity catch as a junior and there were no promises coming into his senior season.

Martin had just one varsity catch as a junior and there were no promises coming into his senior season.

"I said, 'I don't know where I'm going to end up, if I'm going to get to play or not. But I'm going to be the best receiver in the state.' I would run my Massillon Mile, slipping up the street, I'd run up around the stadium, the new high school wasn't there at the time, I'd run down where the old practice field used to be, around the parking lot and stadium, just visualizing what I wanted to do the next year. To get an opportunity my last year as a Massillon Tiger. If I was ever going to play on the Massillon football field, hey, this was going to be my last shot at it. I wanted to make the most of it, so I dedicated myself to say, 'Hey, if I'm going to be successful I'm going to do it by being in shape and being ready to go in this last go around.' I looked at the records and said 'I want to break the single-season record.' The most catches in a season. Bruce Spicer had 56 catches in a ten-game season. I figured that's not hard to do in the passing offense that we had. We should be able to do that.

I should be able to get 60 catches. I should be able to break that 56 mark. That was the driving force. Would it happen? Who knows? But if you're going to dream you might as well dream big."

Martin lived his dream as a senior at Massillon, achieving the goals he had set out to achieve that summer.

"At the end of the season, to be able to break those records, to have 59 catches, close to 900 yards receiving and to be All-Ohio was something.

"My mother didn't doubt me. I told her before the season exactly what I was going to do. She didn't discourage me, she just said, 'Okay, you know what you have to do.' She saw me running, coming back sweaty, laying on the kitchen floor, hurting a little bit.

"I told her my next goal was to break the high jump record. So after the football season, she knew that high jump record was going to be broken. That's one of the records that still stands. Devin Jordan broke the other ones."

CHRIS SPIELMAN

Chris Spielman began playing tackle football at the age of nine.

"I was a little more advanced for my age," he said, "knowing how to hit and the right way to do things. Playing hard was always stressed when you grew up a coach's son. You learned fundamentals at an earlier age. You learned toughness at an earlier age. I was taught to act and play a certain way and that's the way I did it. I knocked the wind out of a lot of kids. But nobody ever got seriously hurt."

Chris Spielman was a two-time All-American at Ohio State.
PHOTO: OHIO STATE ATHLETICS

Spielman liked contact from the beginning. "Yeah. Kids either get turned on or turned off by it. Some kids get turned off by it and never want to play again. But I enjoyed contact. I think I enjoyed competing most of all."

From his earliest childhood memories, Spielman wanted to be a professional football player. "I never thought I *wouldn't* be a pro football player. I was young enough and naive enough to think that you can be a pro football player if you want to. Just like you could be a policeman if you wanted to. I thought that was just a job choice that people made in life.

"I engulfed everything about football. The smell. The feeling. The changing of the leaves. All of that. I still have the same feeling today that I did when I was nine years old."

Early success helped to make Spielman's dreams seem real. "The first game I ever played I scored three touchdowns and intercepted two passes. So I thought, 'I'm pretty good, so I want to play pro football.' I think a lot of kids think that, but I don't know, I was always geared and focused to doing that at a young age. I really didn't have a heckuva lot of other interests."

Spielman didn't find it necessary to share his dreams of playing pro football with others. "I thought people might have taken it for granted that was what I was going to do. I didn't really share. I never cared what people thought, what they told me I could do or couldn't do. It didn't matter. This is what I decided that I was going to do. I made that decision at a young age and never changed my mind about it."

Spielman moved to Massillon as a freshman at Longfellow Junior High when his dad, Sonny Spielman, was hired onto Mike Currence's staff at the high school. Chris' brother, Rick, was a junior when the family moved to Massillon.

Chris played his first football in Massillon at Longfellow. He was a new kid on the freshman team.

"I think that any time somebody moves to Massillon that is a football player, you're kind of under scrutiny a little bit. I wasn't the first guy to move in from out of town to play there. I think they accepted you, but it just takes a little time. It's sacred to them, which it should be. They just wanted to make sure that it means as much to me as it does to them. And once they realize that it did, then, yeah, you're accepted right away."

> **"I engulfed everything about football. The smell. The feeling. The changing of the leaves...I still have the same feeling today that I did when I was nine years old.'"**
>
> **Chris Spielman**

As far as Spielman accepting Massillon, you could say it was love at first sight.

"As soon as I moved over there I got the feeling. Seeing the Massillon Tiger signs in the windows: *A Massillon Tiger player lives here.* Seeing the kids in the junior high wearing Massillon football jerseys every Friday. I just thought that was the greatest thing in the world. It was like one city coming together for one common thing one night a week. And that's the most awesome thing in the world. And I just thought, 'Man, how lucky am I to be a part of something like this? It's like my heaven. My personal utopia.'"

Spielman immediately bonded with his Longfellow teammates. "When I moved there, Kurt Walterhouse was a good player, a kid named Eric Richmond, Mark Marchant and Brian Spicer of the famous Spicer family. We just had a lot of good young players—tough guys. I loved it. We were a good team, because we were tough. Winning meant something to us at that age. I think it means something to every kid at that age. But it meant something more to us. We were going to be part of something that was bigger than everybody. And that's ingrained in us at an early age. That's why I was able to fit in. Because I was of the same mentality as these kids, even though I wasn't even from Massillon."

Throughout his career, Spielman has had to deal with doubters. People doubted him at Ohio State, and he was doubted when he headed into the NFL. It all started when he moved on to the high school as a sophomore.

"I remember people said I couldn't start as a sophomore. *They don't do that at Massillon*." Spielman said. "I just felt that didn't have anything to do with me. I thought for some reason that I'd be startin'. I'd never *not* started, so why wouldn't I start now? Fortunately it ended up going my way."

Currence had a history of *not* starting sophomores. In fact, he rarely *played* sophomores. He didn't have to.

But Spielman was an exception. Currence could tell that he was destined for greatness.

"When he was a sophomore we knew," Currence said. "He could have played for us as a freshman. But freshmen weren't in our building. He was good enough to play some places for us. Yeah, we knew as a sophomore. But I didn't want to make a big thing out of him. Because my seniors are very proud at Massillon. To move a sophomore in front of them would cause a lot of problems. And I don't think Chris was *quite* ready. Not the schedule we had. And he'll probably tell you he had games where he had trouble."

> **"I just thought, 'Man, how lucky am I to be a part of something like this?'"**
>
> **Chris Spielman**

Dale Walterhouse, a longtime assistant at Massillon, was Spielman's first position coach at Massillon. He knows how hard it was to start as a sophomore in Spielman's era. "To start as a sophomore at Massillon, you had to be good and you had to be lucky," Walterhouse said. "You had to be an outstanding person. You had to be lucky in that you better not have a strong person in that position ahead of you.

"Chris could diagnose a play from the first step," Walterhouse said. "It seemed like from the snap of the ball he knew where the ball was going to go and he wanted to get there in the worst way possible. He wasn't the fastest, but he was the quickest guy to the ball. He seemed like he could read the back's mind."

Spielman's first game as a sophomore starter was against Massillon Perry, from Perry Township, which borders Massillon.

"I was excited that I was

playing on special teams and starting on defense," Spielman said. "I don't know, I felt like that was what I was supposed to do. If people wanted to make a big deal out of it, that was fine. I really, even to this day, don't pay much attention to announcers or accolades or bad things said one way or the other. I've always been able to maintain an even keel mentality, I guess. I have a strong belief in myself and a humbleness. Yeah, it might have gone great this game. But what's going to happen next game?

"And I think football is the most humbling sport in the world. As soon as you start thinking you can't be blocked or you can't miss a tackle, 'Whap,' it comes up and smacks you in the face. You never let the highs get too high or the lows get too low."

It usually took more than one man to bring Spielman down.
PHOTO: MIKE CURRENCE COLLECTION

So how *was* that first game at Massillon?

"It felt great. We won the game 33-0. My brother had a great game at quarterback. My dad was on the sideline. Gosh. What more as a player could you want? I think I felt more pride for what my brother did than what I did."

What Spielman did was make an immediate impression on the Massillon populace by making tackles on Massillon's first four kickoffs, all inside the 20-yard line. On the fifth kickoff veteran public address announcer Walt Bronczek said "This time, the tackle was *not* by Spielman." Bronczek's quip immediately became a catch-phrase around Massillon.

"Chris could diagnose a play from the first step."

Dale Walterhouse

Spielman also picked off a pass to set up a touchdown in his Massillon debut.

His brother Rick was three years older than Chris, but two years ahead of him in school.

"He was a big brother who would let me hang around him. As opposed to the kind who didn't want the little guy hanging around. And, by him doing that, by me hanging around tougher guys, and playing football with tougher guys, or playing basketball or baseball with better players than I was, it made me a better player. Because all of a sudden when I hit a little maturity streak, I was getting ahead of all these guys who were two years older than me."

Spielman noticed that the Massillon kids were different. "I think they were a lot more knowledgeable about football. Just the fact that winning was important to them. They understood what tradition was. A lot of people don't have that opportunity to understand what tradition is because they have no tradition."

Two things about his sophomore season stand out in Spielman's memory. First is the 1981 McKinley game, played in front of 22,828 fans in Canton.

"We had 'em beat over there," Spielman said. "It was my brother's last game. Man, I just wanted to beat them over there that year. They won the state championship. My brother actually scored a touchdown for us. He made a 21-yard run. We should have won the game but we didn't. What I took out of it was that I was not going to lose to them again."

Rick Spielman (15) scored Massillon's only touchdown in the 1981 McKinley game.
PHOTO: MIKE CURRENCE COLLECTION

The second big memory for Spielman was a Week 3 game against Cincinnati Moeller, who was considered to be the best team in the nation at the time. The Tigers played gamely before falling, 24-6, in front of 23,950 fans. It was a coming of age game for the sophomore.

"That was up at the Rubber Bowl in Akron. That was a great game. I just remember that we were outmatched. They were a better team than us. I remember I played a real good game. That's when I knew that, absolutely for sure, that if I could play a game like this against the number one team in the nation, as a sophomore, at age 15, that I could, maybe, become a lot better player than I already was. I proved that I wasn't a flash in the pan. I couldn't be tested at a higher level at that age than I was at that time. That's when I knew that I belonged as a starter at Massillon. I'd just played the best team in the country and held my own."

"It was my brother's last game. I just wanted to beat them."

Chris Spielman

Spielman did experience some resentment from teammates as a sophomore at Massillon.

"There were some players that were resentful of Chris," Currence said, "but it was kids that didn't get to play much. We had some disgruntled seniors who really gave him a hard time."

Spielman remembers the resentment, but not from the seniors.

"Not by the seniors, believe it or not, but by the juniors," he said. "I remember one guy urinated in my locker because I was startin'," Spielman said. "He was a linebacker. I couldn't understand why somebody would do that. That was the thing I remembered most. How could a teammate do that to a teammate? I played with teammates over the years that I didn't particularly like, but if somebody took a swat at them I'd be the first one to jump on that somebody. I just didn't comprehend why somebody would do that.

"It was handled so fast. Being a sophomore, I didn't know how to handle it. A lot of the senior captains stood up and took care of the problem. I guess they just talked to him. He got kicked off the team for it, which I felt bad for. I understood the guy's frustration. I just... I don't know. It was an act of frustration. It was obvious. I never took anything personal. I knew I belonged there. That's the way it was."

The townspeople in Massillon fell in love with Spielman. It's hard to imagine that there's ever been a more popular player in the history of the program.

"It started after that first game as a sophomore," Spielman said. "In junior high you're never in the newspapers or talked about on the radio. All of a sudden people would come up and say, 'Hey, I heard about you on the radio,' or 'There was an article about you in the *Akron Beacon Journal* or the *Cleveland Plain Dealer* or the *Canton Repository* or the Massillon *Independent*.' Or people in restaurants, you're out with your buddies at Burger King or something. And people would look at you and whisper or something. 'What, do I have food on my mouth?' I kind of took it in stride. I always have.

"They made such a big deal out of me playing a good game. I don't know why people took to me. I really don't. Maybe because I did what I was supposed to do. I tried to do well in school. I played pretty good every game. Not only for myself, I played for them. I played for Massillon. I played for the town. Consciously, not subconsciously, I played for the town. To represent them. I don't think a lot of kids did at that time. Hey, I didn't want this guy goin' home or goin' to work at Superior's or wherever he worked at, thinking, 'Man, we shouldn't have lost.' I wanted to carry that burden for them and make them go to work happy Monday morning. Make them proud to wear their Tiger stuff around."

From his sophomore season on, Spielman was a hero in Massillon. Fans would line up at football games for his autograph. But Spielman's personality certainly didn't resemble that of a conquering hero.

"He was very backward, quiet," Currence said. "Scared to death to speak to groups. I had to coach him. He would break out into a cold sweat."

Spielman knew his junior season held promise after a couple of disappointing losses. These losses left the 1981 Tigers at 7-3 during his sophomore season.

"We should have been 9-1 with a loss to Moeller," he said. "We had Barberton beat and they ran a kickoff back on the last play. That was frustrating, obviously, to lose to them.

"I knew we had a good team coming back in 1982. I was excited because I was going to play with a lot of guys who were in my class now. I knew that we had a good junior group coming back. I knew that we were going to be a good football team. And we were a *great* football team. We were 12-1 and we got beat by Moeller. Again, we were just outmatched. When they were drawing players the way they were at that time it made it tough to compete against them. But any other school in the state—or in the nation—I believe we would beat handily.

I really believe that. We had great players. Jimmy Bushe, Tom Gruno, Tim Sampsel. Brian DeWitz was a junior quarterback. Jimmy Geiser was a great wide receiver. Tim Swelterwich was a great offensive tackle, Ty Beadle, Charles Calhoun. These guys were all tough, good, solid football players. Big, too. Man we were a good team. I do think, besides Moeller, we were the best team in the country. I think that was one of Massillon's finest teams, the 1982 team."

> **"I played for them. I played for Massillon. I played for the town."**
>
> **Chris Spielman**

Spielman said the Massillon community was excited as the Tigers rolled through the 1982 season undefeated.

"Every game was special," he said, "but I think they knew that our team was 9-0 going into the Canton McKinley game and we thought we were destined for certainly a state championship and maybe a national championship. I believe we were third or fourth at the time in the *USA Today* high school football poll."

Spielman remembers the build- up to the 1982 McKinley game.

"Anticipation and excitement. It's a special week. From the parade to all the festivities that go on before it. The tradition of it. It's basically one town against another town. But Canton's so much bigger with so many more schools than Massillon. You know, Massillon is one city behind this one team. It makes it a little more special. Everyone's just anticipating that game. It's the only thing you talk about. And the great thing is the teachers are all so into it, too. And they understand what's going on. They appreciate the game and they appreciate the tradition and they *honor* that tradition.

"I remember when I was a sophomore and they put us all in the gym to show us how to do the pep rallies. Where you sit and where you go and what goes on. I thought that was kind of neat, you know, being from out of town. In the old gym, the old bull ring I refer to it as, it's nuts. You're down there and you're kind of isolated and everybody's lookin' at ya. The band's there. I remember some townspeople coming over for it. The bonfire on Friday night for the town, which was great, and the parade, where we ride on the truck, which was cool. It's a lot of pressure. But that's how most of those kids are raised. They've prepared their whole lives for that game. They look forward to that time. It's their time to shine. When you have that confidence it's a big advantage for ya.

"I just remember beatin' McKinley 7-0 and how great it felt, bein' from there. Actually scoring the winning touchdown, which was cool. I grew up with all those guys. They were childhood friends. I played midget league football with a lot of those guys. There's always a little more on the table when you play against your friends. They had a great team. A great defensive team. They had some great players, Victor Parks and Garland Rivers, who went on to play at Michigan. They had a running back named Carlos Lewis. A guy named Troy Jenkins.

They were a good team. A real good team. I remember Tommy Manion picking a ball off on the last play of the game in the end zone and sealing the win for us."

Spielman downplayed his touchdown, the only score of the game. "It was an off tackle play to the right side, I was untouched. I knew I was in. I just thought, now we have to hold them defensively. In all my years, at Massillon, Ohio State, Detroit, Buffalo, my whole thought process has always been 'We, we, we, not me, me, me.' But, when you're playing both ways—which was unusual, too, for Massillon, you're just thinking, 'I've gotta get a rest and get ready to go back in on defense.'

"The celebration was big. It was at our place. They were a good team. A tough game. We knew we were 10-0. "The celebration didn't last long because we knew we were headed to the playoffs and the feeling of us being state champs was prevalent everywhere. We went to some guy's house and hung out and talked about the next week's game. How great it was to beat McKinley. We were excited, we were focused for the playoffs.

"We played Sandusky first, and we beat them pretty good (29-7), then we went up to Berea and they were supposed to have a good team and we beat the heck out of them in the Rubber Bowl (31-0). Going into the Moeller game, we knew they were a great, great team, but we felt that we could win. That was the only team that was better than us, and I'll admit that. I remember the townspeople saying, 'Well, we were the best public school.' Which we were."

Spielman felt the Catholic schools had an advantage when he was at Massillon.

"I think they did," he said, "Because at that time they were drawing kids from three states and all over Cincinnati. Compared to drawing kids from a town of 30,000 or 35,000 people. Certainly they're going to have an advantage. But again, we had a great team and we were proud of what we did that year.

"It's a lot of pressure. But that's how most of those kids are raised. They've prepared their whole lives for that game."

Chris Spielman

"The build-up for that game was huge. I remember riding down to Columbus to play that game. It was a great feeling. There were 42,000 people in Ohio Stadium. It was a great, great game. It was exciting. But again, we were a little bit outmatched. I think that was the only time in my career that I felt, you know, that we lost to a better team."

Currence saw a big difference in the play of Spielman against Moeller from his sophomore year to his junior year, in the state title game.

"As a junior he was *quite* ready," Currence said. "He was a leader. Moeller had both Francisco brothers. Chris knocked Hiawatha out of the game. Hiawatha later played at Notre Dame. I had Chris playing both ways. He'd come off the field so tired, he'd say,

'Hey coach, I need a break.' I'd say, 'Chris, you get your ass back in there.' And he said, 'Coach, I'm the only guy tackling anyone.' I said 'Chris, you're the only guy who can catch 'em.' That was the honest to God truth. They were that quick."

Massillon gave Moeller a game, trailing just 21-14 at halftime. The final was Moeller 35, Massillon 14. But 1983 held great promise for Spielman and the Tigers.

"I just knew we had a great team back," Spielman said of the 1983 Tigers. "Another chance to get back to the state championship. Unfortunately our quarterback, Brian DeWitz, got hurt and didn't play against Akron Garfield and they ended up beatin' us. We ended up 9-1 and I think if we would have stayed healthy for the whole season, I really think we would have won the state championship that year. I thought our team was better that year than we were the year before. We had some injury problems and that cost us the game.

"At that time they only took two teams from each division and a 9-1 record wasn't good enough. Certainly today it would have been. Garfield ended up playing in the state championship. We had three Big 10 players out of our backfield. Brian DeWitz went to Indiana, Craig Johnson went to Michigan State and I went to Ohio State. Our fullback, Jim Bushe, went to Toledo. That's four Division I football players in one backfield.

Besides Garfield, we blew everybody else out. We beat McKinley handily, even though the score didn't say that (18-7). We controlled the football game."

It was an empty feeling for Spielman and his teammates, sitting at home when they felt they had the best team in the state.

"It was terrible. There was nothing Currence could say. We felt bad because we couldn't get in the playoffs. That's just the way it went. There was nothing we could do about it. The great thing about our team was that we had great leaders and great competitors while I was there."

"That was the only team that was better than us, and I'll admit that.'"

Chris Spielman

Spielman's legacy in Massillon is important to him.

"In Massillon I want to be remembered as a good kid who did things the right way. I know I probably let people down sometimes."

Spielman's Massillon football resume is the stuff of legends: Two-time first team All-Ohio linebacker, Parade All-American, *USA Today's* Defensive Player of the Year. He was recruited by every major college program in the USA. Currence tried to help get his star pupil ready for the attention.

"I took him all over the country as a senior because he was an All-American as a junior, highly recognized as a sophomore," said Currence. "He was recruited heavily. Everybody wanted him. He visited Ohio State, Michigan, Penn State, UCLA—he really loved UCLA. He wanted to go to UCLA as a kid. Always wore UCLA hats. I think he may have gone to Miami or someplace else to visit. After five visits he ended up loving Bo Schembechler and wanted to go to Michigan.

"The only thing I said to him was, 'You want to live in Michigan, go to Michigan. Want to live in Ohio? You better go to Ohio State.' Because I always thought that if you want to be here and want to be in business here then that is where you should play. He wanted to go play for Bo."

Schembechler knew he had a shot with Spielman. "I loved him," Schembechler said. "He was a tough, hard-working kid. He almost came here. Oh yeah. We made a good run at him."

"The recruiting process was really crazy," Spielman said. "Everybody's wondering where you wanna go. *Everybody*. Not just in Massillon, but Canton. Everywhere you went there was the constant question of where ya goin', what are you doing? What's going on? I didn't know. I tried to enjoy the recruiting process as much a guy can. Going to visit the different campuses and seeing different things.

"The governor called one time. Coming home from a trip from UCLA I had a layover in Dayton and they had a bunch of alumni there chanting "Go to Ohio State, Go to Ohio State," or something like that. There was a lot of pressure for me to go to Ohio State. And if I sit back and think about that, there was nowhere else I was going to go. I'm a Buckeye. I couldn't help but go there. Bo Schembechler, Joe Paterno, Terry Donahue, Howard Schnellenberger. I pretty much got recruited by everybody. I narrowed it down pretty quickly to five schools. Deep in my heart I knew I was going to Ohio State, so it really didn't matter. I wanted to see the schools just in case I would have missed somethin'. This is where I belonged."

Ohio State head coach Earle Bruce scouted Spielman at Massillon.

"I naturally heard about Spielman from my Massillon people," Bruce said, "how good he was. The first game his senior year I got the Ohio State jet and we came to Massillon. Glenn Mason and I came up to watch him play. He kicked off. He received kickoffs. He punted. He received punts. He made about 25 tackles. Ran the ball about 25 times and was the leading ground gainer. I said to Glen, 'I don't believe that's possible. I think that's a one-game show. Get the jet, we're coming up next week and watch the same thing. So we came back. Same thing. Kicked off, returned kicks, did everything. The only difference is, he was selling popcorn at halftime. So he was a complete football player. You get the picture."

Spielman kept Bruce in suspense. "When he decided to come to Ohio State, that was a great day for me," Bruce said. "Funny little story about that. I came up to watch him play the night before the signing. He was supposed to commit to me. He didn't commit. He said, 'I'll call ya after I get home and talk to my parents.'

"About 2:30 in the morning the phone rings. I'm in a dead sleep. I answer the phone. I say, 'Hello.' He says, 'This is Chris Spielman.' And then nothing, and then nothing, and then nothing. I thought, 'Oh my goodness, he's going to tell me he's going to Michigan. Why else would he...' Then he said, 'I've decided to be a Buckeye.' I said, 'Oh golly. You son of a gun. He laughed and I laughed. Then he came and you know the rest. Boy he was a great linebacker for Ohio State."

Spielman's Ohio State career started off on the wrong foot.

"Before he came here I told him to go play in the All-Star game," Bruce said. "He ended up twisting an ankle. Not in practice. Not in the game. He was just stepping off the curb. So he was limping all the time. When he came to Ohio State for August practice he was still limping and he wasn't on the first team. He was second team to Pepper Johnson."

Johnson was a team captain and All-American linebacker at Ohio State.

Spielman remembers his first practice at Ohio State. "I was on the scout team in the first practice and I was so mad I went out and did real good in practice and the next thing I knew I was practicing with the regular defense. I was hitting everything, I didn't care. They said, 'Lay off the quarterback.' I said, 'All right, put me with the regular defense and I won't hit the quarterback,'" Spielman said with a laugh."

Bruce found Spielman was a little different during his first varsity game.

"During the course of the first game, in the first half, I heard someone pounding in back of me in the track area," Bruce said. "Going up and down and yellin', 'I've gotta play, I've gotta play.' I thought, holy man, I've never had anybody do that. A senior or anybody else say he's gotta play. So I tapped Bob Tucker, the defensive coordinator and said, 'Hey Bob, when are you gonna play Chris Spielman?' He said, 'Coach, he's got a bad ankle. He's hurtin'. I don't know whether he's ready to play.' I said, 'He's ready to play, I'll tell you that.'

"We went in at halftime and I think the score was 14-6 in favor of Oregon State. I said, 'I'm ordering you to play him.' He said, 'Do you know what that means?' I said, 'No.' He said, 'I'm going to have to bench Pepper Johnson, because that's the linebacker he plays and I can't switch linebackers right now because of pass cover-

Spielman was a two-time All-American at Ohio State.
PHOTO: DENISE BENNETT

age.' I said, 'Play him.'

"Spielman went in and made the first 10 tackles of the second half for our team. Three and out, three and out, three and out. We took over and drove the ball and scored. We won the game 22-14."

Spielman was named to the Ohio State Football All-Century Team in 2000 by the Touchdown Club of Columbus. He was one of four All-Century captains along with Archie Griffin, Rex Kern and Jack Tatum. Spielman and Tatum were the defensive captains. Spielman was a captain for the Buckeyes in 1987. He finished his career as a two-time first team All-American and a three-time All-Big Ten selection. He was the 1987 Lombardi Award winner as college football's best lineman or linebacker. He was elected to the College Football Hall of Fame in 2010.

Spielman was the 29th player selected in the 1988 NFL draft. He played eight years for the Detroit Lions, leading the team in tackles every season. He is the Lions all-time leader in tackles. He played for the Buffalo Bill for two seasons, setting a team record for tackles in a season (206) in 1996. He led his team in tackles every season he played, except when he was injured in 1997 with Buffalo.

"I take a lot of pride in that because that's my job," Spielman said. "I would have led the Bills in tackles in 1997 if I didn't get hurt."

Spielman was selected to four Pro Bowls in his 10-year NFL career. He tried to come back from a neck injury, and played the 1999 pre-season with the Cleveland Browns until a second neck injury ended his career.

Despite all of his awards, from high school through the professional ranks, Spielman was frustrated by a tag that he was never able to shake.

"I get a little frustrated because I've often been called an over-achiever," Spielman said. "I've achieved exactly what I've set out to achieve. So I don't see how that's over-achieving."

Spielman received nation-wide respect when he sat out the 1998 NFL season to be with his wife when she was diagnosed with breast cancer. Together they formed the Stefanie Spielman Fund for Breast Cancer Research. Stefanie lost her battle with cancer on November 19, 2009.

Spielman currently announces college football games for ESPN and co-hosts a popular radio show in Columbus.

The Boy That Was on the Wheaties Box

No one knew the impact appearing on the Wheaties box would have on Chris Spielman, a shy 16-year-old boy, between his junior and senior year of high school.

When Wheaties sponsored a nation-wide *Search for Champions* contest, Jack Gorius, a local booster, started a citywide campaign to put Spielman—and the town of Massillon—on the Wheaties box.

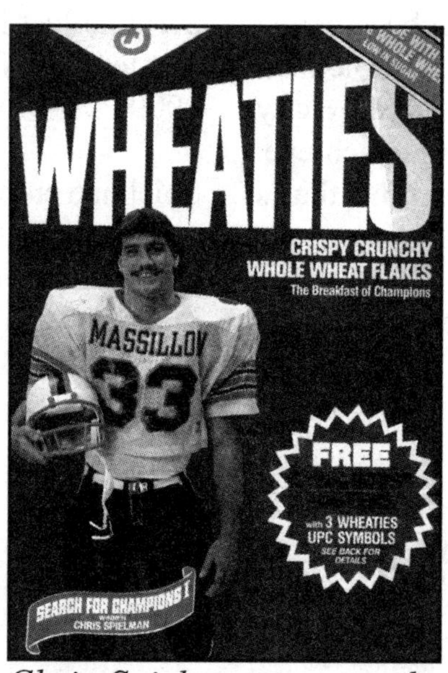

Chris Spielman was on the Wheaties box while he was in high school.

"Jack came up with the idea and presented it to me," Spielman said. "I said 'Sure,' thinking nothing would ever come of it. I should have known better. The town kind of caught fire with it and everybody got behind it. It was just a chance to put Massillon on the map again, to show what a special place it is. I just happened to be the lucky, chosen one at the time.

"Ninety percent of the time it was great, the other ten percent was hard for a kid who's all of a sudden thrust into this position."

There was a defining moment that hurt Spielman.

"We were in a parade or somethin' and I didn't look quick enough for a picture or somethin' and there was a yell from the crowd: 'Hey Spielman, you've gotta look over here. What's a matter with you? Quit acting like that.'"

Spielman wasn't acting cocky, like the heckler suggested.

"I was just tryin' to get by. He yelled, 'Hey, you better straighten up. Massillon *made* you.'

"And you know, I took a little exception to that. I got frustrated.

"I remember lots of times where I basically turned into a loner, a person who really valued privacy, because I had none. I was very shy, and to this day, I think it affects me. Relatively speaking, I kind of dodge the spotlight when I can. I'm basically shy when I'm out amongst people or in a crowd. I shouldn't say shy, I'm a little bit uncomfortable.

"That kicked it off and of course everything got escalated when I came to Ohio State. But it started in Massillon. Then again that experience was a benefit because I was able to handle the pressure when I got down to Columbus. So there's good and bad with the whole thing.

"I want to emphasize that I'm grateful to Jack Gorius and the people of Massillon for giving me that opportunity. It was a wonderful, wonderful experience. But when you have something that is that big—being put on a Wheaties box when you're 16 years old is big—there's going to be some trying times that a young person has to deal with that he might not be *able* to deal with.

"It's the first time people started staring at me, and recognizing me. You feel kind of funny because you feel like, *'Is something wrong with me?'* You don't realize people are thinking, 'That's the kid that might be on the Wheaties box,' or something like that. So you become very self-conscious.

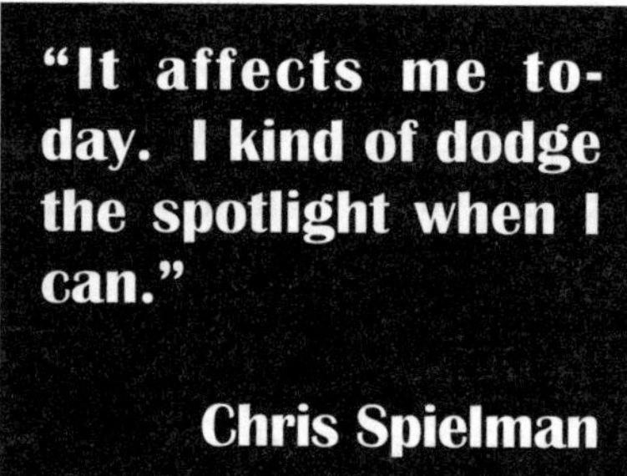

"Everyone thought it was all great and glamorous and glorified. And it *was* great, but it was also very difficult. I became, overnight, a role model for a lot of kids. And that was great. Don't get me wrong about that, if I could go to a hospital and make some kid, a sick kid—even at the young age that I was—feel better or get better or just brighten somebody's day, I certainly didn't mind doing that. But sometimes, if you're not exposed to hospitals, a kid might be in there with pneumonia or something else. For me to go deal with that at 16, when the worst thing I've had is a cold, when you're not prepared for it—it was 'Go here, do this, go here, do that.' I learned, and I grew up fast, and I saw things that a lot of kids didn't see. I think I was a good kid. And I did a lot of good things.

"My parents sensed me going into a shell. They kind of stepped in and took control a little bit. They kind of guarded and protected me a little bit."

Spielman found that his only refuge was time spent with his girlfriend Stefanie, who later became his wife.

"The only place I ever got peace or anonymity would be at my girlfriend's house. She was from Jackson Township. We would walk on Brookside golf course. That was the only time I felt like I could just be Chris. I could have food hanging off of my chin, laugh or giggle or screw around or whatever. Every time in public I felt like I had to constantly live up to 'The Boy that was on the Wheaties Box.' I was afraid to be myself."

Spielman's walks with Stefanie were therapeutic. "We didn't talk about anything," he said. "Not football. Just kid stuff, boyfriend-girlfriend stuff. Sixteen-year-old stuff. What movie we were going to see. How can we sneak past your parents tonight, or something like that. I used to retreat over there—and I think that was the only time I felt that I was able to be myself."

Spielman was surprised when he actually saw himself on the Wheaties box. "I thought, man, I look like a geek (laughs). I thought, I honestly thought, even though there was a big deal made of it, I thought it was not a big deal."

It actually became a *bigger* deal after the cereal box began hitting the grocery shelves.

"Then I started signing all of these Wheaties boxes. And it became *we*. *We* won the contest. Me and the town. Really, once we won, it kind of escalated a little more.

Everybody wanted their boxes signed. Not only did people in Massillon know who I was, so did people in Canton and all over northeast Ohio. I remember going to out of town basketball games and everybody would start chanting things like '*Cheerios!*' or '*Fruit Loops!*,' or '*Wheaties*!' Or like getting off the buses for football or basketball or even track, if there was a crowd, people would throw cereal on me or something like that. I just thought, 'Whatever, man.' Again, things kept compounding and compounding and compounding. That's why by the time I graduated I was ready to get out of Massillon a little bit and come to Columbus."

"The only place I ever got peace or anonymity would be at my girlfriend's house."

Chris Spielman

Did the whole Wheaties thing stop being fun for Spielman?

"It was fun all the time," he insisted. "I probably could have used a break from it once in a while, but I never could get a break from it. As I had more success in college, it helped me to be able to handle all that media pressure. All that other stuff. It's all part of the deal, man."

JOHN MARONTO

Could it be that it was just a case of being in the right place at the wrong time for John Maronto?

John Maronto was 20-10 in three seasons at Massillon.

Maronto succeeded Mike Currence as Massillon's head coach. Currence was fired by Massillon's school board after the 1984 season, but still had a lot of support in Massillon.

Maronto brought in a hard-working, ball-control approach to the job. But it didn't work for him in Massillon. Tiger fans were used to an exciting, wide open attack, not Maronto's grind-it-out style. And the fact that he was 0-3 against Canton McKinley...it was just the wrong time for Maronto in Massillon.

But fast forward to 2003. Maronto is leaving Florida Field in Gainesville after winning the state championship after his 12-1 Mainland Buccaneers defeated Naples, 24-13, for the Class 5A state title. While the state title is certainly the crown jewel in Maronto's career, it's hardly his only success at Mainland.

Maronto has become somewhat of a high school coaching legend in the state of Florida, where, like in Ohio, they play football at a high level. Maronto is definitely in the right place at the right time.

In 13 years at Dayton Beach Mainland his record is 130-34.

In 13 years at Daytona Beach Mainland his record is 130-34. Not many high school coaches average 10 wins a season. He's also been to the playoffs 13 straight seasons, with four Final 4 finishes.

At Massillon, Maronto's three year record was 20-10, and he remains one of the least popular coaches in Massillon history. A lot of it has to do with his record against McKinley. A lot has to do with what fans view as wasted opportunities. Currence felt that Maronto wasted a lot of talent in his three years at the helm, too.

"When they brought Maronto in, he was a tough guy," Currence said. "He made those kids do stuff that there was no rhyme or reason why they would ever win a football game because of it. The training they did. Gaining unnecessary weight and bulkin' up. They were kids that I had and they were my son's best buddies, and they were all bulked up. He had kids that I had trained. Bart Letcavits, a coach's son, went down to Miami and played three years down there as a split end. Never threw a pass to him. Run the ball, run the ball, that's all he did. Whew. The stuff that he did with the talent that he had. There were like 10 Division I players. If my kid had played it would have been 11 Division I players. And then there were some kids who didn't qualify, who went to junior college, who would have run that number up to maybe 15 Division I kids. And Maronto was 7-3. I built that team since they were grade school kids. My son and his buddies were in my little league camps. I knew every position those kids played. He took them out of my positions."

> **"John Maronto was a wonderful man and cared a lot for the kids, but he had like a 90-10/80-20 run-pass ration."**
>
> **Al Hennon**

Al Hennon was an administrator at Washington High School and served on the committee to find Maronto's replacement following the 1987 season. Hennon later became Massillon's Superintendent of Schools.

"John Maronto was a wonderful man and cared a lot for the kids," Hennon said, "but he had like a 90-10/80-20 run-pass ratio. We were looking for an innovative, creative offensive mind."

Maronto agrees that his offense may have been too conservative.

"Yeah, yeah. Probably for that day we were. I came

out of the Detroit Catholic League where we were pretty balanced and we had some weapons. You know (at Massillon) we just had to do what we had to do with what we had. Our style, compared with what Currence had with the run and shoot, we were probably very conservative by those standards."

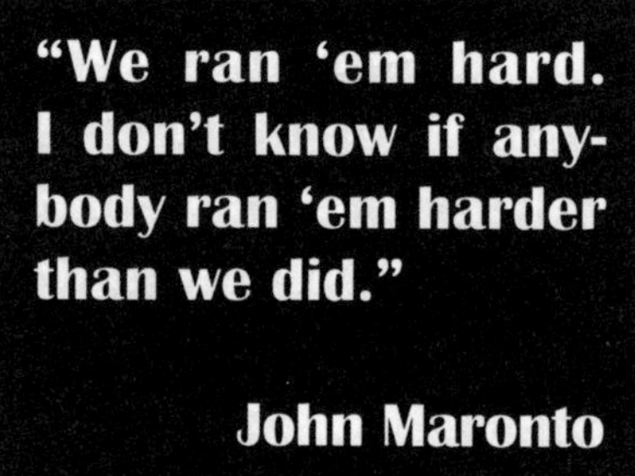

But he objects to criticism that his concentration on strength training and running was a mistake. He is proud of his accomplishments in that area.

"I have to dispute that one," Maronto said. "Any time we did a lift, we did an athletic lift. One thing that has always been my philosophy, when you squat you jump higher, run faster. We had improvement in our speed program. We brought in some of the best speed guys in the country. We were definitely strong. If anything, that is something *good* to be criticized for. I don't think I ever had a team that spent too much time doing the bench press. We spent time doing quickness and agility drills. We were always well-techniqued. I guess our big mission was to develop a great strength program. We ran 'em hard. I don't know if anybody ran 'em harder than we did."

Currence felt that Maronto's philosophy backfired on game day. "Those kids were handling much too much weight for 15, 16 year old kids. A lot of them ended up with back injuries. They should have never, ever been doing that. I never, ever had a kid have an injury in the weight room and lose him for a ball game. I didn't believe in that. He wore 'em out. He would run their ass. He had a running program, his big thing was the Bigger, Faster, Stronger program. They would come to practice and run six quarter (miles), maybe two or three 880s. It was like a track program. Then they would go in and suit up and play football. Why, my God, they couldn't do anything afterwards. He had them so tight and so inflexible that they were like a bunch of overgrown robots out there. A bunch of weightlifters. And I've never seen a weightlifter yet that's been a great football player. Because they lose their flexibility, lose their range of motion. They can't run, they can't catch, they can't do anything. And these kids that he had, my sophomores, who he played as juniors and seniors, and then the class behind them, they were just *outstanding* athletes."

Monte McGuire was a defensive back under Maronto and his replacement, Lee Owens. "I think Coach Maronto was just a little ahead of his time in that category," McGuire said. "If you look back at the program, when he left we kept those same strategies going forward.

"Coach Maronto hired Coach Steve Studer. So that turned the whole weight training program in a better direction. Since then the weight training program has done nothing but flourish because of that model that Coach Studer and Coach Maronto put into the program back then.

"It might have hindered us at first, maybe those first couple of years that Coach Studer implemented that program because a lot of us weren't used to working out with free weights. So when he brought the weight room in, yeah, it was an adjustment period. I felt that we lost a little speed because we were so big. Some people were just so big that we were getting out-quicked against certain teams.

Maronto also faced the challenge of trying to pull together a community fractured by Currence's firing.

"Coach Maronto came to Massillon when football was just switching from the power game to the speed game. He just got caught in the middle of that. It just took some coaches a couple of years to adjust to the speed game."

Maronto also faced the challenge of trying to pull together a community fractured by Currence's firing. But he offers no excuses.

"I felt that we had to bring the community together because of the tough times. There were people who were still loyal to Currence. We were just interested in trying to move forward. That's one thing about coaches, you can have a great coach, a coach everybody loves, and if they're a legend it's hard to follow someone like that. But for the most part coaches have a chance to come in and do it their way. We had all the resources that anybody could ask for."

Bill Caples, a school board member and sportscaster for the Tigers, was involved in

Currence's hiring and firing and Maronto's hiring. Caples felt that Maronto had to battle a lot of off-the-field obstacles.

"John had a decent career here, but nothing outstanding," Caples said. "Not all that was his fault. There were extenuating circumstances, but that's a whole new story, and I'm not going to get into that. Because, believe me, when he came in here he did not always get the best of help from people who should have given it to him. And I'm not talking booster people. There were other people who were in position to help him but didn't. And that's unfortunate."

Like many Massillon head coaches before and after him, Maronto found the job extremely challenging.

"It's an awesome responsibility," he said. "It means so much to the players' families, their neighbors, their teachers and the rest of the community—people they don't even know. Sometimes the players face some ridicule. They may be subject to some things you try to protect them from. You want to give those kids the best kind of experience you can. If I can coach with great enthusiasm every day, no matter how bad I'm feelin' or how bad the weather is or what we're comin' off of. If I can come out there and be absolutely 100% positive, and have something for 'em to challenge 'em, to discipline them. I think that's what they want."

Maronto faced his share of tough times at Massillon. "Sure there were tough times that weren't pleasant," he said. "When I first got there it was a honeymoon. I had to keep telling my family, 'This is just temporary now.' You come into town and there's the signs, 'Welcome Coach Maronto and family.' All of those nice things. And those things really make people feel special. It's a special job. Football is special in the community—it's *critically* important to the community. You've got a lot of people with high hopes. One of our biggest challenges was academics. We tried to create some kind of a balance. Because one thing in Massillon, things can get out of balance sometimes. That can happen any time you have a program the size and scope and magnitude that Massillon has. There aren't many towns that when you're born you get a football in your crib if you're a male. We had players who, if they *hadn't* had that football in their crib, or *hadn't* grown up in Massillon, I'm pretty sure they would have never played football. Now some of them became pretty good players, because of dedication, tradition, some of those good things. But sometimes some of those good things get to the point where there's pressure on kids to play. And maybe there's times when some of those kids don't *want* to play football. There are times where they're put in positions that they shouldn't be put in.

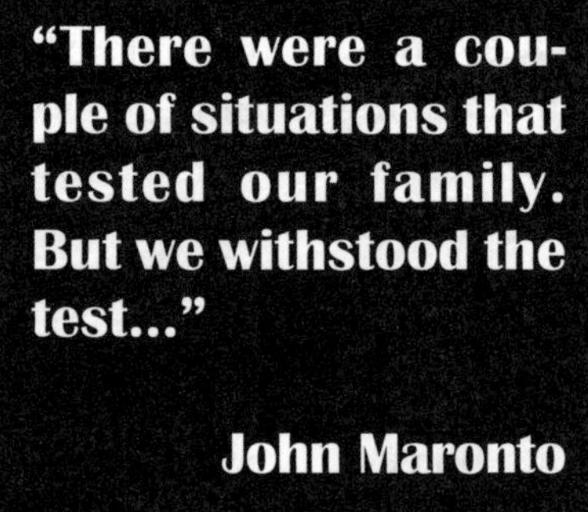

"In Massillon, the principal, the superintendent, the secretaries, everybody that works on the school board, the office workers, I mean the custodians, the support staff, at *every* school, they're all coachin'. Everybody's coaching.

"There were a lot of highs and lows. But 99 percent of the time it was positive. There were some negative times. There were a couple of situations that tested our family. But we withstood the test and that's what we were *supposed* to do. You try to take things for what they are. If you're a leader you have to stand tall sometimes, on your own two feet. I told the kids that in the locker room. 'Hey, this is a big football town. You stand tall and stand proud. As long as you're playin' and preparin' and doing the right things, you're fine. Don't worry about it. I'll take whatever blame's gotta be taken."

One time during the 1985 season, the frustration may have gotten to be a little too much for the coach. Massillon was trailing Barberton 20-9 at halftime.

"They were throwing rotten tomatoes at us and they were beatin' us (on the scoreboard)," Maronto said. "They might have done us a favor. If we had been ahead it might have been different. We just felt we had something to prove after that. So, being emotional, I got pretty emotional there. I got in the locker room and made sure they were all sittin' down. Then I put my fist through the chalkboard. It's one of those games where you have to get your focus where it's needed to be." The players returned to the field and scored 21 unanswered points to win 30-20.

"I love coach Maronto, I truly do," McGuire said. "He was one of those guys who guided me through the times I really needed somebody the most. I went through a situation where I was stabbed my junior year and didn't know if I was going to be able to play football. He was at my hospital bed every day for three weeks, until I was released from the hospital. And at the time he *knew* his contract wasn't getting renewed. But that was just him. He was the ultimate coach and family man. He loved all of us. Without him being a father figure during my sophomore and junior years, I would not be the man I am today, because I would be dead or in prison. Me and my brother Travis grew up without a father. And there's a lot of decisions that we might not have made with a father in our lives. I was lucky to have somebody like Coach Maronto who stepped in and gave me guidance when I needed it."

"When he left here after being fired, he was always so gracious to us—and always has been—in talking about Massillon," Caples said. "He loves Massillon, even though he got fired from here. His final day here when school was out he thanked us for giving him the opportunity. He apologized, 'I'm sorry,' he said, 'I didn't get the job done that was expected of me.' And he sincerely felt bad about that. We told him it wasn't all his fault. But that was John. He did more than any other coach for our kids in getting them into colleges. He was so well known in the college ranks. He was a fine coach. It just didn't work out for him here at the time."

JIM LETCAVITS

It's hard to say whether Jim Letcavits was a better player or a better coach at Massillon. It's easy, however, to say that he is among the best in both areas. But you'd never hear him say that.

Jim Letcavits with star pupil Chris Spielman. Letcavits made his mark in Massillon as an outstanding player and coach.

PHOTO: JIM LETCAVITS COLLECTION

"Real soft-spoken guy," former Massillon head coach Mike Currence (1976-84) said of Letcavits. "Would have loved to have been the head coach. The kids loved him. They'd do anything for him. He could train them to step six inches to the right, take a jab step, lead with the forearm, keep the outside arm free. And they would never, ever fail to do that. Because he would work 'em so much on that technique that they would never be outflanked, never be out of position. They were always where they were supposed to be."

Letcavits was a model of quiet efficiency during his 27 years as an assistant coach at Massillon. He was taught by another longtime Massillon assistant coach.

"Ducky Schroeder was a guy

who very seldom yelled at ya," Letcavits said, "You don't gain anything by yelling at somebody. In fact, when you yell at somebody in front of the other kids you're embarrassing that person. I always told them what they did wrong, then told them what they had to do to get better. I very seldom yelled at the kids. I learned that from Ducky, because he was quiet, too. But he knew his football."

Letcavits enjoyed a five-year career in the CFL.

Letcavits was an All-Ohio end at Massillon in 1953. He was part of a quintet of outstanding ends that Schroeder produced between 1951 and 1955. "Before me there were Bruce Brenner and Bob Khoenle, after me were David Canary and Jim Houston," Letcavits said. "All five were All-Ohio, all in a row."

Letcavits capped his high school career with a career game in the North-South All-Star game. Starring at both offensive and defensive end, Letcavits caught two touchdown passes, recovered a fumble and also punted for the victorious North squad. He was a near-unanimous MVP choice.

Letcavits played college football for his high school coach, Chuck Mather, at The University of Kansas. He won All-Conference honors twice.

He was surprised at the state

of football when both he and Mather arrived at Kansas in 1954.

"When I got out there, those kids didn't know how to block or tackle," he said.

Letcavits played five years of professional football in Canada. He made a memorable play in the first half of the 1960 Grey Cup, Canadian Football's version of the Super Bowl.

Letcavits pulled the ball out of the defender's arms and raced 63 yards to give the Edmonton Eskimos a 6-3 lead.

"I almost won a Corvette," Letcavits said. "I think I caught seven passes, and one for a touchdown in the first half. At halftime I would have been the outstanding player and won the car, but Ottawa went ahead and they ended up beating us 16-6.

"I made it in Canada for five years because of my blocking," Letcavits said. "I had a real nice career in Canada."

Letcavits estimates that he had around 1,000 career receiving yards at Edminton.

He started his career as an assistant football coach at Massillon in 1970 under Head Coach Bob Commings.

"Commings was great with the kids," Letcavits said. "He and Currence were the best I coached with."

Letcavits who was the head track coach at Massillon for 27 years, missed coaching when he retired. "You miss the game, being down on the sidelines with the kids," he said, "I had a great time coaching at Massillon."

Dave Irwin takes the field amid band members in 1999.

19 90s

Ellery Moore

Massillon's All-Ohioans

Duane Scott
1990

Travis McGuire
1991

Eric Wright
1991

Jason Woullard
1991

Steve Miller
1991

Falondo Ashcraft
1991

Dan Hackenbracht
1992

Branden Jackson
1992

B. J. Payne
1993

Trevor Paisley
1993

Lonnie Simpson
1993

Kevin Bouder
1994

Willie Spencer, Jr.
1994

Courtney Herring
1994

Mark Wells
1994

Vinnie Turner
1995

Ben Mast
1996

Milo McGuire
1996

Eric Lightfoot
1996

Josh Krieder
1997

Christian Morgan
1997

Josh Hill
1997

Luke Shilling
1998

Ellery Moore
1998

Ellery Moore
1999

Rocky Dorsey
1999

Jessie Scott
1999

TEAMS 1990s RECORDS

80 WINS 31 LOSSES

6 State Playoff Appearances
1 Final Four

_1990_
8-4
State Quarterfinals
Head Coach: Lee Owens

M	Key Games	Opp.
23	Cin. Moeller	24
7	Canton McKinley	20
21	Jackson	15
335	***Season Totals***	***159***

_1991_
10-3
State Final Four
Head Coach: Lee Owens

M	Key Games	Opp.
42	Canton McKinley	13
42	Toledo St. John's	21
13	St. Ignatius	14
464	***Season Totals***	***182***

_1992_
5-5

Head Coach: Jack Rose

M	Key Games	Opp.
14	Cin. Moeller	24
38	Bloomington South	0
6	Canton McKinley	14
234	***Season Totals***	***153***

_1993_
10-2
State Quarterfinals
Head Coach: Jack Rose

M	Key Games	Opp.
13	Canton McKinley	21
46	Mansfield Senior	6
20	Walsh Jesuit	30
504	***Season Totals***	***133***

1994
10-2
State Quarterfinals
Head Coach: Jack Rose

M	Key Games	Opp.
42	Canton McKinley	41
35	Fremont Ross	28
20	Canton McKinley	27
301	***Season Totals***	***187***

1995
7-3
Head Coach: Jack Rose

M	Key Games	Opp.
21	Cin. Moeller	18
21	Austintown Fitch	14
21	Canton McKinley	24
238	***Season Totals***	***180***

1996
9-2
State Playoffs
Head Coach: Jack Rose

M	Key Games	Opp.
20	Cin. Moeller	15
0	Canton McKinley	21
6	Brunswick	7
277	***Season Totals***	***136***

1997
7-3
Head Coach: Jack Rose

M	Key Games	Opp.
20	Akron Garfield	14
24	Cin. Moeller	28
14	Canton McKinley	27
291	***Season Totals***	***120***

1998
4-6
Head Coach: Rick Shepas

M	Key Games	Opp.
9	Clovis West (CA)	21
0	Glen Mills (PA)	19
20	Canton McKinley	42
150	***Season Totals***	***210***

1999
State Playoffs
10-1
Head Coach: Rick Shepas

M	Key Games	Opp.
35	Perry	14
35	Canton McKinley	7
6	Perry	23
311	***Season Totals***	***164***

Story of the Decade 1990s

100th Massillon-McKinley Game Lives Up to Its Larger than Life Build-up

The build-up for the 100th meeting of the Massillon Tigers and the Canton McKinley Bulldogs was so incredible that it seemed impossible for the game to possibly live up to its hype.

Somehow the game managed to *exceed* expectations, going to overtime, with Massillon winning 42-41 on the last play of the game.

Game program from 100th Massillon-McKinley game.

Sports Illustrated and *ESPN* sent crews to cover the game. Commemorative footballs, watches, coins, hats, t-shirts, and sweatshirts were gobbled up by frenzied fans.

Massillon heroes from bygone days were brought in for the opening of the new Hall of Champions at Washington High School and to ride in the annual *Beat McKinley* parade downtown. Legendary Green Bay Packers Hall of Fame quarterback Bart Starr, who coached Massillon's Steve Luke at Green Bay, was there for the opening coin toss.

Al Paris, Massillon's superintendent of schools at the time, had a lot to do with organizing the festivities.

Tiger captains Steve Griffith, Mark Lightfoot and Willie Spencer, Jr. at the coin toss prior to the 100th game.

"Bart Starr flipped the coin," Paris said. "We had the captains from Massillon and McKinley from 50 years prior on the field that day. There was a lot of to-do about it. Television stations were in. A Hollywood script couldn't have been written any better. To this day, I talk to people from Canton and Massillon and they say that was the greatest high school football game they have ever seen. It'd be hard to top that. Beautiful day. All the balloons.

"They celebrated throughout the night and into the next morning in Massillon," Paris said. "They kept going through town, blowing their horns, hanging out of cars, three in the morning, four in the morning, they couldn't stop celebrating. It was like a war was over. Like World War II was over. Something to that extent.

"The congratulations afterwards, even though I had very little to do with it, it was entirely the players and the coaches, but it felt good to get phone calls in your office and people congratulating you. It made me feel good for Jack Rose and the coaching staff and the kids. I tell you what that did, it had to get a few more scholarships for us. Got kids into school. That was nice. I enjoyed it. I got very many calls after that. You have to realize that I know almost everybody in Massillon. I grew up in Massillon. It wasn't like a superintendent coming into town and you have a group of friends you meet when you come into a community. I've been here since 1934, that's when I was born."

"To this day, I talk to people from Canton and Massillon and they say that was the greatest high school football game they have ever seen"

Al Paris

Massillon, led by All-Ohio quarterback Willie Spencer,

Jr., was an 8-1 team that seemed to get better every week. Canton McKinley was 8-1 and led by third-year starting quarterback Josh McDaniels, son of head coach Thom McDaniels. McDaniels went on to become the offensive coordinator under Bill Belichick with the New England Patriots and was named head coach of the Denver Broncos in 2009.

Steve Luke (l) stands with Green Bay Packers legend Bart Starr prior to the kickoff of the 100th game. Luke was a captain for Starr at Green Bay.

The teams fought to a 14-14 tie through the first half. The remarkable second half saw six touchdowns between the two teams and an unforgettable overtime session

Spencer was the ultimate field general in the 100th game: A calm, cool and collected leader.

"I was just enjoying myself," Spencer said, "I wasn't nervous or anything, because we were basically doing what we wanted to do to them. They were doing what they wanted to do to us, too. It was an offensive game."

The 100th game was the highest-scoring in the history

of the ancient rivalry with 83 points scored between the teams.

The second half started with a bang, with the Tigers dusting off a trick play practically as old as the rivalry itself.

"We scored on a 62-yard flea flicker the second play," Spencer said, "Then they scored, and we scored, and they scored and we scored. It was just really exciting. It's something I'll never forget."

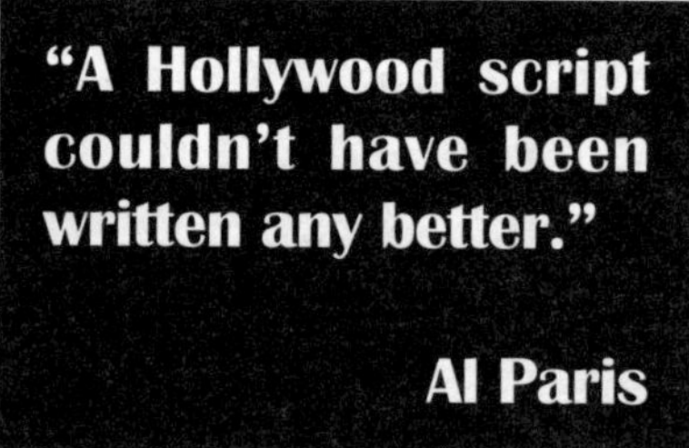

No one in attendance that day will forget Spencer's play in overtime. McKinley got the ball first and scored on a McDaniels touchdown pass. McDaniels, who also kicked for McKinley, missed the extra point, opening the door for Massillon to score and win with a successful extra point.

Then Spencer pulled off the play of the century.

Joe Shaheen was covering the game for Massillon's newspaper *The Independent*. "Maybe the most exciting play I remember in the 100th game was Spencer pitching that ball to Victor Redrick," Shaheen said. "I had never seen a play like that where the receiver became the option pitch man. He lined up as a receiver on the opposite side and here comes Willie Spencer running the option this way and here comes the receiver as the option pitch man. I thought it was a beautifully-designed play. I've watched a lot of football, high school, college, pros and I've never seen a game as exciting as that. And that one play, given what had happened in the context of the game, the fact that it was so key to the outcome of the game, that was as exciting a play as I've ever seen."

The Tigers scored on the Spencer-to-Redrick pitch, but it didn't come without added drama.

Depending on your angle, or your point of view, it either looked like a perfectly-timed pitch from Spencer to Redrick or a forward lateral.

Vaughn Moeller made a sliding touchdown catch in the 100th game.

"It wasn't a forward lateral," Spencer said excitedly. "McKinley says it was a forward lateral. I disagree. The officials didn't call it a forward lateral, so it's not a forward lateral. That's how I look at it. It was a play that we were working on all week. It was the second play of overtime.

"The first play I overthrew the tight end. I just faked the dive up the middle and came around the end and saw the corner there and I faked the pitch and cut up. And then the backside defensive end came up and tackled me and I just pitched it out. I'm glad Victor Redrick continued to stay in

Fans Wait in Line for Hours in a Cold Rain for a Scant Few Tickets

Fans began lining up at 4 a.m., in a cold rain, for their chance to acquire tickets to the 100th Massillon-McKinley game in 1994. The line wound from the ticket office, up the hill, and down the street. Tickets were limited to two per person.

Fans line up at Paul Brown Tiger Stadium.

The game sold out in an hour and a half. Fans in line knew their wait may be fruitless, since tickets were likely to be gone before they made it to the ticket window. But they waited anyway. Many went home empty-handed.

pitch phase with me."

Combining with Redrick for the touchdown had a special meaning for Spencer.

"That's my best friend," Spencer said. "That makes it even better. What happened was our tight end missed the block on their backside defensive end. The backside defensive end was able to run down the line and tackle me. If our tight end had made the block I would have been able to run in and score myself. But I'm glad it happened the way it happened, because I'm happy for Vic. I'm just glad I was able to share something with him that he'll be able to remember for the rest of his life."

All that was left was for Nick Pribich to kick the winning extra point.

"They couldn't stop celebrating. It was like World War II was over."

Al Paris

"All I remember was running out there," Pribich said. "My whole body was pretty numb, I was really nervous. When I got out there Willie Spencer came up to me and grabbed my face mask and said, 'Come on Pribich, come on Pribich, you've gotta make this kick.'"

Pribich's father, Nick, Sr., harkened back to his son's childhood.

"We would practice in the side yard," said Nick, Sr., who started at safety on Earle Bruce's 1964 state championship team. "We had a bush and a telephone pole set up like a goal post. We used to kick in the side yard all the time. Or we'd go over to Jackson or to Tiger stadium to kick. His last kick of every practice was to beat McKinley. We did that for four years. He had seen Josh McDaniels miss that kick. The whole year he never looked up in the stands. After he barely missed a field goal earlier in the 100th game he looked up at me. I said, 'Get your head in the game. You've got to kick again. Forget that kick.' I used to say, 'Good snap, good hold, good kick,' for all of his kicks. A kicker's only as good as his last kick. So in that McKinley game, when we scored in overtime, he's concentrating on his routine. I'm in the stands saying, 'Good snap, good hold.' So they snap to Mark Hiegl. He makes a good hold and Nicky made a good kick and it was history. I squeezed my brother and he fell to the ground. Everybody thought he had a heart attack. I squeezed him so hard I squeezed all the air out of him. I was like in shock.

Nick Pribich kicks the winning point in Massillon's 42-41 victory in the 100th game.

"I don't remember being nervous when I played," Nick, Sr., said. "But when my son played, man I was nervous every snap, every hold, every kick. I'm sure glad Josh McDaniels missed that kick instead of my son. If Nicky missed that kick I'd probably have to leave town. That'd be unbearable. That's something that stays with you your whole life."

Nick, Jr., knew it would be up to him to execute the kick. "I knew it would be a perfect snap and hold," he said. "As soon as I kicked it, it was like the greatest feeling ever. I turned around and ran and just got mobbed by my teammates."

"That was a great victory for Jack Rose," Paris said. "Let me tell you, Jack Rose is a very fine person. He did not have the success that people wanted him to have in Massillon. His biggest thing was not beating McKinley. He didn't have a good record against McKinley. But as an individual, and also as a good football coach, Jack was tops. He was a very good man.

"I was going to retire two years before that. Well, in 1993 I was ready to retire and Jack comes in and says, 'Al, you've got to stick around.' I said, 'What for?' He said 'We've got that 100th game. I want you to be part of that 100th game.' He knew everything that would go along with it, with all the people here. He wanted me to be a part of it because I enjoy sports so much. So I went back to the board of education and asked if they'd have a problem if I stuck around for another couple of years. They said, 'No, you can stick around. We'll give you another five-year contract.' I said, 'No, I just want to go 'til that 100th game, then retire.' Fortunately we won that game and everything came out right for us. We knew we would invite a lot of people in, and we knew a lot of people would *want* to come in. It's a great town, it really is."

Games of the Century

1991's Final 4 loss to Ignatius Among Tigers All-Time Heartbreakers

The 1991 Massillon Tigers were on a roll going into their Final 4 match-up with Cleveland St. Ignatius. They felt their first playoff championship was in hand if they could get by their modern-day nemesis.

"We were the best team in the state at the time," Head Coach Lee Owens said. "There was no question. Maybe not the best Division I talent, or the most players. But we were the best team. We had it together. We were playing by far one of the best teams in the country in Ignatius. But I think we were better."

"We had a special group of guys," said Nick Mossides, who was the Tigers quarterback in 1991. "We had everything, we had the right mix, but somehow, for one reason or another, we couldn't put it all together and put the state championship ring on our fingers. As you get older you think about it a little bit less, but when somebody brings it up it is still pretty difficult to deal with, especially in the manner that we lost against Ignatius.

The Tigers lost, 14-13, in front of 20,150 fans in the Akron Rubber Bowl, when their extra point attempt hit the upright and bounced back.

"It hit the upright," Owens said. "It was a college goal post. It would have gone through on a high school goal post."

"The only thing I remember about that game is losin', really," said Folando Ashcraft. Ashcraft was part of Massillon's dynamic one-two running back punch. Ashcraft and running mate Travis McGuire each ran for over 1,000 yards on the season. But neither running back was healthy heading into the Ignatius game.

Ashcraft was hampered by an ankle injury and McGuire was under the weather.

"I had gotten hurt the week before the McKinley game," Ashcraft said. "It didn't get better during the playoff run. The doctor shot it up and I wrapped it heavily and I just went in there and played."

McGuire was battling flu symptoms.

"I had the flu all week," McGuire said. "I actually got sick before that Ignatius game. I still gave it all I had, but I wasn't 100 percent."

"We were the best team in the state at the time. There was no question."

Lee Owens

Both running backs fumbled the ball against Ignatius.

"There were so many things that didn't go right," Ashcraft said. "I had kind of re-aggravated my ankle a little bit early in the game. I remember takin' a hand-off and goin' through the middle and my ankle turning. I'm tellin' ya it hurt me so bad that when this guy hit my elbow I just kind of dropped the football."

McGuire coughed up the ball against Ignatius, too.

"As the weather got colder, it was a little harder to hold onto the ball," McGuire said. "I put it on the ground against Ignatius."

Folando fumbled once at the 20 and Travis fumbled it once inside the 20," Owens said. "That was the difference in the game. We scored late and tried to pooch kick it.

"The kicker missed it and they got it. That's probably the most criticism I ever received. People thought we were trying an on-side kick. It really wasn't an onside kick. Ignatius had a great kickoff return team. And after our first score we pooched it way from the returner, which means you try to drop it in a hole around the 15-yard line. I thought, 'Let's try to pooch this thing again.' It worked great last time. Let's just drop it in a hole.

"The kicker missed the ball. It went off the side of his foot and it just went out of bounds. It was really poorly executed. It wasn't necessarily the strategy behind it. I would do the same thing again. People look at me like I'm crazy when I say that. But I'd make the same call again. It was my call. It was wet. The special teams coach said the ball was wet. His shoe was wet when he came off of the field. He didn't have as much control over the ball as he did early in the game. So the ball didn't end up going where he wanted it to."

"That kick may have cost us the ball game," McGuire said. "We did have some trouble with our kickoff coverage team. A lot of teams were making big yardage. But in a big game like that, with so little time, you've gotta take your chances. You've gotta kick it deep and at least have them try to drive from the 30-yard line or the 20-yard line.

"We had the better team and we should have won," McGuire said. "That was a state championship game. Whoever won was going to win the state championship. It was pretty much devastating."

"We knew we could play with 'em," Ashcraft said. "We didn't step up to the plate when we needed to. I don't know to this day if Coach Owens told our kicker to squib kick that ball or if he just did that on his own. He says that Coach Owens told him to do that. I don't know. I just didn't understand why Coach Owens would do that. We had probably the best defense in the state of Ohio. You kick the ball deep. Our defense had been stopping them the whole game. You ain't got no confidence in your team to where your defense could stop them for two minutes? I personally wish he would have had the ball kicked deep, but he's the coach of the team, he's our leader, so we did whatever he told us to do.

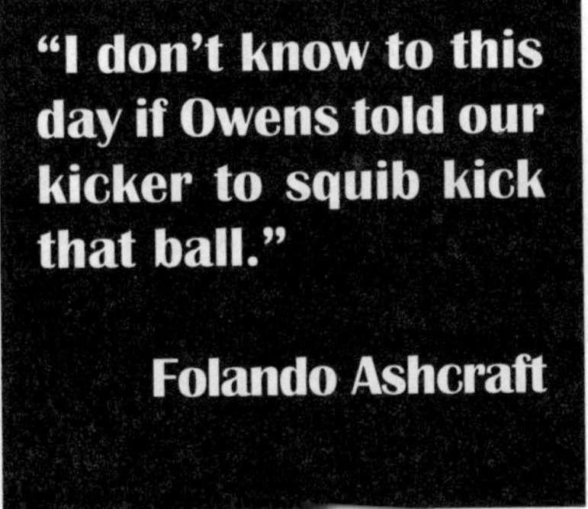

"We can go on the rest of our lives talkin' about how we lost to St. Ignatius and the way we lost. But I would have to put the blame upon myself because I was a leader on that team and you're supposed to lead by example. I didn't bring my A game and we failed.

"At the end of the game I laid on the field for a while," Ashcraft said. "I was like, 'Man, this is how I'm ending my career at Massillon. Just swallowing that whole thing was hard. A guy from Ignatius came and got me up. He told me, ‘I’m telling you right now, I know you’ve been having problems with your ankle, but you’re one of the best running backs I’ve ever seen. You don’t have to put your head down. I know how bad you want to win a championship. But do you know how bad we wanted to beat some running backs like you guys?’ He kind of picked me up off of the ground and said, ‘You keep your head up because you’re gonna go places.’

“I walked back to the locker room and I had this kind of blank feelin’.”

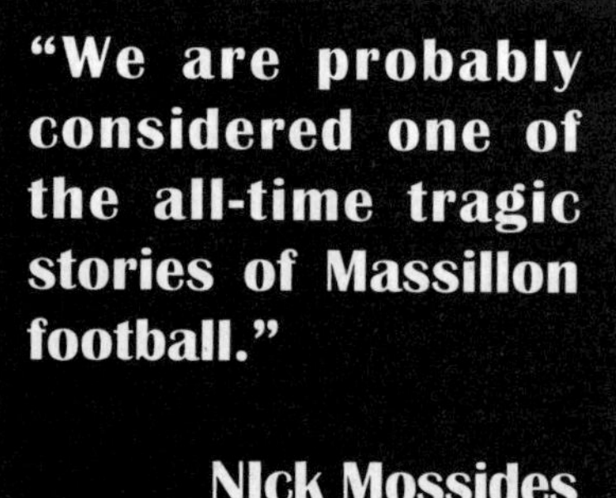

“We are probably considered one of the all-time tragic stories of Massillon football,” said Mossides, who threw two touchdown passes for Massillon’s only scores. “When you think of the most hearbreaking losses in the history of Massillon football, our loss to Ignatius is up there. We are one of the handful of teams since the 1970 team that really had a legitimate shot to win it all. We just came up short.

“It’s almost been like a Curse of the Bambino since the playoff system started. Twenty-two state championships prior to the start of the playoffs,” Mossides’ voice trailed off.

“Maybe if you have so much success early on things have to weigh themselves out. The Yin and Yang of the universe.”

Hollywood Documentary *Go Tigers!* is Critically Acclaimed

Ticket from the premiere of the 2001 documentary Go Tigers! The documentary was well-received by critics.

The year 1999 was a dramatic one in Massillon, but it didn't have anything to do with Y2K.

First of all, the football team was coming off its first losing season (4-6) since 1966. Secondly, a crucial school tax levy that had been defeated in its three previous votes was again on the docket. Finally, Perry Township, a neighboring school district, had sparked a Ohio High School Athletic Association investigation with allegations that Massillon had recruited one of their players.

As fate would have it, a Hollywood film crew was in town getting everything down on high definition film.

Director Ken Carlson, who attended high

school in nearby Jackson Township, wrote and co-produced the documentary *Go Tigers!* about Massillon's 1999 football season.

The Tigers cooperated on the field, producing their first 10-0 regular season since 1982, before falling to Perry in the first round of the playoffs. The town responded by passing the school levy. And Massillon won its court case against the OHSAA, who could not find Massillon guilty of any wrongdoing.

Poster from documentary featuring captains Danny Studer, Ellery Moore and Dave Irwin.

The film debuted in 2001, while the country was in the midst of 9/11 . Despite bad timing at the box office, *Go Tigers!* enjoyed critical success.

The highest praise of all for the documentary came when ESPN hailed it as one of the five best sports documentaries of all time.

Go Tigers! also got favorable reviews from *The New York Times*, *The New York Post*, *The Los Angeles Times*, *Entertainment Weekly*, *The Chicago Tribune*, Roger Ebert and many others. The *Dayton Daily News* described it as almost flawless.

Massillon Head Coach Rick Shepas was okay with the experience. "It wasn't bad," Shepas said. "It was stressful. We didn't know how we'd be portrayed. Ken Carlson did a good job with it."

LEE OWENS

Steve Studer (l) and Joe Studer surround Lee Owens during a happy moment versus Canton McKinley.

Lee Owens was a breath of fresh air for the Massillon Tigers and their fans when he arrived in 1988. The program was going through a down time and the baby-faced coach from Mansfield was just what the town was searching for. It was a job Owens had dreamed of.

"You always aspire to go to the greatest level of coaching that you can," Lee Owens said. "You knew you had reached the top once you coached at Massillon. I always dreamed about it. When I coached in the All-Star game in 1985, a couple of guys pulled me over to the corner of the room and said, 'You're gonna be the next coach here.' That's the first time I thought, 'This might really happen.'"

But Owens was a tough sell for the Massillon job. It took three very influential figures in Massillon history to get him in the fold.

"I talked to Paul Brown and I talked to Earle Bruce. I told Paul Brown that I'd just taken the job in Lancaster. He said, 'That's a good job, but Massillon is the best job I ever had.' I'm thinking, 'Here's a guy who coached the Buckeyes, he coached the Browns and he said, 'If you've got the chance to coach at Massillon, you've really gotta consider it.'"

"I talked to Paul Brown...he said 'If you've got the chance to coach at Massillon, you've really gotta consider it.'"

Lee Owens

Earle Bruce also counseled Owens, who was just 32 when he took the Massillon job. "With Earle Bruce, I said, 'What about my loyalty to Lancaster, I've only been here a year?' He said, 'Don't tell me about loyalty. I stayed with the Buckeyes a year too long.'"

Massillon's superintendent of schools at the time was Al Paris. He, too, gave Owens sage advice, and finally, an ultimatum.

"I give Al Paris the most credit for hiring me. I wanted to work for him. I knew he stood for loyalty. He grew up in Massillon."

Despite the efforts of Brown, Bruce and Paris, Owens still balked. "I turned the job down once or twice. I told 'em I liked the job I had in Lancaster. Then Al said something I'll always remember: 'You won't be asked again.' That was kind of a profound statement. If I turn it down now, it will never happen again."

Owens relented, and was amazed at the welcome he received from the Massillon community.

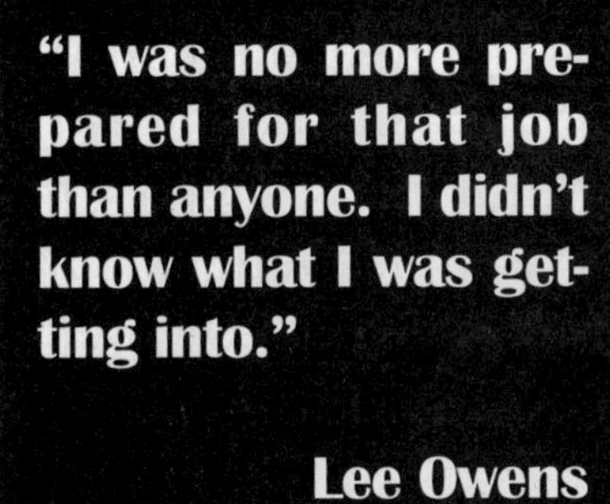

"I was overwhelmed by how important everyone made you feel. They made you feel like you were something special. That was the overwhelming part of it for me."

The enormity of the job hit Owens like a hurricane.

"I was no more prepared for that job than anyone. I didn't know what I was getting in to. Every day was a challenge. On one or two occasions I really questioned whether or not I was worthy of the position. I prayed every day to make me worthy of the opportunity. But I don't think anybody can know what they're getting into until they actually do it. Until they feel the amount of pressure you go through when you play Canton McKinley. And how people want to win that game so much. And you feel a responsibility and an accountability being a coach for trying to find a way to make it happen. And when it doesn't happen, how bad you feel, not necessarily for yourself, but for everyone in the community who builds their sense of worth around that game."

Owens got a surprise during his first practice at Massillon when he looked up in the stands. "I couldn't believe the amount of fans that were there. There were more people at some of our practices than at some of the high school games I had coached. Guys would change their vacation dates to be around for camp. We never went to a practice where the stadium was empty. At Massillon, there were always people at practice. Watching practice. Wanting to know what was going on."

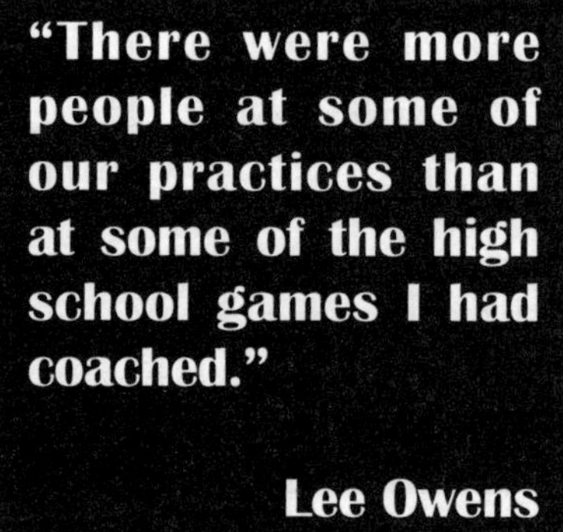

Those stands were a source of inspiration for Owens on game day. "I'll never forget walking onto the field with a couple of guys who I'd coached with for a long time. I said, 'Just take your mind off football for a couple of minutes. Just take a look around this place. It's wild. Look at all these fans. The pageantry. The electricity in the air. This is as good as it gets in high school football. Just suck it in. Take it in.'"

Owens enjoyed working the crowd before games. "People would get there early—always sit in the same seats. So I'd get out of pre-game meetings and walk up in the stands and talk to the folks.

Just make their day. I'd say, 'Look for this. We're going to try to do this tonight.' The people love their team so much, their players so much. You've got to realize, 'Hey, baby, this is *their* team and they're living for it.' You can do a whole lot as a coach to give them the ownership that they want—*that they demand*—and that they're always gonna have."

Sometimes Owens would learn something from the fans.

"A lot of times I'd get pretty good insights from people who would study the team all the time. Outsiders looking in. I'd walk over by the fence and ask, 'What do you think about this guy or that guy?' I'd be shocked at how many times I'd pick up something just by talking to somebody around town who knew something about the team, about one of my players or about a player from another team that we were going to compete against."

Owens was as popular a coach as Massillon has ever had. His days at Massillon are fondly remembered as "happy days" by Tiger fans. A lot of that came through success on the field. Even more was due to Owens' natural feel for public relations.

"It's very important that the public relations isn't taken out of context. A guy who is trying to sell something that isn't really truc or sincere—I don't consider that public relations. For me it was easy to live and die and eat and breath and believe in Massillon football. It will always be a part of me. I'll always root for the Tigers. I think that people talk about me being a good PR guy because I think they can sense a sincere love for Massillon.

"It would be suicide for any coach to go in there and use the program. Massillon fans can just tell if it's not for real."

For Owens, being "for real" meant facing the music during the tough times.

"You know it's hard after a tough loss. You just want to hole up. But that's the worst time to do it. I worked very consciously at being most visible after a loss. I went to church the next day. I wanted to be in the supermarket the following afternoon and at the service club meeting. Because that is when you *had* to.

"You know it's hard after a tough loss. You just want to hole up. But that's the worst time to do it."

Lee Owens

"It's easy to be out in the public after a win. Everybody patting you on the back. I just think that facing up to the people after a tough loss was the most critical time to be out and open. Massillon fans take the losses hard. They want to know why you lost. What are we going to do differently. It's all part of the recovery process we go through. It's horrible, it's so horrible. It's painful. I mean, I'm a terrible loser anywhere, but there, where it's as important as it is, and you're expected to win every game, it even makes it worse. I could never visualize us losing a game there. I could never imagine a reason why we should lose. And the few times we got beat, man it was just death. A little bit of you dies every time."

Owens felt the pressure of being the Massillon coach every day.

"There's no place to hide. Compared to Ohio State or Michigan, you're down there with a million people, it's easy to get lost. But in Massillon, there's no place to get lost. You can't hide. There's no alley dark enough. There's no store you can go to. There's no restaurant you can eat at. You don't ever escape being the coach for a minute. That's the hard part. At times it's hard to keep balanced. I could never get away. I was always answering questions about the program. All year round, 12 months, 365 days of the year, I'm answering questions about the program. It was always on people's minds. Anywhere you go in town somebody would recognize you, somebody would question you. You'd always have to take time and say, 'Here's what's going on, here's what we're doing, here's what's happening.'"

"The Massillon fans applauded like crazy because it was a great contest."

Lee Owens

Along with the attention comes the expectations.

"I knew what the expectations were. We were supposed to win them all, beat McKinley and win the championship. I feel bad about leaving without winning a state title. We had a shot at it."

Owens coached in more than his fair share of heartbreaking losses at Massillon. Owens-coached Tiger teams suffered three one-point losses in four years. Massillon had just 10 one-point losses in its previous 93 seasons. And at Massillon, where winning is the norm, the losses—especially the close ones—are remembered. Owens lost to Austintown Fitch 20-19 in 1988, to Cincinnati Moeller 24-23 in 1990 and in the ultimate heartbreaker, to Cleveland St. Ignatius 14-13 in 1991.

"My first loss was to Austintown Fitch, and it really hurt. We were rolling along at 4-0, ranked in USA Today, and we had a chance to stop their last drive a few times. We dropped an interception. They kicked a 43-yard field goal, and that ball is in the air forever and ever and ever and just crosses the bar. The kid who kicked it goes on to kick for the San Francisco 49ers. Jeff Wilkins. A 43-yard field goal to win it on the last play of the game."

"We lost to Moeller, 24-23, where they throw the pass at the end of the game to win. No turnovers, no penalties by either team. We have three good drives, they have four good drives. They win it in the end with a great play. I felt so terrible for our players. I didn't know what to tell them. The Massillon fans applauded like crazy because it was a great contest. It was one of the greatest high school football games you'd ever witness. It's impossible to get over that.

"The Ignatius loss and Moeller loss were both losses you just don't get over. The McKinley loss (20-7 in 1990) was bad, but it happened. It hurt, but it wasn't like those one-point losses where we played our hearts out. I don't think we really played our hearts out in that McKinley loss.

Owens won the town over

in his first game, a game he remembers well.

"It was one of those things where, 'We've gotta win. We're not going to play it close to the vest. We're going to win these people over from the first get go.' We took the ball down, made a couple of first downs. We got to about midfield and it was fourth down. And I'm thinkin', 'It's now or never.' We called a fake punt and it goes for a big gain. And the people are up on their feet. And I go, 'All right.' And from then on you get a reputation for making that kind of a play call. It was something."

"Lee was kind of a gambler," Paris said, "He was also a very good football coach. He brought in a new type of offense, the run and boot. He was successful with it. He made some quick decisions as far as on-side kicks, quick kicks. Brought a lot of enthusiasm back into the game. And he got a big break when we won the McKinley game his first year here on the muddy field. He was able to win that game, and it really brought the people back together."

"I remember almost every play for that game," Owens said. "We threw a flea flicker for a touchdown with the back-up quarterback, Jamie Slutz. We kicked a field goal in the mud in overtime to win the thing. Our defensive back fell down in the mud in overtime and their quarterback threw the ball to their tight end, who was wide open. The ball went right through his hands or they would have won the game. I remember the rush onto the field. Sliding in the mud. Being hugged by the coaches. Nick Vrotsos and I hugging and rollin' in the mud. Yelling back to the stands,

'I love Massillon!' Those are memories that will last forever. We were the toast of the town. We finally beat McKinley. We passed the school bond issue on Tuesday. We did what we had to do. Ducky Schroeder said, 'You were hired here for one reason, to win this game.' I thought, 'This *is* a big game. We're trying to build a new high school, pass a levy.' It's a lot of pressure on that game. And for it to go into overtime—the first overtime game. To win it in overtime. It was a thrill. It was the thrill of my lifetime.

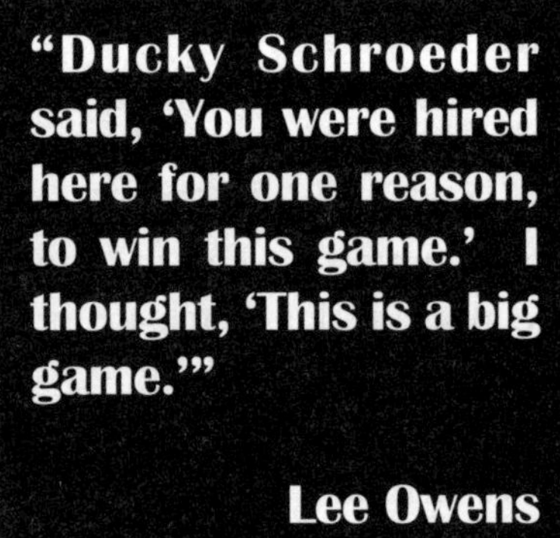

"Lee and I still talk about our most valuable player on that day," Paris said, "the kid who missed the ball in the end zone for McKinley. We laugh about that.

"Lee did a good job. He was a good football coach, a good athletic director. And he was good with public relations. We had some fences to mend at that time. He was able to do that. There were so many people upset with the football program as a whole prior to that. They were very upset that they weren't winning with the previous football coach, John Maronto. Lee had to bring those factions together.

"We received sanctions when Coach Maronto was here. We were on a two-year probation period. And that was

Coach Maronto's last year here and Mr. Owen's first year. The year after that we were able to participate in the playoffs."

"The town was in kind of a renaissance of football," Owens said. "Football had been down. We hadn't been in the playoffs for a while. Now we had the hope of a new high school. We had so many positive things going on. It was a great time. In 1989 we were only 10-3, but our losses were to Cincinnati Moeller, Cleveland St. Joe's and Cleveland St. Ignatius, and I believe they were all state champs. So we lost three games, but they were three great football teams. And we won some big games. We won by some big numbers. It was just a good team. The guys played hard. It was a fun year. In the McKinley game we went over there and scored early, scored on a halfback pass, things just went like they were supposed to go. Whereas the year before we were lucky to win the game, we went over there and it was all us. It was all us from the get-go. It felt good to be able to do that to McKinley. To go over there and kind of just physically grab hold of the game and take it. It's the greatest feeling in the world. You're standing on the sideline. The sun was shining that day. You're just wearin' 'em down and they can't do anything about it. Your kids are playing their hearts out for ya. You paint that picture to them all year long, then it becomes reality. It's a dream come true for you. You just imagine, you want something so bad, then all of a sudden you get it. And you've paid a great price for it. Our kids had really gotten stronger that second year. You could see a difference in the weight room. Steve Studer, the strength training coach, was a big part of what we did.

"We went back to my house and we had a little get together after the game. The phone rings and it's the police. They said, 'Coach, you've gotta come down here.' They had literally emptied out into the streets. I said, 'What can I do?' They said, 'Coach, if you could just come down here and talk to them a little bit and tell them to go on home, we've got a chance.' So I go to the police station, jump up on top of the police car and they run me right down to the middle of town. And I'm saying, 'Hey, this is the greatest football town in American, we've got the greatest football fans in the world, you're all part of this, that's why we're winnin'. But it's probably a good time to go home.' Then they started booing. But, can you imagine, I was a young guy, 33 years old. I'm not very old. You have the police calling you, asking you to move a crowd. Hey, I'm just a ball coach. I'm just a young guy. I'm not anything special. Talk about getting hyped up. It's just amazing."

> **"You just imagine, you want something so bad, then all of a sudden you get it.'"**
>
> **Lee Owens**

Owens' final year at Massillon was 1991. "We made a great run at it," Owens said. "We had a really strong football team. We had a big, big win against McKinley. We had two big playoff wins, one against Akron Ellet and one against Toledo St. John's."

The 42-13 win over McKinley was one of the greatest wins in the historic series. It also included an amazing performance by running back Travis McGuire.

"One of the greatest efforts by a high school player that I ever coached was his 300 yards against McKinley," Owens said.

Massillon knocked off Akron Ellet 28-6 to advance to the regional championship against St. John's. The St. John's game was reminiscent of the Walsh Jesuit playoff game two years earlier. The Tigers fell behind 21-7 before rallying to a 42-21 win. Their next test was Cleveland St. Ignatius.

"All I know is we played them 14-13. It was a great game. We turned the ball over. But it was a good game. It was a *great* game. They just put the drive together at the end to win it. That was for the title, really," Owens said. "You win that game and you're going to win the title. We both knew that. The best two teams in the state—probably the best two teams in the country—were playing that day.

The kicker, Jason Brown, took the loss hard, according to Owens. "He was sad. He was down." Owens said. "Obviously he felt he could have done more to help the team. But we fumbled the ball a couple of times. One play we fumbled, Travis was going to walk into the end zone. There's nobody in the middle of the field. It's perfectly blocked. He can see the end zone. And he mishandled the ball. That would have put the game away."

Owens finished his Massillon career with a 35-13 record. He joined John Cooper's staff at Ohio State, where he served as an assistant for four years. In 1995 he took over at the University of Akron. He led the Zips to a 40-61 record in 9 years as head coach.

Owens inherited an Akron program that had finished 1-10 under Gerry Faust, the former Cincinnati Moeller and Notre Dame head coach. Highlights of Owens' tenure were three winning seasons. Ironically, he was fired after his winningest season in 2003.

"We made a great run at it."

Lee Owens

Tom Stacy, who was head coach at Massillon from 2005-07, was an assistant to Owens at Akron.

"When we came to Akron they had the worst facilities in the MAC," Stacy said. "We were among the lowest-paid coaches in the MAC. I thought Lee did a great job of building that program up. Then a new athletic director came in. A lot of times in Division I the athletic directors are trying to make a name for themselves and move on, and I think that's what happened with Lee. We went 7-5 and got fired. It was a joke in the league. It was a joke."

Owens ended up at Division II Ashland University, where he's built a strong program. In six seasons, Owens was 35-20, including two 9-win seasons and two straight playoff appearances.

TRAVIS McGUIRE

Anyone who was there will never forget it. The greatest rushing performance in a century-old rivalry that has historically featured marquee backs on both sides of the field.

A player playing the game of his life, in *the* game of his life. A childhood dream coming true, unfolding before over 20,000 fans. A once-in-a-century performance that may *never* be matched, in a rivalry that many feel has no match.

Travis McGuire en route to his record-setting 302-yard day against Canton McKinley.
PHOTO: ROBERT C. ERICKSON II, M.D.

When discussing the finest individual performances in the Massillon-McKinley game it's tough to find a more dominating performance than Travis McGuire's on November 2, 1991. McGuire was unstoppable. He powered, spun and sped his way to 302 yards and five touchdowns on that cold and snowy day at Canton's Fawcett Stadium.

Despite sharing carries with another 1,000 yard back, Folando Ashcraft, McGuire picked up 1,976 yards—the all-time Massillon single season rushing record.

McGuire's performance against McKinley is Massillon's single game rushing record. His total outdistances Homer Floyd's 37-year-old single game mark of 263 yards. Floyd's big day also came against McKinley, in 1954.

In terms of career yardage, McGuire rests at number three on the list behind Art Hastings and Ashcraft. Ashcraft and Hastings had an extra year to accumulate their yardage.

McGuire didn't get to play his sophomore season. And his junior season really didn't reveal the success that was in his future.

"We had to boot him (off the team) as a sophomore," coach Lee Owens said. "His junior year he came back and played some, but wasn't really happy. Then he blossomed as a senior. He had to sit out all of his sophomore year. He had some real issues. I think he grew up."

McGuire looks back on his high school years and wonders what if. What if he had more carries? How high could his rushing totals have been?

"My junior year I didn't get to touch the ball as much as I wanted to. That was a little frustrating. Folando got a lot of attention that year as being *the man*. He was their golden boy."

In McGuire's eyes, things didn't really get better his

senior season. He felt he was still in Ashcraft's shadow. "I only touched the ball nine or 10 times the first five games. But I was still gaining 100 yards. I guess they finally realized 'We've got to give him the football.'"

McGuire didn't get the number of carries he felt he deserved until the Canton McKinley game, after Ashcraft had sprained his ankle the week before.

McGuire picks up yardage as a junior against McKinley.

"That's why I touched it 36 times. Then it sunk in to the coaches. Then I touched it 30 and 28 times in the playoffs. But that's what it should have been the whole year. If I would have touched it that much all year, I would have had well over 2,000 yards."

Owens was well aware of the tension caused by the two-back system. But he thinks the system actually *helped* McGuire.

"I know," Owens said, "I had to battle both of those guys all the time because we tried to have a one-two punch at running back. I know Travis was always upset. And it was part of him growing up.

"We had a good one-two punch, so they couldn't just key on him all of the time.

So that worked in his favor. He had a great season. He had some great guys blocking for him. We had a great scheme."

Earning the career rushing title at Massillon was important to McGuire. He feels his limited opportunities, especially as a junior, kept him from reaching that milestone. "I wish I could have done more my junior year so I could be the all-time rushing leader at Massillon," McGuire said. "That should be my record. That's a nice one to have. If I had even a half decent junior year I could have gotten it."

McGuire and Owens ended up going to Ohio State together, though how they both ended up there is a matter of conjecture.

"Coach Owens and I became pretty close," McGuire said. "He started coming over at night taking my recruiting calls. I couldn't study. I was getting call after call. It was outrageous. A couple nights a week he took my calls."

McGuire said he was getting mixed signals from Owens.

"At one time he told me not to go to Ohio State. Then all of a sudden he changed his mind and said to go to Ohio State. When I first was going to take a visit there he was telling me, 'Aww, I don't think you should take a visit there.' So I said, 'I am going to take a visit.' I had a private plane that flew me up there. On Monday he said, 'How'd you like it?' I said 'I liked it.' He said, 'Oh, I don't think that's the place for you.' So I'm thinking I should take my coach's advice. Then all of a sudden it all changed. A week later he said, 'Maybe you should reconsider Ohio State.' You know, maybe they said if Travis comes here we'll make you a coach at Ohio State. You've gotta wonder. He was a great coach at Massillon. But there's been a lot of great coaches that didn't get that opportunity to coach at Ohio State. So I don't know. He says he got the job on his own merits, but it happens all the time that an athlete goes places and the coach goes with him."

Owens is aware of McGuire's feelings, but doesn't agree with them. "I don't know how he feels about me," Owens said, "I know at times he's been critical. He says he went to Ohio State just because I went there or that he helped me go there. Or whatever. Which is totally untrue, but he was just a young kid talking."

Whatever the case, McGuire's career at Ohio State never quite got off the ground. It's another classic case of *what if* for McGuire.

Whatever the case, McGuire's career at Ohio State never quite got off the ground.

Owens sees McGuire's adjustment being a lot like his own at Ohio State. Owens was used to the power and prestige that goes with the head coaching job at Massillon. McGuire was used to being the All-Ohio superstar running back at Massillon. Owens said the adjustment in Columbus was huge for both of them.

"He wasn't patient enough," Owens said of McGuire. "Like a lot of Massillon kids, they're used to being..." Owens stopped and reflected. "He was going through the same withdrawal I was going through. He just didn't handle it very well. If he would have just waited his turn, he might have played in the pros. Every other back from that team is in the pros. Every single one of them.

"When he left Ohio State we went around and around. He quit two or three times and I literally went down and got him back, got him back, got him back. When he quit the last time, I couldn't find him. Jim Tressel signed him up at Youngstown State. It was over. I couldn't do anything for him with Tressel, that didn't work out. He went to Rhode Island, that didn't work out. When I got the Akron job he only had one year of eligibility left and we couldn't make that work out."

McGuire looks back on his decision to attend Ohio State with some regret—mainly because of the opportunities he had coming out of high school. "I got recruited by everybody, Notre Dame, Florida, Florida State, all the Big 10 schools." McGuire said. "I went to visit University of Miami, Indiana, Ohio State and Michigan. I had a visit to Tennessee, but I canceled it. I pretty much could have gone anywhere. I always wanted to play in the Big 10."

McGuire was neck and neck with future Heisman Trophy winner Eddie George when they entered Ohio State together in the spring of 1992.

"I actually played good in the spring. I never knew anything about Eddie George. I had no clue who Eddie was. We were even on the depth charts pretty much through the spring. If I had it to do over again, I probably never would have left. But I got married while I was there, our marriage was kind of—I probably would have been divorced because of the life I had to try to lead. The guys wanted you to go out with them, they *expected* you to do it. It was a strain, going out and coming home early in the morning. It was a strain on my marriage, we had a little baby.

"I know it looks great to everyone else looking in from the outside, but they weren't living in my shoes."

Travis McGuire

"Then starting running back Robert Smith says he's not coming back, then all of a sudden he's coming back. So here I am, I know I'm not going to play. I saw my future. I mean, that's pretty much how it was going to be. We had Raymont Harris, Robert Smith, Butler By'not'e, me and Eddie. I'm the only one of the group who didn't play in the NFL. My redshirt freshman year I actually carried the ball 35 times and Eddie carried it about 40—so we carried it about the same amount of times. I led the team in rushing against Pittsburgh."

Owens remembers the running back situation while McGuire was at Ohio State. "He would have had a chance like those other four guys," Owens said.

"I had a bright future, I just wasn't happy," McGuire said. "I know it looks great to everyone else looking in from the outside, but they weren't living in my shoes. They weren't livin' the life I was livin'. They didn't know how it felt for me bein' there. I don't know. I had a lot of added pressures. They don't give you enough money to survive—even with the scholarship. For your apartment, they only give you $600 a month. And you're not allowed to work,. What was I supposed to do? I have a little baby to feed, I have a wife, full time school. And right after school you have football, whether it's in season or out of season. You had to lift weights. You had to eat with the team. You didn't get home 'til 8 or 9 at night. And that's an every day routine, all year round. It was tough.

"I've got articles from the *Columbus Dispatch* where I dominated the spring. And I didn't even move up on the depth chart. I'm thinkin', 'This is pretty much how it was at Massillon where they sit you down and say, 'You might be better, but you ain't going to play until your time.' That's kind of frustrating. Because I proved I could play every day as a freshman. A lot of times I made our first team defense look stupid. There were articles saying 'McGuire turning it on at running back.'

"Raymont and Butler were one and two. Both played a lot. Then it was me and Eddie, and we hardly ever played. They kind of had Eddie ahead of me, and I'm thinkin', man, if this is the case, I'm not going to play until I'm a senior. If it's no way, if they already know Eddie's going to be the starter next year, what can I do? Even if I do what I did in the spring, where I proved I was just as good if not better, but still was behind him, how was I going to beat him out?"

Owens understood his frustration, but he tried to convince McGuire of the value of sticking around.

"You know, most of those guys had to wait until they were seniors to play," Owens said. "I just could not get into his head. I *knew* how bad he felt. I knew he thought he was getting jerked around, wasn't getting enough turns. But I just had to try to convince him, 'Be patient, wait your turn, it's going to work out. It's going to be fine. You belong here, we want you here.' Then he got married. There were some financial problems. It was kind of one thing compounded onto another. But I wanted so much for him to stay in school there."

"After the bowl game, before I transferred, I talked to coach," McGuire said. "He was like, 'You and Eddie are pretty even, I'm not sure who's going to be the starter in the spring.' But I don't know, I just had a feeling deep inside that Eddie was going to be the starter, and that I was going to play, but not as much as I wanted to. And I wasn't going to get to show my talents until I was a senior. Then I was thinking, 'What if the first game of my senior season I blew out my knee again? And I never got to showcase my talents. I'd never get the chance to make the money I was determined I was going to make like the rest of them. That's why I decided to leave.

"I wish I had the maturity I have now, going into Columbus. It would have been easier. But I think that only grows as you get older."

FOLANDO ASHCRAFT

"The first time I started on the kick return team there must have been 15,000 people in the stands," Folando Ashcraft said. "I was used to playing in junior high where you could count the number of people in the crowd. The ball came to me and I just froze and it hit my chest and fell on the ground. Then I realized and I was like, 'Awe man, I guess I better run it.'"

Ashcraft is Massillon's number two all-time rushing leader.

Ashcraft was a sophomore seeing his first varsity action. By the time his Massillon career was over he had gained 2,794 yards, second best in school history. He also finished second all-time in rushing touchdowns with 39.

Ashcraft loved playing for Massillon.

"I'll tell you, it's electrifying. You can't explain how good it is when you get out there. It's like you're in a professional game. That kickoff return started the whole thing."

Ashcraft was half of the

most productive one-two punch in Massillon history. Along with Travis McGuire, Massillon's number three all-time rusher (2,511 yards), Ashcraft must have given opposing defensive coordinators nightmares.

"When we played, we communicated a lot," Ashcraft said of his relationship with McGuire. "One of us would go out and run first and see how hard that particular defense was hitting and come back and tell the other one. I'd be like, 'Trav, they ain't hittin' real hard, I can smell a 200-yard day.' Or he'd come back to me and say basically the same thing. He'd say, 'Man, these cats are arm tacklin', they're grabbin' your jersey, they ain't hittin' nobody. We're gonna have a big night.' We just knew from the beginning of the game if we were going to have a big game. We'd be in the backfield while Nick Mossides would be up there under center. We'd say, 'Man, they're in the 4-4, we're gonna run right through 'em."

Ashcraft was half of the most productive one-two punch in Massillon history.

The Buddy LaRosa classic in Cincinnati was one of Ashcraft's early highlights as Massillon's feature running back in 1990. "We played Covington Catholic, a team out of Kentucky," Ashcraft said. "They were undefeated for two years. We had an opportunity to not just go down there and end that streak but we were able to show everybody down there what Massillon football is all about. We got to play in

Riverfront stadium. I went out and had a 200-yard day. It felt real good. I got to sit in the press box with Paul Brown. Not everybody on the team, just a couple of guys got to visit with Paul Brown and talk about football and life. I just remember him telling us about his days in Massillon and how he grew up there. How he left and went to Miami of Ohio. He explained how he got into coaching. He was coaching at Massillon and he said out of all that coaching, even in the pros, Massillon was the best for him, because that is where football started, in Canton and Massillon. And that the Cleveland Browns are named the Browns because of him and that he started the Bengals, and that those colors come from the Massillon Tigers. He said he always had the Tigers in his mind in everything he did in his life. That really kind of pumped us up."

Ashcraft and McGuire had the same hero growing up: Jerome Myricks. "My goal as a kid growing up was to be like Jerome Myricks. I wanted to be as good as him or *better* than him. I figured if I could be at least *like* him I'd be good, real good. I still think to this day that he's the best running back to put his hands on the ball.

"I really didn't have any intention of being the number two all-time leading rusher in Massillon history. That never really crossed my mind. I just wanted to wear the *Massillon* across my chest."

McGuire learned the spin move that he made famous from Myricks. "I saw him do it when I was in midget league," McGuire said. "He didn't do it as much as I did, but he did it."

"We grew up together,"

Ashcraft said of he and McGuire.

"We go back to when we were little kids, six to seven years old. I grew up on 16th Street. Everybody in Massillon called them The Projects. Travis grew up off of Pearl, down there through the little woods. Way back in midget league we were on the same football team."

> **"We go back to when we were little kids, six to seven years old."**
>
> **Folando Ashcraft**

While Ashcraft started running the ball as a sophomore, McGuire was struggling. "He had a terrible attitude when he was a sophomore," Ashcraft said. When he was in junior high he ran all over everybody. He was coming off of a knee injury as a sophomore and he really wasn't playing much, so he got a real attitude."

Mossides remembers the same thing. "Travis was a wide receiver as a sophomore. He told everybody where to go. He was not easy to deal with at all, for *anybody*. But his junior year he came back with a different attitude, different mindset, and was a starting running back. Folando got more carries than him and was better than him as a junior. Travis really came into his own that senior year. I mean, the strides that he made personally, more than anything, he became as good a teammate as anybody our senior year. A good guy to be around. It was night and day from the guy he was as a sophomore."

The topic of who was the best back, McGuire or Ashcraft, became a hot topic in the Massillon community in 1991. "They were trying to make a big deal about who was going to gain the most yards, me or Travis," Ashcraft said. "One week he'd have a 150-200-yard game, then I'd have one. I just shut everybody down because I got tired of talking about it. I was at Touchdown Club one week and I said, "Here's the deal right here. I really don't care about how many yards I've got and how many yards Travis has. I will give my yards to Travis if he can get us to a state championship. That's all I'm concerned about. I don't care anything about yards or anything else you guys are talking about.' That used to tick me off when they used to talk about that, because I was never an individual person at all. Anyone on the team will tell you that."

"I will give my yards to Travis if he can get us to a state championship."

Folando Ashcraft

McGuire was very aware of statistics and very much wanted to be the career rushing leader. "Folando got a lot of attention our junior year as being *the man,*" McGuire said. Folando got a lot more credit than I did. He earned it I guess. He touched the ball a lot more, but I thought I was the better player."

Ashcraft felt that McGuire's behavior as a sophomore affected his junior season. "Our junior year he had that mindset that the world was out to get him," Ashcraft said. "Sometimes he would say certain things, and sometimes he'd even say them to me, but usually he'd say them to somebody else and it'd get back to me. So I just had to talk to him. I was tired of hearing about that thing with the yards. He really had this thing in his mind his senior year, 'I'm going to have more yards than Folando.' And I was like, 'That's fine with me; win me a championship. If I've got to ride your coattails, let's do it.' So we used to have some words, some scuffles. It was all in how he thought he got treated his junior year. I think I wound up with something like 1,182 and he had something like 535 yards in 1990). If he would have stepped up to the plate more his junior year, like he did his senior year, who knows, he could be the number one rusher of all time. He's into those individual things, I'm not."

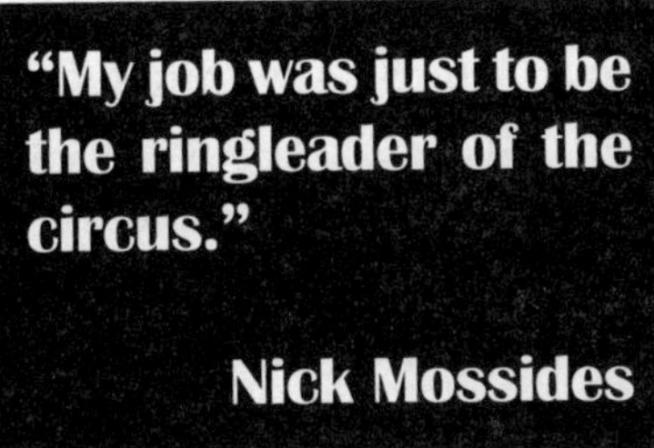
"My job was just to be the ringleader of the circus."

Nick Mossides

Mossides was right in the middle of the two running backs. "My job was just to be the ringleader of the circus," Mossides said. "To make sure everything was going, flowing in the right direction. I got to check off a lot at the line of scrimmage. When you have two great backs like that you basically have a run with Travis one way or a run with Folando the other way. The best two backs in the state were on the same team. And it could have divided our team into factions, a Folando faction, a Travis faction. Because you wouldn't think there were enough balls to go around. But to their credit, they had a great relationship with each other, enjoyed spending time with each other, not just in football, off the field, too. They really developed a good friendship. Folando had such an easy-going, good hearted personality. Liked to joke, liked to mess around, laugh. But when it came time to play, he strapped it on. The guy was a gamer, he came to play. He wanted the ball in his hands and his stats prove that out. Travis had a certain ability that all great running backs have. The vision. The ability to kind of get through creases when it doesn't look like there's much there. To spin, to juke, to do whatever it takes to get extra yards. Folando had that breakaway speed, but he was a lot more physical kind of a guy."

Ashcraft feels McGuire's attitude was his downfall. "And it carried on in college, Ashcraft said. "And that's too bad because I expected to see him step up to even the next level because he had that much potential. I never would tell *him* that. He used to always talk about his agility and all this other kind of stuff, which was true. You know he *was* a good running back. And I believe he could have played anywhere else. If he kept his head on straight we'd be watching him play in the NFL. But things happen sometimes. Some people get a certain amount of success and let it get the best of them."

B. J. PAYNE

B. J. Payne became a Massillon Tiger at age five, playing on the field in Paul Brown Tiger Stadium after a Massillon game in 1980.

"It was an absolutely great experience."

Payne's family moved to Massillon so he and his

B. J. Payne followed a successful football career and a stint in professional wrestling with a promising career as a high school coach. Here he's addressing his Lexington squad.

"We were playing football on the field with a paper cup," Payne said.

brothers could play for the Tigers.

"We actually moved up here

because my brother was going to be a freshman in high school and my other brother was going to be in seventh grade. My mom wanted to find a place to raise her boys to play football.

"We lived in North Carolina and she went on a trip by herself for a week. She visited five schools, Massillon, Canton McKinley, Erie Cathedral Prep, Altoona and Alaquippa. She visited Massillon and absolutely fell in love with it. A month later we were living there."

Payne and his brother, Charles Calhoun, were both first team All-Ohioans at Massillon.

"My first memories were of watching my brother playing for Massillon. I'd sit in the end zone where the cheerleaders put up the banners on the fences. After the games I'd take the banners home and run through them Saturday morning just like the players ran through the paper hoop on Friday night. Like any other kid in Massillon, I wanted to grow up to be a Tiger. It was bred into me from the time we moved up here."

Payne started at defensive tackle in 1992 for a Massillon team that finished 5-5. It was a tough experience.

"Tough, tough," Payne said. "There's so much pride in Massillon football, it was tough having to walk around town and look people in the eye when you're on a .500 team, knowing how much everyone in Massillon cares about the game of football. That was tough to swallow. Having to look the old-timers in the eye, the coaches that you grew up watching and respecting, like Nick Vrotsos or Jim Letcavits, and knowing all that they've given to the program. Looking at them was very tough. I think that everybody knew that when I stepped on the field I gave everything I had and then some. I hope I made those guys proud."

The Tigers bounced back in 1993. Massillon fans were starting to talk about a possible state championship as they worked through the regular season undefeated.

"My mom wanted to find a place to raise her boys to play football...She visited Massillon and fell in love with it."

B. J. Payne

"Going into the McKinley game we were 9-0," Payne said. "We lost that game, then lost in the second round of the playoffs to Walsh Jesuit. We were a group of guys who had been together. I don't think we had one kid miss a workout in our senior year. We were about one or two players away from being a championship team."

Payne credits two coaches for developing him into an All-Ohioan.

"Steve Studer had me ready physically and mentally," Payne said. "Coach Stu got me ready in the off-season and Coach Gary Wells got me ready in-seaosn. Coach Wells is probably the most intense man I ever knew in my life. He was our defensive line coach. He was nuts. And I say that in a good way. He made you *want* to play the game. He made you *love* to play the game.

"I loved playing in Massillon. I loved playing in front of 12,000 people. I loved celebrating after sacks, after big tackles. I used to do dances. I'd do baseball swings. I absolutely loved the show business part of it. Because for me to do that I had to be making big plays. I made a big play and let everybody know I made a big play. I set the record for tackles for loss. My junior year I had 21, my senior year I had 19, which is something I was very proud of. To make a big stop in the backfield was huge for me."

Payne started his college career at Murray State, but transferred to Mount Union. He had become a father, and being close to home, and his son, was paramount.

"I fell in love with Mount Union," Payne said. "My first year there we lost in the national semifinals. We won the national championship the next three years. We were 54-1 my four years there."

Payne recalled an early incident with Mount Union's legendary head coach Larry Kehres.

"We were doing a two minute drill, and you don't mess around with his two minute drill, that's his baby. You just don't mess it up. And one of the offensive linemen pulled me down by my facemask. I got on top of him and just started punching him. I was whalin' on him, beatin' the crap out of him.

"Kehres just grabbed me by the facemask, rammed me into the fence and said, 'This isn't Massillon. You hear me?' And he went off on me for about 10 minutes. I said, 'Yes sir.' I walked away. I said, 'Just don't let him grab me by my facemask again.' "When I said that he had me up against the fence again.' He had seen lots of players from Massillon who had trouble adusting because they were used to the way it was in Massillon. Especially players who went to the small schools. But Larry's a guy who's won 10 national titles. Has ice in his veins. Never got nervous about anything. But he says he still breaks into a sweat any time he comes to Paul Brown Tiger Stadium. Just the aura. He gets nervous coming there to watch a game. He has the utmost respect for the program. When I graduated he said to me, 'Listen, I never told you this, but you have no clue how much I respect Massillon.

"We practiced on Massillon's field for a game we were playing in Wisconsin because Mount didn't have artificial turf at the time. He said that he was more nervous for that practice than he was for the game that week. Just being in Paul Brown Tiger Statdium with all the tradition."

Payne said there were similarities between Mount Union and Massillon.

"I think it's similar. Everybody around school and around town supports the program. Now the tradition hasn't been around as long at Mount as it has at Massillon. The size of the crowd was the biggest difference. It was about half the size of the crowd that was at Massillon. Big games at Mount we got 6,000 people. The national championship game there'd be 8,000 people. We had bigger crowds when we played average teams at Massillon. That was the biggest difference.

"I would give up one of

my national championship rings to beat McKinley. The Massillon-McKinley game is so special. As crazy as it sounds, it's bigger than the national championship game for Division III. That's not taking anything away from Mount Union and the experience we had there. But the Massillon-McKinley games, there's no comparison to it as a player. I never had a chance to experience it as a coach, but as a player it was awesome. All the activities all week long. I was fortunate as a captain at Massillon that I got to go to all the luncheons and the banquests. You got no sleep that week. It's crazy. At Mount it wasn't like that. We did TV and radio, but it wasn't an all day thing. We had practice and it was back to the hotel. It wasn't like that for Massillon-McKinley. You had stuff all day, then you've got practice at night. You try to go out to eat with your family and you see 50 people out and they want to know what is going ot happen, are you guys going to beat McKinley. Then you've got your own family. My whole family, every night, asking me about it. My brother came home from North Carolina for the whole week. It was absolutely nuts.

"I had a very good career at Mount. I was All-American my senior year.

Payne spend four years as a professional wrestler after college.

"It's something I wanted to do since I was five years old," Payne said. "I signed with the WBF, which is now the WWE. I was in it for four years until I injured my neck. It's a lot tougher than people think. For four years I had to watch everything I ate. Had to work out three times a day. You don't have much of a personal life. Everything was so strict.

In high school and college Payne was known for painting his face. Not so in wrestling.

"It's funny, when I got into wrestling I didn't paint my face.

"I was always goofy, goofy, goofy, and then when I put on my paint before the game I was serious. That was my personality. I loved the showmanship part of it.

"Massillon Head Coach Jack Rose loves this story. We're playing St. Vincent my senior year and we're beating them 14-7 at halftime. We weren't playing well in the first half. I remember sitting in the front row in the locker room. Jack starts going off and he looks at me and he says, 'And you, go wipe that stuff off of your face, you're playing terribly.' I looked at him. He said, 'I'm serious. Go wipe it off.' So I went in and wiped it all off.

"After the game Jack came up to me—of course we blew the team out 42-7—and said, 'B. J., I'm sorry. You were the only guy I saw in the front row.' It ended up being the best game of my senior year. I had like 12 tackles in the second half. It motivated me."

Before transferring to Mount Union, Payne told Kehres of his face painting habit.

"I told Kehres, 'I just wanted to let you know that I paint my face for every game.' Kehres thought it was just a little black under the eyes. He used to always call me Gene Simmons. It was just one of those things that made me tick."

JACK ROSE

Life as Massillon's head coach was not easy for Jack Rose.

Rose's record at Massillon from 1992-97 was 48-17. He won 74 percent of the time. That wasn't good enough in Massillon. And Rose understood that.

He committed the unforgiveable crime in Massillon; he failed to beat arch-rival Canton McKinley.

Jack Rose led Massillon to a 48-17 record from 1992-97.

Rose's record against McKinley was 1-6. It was more than the Massillon fan base could stand.

"Your tenure here is judged on that game," Rose said. "I beat Austintown Fitch *at* Fitch. I beat Fitch four years in a row. Well, *nobody* beat Fitch four years in a row. I beat Cincinnati Moeller two years in a row. I've done some things here that haven't been done before. But that's not enough because of that last game."

If you take away Rose's losses in "that last game" his record is a glittering 48-11. Of course, you can't take away those losses. "My detractors said I didn't know how important that game is," Rose said. "I had a guy ask me after the 1993 game, 'Is it better to be 9-1 and lose to McKinley or be 1-9 and beat McKinley?' That's how important this game is.

"McKinley's the season. I don't want to be 1-9, but if you're going to win one of ten, it would be the McKinley game."

The McKinley losses were as hard on Rose as they were on the Massillon fans. "Yeah, it bothered me," Rose said. "It's just something I've got to live with. There's nothing I can do about it.

"In four years (1993-96), we had three 9-1 seasons," Rose said. "We were 34-6, which is pretty good. In most places people'd never want you to leave if you're doing that well. Two of the three 9-1 seasons were bad because we got beat in the last game. We were 9-1 one other time and that was a good 9-1 because we beat McKinley."

"In four years we were 34-6, which is pretty good. In most places people'd never want you to leave if you're doing that well."

Jack Rose

Rose was counseled by legendary Massillon head coach Leo Strang, who led the Tigers to three straight state championships (1959-61) and two national championships (1959, 1961).

"Leo always said, 'Jack, enjoy it, because you've just

got to understand, it's never going to be good enough. Even if you win the state championship here, there will always be people who will complain about something that happens. And you just can't let it get to you.'

"I tried to do that," Rose said "It's tough."

Strang never had it as tough as Rose; he was 6-0 against McKinley from 1958-63.

"Leo always said, 'Jack, enjoy it, because you've just got to understand it's never going to be good enough.'"

Jack Rose

Al Paris was the superintendent of schools who hired Rose in 1992. It wasn't a popular hire from the start. There were rumblings that Rose, who was an assistant on Lee Owens' (1988-91) staff, was not the choice of the hiring committee that was assembled to evaluate and interview the coaching prospects. Paris said that is not true.

"I'll rebut that," Paris asserted. "I don't recall any time we chose a football coach while I was there, whether it was Lee Owens or Jack, when it wasn't recommended through the committee."

Massillon hadn't promoted an assistant coach to the head job since 1945 when Augie Morningstar took over and produced an unusual 5-0-5 record. It became an unwritten rule that Massillon didn't promote assistant coaches to the head job.

"That was tough," Paris said. "We had three people on staff that really wanted that job: Jack Rose, Phil Mauro and Joey Studer. All three were good football coaches. Jack had won the state championship at St. Thomas Aquinas (in Louisville, Ohio)and was runner-up another year. We had some other candidates. Brian Cross was a candidate. I believe Kerry Hodakievic was in on that."

"There were people on the committee who didn't want to hire an assistant coach, they wanted to go outside."

Al Paris

Both Cross and Hodakievic went on to be head coaches at McKinley.

"There were people on the committee who didn't want to hire an assistant coach, they wanted to go outside," said Paris. "After we went through the interview process they thought that Jack could do the job. It helped in a couple ways, because there were no teaching jobs open at the time, so we were able to maintain the same staff. Coach Studer and Coach Mauro said there was no ani-mosity and they were able to stay on board. Jack had a good staff. It went well, other than the fact that we hit McKinley when they were really good."

As Rose's losses to McKinley mounted, the pressure on Paris also increased.

"There were quite a few calls

to my office near the end," Paris said. "You just have to listen to them. I'd tell 'em that he has a contract and we will not break a contract, but when the contract is up, everything you're telling us, plus our evaluation, will be considered in deciding whether we keep him or let him go. And that's the way you handle a situation like that. I would say, 'We'd be very unprofessional not to honor a contract that we ourselves put together and offered to this man. Most of 'em accepted that. *Most* of 'em. Some of 'em wanted me to go right out and fire him right away. Have another law suit like we had in the past with Mike Currence in 1985. That cost us a lot of money. It also split the community. Embarrassed us. Al Hennon did a good job in the closing of Jack's contract, got him out, helped him get a job elsewhere. Things worked out well for us."

"...after that loss to Moeller...we came in...and on our voice mail was the full version of the song 'Hit the Road Jack.'"

Al Hennon

Hennon, superintendent of schools during Rose's final three years at Massillon, remembers Rose's last year at the helm, in 1997.

"There's one thing that I remember during Jack's tenure," said Hennon "It was after that loss to Cincinnati Moeller." Massillon squandered a 24-7 fourth quarter lead and lost 28-24 to heavily-favored Cincinnati Moeller, the state's third ranked team.

"We came in on the Monday morning after that game and on our voice mail was the full version of the song 'Hit the Road Jack,'" Hennon said. "I was devastated to hear that. It really angered me because I was loyal to Jack."

The 1997 season was a death knell for Rose at Massillon. He felt the end was coming prior to the season. "I'm probably not going to be renewed," he said then. "I know that."

"Jack knew what was going on. He knew his time was coming to an end...Jack couldn't beat McKinley."

Al Paris

"Jack knew what was going on," Paris said. "He knew his time was coming to an end. He didn't have a problem with it. No one *likes* to get fired. He knew the situation. You win in Massillon you stay. If you don't win, things get rough. There isn't a coach here who didn't have the same problem. Jack couldn't beat McKinley. He only beat 'em once."

"Rose felt fans' expectations were out of line.

"This is not the Massillon of 40 years ago," Rose said. "There was a lot bigger population then. The town was pumping out steel like crazy. People were coming in and getting jobs. It's a whole socioeconomic difference. But the team's been the one constant. It's always been there. I think that's added more pressure to the kids today. The town has the same expectations.

We just don't have that population base to draw from that a lot of our opponents do."

Rose received counsel from another Massillon coaching legend, Earle Bruce, who won two state championships (1964-65) at Massillon and was head coach at Ohio State (1979-1987).

"When you lose here, it's almost like a death. Especially if you lose to McKinley."

Jack Rose

"When I was up at Kent State as an assistant coach, prior to joining Owens' staff at Massillon, Earle told me that Massillon was the toughest job he ever had. So when I got this job I asked him if that was true. He just said, 'It was the toughest job I ever had.' I said, 'Come on coach, tougher than Ohio State?' He said deliberately, 'I said it was the toughest job I ever had.'

"That's pretty tough," Rose said.

"When you lose here, it's almost like a death. Especially if you lose to McKinley.

"You know it takes so much out of you. By November, I'm a shell of what I am in August. It's almost like an endurance race. It just wears you out. The pressure, the stress. It's a very, very, tough job."

WILLIE SPENCER, JR.

Willie Spencer, Jr. will always be known for two things in Massillon. He'll be known as the son of Willie Spencer, the 1970's star Massillon tailback who beat the odds by run-

Willie Spencer, Jr. is interviewed after leading Massillon to a 42-41 overtime victory over Canton McKinley in 1994.

ning straight from high school football to pro football, then fell into trouble with the law. He'll also be remembered as the quarterback who led Massillon to a scintillating 42-41 overtime victory in the 100th Massillon-McKinley game in 1994. Both remembrances can bring tears to his eyes, but for different reasons.

"I've kind of got the double whammy with my dad," Spencer said. "People are always comparing me to him. It's like I can't shake him. If I do well, they're gonna compare me to him on the football end. If I fail they're gonna compare me to him on the other end. Even my bad knee, just like his. I can't shake this man. But you know what? He blessed me by giving me the genes to go out and play football.

"I've kind of got the double whammy with my dad. People are always comparing me to him."

Willie Spencer, Jr.

"Our relationship isn't where it needs to be. There's a lot of animosity on both ends. My end is, as I get older I understand more. I know he was a young man at the time. He was making a lot of money playing pro football. I understand he was spending a lot and he got hurt and he was used to that lifestyle. He started selling drugs. I know how that is. I've seen guys do that. But I can't understand that he forgot about me and my sister. True, he went to prison. I could care less that he went to prison. That's done with. But he forgot about us. He not only forgot about us then, he's not doing anything now.

"On *his* end he feels like I got this house built for my mom and my stepdad and he's like, 'What have you done for me?'

"I could be a lot further in life if I would have had

some guidance behind me. I didn't have that. I've learned on the run my whole life. He's been where I'm at. He should have been there more. He wasn't there at all. He should have been there."

Willie Jr. has grown up with the celebrity of being Willie Spencer's son.

"I've always been a celebrity," Spencer said. "I've always been known in Massillon because of my father. Everybody knew me regardless of whether I played football or not, because of my father. As far back as I can remember, everybody always talked about my dad. Telling me stories of the things he used to do. They said I'm just like my dad. He kind of paved the way for me. It's nice to follow somebody that did well while they were here. There were a lot of expectations. I met 'em."

Spencer and his father are the only father-son combination to be selected first team All-Ohio in Massillon history. Willie Sr. was a first team All-Ohio running back in 1971. Willie Jr. was a first team All-Ohio quarterback in 1994. Willie Sr. played at 6'4", 220, Willie Jr. at 6'3", 200.

Spencer has fond memories of his playing days and is proud to be remembered for his heroics in the 100th game. He's constantly reminded about it.

"People always talk about that," Spencer said. "I know it's special because every time I watch it I can feel it. I can feel how special it was. I chill up and tear, fightin' tears back. I wish I could have just been a spectator and seen it. Maybe I could view it differently. Maybe if I could have set back and seen myself, maybe I could look at it differently. But I know it was big and it was special and it will be with me the rest of my life."

Spencer calmly led the Tigers in the 100th game.

"I wasn't nervous," Spencer said. "I was just enjoying myself."

The play Spencer will forever be remembered for was a lateral in overtime that led to Victor Redrick's 15-yard touchdown run.

"It was a play we were working on in practice all week," Spencer said. "It was the second play of overtime. All I remember is I just faked the dive up the middle and came around the end and saw the corner there and I faked the pitch and cut up. And then the backside defensive end came up and tackled me and I pitched it out. I'm glad Victor continued to stay in pitch phase with me."

Spencer calls signals in the 100th Massillon-McKinley game.

After committing to the University of Akron, Spencer turned a lot of heads with a spectacular performance in the Big 33 game, which pits the top 33 players in Ohio against the top 33 players in Pennsylvania.

"That game was fun," Spencer said. "It seemed like however I threw the ball it was just on point. I never felt that way ever before. I was in a zone. I never felt that again. It was the first time I could just drop back and throw the ball and it just felt so good."

Spencer played for former Massillon coach Lee Owens, who was the head coach at Akron. It was a rocky road for both individuals.

After redshirting his freshman season, Spencer was given a shot at the starting quarterback job as a redshirt freshman. It lasted four games.

"Coach Owens benched me after the fourth game," Spencer said. "When that happened it wrecked my confidence. I was used to being the man."

"Willie was lazy in the classroom and a hot dog on the field," Owens said. "We knew that when we recruited him. We couldn't keep playing him at quarterback because he was always on the borderline academically. There was no telling for sure if we were going to lose him. I told him if he could just be more solid we'd keep him at quarterback."

Spencer claimed Owens never told him why he was benched.

"That hurt Willie the person and that hurt Willie the player," Spencer said. "The only thing I blame coach Owens for is the way he handled it. He hurt me more than he helped me. I was the best player at that position. I earned it. I just wish Coach Owens would have explained to me why he did what he did. Why did he feel like I wasn't doin' what he expected? He never sat me down and spoke to me."

"We made him a receiver," Owens said. "He kind of had a hard time being a receiver because he's always been the star of the show at quarterback. When he didn't have the ball in his hands he wasn't very good."

"That kind of kills me to this day," Spencer said. "I don't know why I was benched. If he would have explained some things to me I don't think I would have self-destructed like I did. I started drinkin', I started smokin'. It wasn't because I wasn't the man anymore, it wasn't because I got benched. I just didn't *understand*. That ate at me. It killed me in a sense."

Owens felt he did all that he could to help Spencer.

"Coach Owens benched me after the fourth game. When that happened it wrecked my confidence."

Willie Spencer, Jr.

"Nobody was going to take care of Willie better than I was," Owens said. "Everybody knows that."

Despite his problems, Spencer put together a good season for Akron and was mentioned as a potential All-MAC receiver. But his off-the-field problems took their toll and he ended up with academic problems.

"We fought to get him back,"

Owens said, "but his appeal didn't go through."

Spencer got new life when he joined George Whitfield at Tiffin University. Whitfield had followed Spencer at quarterback for Massillon.

"George Whitfield set it all up," Spencer said. "He looked out for me. The coaches looked out for me at Tiffin. I was still at a low point. I was still drinkin' when I got there. But as I started there my life started changin', my grades got better. I was able to play in 1999, had a good season. Then some more problems."

Academic troubles ended Spencer's career at Tiffin. But he did draw the attention of NFL scouts with his talent. He got a look from the San Francisco 49ers.

"John McVay, the San Francisco 49ers' General Manager, flew me out there first class; everything was good. I don't know if it was because he coached my dad in professional football, if that's how it happened. He did what he could for me."

Spencer spent three days with the 49ers and got to observe two of the greatest receivers in NFL history.

"I saw Jerry Rice and I saw his work ethic," Spencer said. "I saw Terrell Owens. I saw their work ethic. You should see those guys, my gosh."

Spencer came ever-so-close to making the roster with the Washington Redskins after signing a $200,000 contract.

"Every time I caught the ball during my workout with Washington I ran all the way to the end zone, just like Jerry Rice did. I was doing real well. Reporters started interviewing me after practice."

One published report from Redskins camp was flattering of Spencer. "Willie Spencer keeps getting better and better. He was one of the highlights of the second week of camp, making play after play. He has good speed and good hands, and also has a tenacious attitude. With his size, speed and toughness, Spencer is making a stronger case for a roster spot than anticipated. He is listed among the top six of 10 wideouts on the depth chart."

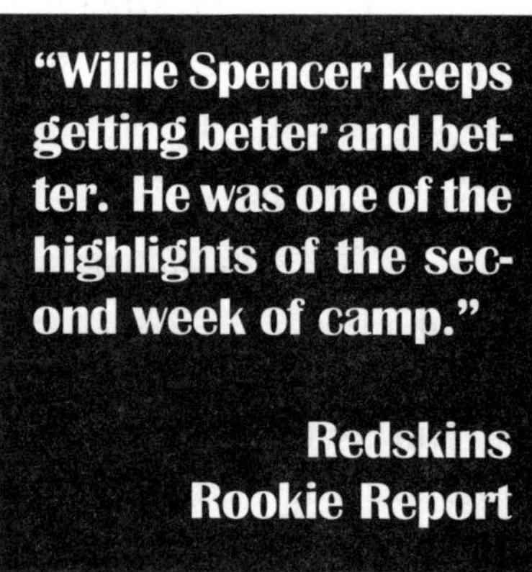
"Willie Spencer keeps getting better and better. He was one of the highlights of the second week of camp."

Redskins Rookie Report

Spencer feels a remark he made in an interview soured head coach Marty Schottenheimer on him.

"They asked me a question and I said that camp reminds me of Tiffin. I didn't mean it like they took it. They took it like I was tryin' to compare Champ Bailey and our guys to Tiffin. What I meant was I was starting to feel comfortable. I was dominating a little bit. If I hadn't said that I feel I would be there right now."

After being cut by the Redskins, Spencer caught on with the Chicago Bears, signing a $225,000 practice squad contract.

A knee injury kept him from ever seeing the field in an NFL regular season game. He had highlights in NFL Europe, but the knee injury effectively ended his football career.

Spencer encourages today's Massillon players to appreciate their high school playing days.

"The guys playin' now need to know and appreciate what they're doin' now, because 85-90 percent of them won't play another game. And if they do play, the couple of guys who do play beyond Massillon, it's probably not going to be at a big time program. It's never going to be the caliber of a Massillon. So they really need to appreciate what they've got.

"I realize I'll never feel that way again. I never felt that at Akron. I never felt that at Tiffin. I never felt that in the pros. Massillon's special. The game is so pure. It's not pure anymore once you leave high school It's not pure in college and it's not pure in the pros. It's not really fun anymore. It's fun, but it's not what it used to be.

"Massillon's special. The game is so pure. It's not pure in college and it's not pure in the pros.

Willie Spencer, Jr.

ELLERY MOORE

Ellery Moore's life has been shaped by poverty, bad choices and teenage incarceration. But it's also been marked by belief, positive role models and an ability to overcome obstacles and ultimately succeed.

Ellery Moore was the Defensive Player of the Year in the State of Ohio in 1999.

Belief has been a constant—and something that's helped Moore through the tough times.

Moore had tough times in a childhood that was poor enough that he couldn't afford to play organized youth football, even though he had great potential.

"I couldn't afford to play midget football because, you know, you have to buy stuff. My family wasn't financially set to put me in that position. But I was always playing backyard football in Shriver Park, so I was always *ready* to play football.

"I didn't start playing football until middle school—at least not *organized* football," Moore said.

But Moore is philosophical about his childhood, which he admits was tough.

"It was the plan that God had for me," he said. "I know there are plenty of children out there that had it harder than me, so I really have no complaints about my childhood. It wasn't a childhood that a child should have, it was drugs, alcohol and divorce, single-parent living. I made it through and I'm doing pretty well now."

> **"It was the plan that God had for me. I know there are plenty of children out there that had it harder than me..."**
>
> **Ellery Moore**

When he was 13, he moved to Canton to live with his father. An incident there could have sent Moore into a downward spiral.

"I went to juvenile detention," Moore said.

"Basically being tricked by a public defender and a prosecutor to say that I did what I did was bad," Moore said. "I was a young kid. My parents weren't in the room. It was lead detectives and prosecutors. I was scared to death. At the age of 13 I had no idea what was going on. It was a scary situation."

Over a year in juvenile detention changed Moore. So did the mentoring of Corrections Officers (COs) in the detention center.

"When I went to juvenile, I just grew up," Moore said. "I knew I wanted to get out and play for Massillon. I wanted to play both ways for Massillon."

The COs said, 'Well, you know, it's going to be hard to play both ways.' They saw the talent in me. They said, 'It's going to be hard, but if you believe in it, you can do it.'

"They were letting me know that they saw a different type of person in me than a lot of the kids they get in there. They told me to stay focused and hopefully things would come together for me.

"It wasn't easy by any means. Any time you're locked away from friends and family and somebody tells you when to wake up and shower and eat, how to wash your face and how to tuck your shirt in, it's not easy.

"The whole thing for me was knowing that I didn't belong there. Knowing I didn't deserve to be there for the specific reason they put me there. I was in a lot of trouble. I was doing a lot of *little* things that my environment enabled me to do. Things I could do and still be okay in my environment. Things like getting in stolen cars, getting in fights. Doing dumb things that I thought it was okay to do because other people were doing it. I made the choice knowing it was wrong, that it *wasn't* right. I was still able to understand right from wrong."

Moore found that organized football was a good outlet for his aggression.

"I got to hit somebody and they said I wasn't going to get in trouble for it," Moore mused. "I thought, let me try this right here."

While Moore was working

to straighten his life out, he was watching his mother struggle.

"She had a personal battle with addiction," he said. "But she tried to make sure my brother and I had a roof over our head, even if it wasn't a nice roof. She tried to make sure we had clothes on our back, shoes on our feet. She sacrificed a lot and she's changed a lot even to this day. She's just a wonderful woman."

"She had a personal battle with addiction, but she tried to make sure my brother and I had a roof over our heads, even if it wasn't a nice roof."

Ellery Moore

Moore met a pivotal person in his life when he entered high school in Massillon.

"When I got there, I was out of shape. I didn't know how to work out. But Stu (strength coach Steve Studer) got hold of me and told me, 'You will be one of the strongest kids, if not the *strongest* kid that ever came out of this school.' Ever since he told me that in the weight room that day, I just worked hard and left as one of the strongest kids ever at Massillon.

"Stu was the closest thing to a father figure that I ever had, inside of football and outside of football," Moore said. "I had Christmas dinners and Thanksgiving dinners with his family. I love them to death. What a wonderful family. That family just embraced me and loved me so much. Stu and I had a very special relationship. He saw the potential in me."

Under Studer's tutelage, Moore developed into a captain by his senior year at Massillon.

I just wanted to represent Massillon to the fullest," Moore said. "We wanted to be the best three captains who ever came to Massillon. We wanted to be the best. Danny Studer, being Stu's son, he had respect from that aspect alone. I knew he loved it and was going to work had. And Dave Irwin took on the role of quarterback, the classic quarterback in high school. The guys wanted to look up to him."

Moore realizes how his life could have turned in the wrong direction.

"I could have gone the other way, used my background as an excuse to continue that bad behavior," he said. "But the thing about life that I've grown to understand is that I'll continue to make mistakes. I will never be perfect. I'm a Christian, so I know this. I can strive and strive and strive, but I'm going to fall short sometimes. And at that young age, I was starting to understand that. That's why I kept pushing and trying to do something better with my life.

"My time in juvenile detention turned me around. I saw just how quickly my life could be taken away. Just how precious time was. Everybody thinks that the next minute is promised to you. It's not. I went in to juvenile detention at 13 and got out at 15. It matured me. It made me realize that I had to make sure that I understood the consequences of every choice.

"I would say that 20-30 percent of my teammates at Massillon came from a rough situation. It might have been drugs, it might have been alcohol, it might have been a lack of financial support, lack of any emotional support. Your father figure's not there supportin' you at a football game or a practice. Or your mother's not there supportin' you. I mean, as a kid that emotional support is almost more important than money. 'If I can look in the stands and I can see my mom cheering for me. Or if I look in the stands and see my uncle there or my grandfather.' That's amazing for a kid. If you get some support from somebody who cares about you it goes a long way in a young man's life."

Moore felt a lot of love and support from the city of Massillon during his senior year of high school.

"The city just embraced us," he said. "Once we got on a roll and were fighting and clawing to get victories, the city, the whole town, just walking down the streets, the love you would get was just amazing. I'd tell my college and professional teammates about that. A lot of people say they understand it because they always hear about Massillon, but they really don't know. I have never had a better feeling than that. We were rock stars in our own right. People knew us *everywhere* we went. Somebody always wanted to talk to you, somebody wanted an autograph, somebody wanted you to meet their son. That's what it was like.

"There was a lot of pressure. But we put 90 percent of the

pressure on ourselves as young kids wanting to be superstars at Massillon. Wanting to represent Massillon and be a Massillon Tigers to the fullest."

A Hollywood team was in town filming a documentary on Massillon football during Moore's senior year. They focused on Moore and Studer and Irwin as the team's captains. They also focused on a school levy that had failed four times and was up for a vote at the end of the football season.

Moore, an outgoing and well-spoken young person, found himself using his football popularity to help campaign for the levy's passage.

"The school levy was huge at that time," Moore said. "It was sad at the beginning. But when we started rolling you could just see the whole demographic change. It was amazing to feel at that age, as a 17-year-old, that you had that much power to do that."

The Tigers finished the regular season 10-0 in 1999, the first time since 1982. Moore was selected first team All-Ohio and named the outstanding defensive player in the state. Joe Paterno recruited him to play at Penn Sate. Everything was going great until one of Moore's choices backfired on him.

"I didn't worry about my SAT scores," Moore said. "I was just like, 'I'm Ellery Moore, I'm from Massillon. People are going to make sure that I'm taken care of.' It was that kind of attitude which ultimately could have destroyed me. I had to wake up. So once I didn't get to attend Penn State I realized, 'Okay, Ellery, you were playing a little too much. You lost track of the things you should have focused on. Let's get back into gear."

Moore spent a semester at Kiski Prep, a college preparatory school in Pennsylvania, after graduating from Massillon. Colleges were still beckoning.

"I was still getting offers from some pretty big time schools," Moore said. "I chose Kentucky. I was planning to play right away and I wanted to leave after three years. I thought that was the best opportunity to play against the type of competition that would get me to the next level. I was playing against Florida, Georgia, Alabama, LSU. I mean these are Top 10 programs every year. I knew I was going to play against that type of talent and really see if I was good enough to go to the next level."

Moore started strong and was named to the SEC's All-Freshman team. But injuries and a coaching change kept him from delivering on the promise of his freshman year.

"I tore my MCL and my meniscus the eighth game of my freshman year against Mississippi. That laid me up for the rest of that season. I came back for the fall. So I bounced back pretty quick from that. I started a couple of games that year.

"Then the coaching staff changed. We went to a 3-4. That kind of took away from my explosiveness and technique. We finished 7-4 my sophomore year. Then we ended up on probation and losing scholarships. It was tough."

At the end of his college career Moore was looking forward to playing in the NFL.

"I thought I was going to be drafted," he said. "That didn't happen."

He did get an opportunity with the Cleveland Browns.

"I went in and worked out for Head Coach Romeo Crennel and signed a free agent contract. I got cut the last week of training camp. I came back to Lexington and played a couple of years of indoor football."

Moore had another chance at the NFL when he participated in a mini-camp with the Cincinnati Bengals.

"I ended up getting cut. NFL camps are very tough. Very intense. You are on edge wondering if you are going to have to see the coach and turn in your playbook. That's tough, walking into a job every day knowing you could be fired for no reason. Not because of poor play, not because of poor performance, just because another guy from another team might have gotten fired. And that happens. But it's part of it. We all understand that. It doesn't stop it from hurting so much."

Moore has continued to toil in the lower ranks of professional football. He's 28 now, and his body has suffered many of the slings and arrows of playing a collision sport like football.

"I'm still enjoying it," he said. "My body's getting a little tired. I'm pretty sure I'm done. I still have an agent. I talked to him just yesterday about going to a United Football League team in Harper, Connecticut. If that comes by, I might try again. I've really still got the itch to play."

Corey Hildreth

Massillon's All-Ohioans

2000
Justin Zwick, David Abdul, Kreg Rothoff, Perry James.

2001
Justin Zwick, David Abdul, Shawn Crable, Devin Jordan, Justin Princehorn.

2002
Devin Jordan, Ricky Johnson, Shawn Crable, J. P. Simon, Marquis Johnson.

2003
Billy Relford.

2004
D'Angelo McClendon.

2005
Andrew Dailey, Troy Ellis, Brian Gamble, Brett Huffman, Antonio James, Paris McCall, Shawn Weisend.

2006
Andrew Dailey, Brian Gamble, Bobby Huth, Steve Schott, Corey Shane.

2007
Corey Hildreth, Steve Shott, Steve Yoder.

2008
Michael Clark, Cooper Ivan, Matt Rose, J. T. Turner.

2009
Bo Grunder, Spencer Leno, Jeff Myers, Robert Partridge, Devin Smith.

TEAMS 2000s RECORDS

81 WINS — **40** LOSSES

7 State Playoff Appearances
1 State Final/4 Final Fours

2000
8-3
State Playoffs
Head Coach: Rick Shepas

M	Key Games	Opp.
21	St. Ignatius	36
13	Canton McKinley	9
13	Marion Harding	17
332	***Season Totals***	***204***

2001
12-2
State Final Four
Head Coach: Rick Shepas

M	Key Games	Opp.
35	Canton McKinley	19
27	North Canton	7
20	St. Ignatius	49
554	***Season Totals***	***237***

2002
11-3
State Final Four
Head Coach: Rick Shepas

M	Key Games	Opp.
34	Canton McKinley	17
23	Perry	21
20	Warren Harding	21
557	***Season Totals***	***151***

2003
4-6
Head Coach: Rick Shepas

M	Key Games	Opp.
12	St. Ignatius	37
6	St. Edward	27
8	Canton McKinley	40
201	***Season Totals***	***269***

2004
4-6

Head Coach: Rick Shepas

M	Key Games	Opp.
13	St. Ignatius	38
7	St. Edward	37
7	Canton McKinley	20
284	***Season Totals***	***227***

2005
13-2
State Championship Game

Head Coach: Tom Stacy

M	Key Games	Opp.
21	Canton McKinley	3
21	St. Edward	17
17	St. Xavier	24
488	***Season Totals***	***204***

2006
7-5
State Quarterfinals

Head Coach: Tom Stacy

M	Key Games	Opp.
10	Canton McKinley	7
41	Massillon Perry	20
10	Toledo Whitmer	14
368	***Season Totals***	***216***

2007
6-4

Head Coach: Tom Stacy

M	Key Games	Opp.
52	Mentor	56
56	Warren Harding	0
23	Canton McKinley	20
320	***Season Totals***	***191***

2008
6-5
State Playoffs

Head Coach: Jason Hall

M	Key Games	Opp.
24	Jordan (UT)	27
17	Canton McKinley	0
7	North Canton Hoover	14
308	***Season Totals***	***195***

2009
10-4
State Final Four

Head Coach: Jason Hall

M	Key Games	Opp.
21	Canton McKinley	35
10	Canton McKinley	7
17	Cleveland Glenville	31
360	***Season Totals***	***248***

Story of the Decade 2000s

Penalty-filled Playoff Loss Leads to Near-Riotous Scene, Arrests, at Tiger Stadium

It seemed like every successful play was penalized. Massillon was flagged 15 times in their first- round playoff game in 2000 after winning a court decision over the Ohio High School Athletic Association. With each successive flag the Massillon fan base seethed, suspecting a fix was in against their team.

The final dagger was a holding penalty on a 53-yard touchdown run by All-American quarterback Justin Zwick with four seconds left in the game. The flag, thrown some 20 yards behind the play, sealed the Tigers loss to Marion Harding, 17-13.

The loss set off a surreal scene at Paul Brown Tiger Stadium that saw fans hurling plastic bottles from the stands. Five people were arrested when fans rushed the field. One irate fan accosted an official.

"I heard rumors that it was Clair's way—because we were in the middle of the Jessie Scott recruiting thing—this was Clair's way of making a statement," said Superintendent of Schools Al Hennon, referring to the officiating during the game. "I don't know if one guy has that much power."

Clair Muscaro was the commissioner of the OHSAA when Massillon was being investigated after neighboring Perry High School accused them of recruiting running back Scott. Muscaro's power as commissioner made him essentially the judge and jury when it came to interpreting the rules and handing down punishment to member schools.

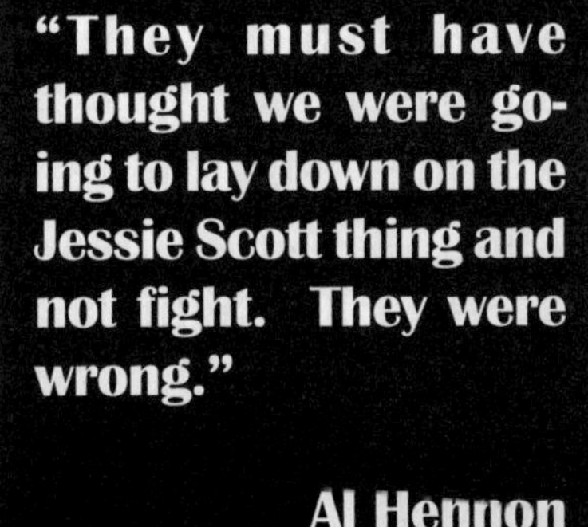

Hennon was a central figure in the drama brought about by the ensuing legal battle that Massillon brought against the OHSAA.

The "statement" Hennon suggested Muscaro was making involved what many Massillon fans felt was an intentional effort to eliminate the Tigers from the playoffs.

"I know that there were a lot of negative feelings across the state toward us," Hennon said. "They must have thought we were going to lay down on the Jessie Scott thing and not fight. They were wrong. I remember it getting back to me that one of the board of control members from northeast Ohio called us a rogue district. A guy named Schumacher. So I knew the negative feelings were out there. Human nature is human nature. There might have been a guy or two on that officiating crew that would have taken the opportunity, if the call was close, it was going to go against us. It was a very difficult time in our athletic life here. It was a tough game to watch. I was standing with Justin's father, Bill Zwick, when the flag comes in behind Zwick's touchdown run. We were standing where Justin passed us and we saw the referee come and pull out the flag. Justin was already crossing the goal line by the time the flag landed on the ground. That is just a call you don't make.

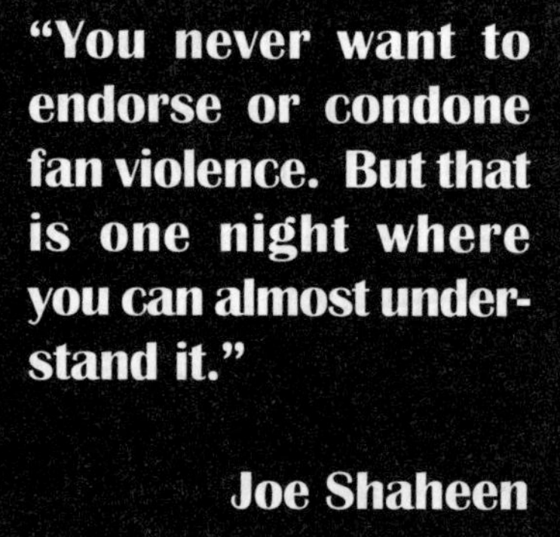

"People could have had a burr for us, or the officials could have been incompetent," Hennon speculated.

"You never want to endorse or condone fan violence. But that is one night where you can almost understand it," said Joe Shaheen, sports editor of Massillon newspaper, *The Independent*. It was clear to me that the officials were out to get Massillon that night. I've never seen anything like it. There were nine holding penalties. I've never seen anything like it in my life. And the final straw was Zwick's scramble at the end of the game. That kind of made me ashamed to be covering high school football. It was clear that the officials or *an official* had an agenda that night, and they were not going to let Massillon win that football game. That might have been, in my mind, Justin Zwick's finest moment. He wasn't gonna let 'em lose that game and the officials literally took it away from him. Because at the end he had run into the end zone. That was like watching a boxing match and they just weren't gonna let the one guy win. Like I say, I would never condone fan violence, but you can definitely understand the frustration because they were not going to let Massillon win that football game. It was so blatant. I'll just never forget, he was running down the field, he was way past it and all of a sudden you see a flag."

"It was kind of ridiculous," Justin Zwick said of the officiating. "We're on the goal line once and punched one in and they call holding on our tight end. It was a quick hitter and they called holding."

It got to the point where the players expected to see a flag every time they made a good play.

"Right after I scored that touchdown I turned around immediately, just to see if there were flags on the field. Of course, there were. You just kind of get that feeling, if something good happens they're going to call something on us."

Zwick recalled the play, which has to go down as one of the most exciting in Massillon history, despite the outcome.

"It was third and long," Zwick said. "It was a pass play. I rolled to my right and saw they were dropping their guys in coverage. They weren't really bringing a lot of pressure. So I just took off. I was trying to get the first down, we needed it. I just cut back across the field. Somehow I got to the end zone. It was weird. I was thinking to myself, 'Don't get knocked out of bounds like you did in the St. Ed's game.' In the St. Ed's game I had a long run and I kind of ran out of gas and the guy caught me. I was telling myself, 'Don't get caught like that.' Then after I scored, I saw the flag and I was upset. That would have gone down as a playoff win. It would have been a pretty big play. I was just in disbelief."

For Hennon, it was an easy decision to fight the OHSAA's ruling that Massillon had recruited Scott.

"Very simple," Al Hennon said, "I did not believe that the OHSAA or Perry had credible evidence to support that we had talked to Jesse Scott."

The investigation was initiated after Perry High School head coach Keith Wakefield wrote a letter to Muscaro alleging people involved with the Massillon football program had talked to Scott about transferring to Massillon.

> **"It was clear to me that the officials were out to get Massillon that night. I've never seen anything like it."**
>
> **Joe Shaheen**

"The letter was a year old before we knew anything about the Jessie Scott situation," Hennon said. "That angered me, and the people around here know that when I get hot and angry, I'm gonna fight. And they were in for a fight from the get go. Because I didn't believe they had evidence to support *anything*. There was a lot of 'He said, she said.' I can't tell you to this day if Jessie Scott was talked to or he wasn't. But they tried to try it in the newspaper. Keith Wakefield tried to try it with the coaches in Stark County. With people like Paul Farrah sending a letter to the OHSAA that said, and I quote, 'I can't tell ya who, but somebody from Massillon's talkin' to my kids.' And this is when he was at Tuslaw. Give me a break. We followed up on every one of those things, either Assistant Superintendent Bob Rohrer or myself. We talked to people to say, 'Hey, what have you got? If you've got something we'll take action. We don't want our reputation tarnished with this. We've been through this before.' But that to me smelled of a set-up. Keith Wakefield had just applied, but didn't get an interview, for the Massillon job. Things just didn't smell right to me. When you think about it, that was both a professional issue and a personal issue with me. Professionally, you're saying we're running a dirty program, but you haven't given me the opportunity to talk to anybody about it.

"The first thing we get called into is a kangaroo court and the second thing we were lookin' at was the death penalty in this thing. Because we knew, given our past history, if this thing didn't go well for us, it would have been like Canton McKinley in 1962 who was forced to forfeit their season. I wasn't going to let that happen. I maintain that I showed how I react to situations. I contend they never gave me anything that said, 'This person's wrong, that person's wrong.' I still don't believe Jeff David did anything. I don't believe Rick Shepas did anything. Because the letter was written while former Massillon head coach Jack Rose was still here. All the rumors flying around, it was ugly. It was mishandled by the OHSAA. *Totally.* I will *never* forget that."

Rose was Massillon's head coach from 1992-97.

"But that to me smelled of a set-up. Keith Wakefield had just applied but didn't get an interview for the Massillon job."

Al Hennon

Jeff David, the chairman of the Paul David Trust, is a former Massillon player (1977-78) who was an assistant coach during the Scott case. He remains close to the football program today. David's father, Paul David, founded Camelot, a national music retailer that at one time had 400 locations across the nation.

Profits from the sale were reportedly $380 million. The foundation is a philanthropic leader in Stark County, Ohio.

In 2008 Jeff David built a $3 million, 80,000 square foot indoor practice facility as part of the $6 million "Dream" project for Massillon's Washington High School. The project includes plans for a new 18,000-square-foot locker room and sports medicine and health sciences complex at the stadium.

It was a "Mr. David" who was alleged in Wakefield's letter to have spoken with Scott.

Shepas was Massillon's head coach (1998-2004) during the court case and playoff loss.

"I wasn't even there when that started," Shepas said. "All of that stuff was prior to me getting there. If I'd have recruited Jessie Scott he'd of had a heckuva lot more yards and carries than he had," Shepas said with a laugh.

"There was a time when I was very close with Clair," Hennon said. "I was the site director for the state championship games for nine years under Clair. He counted on me to make some calls.

"And I'm not sure that his reaction wasn't based on the fact that he had to distance himself from me in that Jesse Scott situation. He may have been fearful of getting tagged with, 'Well, you're close with Al.' I'm sure somebody said that to him. So Clair did a complete turn around. And not that I expected—or anybody here expected—a favor or any kind or a grace period. I just expected fairness. And we didn't get it from start to finish in the Jessie Scott thing. And to this day, I'll fight at the drop of a hat on that thing. Because I still believe that we were mistreated by Keith Wakefield and the Perry administration. We were mistreated by the Ohio High School Athletic Association and some of the coaches in Stark County. It's still upsetting to me.

Shepas wasn't happy with the way things played out in the Scott case.

"Jessie was a great kid," Shepas said. "He won the case and won his right to play. Massillon wasn't absolved, nor was I absolved or vindicated of anything.

I don't think anything good came out of it. I think it was the one thing that tarnished a great season by a bunch of great Massillon kids in 1999. It wasn't a distraction. Our kids rallied around it. Our kids were fine. Jessie Scott was a part of the success. He was a role player. He touched the football. But he wasn't the key guy."

The 1999 Tigers finished the regular season 10-0, then lost to Perry, Scott's old school, in the playoffs.

The Tigers were hoping for a deep playoff run in 2000. The Marion Harding game ended those hopes.

"I don't think there's any question they were out to get us," Shepas said. "It wasn't too far into the game that it became obvious. We had 153 yards in penalties and they had 51. The calls didn't go our way.

"Could I understand why the fans would be upset," Shepas said rhetorically. "Absolutely. I can understand why. Pent up frustration from the entire game. I think it was the release of what had escalated during the course of the game."

Shepas saw the potential for trouble as the game ended.

"I remember just getting the team off the field," he said. "Our number one priority was the safety of our players with all of those Coke bottles flying. We just got 'em the heck off the field."

Rick Ulum was in charge of the game for the Massillon police department.

"We talked as the end of the game approached," Ulum said. "We knew that if there was a call that determined the outcome of the game against Massillon, we could have problems. We made a plan to get the officials off of the field.

"There were so many penalties that the Massillon people were convinced that the officials had it out for them and they were being cheated," Ulum said. "Then there's a play that costs them the game. It wasn't like there was just one play that all of a sudden caused everybody to explode. People were already getting the attitude that the calls were going against Massillon. Then to have a call that determined the game...it was the last straw that the people couldn't take.

"Our number one priority was the safety of our players with all of those Coke bottles flying. We just got 'em the heck off of the field."

Rick Shepas

"I remember when they started throwing bottles. There was an isolated bottle or two thrown at the end of the game. Then everybody started throwing them like crazy. It just got out of control. Then it went from 'Who cares about the bottles,' because we had people on the field trying to confront the officials.

"We were trying to get control of the crowd and get the officials off the field," Ulum said. "I don't know if there were 25 to 50 people who came out on the field. Not any more than that. When they started seeing people getting arrested, that kind of calmed things down.

"We had a person confronting a referee. That was our first concern right there. We had to get the person away from the referee. He got in his face and pushed him. We got in between them and grabbed him and told him he was under arrest.

"We have 20-24 officers working games. We had to call officers from the end zones and the stands to come down to help on the field.

"I grabbed three officers and we kind of circled the officials. These officials' lives were in serious danger. You don't know what these people are liable to do to them. You knew they were probably in danger of some serious physical harm if not worse than that. We made five arrests. We kept the officials surrounded and escorted them off of the field. There might have been one or two people who got close to the officials, but except for the initial person who got on the field and got right in the official's face, I don't think anybody else got that close. We had 'em pretty well surrounded so they were escorted out without any problems. I don't remember any significant group trying to overrun us en mass and trying to get at the officials. There was never any danger of us losing contrrol of them and them being in the situation of being at the mercy of the crowd, which was lucky for us. Because you're aware that if these people want to come down out of the crowd, you've got 10-12,000 people and 10 officers. You realize if a bunch of people decide that they're going to come on the field and try to cause a problem you're going to have a serious issue trying to maintain control and you're going to have to take some drastic measures to make sure nobody gets hurt. We got the officials into the officials' locker room until everybody cleared out of the stadium. People were yellin' as they went past the officials' locker room, pounding on the door or pretending they were trying to get in the door. People were upset as they were leaving the stadium. But the door was shut and we had an officer watching the door.

"I grabbed three officers and we kind of circled the officials. These officials' lives were in serious danger."

Rick Ulum

"We've never had anything like that happen. We never anticipated Massillon people behaving like that. You have a few troublemakers that you know about. But you never expect wholesale bottle throwing and people rushing the field."

While Shepas understood why the Massillon fans reacted like they did, he didn't condone it.

"Just because we're upset about things doesn't mean we can do those things," he said. "I don't think anybody felt differently about that."

"Those are terrible memories," Hennon said. "We had people react to a call. I never wore black and white stripes because, frankly, when I coached, I didn't like them. Some folks reacted wrongly. They weren't good role models for our kids in regard to the bottles that were thrown. I got hit by one. My band director got hit by one. But the two guys who got arrested, one lived in Tuslaw and the other lived in Perry. Neither one of 'em had a Massillon address. Our police were on top of it from the beginning. It was ugly. But Clair took an opportunity to try to jag us again and reprimand us. And what's amazing about that is Clair Muscaro runs those games. So if he reprimands us, he reprimands himself. Because he didn't do a good job of taking care of a crowd. And it wasn't a crowd. It was two people. Our fans are smart football fans. They might be some of the smartest in the nation. And they're the most vocal. If they see something they don't like...you don't throw a flag following a play, you just don't do that. Our fans understand that. And that's what caused the reaction. It was a touchdown. We took a lot of flack for that. That was a black eye for our program. Our detractors outside of Masslllon had a hay day with that one. But we reacted. We worked hand in hand with Judge Elum. It was just an unfortunate incident."

Muscaro, who has since retired, didn't wish to discuss the incident. "That was a long time ago," he said, "I don't really remember. I'd rather not comment. I will say that the Massillon people were very cooperative throughout the whole process."

Games of the Century

Massillon Kicks Perry With 2002's Version of "The Drive"

There was a lot on the line when Massillon and cross-town foe Perry squared off in the second round of the 2002 playoffs.

Perry had a two-game winning streak over the Tigers after losing their previous 10 games to Massillon.

There was also the lingering bad blood from a nasty court case in 2000 when Massillon was found innocent of accusations that they recruited Perry running back Jessie Scott in 1999.

Matt Martin was brilliant in Massillon's 23-21 playoff win over Perry.

Massillon appeared to be in charge, leading 20-7 late in the third quarter. But the real fireworks were still in store for the 17,000 fans at Canton's Fawcett Stadium.

Perry scored to narrow the gap to 20-14, but it looked like the Tigers could run out the clock.

Then a missed handoff between Matt Martin and Tuffy Woods turned things upside down.

"That happened a couple of times during the season," Martin said. "I'd open one way and he'd go the other way. The blame was on both of us.

He went the wrong way and instead of just tucking it and following him I tried to bring it back and we kind of missed the handoff."

"Tuffy turned the ball over," head coach Rick Shepas said. "We were in a tough game. I just remember being on the sidelines thinking, 'We've got to get the ball back to Tuffy. I can't let the season end on a fumble in a place like Massillon.' So we got the ball back to Tuffy a little later on. I just wanted to make sure he knew we were with him."

Perry recovered the fumble and marched the ball downfield and scored with 1:17 left in the game.

"With the magnitude of the game and everything, if you lose you're out. It seemed pretty devastating," Martin said. "When they scored that touchdown it was like, 'Well, we have one last chance.' So we had to make the most of it." Martin responded by putting together one of the greatest drives in Massillon history.

"We went on to execute the two-minute drive specifically to kick a field goal," Shepas said. "I remember how patient Matt Martin was distributing the football."

"Coach Shepas just said to take what the defense gives," Martin said. "Don't try to force anything."

"I said, 'Look, we're not going to go for the touchdown unless they give us the opening. As long as they're sittin' soft on us we're going to just play in front, get our yards, and go for a field goal."

"There were a couple of intermediate routes to Stephon Ashcraft and Billy Relford," Martin said. "Devin Jordan was on the backside by himself and he came up to me after one of the plays and said he could beat the guy deep. He said, 'Just throw it up and I'll go up over him and get it.' So I looked off the safety and waited and threw it up and he went up and got it just like he said he would. That got us in range. We threw a couple of out routes and Max Shafer came in and got the 35-yard field goal at the game's final gun to give us a 23-21 win."

"We put it on the field goal kicker and he made a great kick," Shepas said.

Martin was in line to be the game's star even before leading the dramatic final drive. He finished 21-29 for 294 yards. He also connected on two touchdown passes to Jordan.

The 2002 Tigers went on to defeat a strong Pickerington team 14-0 before a Final 4 match-up with Warren Harding.

Warren had beaten the Tigers 31-27 in Week 9. The rematch at the Rubber Bowl promised to be just as exciting.

Warren ended Massillon's playoff march 21-20 in overtime.

This time Shafer missed the kick.

"One day you're the hero, the next day you're not," Shepas said. "To me that's a great lesson that a young guy only gets to learn every now and then. To find out how short term success really is and how fickle people really are."

"Warren scored in overtime and made the extra point," Martin said. "Then we scored on third down and didn't make the extra point. We thought there was going to be another overtime and we were ready to keep going. It kind of ended to suddenly. Just like that and we were done."

Games of the Century

2005 Tigers Break Iggy Curse with Dramatic Last Second Win

Shawn Weisend scores the winning touchdown. PHOTO: JOE NAGY

Cleveland St. Ignatius had dealt Massillon a couple of serious doses of heartache on their way to a 8-0 series record against the Tigers. A one-point defeat in a Final 4 match-up in 1991 was particularly devastating.

But the 2005 Tigers were determined to end the streak that gnawed at team and the town. "We didn't care about the other teams that never beat Ignatius," said Andrew Dailey, an All-Ohio safety on the 2005 team. "We just cared about the team that was going to play Ignatius that night. We were ready to be the first team to beat 'em."

First year head coach Tom Stacy knew he was inheriting a special team when he accepted the Massillon job: It was proven to him when his team snatched a 29-26 come-from-behind win that night.

"I've never been in a football game where the kids played harder than our kids did that night," Stacy said. "Our guys played extremely hard. And St. Ignatius coach Chuck Kyle said that after the game. 'I can't believe how hard your kids played.' We had to come back and win it."

"I've never been in a football game where the kids played harder than our kids did that night."

Tom Stacy

Massillon was 5-0 heading into the showdown with 4-1 Ignatius. A large contingent of Massillon fans packed Byers Field in Parma, a venue that has not been kind to the Tigers.

"It's a place where Massillon has never really played very well," Stacy said. "It's a tough place to win. It's always windy. The locker rooms are terrible. It's the worst artificial turf in Ohio. It's like concrete. It looks nice, but it's a terrible place to play."

As had happened in the past, Ignatius got off to a fast start against the Tigers.

"We were down 19-7," said Brian Gamble, a junior All-State defensive back and 1,000-yard rusher. "I just remember looking in every player's eyes. Everybody was ready to meet the challenge. Ready to come back. Ready to show everybody that we were the real deal."

Massillon came back in the second half with a 14-play, 77-yard touchdown drive to close the gap to 19-14, with Quentin Nicholson scoring from the one yard line.

Ignatius answered with a touchdown drive to stretch their lead to 26-14.

Then Massillon put together a beautiful 90-yard drive to pull within 26-21. The drive included a dramatic fourth down play involving punter Shawn Weisend, who was also the team's back-up quarterback. "We ran a fake punt and I caught a little 10-yard out route to give us a first down," Dailey said.

A nifty 16-yard run by Gamble and a 25-yard pass from starting quarterback Bobby Huth to Brett Huffman put the ball in scoring position. Gamble scored from the one behind great blocking.

In the fourth quarter, Gamble made a momentum-changing hit on Ignatius' star receiver.

"That was an incredible hit, an incredible play," Dailey said.

"It was third down. We needed the ball back," Gamble said. "It was the fourth quarter, about 10 minutes left. It was just so loud out there and everything was moving fast. I think when I hit Robbie Paris it was the turning point because he was their star. You never go out and try to hurt anybody. It just happened. It wasn't a dirty hit. He was comin' across the middle. He ran a post and I just broke on it and made the hit and unfortunately it ended his season. I know it sounds cruel but it did feel good to be the one to give us the ball back and give us a chance to win the game. When they brought the ambulance out there I went over with the refs and I gave him my best wishes. It was never my intent to hurt him. It happened. It's part of the game. I've talked to him since then. I think everything happens for a reason. It wasn't a good situation for them, but for us—he was killin' us. I can remember one play, him going up over me, I think he pushed off my shoulder but it didn't get called. He was a great player. I think him going out gave us all of the momentum. And it sunk them. That was their man."

Massillon and Ignatius then traded scoreless possessions to set up the Massillon's winning drive. Starting with 2:38 left on the clock, Massillon converted on a fourth and four when Lanale Robinson busted through for 10 yards to put the ball on the Ignatius 37. Two Huth incompletions left the Tigers in a third and 15 situation. Worse yet, Huth was knocked out of the game after taking a hard hit. The Tigers hope laid with Weisend.

"Shawn Weisend is one of the most talented athletes I've ever coached," Stacy said. "We always knew he had the athletic ability. He was a first team all-state punter. He always had the arm strength, the ability. After Bobby beat him out, we told him he had to prepare as if he was a starter.

The team believed in Weisend.

"We knew we had a good backup that was going to be

able to handle it," Dailey said. "We felt good," Gamble agreed. "When Bobby went out and Weisend came in we felt like there was no dropoff. He knew the offense and we knew he was capable of making plays. We were like a machine, everything just kept on rollin'."

"When Bobby Huth went out and Weisend came in we felt like there was no dropoff."

Brian Gamble

Weisend's third down pass to Gamble fell incomplete, setting up a fourth and 15 from the Ignatius 42.

"Stacy had a play where all four guys go vertically downfield, and one guy bends, and that's all you need is one little bender," Dailey said. "He just drew the play up right there. He told me, 'You don't bend this time, you just keep goin'. He told Zach Vanryzin, 'After you get to the first down marker, just come across the middle of the field. Shawn's gonna hit ya.' Shawn hit Vanryzin on that play for the first down."

The 24-yard play put the ball on the 18 yard line. Another Weisend-to-Vanryzin hook-up moved the ball to the 13-yard-line. A pass interference call on Ignatius moved the ball to the two. A running play lost three yards and Massillon had time for one final play.

"We thought they were going to be in man coverage," Stacy said. "It was a pick play, and I think we were trying to free up Brian Gamble. Initally, if you look at the tape, Brian's open early. But Shawn was smart, he thought, 'If I can take this and run it and get in, that's what I have to do.' Shawn had pretty good speed for his size and he was also strong. We thought that would be a good call down there on the goal line. But it wasn't play calling so much. It was desire to win the football game. Not only for himself, but for his teammates more than anything else."

"I just remember Shawn sitting back there looking for guys open and there really was nobody open," Daily said. "They were just on 'em like a glove. I'm like, 'He's gotta make a play here.' And when he took off I think everybody in the stadium just held their breath until he got into the end zone."

"I was just thinking, turn the corner. Turn the corner and get in," Stacy said. "I still wasn't sure he got in, even though he stuck the ball out. I wasn't sure he was in until I saw the referee hold his arms up."

The score, with 10 seconds remaining, put the Tigers ahead for good. Gamble intercepted an Ignatius pass to ice it. "I got the pic and we won the game," Gamble said. "(Teammate) Troy Ellis said I took it from him. I was about to try to take it to the house, but everyone on the sideline was yelling, 'Get down, Get down.'"

"Right after the game you realize, 'We're the first team to beat Ignatius,' Dailey said. "That hits you right after the game and Sunday morning when you wake up."

"I just remember thinking, 'What a great victory. This is going to go down as one of the great ones in the history of the school,'" Stacy said "The kids really wanted that one. I thought, 'This is one for our 1989 team.' They beat us up in the Rubber Bowl (42-21). Their national championship team. They had Joe Pickens. We had a good football team, but we didn't have *great* talent, I didn't think. I thought that was one of the greatest coaching jobs Lee Owens ever did, leading those kids to a state semi-final game. I thought, 'This is one for those guys, that state semi-final team.'"

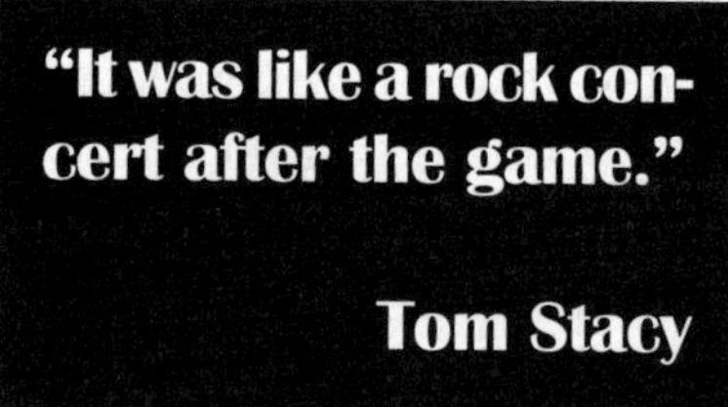

The win also validated the 2005 team in many people's eyes.

"We knew all along we could be going to state," Gamble said. "But, I think the turning point, when we really *knew* we could be going to state, is when we beat Ignatius. I think that's when people started saying, 'If you guys can beat Ignatius you can go to state.'"

"It was like a rock concert after the game," Stacy said. "Those are Massillon fans. That's when they're at their best. That's what makes them special."

The Tigers went on to finish 13-2, after making an exciting playoff run that included wins over unbeaten Canton McKinley Cleveland St. Ed's teams. A tough loss in the state championship game, 24-17, to Cincinnati St. Xavier, ended the magical season.

Games of the Century

Upsets of McKinley, St. Edward, Send 2005 Tigers to State Title Game

Canton McKinley and Lakewood St. Edward seemed invincible as they mowed over their first 12 opponents in the 2005 season. Massillon, who was beaten 38-8 by Canton McKinley in Week 10, was cast in the role of underdog in back-to-back playoff games against the unbeaten titans.

Massillon won their first nine games before their Week 10 loss to McKinley. The loss could have been demoralizing, casting a pall over their first round playoff game against North Canton Hoover. Instead it served as a catalyst for the playoffs—and the inevitable re-match with McKinley.

Bobby Huth threw 18 touchdowns and only six interceptions in 2005. Six of his TD passes came in the playoffs.

Junior co-captain Brian Gamble, who starred as a running back and defensive back all season, summed up the loss to McKinley. "We got beat down," Gamble said. "Nobody saw that comin. A few mistakes, a few guys who weren't ready to play. I just think it was the moment—how *big* that game was. The stage. McKinley thought it was going to be easy. That they weren't capable of playing with us. Our heads were big. They jumped out on us early. Morgan Williams went off on us. They played a great game and we played like garbage."

Massillon's rookie head coach Tom Stacy knew his team would bounce back against Hoover.

"No one was scared to play them. We were ready to play them again. We wanted another shot at them."

Brian Gamble

"They just wanted to get it fixed. The best way to get it fixed was to put one on Hoover. And obviously we were able to do that (45-14). I wasn't surprised. Donny Hertler's team was pretty young. They had barely got in the playoffs. I felt if we were going to move on in the playoffs we had to beat them and we had to *handle* them. It wasn't like we didn't expect to win."

In round two Massillon slipped by Findlay, 27-20, to set up the re-match with McKinley. They may have been looking ahead.

"They could have easily knocked us out," said junior All-Ohio safety Andrew Dailey. "That was a scary game."

"We did two or three things during that game that were uncharacteristic of our team," Stacy said. "Looking back, that tells me that we weren't focused. Those things happen and you're lucky to get out of there with a win."

It didn't take Stacy long to start thinking about his rematch with McKinley. "About 30 seconds after the game ended," he said.

Gamble and Dailey had different experiences in the week leading up to the rematch. "That was probably the most stressful week for me at least, because I knew that we had to get this win," Gamble said. "No one was scared to play them. We were ready to play them again. We wanted another shot at them."

Dailey, conversely, found the rematch a more settling feeling. "It was a totally different ball game," he said. "It wasn't a traditional Week 10 Massillon-McKinley ball game. This is a playoff Massillon-McKinley ball game. It's completely different. You don't go through McKinley Week all week. McKinley Week is a big thing. You have two or three dinners you have to go to. You have breakfasts and church ceremony, you have to go to breakfast with the McKinley team. McKinley week, Week 10, there are a lot of distractions off the field. It really, really is more than a football game that week. It's about town pride. Orange and black and red and black. When you come to the playoffs you don't have all the reminders of Massillon-McKinley week. The parades and all that. You just have the football game. And that's all it was about that week. So we just went out there with a chip on our shoulder."

Stacy recognized that the players were focused for the re-match.

"Our kids were not going to let that second one get away.

You could see it all week in practice. We had great focus. We had great preparation. We had no doubt that the kids were going to be ready to play. We just had to, as coaches, give them a good game plan. Fortunately we were able to do that. The kids executed the plan, not to perfection, but it was very well done."

"I remember Morgan puckering his lips and winkin' at me, being cocky...We felt their cockiness."

Brian Gamble

McKinley was on a roll, scoring at least 35 points against each of their previous five opponents, while giving up less than 10 points a game.

"I remember McKinley's star running back, Morgan Williams, puckering his lips and winkin' at me during the coin toss," Gamble said. "Being cocky. I'm not going to say what I said to him, but they weren't friendly words. It's that rivalry. You grow up Massillon-McKinley. You've got to beat these guys. Period. You beat McKinley. We felt their cockiness. Their little swaggerwas up. People were saying we had no chance. Out of 10 (newspaper) reporters, all ten picked McKinley. We were ready to play that game, and it showed on the field. We came out and we were smackin' 'em in the mouth. From the first kickoff when Andrew Dailey went down and body slammed Brian Williams. From right there it was like 'Yeah. We're ready to play. Let's go.'"

"They came a little bit big-headed," Dailey said, "a little bit cocky. They were laughing at us. They thought we couldn't even hold their jocks. And we just wanted to play football."

In front of 16,111 fans, the Tigers dominated the whole way, winning 21-3.

Dailey wasn't surprised by the outcome.

"It really wasn't a shock to me," he said. "That is what we should have done Week 10. We had a chance to do it and we did. Of course the town was nervous. Week 10 was all they remembered. They didn't remember our first nine wins before that. They remembered our loss to McKinley. They all knew we were going to run into them again. The town just thought, 'Oh gosh.' They were nervous. We stayed away from all that. Coach Stacy did a good job of handling the team that way. Kept us at practice a little later so we weren't screwing around too much after school. He knew how the town was. He knew if you had guys running around town they were going to run into some old-timers and they're going to get into your head. I give credit to Coach Stacy that week."

St. Edward looked like a team on its way to a state title, winning three playoff games after a 9-0 regular season."

"We wanted to play Glenville because we felt that they had athletes, but as far as a scheme goes, we felt that we could outcoach them," Gamble said.

"And St. Ed's, we knew that they had great players *and* a great scheme. It showed when they beat Cleveland

Glenville. We didn't want to play St. Ed's, but we had to."

Stacy thought he was back at the University of Akron when he saw his Tigers line up against St. Edward. "We came out the first series and their offensive line came out and I said to defensive coordinator Steve Kovacs, "Steve, this looks like I'm coaching in the MAC again," Stacy said. "He looked at me and shook his head and just started laughing. They were big, powerful, good-looking guys. They *looked* the part."

Ed's *played* the part, too, stretching a 10-7 lead to 17-7 with seven minutes left in the game. That's when Gamble approached Stacy confidently.

"When we got down 17-7 I told Coach Stacy, 'Give me the ball,'" Gamble said. "That's it. We went four wide for the rest of the game. We spread 'em out and we dished the ball around. In the last two series I had seven catches and two touchdowns. We just spread 'em out and they weren't ready for it. We ran our *Tiger* offense, the two minute offense, and they weren't ready for it."

What happened the remainder of the game was magical. Quarterback Bobby Huth passed the Tigers down the field, hitting Gamble with an 18-yard touchdown strike with just over five minutes left to trim St. Ed's lead to 17-14.

Then it was time for the defense to step up. On first down Paris McCall stuffed Ed's star running back Nate Oliver after a one-yard gain. An incomplete pass made it third and nine. Then Dailey made a big play.

"All game I was playin' with the quarterback," Dailey said. "I would show blitz, I'd drop back in coverage. Then I *wouldn't* show blitz and I'd come. All game that was my thing. It was third down and I was showin' blitz. And I came. I caught him blind-side on the back side and laid him out. I just remember the crowd going absolutely nuts. It was incredible. I had all this adrenaline running through my body. As soon as the ball was snapped and was in his hands—it happens that quick. I'd say it took two seconds. He was looking for a receiver. I was there. I was shocked that he hung onto the football. I think it just landed right in his stomach on the ground. He kind of just sucked it in there. I was just going all out and doing whatever I had to do to get to him. If I had to dive or do absolutely anything, I was gettin' there before he got the ball off. That was a big play."

"We just spread 'em out and they weren't ready for it."

Brian Gamble

Massillon got the ball back at their own 45-yard line with 3:40 left. They needed a touchdown to win.

Huth went to work, hitting Vanryzin and Gamble for first downs. On first down at the St. Edward 29, disaster struck.

"They snapped the ball over Bobby's head, or past him. I thought we were in trouble," Stacy said.

"We tried to call a time out," Gamble said of the muffed snap. "It was so loud in there, our center snapped the ball and it went over his head and Bobby did the smart thing and jumped on it. He didn't try to scoop it up, which could have been even worse."

The play cost Massillon 20 yards of field position. On second and 30, Huth threw incomplete to tight end Brett Huffman, bringing up third and 30 at the St. Edward 49.

"It was third and 30," Gamble said, "the huddle was silent. You could kind of feel that they had momentum."

"The amazing third and 30," Dailey said. "That's a play that probably should have never happened. If they stop us, they win the game."

"I caught him blindside and laid him out. I just remember the crowd going absolutely nuts. It was incredible."

Andrew Dailey

"There was no doubt in my mind we were going to Gamble," Stacy said. "We called a route called Pirate. It was supposed to be a skinny post to him, and he just broke it off to a dig route. We were going to him all the way. See if he could make a play."

"Coach Stacy said, 'They're going to double cover you, but get open.' They did double team me. I knew that Bobby wasn't going to anybody else. He told me, 'I'm throwing to you no matter what, so get it.' So I went to go break it to the post, and

I saw Nate Oliver, who's at Ohio State right now, I saw him playing over the top and I saw Deonte Morrow, who's at Iowa now, playing underneath me. So instead of breaking into the post like the angle, I broke it off and Bobby stepped up in the pocket and fired a rocket. I caught it and made a guy miss. Trey Miller did a great job of *not* blocking the person because it would have been a clip, he put his hands up. We got the first down."

Gamble a made big play after big play against St. Edward.

"I just remember it took a while to develop and all the other receivers, who were kind of like the decoys, were already through their routes and noticed that Brian was coming across the middle, about 25-30 yards downfield," Dailey said. "So after we had all run our routes we could see Brian wide open in the middle of the field. And you could almost take a second and all watch him catch the ball. Then you turn and try to get a block for him. Then he made a move and gained a couple more yards and got the first down. It was like a miracle."

A lot of Massillon players thought there was divine intervention. Beloved strength coach Steve Studer had died of a heart attack suffered at the high school a year earlier. He left a big void in the players' lives. They felt "Coach Stu" was with them during their playoff run. It was never more palpable than on that snowy, battleship gray day at the Akron Rubber Bowl.

"When I got that first down I remember looking up into the stands and I could just see the sun shining over the whole Massillon section."

Brian Gamble

"After I got the first down the sun came out," Gamble said. "Seriously now, you know Coach Studer. Well, when we beat Mansfield, that's the last time we would ever play Mansfield, the contract was up. We beat them 55-0. Coach Studer's number was 55. When we beat Ignatius 29-26, and you add that up, it's 55. So we felt like Coach Stu was on our side. When I got that first down I remember looking up into the stands and I could just see the sun shining over the whole Massillon section. Right there I knew that we were going to punch it in and score. Definitely felt Coach Studer was with us. Not only me, I think *everyone* felt it."

The Huth-to-Gamble connection put the ball on the St. Edward 14.

Huth hit Gamble again on first down to move the ball to the five-yard line. On second down Gamble made a determined run into the end zone, dragging St. Edward defenders with him.

"I drug a couple of guys with me," Gamble said. "I saw teammate Corey Shane pull around and he cleaned one person up and I saw the goal line, because the paint is thicker. I just remember goin' and feeling one guy hit me, then another. I remember I had my eyes closed for sure. I took another three extra high knees to get into the end zone. I just felt exhausted really. I *was* exhausted. I reached and when I looked up, the ball was over the pylon, over the goal line. I remember Bobby Huth and Corey Shane grabbing me and picking me up and telling me they love me and everything else. The crowd was *loud*. They were throwing snow balls up in the air. It was crazy. It was a great feeling.

"When we got in the locker room everyone was like, 'When you got the first down, dude, the sun just came out.' We felt like it was Stu. It was Coach Studer doing it. It was a great feeling."

"Oh my goshm it was a crappy day and the sun comes out right after that happens," Dailey said. "You see it on television now and you think, 'Oh wow, that's a special moment in Tiger history.'"

The Tigers 21-17 win over St. Edward put them in the state title game against Cincinnati St. Xavier. A crowd of 20,227 packed Canton's Fawcett stadium for the final. Massillon fell behind 24-3 and staged a dramatic second half comeback attempt, highlighted by a 80-yard strip and run for a touchdown by Dailey late in the third quarter. But Massillon had run out of miracles, falling 24-17 to a tough St. Xavier team.

RICK SHEPAS

It was the best of times, it was the worst of times...it was the season of darkness, it was the spring of hope, it was the winter of despair. —Charles Dickens, *A Tale of Two Cities*

Rick Shepas led Massillon to back-to-back Final Fours.

Charles Dickens wasn't describing Rick Shepas and his career as head coach at Massillon when he wrote *A Tale of Two Cities,* but he might as well have been.

Shepas made an impression on Massillon football that's

as subtle as a punch in the nose. He was charismatic, controversial, creative and confounding.

The best of times saw Shepas producing a 41-9 record, four straight playoff appearances and back-to-back Final 4 finishes—the first Massillon coach to do so.

Shepas made an impression on Massillon football that's as subtle as a punch in the nose.

The worst of times saw Shepas struggling on the field, with colleagues and in the Massillon community.

On the field, Shepas' three 4-6 finishes represent three of Massillon's four losing seasons since 1932. The only other belongs to Bob Seaman (1966).

Off the field, Shepas' list of detractors grew as the losses mounted.

Shepas felt he inherited problems when he took the job in 1998. "I think the biggest surprise was the condition the football program was in when I came here," Shepas said. "The kids think they're doing what they're supposed to be doing, but they're not workin' half as hard as they need to in order to compete with even the average teams in the state. That was a big shock. It was really a big undertaking to change the process."

His early days at the helm were some of the darkest. Longtime assistants were fired. Students booed him at pep rallies. He trashed sacred traditions. He rattled cages.

"You never feel real good about being the bad guy," Shepas said. "To this day I don't feel real good about it. Unfortunately, as a leader, sometimes you have to make unpopular decisions. That's the way I look at it. You can't make concessions and you can't kiss their rear ends. It's not my fault if people choose not to cooperate. It's not my fault if they don't make the changes that they need to make to adapt to a new coach. It's not the head coach's job to adjust to the group. It's the group's responsibility to adjust to the coach.

Shepas shouts instructions to defensive back Jamaal Ballard during the 2001 Massillon-McKinley game, a 29-26 Massillon win.

"The one thing that's unique to the job here at Massillon that is also unique to the job at Ohio State and with the Cleveland Browns is one thing. We're treated like we are a pro-calibre level here in Massillon. Which is nice. It is exciting for the kids that we get media coverage everyday. We're also criticized for everything. Every little thing. There are a number of distractions that surround the job at Massillon and the job at Ohio State and the job with the Cleveland Browns. They're very similar. And they were all created by the same guy. Paul Brown created such an unbelievable attitude about winning that it's been hard for any coach to follow that. And he did that every place he's been. So no matter what you do, how much you win by, it's not good enough.

"If you measure what I was able to accomplish with the two jobs I had there, I was the athletic director and the football coach, I feel great about what was accomplished. I don't know how they view me. I think some people view everything I've done as very positive and meaningful. Some people were probably offended by the changes that were made and some of the things that have gone on. I don't think you're going to please everybody. It's probably split down the middle.

"I feel great about what was accomplished there. I don't know how they view me."

Rick Shepas

"I tried to eliminate all of the distractions that had caused us problems in the past. Those were major changes. Unfortunately along the way people get offended. People were used to doing things a certain way.

"Paul Brown set up the Booster Club to be accountable to the head football coach. He was the head football coach and the athletic director. He started the Booster Club, he sat at the head of that table. Somewhere along the line in the 70-year history of the organization, we lost that basic philosophy. Some people in the community think if the head coach is only going to be here for a short time and the head coach is going to be gone, why should we give that control to that guy. Why shouldn't a group of people in town control that area. The coach was hired here to lead and run a program and when he actually gets here, instead of him actually setting the direction, leading the program and making the decisions, you had other people trying to set the direction, lead the program and make all the decisions. Some people asked me before I even took the job, 'How are you going to handle that? The program won't be yours.' I told them, 'It will be mine, what are you talking about.'"

Throughout his career Shepas found himself battling the powerful Massillon Tigers Football Booster Club, the school administration and the Massillon fans. It was especially tough his final two years when his 2003 and 2004 teams each finished 4-6 after reaching the Final 4 in 2001 and 2002. Shepas feels people were working against him his final years at Massillon.

"I don't think there was any question," Shepas said. "How could you go from having such a great thing going to such a volatile situation? Things changed. The climate changed. Some things changed politically. It wasn't good administratively. Superintendent of Schools Al Hennon was extremely supportive. He's the guy who hired me. I have a lot of respect for him. It's a shame that things went the way they did. I won't ever discount any stubbornness that I may have added to the equation, either.

"Rick and I had our problems," Hennon said. "And it resulted from my two kids. I would dare anybody to tell me that if they've been a father that, with their kids, they've been a father first. I don't blame Rick or myself for that. I blame the outside influences for comin' in and makin' that thing a bigger thing than it ever was. He was doing what he needed to do and I was doing what I needed to do as a father and as a parent and we both understand that. It was a problem, and it was at the time a huge problem for both of us. But if other people would have kept their noses out of it, and their voices away from it, there would have never been as huge a problem as people perceived it to be."

> **"It was a problem, and it was, at the time, a huge problem for both of us."**
>
> **Al Hennon**

"I'm not everybody's cup of tea as a coach," Shepas said. "I'm a player's coach, but I'm not easy on the kids. It's tough when you add the emotional equation in as well. I think it just got tougher. It got to the point where I had to coach Al Hennon's kids. I enjoyed it but it was a tough expectation on all of us. There was an expectation because he was the superintendent, he had an expectation for his kids. I had an expectation as a coach. Between he and I, I think it would have been fine. It would have been something we would have had to deal with, but it would have been fine. But when you get people who have other political agendas together involved in a school district—when they saw there was a breech in the relationship between Al and I—it ended up causing the majority of the problems. It wasn't really Al, it was other people playing to Al's emotions, ultimately."

Shepas also felt he had to wrestle control of the program from the Booster Club.

"It wasn't an easy situation because the Booster Club had a lot of power and influence," Shepas said. "And some of their power and influence wasn't directed in the right areas. It was about whose interests were at stake. I made several moves at that time to take control of the football program and we did. After a while I think people just had a problem with that."

The back-to-back 4-6 seasons and eroding support finally became more than Shepas could endure.

"Other than the way the last two years had gone, I think the proof was in the pudding. I don't really have a whole lot of regrets. I could have been a little nicer to some people, that was it. The last two years the focus got away from the players, because of the political make-up. We had administrators giving players a hard time in the school Just things that weren't just generally nice. Bob Rohrer was a tremendous principal. That had changed. We just had some issues. We had some sad but true issues. That's why Massillon wasn't Massillon to me anymore. When personal interests start to affect the way the football program is...it was just intolerable at that point. There was no way in the world I wanted to leave that 2005 team that went to the state title game. But at the same time, after that great season, let's say we have the great season and get to the state finals. What happens after that great team graduates? After all those guys go, I'm still gonna be left with the same administrators. That's when I made the decision to leave. I knew we were going to have a great season. I knew exactly what was going to happen. Everything was in place. I made the decision to leave based on what was going to happen after that great season. I didn't see anything changing in the infrastructure of the administration. I saw some resistance and I thought, 'That's enough for me.'"

"I wish Rick would have won those first two games in 2004—and we had our chances," Hennon said. "And 2003 was a tough year for him, too. But I always supported him. I'll always support the guy in that seat."

Hennon had compassion for Massillon's head coaches—he was involved in hiring four of them.

"You have to have the package," Hennon said. "You have to have a strong personality. The ability to coach one of the most diverse group of kids—a melting pot of kids. You have to know how to handle the media. And you have to know how to handle your booster club. It's a monumental task. Guys like former coach Lee Owens could make recommendations to Rick Shepas, because they've been there. But if you haven't sat in the seat, don't make the recommendation because you don't know what's happenin'. That's just the way it is.

Shepas left Massillon with a 53-28 record for the head coaching job at Waynesburg University in Pennsylvania in 2005. His career record is 28-23.

Shepas Coached a Trio of Terrific Quarterbacks at Massillon

While Rick Shepas was enjoying his finest seasons as Massillon's head coach, he also had the pleasure of coaching three of Massillon's finest quarterbacks.

Dave Irwin unloads a bomb against Canton McKinley in 1999.

The quarterbacks, Dave Irwin, Justin Zwick and Matt Martin, lit up opposing defenses for 109 touchdown passes between 1999 and 2002. Massillon outscored its opponents 1,754-756.

"In those years we scored more points than any other team in Massillon history," Shepas said.

Irwin was Shepas' first outstanding quarterback at

Massillon. But the scrappy field general had trouble getting on the field as a junior in 1998.

Shepas was in his first year as Massillon's head coach and Irwin felt he was being overlooked.

"It was bad for me right from the get-go," Irwin said. "I just felt he left me out.

"I was playing well. I worked hard in practice but I wasn't getting the shot. I don't know if he just didn't have a feel for the team. I couldn't figure out what was going on for the life of me. I just knew if I didn't get that shot my junior year I was transferring. I was a Massillon Tiger though and through, but I wanted to play. I felt I should be on the football field. I felt like I was being shafted by my coach. I told Shepas if I didn't get my shot this year I'm not going to play next year under you."

"I always felt early on that Irwin could be the guy."

Rick Shepas

Two other quarterbacks started before Irwin got his chance in Week 8.

"I always felt early on that Irwin could be the guy," Shepas said. "It was his turn and he took advantage of the opportunity."

Joe Shaheen, sports editor for the Massillon newspaper, *The Independent,* was impressed with Irwin early on.

"I remember him throwing the ball real well and saying, 'They can win with this guy.' I didn't realize at that point how good a leader he was and how the kids responded to him on the field. He threw the ball extremely nice, stood in the pocket, he didn't have happy feet in the pocket. I was impressed right away with him."

"I thought he was a great student of the game," Shepas said of Irwin. "I thought he had a lot of football IQ, field savvy. He was a fiery competitor, a good leader. He was definitely the guy the team rallied around. I think the players wanted to win for him. He was a great winner. Not necessarily fundamentally or technically sound. Not the biggest arm. But a winner."

Dave Irwin was the offensive leader of the 1999 team that finished the regular season 10-0, Massillon's first unbeaten regular season since 1982. Massillon's perfect regular season rested on Irwin's right hand in more ways than one.

"Two weeks before the Canton McKinley game I was working on a piece in shop class. The piece fell and I went to grab it. I was making a bolt, it was really a sharp bolt. I'm not sure if the bolt cut it or the machine cut it. It happened so quick. All I knew is that it was cut. The finger was just sitting there, finger flopped over, tendon sticking out. I instantly panicked. I don't know what's going through my mind. Massillon-McKinley is just two weeks away and something like that happens. Every time I think back about that day it just turns my stomach. I remember the feeling I had at that time because I just thought football was over completely. I didn't think there was anything they were going to be able to do. I really thought I was going to lose my finger. I went right over to Dr. Lykins' office, and they numbed it up and sutured it up the best they could. It was swollen. It was a freak accident."

Irwin's finger injury was the talk of the town for the two weeks leading into the McKinley game. The local newspapers contained daily updates.

"I thought he had a lot of football IQ, field savvy."

Rick Shepas

Massillon had lost four in a row to McKinley heading into the 1999 showdown. Shepas felt Irwin was being affected by more than his injured finger.

"He had been a little nervous," Shepas said. "There had been some rumors that one of the coaches over there had offered a steak dinner for knocking him out or something like that. I think he let that get to him a little bit. And I think it did take away a little bit from his performance in the first half."

Irwin acknowledges that he knew of the threats. "They told theirplayers they were going to give them steak dinners if they hurt me," he said. "I wasn't going to let that rattle me. That didn't bother me at all. Cheap shots are a different story."

At the end of the first half Irwin suffered a late hit. "I was running the ball. I was actually starting to get up and the guy spears me.

It was a cheap shot. I had to shake it off. I wanted to come back out in the second half. I wasn't going to let anything stop me."

Irwin came back and threw three second-half touchdown passes and Massillon turned a 7-7 halftime tie into a 35-7 win.

"Being able to go 10-0 was an accomplishment in itself," Shepas said. "It's very hard to do. Especially at Massillon. It hadn't been done in a while. I'll remember that game against McKinley at Fawcett Stadium the rest of my life. Even though Irwin was struggling with that hand, we found a way to overcome that and score a lot of points. He hung in there. Hung tough."

Zwick set Massillon career records for pass attempts, completions and touchdown passes.

Shepas' next star quarterback was Zwick, who transferred into Massillon from nearby Orrville following the 1999 football season. He came in and set nearly every Massillon passing record. After his two seasons at Massillon Zwick had the most pass attempts, completions, yards and touchdown passes in school history. He was also a two-time first team All-Ohio performer at Massillon.

"He's one of those kids who you see that had Division 1 written all over him," Shaheen said. "Big, strong, fast. A kid who, if they would have let him, could have rushed for 1,000 yards. Great arm."

But Shaheen suggests Zwick may not have been Shepas' best quarterback at Massillon.

"Physically, all the tools were there, but I'm not sure he had the pocket presence that a Dave Irwin had. And that leadership and that ability to command respect. In my era of covering the Tigers, Irwin was clearly my favorite quarterback. I don't think Zwick was as good a high school quarterback as Dave Irwin. That's my opinion. Zwick could throw the ball 80 yards, though. He could do it all. He's a super athlete. A super talent."

Zwick signed to play with Ohio State at the end of his junior season at Massillon. In his senior season he delivered 40 touchdown passes, 246 completions and 3,281 passing yards. He is still among the all-time leading passers in Ohio high school history.

Zwick led the Tigers to two playoff appearances, including a Final Four appearance against Cleveland St. Ignatius (a 49-20 loss).

Of all the Massillon quarterbacks, Zwick probably left the biggest shoes to fill when he headed to Columbus in 2002. Matt Martin had the daunting challenge of following Zwick at Massillon. He took it in stride.

"There aren't too many guys

around like him, a 6'4" prototype," Martin said. "You do the best job you can and don't worry about what he did, because he's a special guy."

Martin was pretty special himself.

"Matt Martin was a quarterback that I thought was the greatest accomplishment," said Shepas. "We were graduating Zwick and coming back with a great defense. Matt Martin was probably the most pivotal player in the success of that 2002 team that went to the state semifinals. He was smart."

Matt Martin reads the defense at the line of scrimmage.

Shaheen agreed. "His strength was mental," Shaheen said. "Before the season the big headline was that Martin was following in big footsteps because he was following Justin Zwick.

"He always changed into a good play at the line of scrimmage. He had it upstairs. Rick saw that early in the summer. He had the leadership skills and that toughness. He had that fullback/linebacker build."

Teammate Shawn Crable wasn't sure about Martin at first. "To me he wasn't a Zwick," Crable said. "And

I kind of worried about him when Zwick left. He silenced all that. He played well. He could throw the ball. He was smart. He did all the things our coach asked him to do. My opinion of Matt is that I would take him as my quarterback any day.

"If I could go back and say who would I rather have, him or Zwick, I'd take him. The thing about Matt Martin is that he threw to everybody."

In his only season as Massillon's starting quarterback Martin led the Tigers to their most prolific scoring total. Martin's 2002 Tigers scored 557 points, three more than Zwick's 2001 team. Martin's 26 touchdown passes are second in Massillon history, behind Zwick's 40 in 2001.

Martin led the Tigers to an 11-3 record. The 2002 Tigers three losses were by a combined 13 points.

"I'll always have a special smile on my face thinking about the way he played."

Rick Shepas

"I'll always have a special smile on my face thinking about the way he played," Shepas said of Martin. "The coachin' job that I was able to do with him, the confidence that he showed as he led us through some of those games. That's definitely a proud moment right there, the way he played. He knew our offense as well as anybody's ever known it. He knew our offense better than Zwick knew it."

JUSTIN ZWICK

Justin Zwick was already a football hero when he transferred to Massillon late in his sophomore year of high school.

As a freshman he led nearby small school Orrville to a state title on Massillon's home field. The experience at Paul Brown Tiger Stadium made a strong impression on Zwick.

Zwick went deep often during his Massillon career. He threw 40 TD passes his senior season.

"You play in that stadium, it's hard *not* to be impressed," Zwick said. "You saw what it was about. I just thought, 'Wow, it'd be great to play here.' I was playing Division 4 as a freshman, the next year we moved up to Division 3. I had a lot of success at Orrville."

What Zwick and his family saw in Massillon was an opportunity for their quarterbacking prodigy to be tested at the Division I level.

"It was something my family and I had talked about," Zwick said. "My brother had played at Youngstown State. He said he wasn't ready for all the things they did at Youngstown. So if you're going to play somewhere bigger than Youngstown, you're going to have to get prepared. He's really the one who got it going in my head. As a family we thought it was something that needed to be done.

"I wanted to make myself the best quarterback I could. To prepare myself for the college level. I wanted to play against the best teams in the state, to be in the big game situation with a lot of pressure.

"You hear about the tradition that goes into Massillon football and you really don't understand it until you're actually there. It was a big decision. I spent many nights on the phone with my brother. In the end it was what was what was best for me to test my skills."

While Massillon accepted Zwick with open arms, back in Orrville things got pretty ugly.

"I lost a lot of friends in Orrville," he said. "They weren't too happy with me or my family. I went around to all of my close friends and told them before I left. I went to each of their houses and told them what I was doin' and why I was doin' it. I hoped they'd understand. It didn't go over too well. We had to change our mailbox about every weekend during the season. People were smashing our mailbox. If my car was in the driveway they'd throw eggs at it. If my mom was in the yard planting flowers, people would drive by yelling obscenities. My parents would go to the grocery store and people who were friends wouldn't say hi like they usually would. It was kind of crazy. That's a lot to go through as a young guy like that. You really get to know who you can trust and lean on. A lot of those guys have come back and are great friends today. But at the time they didn't want me to leave. I can't blame 'em."

Thirteen miles away, Massillon became Zwick's sanctuary.

"I think they had heard about me through the grapevine," Zwick said, "Since my freshman year there were rumors that I was coming here.

"My first day at Massillon I went to lunch and sat at the table with the guys at lunch. It wasn't awkward. They made me feel like part of the team from the get-go. I think that here they're going to accept you no matter who you are or where you're from as long as you're willing to go through the same stuff that they do and as long as you're here for the same reason they are. I feel like I grew up with these guys.

"I lost a lot of friends in Orrville...We had to change our mailbox about every weekend during the season."

Justin Zwick

"Jared Frank, Craig Rotthoff, Matt Shem, those were the guys I surrounded myself with at first. They were the guys who kind of took me under their wings a little bit. I started to get close with them.

"The city was great. They took me in. Countless families in Massillon gave me a place to stay. Craig McConnell, who I played with, I was like another son to his parents. Mike Corsale and his family—I had a key to their home. It was really special That just shows you what kind of town it is. For a kid who nobody knew, to take him in like that. To open their homes. It was really something else."

Zwick also had a close relationship with head coach Rick Shepas.

"He and his family kind of took me in. I was like a big brother to his daughters. It was nice to have that. I would sleep at his house on Thursday nights before the games just to get that extra little bit of sleep in the morning. His wife would cook me my pre-game meal. It was really something special that their family did for me, taking me in, basically caring for me as one of their own."

Things worked out beautifully for Zwick at Massillon. He became a two-time first team All-Ohio quarterback, rewriting the passing section of Massillon's prestigious record book.

In two sizzling seasons Zwick threw for 5,741 yards and 63 touchdowns. In his senior season alone he threw for 3,281 yards and 40 touchdowns.

"Justin was just a tremendously confident kid," Shepas said. "Trusted his arm. Trusted the way he threw the ball. I don't think anybody could have enjoyed their time at Massillon any bigger. He was a celebrity. He was the biggest celebrity in the state of Ohio since Art Schlichter."

Schlichter was the ballyhooed quarterbacking recruit out of Washington Courthouse, Ohio. Schlichter starred at Ohio State, but an infamous gambling addiction derailed his football career and inevitably his life. Zwick was widely considered the most heralded quarterbacking recruit at Ohio State since Schlichter.

"I think he's the kid while I was at Massillon who had to deal with the most amount of pressure, most scrutiny," Shepas said. "He came in with the most attention. He had a bull's eye on his back and I think he handled it well. I don't think too many other people could have done as well with the same or similar circumstances. You can't argue with the numbers he put up here."

Zwick thrived in Coach Rick Shepas' wide open offense.

Playing quarterback at Massillon prepared Zwick for what awaited him at Ohio State.

"I think if any high school

could get you ready to go to Ohio State, Massillon did the best that any high school could. I always say this is kind of the mini-Columbus. All the pressure they put on the football team. How crazy all the people are about their football.

"The first game I had chills going down my whole body," Zwick said. "I'm standing there behind the tunnel just waiting to run out. My whole body was just tingling. The crowd was so loud. And there were so many people there. I'd never played in front of a crowd that big before. It was something that's hard to explain. Your body is just tingling, you've go so much excitement running through you. After that game it kind of settled down a little bit. You get used to it after a while. But that first game, it was just crazy."

Zwick overcame his nervousness and threw five touchdown passes in his first game, a 40-7 win over Akron Buchtel.

But it's the Canton McKinley games and the Ignatius games that he remembers most.

"When you get to Massillon and you're playing Ignatius in front of a sell-out crowd and you're playing McKinley, there's nothing that compares to those games and they way the city gets behind it. The Orrville-Wooster game has a lot of history itself, but I don't think any rivalry in the state compares to that Massillon-McKinley game. My senior year playing in the Rubber Bowl against McKinley for the second time that season, playing against Ignatius at the Rubber Bowl, you're not gettin' that experience anywhere else. That's something special. I wanted to go and see what that was like. To play in front of crowds like that and play that kind of competition. I'm glad I did it."

The three wins over McKinley were especially sweet for Zwick.

"You're going to remember those the rest of your life," he said. "Playing a game like that, that's so well-known."

"When you get to Massillon...there's nothing that compares to those game s and the way the city gets behind it."

Justin Zwick

In 2000, in front of 17,957 fans at Tiger Stadium, with Massillon trailing the Bulldogs, 9-7, Zwick led the Tigers on a 91-yard game-winning touchdown march.

"We had done that all year," Zwick said. "If we were ever in that position we always found a way to get down the field or make that drive when we had to get in the end zone. We got it done. It was exciting to see the crowd. I took the knee for the last play of the game. Just looking up in the crowd and seeing everyone going crazy. All your teammates going crazy on the field, gettin' the victory bell and ringing the bell. That's stuff you don't forget. You feel privileged to be in the game. To have a chance to play in something that big."

Zwick's next crack at McKinley came in the teams'

108th meeting, in 2001, in front of 23,815 spectators in Canton. It was another exciting finish. This time the Tigers trailed, 26-22, late in the game.

"That game was kind of crazy," Zwick said, "I thought we had control of it (22-12) and we let them back in it. But it came to crunch time and we had to get it in the end zone." This time it took a 72-yard drive, capped by a beautiful 27-yard touchdown run by Robert Oliver.

"The offensive line started doing a great job and Bob made a great run, breaking a couple of tackles," Zwick said. "Joe Jovingo made a block on the cornerback. That extra effort by Joe to get that block allowed Bob to go in untouched after that. Then Craig McConnell came up with the interception in the end zone with six seconds to play and I got to take a knee again."

Massillon and McKinley met again two weeks later in the Akron Rubber Bowl. This time the Tigers won easily, 35-19, in front of a crowd of 21,203. "It was a lot of fun playing in the Rubber Bowl and beating McKinley for the second time in a season," Zwick said with a laugh.

Massillon dispatched of North Canton the next week, 27-7, to win the regional championship and advance to the Final 4.

Their Final 4 opponent was Cleveland St. Ignatius, who had dealt Massillon its only defeat of the season, 40-26, in Week 4.

"You're playing Ignatius in front of a sell-out crowd," Zwick said. "It's standing room only."

The crowd of 29,871 at the

Rubber Bowl saw Massillon and Ignatius tied 14-14 with four minutes left in the first half. Then the wheels came off for the Tigers.

Ignatius drove 76 yards for a touchdown, then capitalized on a Zwick mistake.

"Right before the half I fumbled the ball and it rolled all the way to the end zone. I don't know how that happened. It rolled 35 yards into the end zone and they fall on it. It's tough when stuff like that happens and you go down by two touchdowns."

Massillon cut the lead to eight points late in the third quarter, but Ignatius scored three unanswered touchdowns to win, 49-20.

Massillon was 20-5 with Zwick at quarterback: Three of those losses were to Ignatius.

"We came out and we fought and fought and fought," Zwick said, "but it wasn't meant to be."

Zwick left Massillon as one the most decorated players in history. Beside his All-Ohio recognition, he was a Parade All-American and was selected to participate in the Elite 11 quarterback camp. The prestigious camp tutors the top quarterbacks in the nation. In its 12 years the camp has tutored five future Heisman Trophy winners.

Zwick could have gone anywhere he wanted to play college football. But Ohio State wanted him and he wanted Ohio State. He signed with the Buckeyes and head coach Jim Tressel after his junior season at Massillon.

"It was great," Zwick said of his signing day. "Coach Shep really set that up nice for me, with the press conference. We did it at Copper's restaurant, it was really nice. It was a crazy day. A lot of people showed up."

Once he committed to Ohio State, Zwick became a statewide celebrity.

"It was nuts after that, the whole Ohio State thing," Zwick said.

Being the most highly anticipated Ohio State recruit in 25 years was not necessarily the joyous situation one might imagine.

"It was fun and tough all at the same time," Zwick said.

Zwick was a regular visitor to the Ohio State sideline during his senior year of high school. "I remember going into a game there and walking by the student section and hearing my name yelled by the students. That's all fun and what not, but it puts it on your shoulders when you're there.

"As a senior, I always had that 'Ohio State recruit Justin Zwick' as a lead in. Ohio State football is special. To be a part of that was great. Being highly anticipated, that was fun. Lookin' back on it, you almost wish it wasn't quite as big as it was. But that's just the way it goes. That was just part of the deal."

There was plenty of talk about Zwick displacing Craig Krenzel as the starting quarterback as a true freshman. Fanning the flame was Zwick's performance in the spring game where he was 19-27 with four touchdown passes.

"That was a great game," Zwick said. "Troy Smith and I got to play a lot in that game. It was a lot of fun.

I'll never forget that game. I always thought once I got that shot I was going to do well. Going into Ohio State everything was rolling and everything was fun. I should have known something was going to happen sooner or later. It's just the law of averages.

"Going into Ohio State everything was rolling and everything was fun. I should have known something was going to happen sooner or later."

Justin Zwick

"There was talk of me starting. Camp was going well. But I injured my shoulder andcouldn't throw for a couple of weeks and they decided to redshirt me. It was one of those freak accidents, one of those weird hits. Craig ended up having a great season and Maurice Clarrett played out of his mind and we ended up winning the whole thing. Timing was never my best thing at Ohio State."

Krenzel was back the next season. Zwick got some playing time against Northwestern.

"I'll never forget throwing my first pass. Louis Irizarry was streaking down the sideline and he drops the ball. My first pass as a college quarterback could have been a nice 45-yard touchdown pass. That's just kind of how it went for me at Ohio State."

Then came his redshirt sophomore year.

"That's when all the fun

started," Zwick quipped. "Troy and I were battling all through spring, all through camp. It was the Thursday before camp let out. I had come back to watch the game at Massillon. They announced over the loud speakers at Tiger Stadium that I'd been named starter for that first game. But we were both going to play."

Zwick in action at Ohio State.

PHOTO: OHIO STATE ATHLETICS

The Buckeyes opened against University of Cincinnati, whose new coach was Mark Dantonio, who just a season before was Ohio State's defensive coordinator.

"He had just gone down there so he know our system and personnel real well. So I was kind of nervous going into that game because he's such a great defensive coach.

"We won, so that kind of started things out. Even though we weren't hitting on all cylinders, we were winning, pulling out games."

Against Marshall, Zwick

threw for 318 yards and three touchdown passes, including an 80-yarder to Santonio Holmes. He also led a field goal drive that helped the Buckeyes eke out a 24-21 win. After the game Tressel was publicly critical of Zwick's two interceptions.

"I knew Coach Tressel's mentality, don't make mistakes, hold onto the ball. I knew he wasn't a big throwing coach. On the other hand Brett Favre has the most touchdown passes in the NFL and he also has the most interceptions. You're gonna get bit on a couple of things here and there because you want to make that throw or complete that ball. We pulled that game out. I put our team in a bad situation with a couple of those throws and we pulled it out and that's all I was focused on. I don't care about picks or touchdowns as long as we win. It's tough because I knew he was going to get on me about it, which he has a right to. But I didn't pay too much more attention to it than that."

"I knew Tressel's mentality, don't make mistakes, hold onto the ball. I knew he wasn't a big throwing coach."

Justin Zwick

The next week Ohio State escaped with a 23-14 win over North Carolina State.

"We went up to Northwestern and didn't play well on either side of the ball," Zwick said. "We gave up a bunch of points and didn't score a lot of points. That kind of was a downward spiral for a couple of games, topped off with the Iowa game, where I had a slight separation of my shoulder during the first series of the game. I tried to play through it because I knew what would happen if I came out—Troy comes in and you're in that position where you're tryin' to keep your job. You don't want to show any kind of pain. I fought through that first half and it was a bad day. At halftime my shoulder just locked up on me. I wasn't able to go out and do what I had to do to help the team get back into it. After the game I could barely get my shoulder pads off. It was pretty bad. For two weeks I couldn't hardly lift my arm up to throw a football. We played Indiana the next week, which would have been a great game to get into and get some rhythm going again. But I was unable to throw and had to sit that game out. The rest of the season Troy ended up getting the team going a little bit and ended up having that monster game against Michigan at the end of the season (341 yards passing, two touchdown passes and 145 yards rushing). It was a breakout game for him. Once he beat Michigan as a starting quarterback (37-21), in a game we weren't supposed to win, in Columbus, that's tough for someone like myself to overcome."

That's about when Zwick turned to his old high school coach for advice.

"We talked about a lot of things during those days," Shepas said, "including transferring out of there. I talked to him and I even talked to Tressel about him transferring."

Shepas played receiver under Tressel at Youngstown

State in the 1980s and is a member of the school's athletic Hall of Fame.

"He clearly wasn't going to win the job. If he had any desire at all to play in the NFL he had to get snaps under his belt. He had to get back to the guy he was. A deal was definitely in the works. He was going to go to Montana. I was working the thing through the proper channels. I knew if Justin was going to make it to the NFL he was going to have to get playing experience."

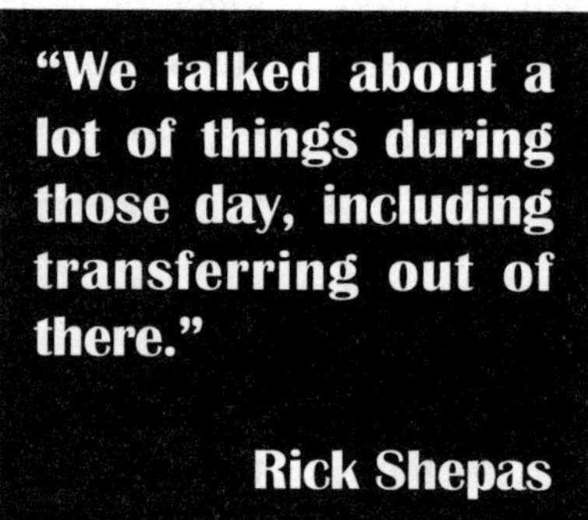

"I talked with Shep about some things," Zwick said. "Thought of maybe going somewhere else and playing, trying to get some film, kind of crossed my mind. It was a big decision to make. To pull the trigger.

"I came to Ohio State with the idea of living in Ohio the rest of my life. If I go to Montana and nothing happens with the NFL, I come back to Columbus and I'm known as the guy who left. That played into it. I know how the people of Ohio love their Buckeyes and that's always something nice to have in your corner. That played a factor in coming to Ohio State and a factor in staying instead of transferring out."

Any thoughts of transferring were suddenly dashed when Zwick was informed that

Smith had been suspended for the Alamo Bowl and the opening game of the 2005 season for accepting $500 from a booster.

"I didn't learn of that until I was home for a little break between bowl practice and leaving for the bowl game," Zwick said. "Troy was being suspended and I was going to be starting the Alamo Bowl. I figured, 'Well, I get another shot to go out and show 'em what I can do.'"

Zwick made the most of his Alamo Bowl opportunity, leading Ohio State to a 33-7 win over Oklahoma State. He completed 17 of 27 passes for 189 yards including a 23-yard touchdown strike to Anthony Gonzalez on his first throw of the game. In fact it was his first throw since injuring his shoulder in the Iowa game.

"You come back and the first pass you throw is a touchdown. I felt pretty good about that. It was just fun being that guy and not having to worry about anything. It was the first game I didn't have to look over my shoulder at all. I just went out and did what I had to do. If I threw an interception they weren't going to go with anybody else. It's easier to play when you know you're the guy no matter what. That was just a lot of fun knowin' that the team was behind me full go."

His Alamo Bowl performance gave Zwick renewed confidence. "I had a great game, the team played well," he said. "We won that game and I knew I was going to get that start the first game the next year because of Troy's suspension. So I knew I had another shot to get my spot back. I knew it was an uphill battle, but, hey, I'm a competitor."

The Ohio State-Texas match-up in Week 2 of the 2005 season was the big story in college football during the off season. Texas was ranked No. 2 and Ohio State No. 4 going into the game. Texas was led by Vince Young, who would go on to win the Heisman Trophy. Texas ended up winning the national championship, too.

> **"A play I'll never forget is Hamby in the end zone—to go up by two scores. Those darn tight ends..."**
>
> **Justin Zwick**

But first Zwick had the opportunity to face Miami. "We played Miami that first game, we beat them, I had a good game."

Zwick was 17-23 for 155 yards with a 20-yard touchdown pass to Santonio Holmes against Miami. But was it good enough to earn him the start against Texas?

"We didn't know who was going to start until the Thursday or Friday before the game. I got the nod and took the first two series."

The game entire game was played at a fever pitch. The opening series were especially tense.

"You know a game like that, the first couple of series everybody has to get into the game a little bit, that big of a night game. It's one of those games where everybody's moving a little too quick, not relaxed, playing the way they usually are. So we stalled the first couple of series. In my second series, it was third and six and

I threw a nice little pass to Gonzalez. We ran that play a lot, and he just took off to run a little early—and that happens. Everybody wants to make plays. He takes his eye off of the ball and that's a third down that we didn't get. I remember that same play being called later in the game and I'm not in the game and it workin' fine. For whatever reason it wasn't meant for me to have that happen.

"I remember not getting to play much the rest of the first half. I was thinkin, 'Here we go again.'

"But we came out and I got to play a little bit in the second half. A play I'll never forget is Ryan Hamby in the end zone—to go up by two scores. Those darn tight ends keep gettin' me," Zwick said with a laugh, referring to his first pass as a Buckeye that was dropped by tight end Irizarry.

"That was tough. And he wanted to catch that ball as much as I wanted him to. It was a great little route. Great little call down there at the goal line. They sent it in from the sideline. It's something we practiced all week for him at the goal line area. It was wide open. Hit him in the numbers. It was one of those freak things. He usually catches that ball ten out of ten times. He has great hands. It's just one of those things that happens. He almost catches it three different times. That would have put us up two scores and even if they score we're just trying to run the clock out at the end of the game. It didn't happen. That was kind of the dagger for me.

"It came down to that last series and Troy and I are both kind of standing there waiting to see what was going to happen. Who was Tressel going to go with? He looked at me and he said, 'You're in.'"

With 2:31 left in the game, and the Buckeyes trailing 23-22, Zwick had a chance to lead the Buckeyes to victory. On first down Zwick was forced to scramble. As he headed for the sideline he attempted to switch the ball to his outside hand. "I got hit by two people at the same time," Zwick said. "I was trying to switch hands. I was tryin' to go to my left. Changing hands and getting hit, it was just a bad combination. You've gotta take care of the ball, and I didn't there and that's what happens. What are you gonna do, I guess. So I went in and things didn't go the way I wanted them to with the fumble at the end of the game. You know, I can't do anything about that now. Everybody wants to blame somethin'. That fumble was the last thing they saw me do. And that hurt us at the end of the game. I felt I put us in position earlier in the game to get that win. Going into the next week we didn't know what was going to happen.

"It came down to that last series and Troy and I are both kind of standing there waiting to see what was going to happen. Who was he going to go with?"

Justin Zwick

"That Monday I was doing an interview and watching the TV after practice and saw Coach Tressel's press conference. That's where he said that Troy was going to be the starter from now on. That's how I learned about that. That was tough. Mostly because I had to watch it on TV instead of being sat down and told the direction they were going to go and why. That's something that kind of sprung up on me. I'm sitting there doing an interview and all of a sudden the TV comes on and Tress is having a press conference and this is what he said. And I'm like, 'Whoa. All right.' It was tough for a couple of weeks to deal with. I probably talked to Shep every other night during that time. He really helped me through that. I realized I was only one play away from going back in the game. I had to be ready. So I continued to prepare like I was going to be the guy. It was another one of those time things. You're watching from the sideline instead of being in there. That was tough because I didn't think I did bad enough to play myself out of the position in that Texas game. If a couple of different things happen, you get a couple of different catches here, you hold onto the ball and drive your team down, it's hard to see them sittin' you the next week. That's what I had trouble with. They made a decision, that's what they get paid all the money to do. And that's just the way things go."

Zwick's relationship with Smith had its rough times. "We butted head, of course, as any competitors would, going after the same thing. Going into our senior year is probably the best our relationship had ever been because we didn't have that constant reminder that we were battling against each other. He was the Heisman candidate and I was his back-up. We weren't the best of friends, but we were teammates and we had the same goals in mind for the team. When you're competing with somebody and there's only one position available to play, it creates a little tension. A couple of times it got heated, but nothing too serious."

Zwick's Ohio State career certainly did not unfold like anyone could have predicted. But he handled himself with dignity, and that has earned him respect among the Ohio State fan base. "I've had numerous people come up to me my senior year and even now who thank me for being the way I was. They'll come up to me and thank me for handling things the way I did. I have moms and dads coming up thanking me for being a good role model for their kids. That touches you a little bit. People recognize that kind of stuff. As you go through something like that as a kid, you don't think about it. I probably still don't grasp it all together, even being 27 years old. People just appreciate how I acted, how I handled things. It's all about timing and the situations you get put in. That's what I've realized."

Zwick had try-outs with the Indianapolis Colts and the Carolina Panthers, but nothing materialized. He threw one pass for the Columbus Destroyers in the Arena Football League. "Threw one pass, a 48-yard touchdown pass," he said. "I was 1-1. It has to be one of the best quarterback rating in Arena Football history," he said with a laugh. "I was signed for the next season and the team went under, so I was left with no option but finding a job and going to work."

DEVIN JORDAN

The all-time-leading receiver in Massillon Tigers history almost decided against playing football during his freshman year of high school. It was a newspaper article that changed his mind.

He read an article about Justin Zwick transferring to Massillon to play quarterback. At the time Devin Jordan was a frustrated freshman at Perry High School.

Jordan had pretty much given up on football after a bad experience on the Perry freshman team.

Jordan's numbers as a junior were dizzying: 98 catches, 1,492 yards, 18 touchdowns.

"They wanted me to play quarterback, and they wouldn't even allow me to play receiver, so I didn't want to play anymore," Jordan said. "I read an article in the paper that said Justin Zwick of Orrville was going to play at Massillon. I thought, 'Hey, if I want to play receiver I want to go to Massillon.' After my freshman year of high school I transferred to Massillon."

Jordan only started to realize his dream during his sophomore year at Massillon. "I had a decent sophomore year, but I guess my junior year was my break-out year because I was the number one target. I knew going into my junior year I was going to be the guy.

"Me and Zwick would stay after practice and work on our timing. I think that really paid off. We'd do early morning workouts. He'd say, 'Meet me at the stadium at eight o'clock in the morning, we'll do some routes.' I think it paid off."

Jordan's break-out junior season rocketed him to the top of Massillon's all-time receiving records.

The extra work clearly paid off as Jordan's junior season rocketed him to the top of the of the all-time Massillon receiving records. In a single season Jordan broke the Tigers *career* marks for pass receptions (98), receiving yards (1,492) and he tied the record for touchdown receptions (18).

"He was my go-to guy," Zwick said, "He helped me get to where I was. He was a great athlete, great hands, smart kid, hard worker."

As the yardage and touchdown catches started adding up, everyone noticed.

"You're seeing articles written about you, people hyping you up, saying 'Devin Jordan's really good.' I didn't really realize it. The coach would say, 'Devin, do you realize you had 150 yards the other day?' It wasn't like a big deal to me. I didn't really care about stats, I just wanted to have fun. People would say, 'Devin, you're averaging over 120 yards a game as a receiver, that doesn't happen in high school, especially at Massillon, where you're playing top-notch competition all the time.' I think the moment I realized it was when we were going down to Ohio State the week before we played Dayton Chaminade. I was reading the paper on the way down to Columbus and it said, 'Massillon's Jordan Eclipses 1,000 Yards.' That's when it really hit me. It made me feel good. That's when I really realized what I had done. When I realized I was one of the best ever, stats-wise, in Stark County history, that's amazing. Eclipsing 1,000 yards was really cool."

After his record-setting junior season Jordan said goodbye to Zwick, who took his golden arm to Ohio State.

But Jordan didn't let his success go to his head. His Christian upbringing helped.

"Being raised by my mom and dad, my dad is a Baptist minister, I'm just a humble person. To other people I was big time, but to me I was just Devin, a regular person. I think people appreciated that.

"I was getting recruiting letters from all these Division I colleges after my junior year. After my junior year Joe Daniels, who was the receivers coach at Ohio State at the time, came into one of my basketball practices and offered me a scholarship to Ohio State."

After his record-setting junior season Jordan said goodbye to Zwick, who took his golden right arm to Ohio State. Matt Martin took over for Zwick.

"My senior year was a great experience, just being at Massillon prepared me for Ohio State because it's such a football-crazy town. Ohio State's the same way.

"I thought Matt Martin was a heckuva quarterback for us," Jordan said

Besides the challenge of adjusting to a new quarterback, Jordan had to adjust to the ball being thrown from a lefthanded quarterback in Martin.

"A spiral coming from a right-handed quarterback is totally different than a spiral coming from a lefthanded quarterback," Jordan said. "You catch the ball a lot differently. At the beginning of the season at football camp I was dropping a lot of passes because the spirals were coming at me differently. It took me a while to get used to it.

"I remember Coach Rick Shepas being really hard on me my senior year. My senior year I didn't have the stats—I wasn't having the type of season I thought I'd have bein' an Ohio State recruit. I wasn't really performing.

"As a player I was wondering, 'Why are you yelling at me?' He was really tough on me. One time during my senior year I wasn't really performing the best and he said, 'I'm going to call up Ohio State Head Coach Jim Tressel and tell him to take away your scholarship.' I kind of took that personally. How would you do that? He was serious. It was almost like he was scaring me. Why would you tell me that? After the Ignatius game he called me out. Told me I played horrible. He said 'The game was lost because of you. You didn't show up today. You let Tony Gonzalez outplay you.' It made me feel horrible. We had just lost. It kind of gave me a hard feeling toward him."

Making things even harder, Jordan had suffered an injury in the Ignatius game.

"I went up for a pass and came down on my chest. I actually still have the mark today. After the game that night, it was four in the morning, I went to the hospital because I couldn't breath. I was in the hospital after the St. Ignatius game, people don't know that. It was a wake-up call for me, because that was the first time I had ever been hurt playing football. It really affected me. That's one reason I didn't really have a really good season. That affected me, really, until the McKinley game."

Joe Shaheen, sports editor for *The Independent,* remembered talking to Jordan following the football season.

"I saw him early in the basketball season," Shaheen said. "Massillon had won a pretty important basketball game and in the locker room Jordan pulled off his jersey. His chest, you could see it was swollen where his sternum would be. I mean it scared me just seeing that. He had a chest bruise and being a football guy, Rick Shepas didn't really make a lot of it. A good three weeks after the football season I saw how his chest looked and it almost made me sick to my stomach. It was discolored, it was purple."

The highlight of Jordan's Massillon career came when Massillon and Perry clashed in the second round of the 2002 playoffs.

"I remember my house getting toilet papered before the game. My mom made me clean up the mess. That really put me over the edge to where I *really* wanted to beat 'em. I think I had one of my best games in high school against them."

"After the Ignatius game, it was four in the morning, I went to the hospital because I couldn't breath."

Devin Jordan

Jordan caught seven passes for 170 yards and two touchdowns against Perry, including a 40-yard reception in the final drive that put the Tigers in position to kick the game-winning field goal as time expired to beat Perry 23-21.

"It was funny, on Monday after the game, Mrs. Snodgrass, she was one of my favorite teachers, she said 'Devin, I'm not going to lie, we thought the game was over, we were walking out of the stadium. All of a sudden we hear all of these cheers and the announcer says Devin Jordan makes a 40-yard gain.' That was one of my most memorable games because it kept us alive in the playoffs and it was against my old junior high school teammates.

"At Pickerington, it was 0-0, muddy game, the worst conditions I ever played in. I remember being in the locker room at halftime and Marquis Johnson kind of stood up and let his emotions show and kind of sparked us all. It lit me on fire. We didn't want to lose. I scored our two touchdowns in the third quarter. We won 14-0. It was kind of good for me, being a captain and not really producing the way I hoped to (during the regular season), but when it came to the playoffs I kind of stood up and made some big plays and helped us have a memorable season."

Devin Jordan as an Ohio State Buckeye.

PHOTO: OHIO STATE ATHLETICS

While Jordan's senior season paled in comparison to his incredible junior season, it was nonetheless impressive. He ended up with a team-leading 45 catches for 893 yards and 12 touchdowns. His 19.8 yards per catch was actually an improvement over his junior season (15.2).

Being a minister's son helped Jordan keep things in perspective as he gained the fame that starring at Massillon and signing with Ohio State can bring.

"Growing up with a family like that kept me humble. I had my limitations, I couldn't be everywhere every night. Being raised like that kept me who I was. I didn't get a big head just because I was a good football player. When you have a good game and your mom tells you, 'Hey, you've gotta do the dishes, you've gotta take out the trash, it brings you back to reality. I think their spirituality was very helpful to me as a person."

"I told my receivers coach I wanted to stay around. I wanted to help the team."

Devin Jordan

Jordan's career at Ohio State was full of promise, but injuries continually derailed his opportunities to get on the field.

"First thing that happened I had to get knee surgery," he said.

"His redshirt freshman camp he was playing really well and doing the things he needed to do to get in there and make some plays during the season," Zwick said.

"I led the receivers in the jersey scrimmage my redshirt freshman year, I had the most yards receiving," Jordan said. "I was backing up Santonio Holmes, I thought things were going really good. I was in the best shape of my life."

"Then he broke that ankle," Zwick said. "I'll never forget that play, he was blocking and someone just rolled up on his ankle and it was a bad break.

"It broke my fibula and dislocated my ankle," Jordan said. "It basically ended my career on that play. I was never the same. Coming into my junior year I just hung it up. My body couldn't take it anymore.

"I told my receivers coach I wanted to stay around. I wanted to help the team. When my senior year came along I got to mentor Brian Hartline, Brian Robiskie, Ray Small, all those guys. They all came in and I coached 'em up."

"He took advantage of his opportunities," Zwick said, "He was basically like a coach. He really took advantage of things."

Jordan continued to follow his coaching instincts after graduating from Ohio State.

"I went to Wittenberg and coached their for a year. I really wanted to come back to Columbus and there was an opening at Otterbein. I'm coaching there now and having a great time.

"My goal is to progress. I want to be an inspiration in other kids' lives. I want to beat Mount Union. I think we have a pretty good shot this year. We just have to find a way to get over that hump.

My personal goal is to be the receivers coach at Ohio State. I know it's going to take a lot of work, but I want to be back at Ohio State one day."

SHAWN CRABLE

Shawn Crable beat the odds. "Shawn was a projects kid," Ella Kirkland said of her prize foster child, who has experienced some of life's toughest times.

Shawn Crable at Michigan.

PHOTO: U-M ATHLETIC DEPARTMENT

"I went from foster home to foster home," Crable said, reflecting on his early childhood. The foster home situation was bad. I was in a couple of situations, a couple of places, where I didn't want to be."

At age 11, Crable had nowhere to turn. "He needed a place to stay," Kirkland said. "A friend of mine said they had a little boy on emergency placement and they said that he was at the park. I said I would stop by and see him. I didn't have a lot of history on him. I just knew that he was neglected and he was in foster care."

Crable was playing basketball at the Pearl Street Park on Massillon's southeast side when Kirkland pulled up. "She got out of the car," Crable said, "so I walked over there."

"He was tall and thin and he smiled real easy," Kirkland said of her first meeting with Crable. "I asked him if he would like to live with me and he said 'Yes.' So I gave him a hug and we came home."

"She got out of the car and gave me the biggest hug in the world," Crable said. "I looked at her like, 'Who are you,'" he said with a laugh.

"I think it surprised him when I hugged him," Kirkland said.

"Later on that evening I got my stuff and I moved over there," Crable said. "She had a beautiful house. Nice swimming pool and things like that. And I think she needed me as much as I needed her."

"I was getting in fights all the way through seventh grade."

Shawn Crable

Kirkland had parenting experience. Besides raising her biological son, she had worked with four foster children before Crable. Her success was not immediate.

"He was very, very angry," she said. "He was hurt. Shawn felt abandoned. He felt everybody had lied to him. He had some problems at school. So we had quite a few trips up to the school."

"I was getting in fights all

the way through seventh grade," Crable said, "and even into eighth grade. I was very angry. That's why I got into fights at school all the time. But me and her never, never argued. Never got into a battle. I never tested her."

Kirkland agreed, "He's always been very polite to me. He's never given me a hard time. Whenever there was a problem, I was always there to stand by him. I think that was the exception rather than the rule in his life. We kind of bonded that way."

Crable in action against Canton McKinley.

Crable could have gone the way of many "projects kids" who become casualties of the street. "I know where I came from and I know that I don't want to go back there" Crable said, "You don't have to turn to the streets. There's nothing that's going to keep you in a hole. There's nothing that's going to make you sell drugs, make you not want to go to school or do your homework. There's no *thing* or *nobody* that's going to make you do that. It's your decision. Anybody can make it out of where I made it from. I burnt my stress and anger off playing sports. You can do whatever you want to do. But you need to do *something*. You don't have to turn to the streets.

"I understand I am gifted. I'm tall and muscular and I can play. But everybody can do something. You've just got to put your mind to it."

Crable learned a valuable lesson while playing football in seventh grade. "I got kicked off the team. I was a trouble maker. I was yellin' and arguing. I had a little attitude. I was a problem child. My attitude got me kicked off the team. I didn't really understand what teamwork was. I really wasn't a team player, so I don't think very many people liked me."

"I got kicked off the team. I was a trouble maker...I had a little attitude. I was a problem child."

Shawn Crable

Away from the football field, Crable had a great advocate in Kirkland.

"He needed someone to reach out and give him a hug now and then," Kirkland said. "And say good job. He just needed somebody to care about him. To go to his game. Somebody to be there to put a crease in his pants when they need it. To sew on a button. Regular everyday things.

"Early on we spent a lot of time talking. He was just very sad. Angry. We talked for hours. And I wasn't sure I was getting through. We'd go over and over the same things. He didn't think he was going to be able to be a good boy. Those were the saddest times, when I didn't think I was reaching him. I would read books and I would go to classes that I thought would help me relate to him and his problems. For months and years we spent time at that kitchen table talking and trying to get him to realize that it's really not the end of the world. You can overcome this, you can move on. There is life after foster care. You can have a great life. All you have to do is pursue it. Evidently he listened and realized. There were times I'd pass by his room and he'd be on his knees saying prayers. That was a good thing that he found some comfort in saying prayers. But you know I'd go to his room and I'd have to cry a little bit because it was very sad. He was just so young. But evidently it all came together and made a bigger, better person of him. I really don't know when the light went on for him. Just one day he was my son. He just evolved."

Shawn Crable before the Massillon-McKinley game, 2002.

Things changed for Crable when he entered high school. "I got in this big school and everybody was bigger than me. I had guys like Ellery Moore walking around and I'm like, 'Oh, MAN.' I just kind of shut up and started observing and learning. Watching those guys play and seeing what they were doing on the field,

I wanted to do that. I think I started realizing that some of the things I was doing could stop me from doing that.

"I remember (assistant principal) Mr. (Tim) Cocklin coming up to me and saying, 'Out of the years I've been at this high school, the first time I got a report that Shawn Crable was coming to this high school they told me to watch out because you were going to be in my office every day. That you were a problem child.' He said 'I'm just proud of you that you've never been in my office.'"

Cocklin, a 32-year veteran of Washington High School, counts discipline among his responsibilities. He remembers counseling Crable. "He did have a reputation," Cocklin said, "he was a big kid who had a hard life growing up." Cocklin told Crable what was expected of him. "We kind of got an understanding from the get-go at freshman orientation. I told him that things aren't going to be like middle school. This is where you grow up. We expect a lot out of you. He had tremendous potential and I just didn't want to see him waste it, go down that wrong road. And he lived up to his potential. I never had any problem with him, ever."

Crable was part of a strong freshman football class at Massillon. They were also a little headstrong. "We wanted to play the varsity," Crable said. "We thought we could beat them. The varsity players went to Head Coach Rick Shepas and said they wanted to scrimmage us because we were talking so much. Coach Shepas came in throwing things and yelling at us. He asked us if we really wanted to play the varsity. He moved all of the good freshman players to the varsity after the freshman season was over. That was a real eye opener for us. They were thumping us. After the first day of practice our whole freshman team was like, 'We don't want to move up anymore.' They were teeing off on us."

"Shawn Crable is a kid that will always be close to my heart because we worked on him from a psychological standpoint from the time he was in the eighth grade," Shepas said.

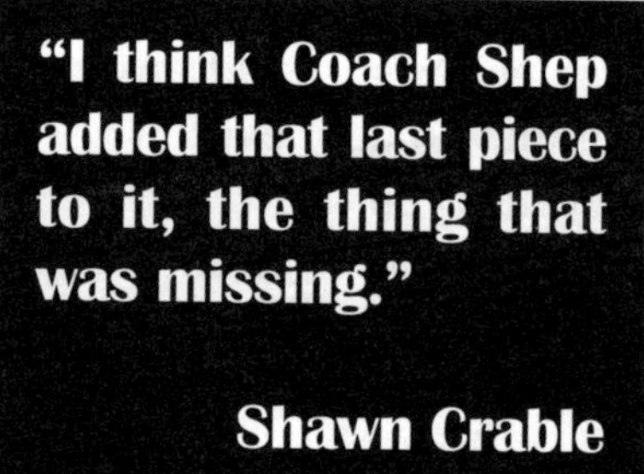

"He's a group home kid that really made a lot of strides. Athletically and physically he has all the God-given ability. But the strength in his game now is coming from his maturity as a young individual sorting out who he wants to be. I probably had something to do with his vision about football and how he felt about football as a vehicle to an education and to the NFL. He's a very smart kid. He's smarter than a lot of people give him credit for. He was very youthful and at times immature early on in his career. A jokester, a prankster. And he had to learn more about focusing. But when you get to a place like Michigan you have a lot of great players around you. You get focused or you're out of there. He's doing an outstanding job and those are the victories that I want to be a part of."

"I loved him," Crable said of Shepas. "I went over to his

house and ate. I think he was the first coach that really got me to calm down and think about football. I think Coach Shep added that last piece to it, the thing that was missing. He knew how to talk to me. He knew how to get through to me."

Crable had a few tiffs with Shepas along the way, however. As a sophomore Crable was unhappy that he wasn't playing, so he quit the team.

"Coach Shep came to my house, came and got me. He said, 'Why'd you quit?' I said, 'This is a bunch of crap. I should be playing.' He said, 'You just need to wait your turn. Learn how to wait things out.' I told him that I felt like I was just wasting my time. At the end of the conversation I ended up back on the team and he put me on the JV team for a game. Then starting linebacker Jason Abbott got hurt, messed up his shoulder, and I got to start.

"It was the game they brought Denny Franklin down to be put in the Hall of Champions and they had former Michigan coach Bo Schembechler there to introduce him. That was the Cleveland St. Ignatius game. Right after the game Coach Schembechler came down wanting to talk to me. He said, 'I want to know who number 2 is.' He came over and told me, 'I just want to let you know son, you have a scholarship to play at Michigan if you ever want it.' It was my first game ever playin' varsity. I thought to myself, 'Things are weird. The Lord works in strange ways. If I'd have just quit and been done with it I would have never had that opportunity. That was an exciting thing for me.

"From that time on Shepas

and I were buddies, until we named captains my senior year. We had an explosion. I was pretty sure I was going to be the captain. They had brought former Massillon star Steve Luke in to talk to us. Steve asked who was the leader out of all of us and everybody pointed to me. I'm like, 'Whoa.' It was a real eye opener to me that everybody thought of me like that. So then it came time to pick captains and Coach Shep came in and gave this great speech about what a captain should be and don't pick a guy just because he's popular. It's not the poster boy of the team. It doesn't have to be the best athlete. He just said a bunch of things that just blew me out of the water. The whole time he's giving this speech I'm thinking, 'You're talking about me.' It ended up that everybody else took it that way, too, and didn't vote me captain. It was a shock to a lot of us. Well, the team listened to him and they picked all kinds of other people. I was kind of upset with that. I was like, 'You come in here and give this great speech and I don't get voted captain.' We had a big dispute. I said, 'Why would you come in and give a big speech like that?' So he pulls me in his office and tells me, 'You know you're really the captain of this team. I didn't mean for everything to turn out like this.'

"Then we started practice and when the team started playing bad he'd say, 'Shawn, get this under control.' I said, 'I'm not your captain. Maybe you should yell at the captains.' We had a big falling out about it. But after a week or so it started to mellow down. We had a lot of talks and a lot of sit-downs. We kind of just understood that those things just kind of happen. The bottom line was that we both wanted to win. He told me, 'Even if you're not the captain you have the most input on the team. You and I arguing all the time is tearing the team apart.'"

Kirkland remembers Crable's disappointment in not being named captain at Massillon. But she also remembers his happiest moment at Massillon.

"The happiest I ever saw Shawn was when he got his letterman jacket. When he got his letterman jacket it was a real kick for him. He had a great time. He was prancin' around."

"That was a big eye opener for me that they went out and did something like that," Crable said. "I did not expect it. I put it right on. That was a very special time for me. I was gettin' after it. Lovin' it."

After Crable decided to attend the University of Michigan, he felt insecure about leaving Kirkland.

"A couple of days before he left for school he said, 'When I go to school, Mom, when I come home for breaks, where will I go?' I said, 'You'll come home. This is your home.' That never entered my mind, but it did his."

Crable started slowly at the University of Michigan. He redshirted his first season. His next two years he saw spot duty. Finally, Michigan head coach Lloyd Carr called Crable into his office.

"It's never good when he calls you to his office," Crable said. "Unless you're the captain or something, there's never anything positive about being called into his office. I went in there knowing it was going to be something bad, that I was going to get yelled at or something like that."

"He got kicked to the curb," Kirkland said. "Coach kicked him to the curb. Coach told him either put up or shut up. That was exactly what he needed to do. And he knew he couldn't come back here a failure. I would have had a fit. We don't have any quitters in this house. You have to see the job through. You have to complete the task."

"He sat there for a minute and said, 'What's on your mind, what's going on with you?'" Crable said. "I said, 'Nothing. Everything's cool.' He said, 'If everything's cool you won't have any problem with this.' It kind of caught me off guard when he slid the transfer papers to me and said, 'I think you should think about transferring.'

"I don't think he really wanted me to transfer. I think it was just a tactic to help me understand that I either needed to start playin' or I needed to start thinking about leaving. I think it all boiled down to them having an expectation for me and I wasn't meeting it.

"I found out that you *can* go harder. When I look at how I played as a sophomore and how I play now, I'm two totally different people. It was just my perception. He opened my eyes to a lot of things. He said just because you have more potential than somebody, you've gotta show that you play harder than them, work harder than them, every day. That's the only way you'll start."

Crable cracked the starting lineup as a junior. His senior season turned out to be a break out year for him. It all started when he received an honor that eluded him at Massillon.

"Shawn called me and he was kind of hem-hawin' around," Kirkland said. "I had heard it through the grapevine that he was named defensive captain at Michigan, but I didn't tell anybody I knew. Then he said, 'Oh, I'm doing pretty good for being the captain of the team' You could just feel his smile. He was just real pleased. He deserved it. He really worked hard."

Crable had a dominating senior season at Michigan. He set the school record with 28 tackles for loss in a season. He was recognized for his outstanding play when he was a second team All-American pick by the Walter Camp Football Foundation. He was also a semi-finalist for the Butkus and Bednarik awards.

Crable was a third round draft pick of the New England Patriots. After an outstanding rookie camp he spent the first half of his rookie season as gameday inactive before a shin injury sidelined him for the season. In his second season he was again injured and spend the entire season on injured reserve.

Like at Michigan, Crable will have to prove himself to make it in the NFL.

Shepas thinks it's all up to Crable whether he succeeds in the NFL. "I think everybody sees the high football IQ and the talent," Shepas said. "It just comes down to a decision of when he wants to play, that's all."

Crable's Hit on Troy Smith Part of Michigan-Ohio State Lore

The 2006 version of the Ohio State-Michigan game was billed as the "Game of the Century." Both teams were 11-0 and were ranked number one and two in the country.

> "That was a bogus call. They made two different calls."
>
> Shawn Crable

Ohio State was clinging to a 35-31 lead late in the fourth quarter and faced a third and 15 on the Michigan 38. Troy Smith, who weeks later won the Heisman Trophy, avoided a sack and was rolling toward the Ohio State sideline. Michigan noseguard Terrence Taylor and Shawn Crable had the angle on Smith and were closing fast.

"Terrence was behind me and he wasn't slowing down," Crable said. "When I hit Troy, Terrence hit me. I didn't try to wrap up, I didn't try to take him to the ground. I just hit him." Crable hit Smith high and hard, sending him hurtling into his teammates on the sideline. A penalty flag flew.

"That was a bogus call," Crable said. "They made two different calls. The referee that threw the flag said that I hit him while he was out of bounds—that it was a late hit. The other referee ran in and said it wasn't a late hit, that he was in bounds. He said it was a helmet-to-helmet hit. But as often as you see Troy runnin' down the sidelines on teams and skippin' and stuff like that, you're telling me I need to watch where I hit him? If the quarterback leaves the pocket and is running, he's a running back. I'm 6'6" and he's 5'11". If he's crouching and I'm crouching, I'm going to hit him helmet-to-helmet. That's what I'm upset about. I could understand if he had his back to me and he was sittin' in the pocket and didn't see me and I came in and just smacked him helmet-to-helmet, I can see the referee protecting him. But when he takes off running, why should I treat him any different than a running back? If we wouldn't have been playing at Ohio State and it hadn't happened on the Ohio State sideline, there wouldn't have been a call."

"If the quarterback leaves the pocket and is running, he's a running back. I'm 6'6" and he's 5'11". If he's crouching and I'm crouching, I'm going to hit him helmet-to-helmet."

Shawn Crable

Ohio State took advantage of the call, scoring a minute later and eventually winning the game, 42-39. ABC cameras zoomed in on Crable and replayed the hit several times. "Our coaches sent the play into the NCAA for review," Crable said. "My coaches didn't blame me, my teammates didn't blame me. They said if I was ever in that position again, hit him."

Comments about Heisman-Winner Tebow put Crable in the Headlines

All of the talk leading up to the 2008 Capital One Bowl in Orlando seemed to focus on the University of Florida's Heisman Trophy winner, Tim Tebow. Michigan's defensive captain Shawn Crable had finally heard enough.

"We had been going to banquets with the team and everybody was like, 'It's Tebow Time' and stuff like that. It got to the point where I was doin' an interview and a guy asked me how I felt about Tebow. I said 'He's a good

Crable beats his man and has his eyes on Heisman Trophy winner Tim Tebow during the 2007 Captial One Bowl. Crable was Michigan's defensive captain.

PHOTO: U-M ATHLETIC DEPARTMENT

quarterback.' The next words out of the reporter's mouth were, 'Tebow has a habit of running over linebackers. Are you in any way intimidated about that?' That made me upset. I said 'He's just a quarterback. He's nothin' special. He's not going to run me over. He's not going to do all of that stuff that you all are talking about. He's an average quarterback, but he's good for the scheme that they have him in. He runs that scheme to perfection.'

"Down there he's Superman and everything. He's like *The Man. He can't be stopped. He's intense. He does everything.* And in the first quarter of our game he *was* intense, he *was* talkin'. He was telling everybody, 'I just love football, I just love it.' But by the end of the first quarter he didn't say a word. Not a word. He didn't say a word the rest of the game. He didn't make a peep, because we were hittin' him. Our plan all week in practice was to hit him in the mouth. We're going to hit him in the face and stand him up. If he wants to fight for yards, we're going to tattoo him. He's going to start feelin' people hittin' him. And that started working in the game. He'd get hit the first time and he'd go down, because he knew somebody else would be coming to hit him. We minimized him."

In the end, Michigan prevailed 41-35 in what many considered the most entertaining game of the bowl season. Michigan fans, greatly outnumbered by Gator supporters, rejoiced along with the players on the field.

"Our little bit of fans that were there to support us, they stayed," Crable said. "They cheered. After all that Gator talk, Gator chompin', at the end it was *our* stadium."

TOM STACY

Tom Stacy has experienced a lot of highlights in his coaching career. He's developed Division I quarterbacks into NFL prospects and led Massillon to the division I state championship game in his rookie year as head coach in 2005. So picking a career highlight should be pretty easy.

Tom Stacy confers with quarterback Chris Willoughby.

Maybe it was working with Charlie Frye, his former Akron prodigy who became the starting quarterback for the Cleveland Browns. Perhaps it was Massillon's big win over Cleveland St. Ignatius or Cleveland St. Edwards during the 2005 title run? How about one of his three coveted wins over Canton McKinley?

"Probably the best coaching experience of my life was being an assistant at Massillon from 1988-1990," Stacy said. "It was the most fun I ever had in coaching. It was a blast. An unbelievable atmosphere. The 1988 McKinley game was called the *$20 Million*

Dollar Game. If we win it, we probably build the new high school. That was exciting. We beat McKinley that year in overtime, 10-7. My kids were very young, and my wife and I lived in a little house on 16th Street northwest. We just had a ball. Our neighbors were all big Massillon fans. I think that was the best coaching experience of my career."

But Stacy's legacy in Massillon will certainly be tied to the job he did with the 2005 Tigers.

Stacy inherited a hungry team from his predecessor, Rick Shepas, who moved on to become the head coach at Waynesburg University in Pennsylvania after posting the first back-to-back losing seasons in Massillon's modern history (4-6 both seasons).

"They were hungry for a lot of things we wanted to bring in," Stacy said. "The leaping tiger on the helmet, the shorter practices. They were hungry for change. And that's no slam on Rick. The kids were ready for change. There's no question."

The football savvy town of Massillon knew the 2005 team was loaded. They'd been following the players since youth leagues.

"When we were in fifth grade people used to tell us that our class (2006) and the class ahead of us (2005) were going to win state," said Brian Gamble, who was a captain on both the 2005 and 2006 teams. "So everyone knew our year was comin'. Everybody around town already knew who we were."

Support had eroded for

Shepas, and Superintendent Al Hennon knew a change needed to be made with the heralded 2005-2006 classes becoming upper classmen.

"The communication totally broke down during the Shepas era," Hennon said. "When communication breaks down, everything breaks down.

"This hire had to be the right person. It wasn't just X's and O's. We had to bring the community back, in some way, shape or form."

Stacy came recommended by Lee Owens, Massillon's version of "The Great Communicator." It was on Owens' Massillon staff that Stacy enjoyed the best years of his career as a Massillon assistant. He also coached with Owens at University of Akron and Ashland University. All told, the pair worked together for 15 years.

Stacy knew that he was inheriting a special group of players. He also knew that he had to repair relationships in the community. He understood that Shepas' job wasn't easy.

"I feel every coach who has ever been there added to the program in some way," Stacy said. "Rick Shepas did some great things there. Won some big games. I went in with the attitude that I wasn't going to slam Rick. Until you walk in those shoes you don't understand the pressure and expectations that are on the head coach in Massillon. There were some problems. But with that job you're going to have some problems."

Stacy proved to the right man at the right time.

"With Stacy comin' in, no one really knew what to expect," Gamble said. "All the older guys, the boosters, were telling us he was a good coach. It was like when he came in, *we* knew what we had, but *he* didn't know what we had. But it was good in a way because his offense was much simpler to learn. Coach Steve Kovacs was another key to our success because he brought something to our defense that was crazy, it just had everybody on the same page. We were like dogs off the leash on the field. I think everybody just bought into what he was selling, Coach Stacy and all of the other coaches. Because we wanted to be good. We wanted to win. Because we had come off a 4-6 season. It turned out good for us."

Stacy, in the heat of battle.

One thing that Stacy changed when he arrived on the job was the team's language. Stacy, who describes himself as a Christian ("Yes sir, very much so."), was shocked at the profanity being used by the players. "I said, 'Listen guys, the profanity thing has been a problem. You know it and I know it. And we're going to fix it. That's not Massillon football. That's not what John Muhlbach did. That's not what Chris Spielman did. The players that played here in the past didn't do that.' What we started doing is Tiger Reminders. It's an up-down every five yards for 100 yards. We started doing those every time somebody used profanity. I'd say, 'Hey, you've got to do a Tiger Reminder.' The good thing is the kids would remind us after practice. 'Hey Coach, I've got a Tiger Reminder, don't forget.' I knew then we were turning the corner. Our kids knew they shouldn't be doing it, they knew it wasn't right and they did a good job of fixing it. Was it perfect? Absolutely not. But I'll tell you, we made great in-roads in that respect. And I think our performance in 2005 reflected that."

On the field, the Tigers roared out of the gate in 2005. A 35-31 win over Cincinnati Elder in Paul Brown Stadium in Cincinnati got statewide attention. Elder had won back-to-back state championships in 2002-2003.

Then came a showdown with Cleveland St. Ignatius, who Massillon had never beaten in eight tries.

"I knew that would be a key game for us, win or lose," Stacy said. "When we won that game we thought as a staff, 'Hey, we've got a chance to do something special here.' Shawn Weisend's heroic play when Bobby Huth got hurt...Brian Gamble's hit on Robby Paris put him out for the season. We had to come back and win it. That drive at the end was something, to have enough gas in the tank."

Massillon had to battle back from deficits of 19-7 and 26-14 against St. Ignatius.

Then Huth was knocked out of the game. Back-up quarterback Weisend became the hero.

Huth didn't want to come out. "He wanted to go right back in," Stacy said. "I said, 'Bobby we can't put you in. We think you have a concussion. You're not 100 percent, mentally.' That's just the kind of kid he is."

"Brian Gamble's hit on Robby Paris put him out for the season."

Tom Stacy

After the game, a 29-26 win, Massillon celebrated as if it had won the state championship.

Massillon rolled through their next three games, including a 13-0 shutout of Warren Harding.

"That game meant a lot to me because I have so much respect for Thom McDaniels," Stacy said. "I knew they were going to come in here and play their tails off. Thom always does a great job against Massillon, whether it's with Warren or McKinley."

Both Massillon and McKinley came into the regular season finale undefeated. McKinley won 38-8. "They outplayed us," Stacy said flatly. "They outcoached us. They deserved to win. They took it to us."

But the Tigers rebounded.

Stacy knew they would. "That was the thing about that team, they knew they were good," Stacy said. "They knew they could turn the page."

The Tigers took out their frustrations on Canton Hoover in Week 1 of the playoffs, 45-14. Then it was a thriller against Findlay that wasn't decided until the final seconds.

"That game scared me because our kids don't know who Findlay is," Stacy said. "We had a lack of focus."

Findlay almost tied the game at the end. "They ran the hook and ladder play and Mr. Gamble made that stop.

"We knew they did it, but we didn't get the information to our kids fast enough to warn them that this might be a time they might try it. When that kid went down the sideline I thought, 'Oh geeze, they're gonna score.' Then I saw Gamble come from the middle of the field and make the tackle. That might be the most underrated play of that season. That was a great play."

"I knew I was going to catch him," Gamble said, "I had the angle on him. But could I knock him out of bounds? He was 240 pounds. When I got there I just laid everything I had into him. He didn't fall down but he stumbled out of bounds. I did enough."

Findlay had the ball at the Massillon three with less than a minute left. "That goal line stand was huge," Stacy said.

"They had the ball on the one-inch line," Gamble said.

"We knew they were going to sneak it. I just remember me, Andrew Dailey and Paris McCall just stuffed 'em. The clock ran out and we won. Once again we stepped up to the challenge. Football is a game of inches, and they're one inch from the goal line and we stopped 'em. I think that's one of the greatest moments of the season."

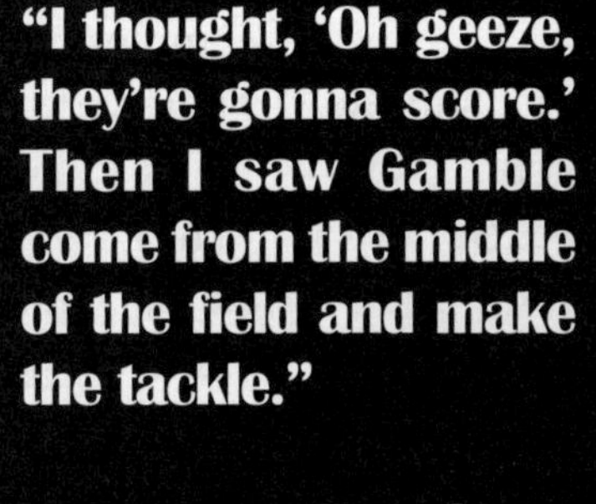

That set up a rematch with McKinley in the Rubber Bowl. The Massillon crowd was there early.

"It's like going to a college football game," Stacy said. "It's really special. I think that's what sets Massillon apart from maybe any other high school in the country. I haven't coached in Texas or Florida, but I can't imagine a school having the following at away games that Massillon has. It makes a big difference in the game. It intimidates the other team. It's really unique."

"Our kids were not going to let that second one get away," Stacy said. "You could see it all week in practice. We had great focus. We had great preparation."

"The guy I thought made a really big difference in that game was Lanelle Robinson," Stacy said. "He really made some big runs. He was fast, powerful. And that kid had one of the best attitudes, as far as being a team player, than any kid I've ever been around. He would have been the starting tailback and rushed for 1,000 yards for a lot of teams in the area. And he almost ended up rushing for 1,000 yards for us as a backup (907).

Massillon beat McKinley 21-3 in the rematch. Next up was Lakewood St. Edward in the state semi-final.

"I think that was one of the Brian Gamble games. I think he said, 'Hey, I'm not going to let us lose. I'm going to make some plays that are going to be the difference in this football game.' It was one of those games.

Massillon got past St. Edward, 21-17, setting up a date with Cincinnati St. Xavier in the state final.

In the state championship game, Stacy and his Tigers had their work cut out for them.

"St. Xavier was the best football team we played," Stacy said. "They were very similar to St. Edward. The biggest difference was that St. Xavier had a much more complex defensive scheme. They were hard to run on."

"They were just a great team," Gamble said. "They made no mistakes and we made a few mistakes. That was the difference. What did it was before the half when they took the punt return to the house. The score at that time was 10-7. It ended up being 17-7 going into halftime. It deflated us, but we came back."

Stacy wishes he could change his decision on the punt call. "You know, the funny thing is, the kid wasn't supposed to catch it. We had been so good on punt coverage that year. And there's a chance that kid might drop it. A guy like Brian Gamble might pick it up..." Stacy mused.

St. Xavier withstood a spirited Massillon comeback in the second half to win, 24-17.

Stacy spent two additional seasons at Massillon, but couldn't match the success of the 2005 season.

"I think the expectations are always too high," Stacy said. "The expectations are to win a state championship every year. But that's what makes Massillon unique. We lost some good kids after 2005. That made a big difference in our team. We weren't as good a football team.

"I can't imagine a school having the following at away games that Massillon has. It intimidates the other team."

Tom Stacy

Stacy was able to beat McKinley in 2006 and 2007. Overall his teams finished 7-5 and 6-4. In 2006, McKinley came into the game undefeated.

"The win over McKinley when they were undefeated was a big one," Stacy said. "In my 10 years as a head coach, I'd say that was my most underrated win ever. There's a lot of people who didn't give us a chance to win that football game.

"Another big win was beating Hamilton Chandler, who went on to win the state championship in Arizona. They were a heckuva team. Might have been the fastest team we played while I was at Massillon. That was another underrated win."

Stacy felt he had a hard time living up to the success of the 2005 team. "There's a lot of pressure to win the state championship. Especially when you got as close as we did. I think that's what made it so tough on me and my staff in 2006 and 2007. When you have great success early, then you don't have as good a football team, they still expect you to win. And I think that's why I'm not still there. Those expectations are there and when you can't produce there's a good chance you're not going to be there. I had to decide if I'm going to bring a lawyer in there to fight for my job. Would I have done that? I don't think I would have. The last thing I wanted to do was hurt those kids, that community or that program. They had gone through that with Mike Currence. I have a great respect for Mike, but I was not going to let it get that far. All I'm saying is I don't know if they would renew me or not. When Superintendent of Schools Fred Blosser left, I decided I didn't want to go back."

BRIAN GAMBLE

Brian Gamble's first memory of Massillon football was at the 100th game against Canton McKinley. "Willie Spencer is my first memory," Gamble said. "He was a beast. He was a hero, someone to look up to as a young guy. I just remember us winning the 100th game. The excitement. I remember it being crazy. I was only five or six years old."

Brian Gamble was a two-year captain. two-way starter and two-time All-Ohioan.

PHOTO: JOE NAGY

Ten years later, it was Gamble in the role of hero for Massillon children. "You look up in the stands and see the number 26 jerseys. You like that, because they look up to you. I think it helps you off the field, too. Because when you see little kids, you know they know who you are. And it's fun to be their role model. Like my first memory of Massillon football was Willie Spencer, for a lot of little kids it's going to be Brian Gamble."

Gamble was a captain at Massillon in both his junior and senior seasons. Head coach Tom Stacy said he deserved the honor. "He was the leader," Stacy said. "He was the emotional leader. I can honestly tell you this, he was the leader of our football team both his junior and senior seasons. No question about it. I've never had a junior that had that much influence in high school or college."

Gamble embraced his leadership role. "I liked it because I like it bein' on my shoulders. It was the leader's fault. I took it as '*You have to go out there and take care of business.*' They're lookin' at you like they expect you to be the one to produce. It's a business. Even though it's Massillon, it's a high school, it's still like it's a college or a pro team. Because you have to *produce*. It's all about winning at Massillon. It's not all about having fun. It's really not.

"It was good being one of the stars. You go out there and play and all of the sudden you're in the newspapers all of the time. It wasn't just me. I thought everyone on the team was a star.

"You definitely feel responsible. You feel like the city's fate is in your hands. Because you know how Massillon is. It's all about football. Everyone's at the games. Everyone wants us to win. It's a pride thing. You want to go out there and produce for your city. You want to represent Massillon."

Stacy became Gamble's head coach in 2005. Gamble played under head coach Rick Shepas as a sophomore. He was part of the second of back-to-back 4-6 seasons.

Shepas suffered three 4-6 seasons in his seven seasons at Massillon.

"He put fear in a lot of people, but not me," Gamble said of Shepas. "I guess it was respect. I respected him and I think he respected me because he saw that I was a hardnosed-type of dude. Basically he just wanted to win football games and he wanted everybody to play to the best of their ability. If you're not playing to where he thinks you're capable of playin' he's going to call you out on it. Shepas tries to push the better players so hard that he wants you to hate him and resent him so much that you want to go out there and prove him wrong. He was that type of guy. He played a lot of mind games. And you can't do that with certain people in high school. They don't have that mental strength, that toughness, that ability to take that verbal abuse. Other players he brought out the best in. He definitely brought out the best in me.

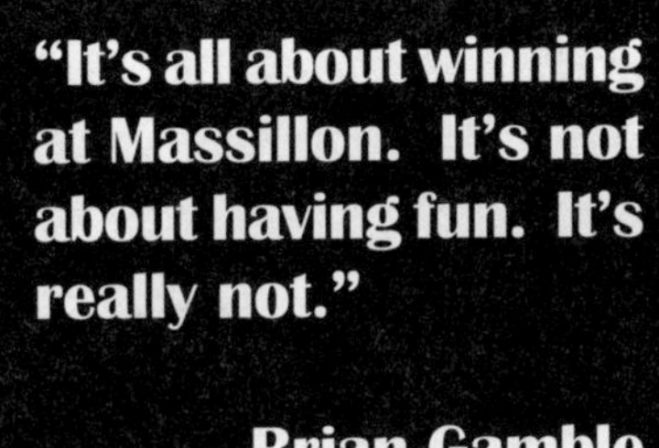

"I remember playing basketball with him. He was foulin' everybody, he would cheat. And you better not call a foul on him. I remember I was guarding him once and he tried to post me up and I just started giving him elbows. I just started fouling him because that's what he was doing to everyone else. He just looked at me and said, 'Yeah, you see, that's what

I'm lookin' for right there.' He just wanted somebody to push him back. He saw that I wasn't going to take it. He and I never had a problem. I know he had problems with a lot of people, but me and him never had a problem."

Gamble was the second-leading tackler for Massillon as a sophomore. "I just remember rockin' people, really," Gamble said. "Just goin' out there playing unconscious. They had me at linebacker and I was like 170 pounds. So I was undersized. I still loved the challenge. I still got to the ball and made plays. It was just about provin' a point, gettin' on the field."

Gamble was a star on offense, but he preferred defense.

While everyone in Massillon knew that Shepas was on shaky ground following the 2004 season, the players did not expect to lose their head coach.

"We didn't know," Gamble said. "He sprung it on us after the last summer workout before camp. Everybody was sort of mad. I felt like he kind of abandoned us, betrayed us. But in the long run I can see that he had to look out for the best interests of his family."

Shepas left to become head coach of Waynesburg University, a Division III school in Pennsylvania.

Stacy inherited a hungry team in 2005. “It’s easy to coach a team that’s hungry, that’s mad, that’s ready to get in there and tear it up,” Gamble said. “It was just a guy comin’ in there with a good plan and the right bunch of kids to execute it. Everyone wanted to win. Everybody was on the same page. There was no one off to the side who was a distraction. We knew the goal.”

Gamble starting noticing the attention that comes with being Massillon’s star player during the summer leading into his junior season.

“I was known as the star,” Gamble said. “People would say ‘What’s up’ to you and talk to you and you wouldn’t even know who you were talking to. That started happening the summer of my sophomore year heading into my junior year. Sometimes you just wouldn’t want to be bothered but you didn’t want to come off like a jerk so you talk with ’em. It was fun for a while. Some people buy into that and get big heads. You could see it with some of the players. But I think everyone’s focus was there. We knew growing up that was a part of it. So when it came, it was great. You felt like a king. You’re really just now getting into the real Massillon Tiger program. Varsity football. You’re getting a taste of the boosters and everything that goes along with it.”

The 2005 season holds the fondest memories for Gamble. It was a Week 6 win over Cleveland St. Ignatius that signaled that big things could be on the way.

“I think the turning point, when we really knew we could be going to state is when we beat Ignatius," Gamble said. "That was the hump on our back, we were 0-8 against them. I think that's when people started to say, 'If you guys can beat Ignatius you can go to state.'

Massillon rolled into Week 10 undefeated. Canton McKinley was undefeated, too. It turned out to be McKinley's day.

"They just took it to us," Gamble said. "Nobody saw that comin'. Morgan Williams (McKinley's star running back) went off on us."

It was not a happy locker room after the game. "Everybody was pissed," Gamble said. "Not tears. We knew that we were in the playoffs. We knew our coaching staff was going to get us ready to play them again if necessary."

Massillon and McKinley won their next two playoff games to set up a rematch at the Rubber Bowl in Akron.

"We got another shot at McKinley," Gamble said.

Massillon beat McKinley 21-3. Next up was 12-0 Lakewood St. Edward. Massillon was again the underdog.

Gamble was the star of the St. Ed's game, gaining a combined 160 yards rushing and receiving and scoring the game's final two touchdowns. The win put the Tigers in the state championship game for the first time since 1982.

Gamble remembers all of the activities leading up to the championship game with Cincinnati Xavier.

"We talked to all of the elementary schools. We had the new middle school then.

We talked to them. The whole town was just electric.

The Tigers fell behind 17-7 after Xavier returned a punt for a touchdown at the end of the first half. A second half comeback made things interesting.

"Andrew Dailey stripped Darius Ashley and I led him to the end zone for 80 yards. We felt we had the momentum," Gamble said.

"I think we panicked. Tried to pass the ball a little too much. I don't blame it on anyone, it was a team effort. But I think if we could have played like we'd been playing, doing the same things we'd been doing, we would have had a good chance of winning. I had averaged 15 carries a game and I only had nine carries for 16 yards in the championship game."

Massillon lost, 24-17.

The 2006 season held high expectations for the Tigers, with most of their skill players returning.

"My senior season was disappointing," Gamble said. "I don't think we were as close knit. I was still first team All-Ohio my junior and senior year. I had a lot of achievements."

Gamble was hotly recruited. "I talked to everyone, Ohio State, Penn State, West Virginia, Tennessee, Virginia Tech, Cincinnati, Pittsburgh, Louisville, Miami, Minnesota, Michigan, Michigan State. I had a lot of people who were calling my phone every day. Coach Ron Zook at Illinois is a sweet talker."

Gamble was slated to start at nickle back for the University of Illinois as a true freshman. "In camp one of our receivers tore his ACL. Coach Zook asked, 'Who do you want from our defense, who do you think could go out there and play?' They wanted me. So I went out and started at inside receiver. And it worked out pretty good."

Gamble caught a touchdown pass to give Illinois a 21-14 lead against Ohio State in 2007. Ohio State was 10-0 and number one in the country.

"It was real quiet," Gamble said, describing Ohio Stadium after his touchdown catch, that came with 17 seconds left in the first half. "That was a great feeling. I had all my family in the stands. It just felt good to get my touchdown against Ohio State. We came in there and upset them. The play was called for me. They put me in single coverage and ran trips opposite me. I came wide open. The ball seemed like in was in the air forever, but I knew I was gonna catch it. I love the big situation. I want the ball in my hands."

Gamble made another important move late in the game, but this one was on the sidelines, not on the field. In fact the incident was featured in *Sports Illustrated.*

Illinois faced a fourth and inches from their own 34 yard line. There was 6:36 remaining in the game. Illinois led 28-21.

Illinois was in punt formation when Ohio State coach Jim Tressel called a time out.

Sports Illustrated reported that Gamble talked quarterback Juice Williams into approaching Zook about going for the first down during the time out. Gamble said it unfolded differently.

"Everyone wanted to go for it, but no one was man enough to go tell coach," Gamble said. "I was saying it before Tressel called the time out. Then when he called the time out I was like, 'Yeah, that's the green light to go up there.' I went to Juice and I'm like, 'Man, we need to go for this, you know what I mean?' He didn't really say anything, but I could tell he wanted to go for it. So I went over to Zook and I said, 'Coach, man, we need to keep the ball in our hands. We don't want to give them back the ball.' Juice was behind me. I said, 'We've got to go for it. We've got the momentum. We need to keep this momentum. If we get this first down we can keep the ball.' I remember he looked at Juice and said, 'Can you get it?' Juice said, 'Yeah, I'm gonna get it.' And we got it and kept the ball for the rest of the game."

> **"The whole town was just electric."**
>
> **Brian Gamble**

Illinois went to the Rose Bowl where they faced USC. While it wasn't a pleasant game for Illinois, 49-17 losers, there was another *Sports Illustrated* surprise for Gamble.

"I got a couple of calls from my buddies saying that my picture was in *Sports Illustrated* catching the ball against USC with the mountains in the background. I hadn't seen it yet. My mom ordered a copy of it. I just liked the background of it, the sun was setting. It was pretty."

Gamble's promising start at Illinois came to an abrupt halt after his freshman year. "I got in trouble," he said. "I got in a fight. That's basically what happened. I got kicked off the team for a semester. I did my little anger management. When I got kicked out, my son was born. When I went back after I did all I had to do, I just realized that I couldn't be away from my son. So I went to Zook and we talked. I said I thought it'd be better if I left and went somewhere closer to home. There's no hard feelings between me and Zook. Everything's good still. Kids change your life.

"I love the game of football. I think that football teaches you a lot of things in life. I've had a ride. I'm not done. I'm still playing. Monte McGuire (a former Massillon player from 1986-88) actually called me. He told me Coach (Lee) Owens wanted to talk. So we're going to try to win a Division II national championship at Ashland University.

Playing at Massillon was definitely the best years of my life. You grow up with all of that. You grow up Massillon. It's a big deal to you. Running out for the Massillon-McKinley game was a way better feeling than running out for the Rose Bowl. You grow up here. That's just what you know. You grow up Massillon."

ANDREW DAILEY

Like so many players who came before him, Andrew Dailey's dream of being a Massillon Tiger started in grade school.

Dailey's dreams came to fruition as he became a two-time first team All-Ohioan and a Penn State signee. But the dream started when a bright-eyed boy was sitting among a crowd of 20,000 fans watching a Massillon-Canton McKinley game.

Andrew Dailey was a two-time first team All-Ohioan.
PHOTO: JOE NAGY

"I was in third grade, watching the traditional balloons they release before the game, watching the players come out of the tunnel," Dailey said.

A few years later, as a middle-schooler, Dailey was impressed by an undersized Tiger star.

"I remember Billy Relford coming down on kickoffs his sophomore year and making plays," Dailey said. "I said, 'I'll do anything it takes some day to make a play on special teams for the Tigers. I don't think there are many kids across the country who grow up just wanting to make plays on special teams for their high school. Billy inspired me. I wanted to start off making plays on special teams just like Billy Relford did. He brought another element to the team. He sparked a lot of other guys to play with more tenacity and enthusi-asm."

"I said, 'I'll do any-thing to make a play on special teams for the Tigers.'"

Andrew Dailey

Relford was a playmaker throughout his Massillon ca-reer. His 17 interceptions set a Massillon record. While Relford was small at 5'8", Dailey was never small for his age. Although he was the fastest player on his youth football team, he had to play guard because he was above the weight limit to be a ball carrier.

As a fourth grader Dailey was aching to play tackle. "I played flag football through third grade. I couldn't put on the pads until fifth grade. So I ended up being a wa-ter boy for St. Mary's eighth grade team. At the end of practice the eighth graders got to call out one seventh grader to go against head up. One guy was the ball carrier and the other guy was the defender. I had some little tike's pads. I had dad's old Lorin Andrews Junior High helmet. I went to practice with my pads and just put 'em on with all of the seventh graders, just seeing if someone would call me out. And someone did call me out. He lit me up. It was actually my first taste of pads in a football environment. It was pretty shocking. The kid was four years older than me. He got me pretty good. Banged my knee up a little bit. I thought, 'Hey, if this is what football's all about, I'm still gonna love it.'"

It didn't take Dailey long to learn that he was part of a special group of young athletes growing up in Massillon. Many Massillon fans follow the players from the time they start playing flag football. Star players are identified before they're out of grade school. Dailey and his teammates were identified as a strong class.

Dailey celebrates a big play.

"It goes all the way back to fifth or sixth grade," Dailey said. "You could say it was the town, all the hype and pressure they were givin' us at such a young age. Maybe the town was building us into these kids that were ready to go to work and have one goal (of winning a state championship).

"By my freshman year they were saying, 'Wait until this freshman class gets to be juniors. And the class above us was hearing the same thing. It really was incredible. You don't notice all the hype and pressure while you're growing up. I guess you see it somewhat, but you think it's normal then. When you look back you say, 'That was not normal.'

"There was a ton, *a ton*, of pressure on our shoulders, on everyone on our team's shoulders. But to be honest, I didn't feel as much of it then because it was all natural, it was what we were born and raised to do. We were born and raised to go play football for Massillon and to win football games. You didn't feel as much pressure then because that's just the attitude we had: Just go out there and play the game full out and you'll be fine. Now you look back at it and say, 'Holy cow, there were 20,000 people rooting for me that game. That's pretty incredible.'"

"We were born and raised to go play football for Massillon. And to win football games."

Andrew Dailey

Rick Shepas was Dailey's first high school coach at Massillon. "I really like coach Shep," Dailey said. "He was just a hardnosed guy. Very blunt. He was just going to tell you how it is. You need a coach that's not going to beat around the bush with you. He'd tell you what you needed to work on and where you stood. If it comes out of his mouth that where you stand is not where you want to be, you need to do something. You need to work harder to make yourself better in his eyes.

"When Coach Shep told us

he was leaving Massillon there were a lot of players who were very, very upset. Coach Shep left us at the end of my sophomore year. There were some guys on the team that said this is coach Shep's team. We'd been running his offense and his plays since seventh grade."

Shepas was replaced by Tom Stacy after suffering back-to-back 4-6 seasons. Despite the fact he liked Shepas, Dailey thought the move made sense.

"There was too much talk around town about Coach Shep as a coach. It was beginning to affect the football team. So it was best at the time for coach Shep to leave. Not saying that it was his fault or anything. It's just how the town controls the Massillon football team. Once the town starts hootin' and hollerin' about one thing, there's going to be a change. The town kind of got what they wanted. I would say coach Shepas was forced out."

Stacy brought a different approach. "I thought his offense was brilliant," Dailey said of Stacy. "He had some tricks up his sleeve.

"We just knew we were going to be a special team and that we were going to be able to have one of the best records in Massillon history.

"It was a very special team to be a part of," Dailey said. "I've never been a part of any team, at any level, even at the collegiate level, that was so well gelled and so hardnosed and ready to attack one goal—and I played on a Rose Bowl team at Penn State.

The 2005 Tigers finished 13-

2, losing 24-17 to Cincinnati Xavier in the championship game after making a dramatic run through the playoffs. It was Massillon's first trip to the state championship game since 1982. It was also the first Massillon team to win 13 games.

Dailey on the run against Cincinnati Moeller in 2006.

The loss to St Xavier was devastating to Dailey and his teammates. "After the game a lot of guys on the team were cryin'. You saw a lot of emotion."

What happened after the game surprised Dailey.

"We go downtown and there's a truck with an open bed down there for us. We get on the back of this truck and there's probably 8,000-10,000 people just standing there in 28 degree weather, snow pouring down on them. We'd just lost the state championship and they were cheering us on, giving us a standing ovation. It was just incredible. Even with the loss in the championship game. It was incredible to see how much appreciation we had from our fans."

Dailey's senior year was disappointing. First, he was switched away from the safety position that he loved.

"It was tough, it really was," he said. "I thought I made more plays playing the safety spot. My senior year they put me in a position where I was just absorbing blockers and not being given the chance to make the plays I should be making. At safety you can kind of roam the field and play both sides of the field. You can play all over the place. My senior year I was playing outside linebacker—almost a defensive end. It was frustrating because teams were running the ball the other way. Never running the ball to my side. They really took me out of the game plan. But there's nothing you can do about it except help the team the best way you can. I did play a lot more offense my senior year.

"We beat McKinley, got the victory bell back, squeezed into the playoffs. The second round we played Toledo Whitmer. Nobody had ever heard of them. We were in tough weather conditions. Brian Gamble (Massillon's star running back and defensive back) had an ankle injury."

Massillon trailed 14-10 late in the game. All Whitmer had to do was run out the clock.

"There was probably a minute thirty left in the game and they're running the ball," Dailey said. "I'm the kind of kid who's always saying the game's never over. But I couldn't help but think it was over. Just standing out on the field trying to make every play I could. Watching these guys running the ball, running the clock out. Me and Brian, I remember the two of us, right there on the field, we just started breakin' down. I never cried so much in my life as right there, the last

25 seconds of the game. I just could not believe it was over. It wasn't just the season and the game. My high school career had just come to an end. It was really, really unbelievable."

Dailey was highly sought after by major universities. He narrowed his list down to Notre Dame, Penn State and the University of Florida. He was fascinated with Notre Dame.

"I was actually a big Notre Dame fan. I don't really know why, but I was. They said, 'We've got one scholarship left for a linebacker and we already offered it to this kid from Tennessee.' So they weren't going to offer me. They were waiting on him. I decided to move on. I looked at Florida and Penn State. Florida offered me, and I really did like Florida. Coach Urban Meyer took me into his office, it was just me and him personally. It was exciting to get that offer.

"I never cried so much in my life as right there, the last 25 seconds of the game. I could not believe it was over."

Andrew Dailey

"Penn State told me, 'Andrew, take your time. It's a big decision. Your offer will always be here.' But on one of my later visits Coach Joe Paterno sat me down and said, 'Andrew, we're getting worried. We don't know what it is you don't see in us. You haven't committed yet. Andrew, I'm going to give you another 7-10 days and I'm going to offer this other kid.'"

After driving back to Massillon, Dailey called Paterno and told him he'd decided to be a Penn State Nittany Lion.

A week later Notre Dame called. The Tennessee linebacker had backed out. They were ready to offer Dailey.

"I think I was at the point with Notre Dame that I realized I didn't like them as much as I thought I did. I was just fighting for that offer I think. I wasn't planing on committing to Notre Dame. It really came down to Penn State and Florida. I just felt absolutely the most comfortable at Penn State."

Dailey recently brought several of his Penn State teammates home with him for his 21st birthday. Discovering Massillon was an eye opener for them.

"I just showed 'em the weight room, the stadium and stuff," Dailey said. "They were just in awe. They couldn't believe the facilities we have. The tradition in the town. We think it's normal to have Tiger Rags (Massillon memorabilia store) downtown with thousands of Massillon t-shirts. I mean you can get anything you want down there. We have absolutely everything you need, from a bumper sticker to a coffee mug with Obie on it. It really is impressive."

Dailey said the training he received in Massillon prepared him for Penn State.

"In college I have teammates from a lot of different areas. Looking back on how hard we trained at Massillon, it's actually incredible. It's really pretty amazing what a strict program we have. I don't know of many kids at all at Penn State that grew up going through the kind of program that I went through. There's a distinct advantage coming from Massillon."

But the Penn State experience has not been easy for Dailey. As a redshirt junior he is fighting for a starting position.

"I said, 'Coach Paterno, I'm getting frustrated here. Can I get another shot? Can I show you I can play safety?"

Andrew Dailey

"It's been up and down," he said. "I got recruited as a linebacker and Penn State is Linebacker-U. I was looking for a school that was saying 'We think you can play safety.' But most of the schools were saying linebacker, linebacker. So I got there and gave linebacker a try. It was different than playing linebacker at Massillon. I never really caught up on it. I got a call from Coach Paterno after my freshman year and he said, 'Come to my office and have a talk.' He said, 'Andrew, we have a situation on the team where we'd like to switch you to slot receiver. I heard you played that in high school.' I said, 'Coach, I'm willing to do whatever is needed for the team. I just want to get on the field and start being a part of this team and making plays.'"

The switch to slot receiver didn't work for Dailey.

"Right after camp they sent

me back to linebacker. I played linebacker for two weeks and I went back to him and I said, 'Coach, I tried to help better the team, I went to offense for you. I've been at linebacker for a year, going on another half of year here. I'd really like to try safety. I just feel more comfortable at that position. I'll lose a couple pounds. I'd like to show you that I can play there.'

"He said, 'We'll see, we'll see. We know you have the athletic ability and you can do that. We'll see, we'll see.'"

But Dailey continued to toil in a deep linebacker rotation after his meeting with Paterno.

Finally he scheduled another meeting with his head coach.

"I said, 'Coach Paterno, I'm getting frustrated here. Can I get another shot? Can I show you I can play safety?'"

After Dailey's second plea, Paterno agreed to make a change.

"The next practice he said, 'Go to the safety meetings.'

"They put me at free safety because that's where they needed me at the time. I spent my redshirt freshman season just learning behind the guys, playing a little bit of nickel. I was getting a lot of work done, practicing with them. I went into my redshirt sophomore year competing for a spot and ended up winning the nickel spot."

Dailey made two big plays in his first start.

"I made a pick against Akron in Week 1. It felt really

good. I was on cloud nine. I felt like I was back at the beginning of football again. It felt real good to be a part of something and show the coaches that I can play."

Dailey also took a fake punt 37 yards for a first down. Unfortunately, he injured his shoulder on the play.

"My shoulder was giving me problems and they told me, 'Get your shoulder fixed up and we're going to put another guy at nickel until then.'"

Of course all football players know that your position isn't safe when you're injured. Dailey was unable to reclaim the nickel back job following his shoulder rehabilitation.

"It was just too tough to catch back up after being out that long," he said. "The rest of the year I just played special teams."

This year Dailey is entering his redshirt junior season. He spent spring ball at his favorite position, strong safety.

"Going into this spring they moved me to strong safety, which is where I thought I should be all the time," Dailey said. "Penn State calls it the hero, kind of the same position I played my junior year at Massillon. I started the spring game with the first team defense. Had a pretty good game, made a couple of tackles, had a pass break up, knocked a pass down. Now I'm just ready for camp. Hopefully I'll be able to clinch that spot. I think I have a pretty good chance. There are three safety spots because we play a lot of nickel. I think I have a pretty good shot at being the hero or nickel for sure."

BO GRUNDER

Most two-way players prefer to play offense or defense. But it really didn't matter to Bo Grunder.

Grunder epitomized the hard-nosed player that Massillon fans love. His passion while playing on both sides of the ball earned Grunder legendary status in his hometown.

"Wherever I'm needed that's where I'm going to play," Grunder said, "There's ups and downs to both sides of the ball. On offense you can deliver the hit, too."

Bo Grunder was Co-Defensive Player of the Year in the state of Ohio in 2009.

Grunder certainly delivered on offense and defense. His varsity debut got everyone's attention.

"My junior year I scored four touchdowns the first game," Grunder said. "I never thought I'd be doing something like that. People kind of knew who I was after that.

By the time he finished his

Massillon career, Grunder was known statewide The 5'9", 165 pound defensive back was named first team All-Ohio and Co-Defensive Player of the Year for the state of Ohio after helping to lead the Tigers to the State Final Four.

Grunder picked off 12 passes in his Massillon career—nine in his senior year alone. He was also dangerous as a return man, bringing back three punts for touchdowns, the most in Massillon history. Grunder was also one of the Tigers top targets at receiver in both his junior and senior seasons.

While his junior season saw the Tigers finish 6-5 while adjusting to new head coach Jason Hall, Grunder and his teammates expected success in 2009.

"I was pretty confident, actually," Grunder said. "I thought we had a pretty good team. A lot of starters coming back. We had a senior meeting and we said we were going to do whatever we had to do to win a state championship."

The 2009 Tigers were undefeated before losing a controversial decision to Cleveland St. Ignatius in Week 6.

Leading 21-20, Massillon appeared to wrap up the win when Tyler Miller intercepted an Ignatius pass with two minutes remaining. Amid the celebration was a late penalty flag for defensive holding. Given new life, Ignatius scored and went on to win, 26-21.

"We had the win over Ignatius in our hands and we just let it go," Grunder said.

Massillon lost again in Week 7, to Steubenville, another of the top teams in the state.

"That was a crazy atmosphere," Grunder said of the game, played at Steubenville. The two teams, traditional rivals dating to the 1930s, hadn't played since 1978. Steubenville prevailed 13-3.

"We couldn't give up and let everything go," Grunder said. "We had to keeping goin' and keep winnin' games to get a good seed in the playoffs."

Grunder, a two-way star at Massillon rarely on the bench.
PHOTO: JOE NAGY

Massillon won two straight, then ended the regular season with a disheartening loss to Canton McKinley, 35-21.

"We just made mistakes and they took advantage," Grunder said.

The Tigers made a great playoff run, including a 10-7 revenge win over McKinley.

"There was a lot of people doubting us," Grunder said. "It just made me all the more ready to play them again.

Grunder loved playing for Massillon. "There's not too many places in America that are anything like Massillon, where the whole community supports you."

JASON HALL

Jason Hall may just have what it takes to lead the Massillon Tigers to the state championship.

Hall is the latest coach to come to Tigertown with dreams of leading the Tigers to their first state playoff title.

Jason Hall led Massillon to a state Final Four appearance in his second year on the job.

He almost did it in his second year at the helm before bowing to Cleveland Glenville, 31-17, in the State Final 4.

The semi-final loss to Glenville followed an exciting playoff run that saw the Tigers knock off North Canton Hoover, Twinsburg, and avenge a regular season loss to Canton McKinley.

Hall is a nice guy who won't let anybody push him around. He treats people well, but he's not afraid to make unpopular decisions.

The old guard at Massillon was offended when he chose to close practices to the public. They let him know about it. He stuck to his guns. He won't be pushed around.

But don't think he doesn't understand the Massillon community. He found out how passionate the community is about football at his first scrimmage.

"Our first scrimmage, there were about 5,000 people there," Hall said. "That was eye opening."

It was also during Hall's first year as head coach that Massillon was named a finalist in *ESPN's* Title Town USA competition. When the sports network came to town they were greeted by a raucous crowd at Tiger Stadium.

"We packed the stadium for the Title Town USA program," Hall said. "It put goosebumps on me. I tell people, 'You don't understand how important it is, how special it is, until you're a part of it. What it means to the people in this town, who live here and are part of it. It's truly something special.' I got a quick education on how important it really is to the town, to its people."

"My philosophy is that you've got to build it from the ground up."

Jason Hall

Hall has a plan to build Massillon into a state champion. But it doesn't start at the high school level, or even the middle school level.

"My philosophy is that you've got to build it from the ground up. We've done a lot with the youth program. We've gone back to runnin' it through the elementary school, the way it was done many years ago. We've restructured our middle school program. Myself and a lot of the coaches and players have been going into the middle school all year long. You build at the lower levels, introducing study tables along with practice. We're big on getting the academic piece started at the lower level. I want to be here for a long time and I hope the community wants me here for a long time. If you want that kind of long-term success you've gotta attack your young kids. It's a K-12 program. I think that's how you build a program. It's gotta be our community, K-12, bulding a football program and maintaining it."

> **"I'm not a big fan of private schools because I think they get away with murder."**
>
> **Jason Hall**

Hall is infusing a lot of what he learned during his All-American career at Mount Union. He played under the legendary Larry Kehres, who has won 10 NCAA Division III National Championships in his 25 seasons as head coach.

"Larry Kehres, I'm always talking to him. I was a part of the start of his championship run at Mount Union. We're taking the same approach, the same type of philosophy in Massillon, I know that. It would be nice if we got it going here like Mount's got it going.

"I always use the term 'Players, Formation, Plays,' from a coaching standpoint. I try to put the players in the right formation to run the plays that make them successful. To me, that's football. I learned that from Larry Kehres.

"My roommate at Mount Union was B. J. Payne, who had a very successful career here and had a very successful career at Mount Union. Now he's a successful head coach. As players at Mount we came here to watch Massillon. So I was around it. I knew exactly the traditions and expectations of Massillon.

Hall believes Massillon needs to concentrate on competing with the state's public school programs during the regular season. He feels the playoffs are the time to tangle with the state's parochial powers.

Hall shown during Massillon's 2009 game at Steubenville. Part of Hall's philosophy is to build a regular season schedule that features the state's best public school programs.

"I'm not a big fan of private schools because I think they get away with murder," Hall said. "We're not on a level playing field. Now I'll take my kids and we'll play anybody, I'm not saying that. But at the same time you'd like a level playing field. I've proposed several times that I think there should be a Catholic League playoff system. Put them on a playing field that is level. To consistently put us in a classification with Cincinnati Xavier, Cincinnati Moeller, Cleveland St. Ignatius, Lakewood St. Edward, the big enrollment private schools, year in, year out, you're not going to be on a level playing field. It doesn't matter how you say it, year in, year out, you're *not* going to be on a level playing field. It doesn't mean that you can't put a team together that can play with them. It's hard to compete with someone who can go out and recruit their team. The proof's in the pudding. Ignatius has six games out of state right now because everybody is like, 'Hey, we're not going to play you guys.'

"We're a public school, and we're going to do our best to play a public school schedule. Mentor, Strongsville, we'll play any of those guys. And they're great, quality teams. Great coches. We'll sign any public school right now. We have a long-standing relationship with Warren Harding. A pretty long relationship with Mentor now. We're bringing back an histroic game in Steubenville that means a lot to both communities. We're playing GlenOak, a Stark County team that has a huge enrollment. All of those teams are on the same playing field as us."

Hall would like to become an institution at Massillon.

"I want to be here for the long haul," Hall said. "I'm lookin' forward to that. I think our community, our kids, our fourth graders, need to know that Coach Hall's going to be there when they're seniors in high school."

About the Author

Scott H. Shook is the author of 1998's Best Seller *Massillon Memories*, his first book on the Massillon Tigers.

Scott was born in Massillon, Ohio, and lived there before moving to Marco Island, Florida in 1973. As a 15-year-old, he began his sportswriting and photography career at two local newspapers in the Marco Island-Naples area.

He continues to reside in Marco Island, where he works in resort management in addition to his writing and photographic pursuits.

A graduate of The University of Florida, Scott has had hundreds of newspaper and magazine articles and photographs published worldwide. A tennis professional, his tennis features have appeared in *Tennis* magazine.

Despite leaving Massillon as a teenager, Scott shares the cradle-to-grave interest in football that is bred into its citizenry. He attends several Massillon football games each fall.

Order Additional Copies

Order additional copies of A Century of Heroes today.
Send check or money order to A Century of Heroes, 100 Stevens' Landing Drive, Suite 403, Marco Island, FL 34145. Phone 239-394-6615.

Please send me ______ books at $21 plus $4.95 shipping per book (Shipping charges subject to change).

____
Name

____
Address

____
City, State, Zip